D1216886

Modern English-Canadian Prose

AMERICAN LITERATURE, ENGLISH LITERATURE, AND WORLD LITERATURES IN ENGLISH: AN INFORMATION GUIDE SERIES

Series Editor: Theodore Grieder, Curator, Division of Special Collections, Fales Library, New York University

Associate Editor: Duane DeVries, Associate Professor, Polytechnic Institute of New York, Brooklyn

Other books on world literatures in this series:

BLACK AFRICAN LITERATURE IN ENGLISH—*Edited by Bernth Lindfors*

ASIAN LITERATURE IN ENGLISH—*Edited by G.L. Anderson*

AUSTRALIAN LITERATURE TO 1900—*Edited by Barry G. Andrews and William H. Wilde*

MODERN AUSTRALIAN POETRY, 1920-1970—*Edited by Herbert C. Jaffa*

MODERN AUSTRALIAN PROSE, 1901-1975—*Edited by A. Grove Day*

ENGLISH-CANADIAN LITERATURE TO 1900—*Edited by R.G. Moyles*

MODERN ENGLISH-CANADIAN POETRY—*Edited by Peter Stevens*

INDIAN LITERATURE IN ENGLISH, 1827-1979—*Edited by Amritjit Singh, Rajiva Verma, and Irene Joshi*

IRISH LITERATURE, 1800-1875—*Edited by Brian McKenna*

NEW ZEALAND LITERATURE TO 1977—*Edited by John Thomson*

SCOTTISH LITERATURE IN ENGLISH AND SCOTS—*Edited by W.R. Aitken*

AUTHOR NEWSLETTERS AND JOURNALS—*Edited by Margaret Patterson*

The above series is part of the
GALE INFORMATION GUIDE LIBRARY

The Library consists of a number of separate series of guides covering major areas in the social sciences, humanities, and current affairs.

General Editor: Paul Wasserman, Professor and former Dean, School of Library and Information Services, University of Maryland

Managing Editor: Denise Allard Adzigian, Gale Research Company

Modern English-Canadian Prose

A GUIDE TO INFORMATION SOURCES

*Volume 38 in the American Literature, English
Literature, and World Literatures in English
Information Guide Series*

Helen Hoy

*Associate Professor of English
University of Lethbridge
Lethbridge, Alberta*

Gale Research Company
Book Tower, Detroit, Michigan 48226

Library of Congress Cataloging in Publication Data

Hoy, Helen.
  Modern English-Canadian prose.

  (American literature, English literature, and
world literatures in English information guide
series ; v. 38)
  Includes indexes.
  1. Canadian fiction—20th century—Bibliography.
2. Canadian prose literature—20th century—
Bibliography. I. Title. II. Series: Gale information
guide library. American literature, English literature,
and world literatures in English ; v. 42.
Z1377.F4H69 1983 [PR9192.5] 016.818'508 73-16996
ISBN 0-8103-1245-X

For my parents, with love

VITA

Helen Hoy is associate professor of English at the University of Lethbridge, Lethbridge, Alberta. She received her Ph.D. from the University of Toronto and has taught at the University of Toronto and the University of Manitoba. She reviews Canadian fiction for UNIVERSITY OF TORONTO QUARTERLY's "Letters in Canada" and has published articles on Robertson Davies, Hugh MacLennan, Alice Munro, and Gabrielle Roy.

CONTENTS

Contents

Contents

ACKNOWLEDGMENTS

I wish to thank the staff of the Robarts Library and the Massey College Library, University of Toronto; the secretarial staff of University College, University of Toronto (especially Rosalie Cooke); and my sister Teresa for their assistance over the past several years. The clerical assistance of Brenda Oleksy and Cindy Verwer, computer services of Pete Madany and the University of Lethbridge Computing Centre, and the library services of the University of Lethbridge (Rosemary Howard, in particular) were also invaluable. Finally, I would like to acknowledge the University of Lethbridge Research Grant which helped to support the final stages of manuscript preparation.

INTRODUCTION

MODERN ENGLISH-CANADIAN PROSE: A GUIDE TO INFORMATION SOURCES is a checklist of twentieth-century Canadian fiction and nonfiction prose written in English. It is intended both for readers relatively unfamiliar with Canadian literature and for scholars in the field. The guide includes writers whose work rests squarely within the twentieth century, omitting those like Sara Jeannette Duncan, Ralph Connor, and Gilbert Parker who may have published in this century but only as the continuation of an established literary career (and who are already included in a companion volume in the Gale series, R.G. Moyles' ENGLISH-CANADIAN LITERATURE TO 1900: A GUIDE TO INFORMATION SOURCES [Vol. 6, 1976]). Emphasis is on novelists and short story writers; nonfiction prose writers chosen (a more highly selected group) include figures who have established reputations in closely related literary pursuits: essay writers, literary critics, nature writers, biographers, writers of memoirs, and humorists.

The checklist begins with entries for general reference sources available to students of Canadian literature--general bibliographies and reference sources, biographical references, and indexes to serials, anthologies, collections, and theses. There follows information on manuscripts and other special collections devoted to Canadian prose. Next, entries for books and articles of literary history, criticism, and theory provide background material for a study of English-Canadian prose.

The compilation of information sources for individual authors (and particularly for fiction writers) is the heart of this guide. To avoid creating artificial divisions when the canon is still in the process of being established, I list authors alphabetically rather than dividing them into major and minor figures or listing them by period. The only division is between fiction and nonfiction writers, and even that is sometimes unavoidably arbitrary. For example, authors such as Bodsworth, Glassco, Hiebert, Horwood, and Leacock could readily appear in either category.

Among the fiction writers represented are all of the major novelists and short story writers, as well as writers of single masterpieces, novelists of interest to the literary historian, and novelists who have made a sustained if minor contribution to the field. There is considerable controversy about whether writers like Brian Moore and Malcolm Lowry can rightfully be considered Canadian, but I have included them for those readers expecting to find them in such a guide as the present one. Although I have attempted to reflect the general scholarly consensus regarding significant Canadian prose writers, some idiosyncracy of choice is inevitable. Names of candidates who have been excluded--Elizabeth Brewster, John Buell, Juan Butler, Frank Parker Day, Selwyn Dewdney, George Elliott, Hubert Evans, Shirley Faessler, Lawrence Garber, Margaret Gilboord, Roderick Haig-Brown, Robert Harlow, Charles Yale Harrison, James Houston, Robert Hunter, William Kinsella, David Knight, Douglas LePan, Norman Levine, Alistair McLeod, Colin McDougall, John Marlyn, Fredelle Bruser Maynard, Martin Myers, Alden Nowlan, Chris Scott, Elizabeth Smart, Peter Such, Carol Shields, W.D. Valgardson --spring readily to mind. The listing of nonfiction prose writers is restricted to established figures in a range of literary pursuits within the field of belles lettres. Historians, political economists, philosophers, and members of such other separate disciplines are excluded.

Following a brief biographical sketch, the listing of materials for each individual author is divided into two general parts, the primary and the secondary, each with internal subdivisions:

1. Primary material: the primary material is in chronological order, within each of the following subsections:

a. Monographs: except for the nonfiction writers, books of fiction precede other monographs by the author--nonfiction prose, poetry, drama, or edited works. Reprints and translations (a daunting number in the case of an author like Leacock) are excluded.

b. Short work: uncollected short stories and significant nonfiction articles, particularly literary criticism or theory, appear here. Juvenilia, journalism, articles in newspapers or college papers, encyclopedia entries, and book reviews by these authors are excluded. The original appearance of material subsequently reprinted in collections of the author's work is also omitted; only the first appearance of uncollected material is noted.

c. Manuscripts: listed here are libraries holding collections of the author's manuscripts.

2. Secondary material: the secondary material is arranged alphabetically, by author for criticism and by journal title for book reviews, within each of the following subsections:

a. Bibliographies.

b. Criticism: although not exhaustive, the checklist of criticism attempts to be a comprehensive survey of serious scholarship in English. It does not, for the most part, include criticism of poetry or drama, obituaries, newspaper articles, encyclopedia articles, profiles in popular magazines, films, tapes, or theses. Reprints are noted only for major critical anthologies.

c. Book reviews: the list of book reviews is very selective, eliminating, in general, brief reviews, newspaper reviews, and those in obscure and minor periodicals. To best utilize space, entries for book reviews appear in an abbreviated form (refer to the list of abbreviations of journal titles).

Although aiming for comprehensiveness, this present guide is necessarily selective, being a distillation from over eleven thousand entries (and another eight thousand book reviews). Whenever possible, monographic entries contain such information as pagination, illustrators, and the presence of bibliographies and indexes. In titles, I have retained ampersands when they appear in the original. Please note that entries in this guide are numbered and so cited in cross-references and indexes. Corrections and additions are welcome. Although the majority of entries are for the period through 1979, I have tried to keep the material current. The cut-off date for entries is January 1, 1981, although entries for monographs continue through 1981 and, in some cases, into 1982.

ABBREVIATIONS OF JOURNAL TITLES

AA	AMERICAN ANTHROPOLOGIST
AAPSS	ANNALS OF THE AMERICAN ACADEMY OF POLITICAL AND SOCIAL SCIENCE
AHR	AMERICAN HISTORICAL REVIEW
AIHR	ALBERTA HISTORICAL REVIEW
AmR	AMERICAN REVIEW
AntiqR	ANTIGONISH REVIEW
APBR	ATLANTIC PROVINCES BOOK REVIEW
APSR	AMERICAN POLITICAL SCIENCE REVIEW
AR	ANTIOCH REVIEW
ARCS	AMERICAN REVIEW OF CANADIAN STUDIES
ArQ	ARIZONA QUARTERLY
ASch	AMERICAN SCHOLAR
Atl	ATLANTIC MONTHLY
AtlA	ATLANTIC ADVOCATE
BCan	BOOKS IN CANADA
BCHQ	BRITISH COLUMBIA HISTORICAL QUARTERLY
BCLQ	BRITISH COLUMBIA LIBRARY QUARTERLY
BCStud	BRITISH COLUMBIA STUDIES
BForum	BOOK FORUM
BJA	BRITISH JOURNAL OF AESTHETICS
BLM	BONNIERS LITTERÄRA MAGASIN
BOT	BOOKS OF THE TIMES
BrBN	BRITISH BOOK NEWS
BrO	BRANCHING OUT
Boundary	BOUNDARY 2

CA	CANADIAN AUTHOR
CAB	CANADIAN AUTHOR AND BOOKMAN
CamJ	CAMBRIDGE JOURNAL
CamR	CAMBRIDGE REVIEW
CanA	CANADIAN AUDUBON
CanL	CANADIAN LITERATURE
CanP	CANADIAN POETRY
CanR	CANADIAN REVIEW
CArt	CANADIAN ART
CB	CANADIAN BOOKMAN
CBRA	CANADIAN BOOK REVIEW ANNUAL
CCL	CANADIAN CHILDREN'S LITERATURE
CDim	CANADIAN DIMENSION
CE	COLLEGE ENGLISH
CEStudies	CANADIAN ETHNIC STUDIES
CFM	CANADIAN FICTION MAGAZINE
CFor	CANADIAN FORUM
CGJ	CANADIAN GEOGRAPHICAL JOURNAL
CHist	CURRENT HISTORY
CHJ	CANADIAN HISTORY JOURNAL
CHR	CANADIAN HISTORICAL REVIEW
CJEPS	CANADIAN JOURNAL OF ECONOMIC AND POLITICAL SCIENCE
CJIP	CANADIAN JOURNAL OF IRISH STUDIES
CJPS	CANADIAN JOURNAL OF POLITICAL SCIENCE
CJR	COLUMBIA JOURNALISM REVIEW
CL	COMPARATIVE LITERATURE
ClassR	CLASSICAL REVIEW
CLS	COMPARATIVE LITERATURE STUDIES
CM	CARLETON MISCELLANY
ConL	CONTEMPORARY LITERATURE
ContempR	CONTEMPORARY REVIEW
CRCL	CANADIAN REVIEW OF COMPARATIVE LITERATURE
CRead	CANADIAN READER
CRevAS	CANADIAN REVIEW OF AMERICAN STUDIES

Crit	CRITIQUE
CritQ	CRITICAL QUARTERLY
CSS	CANADIAN SLAVIC STUDIES
DK	DER KUNSTWART
DQ	DENVER QUARTERLY
DR	DALHOUSIE REVIEW
EA	ÉTUDES ANGLAISES
EC	ÉTUDES CANADIENNES/CANADIAN STUDIES
ECW	ESSAYS ON CANADIAN WRITING
EF	ÉTUDES FRANÇAISES
EJ	ENGLISH JOURNAL
ELH	ELH
ELN	ENGLISH LANGUAGE NOTES
EQ	ENGLISH QUARTERLY
ES	ENGLISH STUDIES
ESC	ENGLISH STUDIES IN CANADA
ETC	ETC.
FSt	FIRST STATEMENT
GeoJ	GEOGRAPHICAL JOURNAL
HAB	HUMANITIES ASSOCIATION REVIEW (or BULLETIN)
HiT	HISTORY TODAY
HM	HARPER'S
HudR	HUDSON REVIEW
IFR	INTERNATIONAL FICTION REVIEW
IJ	INTERNATIONAL JOURNAL
IUR	IRISH UNIVERSITY REVIEW
JA	JOURNAL OF AESTHETICS
JAAC	JOURNAL OF AESTHETICS AND ART CRITICISM
JAH	JOURNAL OF AMERICAN HISTORY
JAF	JOURNAL OF AMERICAN FOLKLORE

JCanS	JOURNAL OF CANADIAN STUDIES
JCF	JOURNAL OF CANADIAN FICTION
JCL	JOURNAL OF COMMONWEALTH LITERATURE
JEGP	JOURNAL OF ENGLISH AND GERMAN PHILOLOGY
JES	JOURNAL OF EUROPEAN STUDIES
JJQ	JAMES JOYCE QUARTERLY
JML	JOURNAL OF MODERN LITERATURE
JP	JOURNAL OF PHILOSOPHY
JPE	JOURNAL OF POLITICAL ECONOMY
JQ	JOURNALISM QUARTERLY
KR	KENYON REVIEW
LaUR	LAKEHEAD UNIVERSITY REVIEW
LHY	LITERARY HALF-YEARLY
MASJ	MIDCONTINENT AMERICAN STUDIES JOURNAL
MassR	MASSACHUSETTS REVIEW
MCMT	MAIN CURRENTS IN MODERN THOUGHT
ME	MYSTERIOUS EAST
MFS	MODERN FICTION STUDIES
MHRev	MALAHAT REVIEW
MLJ	MODERN LANGUAGE JOURNAL
MLN	MODERN LANGUAGE NOTES
MLQ	MODERN LANGUAGE QUARTERLY
MLR	MODERN LANGUAGE REVIEW
MP	MODERN PHILOLOGY
MQR	MICHIGAN QUARTERLY REVIEW
NAR	NEW AMERICAN REVIEW
NatF	NATIONAL FORUM
Nation&A	NATION AND ATHENAEUM
NatR	NATIONAL REVIEW
Neophil	NEOPHILOLOGUS
NER	NEW ENGLAND REVIEW
NewR	NEW REPUBLIC

NLI	NEW LITERATURE AND IDEOLOGY
NMQ	NEW MEXICO QUARTERLY
NoR	NORTHERN REVIEW
N&Q	NOTES AND QUERIES
NQ	NEWFOUNDLAND QUARTERLY
NS	NEW STATESMAN
NS&N	NEW STATESMAN AND NATION
NSoc	NEW SOCIETY
NWR	NEWEST REVIEW
NY	NEW YORKER
NYRB	NEW YORK REVIEW OF BOOKS
NYTBR	NEW YORK TIMES BOOK REVIEW
NYTSR	NEW YORK TIMES SATURDAY REVIEW
OntarioR	ONTARIO REVIEW
OpenL	OPEN LETTER
PacA	PACIFIC AFFAIRS
Person	PERSONALIST
PFor	PRAIRIE FORUM
PHR	PACIFIC HISTORICAL REVIEW
PoetR	POETRY REVIEW
PQ	PHILOLOGICAL QUARTERLY
PR	PARTISAN REVIEW
PrS	PRAIRIE SCHOONER
PSQ	POLITICAL SCIENCE QUARTERLY
QJS	QUARTERLY JOURNAL OF SPEECH
Q&Q	QUILL AND QUIRE
QQ	QUEEN'S QUARTERLY
QR	QUARTERLY REVIEW
RAn	REVIEWS IN ANTHROPOLOGY
RES	REVIEW OF ENGLISH STUDIES
ROO	ROOM OF ONE'S OWN

Abbreviations of Journal Titles

ROR	REVIEW OF REVIEWS
RUL	REVUE DE L'UNIVERSITÉ DE LAVAL
RUO	REVUE DE L'UNIVERSITÉ D'OTTAWA
RusR	RUSSIAN REVIEW
SAQ	SOUTH ATLANTIC QUARTERLY
SaskH	SASKATCHEWAN HISTORY
SatN	SATURDAY NIGHT
SatR	SATURDAY REVIEW
SCL	STUDIES IN CANADIAN LITERATURE
SCN	SEVENTEENTH-CENTURY NEWS
SCR	SOUTH CAROLINA REVIEW
SELit	STUDIES IN ENGLISH LITERATURE
SHR	SOUTHERN HUMANITIES REVIEW
ShStud	SHAKESPEARE STUDIES
SlavR	SLAVIC REVIEW
SN	STUDIA NEOPHILOLOGICA
SNNTS	STUDIES IN THE NOVEL
SocS	SOCIAL STUDIES
SoR	SOUTHERN REVIEW
SQ	SHAKESPEARE QUARTERLY
SR	SEWANEE REVIEW
SSF	STUDIES IN SHORT FICTION
TamR	TAMARACK REVIEW
TC	TWENTIETH CENTURY
TES	TIMES EDUCATIONAL SUPPLEMENT
ThisM	THIS MAGAZINE
TLS	TIMES LITERARY SUPPLEMENT
UTQ	UNIVERSITY OF TORONTO QUARTERLY
UWR	UNIVERSITY OF WINDSOR REVIEW
VQR	VIRGINIA QUARTERLY REVIEW
WAL	WESTERN AMERICAN LITERATURE

WascanaR	WASCANA REVIEW
WatR	WATERLOO REVIEW
WCR	WEST COAST REVIEW
WHQ	WESTERN HISTORICAL QUARTERLY
WHR	WESTERN HUMANITIES REVIEW
WLT	WORLD LITERATURE TODAY
WLWE	WORLD LITERATURE WRITTEN IN ENGLISH
WR	WESTERN REVIEW
YR	YALE REVIEW
YWES	YEAR'S WORK IN ENGLISH STUDIES
ZAA	ZEITSCHRIFT FÜR ANGLISTIK UND AMERIKANISTIK

1. REFERENCE SOURCES

A. BIBLIOGRAPHIES AND GENERAL REFERENCE WORKS

International reference sources--such as the MODERN LANGUAGE ASSOCIATION BIBLIOGRAPHY, the MHRA ANNUAL BIBLIOGRAPHY OF ENGLISH LANGUAGE AND LITERATURE, SOCIAL SCIENCES AND HUMANITIES INDEX, READER'S GUIDE TO PERIODICAL LITERATURE, THE YEAR'S WORK IN ENGLISH STUDIES, ABSTRACTS OF ENGLISH STUDIES, the British Museum and Library of Congress, National Union catalogs, BOOK REVIEW DIGEST, BOOK REVIEW INDEX, and INDEX TO BOOK REVIEWS IN THE HUMANITIES--are not listed here but should also be consulted.

1   Amtmann, Bernard, comp. CONTRIBUTIONS TO A DICTIONARY OF CANADIAN PSEUDONYMS ۧAND ANONYMOUS WORKS RELATING TO CANADA/CONTRIBUTION À UN DICTIONNAIRE DES PSEUDONYMES CANADIENS ET DES OUVRAGES ANONYMES RELATIFS AU CANADA. Montreal: B. Amtmann, 1973. 144 p.

2   _____. CONTRIBUTIONS TO A SHORT TITLE CATALOGUE OF CA-NADIANA. 4 vols. Montreal: Author, 1971-73.

        Catalog of a bookseller's holdings.

3   "Annual Bibliography of Commonwealth Literature." JOURNAL OF COM-MONWEALTH LITERATURE, 1965-- .

        Includes a section on Canada; lists books and articles, pri-mary and secondary material, all genres and periods.

4   ATLANTIC PROVINCES CHECKLIST: A GUIDE TO CURRENT INFOR-MATION IN BOOKS, PAMPHLETS, GOVERNMENT PUBLICATIONS, MAGAZINE ARTICLES AND DOCUMENTARY FILMS RELATING TO THE FOUR ATLANTIC PROVINCES, 1957-1965, 1972. Halifax: Atlantic Provinces Library Association, 1958-66, 1973. Annual.

5   Bell, Inglis Freeman, ed. "Canadian Literature: A Checklist." CA-
    NADIAN LITERATURE, 1960-71. Annual.

>   Checklist of Canadian literature and criticism in books and
    articles, 1959 through 1970; edited by Rita Butterfield, 1964
    and on; continued by nos. 42 and 73.

6   Bell, Inglis Freeman, and Jennifer Gallup, eds. A REFERENCE GUIDE
    TO ENGLISH, AMERICAN, AND CANADIAN LITERATURE: AN AN-
    NOTATED CHECKLIST OF BIBLIOGRAPHICAL AND OTHER REFERENCE
    MATERIALS. Vancouver: University of British Columbia Press, 1971.
    xii, 139 p. Indexes.

>   Includes some basic Canadian reference materials.

7   Bell, Inglis Freeman, and Susan W. Port, eds. CANADIAN LITERATURE/
    LITTÉRATURE CANADIENNE 1959-1963: A CHECKLIST OF CREATIVE
    AND CRITICAL WRITINGS/BIBLIOGRAPHIE DE LA CRITIQUE ET DES
    OEUVRES D'IMAGINATION. Vancouver: Publications Centre, University
    of British Columbia, 1966. 140 p.

>   Lists books and articles.

8   BOOKS IN CANADA. Toronto: Canadian Review of Books, 1972-- .
    Monthly.

>   Announces and reviews current publications.

9   CANADIANA. Ottawa: National Library, 1951-- . Annual.

>   Listing of "publications of Canadian origin or interest"; con-
    tinues from no. 11. Standard reference.

10 CANADIAN BOOKS IN PRINT/CATALOGUE DES LIVRES CANADIENS
    EN LIBRAIRIE. Toronto: University of Toronto Press, 1968-- . Annual.

>   Author and title index, and subject index; subject guide be-
    gins 1974. Essential reference.

11 CANADIAN CATALOGUE OF BOOKS PUBLISHED IN CANADA, ABOUT
    CANADA, AS WELL AS THOSE WRITTEN BY CANADIANS, WITH IM-
    PRINT, 1921-1949. (CONSOLIDATED ENGLISH LANGUAGE REPRINT
    EDITION) WITH CUMULATED AUTHOR INDEX. 2 vols. [Toronto]:
    Toronto Public Libraries, 1959. Vol. 1, (1921-39); Vol. 2, (1940-49).
    Index.

>   Continued by no. 9.

12 "Canadian Newspapers on Microfilm." Compiled by the Microfilm Com-
    mittee of the Canadian Library Association under the Supervision of Sheila

A. Egoff. 3 vols. Mimeographed. Ottawa: Canadian Library Association, 1959. Index.

In three-ring binders; revisions added.

13 CANADIAN PUBLICATIONS, BOOKS--PERIODICALS, OUT OF PRINT, 1967-1972/PUBLICATIONS CANADIENNES, LIVRES--PÉRIODIQUES, ÉPUISÉE, 1967-1972. Vancouver: Versatile Publishing, 1974. xxxiv, 651, 185 p. Index.

Lists the holdings of the antiquarian book market.

14 Colombo, John Robert. COLOMBO'S CANADIAN REFERENCES. Toronto: Oxford University Press, 1976. viii, 576 p. Index.

Encyclopedia of "people, places, and things of Canadian interest."

15 _____, ed. COLOMBO'S CANADIAN QUOTATIONS. Edmonton: Hurtig, 1974. x, 735 p. Index.

Quotations listed by author.

16 _____, et al., comps. CDN SF & F: A BIBLIOGRAPHY OF CANADIAN SCIENCE FICTION AND FANTASY. Toronto: Hounslow, 1979. viii, 85 p.

17 Crombie, Jean Breakell, and Margaret Alice Webb, comps. "Bibliography of Canadiana, 1944." Mimeographed. Montreal: Sir George Williams College, 1945. 322 p. Index. SUPPLEMENT, 1944-1946. 1946. N. pag. Index.

Lists books in the possession of Sir George Williams College, now Concordia University, Montreal.

18 Cuddy, Mary Lou, and James J. Scott, comps. BRITISH COLUMBIA IN BOOKS: AN ANNOTATED BIBLIOGRAPHY. Vancouver: J.J. Douglas, 1974. 144 p. Index.

19 Daiches, David, ed. THE PENGUIN COMPANION TO LITERATURE IN BRITAIN AND THE COMMONWEALTH. London: Penguin Books, 1971. 576 p.

20 Edwards, Margaret H., John C.R. Lort, and Wendy J. Carmichael, comps. A BIBLIOGRAPHY OF BRITISH COLUMBIA: YEARS OF GROWTH, 1900-1950. Victoria, B.C.: Social Sciences Research Centre, University of Victoria, 1975. ix, 446 p. Index.

Lists books about British Columbia.

21   Fee, Margery, and Ruth Cawker, eds. CANADIAN FICTION: AN AN-
       NOTATED BIBLIOGRAPHY. Toronto: Peter Martin, 1976. xiii, 170 p.
       Index.

              Annotated guide to books by and about Canadian fiction
              writers.

22   Fulford, Robert, Dave Godfrey, and Abraham Rotstein, eds. READ CA-
       NADIAN: A BOOK ABOUT CANADIAN BOOKS. Toronto: James
       Lewis and Samuel, 1972. xi, 275 p. Bibliog.

              Handbook of bibliographical essays including W.H. New,
              "Modern Fiction," pp. 219-27.

23   Gnarowski, Michael, comp. A CONCISE BIBLIOGRAPHY OF ENGLISH-
       CANADIAN LITERATURE. 1973. Rev. ed. Toronto: McClelland and
       Stewart, 1978. 145 p.

              Useful introduction to primary and secondary material in books
              and articles; covers all genres and periods.

24   _____. "A Reference and Bibliographical Guide to the Study of English-
       Canadian Literature." Diss. University of Ottawa 1967. iii, 158 1.

25   Goggio, Emilio, Beatrice Corrigan, and Jack H. Parker, comps. A BIB-
       LIOGRAPHY OF CANADIAN CULTURAL PERIODICALS (ENGLISH AND
       FRENCH FROM COLONIAL TIMES TO 1950) IN CANADIAN LIBRARIES.
       Toronto: University of Toronto, Department of Italian, Spanish and Por-
       tuguese, 1955. 44 p.

26   Gottleib, Lois C., and Wendy Keitner, comps. "Bird at the Window:
       An Annotated Bibliography of Canadian Fiction Written by Women, 1970-
       1975." AMERICAN REVIEW OF CANADIAN STUDIES, 9 (Aut. 1979),
       3-56. Index.

27   Hamilton, Robert M., comp. CANADIAN QUOTATIONS AND PHRASES:
       LITERARY AND HISTORICAL. Introd. Bruce Hutchison. 1952. Rev.
       and enl., with Dorothy Shields. Toronto: McClelland and Stewart,
       1979. 1,063 p. Index.

              Organized by subject.

28   Harvard University. Library. CANADIAN HISTORY AND LITERATURE:
       CLASSIFICATION SCHEDULE, CLASSIFIED LISTING BY CALL NUMBER,
       ALPHABETICAL LISTING BY AUTHOR OR TITLE, CHRONOLOGICAL
       LISTING. Widener Library Shelflist, 20. Cambridge, Mass.: Harvard
       University, Library, distributed by Harvard University Press, 1968. 411 p.

29   Hayne, David M., and Antoine Sirois, comps. "Preliminary Bibliography of Comparative Canadian Literature." CANADIAN REVIEW OF COMPARATIVE LITERATURE, 1976-- . Annual.

30   Henderson, Diane, ed. GUIDE TO BASIC REFERENCE MATERIALS FOR CANADIAN LIBRARIES. 5th ed. Toronto: University of Toronto Press, for the Faculty of Library Science, 1977. 250 p. Index.

        In a three-ring binder.

31   Jarvi, Edith, Isabel McLean, and Catharine MacKenzie, comps. CANADIAN SELECTION: BOOKS AND PERIODICALS FOR LIBRARIES. [Toronto]: University of Toronto Press, for the Centre for Research in Librarianship, Faculty of Library Science, 1978. xii, 1,060 p. Index.

        Annotated.

32   Klinck, Carl F. CANADIAN LITERATURE IN ENGLISH: A SELECT READING LIST. Association for Commonwealth Literature and Language Studies, Bulletin no. 4, 1967. Leeds, Engl.: University of Leeds, 1968. 32 p.

33   Lecker, Robert A., and Jack David, eds. THE ANNOTATED BIBLIOGRAPHY OF CANADA'S MAJOR AUTHORS. Downsview, Ont.: ECW, 1979-- . Index.

        Volume 1 (1979) provides comprehensive bibliographies of primary and secondary material for Atwood (fiction), Laurence, MacLennan, Richler, and Gabrielle Roy. Volume 2 (1980), on five poets, includes Atwood and Leonard Cohen. Volume 3 (1981) treats Buckler, Davies, Knister, Mitchell, and Ross, while Volume 4 (1982), on four poets, includes Birney.

34   "Letters in Canada." UNIVERSITY OF TORONTO QUARTERLY, 1936-- . Annual.

        Review of Canadian writing. Also in book form, 1981-- .

35   Lochhead, Douglas, comp. BIBLIOGRAPHY OF CANADIAN BIBLIOGRAPHIES/BIBLIOGRAPHIE DES BIBLIOGRAPHIES CANADIENNES. 2nd ed., rev. and enl. Index comp. by Peter E. Grieg. Toronto: University of Toronto Press, published in association with the Bibliographic Society of Canada, 1972. xiv, 312 p. Index.

        A revision of no. 62.

36   McDonough, Irma, ed. CANADIAN BOOKS FOR CHILDREN/LIVRES CANADIENS POUR ENFANTS. 1976. Rev. ed. as CANADIAN BOOKS FOR YOUNG PEOPLE/LIVRES CANADIENS POUR LA JEUNESSE. Toronto: University of Toronto Press, 1978. x, 150 p.

        Annotated.

37   MANITOBA AUTHORS/ÉCRIVAINS DE MANITOBA. Pref. Guy Sylvestre. Introd. Wilfred Eggleston. Ottawa: National Library, 1970. N. pag. Index.

Provides biographical information and annotates the works of Manitoba writers.

38   Matthews, William, comp. CANADIAN DIARIES AND AUTOBIOGRAPHIES. Berkeley: University of California Press, 1950. 130 p. Index.

With brief annotations.

39   Miska, John. CANADIAN PROSE WRITTEN IN ENGLISH, 1833-1980: A BIBLIOGRAPHY OF SECONDARY MATERIAL. Lethbridge, Alta.: Microform Biblios, 1980. 292 p.

On microfiche.

40   Morley, Marjorie, comp. A BIBLIOGRAPHY OF MANITOBA FROM HOLDINGS IN THE LEGISLATIVE LIBRARY OF MANITOBA. Winnipeg: Legislative Library, 1970. 267 p.

41   Moyles, Robert G., and Catherine Siemens, comp. ENGLISH-CANADIAN LITERATURE: A STUDENT GUIDE AND ANNOTATED BIBLIOGRAPHY. Edmonton, Alta.: Athabascan, 1972. 44 p. Index.

Guide to basic reference tools.

42   Nesbitt, Bruce, ed. "Canadian Literature: An Annotated Bibliography/ Littérature Canadienne: Une Bibliographie avec Commentaire." JOURNAL OF CANADIAN FICTION, 1973-- . Annual.

Checklist of primary and secondary material in books and articles, continuing from no. 5; see also no. 73.

43   New, William H., comp. CRITICAL WRITINGS ON COMMONWEALTH LITERATURE: A SELECTIVE BIBLIOGRAPHY TO 1970, WITH A LIST OF THESES AND DISSERTATIONS. University Park: Pennsylvania State University Press, 1975. 333 p.

Lists books and articles.

44   PAPERS OF THE BIBLIOGRAPHICAL SOCIETY OF CANADA/CAHIERS DE LA SOCIÉTÉ BIBLIOGRAPHIQUE DU CANADA. Toronto: The Society, 1962-- . Annual.

45   Peel, Bruce Braden, comp. A BIBLIOGRAPHY OF THE PRAIRIE PROVINCES TO 1953 WITH BIBLIOGRAPHICAL INDEX. 1956. 2nd ed., rev. and enl. Toronto: University of Toronto Press, 1973. xxviii, 780 p. Indexes.

Lists books and pamphlets; author index includes biographical notes.

46   PERIODICALS IN THE SOCIAL SCIENCES AND HUMANITIES CURRENTLY RECEIVED BY CANADIAN LIBRARIES/INVENTAIRE DES PÉRIODIQUES DE SCIENCES SOCIALES ET D'HUMANITÉS QUE POSSÈDENT LES BIBLIO-THÈQUES CANADIENNES. 2 vols. Ottawa: National Library of Canada, 1968.

47   Pluscauskas, Martha, comp. CANADIAN SERIALS DIRECTORY/RÉPER-TOIRE DES PUBLICATIONS SÉRIÉES CANADIENNES. 1972. Rev. ed. Toronto: University of Toronto Press, 1977. xii, 534 p.

48   Robbins, John E., ed. ENCYCLOPEDIA CANADIANA. 1957-58. Rev. ed. 10 vols. Toronto: Grolier, 1975.

49   QUILL AND QUIRE. Toronto: Current Publications, 1935-- . Monthly.

Announces and reviews current publications.

50   Rhodenizer, Vernon Blair. CANADIAN LITERATURE IN ENGLISH. Mon-treal: Quality, 1965. 1,055 p.

A biobibliographical survey; for index, see no. 63.

51   Robinson, Jill M., ed. SEAS OF EARTH: AN ANNOTATED BIBLIOG-RAPHY OF SASKATCHEWAN LITERATURE AS IT RELATES TO THE EN-VIRONMENT. Canadian Plains Reports, 2. Regina: Canadian Plains Research Center, University of Regina, 1977. x, 139 p. Index.

Includes fiction (emphasizing Hiebert, McCourt, Mitchell, and Ross), travel literature, biography, and literary criticism.

52   Robinson, Paul. AFTER SURVIVAL: A TEACHER'S GUIDE TO CANADIAN RESOURCES. Toronto: Peter Martin, 1977. 329 p.

53   Rogers, Amos R. "American Recognition of Canadian Authors Writing in English." Diss. University of Michigan 1964. 818 l.

Includes a bibliography of book reviews, pp. 670-813.

54   Rogers, Helen, ed. INDIAN-INUIT AUTHORS: AN ANNOTATED BIB-LIOGRAPHY/AUTEURS INDIENS ET INUIT: BIBLIOGRAPHIE ANNOTÉE. Introd. Guy Sylvestre. Ottawa: National Library, 1974. 108 p.

Lists primary material, books and articles.

55   Rome, David. JEWS IN CANADIAN LITERATURE: A BIBLIOGRAPHY. 1962. Rev. ed. 2 vols. Montreal: Canadian Jewish Congress and Jewish Public Library, 1964.

Bibliographical essays on primary and secondary material; for supplement, see no. 56.

56   . RECENT CANADIAN JEWISH AUTHORS AND LA LANGUE FRANÇAISE: SUPPLEMENTARY TO JEWS IN CANADIAN LITERATURE. Pref. Joseph Kage. Montreal: Jewish Public Library, 1970. N. pag.

Supplement to no. 55.

57   , comp. A SELECTED BIBLIOGRAPHY OF JEWISH CANADIANA. Montreal: Canadian Jewish Congress and Jewish Public Library, 1959. N. pag.

58 Ryder, Dorothy E., ed. CANADIAN REFERENCE SOURCES: A SELECTIVE GUIDE. Ottawa: Canadian Library Association, 1973. x, 185 p. Index. Supplement, 1975. xi, 121 p.

Further annual supplements in CANADIAN LIBRARY JOURNAL.

59 Story, Norah. THE OXFORD COMPANION TO CANADIAN HISTORY AND LITERATURE. Toronto: Oxford University Press, 1967. xi, 935 p.

"Articles and bibliographical commentaries"; for supplement, see no. 65.

60 Stratford, Philip, comp. BIBLIOGRAPHY OF CANADIAN BOOKS IN TRANSLATION: FRENCH TO ENGLISH AND ENGLISH TO FRENCH/ BIBLIOGRAPHIE DE LIVRES CANADIENS TRADUITS DE L'ANGLAIS AU FRANÇAIS ET DU FRANÇAIS À L'ANGLAIS. 1975. 3rd ed. Ottawa: Canadian Federation for the Humanities, 1981.

61 Strickland, David, ed. "QUOTATIONS" FROM ENGLISH CANADIAN LITERATURE. Toronto: Modern Canadian Library, 1973. 189 p. Index.

Quotations organized by subject.

62 Tanghe, Raymond, comp. BIBLIOGRAPHY OF CANADIAN BIBLIOGRAPHIES/BIBLIOGRAPHIE DES BIBLIOGRAPHIES CANADIENNES. Toronto: University of Toronto Press, 1960. 206 p. Indexes.

With supplements in 1962, 1964, and 1966; revised as no. 35.

63 Thierman, Lois Mary, comp. INDEX TO VERNON BLAIR RHODENIZER'S CANADIAN LITERATURE IN ENGLISH. Edmonton: La Survivance, [1968]. ix, 469 p.

Author, title, and subject index to no. 50.

64   Tod, Dorothea D., and Audrey Cordingley, comps. "A Check List of
      Canadian Imprints/Catalogue d'Ouvrages Imprimés au Canada, 1900-1925."
      Mimeographed. Ottawa: Canadian Bibliographic Centre, Public Archives
      of Canada, 1950. 370 p.

65   Toye, William, gen. ed. SUPPLEMENT TO THE OXFORD COMPANION
      TO CANADIAN HISTORY AND LITERATURE. Toronto: Oxford Univer-
      sity Press, 1973. v, 318 p.

      Supplement to no. 59.

66   UNION LIST OF CANADIAN NEWSPAPERS HELD BY CANADIAN LI-
      BRARIES/LISTE COLLECTIVE DES JOURNAUX CANADIENS DISPONIBLES
      DANS LES BIBLIOTHÈQUES CANADIENNES. Ottawa: National Library,
      1977. 483 p. Index.

67   Wallace, William Stewart, comp. THE RYERSON IMPRINT: A CHECK-
      LIST OF THE BOOKS AND PAMPHLETS PUBLISHED BY THE RYERSON
      PRESS SINCE THE FOUNDATION OF THE HOUSE IN 1829. Toronto:
      Ryerson, 1954. 141 p.

68   _____, gen. ed. ENCYCLOPEDIA OF CANADA. 6 vols. Toronto:
      University Associates of Canada, 1935-37. NEWFOUNDLAND: SUP-
      PLEMENT. 1949. 104 p.

69   Watters, Reginald Eyre, comp. "Bibliography." In CANADIAN AN-
      THOLOGY. Ed. Carl F. Klinck and Reginald E. Watters. 1955. 3rd
      ed., rev. and enl. Toronto: Gage, 1974, pp. 646-721.

      A brief introduction to primary and secondary material in
      books and articles, covering all genres and periods.

70   _____, ed. A CHECKLIST OF CANADIAN LITERATURE AND BACK-
      GROUND MATERIALS 1628-1950: BEING A COMPREHENSIVE LIST OF
      THE BOOKS WHICH CONSTITUTE CANADIAN LITERATURE WRITTEN
      IN ENGLISH, TOGETHER WITH A SELECTIVE LIST OF OTHER BOOKS
      BY CANADIAN AUTHORS WHICH REVEAL THE BACKGROUNDS OF
      THAT LITERATURE. 1959. 2nd ed., rev. and enl. Toronto: University
      of Toronto Press, 1972. xxiv, 1,085 p. Indexes.

      Essential reference tool. The second edition increases coverage
      through 1960.

71   Watters, Reginald Eyre, and Inglis Freeman Bell, comps. ON CANADIAN
      LITERATURE 1806-1960: A CHECK LIST OF ARTICLES, BOOKS, AND
      THESES ON ENGLISH-CANADIAN LITERATURE, ITS AUTHORS, AND
      LANGUAGE. Toronto: University of Toronto Press, 1966. ix, 165 p.

      Essential reference tool.

72   Woodsworth, A., comp. THE "ALTERNATIVE" PRESS IN CANADA: A CHECKLIST OF UNDERGROUND, REVOLUTIONARY, RADICAL, AND OTHER ALTERNATIVE SERIALS FROM 1960. Toronto: University of Toronto Press, 1972. xi, 74 p. Bibliog. Indexes.

73   Zimmering, Suzann, Bruce Nesbitt, et al., comps. "Canadian Literature 1971: An Annotated Bibliography." ESSAYS ON CANADIAN WRITING, 9 (1977-78), 190-326. Index.

       Fills the gap in coverage created by the transition from no. 5 to no. 42.

B. BIOGRAPHICAL REFERENCES

International biographical dictionaries such as CONTEMPORARY AUTHORS and CONTEMPORARY WRITERS are not listed here but should also be consulted.

74   Brown, George W., David M. Hayne, and Francess G. Halpenny, eds. DICTIONARY OF CANADIAN BIOGRAPHY. Toronto: University of Toronto Press, 1966-- .

       An essential reference tool. Volumes 1-4 (1000-1800) and 9-10 (1861-1880) have been published. By 1985, the DICTIONARY should be complete to the end of the 1880s.

75   "Canadian Biographies: Artists, Authors, and Musicians." 3 vols. Mimeographed. Ottawa: Canadian Library Association, 1948-52.

       First volume entitled simply "Canadian Biographies: Artists and Authors."

76   THE CANADIAN WHO'S WHO, WITH WHICH IS INCORPORATED CANADIAN MEN AND WOMEN OF THE TIME: A BIOGRAPHICAL DICTIONARY OF NOTABLE LIVING MEN AND WOMEN. 1910. 14th ed. Toronto: University of Toronto Press, 1979. 1,089 p. Triennial. Semi-annual supplements.

77   CREATIVE CANADA: A BIOGRAPHICAL DICTIONARY OF TWENTIETH-CENTURY CREATIVE AND PERFORMING ARTISTS. 2 vols. Toronto: University of Toronto Press, 1971-72. Index.

78   Hind-Smith, Joan. THREE VOICES: THE LIVES OF MARGARET LAURENCE, GABRIELLE ROY, AND FREDERICK PHILIP GROVE. Toronto: Clarke, Irwin, 1975. xii, 235 p. Bibliog. Index.

79   Jones, Joseph, and Johanna Jones. AUTHORS AND AREAS OF CANADA.

People and Places in World-English Literature, no. 1. Austin, Tex.: Steck-Vaughn, 1970. xiv, 82 p.

Brief biobibliographical sketches.

80   Lonn, George. CANADIAN PROFILES: PORTRAITS IN CHARCOAL AND PROSE, OF CONTEMPORARY CANADIANS OF OUTSTANDING ACHIEVEMENT. Introd. Louis St. Laurent. Toronto: Pitt, 1965. 256 p.

Includes only a few authors.

81   Melanson, Lloyd J. THIRTY-FOUR ATLANTIC PROVINCES AUTHORS. Halifax: Atlantic Provinces Library Association, 1979. 38 p.

Includes Buckler, Horwood, Montgomery, and Raddall.

82   Middleton, Jesse Edgar, and W. Scott Downs, eds. NATIONAL ENCY-CLOPEDIA OF CANADIAN BIOGRAPHY. 2 vols. Toronto: Dominion, 1935–37. Index.

83   Milner, Philip, ed. NOVA SCOTIA WRITES: A DESCRIPTIVE LISTING OF CONTEMPORARY NOVA SCOTIA WRITERS. Antigonish, N.S.: FORMAC, 1979. 100 p.

Brief biobibliographical entries.

84   Rhodenizer, Vernon B. AT THE SIGN OF THE HAND AND PEN: NOVA-SCOTIAN AUTHORS. 2nd ed. Toronto: Canadiana House, 1968. 42 p.

Brief biobibliographical sketches.

85   Roberts, Charles G.D., and Arthur L. Tunnell, eds. A STANDARD DICTIONARY OF CANADIAN BIOGRAPHY: THE CANADIAN WHO WAS WHO. 2 vols. Toronto: Trans-Canada, 1934–38.

Biographies of Canadians dead before 1937.

86   Sylvestre, Guy, Brandon Conron, and Carl F. Klinck, eds. CANADIAN WRITERS: A BIOGRAPHICAL DICTIONARY/ÉCRIVAINS CANADIENS: UN DICTIONNAIRE BIOGRAPHIQUE. 1964. Rev. and enl. Toronto: Ryerson, 1966. xviii, 186 p. Index.

Standard reference.

87   Taylor, Charles. SIX JOURNEYS: A CANADIAN PATTERN: BRIGA-DIER JAMES SUTHERLAND BROWN, BISHOP WILLIAM WHITE, JAMES HOUSTON, HERBERT NORMAN, EMILY CARR, SCOTT SYMONS. To-ronto: Anansi, 1977. vi, 254 p. Bibliog.

88   Thomas, Clara. CANADIAN NOVELISTS, 1920-25. Toronto: Longmans, Green, 1946. 129 p. Index.

      Brief biobibliographical sketches, with some reference to the writings.

89   Wallace, W. Stewart. THE DICTIONARY OF CANADIAN BIOGRAPHY. 1926. 4th ed., rev. and enl. by W.A. McKay as THE MACMILLAN DICTIONARY OF CANADIAN BIOGRAPHY. Toronto: Macmillan, 1978. 914 p. Bibliog.

90   _____. A DICTIONARY OF NORTH AMERICAN AUTHORS DECEASED BEFORE 1950. Toronto: Ryerson, 1951. 525 p.

91   Whittaker, Ted, ed. THE WRITERS' UNION OF CANADA: A DIRECTORY OF MEMBERS. Toronto: The Union, 1981. xv, 293 p.

92   WHO'S WHO IN CANADA: AN ILLUSTRATED BIOGRAPHICAL RECORD OF MEN AND WOMEN OF THE TIME. Toronto: International Press, 1911-- . Biennial.

For biographical references, see also nos. 37, 50, 135, and 203.

C. INDEXES TO SERIAL PUBLICATIONS, ANTHOLOGIES, AND COLLECTIONS

93   Adshead, G.R., comp. CANADIAN FORUM, A MONTHLY JOURNAL OF LITERATURE AND PUBLIC AFFAIRS. INDEX, VOLS. 1-9, 1920-29. Ottawa: Canadian Library Association, 1973. 84 p.

94   Armitage, Andrew, and Nancy Tudor, eds. CANADIAN ESSAY AND LITERATURE INDEX. 1973-1975. 3 vols. Toronto: University of Toronto Press, 1975-77.

      Indexes selected books and periodicals; continues from no. 107.

95   CANADIAN PERIODICAL INDEX/INDEX DE PÉRIODIQUES CANADIENS. Ottawa: Canadian Library Association, 1938-- . Monthly.

      Title varies; sometimes CANADIAN INDEX TO PERIODICALS AND DOCUMENTARY FILMS. Essential reference tool; for earlier material, see no. 97.

96   Clever, Glenn, Burris Devanney, and George Martin, comps. AN INDEX TO THE CONTENTS OF CANADIAN LITERATURE NUMBERS 1-50 WITH AN ADDENDUM (P. 153) FOR NUMBERS 51-54. Ottawa: Golden Dog, 1973. 170 p.

97   Faxon, Frederick W., Mary E. Bates, and Anne C. Sutherland, eds.
       CUMULATED MAGAZINE SUBJECT INDEX, 1907-1949: A CUMULA-
       TION OF THE F.W. FAXON COMPANY'S ANNUAL MAGAZINE SUB-
       JECT INDEX. 2 vols. Boston: G.K. Hall, 1964.

       For the period preceding that covered by no. 95.

98   Harris, J. Robert, ed. THE MALAHAT REVIEW: INDEX 1967-1971,
       WITH A BRIEF HISTORICAL NOTE BY ROBIN SKELTON. Victoria:
       Morriss Printing Co., 1972. 45 p.

99   Ho, Kwai Yiu, ed. THE CANADIAN NEWSPAPER INDEX. Toronto:
       Information Access, 1977-- . Monthly, cumulated.

100   "Index for Issue 1: Autumn 1956 to Issue 20: Summer 1961." TAMA-
       RACK REVIEW, 21 (Sum. 1961), 92-116; "Index for Issue 21: Autumn
       1961 to Issue 41: Autumn 1966." TAMARACK REVIEW, 42 (Wint. 1967),
       95-112.

101   Leverette, Clarke E., comp. "An Index to Little Magazines of Ontario."
       3 vols. Mimeographed. London, Ont.: Killaly, 1972-74.

102   McLaren, Duncan, ed. QUILL AND QUIRE INDEX. Toronto: McLaren
       Micropublishing, 1973. 93 p.

103   Mitchell, Peter, comp. "An Index to MACLEAN'S MAGAZINE 1914-
       1937." Mimeographed. Ottawa: Canadian Library Association, 1965.
       140 p.

104   QUEEN'S QUARTERLY: 1893-1953. INDEX, VOLS. I-LX. Kingston,
       Ont.: Queen's Quarterly Office, Queen's University, 1956. 132 p.
       CUMULATIVE INDEX 1954-1968. N.p.: n.p., n.d. 42 p.

105   Reeve, Phyllis, comp. "Index to Numbers 1-18." CANADIAN FICTION
       MAGAZINE, No. 19 (Aut. 1975), pp. 105-22; Jones, Joe, comp. "Index--
       Numbers 19-22." CANADIAN FICTION MAGAZINE, No. 23 (Aut.
       1976), pp. 139-44.

106   SHORT STORY INDEX: COMPILED FROM THE CANADIAN PERIODICAL
       INDEX 1938-47. Ottawa: Canadian Library Association, 1967.

107   Sowby, Joyce, et al., eds. CANADIAN ESSAYS AND COLLECTIONS
       INDEX, 1971-1972. Ottawa: Canadian Library Association, 1976. 219 p.

       Subject, author, and title index for selected works; continued
       by no. 94.

D. INDEXES TO THESES

International indexes like DISSERTATION ABSTRACTS INTERNATIONAL are not listed here but should also be consulted.

108   Bruchet, Susan Jaques, and Gwynneth Evans, comps. THESES IN CANADA: A GUIDE TO SOURCES OF INFORMATION ABOUT THESES COMPLETED OR IN PREPARATION/THÈSES AU CANADA: GUIDE SUR LES SOURCES DOCUMENTAIRES RELATIVES AUX THÈSES COMPLÉTÉES OU EN COURS DE RÉDACTION. Ottawa: National Library of Canada, 1978. 25 p.

109   CANADIAN THESES ON MICROFILM/THÈSES CANADIENNES SUR MI-CROFILM. Ottawa: National Library, 1969. 251 p.

110   CANADIAN THESES/THÈSES CANADIENNES 1947-1960. 2 vols. Ottawa: National Library, 1973. Index. Annual supplement.

> Continues from no. 113.

111   Gnarowski, Michael, comp. THESES AND DISSERTATIONS IN CANADIAN LITERATURE (ENGLISH): A PRELIMINARY CHECK LIST. Ottawa: Golden Dog, 1975. 41 p.

> Listed according to author studied and according to theme.

112   Klinck, Carl F., comp. "Theses in Canadian Literature." CANADIAN LITERATURE, 1960-71. Annual.

> Continued by no. 116.

113   Lamb, W. Kaye, ed. CANADIAN GRADUATE THESES IN THE HUMANITIES AND SOCIAL SCIENCES, 1921-46/THÈSES DES GRADUÉS CANADIENS DANS LES HUMANITÉS ET LES SCIENCES SOCIALES. Ottawa: Canadian Bibliographic Centre, 1948. 194 p.

> Continued by no. 110.

114   Mills, Judy, and Irene Dombra, comps. UNIVERSITY OF TORONTO DOCTORAL THESES, 1897-1967. Toronto: University of Toronto Press, 1968. xi, 186 p. SUPPLEMENT for 1968-75. 1977. 166 p.

115   Naaman, Antoine, comp. RÉPERTOIRE DES THÈSES LITTÉRAIRES CA-NADIENNES DE 1921 À 1976. Sherbrooke, Que.: Éditions Naaman, 1978. 453 p. Index.

> Lists theses on French- and English-Canadian literature.

116   "Post-Graduate Theses in Canadian Literatures: English and English-French Comparative." JOURNAL OF CANADIAN FICTION, 1972-- .

   Continues from no. 112.

For indexes to theses, see also no. 43.

E. MANUSCRIPTS AND SPECIAL COLLECTIONS

117   Association of Canadian Archivists. DIRECTORY OF CANADIAN RECORDS AND MANUSCRIPT REPOSITORIES. Ottawa: Bonanza, 1977. iii, 115 p. Index.

118   Fyfe, Janet, and Raymond H. Deutsch, comps. "Directory of Special Collections in Canadian Libraries." 2 vols. Mimeographed. Ottawa: Canadian Library Association, 1968.

119   Harlowe, Dorothy, comp. A CATALOGUE OF CANADIAN MANUSCRIPTS COLLECTED BY LORNE PIERCE AND PRESENTED TO QUEEN'S UNIVERSITY. Toronto: Ryerson, 1946. xii, 164 p. Index.

120   Morse, William Inglis, ed. THE CANADIAN COLLECTION AT HARVARD UNIVERSITY. 6 vols. Cambridge, Mass.: Harvard University, 1944-49.

121   UNION LIST OF MANUSCRIPTS IN CANADIAN REPOSITORIES/CATALOGUE COLLECTIF DES MANUSCRITS DES ARCHIVES CANADIENNES. 1968. Rev. ed. 2 vols. Ottawa: Public Archives, 1975. Supplements 1976, 1977-78.

   Lists and describes manuscripts and records in Canadian archives; useful reference tool.

2. LITERARY HISTORY, CRITICISM, AND THEORY

A. MONOGRAPHS

122   Ballstadt, Carl, ed. with introd. THE SEARCH FOR ENGLISH-CANADIAN
       LITERATURE: AN ANTHOLOGY OF CRITICAL ARTICLES FROM THE
       NINETEENTH AND EARLY TWENTIETH CENTURIES. Literature of Canada:
       Poetry and Prose in Reprint, 16. Toronto: University of Toronto Press,
       1975. I, 214 p.

>   Little on twentieth-century literature but includes a previously
>   unpublished piece by Knister.

123   Brown, Edward Killoran. RESPONSES AND EVALUATIONS: ESSAYS
       ON CANADA. Ed. with introd. by David Staines. New Canadian
       Library, no. 137. Toronto: McClelland and Stewart, 1977. xviii,
       314 p.

>   Reprints newspaper articles on Grove, de la Roche, and
>   Callaghan, and general articles on Canadian literature. In-
>   cludes nos. 237-39.

124   Cameron, Donald A. CONVERSATIONS WITH CANADIAN NOVELISTS.
       1 vol. in 2 parts. Toronto: Macmillan, 1973. 159, 160 p. Bibliog.

>   Interviews with twenty English- and French-Canadian novelists.

125   CANADIAN LITERATURE TODAY: A SERIES OF BROADCASTS SPON-
       SORED BY THE CANADIAN BROADCASTING CORPORATION. Toronto:
       University of Toronto Press, 1938. 70 p.

>   Includes Child on fiction, Grove on literary criticism, and
>   others on contemporary literature, biography, humor, the lit-
>   erature of new Canadians, and other topics.

126   Capone, Giovanna. CANADA, Il VILLAGGIO DELLA TERRA: LETTER-
       ATURA CANADESE DI LINGUA INGLESE. Bologna: Pàtron Editore,
       1978. 213 p. Index.

Includes general discussion and an examination of McLuhan, MacLennan, Richler, Leonard Cohen, and Atwood.

127   Cappon, Paul, ed. IN OUR HOUSE: SOCIAL PERSPECTIVES ON CA-
        NADIAN LITERATURE. Toronto: McClelland and Stewart, 1978. 207 p.
        Bibliog.

        Attempts to provide "a sociology of Canadian literature."

128   Chadbourne, Richard, and Hallvard Dahlie, eds. THE NEW LAND: STUDIES
        IN A LITERARY THEME. Calgary: Wilfrid Laurier University Press, for
        Calgary Institute for the Humanities, 1978. viii, 160 p.

        Discusses English- and French-Canadian literature; includes
        an article by Wiebe and one on Lowry.

129   Codignola, Luca, ed. CANADIANA: ASPETTI DELLA STORIA E DELLA
        LETTERATURA CANADESE. Venice: Marsilio, 1978. 159 p.

        Includes articles on Atwood and MacLennan.

130   Collin, William Edward. THE WHITE SAVANNAHS. Toronto: Macmillan,
        1936. 288 p.; rpt., Introd. Germaine Warkentin. Literature of Canada:
        Poetry and Prose in Reprint, 15. Toronto: University of Toronto Press,
        1975. 329 p.

        Mainly on poetry; includes an appendix on Grove.

131   CONNECTIONS: WRITERS AND THE LAND. Winnipeg: Manitoba
        School Library Audio-Visual Association, 1974. viii, 136 p. Index.

        Includes articles on Hiebert, McClung, Niven, Wiebe, and
        Wiseman.

132   CREATIVE LITERATURE IN CANADA: SYMPOSIUM. Toronto: Ontario
        Ministry of Colleges and Universities, 1974. 56 p. Bibliog.

        Includes Marion Engel, "Canadian Writing Today," pp. 2-9.

133   Cude, Wilfred. A DUE SENSE OF DIFFERENCES: AN EVALUATIVE
        APPROACH TO CANADIAN LITERATURE. Lanham, Md.: University
        Press of America, 1980. xix, 216 p.

        Includes articles on Canadian literature and criticism, on
        Ross (3784-85), Davies (1341-43), Atwood (656), and
        Richler (3727).

134   Dahlie, Hallvard. STRANGE TRAFFICKING AND CURIOUS MERCHAN-
        DISE: THE STATE OF CANADIAN FICTION. AN INAUGURAL PRO-
        FESSORIAL LECTURE IN THE FACULTY OF HUMANITIES UNIVERSITY

OF CALGARY PRESENTED ON JANUARY 16, 1979. Calgary: Faculty of Humanities, 1979. 16 p.

135   Davey, Frank. FROM THERE TO HERE: A GUIDE TO ENGLISH-CANADIAN LITERATURE SINCE 1960. Our Nature--Our Voices, 2. Erin, Ont.: Porcépic, 1974. 288 p. Bibliog. Index.

        Biographical-critical sketches of individual authors, with check-lists of primary and secondary material; a sequel to no. 203.

136   Daymond, Douglas, and Leslie Monkman, eds. CANADIAN NOVELISTS AND THE NOVEL. Ottawa: Borealis, 1981. 284 p.

        Includes nos. 453, 637, 1065, 1243, 2237, 2302, 2916, 2979, 3651, 4228, 4230, 4279, and 5186.

137   Deacon, William Arthur. POTEEN: A POT-POURRI OF CANADIAN ESSAYS. Ottawa: Graphic, 1926. 241 p.

        Includes some discussion of "The Modern Era" and of "The First Histories of Canadian Literature."

138   Dimić, Milan V., and Juan Ferraté, eds. ACTES DU VII^{e}CONGRÈS DE L'ASSOCIATION INTERNATIONALE DE LITTÉRATURE COMPARÉE/ PROCEEDINGS OF THE 7TH CONGRESS OF THE INTERNATIONAL COMPARATIVE LITERATURE ASSOCIATION, I: LITTÉRATURES AMERI-CAINES: DÉPENDANCE, INDÉPENDANCE, INTERDÉPENDANCE/LITER-ATURES OF AMERICA: DEPENDENCE, INDEPENDENCE, INTERDEPEN-DENCE. Stuttgart: Bieber, 1979. 562 p.

        Includes articles on English-Canadian literature in a comparative context.

139   Dooley, David Joseph. MORAL VISION IN THE CANADIAN NOVEL. Toronto: Clarke, Irwin, 1979. 184 p. Index.

        Includes analyses of Leacock, Grove, Sara Jeannette Duncan, Ross, Callaghan, MacLennan, Richler, Davies, Laurence, and Atwood; reprints nos. 286 and 980.

140   Dudek, Louis. SELECTED ESSAYS AND CRITICISM. Ottawa: Tecumseh, 1978. ix, 380 p.

        Includes nos. 290-91, 1843, and 4601.

141   Duffy, Dennis. GARDENS, COVENANTS, EXILES: LOYALISM IN THE LITERATURE OF UPPER CANADA/ONTARIO. Toronto: University of Toronto Press, 1982. x, 160 p. Index.

        Nineteenth- and twentieth-century writers, including de la Roche, Hood, and Symons.

142   Eggleston, Wilfred. THE FRONTIER & CANADIAN LETTERS. Toronto: Ryerson, 1957. viii, 164 p. Index.; rpt., Introd. Douglas O. Spettigue. Carleton Library, no. 102. Toronto: McClelland and Stewart, 1977. xxi, 164 p. Index.

Discusses the literary environment, particularly of nineteenth-century Canada but with some reference to the twentieth century.

143   Egoff, Sheila A. THE REPUBLIC OF CHILDHOOD: A CRITICAL GUIDE TO CANADIAN CHILDREN'S LITERATURE IN ENGLISH. Toronto: Oxford University Press, 1967. 287 p. Bibliog. Index.

144   Golysheva, Alisa Ivanovna. SOVREMENNAĬA ANGLO-KANADSKAĬA LITERATURA. Moscow: Vysshaja shkola, 1973. 125 p.

145   Granatstein, J.L., and Peter Stevens, eds. FORUM: CANADIAN LIFE AND LETTERS 1920-70: SELECTIONS FROM THE CANADIAN FORUM. Toronto: University of Toronto Press, 1972. xv, 431 p.

Reprints over 250 poems, short stories, and articles, providing information on political and cultural background with some literary analysis--mainly of poetry.

146   Halpenny, Francess G., ed. EDITING CANADIAN TEXTS: PAPERS GIVEN AT THE CONFERENCE ON EDITORIAL PROBLEMS, UNIVERSITY OF TORONTO, NOVEMBER 1972. Toronto: A.M. Hakkert, 1975. 97 p.

Includes general discussion, nineteenth-century examples, and D. Pacey on the editing of Grove's letters.

147   Harger-Grinling, Virginia, and Terry Goldie, eds. PAPERS FROM THE CONFERENCE ON VIOLENCE IN THE CANADIAN NOVEL SINCE 1960. St. John's, Nfld.: Memorial University, 1982.

148   Harrison, Dick. UNNAMED COUNTRY: THE STRUGGLE FOR A CANADIAN PRAIRIE FICTION. Edmonton: University of Alberta Press, 1977. 250 p. Bibliog.

Traces the development of prairie fiction from the nineteenth century to the contemporary period.

149   _____, ed. CROSSING FRONTIERS: PAPERS IN CANADIAN AND AMERICAN WESTERN LITERATURE. Edmonton: University of Alberta Press, 1979. 174 p.

Includes material by Kroetsch (no. 2241) and Kreisel.

150 Heath, Jeffrey M., ed. PROFILES IN CANADIAN LITERATURE. 2 vols. Toronto: Dundurn, 1980. Bibliog.

Introductions to twenty-seven Canadian writers.

151 Jones, Douglas G. BUTTERFLY ON ROCK: A STUDY OF THEMES AND IMAGES IN CANADIAN LITERATURE. Toronto: University of Toronto Press, 1970. 197 p. Index.

"The approach here is cultural and psychological rather than purely aesthetic or literary."

152 Jones, Joseph, and Johanna Jones. CANADIAN FICTION. Twayne's World Authors Series, 630. Boston: Twayne, 1981. 180 p. Bibliog. Index.

153 Kesterton, Wilfred H. A HISTORY OF JOURNALISM IN CANADA. Foreword by Wilfred Eggleston. Carleton Library, no. 36. Toronto: McClelland and Stewart, 1967. ix, 304 p. Bibliog. Index.

154 Klinck, Carl Frederick, gen. ed. LITERARY HISTORY OF CANADA: CANADIAN LITERATURE IN ENGLISH. 1965. 2nd ed., rev. and enl. 3 vols. Toronto: University of Toronto Press, 1976. Bibliog. Index.

Standard literary history of English Canada.

155 Liljegren, Sten Bodvar. CANADIAN STUDIES IN SWEDEN. Canadian Essays and Studies, 6. Upsala, Sweden: A.-B. Lundequistska Bokhandeln, 1961. 39 p.

Discusses mainly nineteenth-century and native-language writing.

156 Logan, John Daniel, and Donald G. French. HIGHWAYS OF CANADIAN LITERATURE: A SYNOPTIC INTRODUCTION TO THE LITERARY HISTORY OF CANADA (ENGLISH) FROM 1760 TO 1924. Toronto: McClelland and Stewart, 1924. 418 p. Index.

Includes a brief consideration of some early twentieth-century writers.

157 McClung, Mollie G. WOMEN IN CANADIAN LIFE: LITERATURE. Introd. George Woodcock. Toronto: Fitzhenry and Whiteside, 1977. 96 p. Bibliog. Index.

Discusses writers and their works, with special emphasis on Laurence and Atwood; for use in high schools.

158 MacCulloch, Clare. THE NEGLECTED GENRE: THE SHORT STORY IN CANADA. Guelph, Ont.: Alive, 1973. 100 p. Bibliog.

Examines stories by E.W. Thomson, C.G.D. Roberts, D.C. Scott, Leacock, Grove, Callaghan, P.K. Page, Ralph Gustafson, and Irving Layton, and criticism by Frye, Desmond Pacey, and D.G. Jones.

159   MacMechan, Archibald McKellar.   HEAD-WATERS OF CANADIAN LIT-ERATURE.   Toronto: McClelland and Stewart, 1924.   247 p.   Index; rpt. Toronto: Canadiana House, 1968.   247 p.   Index.

Mainly nineteenth-century literature.

160   Mandel, Eli.   ANOTHER TIME.   Three Solitudes: Contemporary Literary Criticism in Canada, 3.   Erin, Ont.: Porcépic, 1977.   iv, 160 p.

Includes discussion of Kroetsch, Laurence, Mitchell, Grove, Watson, ethnic writers, and literary criticism.

161   _____, ed. with introd.   CONTEXTS OF CANADIAN CRITICISM.   Patterns of Literary Criticism.   Toronto: University of Toronto Press, 1971.   vii, 304 p.   Bibliog.   Index.

Reprints significant essays revealing "The Social and Historical Context," "The Theoretical Context," and "Patterns of Criticism"; includes nos. 380, 540-41, and material by Frye, McLuhan, and Kreisel (no. 2200).

162   Marshall, Tom.   HARSH AND LOVELY LAND: THE MAJOR CANADIAN POETS AND THE MAKING OF A CANADIAN TRADITION.   Vancouver: University of British Columbia Press, 1979.   184 p.   Index.

The chapters on Douglas LePan, Leonard Cohen, Ondaatje, MacEwen, Atwood, and Helwig include discussion of their fiction.

163   Mathews, Robin D.   CANADIAN LITERATURE: SURRENDER OR REVO-LUTION.   Ed. G. Dexter.   Toronto: Steel Rail, 1978.   xi, 250 p. Index.

Includes articles on Grove, MacLennan (no. 3062), Callaghan (no. 1099), Mitchell, Atwood (no. 705), and on the political and cultural context of Canadian literature (nos. 413, 415).

164   Mensenkampff, Ursula V.   DIE "GRENSE" IN DER ANGLOKANADISCHEN LITERATUR.   Riga, USSR: Ernst Plates, 1935.   89 p.   Bibliog.   Index.

Includes early twentieth-century novelists.

165   Moisan, Clement.   L'ÂGE DE LA LITTÉRATURE CANADIENNE: ESSAI. Montreal: HMH, 1969.   ix, 193 p.   Bibliog.   Index.

Includes French- and English-Canadian writers.

166   Monkman, Leslie. A NATIVE HERITAGE: IMAGES OF THE INDIAN IN ENGLISH-CANADIAN LITERATURE. Toronto: University of Toronto Press, 1981. xiii, 193 p. Index.

167   Morgan-Powell, Samuel. THIS CANADIAN LITERATURE: BEING AN ADDRESS DELIVERED BEFORE THE TORONTO BRANCH OF THE CA-NADIAN AUTHORS' ASSOCIATION AT TORONTO, ON MAY 11TH, 1940. [Toronto]: Macmillan, [1940]. 14 p.

168   Moss, John G. PATTERNS OF ISOLATION IN ENGLISH CANADIAN FICTION. Toronto: McClelland and Stewart, 1974. 256 p. Bibliog. Index.

> Discusses Raddall, Wilson, Ross, Watson, Bruce, Grove, Garner, Callaghan, MacLennan, and others.

169   _____. A READER'S GUIDE TO THE CANADIAN NOVEL. Toronto: McClelland and Stewart, 1981. 399 p. Index.

> Introduces two hundred Canadian novels.

170   _____. SEX AND VIOLENCE IN THE CANADIAN NOVEL: THE AN-CESTRAL PRESENT. Toronto: McClelland and Stewart, 1977. 326 p. Bibliog. Index.

> General discussion, and chapters on Munro, Laurence, Davies, Atwood and Richler, Leonard Cohen, Matt Cohen, Godfrey, Peter Such and Wiebe, Simpson and Kroetsch.

171   _____, ed. THE CANADIAN NOVEL: HERE AND NOW, A CRITICAL ANTHOLOGY. Toronto: NC, 1978. 204 p.

> Includes original and reprinted articles on Atwood, Davies, Laurence, Munro, Richler, and Wiebe; reprints nos. 697, 1374, 1380, 2370, 2386, 3441, and 4256.

172   _____, ed. with introd. BEGINNINGS: A CRITICAL ANTHOLOGY. The Canadian Novel, Vol. 2. Toronto: NC, 1980. 191 p.

> Both new and reprinted articles on early Canadian fiction up to and including Leacock. Reprints nos. 2557, 4547, and 5170 among others.

173   New, William H. ARTICULATING WEST: ESSAYS ON PURPOSE AND FORM IN MODERN CANADIAN LITERATURE. Toronto: New, 1972. xxvi, 282 p. Index.

> Includes general discussion (nos. 435, 440), a new article on Kroetsch, and reprinted articles on Niven (no. 3497), Mitchell (no. 3199), Ross (no. 3796), Wilson (nos. 4295-96), MacLennan

(nos. 3065–66), Richler (no. 3743), Lowry (nos. 2762–63), and Laurence (no. 2365).

174 Northey, Margot. THE HAUNTED WILDERNESS: THE GOTHIC AND GROTESQUE IN CANADIAN FICTION. Toronto: University of Toronto Press, 1976. 131 p. Bibliog. Index.

Includes chapters on Ostenso's WILD GEESE (1925) and Atwood's SURFACING (1972), Watson's DOUBLE HOOK (1959), Richler's COCKSURE (1968), and Leonard Cohen's BEAUTIFUL LOSERS (1966).

175 O'Flaherty, Patrick. THE ROCK OBSERVED: STUDIES IN THE LITERA-TURE OF NEWFOUNDLAND. Toronto: University of Toronto Press, 1979. xxx, 222 p. Index.

176 Pacey, Desmond. CREATIVE WRITING IN CANADA: A SHORT HISTORY OF ENGLISH-CANADIAN LITERATURE. 1952. Rev. and enl. ed. Toronto: Ryerson, 1961. 314 p. Bibliog. Index.

Includes chapters on early twentieth-century fiction and fiction since 1920.

177 _____. ESSAYS IN CANADIAN CRITICISM 1938-1968. Toronto: Ryerson, 1969. 294 p. Index.

Reprints general articles on Canadian literature (nos. 446, 448–50, 453–54, 457) and articles on Grove (no. 1869), Leacock (no. 2560), Wilson (no. 4299), and Leonard Cohen (no. 1213).

178 Paolucci, Ann, and R.J. Schoeck, eds. CANADA. Review of National Literatures, vol. 7. New York: Griffon House, for the Council on National Literatures, 1976. 164 p.

Includes nos. 257, 461, 531, 2384, and 4196.

179 Park, Julian, ed. THE CULTURE OF CONTEMPORARY CANADA. Ithaca, N.Y.: Cornell University Press, 1957. xv, 404 p. Bibliog. Index.

Includes Roy Daniells, "Poetry and the Novel," pp. 1–80.

180 Parr, John, ed. with introd. SPEAKING OF WINNIPEG. Winnipeg: Queenston House, 1974. 151 p.

Interviews with McLuhan, Laurence, Ludwig and others.

181 Pearce, Jon, ed. TWELVE VOICES: INTERVIEWS WITH CANADIAN POETS. Ottawa: Borealis, 1981. vii, 202 p.

Includes Helwig, MacEwen, and Ondaatje.

182   Phelps, Arthur Leonard. CANADIAN WRITERS. Toronto: McClelland and Stewart, 1951. vii, 119 p. Bibliogs.

>   Includes chapters on Callaghan, Grove, Raddall, Leacock, MacLennan, Montgomery, Mitchell, Birney (as poet).

183   Pierce, Lorne Albert. A CANADIAN NATION. Toronto: Ryerson, 1960. 42 p.

>   Includes some discussion of literature.

184   _____. ENGLISH CANADIAN LITERATURE 1882-1932. Ottawa: [Royal Society of Canada], 1932. 7 p.

185   _____. AN OUTLINE OF CANADIAN LITERATURE (FRENCH AND ENGLISH). Toronto: Ryerson, 1927. 251 p. Index.

>   Includes early humorists, journalists, novelists.

186   _____. UNEXPLORED FIELDS OF CANADIAN LITERATURE. Toronto: Ryerson, 1932. 31 p.

>   Discusses literary criticism, biography, autobiography, belles lettres.

187   Raudsepp, Enn. "Canadian Prairie Fiction." Mimeographed. Montreal: McGill University, 1975. 43 p. Bibliog.

188   RESOURCE GUIDES FOR THE TEACHING OF CANADIAN LITERATURE. N.p.: Coach House, for Writers' Development Trust, 1977.

>   A series of booklets, from thirty to two hundred pages each; bibliographic teaching tools for elementary and secondary school teachers. The series is organized by such themes as the north, immigrant experience, women, and biculturalism.

189   Rhodenizer, Vernon Blair. A HANDBOOK OF CANADIAN LITERATURE. Ottawa: Graphic, 1930. 295 p.

>   Emphasis is on nineteenth-century writers.

190   Ricou, Laurence. VERTICAL MAN/HORIZONTAL WORLD: MAN AND LANDSCAPE IN CANADIAN PRAIRIE FICTION. Vancouver: University of British Columbia Press, 1973. xii, 163 p. Bibliog. Index.

>   Individual chapters on Stead, Grove, Ostenso, Ross, and Mitchell; discussion of other prairie writers and of the critics; reprints nos. 474-75 in a different form.

190a   Riedel, Walter E. DAS LITERARISCHE KANADABILD: EINE STUDIE ZUR REZEPTION KANADISCHER LITERATUR IN DEUTSCHER ÜBERSETZUNG. SGAK, 92. Bonn: Bouvier, 1980. 140 p.

191   Ross, Malcolm, ed. THE ARTS IN CANADA: A STOCK-TAKING AT MID-CENTURY. Toronto: Macmillan, 1958. v, 176 p. Index.

Includes discussion of the novel and creative scholarship.

192   _____. OUR SENSE OF IDENTITY: A BOOK OF CANADIAN ESSAYS. Toronto: Ryerson, 1954. xv, 346 p.

One section on arts and letters including nos. 492 and 501; includes material by Klein, Callaghan, MacLennan, Frye, McLuhan (no. 4795), Leacock, and Carr, and articles on Leacock (no. 2544) and Stringer (no. 4082).

193   Sirois, Antoine R. MONTRÉAL DANS LE ROMAN CANADIEN. Montréal: Marcel Didier, 1968. 195 p. Bibliog. Index.

Comparative study of English- and French-Canadian literature.

194   Smith, Arthur James Marshall. TOWARDS A VIEW OF CANADIAN LETTERS: SELECTED CRITICAL ESSAYS, 1928-1971. Vancouver: University of British Columbia Press, 1973. xi, 230 p.

Mainly on poetry; some discussion of Canadian criticism.

195   _____, ed. with introd. MASKS OF FICTION: CANADIAN CRITICS ON CANADIAN PROSE. New Canadian Library Original, 02. Toronto: McClelland and Stewart, 1961. xi, 175 p.

Reprints articles by Davies (no. 1304), Grove (from no. 1763), Wilson (no. 4278), MacLennan (no. 3002), McCourt (no. 2915), and Woodcock (no. 5145), and about Leacock (no. 1304), Callaghan (no.1111), MacLennan (no. 5145), Lowry (no. 2746), Klein (no. 2142), Davies (no. 1358), and Canadian literature (no. 239).

196   Staines, David, ed. with introd. THE CANADIAN IMAGINATION: DIMENSIONS OF A LITERARY CULTURE. Cambridge, Mass.: Harvard University Press, 1977. viii, 265 p. Index.

Includes Frye on Canadian poetry, Woodcock on Canadian fiction, Atwood on the supernatural in Canadian fiction, Douglas Bush on Stephen Leacock, and McLuhan on the Canadian border.

197   Stephens, Donald G., ed. WRITERS OF THE PRAIRIES. Canadian Literature Series. Vancouver: University of British Columbia Press, 1973. 208 p.

Includes new articles on Ostenso, Wiseman, Kroetsch and Gabrielle Roy, and reprinted articles on Ralph Connor, Stead (no. 3981), Grove (nos. 1839, 1848, 1858), Mitchell (no. 3199), Laurence (nos. 2316, 2374), Ross (nos. 3788, 3796,

3799), and prairie fiction (no. 345). Also articles by Wiebe (no. 4228) and Laurence (no. 2295).

198   Stevenson, Lionel. APPRAISALS OF CANADIAN LITERATURE. Toronto: Macmillan, 1926. xviii, 272 p. Index.

Some mention of early twentieth-century novelists.

199   Stokes, Roy Bishop. I HAD FORGOTTEN ABOUT THE WIND. Regina: Saskatchewan Library Association, 1975. iv, 13 p.

200   Sutherland, Ronald. THE NEW HERO: ESSAYS IN COMPARATIVE QUEBEC/CANADIAN LITERATURE. Toronto: Macmillan, 1977. xv, 118 p. Bibliog. Index.

Articles on Grove (no. 1904) and Davies (no. 1378) as well as more general discussion of the Canadian protagonist, cultural nationalism, the war novel, and the Canadian literary mainstream; reprints nos. 535–36.

201   _____. SECOND IMAGE: COMPARATIVE STUDIES IN QUÉBEC/ CANADIAN LITERATURE. Toronto: New, 1971. 189 p. Bibliog. Index.

Explores interconnections between the two literatures; includes nos. 528–29, 532–34, and 537.

202   Swyripa, Frances. UKRAINIAN CANADIANS: A SURVEY OF THEIR PORTRAYAL IN ENGLISH-LANGUAGE WORKS. Edmonton: University of Alberta Press for the Canadian Institute of Ukrainian Studies, 1978. xiii, 169 p. Bibliog. Index.

Some references to creative writing.

203   Thomas, Clara. OUR NATURE--OUR VOICES: A GUIDEBOOK TO ENGLISH-CANADIAN LITERATURE. Vol. 1. Toronto: New, 1972. ix, 175 p. Bibliog.

Introduction to individual writers and their works, with brief checklists of primary and secondary material; from the beginnings of Canadian literature to 1970. For the sequel, see no. 135.

204   Tweedie, R.A., Fred Cogswell, and W. Stewart MacNutt, eds. ARTS IN NEW BRUNSWICK. Fredericton, N.B.: Brunswick, 1967. 280 p. Index.

Includes "Literature in New Brunswick" by various contributors, pp. 17-118.

205   Twigg, Alan. FOR OPENERS: CONVERSATIONS WITH 24 CANADIAN
      WRITERS. Madiera Park, B.C.: Harbour, 1981. 200 p.

      Includes interviews with Atwood, Leonard Cohen, Matt Cohen,
      Davies, Engel, Fraser, Hodgins, Kroetsch, Laurence, Mac-
      Lennan, Munro, Rule, and Wiebe.

206   Walsh, William, ed. READINGS IN COMMONWEALTH LITERATURE.
      Oxford: Clarendon, 1973. xxi, 448 p. Bibliog. Index.

      The section on Canada reprints general discussions by Wood-
      cock (no. 5149), Atwood (from no. 591), Jones (no. 347),
      and New (no. 440), and specific analysis of Klein (no. 2127).

207   Waterston, Elizabeth. SURVEY: A SHORT HISTORY OF CANADIAN
      LITERATURE. Methuen Canadian Literature Series. Toronto: Methuen,
      1973. 215 p. Bibliog. Index.

      An introductory work organized by general topics such as
      "Terrain," "Native Peoples," "French and English Canada";
      includes a chronological chart of historical and literary events.

208   Webster, Judith, ed. VOICES OF CANADA: AN INTRODUCTION TO
      CANADIAN CULTURE. Introd. William Metcalfe. Burlington, Vt.:
      Association for Canadian Studies in the United States, 1977. xi, 56 p.
      Bibliog.

      Includes articles by Frye, MacLennan, and Davies, and a
      discussion, "Is There a Distinctive Canadian Prose?"

209   Whalley, George, ed. WRITING IN CANADA: PROCEEDINGS OF
      THE CANADIAN WRITERS' CONFERENCE, QUEEN'S UNIVERSITY, 28-
      31 JULY, 1955. Introd. F.R. Scott. Toronto: Macmillan, 1956. xii,
      147 p.

      On the writer, the writer's media, the writer and the public;
      includes Callaghan, "Novelist," pp. 24-32.

210   Wilson, Edmund. O CANADA: AN AMERICAN'S NOTES ON CANADIAN
      CULTURE. New York: Farrar, Straus and Giroux, 1965. 245 p.

      Includes a discussion of Callaghan and MacLennan; reprints
      nos. 577 and 1113.

211   Winks, Robin W. THE MYTH OF THE AMERICAN FRONTIER: ITS RELE-
      VANCE TO AMERICA, CANADA AND AUSTRALIA. London, Engl.:
      Leicester University Press, 1971. 39 p.

For literary criticism, see also nos. 88, 591, 809, 1281, 1701, 1942, 1944, 2889,
4511, 5063, 5081, 5085-86, 5102, 5106, 5112-13.

B. ARTICLES

212   Adamson, Arthur. "Identity through Metaphor: An Approach to the Question of Regionalism in Canadian Literature." STUDIES IN CANADIAN LITERATURE, 5 (Spr. 1980), 83-99.

213   Andrusyshen, C.H. "Canadian Ethnic Literary and Cultural Perspectives." In THE UNDOING OF BABEL: WATSON KIRKCONNEL, THE MAN AND HIS WORK. Ed. J.R.C. Perkin. Toronto: McClelland and Stewart, 1975, pp. 31-49.

214   Arnason, David. "Some Propositions about Canadian Literature." JOURNAL OF CANADIAN FICTION, 3 (Wint. 1974), 1-2.

215   Aspinal, Dawn, and Danny Drache. "Writing in Canada: The Defeatist Tradition in Canadian Literature." CANADIAN DIMENSION, 8 (Mar.-Apr. 1972), 43-45.

216   August, Raymond. "Babeling Beaver Hunts for Home Fire: The Place of Ethnic Literature in Canadian Culture." CANADIAN FORUM, 54 (Aug. 1974), 8-13.

217   Barnard, Leslie Gordon. "Distinctively Canadian." CANADIAN AUTHOR, 10 (Sept. 1932), 33-36.

218   Barr, Arlee. "On the Nature and Purpose of Canadian Literature." ALIVE, 35 ([1974]), 14.

       Reply to no. 480.

219   Bassett, Isabel. "The Transformation of Imperialism: Connor to MacLennan." JOURNAL OF CANADIAN FICTION, 2 (Wint. 1973), 58-62.

220   Benazon, Michael. "Blessed are the Guilty." CANADIAN LITERATURE, No. 82 (Aut. 1979), pp. 130-33.

221   Bennett, Donna A., and Russell M. Brown. "In Place of Job: The Emergence of the Trickster in Canadian Fiction." JOURNAL OF COMMONWEALTH LITERATURE, 14 (Aug. 1979), 28-38.

222   Birbalsingh, Frank M. "National Identity and the Canadian Novel." JOURNAL OF CANADIAN FICTION, 1 (Wint. 1972), 56-59.

223   _____. "Novelists and the Nation." CANADIAN LITERATURE, No. 61 (Sum. 1974), pp. 125-28.

224   Bissell, Claude T. "A Common Ancestry: Literature in Australia and Canada." UNIVERSITY OF TORONTO QUARTERLY, 25 (Jan. 1956), 131-42.

225   _____. "The Novel." In THE ARTS IN CANADA: A STOCKTAKING AT MID-CENTURY. Ed. Malcolm Ross. Toronto: Macmillan, 1958, pp. 92-96.

226   Blanco Amor, José. "Influencia de la literatura europea sobre la del Continente americano: El caso del Canadá." CUADERNOS AMERICANOS, 199 (Mar.-Apr. 1975), 230-38.

227   Blodgett, E.D. "Canadian as Comparative Literature." CANADIAN REVIEW OF COMPARATIVE LITERATURE, 6 (Spr. 1979), 127-30.

228   _____. "The Canadian Literatures in a Comparative Perspective." ESSAYS ON CANADIAN WRITING, No. 15 (Sum. 1979), pp. 5-24.

229   _____. "Cold Pastorals: A Prolegomenon." CANADIAN REVIEW OF COMPARATIVE LITERATURE, 6 (Spr. 1979), 166-94.

230   Boekelman, Marinus. "Towards a Revolutionary Literature." ALIVE, 36 ([1974]), 20-21.

231   Entry deleted.

232   Bonenfant, Jean-Charles. "L'Influence de la Littérature Canadienne-Anglaise au Canada Français." CULTURE, 17 (Sept. 1956), 251-60.

233   _____. "Littérature Canadienne d'Expression Anglaise." REVUE DE L'UNIVERSITÉ LAVAL, 4 (Apr. 1950), 736-52; (May 1950), 812-26; (June 1950), 932-49; 5 (Sept. 1950), 59-73; (Oct. 1950), 159-74; (Nov. 1950), 249-65; (Dec. 1950), 361-69; (Jan. 1951), 457-64; (Feb. 1951), 554-61; (Mar. 1951), 639-49; 6 (Sept. 1951), 51-58; (Oct. 1951), 139-46; (Nov. 1951), 228-33; (Dec. 1951), 310-15; (Jan. 1952), 400-405; (Feb. 1952), 478-83; 7 (Oct. 1952), 180-90; (Nov. 1952), 273-80.

234   Bouraoui, Hedi. "The Canadian Literary Paradox." WAVES, 2 (Aut. 1973), 8-12.

235   Boutelle, Ann. "The Dorian Gray Phenomenon in Canadian Literature." DALHOUSIE REVIEW, 57 (Sum. 1977), 265-76.

       See no. 373 for a reply.

236   Bowering, George. "Modernism Could Not Last Forever." CANADIAN FICTION MAGAZINE, Nos. 32-33 (1979-80), pp. 4-9.

237   Brown, Edward Killoran. "The Immediate Present in Canadian Literature." SEWANEE REVIEW, 41 (Oct. 1933), 430-42.

       Reprinted in no. 123.

238   _____. "The Neglect of Canadian Literature." ECHOES, No. 176 (Oct. 1944), pp. 12, 48.

       Reprinted in no. 123.

239   _____. "The Problem of a Canadian Literature." In his ON CANADIAN POETRY. Toronto: Ryerson, 1943, pp. 1-26.

       Reprinted in nos. 123 and 195.

240   Brown, Russell M. "Critic, Culture, Text: Beyond Thematics." ESSAYS ON CANADIAN WRITING, 11 (Sum. 1978), 151-83.

241   _____. "In Search of Lost Causes: The Canadian Novelist as Mystery Writer." MOSAIC, 11 (Spr. 1978), 1-15.

242   Brydon, Diana. "Australian Literature and the Canadian Comparison." MEANJIN, 38 (July 1979), 154-65.

243   Burns, D.R. "The Move to the Middle Ground: A Reading of the English Canadian Novel." MEANJIN, 37 (July 1978), 178-85.

244   Burpee, Lawrence Johnstone. "The National Note in Canadian Literature." CANADIAN BOOKMAN, 7 (Feb. 1925), 34-35.

245   Burton, Lydia, and Morley, David. "A Sense of Grievance: Attitudes towards Men in Contemporary Fiction." CANADIAN FORUM, 55 (Sept. 1975), 57-60.

246   Bush, Douglas. "Is There a Canadian Literature?" COMMONWEAL, 6 Nov. 1929, pp. 12-14.

247   Cameron, Barry. "Criteria of Evaluation in the Canadian Novel: A Response to Robert Kroetsch." ESSAYS ON CANADIAN WRITING, No. 20 (Wint. 1980-81), pp. 19-31.

       A reply to no. 2243.

248 Cameron, Barry, and Michael Dixon. "Introduction: Mandatory Subversive Manifesto: Canadian Criticism vs. Literary Criticism." STUDIES IN CANADIAN LITERATURE, 2 (Sum. 1977), 137-45.

249 Cameron, Donald A. "Letter from Halifax." CANADIAN LITERATURE, No. 40 (Spr. 1969), pp. 55-60.

250 _____. "Letter from London." CANADIAN LITERATURE, No. 27 (Wint. 1966), pp. 53-58.

251 _____. "The Maritime Writer and the Folks Down Home." CANADIAN LITERATURE, Nos. 68-69 (Spr.-Sum. 1976), pp. 113-21.

252 _____. "Novelists of the Seventies: Through Chaos to the Truth: The Bizarre Images of a New Generation in Canadian Fiction." SATURDAY NIGHT, 87 (July 1972), 9-13.

253 "Canadian Publishing: Answers to a Questionnaire." CANADIAN LIT-ERATURE, No. 33 (Sum. 1967), pp. 5-15.

254 Carpenter, David C. "Alberta in Fiction: The Emergence of a Provincial Consciousness." JOURNAL OF CANADIAN STUDIES, 10 (Nov. 1975), 12-23.

255 Cavell, Richard. "Canadian Literature in Italy." CANADIAN LITERA-TURE, No. 87 (Wint. 1980), pp. 153-56.

256 Chambers, Robert D. "Notes on Regionalism in Modern Canadian Fiction." JOURNAL OF CANADIAN STUDIES, 11 (May 1976), 27-34.

257 Clark, Richard C. "Bibliographical Spectrum and Review Article: Is There a Canadian Literature?" REVIEW OF NATIONAL LITERATURES, 7 (1976), 133-64.

    Reprinted in no. 178.

258 Clifton, Merritt. "The Great White Hoax." CANADIAN LITERATURE, No. 75 (Wint. 1977), pp. 108-11.

259 Cogswell, Frederick. "Literary Traditions in New Brunswick." PRO-CEEDINGS AND TRANSACTIONS OF THE ROYAL SOCIETY OF CANADA, 15 (1977), 287-99.

260 Cohn-Sfetcu, Ofelia. "To Live in Abundance of Life: Time in Canadian Literature." CANADIAN LITERATURE, No. 76 (Spr. 1978), pp. 25-36.

261   Cole, Wayne H. "The Railroad in Canadian Literature." CANADIAN
       LITERATURE, No. 77 (Sum. 1978), pp. 124-30.

262   Colson, Theodore. "The Theme of Home in the Fiction of Canada, the
       United States, and the West Indies." ENGLISH STUDIES IN CANADA,
       4 (Fall 1978), 351-61.

263   Conron, Brandon. "A Bountiful Choice of Critics of English Canadian
       Literature." LITERARY HALF-YEARLY, 13 (July 1972), 44-55.

264   _____. "The Function of the Critic in Canada Today." In COMMON-
       WEALTH LITERATURE: UNITY AND DIVERSITY IN A COMMON CUL-
       TURE. Ed. John Press. London: Heinemann, 1965, pp. 192-200.

265   Dahlie, Hallvard. "The International Theme in Canadian Fiction." In
       COMMON WEALTH. Ed. Anna Rutherford. Aarhus, Denmark: Akademisk
       Boghandel, [1972], pp. 177-89.

266   _____. "New Directions in Canadian Fiction." In COMMONWEALTH
       LITERATURE AND THE MODERN WORLD. Ed. Hena Maes-Jelinek.
       Brussels: Didier, 1975, pp. 169-74.

267   _____. "Self-Conscious Canadians." CANADIAN LITERATURE, No.
       62 (Aut. 1974), pp. 6-16.

268   Daniells, Roy. "Canadian Prose Style." MANITOBA ARTS REVIEW, 5
       (Spr. 1947), 3-11.

269   _____. "National Identity in English-Canadian Writing." In NATIONAL
       IDENTITY: PAPERS DELIVERED AT THE COMMONWEALTH LITERATURE
       CONFERENCE, UNIVERSITY OF QUEENSLAND, BRISBANE, 9TH-15TH
       AUGUST, 1968. Ed. K.L. Goodwin. London: Heinemann, 1970, pp.
       76-88.

270   Davey, Frank. "The Explorer in Western Canadian Literature." STUDIES
       IN CANADIAN LITERATURE, 4 (Sum. 1979), 91-100.

271   _____. "Surviving the Paraphrase." CANADIAN LITERATURE, No. 70
       (Aut. 1976), pp. 5-13.

272   Davies, Gwendolyn. "East Coast Writing." BOOK FORUM, 4, No. 1
       (1978), 79-86.

273   Davis, Cree. "Reply to R.L. Rodensky." ALIVE, 36 (1974), 18.
        Reply to no. 480.

274   Dawe, Alan. "Untaped Interviews." EVENT, 4, No. 1 (1975), 33-40.

275   Dawson, Anthony B. "Coming of Age in Canada." MOSAIC, 11 (Spr. 1978), 47-62.

276   Deacon, William Arthur. "Canada's Literary Revolution." CANADIAN AUTHOR AND BOOKMAN, 23 (Dec. 1947), 21-25.

277   _____. "Canadian Literature." LITERARY REVIEW, 29 Mar. 1924, p. 634.

278   _____. "Critic Speaks: Significance of Canadian Literature." CANADIAN AUTHOR, 15 (Sept. 1937), 13-16.

279   _____. "Literature in Canada--In Its Centenary Year." In YEARBOOK OF THE ARTS IN CANADA 1928/29. Ed. Bertram Brooker. Toronto: Macmillan, 1929, pp. 21-36.

280   Djwa, Sandra. "Biblical Archetype in Western Canadian Fiction." In WESTERN CANADA: PAST AND PRESENT. Ed. Anthony W. Rasporich. Calgary: University of Calgary and McClelland and Stewart, 1975, pp. 193-203.

281   _____. "Canadian Contexts." WEST COAST REVIEW, 7 (Jan. 1973), 46-50.

282   _____. "The CANADIAN FORUM: Literary Catalyst." STUDIES IN CANADIAN LITERATURE, 1 (Wint. 1976), 7-25.

283   Dobbs, Bryan Griffith. "The Case for Canadian Literature." WESTERN CANADIAN STUDIES IN MODERN LANGUAGES AND LITERATURE, 1 (1969), 44-50.

284   Dooley, David Joseph. "The Canadian Adam." ENGLISH STUDIES IN CANADA, 1 (Fall 1975), 344-52.

285   _____. "The Satiric Novel in Canada Today: A Failure Too Frequent?" QUEEN'S QUARTERLY, 64 (Wint. 1957-58), 576-90.

        Excerpts reprinted in no. 872.

286   _____. "Simulating the Stars: Canadian Literature and the Legacy of Nietzsche." JOURNAL OF CANADIAN STUDIES, 12 (Spr. 1977), 83-92.

Reprinted in no. 139.

287   Downey, Deane E.D. "The Canadian Identity & African Nationalism." CANADIAN LITERATURE, No. 75 (Wint. 1977), pp. 15-26.

288   Doyle, James. "The Image of Northern Ontario in English-Canadian Literature." LAURENTIAN UNIVERSITY REVIEW, 8 (Nov. 1975), 103-16.

289   Dudek, Louis. "Canada's Literature of Revolt." NATION, 27 Oct. 1962, pp. 269-72.

290   _____. "The Mirror of Art: Relations between French and English Literature in Canada." CULTURE, 31 (Sept. 1970), 225-31.

Reprinted in no. 140.

291   _____. "The Misuses of Imagination: A Rib-Roasting of Some Recent Canadian Critics." TAMARACK REVIEW, No. 60 (1973), pp. 51-67.

Discusses Frye, D.G. Jones, and McLuhan, among others; reprinted in no. 140.

292   _____. "The Two Traditions: Literature and the Ferment in Quebec." CANADIAN LITERATURE, No. 12 (Spr. 1962), pp. 44-51.

293   Durand, Régis. "La Littérature Canadienne de Langue Anglaise dans la Modernité Nord-Americaine (1)." ÉTUDES CANADIENNES/CANADIAN STUDIES, 2 (1976), 63-69.

294   Edgar, Pelham. "Canadian Literature." LITERARY REVIEW, 19 Nov. 1921, pp. 101-102.

295   _____. "Our Literary Tendencies." CANADIAN AUTHOR, 12 (June 1935), 2, 19.

296   Ferres, John. "From Survival to Affirmation: New Perspectives in Canadian Literary Criticism." AMERICAN REVIEW OF CANADIAN STUDIES, 3 (Spr. 1973), 122-33.

297   Fiedler, Leslie. "Some Notes on the Jewish Novel in English or Looking Backward from Exile." RUNNING MAN, 1 (July-Aug. 1968), 18-21.

Discusses Leonard Cohen and, especially, Richler; excerpt reprinted in no. 3755.

298   Francis, Wynne. "Literary Underground: Little Magazines in Canada." CANADIAN LITERATURE, No. 34 (Aut. 1967), pp. 63-70.

299   Fraser, Nancy W. "The Development of Realism in Canadian Literature during the 1920's." DALHOUSIE REVIEW, 57 (Sum. 1977), 287-99.

300   Frazer, Frances M. "Island Writers." CANADIAN LITERATURE, Nos. 68-69 (Spr.-Sum. 1976), pp. 76-87.

301   French, W. "The Women in Our Literary Life." CANADIAN AUTHOR AND BOOKMAN, 51, No. 3 (1976), 1-6.

302   Friesen, Victor Carl. "The Rural Prairie Novel and the Great Depression." PRAIRIE FORUM, 2 (May 1977), 83-96.

303   Frum, Barbara. "Great Dames." MACLEAN'S, 86 (Apr. 1973), 32, 38.

304   Fulford, Robert. "Good News from the Libraries." ONTARIO LIBRARY REVIEW, 44 (May 1960), 77.

305   _____. "Thrills: Marvel as Writers Display Real Bile, Guile, and Scabrous Outrage under the Guise of Darkest Fiction." SATURDAY NIGHT, 91 (Nov. 1976), 38-39.

306   Fulton, E. Margaret. "Out of Our Past: A New Future." LAUREN-TIAN UNIVERSITY REVIEW, 9 (Nov. 1976), 87-102.

307   Gane, Margaret Drury. "'Do You Use Real People in Your Fiction?'" SATURDAY NIGHT, 90 (Nov. 1975), 39-43.

308   Geddes, Gary. "The Shapes of Our Content." LAURENTIAN UNIVER-SITY REVIEW, 8 (Nov. 1975), 1-5.

309   Godard, Barbara. "The Avant-Garde in Canada: OPEN LETTER and LA BARRE DU JOUR." ELLIPSE, 23-24 (1979), 98-113.

310   _____. "The Geography of Separatism." LAURENTIAN UNIVERSITY REVIEW, 9 (Nov. 1976), 33-50. Bibliog.

311   _____. "God's Country: Man and the Land in the Canadian Novel." REVUE DE LITTÉRATURE COMPARÉE, 47 (Apr.-June 1973), 225-41.

312   _____. "The Oral Tradition and Contemporary Fiction." ESSAYS ON CANADIAN WRITING, Nos. 7-8 (Fall 1977), pp. 46-62.

313   Goetsch, Paul. "Der literarische Nationalismus in Kanada seit 1960." In LITERATUREN IN ENGLISCHER SPRACHE: EIN ÜBERBLICK ÜBER EN- GLISCHSPRACHIGE NATIONALLITERATUREN AUSSERHALB ENGLANDS. Ed. Heinz Kosok and Horst Priessnitz. Bonn, W. Germany: Bouvier, 1977, pp. 122-40.

314   Gottlieb, Lois C., and Wendy Keitner. "Demeter's Daughters: The Mother-Daughter Motif in Fiction by Canadian Women." ATLANTIS, 3 (Fall 1977), 131-42.

315   _____. "Images of Canadian Women in Literature and Society in the 1970's." INTERNATIONAL JOURNAL OF WOMEN'S STUDIES, 2 (1979), 513-27.

316   _____. "Mothers and Daughters in Four Recent Canadian Novels." SPHINX, 1 (Sum. 1975), 21-34.

317   Grace, Sherrill E. "Duality and Series: Forms of the Canadian Imagi- nation." CANADIAN REVIEW OF COMPARATIVE LITERATURE, 7 (Fall 1980), 438-51.

318   Granatstein, J.L. "Poets and Novelists on Politicians: The Case of Mackenzie King." TAMARACK REVIEW, 65 (Mar. 1975), 30-37.

319   Grayson, J. Paul, and L.M. Grayson. "The Canadian Literary Elite: A Socio-Historical Perspective." CANADIAN JOURNAL OF SOCIOLOGY, 3 (Sum. 1978), 291-308.

320   Greene, Donald. "Western Canadian Literature." WESTERN AMERICAN LITERATURE, 2 (Wint. 1968), 257-80.

321   Greening, W.E. "Wanted: Reciprocity in Canadian Literature." DAL- HOUSIE REVIEW, 29 (Oct. 1949), 271-74.

322   Greenwood, Thomas. "Évolution de la Littérature Canadienne Anglaise." ÉTUDES ANGLAISES, 11 (Jan.-Mar. 1958), 23-30.

323   Gros-Louis, Dolores. "Pens and Needles: Daughters and Mothers in Recent Canadian Literature." KATE CHOPIN NEWSLETTER, 2, No. 3 (1976-77), 8-13.

324   Gross, Konrad. "Looking Back in Anger? Frederick Niven, W.O.
Mitchell, and Robert Kroetsch on the History of the Canadian West."
JOURNAL OF CANADIAN FICTION, 3, No. 2 (1974), 49-54.

325   Gustafson, Ralph. "Writing and Canada." NORTHERN REVIEW, 3
(Feb.-Mar. 1950), 17-22.

326   Gwyn, Sandra. "The Literary Arts." In her WOMEN IN THE ARTS IN
CANADA. Studies of the Royal Commission on the Status of Women in
Canada, 7. Ottawa: Information Canada, 1971, pp. 60-98. Bibliog.

327   Hamilton, L. "Some Aspects of Anglo-Canadian Literature." NEUPHILO-
LOGISCHE MONATSSCHRIFT, 3 (1932), 227-37.

328   Hancock, Geoffrey. "CanLit: Plugged In? Or Burned Out? An Interview with Geoff Hancock." CANADIAN FICTION MAGAZINE, Nos.
30-31 (1979), pp. 5-14.

329   _____. "HERE AND NOW: Innovation and Change in the Canadian
Short Story." CANADIAN FICTION MAGAZINE, No. 27 (1977), pp.
4-22.

330   _____. "Magic Realism, or, the Future of Fiction." CANADIAN FIC-
TION MAGAZINE, Nos. 24-25 (Spr.-Sum. 1977), pp. 4-6.

331   Harlow, Robert. "Bastard Bohemia: Creative Writing in the Universities."
CANADIAN LITERATURE, No. 27 (Wint. 1966), pp. 32-43.

332   Harrison, Dick. "Across the Medicine Line: Problems in Comparing Canadian and American Western Fiction." In THE WESTERING EXPERIENCE
IN AMERICAN LITERATURE: BICENTENNIAL ESSAYS. Ed. Merrill Lewis
and L.L. Lee. Bellingham: Western Washington University, Bureau for
Faculty Research, 1977, pp. 48-56.

333   _____. "The American Adam and the Canadian Christ." TWENTIETH
CENTURY LITERATURE, 16 (Jan.-Oct. 1970), 161-67.

334   _____. "Cultural Insanity and Prairie Fiction." In FIGURES IN A
GROUND: CANADIAN ESSAYS ON MODERN LITERATURE COLLECTED
IN HONOR OF SHEILA WATSON. Ed. Diane Bessai and David Jackel.
Saskatoon: Western Producer Prairie Books, [1978], pp. 278-94.

335   _____. "The Imperial Heritage in Canadian Prairie Fiction."
KUNAPIPI, 2, No. 1 (1980), 107-16.

336   _____. "Popular Fiction of the Canadian Prairies: Autopsy on a Small Corpus." JOURNAL OF POPULAR CULTURE, 14 (1980), 326-32.

337   Hassan, Ihab. "Canadian Literature." In WORLD LITERATURE SINCE 1945: CRITICAL SURVEYS OF THE CONTEMPORARY LITERATURE OF EUROPE AND THE AMERICAS. Ed. Ivar Ivask and Gero von Wilpert. New York: Frederick Ungar, 1973, pp. 128-35. Bibliog.

338   Hedenstrom, Joanne. "Puzzled Patriarchs and Free Women: Patterns in the Canadian Novel." ATLANTIS, 4 (Fall 1978), 2-9.

339   Hertzel, Leo J. "Some Commonplace Thoughts on Canadian Fiction and Culture." NORTH AMERICAN REVIEW, NS 8 (Fall 1971), 36-40.

340   Hicks, Granville. "Novelists in the Fifties." SATURDAY REVIEW, 24 Oct. 1959, pp. 18-20.

341   Hirano, Keiichi. "The Aborigene in Canadian Literature: Notes by a Japanese." CANADIAN LITERATURE, No. 14 (Aut. 1962), pp. 43-52.

342   Hosek, Chaviva. "Romance and Realism in Canadian Fiction of the 1960's." JOURNAL OF CANADIAN FICTION, No. 20 (1977), pp. 125-39.

343   Irvine, Lorna. "Hostility and Reconciliation: The Mother in English Canadian Fiction." AMERICAN REVIEW OF CANADIAN STUDIES, 8 (Spr. 1978), 56-64.

344   _____. "A Psychological Journey: Mothers and Daughters in English-Canadian Fiction." In THE LOST TRADITION: MOTHERS AND DAUGHTERS IN LITERATURE. Ed. Cathy N. Davidson and E.M. Broner. New York: Ungar, 1980, pp. 242-52.

345   Jackel, Susan. "The House on the Prairies." CANADIAN LITERATURE, No. 42 (Aut. 1969), pp. 46-55.

           Reprinted in no. 197.

346   Jacob, Fred. "Canadian Literati." AMERICAN MERCURY, 8 (June 1926), 216-21.

347   Jones, Douglas G. "Adam's Inventory: Aspects of Contemporary Canadian Literature." SOCIAL EDUCATION, 35 (Oct. 1971), 595-601.

           Reprinted in no. 206.

348 _____. "Myth, Frye and Canadian Writers." CANADIAN LITERATURE, No. 55 (Wint. 1973), pp. 7-22.

349 Karr, Clarence. "What is Canadian Intellectual History?" DALHOUSIE REVIEW, 55 (Aut. 1975), 431-48.

350 Kattan, Naïm. "Le Roman Canadien Anglais." LETTRES NOUVELLES, Dec. 1966-Jan. 1967, pp. 21-30.

351 _____. "L'Espace dans la Littérature Canadienne." PROCEEDINGS AND TRANSACTIONS OF THE ROYAL SOCIETY OF CANADA, 4th ser., 14 (1976), 127-29.

352 _____. "Montreal and French-Canadian Culture: What They Mean to English-Canadian Novelists." TAMARACK REVIEW, 40 (Sum. 1966), 40-53.

353 _____. "Romanciers Canadiens-Anglais et Canadiens-Français." LIBERTÉ, 7 (Nov.-Dec. 1965), 479-83.

354 _____. "Space in the Canadian Novel of the West." Trans. Joyce Marshall. ARIEL, 4 (July 1973), 103-10.

355 _____. "Ten Years of Literature: A Writer at the Canada Council." Trans. I.M. Owen. In THE HUMAN ELEMENTS: CRITICAL ESSAYS. Ed. David Helwig. [Ottawa]: Oberon, 1978, pp. 68-77.

356 Kennedy, Leo. "The Future of Canadian Literature." CANADIAN MERCURY, 1 (Apr.-May 1929), 99-100.

357 Kent, David A. "Two Attitudes: Canadian Short Stories." ESSAYS ON CANADIAN WRITING, 16 (1979-80), 168-78.

358 Ketterer, David. "Canadian Science Fiction." In OTHER CANADAS: AN ANTHOLOGY OF SCIENCE FICTION AND FANTASY. Ed. John Robert Colombo. Toronto: McGraw-Hill Ryerson, 1979, pp. 326-33.

359 Kilgallin, Anthony R. "The Beaver and the Elephant." TIMES LITERARY SUPPLEMENT, 26 Oct. 1973, p. 1300.

360 Kirkconnell, Watson. "Towards a National Literature." CANADIAN AUTHOR, 9 (May 1932), 23-24.

361 _____. "Writing on the Prairie." CANADIAN AUTHOR, 10 (Sept. 1932), 26-29.

362   Kröller, Eva-Marie. "Comparative Canadian Literature: Notes on its Definition and Method." CANADIAN REVIEW OF COMPARATIVE LITERATURE, 6 (Spr. 1979), 139-50.

363   LaBonté, Ronald. "Social Realism, or, The Future of Fiction." CANADIAN FICTION MAGAZINE, No. 27 (1977), pp. 123-36.

364   La Bossière, Camille R. "Similitude and Differentiation: Contexts for the Comparative Study of Canadian Literature." PROCEEDINGS OF THE PACIFIC NORTHWEST CONFERENCE ON FOREIGN LANGUAGES, 30, Nos. 1-2 (1979), 20-21.

365   LePan, Douglas. "The Dilemma of the Canadian Author." ATLANTIC MONTHLY, 214 (Nov. 1964), 160-64.

366   Lillard, Charles. "Daylight in the Swamp: A Guide to the West Coast Renaissance." MALAHAT REVIEW, 45 (1978), 319-40.

367   _____. "The Past Rising from Our Midst." MALAHAT REVIEW, No. 50 (Apr. 1979), pp. 8-22.

368   "Literature." In REPORT. ROYAL COMMISSION ON NATIONAL DEVELOPMENT IN THE ARTS, LETTERS, AND SCIENCES, 1949-1951. Ottawa: King's Printer, 1951, pp. 222-27.

369   Livesay, Dorothy. "The Native People in Our Canadian Literature." ENGLISH QUARTERLY, 4 (Spr. 1971), 21-32.

370   Lochhead, Douglas. "The Literary Heritage: The Place, the Past, the Prospect." In ATLANTIC PROVINCES LITERATURE COLLOQUIUM PAPERS/ COMMUNICATIONS DU COLLOQUE SUR LA LITTÉRATURE DES PROVINCES ATLANTIQUES. Ed. Kenneth MacKinnon. Marco Polo Papers 1. Saint John, N.B.: Atlantic Canada Institute, 1977, pp. 3-9.

371   Loomer, L.S. "First World War in Canadian Fiction." CANADIAN NOTES AND QUERIES, No. 10 (1972), p. 7.

372   Lower, Arthur R. "Canadian Values and Canadian Writing." MOSAIC, 1 (Oct. 1967), 79-93.

373   _____. "'The Dorian Gray Phenomenon': Explained?" DALHOUSIE REVIEW, 58 (Aut. 1979), 541-46.

       Reply to no. 235.

374 Lucas, Alec. "The Anthology: A Notable and Unacclaimed Achievement of Canadian Literature." LITERARY HALF-YEARLY, 13 (July 1972), 111-19.

375 _____. "Canadian Short Story Anthologies: Notes on Their Function and Form." WORLD LITERATURE WRITTEN IN ENGLISH, 11 (Apr. 1972), 53-59.

376 McCarthy, A.H. "Literary Revolution--Its Causes and Effects." CANADIAN AUTHOR AND BOOKMAN, 53 (Jan. 1978), 14-18.

377 McClelland, John. "Is There an English Canadian Literature?" CANADIAN FORUM, 50 (Oct. 1970), 240-41.

378 McCormack, Thelma. "Writers and the Mass Media." CANADIAN LITERATURE, No. 20 (Spr. 1964), pp. 27-40.

379 MacCulloch, Clare. "Canadian Neo-Romanticism." ALIVE, 34 ([1974]), 20.

380 McDougall, Robert L. "The Dodo and the Cruising Auk: Class in Canadian Literature." CANADIAN LITERATURE, No. 18 (Aut. 1963), pp. 6-20.

    Reprinted in no. 161.

381 _____. "A Perceptive Scenario for Cultural History." LITERARY HALF-YEARLY, 13 (July 1972), 120-36.

382 _____. "University Quarterlies." CANADIAN FORUM, 38 (Feb. 1959), 253-55.

383 MacIver, I.D. "Prose Writers of Nova Scotia." ACADIA ATHENAEUM, 63 (Jan. 1937), 33-40.

384 McKenna, Isobel. "Women in Canadian Literature." CANADIAN LITERATURE, No. 62 (Aut. 1974), pp. 69-78.

385 McKenzie, Ruth. "Life in a New Land: Notes on the Immigrant Theme in Canadian Fiction." CANADIAN LITERATURE, No. 7 (Wint. 1961), pp. 24-33.

386 _____. "Proletarian Literature in Canada." DALHOUSIE REVIEW, 19 (Apr. 1939), 49-64.

387 McLean, Ken. "Evangelical and Ecclesiastical Fiction." JOURNAL OF CANADIAN FICTION, No. 21 (1977-78), pp. 105-19.

388 MacLulich, T.D. "Canadian Exploration as Literature." CANADIAN LITERATURE, No. 81 (Sum. 1979), pp. 72-85.

389 _____. "Novel and Romance." CANADIAN LITERATURE, No. 70 (Aut. 1976), pp. 42-50.

390 _____. "The Rohmer Syndrome: A Kidnapping of the Mind." ESSAYS ON CANADIAN WRITING, No. 4 (Spr. 1976), pp. 11-15.

391 _____. "Society in Transition: Fiction and Canadian Society 1890-1940." STUDIES IN CANADIAN LITERATURE, 3 (Sum. 1978), 211-31.

392 McMullen, Lorraine. "Images of Women in Canadian Literature: Woman as Hero." ATLANTIS, 2 (Spr. 1977), Part 2, 134-42.

393 McMullin, Stanley E. "A Search for the Promised Land: Notes on the New World Hero in the Canadian Novel." REVISTA DE LETRAS, 3 (Dec. 1971), 480-94.

394 McPherson, Hugo. "Canadian Writing: Present Declarative." ENGLISH, 15 (Aut. 1965), 212-16.

395 MacPike, E.F. "American and Canadian Diaries, Journals, and Note-books." BULLETIN OF BIBLIOGRAPHY, 18 (May-Aug. 1945), 156-58.

396 Magee, William H. "Alberta as a Literary Imagination." ENGLISH TEACHER, 3 (Oct. 1963), 18-30.

397 _____. "Local Colour in Canadian Fiction." UNIVERSITY OF TORONTO QUARTERLY, 28 (Jan. 1959), 176-89.

398 _____. "Ontario in Recent Canadian Literature." ONTARIO HISTORY, 55 (June 1963), 105-15.

399 _____. "Trends in the Recent English-Canadian Novel." CULTURE, 10 (Mar. 1949), 29-42.

400 Mandel, Ann. "Useful Fictions: Legends of the Self in Roth, Blaise, Kroetsch, and Nowlan." ONTARIO REVIEW, No. 3 (Fall-Wint. 1975-76), pp. 26-32.

401   Mandel, Eli. "Criticism as Ghost Story." IMPULSE, 3, No. 2 (1974), 1-6.

402   _____. "The Ethnic Voice in Canadian Writing." In FIGURES IN A GROUND: CANADIAN ESSAYS ON MODERN LITERATURE COLLECTED IN HONOR OF SHEILA WATSON. Ed. Diane Bessai and David Jackel. Saskatoon: Western Producer Prairie Books, 1978, pp. 264-77.

403   _____. "Images of Prairie Man." In A REGION OF THE MIND: INTERPRETING THE WESTERN CANADIAN PLAINS. Ed. Richard Allen. Regina: University of Saskatchewan, Canadian Plains Studies Centre, 1973, pp. 201-09.

404   _____. "The Politics of Art." CANADIAN FORUM, 57 (Sept. 1977), 28-29.

405   _____. "Romance and Realism in Western Canadian Fiction." In PRAIRIE PERSPECTIVES 2. Ed. Anthony W. Rasporich and Henry C. Klassen. Toronto: Holt, Rinehart and Winston, 1973, pp. 197-211.

406   _____. "Writing West: On the Road to Wood Mountain." CANADIAN FORUM, 57 (June-July 1977), 25-29.

407   Marchessou, Hélène. "Identité et Méconnaissance ou Reconnaissance de l'Altérité chez Margaret Laurence, Leonard Cohen, Joe Rosenblatt, et A.M. Klein: Pluralité Ethnique Canadienne et Littérature." ÉTUDES CANADIENNES/CANADIAN STUDIES, 4 (1978), 65-76.

408   Marquis, Thomas Guthrie. "Fiction." In CANADA AND ITS PROVINCES. Vol. 12. Ed. Adam Shortt. Toronto: Glasgow Brook, 1913, pp. 534-66.

409   Marsland, Elizabeth. "La Chaîne Tenue: Roads and Railways in the Prairie Novel." CANADIAN LITERATURE, No. 77 (Sum. 1978), pp. 64-72.

410   Martin, Sandra. "The Book that Changed My Life." SATURDAY NIGHT, 91 (May 1976), 31-39.

411   Mathews, Robin D. "Canadian Literature: The Necessary Revolution." THIS MAGAZINE IS ABOUT SCHOOLS, 6 (Fall 1972), 53-66.

412   _____. "The Canadian Problem." In COMMONWEALTH LITERATURE: UNITY AND DIVERSITY IN A COMMON CULTURE. Ed. John Press. London: Heinemann, 1965, pp. 157-67.

413 _____. "Le Roman Engagé--The Social/Political Novel in English Canada." LAURENTIAN UNIVERSITY REVIEW, 9 (Nov. 1976), 15-31.

Reprinted in no. 163.

414 _____. "U.S. Expansionism, Canadian Literature, and Canadian Intellectual History." JOURNAL OF CANADIAN STUDIES, 6 (Nov. 1971), 30-41.

415 _____. "The Wacousta Factor." In FIGURES IN A GROUND: CANADIAN ESSAYS ON MODERN LITERATURE COLLECTED IN HONOR OF SHEILA WATSON. Ed. Diane Bessai and David Jackel. Saskatoon: Western Producer Prairie Books, 1978, pp. 295-315.

Also in no. 163.

416 Matthews, John. "Canada: Introductory." In COMMONWEALTH LITERATURE IN THE CURRICULUM. Ed. K.L. Goodwin. St. Lucia: Southern Pacific Association for Commonwealth Literature and Language Studies, 1980, pp. 79-85.

417 _____. "The Canadian Experience." In COMMONWEALTH LITERATURE: UNITY AND DIVERSITY IN A COMMON CULTURE. Ed. John Press. London: Heinemann, 1965, pp. 21-31.

418 _____. "Colonial Societies in Search of Identity: Lifeboats for the Titanic: Patterns of Identity in Commonwealth Literature." HUMANITIES ASSOCIATION BULLETIN, 30 (1979), 239-54.

419 _____. "The Inner Logic of a People: Canadian Writing and Canadian Values." MOSAIC, 1 (Apr. 1968), 40-50.

420 Matthiasson, John S. "The Icelandic Canadians: The Paradox of an Assimilated Ethnic Group." In TWO NATIONS, MANY CULTURES: ETHNIC GROUPS IN CANADA. Ed. Jean Leonard Elliott. Scarborough, Ont.: Prentice-Hall, 1979, pp. 195-205.

421 Merivale, Patricia. "The Biographical Compulsion: Elegaic Romances in Canadian Fiction." JOURNAL OF MODERN LITERATURE, 8, No. 1 (1980), 139-52.

422 Mitcham, Allison. "The Isolation of Protesting Individuals Who Belong to Minority Groups: A Comparative Study in Contemporary Canadian Fiction." WASCANA REVIEW, 7, No. 1 (1972), 43-50.

423 _____. "The Isolation of the Immigrant and Expatriate." LAKEHEAD UNIVERSITY REVIEW, 5 (Fall 1972), 87-103.

424 _____. "Northern Mission. Priest, Parson and Prophet in the North: A Study in French and English-Canadian Contemporary Fiction." LAURENTIAN UNIVERSITY REVIEW, 7 (Nov. 1974), 25-31.

425 _____. "Northern Utopia." CANADIAN LITERATURE, No. 63 (Wint. 1975), pp. 35-39.

426 _____. "The Violence of Isolation: A Theme in Canadian Literature." LAURENTIAN UNIVERSITY REVIEW, 4 (Nov. 1971), 15-22.

427 _____. "The Wild Creatures, the Native People, and Us: Canadian Literary-Ecological Relationships." ALTERNATIVES: PERSPECTIVES ON SOCIETY AND ENVIRONMENT, 7 (Wint. 1978), 20-23.

428 Mitcham, Elizabeth. "The Canadian Matriarch: A Study in Contemporary French-English Fiction." REVUE DE L'UNIVERSITÉ DE MONCTON, 7 (Jan. 1974), 37-42.

429 Monk, Patricia. "Shadow Continent: The Image of Africa in Three Canadian Writers." ARIEL, 8 (Oct. 1977), 3-25.

430 Morley, Patricia. "Engel, Wiseman, Laurence: Women Writers, Women's Lives." WORLD LITERATURE WRITTEN IN ENGLISH, 17 (Apr. 1978), 154-64.

431 Moss, John G. "Canadian Frontiers: Sexuality and Violence from Richardson to Kroetsch." JOURNAL OF CANADIAN FICTION, 2 (Sum. 1973), 36-41.

432 Mullins, Stanley G. "The Didactic Novel in Post-War Canadian Fiction." CULTURE, 23 (June 1962), 137-53.

433 Muntean, George. "Relations Culturelles Roumano-Canadiennes." REVISTA DE ISTORIE SI THEORIE LITERARĂ, 22, No. 3 (1973), 377-86.

434 Nadel, Ira. "The Absent Prophet in Canadian Jewish Fiction." ENGLISH QUARTERLY, 5 (Spr. 1972), 83-92.

435 New, William H. "Afrocanadiana: The African Setting in Canadian Literature." JOURNAL OF CANADIAN STUDIES, 6 (Feb. 1971), 33-38.

   Reprinted in no. 173.

436 _____. "Canada: Home Ground, Foreign Territory." In his AMONG WORLDS: AN INTRODUCTION TO MODERN COMMONWEALTH AND

SOUTH AFRICAN FICTION. Erin, Ont.: Porcépic, 1975, pp. 101-29. Bibliog., pp. 244-50.

437   _____. "Canadian Literature and Commonwealth Responses." CANADIAN LITERATURE, No. 66 (Aut. 1975), pp. 14-30.

438   _____. "In Defence of Private Worlds: An Approach to Irony in Canadian Fiction." JOURNAL OF COMMONWEALTH LITERATURE, No. 10 (Dec. 1970), pp. 132-44.

439   _____. "A Wellspring of Magma: Modern Canadian Writing." TWENTIETH CENTURY LITERATURE, 14 (Oct. 1968), 123-32.

440   _____. "The Writing of the Decade: The Novel in English." CANADIAN LITERATURE, No. 41 (Sum. 1969), pp. 121-25.

    Reprinted in nos. 173, 206, and 5106.

441 Newton, Norman. "Wilderness No Wilderness." CANADIAN LITERATURE, No. 63 (Wint. 1975), pp. 18-34.

442 Noonan, Gerald. "Aldous Huxley and the Critical Path in Canadian Literature, or How Imperious Fashion Screws Up Local Art--Everywhere." JOURNAL OF CANADIAN FICTION, 2 (Wint. 1973), 73-76.

443 O'Broin, Padraig. "Fire-Drake: Report of a Talk by Irving Layton on Jewish Writers in Canadian Literature." TEANGADOIR, 2nd ser., 1 (Nov. 1961), 73-80.

444 O'Connor, John J. "Saskatchewan Sirens: The Prairie as Sea in Western Canadian Literature." JOURNAL OF CANADIAN FICTION, 28-29 (1980), 157-71.

445 O'Flaherty, Patrick. "Newfoundland Writing: 1949-74: A Comment." CANADIAN FORUM, 53 (Mar. 1974), 28-30.

446 Pacey, Desmond. "Areas of Research in Canadian Literature." UNIVERSITY OF TORONTO QUARTERLY, 23 (Oct. 1953), 58-63.

    Reprinted in no. 177.

447   _____. "Areas of Research in Canadian Literature: A Reconsideration Twenty Years Later." QUEEN'S QUARTERLY, 81 (Spr. 1974), 62-69.

448   _____. "At Last--A Canadian Literature?" CAMBRIDGE REVIEW, 2 Dec. 1938, pp. 146-47.

    Reprinted in no. 177.

449   _____. "The Canadian Imagination." LITERARY REVIEW, 8 (Sum. 1965), 437-44.

        Reprinted in no. 177.

450   _____. "The Canadian Writer and His Public, 1882-1952." In STUDIA VARIA: ROYAL SOCIETY OF CANADA LITERARY AND SCIENTIFIC PAPERS. Ed. E.G.D. Murray. [Toronto]: University of Toronto Press, 1957, pp. 10-20.

        Reprinted in no. 177.

451   _____. "Introduction." In his A BOOK OF CANADIAN STORIES. Toronto: Ryerson, 1947, pp. xi-xxxvii.

452   _____. "Literary Criticism in Canada." UNIVERSITY OF TORONTO QUARTERLY, 19 (Jan. 1950), 113-19.

453   _____. "The Novel in Canada." QUEEN'S QUARTERLY, 52 (Aut. 1945), 322-31.

        Reprinted in nos. 136 and 177.

454   _____. "The Outlook for Canadian Literature." CANADIAN LITERA-TURE, No. 36 (Spr. 1968), pp. 14-25.

        Reprinted in no. 177.

455   _____. "'Summer's Heat, and Winter's Frigid Gales': The Effects of the Canadian Climate Upon Canadian Literature." PROCEEDINGS AND TRANSACTIONS OF THE ROYAL SOCIETY OF CANADA, 4th ser., 8 (1970), 3-23.

456   _____. "Two Accents, One Voice." SATURDAY REVIEW, 7 June 1952, pp. 15-16, 50-51.

457   _____. "The Young Writer and the Canadian Milieu." QUEEN'S QUAR-TERLY, 69 (Aut. 1962), 378-90.

        Reprinted in no. 177.

458   Pache, Walter. "Auf der Suche nach Identität: Zur Situation der englisch-kanadischen Literatur." AKZENTE, 23, No. 3 (1976), 196-216.

459   _____. "English-Canadian Fiction & the Pastoral Tradition." CANADIAN LITERATURE, No. 86 (1980), pp. 15-28.

460   . "Formen der Idylle in der modernen Erzählliteratur Kanadas." ARCADIA, 15 (1980), 29-43.

461   Paolucci, Anne, and Henry Paolucci. "Canada's 'Two Solitudes': Foci of a National Ellipse." REVIEW OF NATIONAL LITERATURES, 7 (1976), 38-66.

      Reprinted in no. 178.

462   Parker, George. "The Canadian Author and Publisher in the Twentieth Century." In EDITOR, AUTHOR, AND PUBLISHER: PAPERS GIVEN AT THE EDITORIAL CONFERENCE, UNIVERSITY OF TORONTO, NOVEMBER 1968. Ed. William J. Howard. Toronto: University of Toronto Press, 1969, pp. 28-46.

463   Paustian, Shirley Irene. "Saskatchewan in Fiction." SASKATCHEWAN HISTORY, 1 (Oct. 1948), 23-26.

464   Phelps, Arthur L. "Canadian Literature and Canadian Society." NORTHERN REVIEW, 3 (Apr.-May 1950), 23-26, 31-35.

465   Pierce, Lorne Albert. "A Survey of English Canadian Literature (1882-1932)." In FIFTY YEARS RETROSPECT, ROYAL SOCIETY OF CANADA ANNIVERSARY VOLUME, 1882-1932. Toronto: Ryerson, 1932, pp. 55-62.

466   . "To Canadian Authors, without Prejudice." CANADIAN BOOK-MAN, 20 (Aug. 1938), 22-24.

467   Pivato, Joseph. "Eight Approaches to Canadian Literary Criticism." JOURNAL OF COMMONWEALTH LITERATURE, 13, No. 3 (1979), 43-53.

468   . "Italy in French and English-Canadian Literature." SELECTA, 1 (1980), 19-22.

469   Polk, James. "Lives of the Hunted." CANADIAN LITERATURE, No. 53 (Sum. 1972), pp. 51-59.

470   Pynsent, R. "Nationaler Sensualismus: Dreizehn kanadische Dichter." AKZENTE, 23, No. 3 (1976), 242-55.

471   Reaney, James. "A Hut in the Global Village." PROCEEDINGS AND TRANSACTIONS OF THE ROYAL SOCIETY OF CANADA, 4th ser., 5 (1967), 51-56.

472   Reid, J. Addison. "The Canadian Novel." CANADIAN FORUM, 2 (June 1922), 658-660.

473   Reid, Verna. "The Small Town in Canadian Fiction." ENGLISH QUAR-
TERLY, 6 (Sum. 1973), 171-81.

474   Ricou, Laurence. "Empty as Nightmare: Man and Landscape in Recent
Canadian Prairie Fiction." MOSAIC, 6 (Wint. 1973), 143-60.

      Reprinted in a different form in no. 190.

475   _____. "From King to Interloper: Man on the Prairie in Canadian
Fiction 1920-1929." In THE TWENTIES IN WESTERN CANADA. Ed.
Susan Trofimenkoff. Ottawa: National Museum of Man, 1972, pp.
5-31.

      Reprinted in a different form in no. 190.

476   Entry deleted.

477   Riedel, Walter E. "Kanadische Kurz-Prosa in Deutscher Übersetzung."
DEUTSCHKANADISCHES JAHRBUCH, 4 (1978), 205-14.

478   Rimanelli, Giose. "Canadian Literature: An Italian View." CANADIAN
LITERATURE, No. 21 (Sum. 1964), pp. 13-20.

479   Robertson, R.T. "Another Preface to an Uncollected Anthology: Canadian
Criticism in a Commonwealth Context." ARIEL, 4 (July 1973), 70-81.

480   Rodensky, R.L. "On the Nature and Purpose of Canadian Literature."
ALIVE, 34 ([1974]), 15.

      See nos. 218 and 273 for replies.

481   Ross, Catherine Sheldrick. "Calling Back the Ghost of the Old-Time
Heroine: Duncan, Montgomery, Atwood, Laurence, and Munro." STUDIES
IN CANADIAN LITERATURE, 4 (Wint. 1979), 43-58.

482   _____. "'A Singing Spirit': Female Rites of Passage in KLEE WYCK,
SURFACING and THE DIVINERS." ATLANTIS, 4 (Fall 1978), 87-94.

483   Rubinger, Catherine. "Two Related Solitudes: Canadian Novels in
French and English." JOURNAL OF COMMONWEALTH LITERATURE,
No. 3 (July 1967), pp. 49-57.

484   Sandwell, Bernard K. "Professional Conspiracy to Destroy Canadian Literature." SATURDAY NIGHT, 27 July 1946, p. 11.

485 _____. "The Social Function of Fiction." QUEEN'S QUARTERLY, 49 (Wint. 1942), 322-32.

486 Schoemperlen, Diane. "The Role of the House in Canadian Fiction." MALAHAT REVIEW, No. 51 (July 1979), pp. 17-32.

487 Scobie, Stephen. "Scenes from the Lives of the Saints: A Hagiology of Canadian Literature." LAKEHEAD UNIVERSITY REVIEW, 7 (Sum. 1974), 3-20.

488 Seaman, Andrew Thompson. "Fiction in Atlantic Canada." CANADIAN LITERATURE, Nos. 68-69 (Spr.-Sum. 1976), pp. 26-39.

489 Selby, Joan. "The Transmutation of History: Landmarks in Canadian Historical Fiction for Children." CANADIAN LITERATURE, No. 6 (Aut. 1960), pp. 32-40.

490 Sharp, D.L. "Quality of Canadian Writing." COMMENTATOR, 15 (Jan. 1971), 16-17.

491 Shoolman, Regina. "Is There a Canadian Literature?" STORY, 10 (Mar. 1937), 2-3, 5-7, 119.

492 Sinclair, Lister S. "The Canadian Idiom." HERE AND NOW, 2 (June 1949), 16-18.

          Reprinted in no. 192.

493 Sirois, Antoine. "Conquête Horizontale et Verticale de la Ville." CA-NADIAN LITERATURE, No. 72 (Spr. 1977), pp. 45-48.

494 _____. "'Le Mont-Royal.'" In MÉLANGES DE CIVILISATION CANADIENNE-FRANÇAISE OFFERTS AU PROFESSEUR PAUL WYCZYNSKI. Cahiers du Center de Recherche en Civilisation Canadienne-Française. Ottawa: Éditions de l'Université d'Ottawa, 1977, pp. 267-73.

495 _____. "L'Identité Nationale dans le Roman et le Théâtre Canadiens-Anglais." PROCEEDINGS AND TRANSACTIONS OF THE ROYAL SO-CIETY OF CANADA, 4th ser., 16 (1978), 261-68.

496 _____. "L'Image de la Ville dans le Roman du Terroir D'Expression Française et d'Expression Anglaise." CANADIAN REVIEW OF COM-PARATIVE LITERATURE, 3 (Fall 1976), 269-85. Bibliog.

497 Skelton, R. "Forget CanLit and Concentrate on LitCan." BOOKS IN CANADA, 7 (Mar. 1978), 7-8.

498   Smith, A. "Continental Dimension in the Evolution of the English-Canadian Mind." INTERNATIONAL JOURNAL, 31 (Sum. 1976), 442-69.

499   Smith, Arthur James Marshall. "Canadian Literature of Today and Tomorrow." PROCEEDINGS OF THE CANADIAN LIBRARY ASSOCIATION, June 1947, pp. 32-38.

500   _____. "Evolution and Revolution as Aspects of English-Canadian and American Literature." In PERSPECTIVES ON REVOLUTION AND EVOLUTION. Ed. Richard A. Preston. Duke University Center for Commonwealth and Comparative Studies, 46. Durham, N.C.: Duke University Press, 1979, pp. 213-37.

501   _____. "Wanted--Canadian Criticism." CANADIAN FORUM, 8 (Apr. 1928), 600-601.

        Reprinted in no. 192.

502   Staines, David. "Introduction: Canada Observed." In his THE CANADIAN IMAGINATION: DIMENSIONS OF A LITERARY CULTURE. Cambridge, Mass.: Harvard University Press, 1977, pp. 1-21.

503   Stephen, A.M. "Views on Canadian Literature." INTERNATIONAL FORUM, 1 (May 1926), 25-30.

504   Stephens, Donald. "Lilacs out of the Mosaic Land: Aspects of the Sacrificial Theme in Canadian Fiction." DALHOUSIE REVIEW, 48 (Wint. 1968-69), 500-509.

505   _____. "A Quality of Negatives." CANADIAN LITERATURE, No. 27 (Wint. 1966), pp. 3-4.

506   _____. "Recent Canadian Short Fiction." LITERARY HALF-YEARLY, 13 (July 1972), 181-84.

507   _____. "The Recent English Short Story in Canada and Its Themes." WORLD LITERATURE WRITTEN IN ENGLISH, 2 (Apr. 1972), 49-52.

508   _____. "The Writing of the Decade: 4. The Short Story in English." CANADIAN LITERATURE, No. 41 (Sum. 1969), pp. 126-30.

        Reprinted in no. 5106.

509   Stevens, Peter. "Canada." In LITERATURES OF THE WORLD IN ENGLISH. Ed. Bruce King. London: Routledge and Kegan Paul, 1974, pp. 42-60.

510 _____. "Canadian Artists as Writers." CANADIAN LITERATURE, No. 46 (Aut. 1970), pp. 19-34.

511 _____. "The Writing of the Decade. 5. Criticism." CANADIAN LITERATURE, No. 41 (Sum. 1969), pp. 131-38.

Reprinted in no. 5106.

512 Stevenson, Lionel. "Canadian Fiction: Then and Now." CANADIAN AUTHOR AND BOOKMAN, 39 (Aut. 1963), 11-13, 23-24.

513 _____. "The Outlook for Canadian Fiction." CANADIAN BOOKMAN, 6 (July 1924), 157-58.

514 _____. "Overseas Literature: From a Canadian Point of View." ENGLISH REVIEW, 39 (Dec. 1924), 876-86.

515 Stich, K.P. "The Country Beyond: Some Aspects of Canadian Literature in France: 1900-1930." LAURENTIAN UNIVERSITY REVIEW, 9 (Nov. 1976), 71-79.

516 Stock, Brian. "A Culture in Search of an Economy." TIMES LITERARY SUPPLEMENT, 26 Oct. 1973, pp. 1311-13.

517 _____. "English Canada: The Visible and Invisible Cultures." CANADIAN FORUM, 52 (Mar. 1973), 29-33.

518 Stockdale, J.C. "The Time is Now or Not Yet: Attitudes towards Exploration in the French and English Canadian Novel." STUDIES IN CANADIAN LITERATURE, 4 (Sum. 1979), 62-73.

519 Stouck, David. "Notes on the Canadian Imagination." CANADIAN LITERATURE, No. 54 (Aut. 1972), pp. 9-26.

520 Strange, K.M. "Quantity and Quality in Canadian Writing." SATURDAY NIGHT, 1 Nov. 1947, pp. 18, 22.

521 Stratford, Philip. "Canada's Two Literatures: A Search for Emblems." CANADIAN REVIEW OF COMPARATIVE LITERATURE, 6 (Spr. 1979), 131-38.

522 Strong-Boag, Veronica. "Cousin Cinderella: A Guide to Historical Literature Pertaining to Canadian Women." In WOMEN IN CANADA. Ed. Marylee Stephenson. Toronto: New, 1973, pp. 262-90.

523   Struthers, J.R. (Tim). "Myth and Reality: A Regional Approach to the Canadian Short Story." LAURENTIAN UNIVERSITY REVIEW, 8 (Nov. 1975), 28-48.

524   Sullivan, Rosemary. "Beyond SURVIVAL." CANADIAN FORUM, 57 (Mar. 1978), 6-7.

525   Sutherland, Fraser. "Home Truths." CANADIAN LITERATURE, Nos. 68-69 (Spr.-Sum. 1976), pp. 102-06.

526   _____. "Nada in Canada." NORTHERN JOURNEY, 2 (1972-73), 6-16.

527   Sutherland, John. "Critics on the Defensive." NORTHERN REVIEW, 2 (Oct.-Nov. 1947), 18-23.

528   Sutherland, Ronald. "The Body-Odour of Race." CANADIAN LITERATURE, No. 37 (Sum. 1968), pp. 46-67.

            Reprinted in no. 201.

529   _____. "The Calvinist-Jansenist Pantomime: An Essay in Comparative Literature." JOURNAL OF CANADIAN STUDIES, 5 (May 1970), 10-21.

            Reprinted in no. 201.

530   _____. "Canada's Elizabethan Age." TIMES LITERARY SUPPLEMENT, 26 Oct. 1973, pp. 1295-96.

531   _____. "Canadian Fiction: Comparatively Speaking." REVIEW OF NATIONAL LITERATURES, 7 (1976), 13-37.

            Reprinted in no. 178.

532   _____. "Children of the Changing Wind." JOURNAL OF CANADIAN STUDIES, 5 (Nov. 1970), 3-11.

            Reprinted in no. 201.

533   _____. "Cornerstone for a New Morality: The Existential Vacuum and the Canadian Novel in English and French." WASCANA REVIEW, 4, No. 2 (1969), 39-52.

            Reprinted in no. 201.

534   _____. "The Fourth Separatism." CANADIAN LITERATURE, No. 45 (Sum. 1970), pp. 7-23.

            Reprinted in no. 201.

535 _____. "The Mainstream." CANADIAN LITERATURE, No. 53 (Sum. 1972), pp. 30-41.

>Reprinted in no. 200.

536 _____. "Tabernacles à Douze Étages: The New Multi-Cultural Nationalism in Canada." JOURNAL OF CANADIAN FICTION, 2 (Spr. 1973), 72-77.

>Reprinted in no. 200.

537 _____. "Twin Solitudes." CANADIAN LITERATURE, No. 31 (Wint. 1967), pp. 5-24.

>Reprinted in no. 201.

538 Swainson, Donald. "Trends in Canadian Biography: Recent Historical Writing." QUEEN'S QUARTERLY, 87 (Aut. 1980), 413-29.

539 Swan, Susan. "Why Women Write the Most Interesting Books: The Astonishing Matriarchy in Canadian Letters." SATURDAY NIGHT, 93 (Nov. 1978), 21-23.

540 Tallman, Warren. "Wolf in the Snow. Part One: Four Windows on to Landscapes." CANADIAN LITERATURE, No. 5 (Sum. 1960), pp. 7-20.

>Reprinted in nos. 161, 978, and 5102.

541 _____. "Wolf in the Snow. Part Two: The House Repossessed." CANADIAN LITERATURE, No. 6 (Aut. 1960), pp. 41-48.

>Reprinted in nos. 161, 978, 3755, and 5102.

542 Thacker, Robert. "Canada's Mounted: The Evolution of a Legend." JOURNAL OF POPULAR CULTURE, 14 (1980), 298-312.

543 Thiessen, J. "Canadian Mennonite Literature." CANADIAN LITERATURE, No. 51 (Wint. 1972), pp. 65-72.

544 Thomas, Clara. "Crusoe and the Precious Kingdom: Fables of our Literature." JOURNAL OF CANADIAN FICTION, 1 (Spr. 1972), 58-64.

545 _____. "Happily Ever After: Canadian Women in Fiction and Fact." CANADIAN LITERATURE, No. 34 (Aut. 1967), pp. 43-53.

546 _____. "Heroinism, Feminism and Humanism: Anna Jameson to Margaret Laurence." ATLANTIS, 4 (Fall 1978), 19-29.

547 _____. "Seeing Niagara and After." ÉTUDES CANADIENNES/CANADIAN STUDIES, 2 (1976), 47-61.

548 _____. "The Town--Our Tribe." LITERARY HALF-YEARLY, 13 (July 1972), 210-26.

549 Thompson, Eric. "Prairie Mosaic: The Immigrant Novel in the Canadian West." STUDIES IN CANADIAN LITERATURE, 5 (Fall 1980), 236-59.

550 Thompson, Kent. "The Canadian Short Story in English and the Little Magazines: 1971." WORLD LITERATURE WRITTEN IN ENGLISH, 11 (Apr. 1972), 15-24.

551 "Towards a Methodology of Comparative Canadian Studies/À la Recherche d'une Méthodologie en Études Comparées Canadiennes." CANADIAN REVIEW OF COMPARATIVE LITERATURE, 6 (1979), 115-30.

552 Tretheway, David. "Alienated Adam: The Voyageur." COPPERFIELD, 5 (1974), 9-33.

553 Varcoe, George. "Den nutida romanen i kanadensisk literatur." BON-NIERS LITTERÄRA, 43 (1974), 67-75.

554 Vipond, Mary. "Best Sellers in English Canada, 1899-1918: An Overview." JOURNAL OF CANADIAN FICTION, No. 24 ([1979]), pp. 96-119. Bibliog.

555 _____. "The Image of Women in Mass Circulation Magazines in the 1920s." MODERNIST STUDIES, 1 (1974-75), 5-13.

556 Waddington, Miriam. "Canadian Tradition and Canadian Literature." JOURNAL OF CANADIAN FICTION, No. 8 (Dec. 1969), pp. 125-41.

557 Walsh, William. "Canada." In his COMMONWEALTH LITERATURE. London: Oxford University Press, 1973, pp. 67-92.

558 Warwick, Jack. "The Call of the Wild in French and English Canadian Literature." ÉTUDES CANADIENNES/CANADIAN STUDIES, 2 (1976), 79-89.

559 _____. "Le Nord Canadien: Deux Cultures, un Mythe?" In MÉLANGES DE CIVILISATION CANADIENNE-FRANÇAISE OFFERTS AU PROFESSEUR PAUL WYCZYNSKI. Cahiers du Centre de Recherche en Civilisation Canadienne-Française. Ottawa: Éditions de l'Université d'Ottawa, 1977, pp. 293-302.

560   Waterston, Elizabeth. "The Lowland Tradition in Canadian Literature."
       In THE SCOTTISH TRADITION IN CANADA. Generations: History of
       Canada's Peoples. Ed. W. Stanford Reid. Toronto: McClelland and
       Stewart, 1976, pp. 203-31.

561   Watson, J. Wreford. "Canadian Regionalism in Life and Letters." GEO-
       GRAPHICAL JOURNAL, 131 (Mar. 1965), 21-33. Bibliog.

562   Watt, Frank W. "Climate of Unrest: Periodicals in the Twenties and
       Thirties." CANADIAN LITERATURE, No. 12 (Spr. 1962), pp. 15-27.

563   _____. "The Growth of Proletarian Literature in Canada, 1872-1920."
       DALHOUSIE REVIEW, 40 (Sum. 1960), 157-73.

564   _____. "The Literature of Canada." In THE COMMONWEALTH PEN:
       AN INTRODUCTION TO THE LITERATURE OF THE BRITISH COMMON-
       WEALTH. Ed. Alan Lindsey McLeod. Ithaca, N.Y.: Cornell University
       Press, 1961, pp. 11-34.

565   _____. "The Theme of 'Canada's Century,' 1896-1920." DALHOUSIE
       REVIEW, 38 (Sum. 1958), 154-66.

566   Watters, Reginald Eyre. "Original Relations: A Genographic Approach
       to the Literatures of Canada and Australia." CANADIAN LITERATURE,
       No. 7 (Wint. 1961), pp. 6-17.

567   _____. "A Quest for National Identity." PROCEEDINGS OF THE
       THIRD CONGRESS OF THE INTERNATIONAL COMPARATIVE LITERATURE
       ASSOCIATION, 1962, pp. 224-41.

568   _____. "The Study of Canadian Literature, Since 1940." WORLD LIT-
       ERATURE WRITTEN IN ENGLISH, No. 13 (Apr. 1968), pp. 1-9.

569   _____. "Unknown Literature." SATURDAY NIGHT, 17 Sept. 1955,
       pp. 33, 35-36.

       Reprinted in no. 978.

570   Weaver, Robert Leigh. "The Economics of Our Literature." QUEEN'S
       QUARTERLY, 60 (Wint. 1953-54), 476-85.

571   _____. "Notes on Canadian Literature." NATION, 16 Feb. 1946,
       pp. 198-200.

572   _____. "A Sociological Approach to Canadian Fiction." HERE AND
       NOW, 2 (June 1949), 12-15.

573   Westfall, William. "On the Concept of Region in Canadian History and Literature." JOURNAL OF CANADIAN STUDIES, 15 (Sum. 1980), 3-15.

574   Whalley, George. "The Great Canadian Novel." QUEEN'S QUARTERLY, 55 (Aut. 1948), 318-26.

575   Whitaker, Muriel. "Tales of the Wilderness: The Canadian Animal Story." CANADIAN CHILDREN'S LITERATURE, 1 (Sum. 1975), 38-45.

576   Williams, David. "The Indian Our Ancestor: Three Modes of Vision in Recent Canadian Fiction." DALHOUSIE REVIEW, 58 (Sum. 1978), 309-28.

577   Wilson, Edmund. "Reporter at Large." NEW YORKER, 14 Nov. 1964, pp. 63-140.

       Discusses Canadian literature with emphasis on MacLennan; reprinted in no. 210.

578   Winks, Robin W. "The American Exile." In AMERICA AND IRELAND, 1776-1976: THE AMERICAN IDENTITY AND THE IRISH CONNECTION. Ed. David Noel Doyle and Owen Dudley Edwards. Westport, Conn.: Greenwood, 1980, pp. 43-56.

579   Wood, Susan. "God's Doormats: Women in Canadian Prairie Fiction." JOURNAL OF POPULAR CULTURE, 14 (1980), 350-59.

580   Young, Scott. "What's Wrong with the Canadian Novel?" SATURDAY NIGHT, 29 May 1954, pp. 16-17.

581   Zezulka, Joseph M. "Passionate Provincials: Imperialism, Regionalism and Point of View." JOURNAL OF CANADIAN FICTION, No. 22 (1978), pp. 80-92.

582   Zonailo, C. "The Wilderness Metaphor: A Study of Four Novels." ROOM OF ONE'S OWN, 2, No. 1 (1976), 76-78.

583   Zureik, Elia T., and Alan Frizzell. "Values in Canadian Magazine Fiction: A Test of the Social Control Thesis." JOURNAL OF POPULAR CULTURE, 10 (Fall 1976), 359-76.

For articles in literary criticism, see also nos. 629, 700, 761, 846-47, 861, 863, 1063, 1065, 1243, 1298, 1302, 1312, 1317-18, 1528, 1530, 1716, 1718, 1830, 1984, 2021, 2152, 2173-74, 2200, 2236-37, 2240-41, 2243, 2916, 2920, 2924, 2989, 2991-92, 3003, 3012, 3076, 3156, 3185, 3974, 4122, 4229, 4320, 4570, 4573, 5068, 5078, 5124, 5135, 5149-50, 5166, 5173, 5177, 5182, 5201, 5204, 5208, and 5210.

INDIVIDUAL AUTHOR GUIDE

Each of the following author guides is divided into two major parts: primary material and secondary material, preceded by a brief biographical note. The primary material is arranged chronologically, the secondary material alphabetically. The two parts are further subdivided as follows:

Primary Material:

    Monographs:
        Fiction
        Nonfiction Prose
        Poetry
        Drama
        Edited Work
        Translations

    Shorter Work:
        Short Stories
        Articles

    Manuscripts

Secondary Material:

    Bibliographies
    Criticism
    Book Reviews

It should be noted that, because of their genres, Leacock's prose monographs are somewhat arbitrarily divided into humor, other works, and edited work. The work of the various authors working in nonfiction prose will require fewer subdivisions than that of the authors working both in fiction and nonfiction.

A. FICTION

ATWOOD, MARGARET (1939--   )

Margaret Eleanor Atwood was born in Ottawa and grew up in Ontario with summers in the northern Ontario and Quebec bush. She received a B.A. in 1961 from the University of Toronto, an A.M. in 1962 from Harvard, and completed the course work for a Ph.D. in English at Harvard. She has taught English at the University of British Columbia, Sir George Williams (Montreal), the University of Alberta, and York University (Toronto). She has also been a writer-in-residence for the University of Toronto, and has been board member and editor for the House of Anansi Press. In 1981 she received the $20,000 Molson Prize. Atwood established her reputation first as a poet; her nationalism and SURVIVAL, her controversial reading of Canadian literature, brought her to prominence as a public figure. In her fiction she displays a cerebral, often witty, acuteness and explores many of the themes and images found also in her poetry and criticism.

PRIMARY MATERIAL

Monographs

FICTION

584   THE EDIBLE WOMAN. Boston: Little, Brown, 1969. 281 p.

585   SURFACING. Toronto: McClelland and Stewart, 1972. 192 p.

586   LADY ORACLE. Toronto: McClelland and Stewart, 1976. 345 p.

587   DANCING GIRLS AND OTHER STORIES. Toronto: McClelland and Stewart, 1977. 254 p.

588   LIFE BEFORE MAN. Toronto: McClelland and Stewart, 1979. 317 p.

589   ANNA'S PET. By Margaret Atwood and Joyce Barkhouse. Illus. Ann Blades. Toronto: James Lorimer, 1980. N. pag.
          For children.

590   BODILY HARM. Toronto: McClelland and Stewart, 1981. 301 p.

NONFICTION PROSE

591   SURVIVAL: A THEMATIC GUIDE TO CANADIAN LITERATURE. Toronto:
       Anansi, 1972. 287 p. Bibliog. Index.

592   DAYS OF THE REBELS: 1815/1840. Canada's Illustrated Heritage. Toronto:
       Natural Science of Canada, 1977. 128 p. Index.

POETRY

593   DOUBLE PERSEPHONE. Toronto: Hawkshead, 1961. 16 p.

594   THE CIRCLE GAME. Illus. Charles Pachter. Toronto: Contact, 1966.
       80 p.

595   THE ANIMALS IN THAT COUNTRY. Toronto: Oxford University Press,
       1968. viii, 69 p.

596   THE JOURNALS OF SUSANNA MOODIE. Toronto: Oxford University
       Press, 1970. 64 p.

597   PROCEDURES FOR UNDERGROUND. Toronto: Oxford University Press,
       1970. 79 p.

598   POWER POLITICS. Toronto: Anansi, 1971. 58 p.

599   YOU ARE HAPPY. Toronto: Oxford University Press, 1974. 96 p.

600   SELECTED POEMS. Toronto: Oxford University Press, 1976. 240 p.

601   TWO-HEADED POEMS. Toronto: Oxford University Press, 1978. 112 p.

602   UP IN THE TREE. Toronto: McClelland and Stewart, [1978]. N. pag.
          For children.

603   TRUE STORIES. Don Mills, Ont.: Oxford University Press, 1981. 103 p.

Shorter Work

SHORT STORIES

604   "The Glass Slippers." ACTA VICTORIANA, 82 (Mar. 1958), 16-17.

605   "The Pilgrimage." ACTA VICTORIANA, 83 (Dec. 1958), 34-36.

606   "A Cliché for January." ACTA VICTORIANA, 83 (Feb. 1959), 7-9.

607   "The Child is Now." SHEET, 1 (Jan. 1960), 10-12.

608   "Insula Insularum." ACTA VICTORIANA, 85 (Feb. 1961), 6-11.

609   "Testament Found in a Bureau Drawer." PRISM INTERNATIONAL, 5 (Aut. 1965), 58-65.

610   "Going to Bed." EVIDENCE, No. 9 (1965), pp. 5-10.

611   "Encounters with the Element Man." IMPULSE, 1 (Wint. 1972), 24-31.

612   "Marrying the Hangman." CAPILANO REVIEW, No. 7 (Spr. 1975), pp. 17-19.

613   "Betty." CHATELAINE, 51 (Feb. 1978), 41, 84, 86-88, 90, 92-94.

614   "The Festival of Missed Crass." CHATELAINE, 52 (Dec. 1979), 44-45, 84, 90, 92, 94, 96.

       For children.

615   Entry deleted.

616   "Anglo-Saxon and I." ACTA VICTORIANA.

       No publishing details. Reprinted in THE TREASURY OF GREAT CANADIAN HUMOUR. Ed. Alan Walker. Toronto: McGraw-Hill Ryerson, 1974, pp. 393-96.

ARTICLES

617   "Superwoman Drawn and Quartered: The Early Forms of SHE." ALPHA-BET, No. 10 (July 1965), pp. 65-82.

618   "MacEwen's Muse." CANADIAN LITERATURE, No. 45 (Sum. 1970), pp. 24-32.

        Reprinted in no. 5112.

619   "Nationalism, Limbo and the Canadian Club." SATURDAY NIGHT, 86 (Jan. 1971), 10-11.

620   "Eleven Years of ALPHABET." CANADIAN LITERATURE, No. 49 (Sum. 1971), pp. 60-64.

621   "Travels Back: Refusing to Acknowledge Where You Come From Is an Act of Amputation." MACLEAN'S, 86 (Jan. 1973), 28-31, 48.

622   "How Do I Get Out of Here: The Poetry of John Newlove." OPEN LETTER, 2nd ser., No. 4 (Spr. 1973), pp. 59-70.

623   "Notes on POWER POLITICS." ACTA VICTORIANA, 97 (Apr. 1973), 6-19.

624   "Surviving the Critics: Mathews and Misrepresentation." THIS MAGA-ZINE, 7 (May-June 1973), 29-33.

        A reply to no. 705.

625   "Poetry in the Buffer Zone." TIMES LITERARY SUPPLEMENT, 26 Oct. 1973, pp. 1305-06.

626   "Getting Out from Under." In THE EMPIRE CLUB OF CANADA: AD-DRESSES 1972-1973. Toronto: Empire Club Foundation, 1973, pp. 353-67.

627   Introd., THE SUN AND THE MOON AND OTHER FICTIONS, by P.K. Page. Toronto: Anansi, 1973, n. pag.

628   "Face to Face: Margaret Laurence as Seen by Margaret Atwood." MAC-LEAN'S, 87 (May 1974), 38-39, 43-44, 46.

629   "What's So Funny?: Notes on Canadian Humour." THIS MAGAZINE, 8 (Aug.-Sept. 1974), 24-27.

630   "Un Petit Rat Heureux."   LE MACLEAN, Sept. 1974, pp. 19-21, 43.
         An interview with Marie-Claire Blais.

631   "Marie-Claire Blais Is Not for Burning: The Novelist Must Suffer but
Not Constantly."   MACLEAN'S, 88 (Sept. 1975), 26-29.

632   Introd., ST. LAWRENCE BLUES, by Marie-Claire Blais.   Trans. R. Manheim.
Toronto: Bantam, 1976, pp. vii-xvi.

633   "Paradoxes and Dilemmas: The Woman as Writer."   In WOMEN IN THE
CANADIAN MOSAIC.   Ed. Gwen Matheson.   Toronto: Peter Martin,
1976, pp. 256-73.

634   "Canadian Monsters: Some Aspects of the Supernatural in Canadian Fiction."
In THE CANADIAN IMAGINATION: DIMENSIONS OF A LITERARY
CULTURE.   Ed. David Staines.   Cambridge, Mass.:   Harvard University
Press, 1977, pp. 97-122.

635   "'My Craft and Sullen Art':   The Writers Speak."   ATLANTIS, 4 (Fall
1978), 161-63.

636   "Production Problems."   CANADIAN LITERATURE, No. 78 (Aut. 1978),
pp. 13-15.

         Discusses UP IN THE TREE.

637   "The Curse of Eve--Or, What I Learned in School."   In WOMEN ON
WOMEN.   Ed. with introd. by Ann B. Shteir.   Gerstein Lecture Series,
1976.   Toronto: York University, 1978, pp. 13-26.

         Reprinted in no. 136.

Manuscripts

638   University of Toronto Library.

SECONDARY MATERIAL

Bibliographies

639   Fairbanks, Carol.   "Margaret Atwood: A Bibliography of Criticism."
BULLETIN OF BIBLIOGRAPHY, 36 (1979), 85-90, 98.

640   Horne, Alan J., comp. "Margaret Atwood: An Annotated Bibliography
        (Prose)." In THE ANNOTATED BIBLIOGRAPHY OF CANADA'S MAJOR
        AUTHORS. Ed. Robert Lecker and Jack David. Downsview, Ont.:
        ECW, 1979, pp. 13-46. Index

641   _____. "A Preliminary Checklist of Writings by and about Margaret At-
        wood." CANADIAN LIBRARY JOURNAL, 31 (Nov.-Dec. 1974), 576-92.
        Dec. 1974), 576-92.

        Reprinted in no. 661.

642   _____. "A Preliminary Checklist of Writings by and about Margaret
        Atwood." MALAHAT REVIEW, No. 41 (Jan. 1977), pp. 195-222.

        A supplement to no. 641; reprinted in no. 661.

Criticism

643   Allen, Carolyn. "Failures of Word, Uses of Silence: Djuna Barnes,
        Adrienne Rich and Margaret Atwood." REGIONALISM AND THE FEMALE
        IMAGINATION, 4, No. 1 (1978), 1-7.

644   _____. "Margaret Atwood: Power of Transformation, Power of Knowl-
        edge." ESSAYS ON CANADIAN WRITING, No. 6 (Spr. 1977), pp.
        5-17.

645   "An ATLANTIS Interview with Margaret Atwood." ATLANTIS, 5 (Spr.
        1980), 202-11.

646   Belkin, Roslyn. "The Worth of the Shadow: Margaret Atwood's LADY
        ORACLE." THALIA, 1 (Wint. 1979), 3-8.

647   Bjerring, Nancy E. "The Problem of Language in Margaret Atwood's
        SURFACING." QUEEN'S QUARTERLY, 83 (Wint. 1976), 597-612.

648   Brady, Elizabeth. "Towards a Happier History: Women and Domination."
        In DOMINATION: ESSAYS EDITED FOR THE UNIVERSITY LEAGUE FOR
        SOCIAL REFORM. Ed. Alkis Kontos. Toronto: University of Toronto
        Press, 1975, pp. 17-31.

649   Braendlin, Bonnie Hoover. "Alther, Atwood, Ballantyne, and Gray:
        Secular Salvation in the Contemporary Feminist Bildungsroman." FRONTIERS,
        4, No. 1 (1979), 18-22.

650   Brown, Russell M. "Atwood's Sacred Wells." ESSAYS ON CANADIAN
        WRITING, No. 17 (Spr. 1980), pp. 5-43.

651   Cameron, Elspeth. "Margaret Atwood: A Patchwork Self." BOOK
       FORUM, 4, No. 1 (1978), 35-45. Bibliog.

       Discusses LADY ORACLE and DANCING GIRLS.

652   Campbell, Josie P. "Woman as Hero in Margaret Atwood's SURFACING."
       MOSAIC, 11 (Spr. 1978), 17-28.

653   Christ, Carol P. "Margaret Atwood: The Surfacing of Women's Spiritual
       Quest and Vision." SIGNS, 2 (Wint. 1976), 316-30; Reply: Atwood,
       2 (Wint. 1976), 340.

654   _____. "Refusing to Be Victim: Margaret Atwood." In her DIVING
       DEEP AND SURFACING: WOMEN WRITERS ON SPIRITUAL QUEST.
       Boston: Beacon, 1980, pp. 41-53.

655   Colman, S.J. "Margaret Atwood, Lucien Goldmann's Pascal, and the
       Meaning of 'Canada.'" UNIVERSITY OF TORONTO QUARTERLY, 48
       (Spr. 1979), 245-62.

656   Cude, Wilfred. "Nobody Dunit: The Loose End as Structual Element in
       LADY ORACLE." JOURNAL OF CANADIAN STUDIES, 15 (Spr. 1980),
       30-44.

       Reprinted in no. 133.

657   Davey, Frank. "Atwood Walking Backwards." OPEN LETTER, 2nd ser.,
       No. 5 (Sum. 1973), pp. 74-84.

658   _____. "LADY ORACLE'S Secret: Atwood's Comic Novels." STUDIES
       IN CANADIAN LITERATURE, 5 (Fall 1980), 209-21.

659   Davidson, Arnold E., and Cathy N. Davidson. "The Anatomy of Margaret
       Atwood's SURFACING." ARIEL, 10 (July 1979), 38-54.

660   _____. "Margaret Atwood's LADY ORACLE: The Artist as Escapist and
       Seer." STUDIES IN CANADIAN LITERATURE, 3 (Sum. 1978), 166-77.

661   _____, eds. THE ART OF MARGARET ATWOOD: ESSAYS IN CRI-
       TICISM. Toronto: Anansi, 1981. 304 p. Bibliog. Index.

       Articles on Atwood's poetry and prose, including one by
       Woodcock.

662   Davidson, Cathy N. "Canadian Wry: Comic Vision in Atwood's LADY ORACLE and Laurence's THE DIVINERS." REGIONALISM AND THE FE- MALE IMAGINATION, 3, Nos. 2-3 (1977-78), 50-55.

663   _____. "Chopin and Atwood: Woman Drowning, Woman Surfacing." KATE CHOPIN NEWSLETTER, 1, No. 3 (1975-76), 6-10.

664   Davidson, Jim. "Interview: Margaret Atwood." MEANJIN, 37 (July 1978), 189-206.

665   Dawe, Alan. Introd., THE EDIBLE WOMAN. New Canadian Library, no. 93. Toronto: McClelland and Stewart, 1973, n. pag.

666   Drummond, Ian. "Fairy Tales of Canada: II, The Lady of the Lake: Or How the Octopus Got Its Tentacles." CANADIAN FORUM, 54 (May- June 1974), 68-69.

667   Durand, Régis. "L'Individuel et le Politique: Notes Sur les Romans de Margaret Atwood et Leonard Cohen." ÉTUDES CANADIENNES/CANADIAN STUDIES, 1 (1975), 63-72.

668   Frankel, Vivian. "Margaret Atwood: A Personal View." BRANCHING OUT, 2 (Jan.-Feb. 1975), 24-27.

669   Fraser, D.M. "Margaret Atwood's SURFACING: Some Notes." 3¢ PULP, 1 May 1974, n. pag.

670   Fulford, Robert. "The Images of Atwood." MALAHAT REVIEW, No. 41 (Jan. 1977), pp. 95-98.

671   Galt, George. "SURFACING and the Critics." CANADIAN FORUM, 54 (May-June 1974), 12-14.

672   Garebian, Keith. "SURFACING: Apocalyptic Ghost Story." MOSAIC, 9 (Spr. 1976), 1-9.

673   Gerson, Carole. "Margaret Atwood and Quebec: A Footnote on SUR- FACING." STUDIES IN CANADIAN LITERATURE, 1 (Wint. 1976), 115- 19.

674   Gerstenberger, Donna. "Conceptions Literary and Otherwise: Women Writers and the Modern Imagination." NOVEL, 9 (Wint. 1976), 141-50.

675   Gibson, Mary Ellis. "A Conversation with Margaret Atwood." CHICAGO REVIEW, 27 (Spr. 1976), 105-13.

676   Gottlieb, Lois C., and Wendy Keitner. "Colonialism as Metaphor and Experience in THE GRASS IS SINGING and SURFACING." In AWAKENED CONSCIENCE: STUDIES IN COMMONWEALTH LITERATURE. Ed. C. D. Narasimhaiah. New Delhi: Sterling, 1978, pp. 307-14.

677   Grace, Sherrill E. VIOLENT DUALITY: A STUDY IN MARGARET ATWOOD. Montreal: Véhicule, 1980. 154 p. Index.

678   Griffith, Margaret. "Verbal Terrain in the Novels of Margaret Atwood." CRITIQUE, 21, No. 3 (1980), 85-93.

679   Gutteridge, Don. "Surviving the Fittest: Margaret Atwood and the Sparrow's Fall." JOURNAL OF CANADIAN STUDIES, 8 (Aug. 1973), 59-64.

680   Hammond, Karla. "An Interview with Margaret Atwood." AMERICAN POETRY REVIEW, 8, No. 5 (1979), 27-29.

681   _____. "A Margaret Atwood Interview." CONCERNING POETRY, 12, No. 2 (1979), 73-81.

682   Hancock, Geoffrey. "This Little Peggy Went to Market: Atwood on Being an International Literary Success." BOOKS IN CANADA, 6 (1980), 30-31.

         An interview.

683   Harrison, J. "The 20,000,000 Solitudes of SURFACING." DALHOUSIE REVIEW, 59 (Spr. 1979), 74-81.

684   Hinz, Evelyn J. "Contemporary North American Literary Primitivism: DELIVERANCE and SURFACING." In HEMISPHERIC PERSPECTIVES ON THE UNITED STATES: PAPERS FROM THE NEW WORLD CONFERENCE. Ed. Joseph S. Tulchin. Contributions in American Studies, 36. Westport, Conn.: Greenwood, 1978, pp. 150-71.

685   Hinz, Evelyn J., and J.J. Teunissen. "SURFACING: Margaret Atwood's Nymph Complaining." CONTEMPORARY LITERATURE, 20 (Spr. 1979), 221-36.

686   Hulley, Kathleen. "Margaret Atwood and Leonard Cohen: The Feminine Voice." ÉTUDES CANADIENNES/CANADIAN STUDIES, 1 (1975), 73-78.

687   Hutcheon, Linda. "Atwood and Laurence: Poet and Novelist." STUDIES IN CANADIAN LITERATURE, 3 (Sum. 1978), 255-63.

         Discusses THE EDIBLE WOMAN and THE STONE ANGEL.

688   Jones, Anne G. "Margaret Atwood: Songs of the Transformer, Songs of the Transformed." HOLLINS CRITIC, 16 (June 1979), 1-15.

689   Kaminski, Margaret. "Interview with Margaret Atwood." WAVES, 4 (Aut. 1975), 8-13.

690   King, Bruce. "Margaret Atwood's SURFACING." JOURNAL OF CA- NADIAN FICTION, 12 (Aug. 1977), 23-32.

691   Ladousse, Gillian Porter. "The Unicorn and the Booby Hatch: An In- terview with Margaret Atwood." ÉTUDES CANADIENNES/CANADIAN STUDIES, 5 (1978), 97-111.

692   Landsberg, M. "Margaret Atwood." CHATELAINE, 50 (Oct. 1977), 120-21.

693   Levenson, Christopher. "Interview with Margaret Atwood." MANNA, No. 2 (1972), pp. 46-54.

694   Lyons, Bonnie. "'Neither Victims nor Executioners' in Margaret Atwood's Fiction." WORLD LITERATURE WRITTEN IN ENGLISH, 17 (Apr. 1978), 181-87.

695   McCombs, Judith. "Atwood's Nature Concepts: An Overview." WAVES, 7 (Fall 1978), 68-78.

696   McDowell, J.H. "Margaret Atwood: LADY ORACLE." WORLD LIT- ERATURE WRITTEN IN ENGLISH, 16, No. 1 (1977), 82-86.

697   McLay, Catherine. "The Divided Self: Theme and Pattern in Margaret Atwood's SURFACING." JOURNAL OF CANADIAN FICTION, 4, No. 1 (1975), 82-95.

       Reprinted in no. 171.

698   MacLean, Susan. "LADY ORACLE: The Art of Reality and the Reality of Art." JOURNAL OF CANADIAN FICTION, 28-29 (1980), 179-97.

699   MacLulich, T.D. "Atwood's Adult Fairy Tale: Levi-Strauss, Bettelheim, and THE EDIBLE WOMAN." ESSAYS ON CANADIAN WRITING, 11 (Sum. 1978), 111-29.

700   _____. "The SURVIVAL Shoot-Out." ESSAYS ON CANADIAN WRITING, No. 1 (Wint. 1974), pp. 14-20.

701 Macri, F.M. "Survival Kit: Margaret Atwood and the Canadian Scene." MODERN POETRY STUDIES, 5 (Aut. 1974), 187-95.

702 Mandel, Eli. "Atwood Gothic." MALAHAT REVIEW, No. 41 (Jan. 1977), pp. 165-74.

703 Mansbridge, Francis. "Search for Self in the Novels of Margaret Atwood." JOURNAL OF CANADIAN FICTION, No. 22 (1978), pp. 106-17.

704 Marshall, Tom. "Atwood under and above Water." MALAHAT REVIEW, No. 41 (Jan. 1977), pp. 89-94.

705 Mathews, Robin D. "Survival and Struggle in Canadian Literature." THIS MAGAZINE IS ABOUT SCHOOLS, 6 (Wint. 1972-73), 109-24.

    Reprinted in no. 163; see Atwood's reply, no. 624.

706 Miller, Hugh. "Surfacing to No Purpose: Margaret Atwood's Apparent Survival." ANTIGONISH REVIEW, No. 24 (Wint. 1975), pp. 59-61.

    Discusses SURFACING.

707 Miner, Valerie. "Atwood in Metamorphosis: An Authentic Canadian Fairy Tale." In HER OWN WOMAN: PROFILES OF TEN CANADIAN WOMEN. By Myrna Kostash et al. Toronto: Macmillan, 1975, pp. 173-94.

708 Mitcham, Allison. "Woman in the North." ALIVE, No. 39 ([1974]), p. 7.

    Discusses SURFACING.

709 Mitchell, Leila G. "The External World in the Novels of Margaret Atwood." JOURNAL OF CANADIAN STUDIES, 15 (Spr. 1980), 45-55.

710 Morley, Patricia. "Survival, Affirmation, and Joy." LAKEHEAD UNIVERSITY REVIEW, 7 (Sum. 1974), 21-30.

711 Nodelman, Perry. "Trusting the Untrustworthy." JOURNAL OF CANADIAN FICTION, No. 21 (1977-78), pp. 73-82.

    Discusses THE EDIBLE WOMAN.

712 Norris, Ken. "Survival in the Writings of Margaret Atwood." CROSS COUNTRY, No. 1 (Wint. 1975), pp. 18-29.

713   Oates, Joyce Carol. "A Conversation with Margaret Atwood." ONTARIO REVIEW, No. 9 (Fall-Wint. 1978-79), pp. 5-18.

714   _____. "An Interview with Margaret Atwood." NEW YORK TIMES BOOK REVIEW, 21 May 1978, pp. 15, 43-55.

715   Onley, Gloria. "Margaret Atwood: Surfacing in the Interests of Survival." WEST COAST REVIEW, 7 (Jan. 1973), 51-54.

716   _____. "Power Politics in Bluebeard's Castle." CANADIAN LITERATURE, No. 60 (Spr. 1974), pp. 21-42.

       Reprinted in no. 5112.

717   Page, Sheila. "Supermarket Survival: A Critical Analysis of Margaret Atwood's THE EDIBLE WOMAN." SPHINX, 1 (Wint. 1974), 9-19.

718   Piercy, Marge. "Margaret Atwood: Beyond Victimhood." AMERICAN POETRY REVIEW, 2 (Nov.-Dec. 1973), 41-44.

719   Purdy, Alfred W. "An Unblemished One-Tenth of One Per Cent of an Event." MALAHAT REVIEW, No. 41 (Jan. 1977), pp. 61-64.

720   Quigley, Theresia. "SURFACING: A Critical Study." ANTIGONISH REVIEW, No. 34 (Sum. 1978), pp. 77-87.

721   Reid, Joanne. "Margaret Atwood: Our Lady of Letters." CANADIAN REVIEW, 2 (Sept.-Oct. 1975), 35, 37-38.

722   Rigney, Barbara Hill. "'After the Failure of Logic': Descent and Return in SURFACING." In her MADNESS AND SEXUAL POLITICS IN THE FEMINIST NOVEL: STUDIES IN BRONTË, WOOLF, LESSING, AND ATWOOD. Madison: University of Wisconsin Press, 1978, pp. 91-115.

723   Rocard, Marcienne. "La Femme objet-de-consommation dans THE EDIBLE WOMAN de Margaret Atwood." CALIBAN, 17 (1980), 111-20.

724   Rogers, Linda. "Margaret the Magician." CANADIAN LITERATURE, No. 60 (Spr. 1974), pp. 83-85.

725   Rosenberg, Jerome H. "On Reading the Atwood Papers in the Thomas Fisher Library." MALAHAT REVIEW, No. 41 (Jan. 1977), pp. 191-94.

726   _____. "Woman as Everyman in Atwood's SURFACING: Some Observations on the End of the Novel." STUDIES IN CANADIAN LITERATURE, 3 (Wint. 1978), 127-32.

727   Ross, Catherine Sheldrick. "'Banished to this Other Place': Atwood's LADY ORACLE." ENGLISH STUDIES IN CANADA, 6 (Wint. 1980), 460-74.

728   _____. "Nancy Drew as Shaman: Atwood's SURFACING." CANADIAN LITERATURE, No. 84 (Spr. 1980), pp. 7-17.

729   Rubenstein, Roberta. "SURFACING: Margaret Atwood's Journey to the Interior." MODERN FICTION STUDIES, 22 (Aut. 1976), 387-99.

730   Salutin, Rick. "A Note on the Marxism of Atwood's SURVIVAL." MALAHAT REVIEW, No. 41 (Jan. 1977), pp. 57-60.

731   Sandler, Linda. "Interview with Margaret Atwood." MALAHAT REVIEW, No. 41 (Jan. 1977), pp. 7-27.

732   Savage, David. "Not Survival but Responsibility." DALHOUSIE REVIEW, 55 (Sum. 1975), 272-79.

       A reply to SURVIVAL.

733   Schaeffer, Susan Fromberg. "'It Is Time That Separates Us': Margaret Atwood's SURFACING." CENTENNIAL REVIEW, 18 (Fall 1974), 319-37.

734   Schiller, W.A. "Interview with Margaret Atwood." POETRY WINDSOR POÉSIE, 2, No. 3 (1976), 2-15.

735   Shapcott, Tom. "Margaret Atwood's SURFACING." In COMMON-WEALTH LITERATURE IN THE CURRICULUM. Ed. K.L. Goodwin. St. Lucia: Southern Pacific Association for Commonwealth Literature and Language Studies, 1980, pp. 86-96.

736   Sillers, P. "Power Impinging: Hearing Atwood's Vision." STUDIES IN CANADIAN LITERATURE, 4 (Wint. 1979), 59-70.

737   Slinger, Helen. "Interview with Margaret Atwood." MACLEAN'S, 6 Sept. 1976, pp. 4, 6-7.

738   Smith, Rowland J. "Margaret Atwood: The Stoic Comedian." MALAHAT REVIEW, No. 41 (Jan. 1977), pp. 134-44.

739   Steele, James. "The Literary Criticism of Margaret Atwood." In IN OUR OWN HOUSE: SOCIAL PERSPECTIVES ON CANADIAN LITERATURE. Ed. Paul Cappon. Toronto: McClelland and Stewart, 1978, pp. 73-81.

740 Struthers, J.R. (Tim). "An Interview With Margaret Atwood." ESSAYS ON CANADIAN WRITING, No. 6 (Spr. 1977), pp. 18-27.

741 Sullivan, Rosemary. "Breaking the Circle." MALAHAT REVIEW, No. 41 (Jan. 1977), pp. 30-41.

742 _____. "SURFACING and DELIVERANCE." CANADIAN LITERATURE, No. 67 (Wint. 1976), pp. 6-20.

743 Swan, Susan. "Margaret Atwood: The Woman as Poet." COMMUNIQUÉ, 8 (May 1975), 8-11, 45-46.

　　　An interview.

744 Sweetapple, Rosemary. "Margaret Atwood: Victims and Survivors." SOUTHERN REVIEW (University of Adelaide), 9 (Mar. 1976), 50-69.

745 Texmo, Dell. "Image and Identity in Margaret Atwood's THE EDIBLE WOMAN." ATLANTIS, 2 (Spr. 1977), Part 1, 64-76.

746 Thompson, J. Lee. "Can Canada Survive SURVIVAL? An Article on SUR-VIVAL: A THEMATIC GUIDE TO CANADIAN LITERATURE." AMERICAN REVIEW OF CANADIAN STUDIES, 3 (Aut. 1973), 101-07. Bibliog.

747 Van Varsveld, Gail. "Talking with Atwood: Excerpts from an Interview Conducted by Gail Van Varsveld." ROOM OF ONE'S OWN, 1 (Sum. 1975), 66-70.

748 Vincenti, Fiora. "Quattro Domande alla Scrittrice Margaret Atwood." UOMINE E LIBRI, 66 (Nov.-Dec. 1977), 48-49.

　　　An interview.

749 Webb, Phyllis. "Letters to Margaret Atwood." OPEN LETTER, 2nd ser., No. 5 (Sum. 1973), pp. 71-73.

For criticism on Atwood, see also nos. 126, 129, 133, 139, 157, 162, 170-71, 174, 205, 481-82, 1701, 3840, 5161, 5172, 5184, and 5188.

Book Reviews

750 THE EDIBLE WOMAN: BCan, 2 (July 1973), 54; CanL, 42 (Aut. 1969), 98-100; CFor, 49 (Feb. 1970), 267; COMMONWEAL, 7 Jan. 1972, p. 328; JCF, 2 (Fall 1973), 113-14; LISTENER, 28 Aug. 1969, p. 287; MHRev, 13 (Jan. 1970), 108-09; NYTBR, 18 Oct. 1970, p. 51; QUARRY,

19 (Spr. 1970), 55-56; SaTN, 84 (Nov. 1969), 54, 56, 58; SatR, 3 Oct. 1970, p. 40; SPHINX, 1 (Wint. 1974), 9-19; TamR, 54 (1970), 75-77; TLS, 2 Oct. 1969, p. 1122; UTQ, 39 (July 1970), 341; WCR, 5 (Oct. 1970), 68-70.

751   SURFACING: AntigR, 11 (Aut. 1972), 113-14; Atl, 231 (Apr. 1973), 127; BCan, 1 (Nov. 1972), 45-46; BCLJ, 36 (Apr. 1973), 80-81; BrBN, Oct. 1973, p. 696; CAB, 48 (Wint. 1972), 23; CanL, 55 (Wint. 1973), 108-10; CFM, 9 (Wint. 1973), 74-79; CFor, 52 (Jan. 1973), 34; CFor, 54 (May 1974), 12-14; COMMONWEAL, 7 Sept. 1973, p. 483; CRead, 14, No. 1 (1973), 2-3; DESCANT, 6 (Spr. 1973), 70-73; DR, 52 (Wint. 1972-73), 679-82; EJ, 63 (Spr. 1974), 90; FIDDLEHEAD, 97 (Spr. 1973), 114-16; JCF, 1 (Fall 1972), 99-100; JCF, 3, No. 3 (1974), 43-44; JCF, 4, No. 1 (1975), 82-95; LaUR, 6 (Fall 1973), 255-57; LISTENER, 24 May 1973, p. 696; LISTENER, 14 Mar. 1974, p. 342; MACLEAN'S, 85 (Sum. 1972), 88; NATION, 19 Mar. 1973, p. 374; NatR, 3 Aug. 1973, p. 852; NewR, 28 Apr. 1973, p. 27; NY, 14 Apr. 1973, p. 154; NYTBR, 4 Mar. 1973, p. 5; NYTBR, 10 June 1973, p. 40; NYTBR, 11 Aug. 1974, pp. 20-21; NYTBR, 17 July 1977; OpenL, 2nd ser., 5 (Sum. 1973), 74-81; Q&Q, 38, No. 10 (1972), 11; QQ, 80 (Sum. 1973), 278-81; QUARRY, 22 (Spr. 1973), 62-64; TLS, 1 June 1973, p. 604; TLS, 23 Nov. 1979, p. 42; UTQ, 42 (Sum. 1973), 344-45; WCR, 7 (Jan. 1973), 51-54.

752   LADY ORACLE: BCan, 5 (Sept. 1976), 3-5; CanL, 72 (Spr. 1977), 84-87; CanR, 3 (Dec. 1976), 52; CBRA, 1976, p. 137; CFor, 56 (Dec. 1976), 49-50; CRead, 17 (Sept. 1976), 2-4; ECW, 6 (Spr. 1977), 28-31; FIDDLEHEAD, 112 (Wint. 1977), 133-37; HudR, 30 (Spr. 1977), 149; LISTENER, 14 July 1977, p. 62; MACLEAN'S, 6 Sept. 1976, p. 68; NYRB, 28 Oct. 1976, p. 30; NYTBR, 26 Sept. 1976, p. 7; NYTBR, 15 Jan. 1978, p. 27; OntarioR, 5 (Fall 1976-77), 96-97; Q&Q, 42, No. 11 (1976), 6; QQ, 84 (Spr. 1977), 102-04; QUARRY, 26 (Spr. 1977), 49-51; SatN, 91 (Sept. 1976), 59; SatN, 91 (Nov. 1976), 46; SatR, 18 Sept. 1976, pp. 28-30; SPHINX, 2 (Wint. 1977), 81-85; TamR, 69 (Sum. 1976), 94-96; TLS, 15 July 1977, p. 872; UTQ, 46 (Sum. 1977), 343-44; WLWE, 16 (Apr. 1977), 82, 84-86.

753   DANCING GIRLS: BCan, 6 (Nov. 1977), 27-28; BrO, 5, No. 1 (1978), 44-45; CAB, 53 (Jan. 1978), 31, 33; CFor, 57 (Dec. 1977-Jan. 1978), 35; CRead, 18 (Aug. 1977), 5-6; FIDDLEHEAD, 117 (Spr. 1978), 134-35; Q&Q, 43, No. 14 (1977), 7; QQ, 85 (Aut. 1978), 517-18; SatN, 92 (Nov. 1977), 60-61, 67; UTQ, 47 (Sum. 1978), 329-31; WAVES, 6, No. 3 (1978); WLWE, 17 (Apr. 1978), 188-90.

754   LIFE BEFORE MAN: AMERICA, 28 June 1980, pp. 545-46; Atl, 245 (Apr. 1980), 123, BCan, 8 (Oct. 1979), 10-11; BCan, 8 (Nov. 1979), 33; BCan, 9 (Dec. 1980), 28; BOT, 3 (Feb. 1980), 71; BrO, 7, No. 1 (1980), 48-49; CanL, 86 (Aut. 1980), 136-38; CDim, 14 (May 1980), 47-48; CFor, 59 (Nov. 1979), 28-29; CRead, 20, No. 9

(1978), [1-2]; DR, 59 (Aut. 1979), 561-63; ECW, 20 (Wint. 1980-81), 165-67; FIDDLEHEAD, 124 (Wint. 1980), 111-12; HudR, 33 (Sum. 1980), 257-70; JCanS, 15 (Spr. 1980), 122-23; LISTENER, 13 Mar. 1980, p. 350; MACLEAN'S, 15 Oct. 1979, pp. 66, 68; NS, 9 May 1980, p. 715; NY, 7 July 1980, pp. 98-100; NYRB, 3 Apr. 1980, pp. 34-35; NYTBR, 3 Feb. 1980, p. 1; Q&Q, 45 (Oct. 1979), 31; QQ, 87 (Sum. 1980), 343-45; QUARRY, 29 (Wint. 1980), 90-92; SatN, 94 (Nov. 1979), 37-39; SatR, 2 Feb. 1980, p. 33-35; SPEC-TATOR, 15 Mar. 1980, p. 20; ThisM, 14 (Mar. 1980), 31-32; TLS, 14 Mar. 1980, p. 289; UTQ, 49 (Sum. 1980), 329-31.

755   SURVIVAL: ALIVE, 3, No. 6 (1973), 12-14; ARCS, 3 (Aut. 1973), 101-07; BCan, 1 (Oct. 1972), 10-11; BCan, 1 (Nov. 1972), 45; CanL, 55 (Wint. 1973), 3-6; CFM, 10 (Spr. 1973), 117-20; CFor, 53 (May 1973), 39-41; DR, 53 (Spr. 1973), 159-60; EVENT, 2, No. 3 (1973), 81-85; FIDDLEHEAD, 97 (Spr. 1973), 114-16; JCanS, 8 (Aug. 1973), 59; JCF, 3 (Wint. 1974), 112-13; JML, 4, No. 5 (1976), 917; LaUR, 6 (Fall 1973), 275-76; LISTENER, 14 Mar. 1974, p. 342; MACLEAN'S, 86 (Aug. 1973), 11, 14; MHRev, 26 (Apr. 1973), 233-34; NLI, 20 (1976), 71; NS, 24 Aug. 1973, pp. 254-55; OpenL, 2nd ser., 5 (Sum. 1973), 81-84; Q&Q, 38, No. 9 (1972), 8; QQ, 81 (Spr. 1974), 123-24; QUARRY, 22 (Sum. 1973), 75-77; SatN, 88 (Jan. 1973), 32-33; UTQ, 42 (Sum. 1973), 440-41; WCR, 7 (Jan. 1973), 51-54.

BACQUE, JAMES (1929--)

James Bacque, a Toronto native and resident, received a B.A. from the University of Toronto in 1952. He has been a Stratford newspaper reporter, assistant editor of SATURDAY NIGHT and several small magazines, a CBC stagehand for three years, and an editor for Macmillan publishers from 1961 to 1968. Bacque was cofounder of New Press in 1969 and the Association of Canadian Publishers in 1970.

PRIMARY MATERIAL

Monographs

FICTION

756   THE LONELY ONES. Toronto: McClelland and Stewart, 1969.   189 p.; rpt. as BIG LONELY. Toronto: New, 1971. 189 p.

757   A MAN OF TALENT. Toronto: New, 1972. 207 p.

758   THE QUEEN COMES TO MINNICOG. Toronto: Gage, 1979. 177 p.

Shorter Work

SHORT STORIES

759   "Turkey Feathers." HARROWSMITH, 3, No. 4 (1978), 86-87, 89-92ff.

760   "Forbidden Words." CHATELAINE, 52 (Oct. 1979), 50, 106ff.

For other stories and an interview by Bacque, see also no. 2225.

ARTICLES

761　"Canadian Publishing: Through the Hoop?" CANADIAN FORUM, 47 (Aug. 1967), 97-99.

762　"An Allegory for Our Times." CANADIAN DIMENSION, 8 (June 1971), 63-64.

SECONDARY MATERIAL

Criticism

763　Bentley, D.M.R. Introd., BIG LONELY. New Canadian Library, no. 148. Toronto: McClelland and Stewart, 1978, pp. v-xii.

Book Reviews

764　THE LONELY ONES: CanL, 45 (Sum. 1970), 74-75; CFor, 50 (Feb. 1971), 403-04; FIDDLEHEAD, 85 (May 1970), 105-07; SatN, 84 (Nov. 1969), 54, 56, 58; TLS, 12 Feb. 1970, p. 184; WCR, 5 (June 1970), 35-37.

765　A MAN OF TALENT: BCan, 1 (Nov. 1972), 4, 58; CanL, 62 (Aut. 1974), 113-14; FIDDLEHEAD, 97 (Spr. 1973), 113-14; JCF, 2 (Fall 1973), 91-92; LaUR, 6 (Fall 1973), 251-52; MHRev, 25 (Jan. 1973), 164-65; SatN, 88 (Feb. 1973), 33; UTQ, 42 (Sum. 1973), 347; UWR, 8 (Spr. 1973), 98-99.

766　THE QUEEN COMES TO MINNICOG: BCan, 9 (Jan. 1980), 18-19; MACLEAN'S, 28 Jan. 1980, pp. 46-47; Q&Q, 46, No. 2 (1980), 43.

BAIRD, IRENE (1901--)

Born in Cumberland, England, Irene Baird came to Canada in 1919 and spent ten years on the West Coast, writing for the Vancouver SUN and then the Vancouver DAILY PROVINCE. During World War II, she travelled extensively as a representative of the National Film Board and later spent a number of years as an information officer with the Canadian government's Northern Affairs Department. Her most significant novel, WASTE HERITAGE, is based on an actual 1938 sitdown strike in British Columbia.

PRIMARY MATERIAL

Monographs

FICTION

767   JOHN. Philadelphia: J.B. Lippincott, 1937. 235 p.

768   WASTE HERITAGE. Toronto: Macmillan, 1939. 329 p.

769   HE RIDES THE SKY. Toronto: Macmillan, 1941. 241 p.

770   THE CLIMATE OF POWER. Toronto: Macmillan, 1971. 255 p.

NONFICTION PROSE

771   THE NORTH AMERICAN TRADITION. Macmillan War Pamphlets. Canadian Series, no. 2. Toronto: Macmillan, 1941. 32 p.

Shorter Work

SHORT STORY

772   "Learning Situation." NORTH, 14 (Nov.-Dec. 1967), 10-16.

ARTICLE

773   "Sidown, Brother, Sidown." LAURENTIAN UNIVERSITY REVIEW, 9
       (Nov. 1976), 81-86.

            Discusses WASTE HERITAGE.

SECONDARY MATERIAL

Criticism

774   Horne, Michael. "Transient Men in the Depression." CANADIAN FORUM,
       54 (Oct. 1974), 36-38.

            Discusses WASTE HERITAGE.

Book Reviews

775   JOHN: CFor, 17 (Jan. 1938), 364; NYTBR, 17 Oct. 1937, p. 27;
       SatR, 9 Oct. 1937, p. 32; TLS, 11 Dec. 1937, p. 945.

776   WASTE HERITAGE: BCan, 3 (June 1974), 35-36; CFor, 19 (Feb. 1940),
       364-65; CFor, 54 (Oct. 1974), 36-38; MACLEAN'S, 87, No. 4 (1974),
       96; NYTBR, 10 Dec. 1939, p. 7; Q&Q, 40 (June 1974), 6; QQ, 47
       (Spr. 1940), 117; SatN, 16 (Dec. 1939), p. 21; SatR, 16 Dec. 1939,
       p. 7; UTQ, 9 (Apr. 1940), 293-94.

777   THE CLIMATE OF POWER: MACLEAN'S, 84, No. 5 (1971), 80; SatN,
       86 (May 1971), 29-30.

BERESFORD-HOWE, CONSTANCE (1922--)

Constance Beresford-Howe grew up in Montreal, receiving a B.A. from McGill University in 1945. In the same year she won the Dodd-Mead Intercollegiate Fellowship Award for her first novel. With an M.A. from McGill in 1946 and a Ph.D. from Brown University in 1950, she taught in the English department at McGill (1948 to 1968) and more recently at Ryerson Polytechnical Institute, Toronto. Beresford-Howe's early fiction includes historical romance. More recently, she has explored, in realistic terms, the modern dilemmas of female protagonists.

PRIMARY MATERIAL

Monographs

FICTION

778   THE UNREASONING HEART. New York: Dodd, Mead, 1946. 236 p.

779   OF THIS DAY'S JOURNEY. New York: Dodd, Mead, 1947. 240 p.

780   THE INVISIBLE GATE. New York: Dodd, Mead, 1949. 241 p.

781   MY LADY GREENSLEEVES. New York: Ballantine Books, 1955. 217 p.

782   THE BOOK OF EVE: A NOVEL. Toronto: Macmillan, 1973. 170 p.
        Volume 1 in a trilogy, "The Voices of Eve."

783   POPULATION OF ONE: A NOVEL. Toronto: Macmillan, 1977. 201 p.
        Volume 2 in a trilogy, "The Voices of Eve."

784   THE MARRIAGE BED. Toronto: Macmillan, 1981. 232 p.
        Volume 3 in a trilogy, "The Voices of Eve."

Shorter Work

SHORT STORIES

785   "Martha and God and the Bright Blue Marble on a Dusty Road." SATURDAY
       NIGHT, 13 Jan. 1945, p. 27.

786   "House to Let--Furnished." CANADIAN HOME JOURNAL, 42 (Mar.
       1946), 5-7, 46, 48-49.

787   "One Plus One." MACLEAN'S, 1 Dec. 1947, pp. 10-11, 35-36, 41.

788   "The Second Mrs. Lindsay." CHATELAINE, 52 (Nov. 1979), 64-65, 93,
       96, 98, 101, 105-06, 108.

789   "Jeanne." CHATELAINE, 53 (Apr. 1980), 50-51, 68, 70, 72, 74, 76,
       78, 80-81, 84-86.

ARTICLES

790   "Character is the Cornerstone." WRITER, 59 (Nov. 1946), 361-63.

791   "Shaping a Novel." WRITER, 61 (May 1948), 149-50.

792   "Character and Incident." WRITER, 68 (Aug. 1955), 264-67.

Manuscripts

793   McGill University Library, Montreal.

SECONDARY MATERIAL

Criticism

794   Martin, Sandra. "Eve, Well Enough Alone." QUILL AND QUIRE, 40
       (Aug. 1974), 16.

795   Mulhallen, Karen. "A Funny Thing Happened to Constance Beresford-
       Howe on Her Way to Freedom." BOOKS IN CANADA, 7 (Jan. 1978),
       31-32.

       An interview.

Book Reviews

796   THE UNREASONING HEART: CFor, 26 (June 1946), 68–69; SatN, 6 Apr. 1946, p. 24; SatR, 11 May 1946, p. 16.

797   OF THIS DAY'S JOURNEY: SatR, 14 June 1947, p. 16; UTQ, 17 (Apr. 1948), 273.

798   THE INVISIBLE GATE: SatN, 9 May 1950, pp. 17–18; SatR, 24 Dec. 1949, p. 18; UTQ, 19 (Apr. 1950), 271–72.

799   MY LADY GREENSLEEVES: SatR, 3 July 1954, p. 27; UTQ, 25 (Apr. 1956), 311.

800   THE BOOK OF EVE: BCan, 2 (Oct. 1973), 23–24; CanL, 61 (Sum. 1974), 79–80; CFor, 53 (Nov. 1973), 31–32; FIDDLEHEAD, 101 (Spr. 1974), 82, 84–86; JCF, 3, No. 3 (1974), 90; LaUR, 7, No. 2--8, Nos. 1–2 (1974–75), 86–87; SatN, 88 (Nov. 1973), 57–59.

801   POPULATION OF ONE: BCan, 6 (Aug. 1977), 16–17; BrO, 5, No. 1 (1978), 46–47; CanL, 80 (Spr. 1979), 80, 82; CFor, 57 (Feb. 1978), 38–39; FIDDLEHEAD, 117 (Spr. 1978), 129–31; MACLEAN'S, 19 Sept. 1977, pp. 80, 82; Q&Q, 13 (1977), 49; SatN, 92 (Sept. 1977), 69.

BIRNEY, EARLE (1904--)

Earle Birney was born in Calgary, Alberta, and grew up in Alberta and British Columbia. He received a B.A. from the University of British Columbia and an M.A. and Ph.D. from the University of Toronto (after graduate work at the University of California and University of London). He taught English at the Universities of Utah, California, and Toronto, and served with the personnel-selection office of the Canadian army in World War I and briefly with the CBC after the war, before becoming a professor of English at the University of British Columbia in 1946. He remained with UBC until his retirement from teaching in 1965, founding the department of creative writing in 1963 and acting as its first head.

Birney has edited CANADIAN FORUM, CANADIAN POETRY MAGAZINE, and PRISM INTERNATIONAL, and been writer-in-residence at several universities. He has travelled very widely and received numerous literary awards, including the Lorne Pierce Gold Medal for Literature, the Leacock Medal for Humour (for TURVEY), the Canada Council Medal, and Medal of Service of the Order of Canada. Known mainly as a major Canadian poet, Birney has also written several comic novels.

PRIMARY MATERIAL

Monographs

FICTION

802   TURVEY: A MILITARY PICARESQUE. Toronto: McClelland and Stewart, 1949. 288 p.; rpt. as THE KOOTENAY HIGHLANDER. A Four Square Book, no. 207. London: Landsborough Publications, 1960. 253 p. Rev. ed. Toronto: McClelland and Stewart, 1976. 288 p. "Unexpurgated."

803   DOWN THE LONG TABLE. Toronto: McClelland and Stewart, 1955. 298 p.

804   BIG BIRD IN THE BUSH: SELECTED STORIES AND SKETCHES. Oakville, Ont.: Mosaic, 1978. 95 p.

NONFICTION PROSE

805   CONVERSATIONS WITH TROTSKY. By E. Robertson, pseud. London: Author, 1935.

806   "Chaucer's Irony." Diss., University of Toronto, 1936. 2 vols.

807   THE CREATIVE WRITER. [Toronto]: Canadian Broadcasting Corporation, 1966. 85 p.

808   THE COW JUMPED OVER THE MOON: THE WRITING AND READING OF POETRY. Aspects of English. Toronto: Holt, Rinehart and Winston, 1972. 112 p. Bibliog.

809   SPREADING TIME: REMARKS ON CANADIAN WRITING AND WRITERS. BOOK I: 1904-1949. Montreal: Véhicule, 1980. 163 p. Index.

810   DYLAN THOMAS AND MALCOLM LOWRY IN CANADA: MEMORIES OF TWENTIETH-CENTURY WRITERS AND WRITING. Toronto: McClelland and Stewart, 1981. 288 p. Bibliog. Index.

POETRY

811   DAVID AND OTHER POEMS. Toronto: Ryerson, 1942. 40 p.

812   NOW IS THE TIME: POEMS. Toronto: Ryerson, 1945. 56 p.

813   THE STRAIT OF ANIAN: SELECTED POEMS. Toronto: Ryerson, 1948. viii, 84 p.

814   TRIAL OF A CITY AND OTHER VERSE. Toronto: Ryerson, 1952. 71 p.

815   ICE COD BELL OR STONE: A COLLECTION OF NEW POEMS. Toronto: McClelland and Stewart, 1962. viii, 62 p. Indexes.

816   NEAR FALSE CREEK MOUTH: NEW POEMS. Toronto: McClelland and Stewart, 1964. 35 p.

817   SELECTED POEMS, 1940-1966. Illus. Leonard Brooks. Toronto: McClelland and Stewart, 1966. xii, 222 p.

818   MEMORY NO SERVANT. Trumansburg, N.Y.: New Books, 1968. 52 p.

819   PNOMES JUKOLLAGES & OTHER STUNZAS. GrOnk, ser. 4, no. 3. Introd. b.p. nichol. Toronto: Ganglia, 1969. N. pag.

820   THE POEMS OF EARLE BIRNEY. Introd. Earle Birney. New Canadian Library Original, no. 06. Toronto: McClelland and Stewart, 1969. 64 p.

821   RAG & BONE SHOP. Toronto: McClelland and Stewart, 1971. N. pag.

822   THE BEAR ON THE DELHI ROAD: SELECTED POEMS. London: Chatto and Windus, 1973. 64 p.

823   WHAT'S SO BIG ABOUT GREEN? Toronto: McClelland and Stewart, 1973. N. pag.

824   THE COLLECTED POEMS OF EARLE BIRNEY. 2 vols. Toronto: McClelland and Stewart, 1975. Index.

825   ALPHABEING & OTHER SEASYOURS. London, Ont.: Pikadilly, 1976. 32 p.

826   THE RUGGING AND THE MOVING TIMES: POEMS NEW AND UN-COLLECTED 1976. Coatsworth, Ont.: Black Moss, 1976. 42 p.

827   THE DAMNATION OF VANCOUVER. Introd. Wai Lan Low. New Canadian Library, no. 011. Toronto: McClelland and Stewart, 1977. 79 p. Appendix.

828   GHOST IN THE WHEELS: SELECTED POEMS. Toronto: McClelland and Stewart, 1977. 159 p. Index.

829   FALL BY FURY & OTHER MAKINGS. Toronto: McClelland and Stewart, 1978. 96 p.

EDITED WORK

830   CONTEMPORARY CANADIAN POETRY. Manchester, Engl.: Meridian, 1948. 21 p.

831   TWENTIETH CENTURY CANADIAN POETRY: AN ANTHOLOGY. Ed. with introd. and notes by Earle Birney. Toronto: Ryerson, 1953. xvii, 169 p.

832   NEW VOICES: CANADIAN UNIVERSITY WRITING OF 1956. Ed. Earle Birney, Ira Dilworth, Desmond Pacey, Jean-Charles Bonenfant, and Roger Duhamel. Foreword Joseph McCulley. Toronto: J.M. Dent and Sons, 1956. vii, 184 p.

For work edited by Birney, see also nos. 2614 and 2620.

Shorter Work

SHORT STORY

833   "Enigma in Ebony." MACLEAN'S, 15 Oct. 1953, pp. 16-17, 104, 106-08.

ARTICLES

834   "Aldous Huxley." In THE ART OF THE NOVEL: FROM 1700 TO THE PRESENT TIME. By Pelham Edgar. New York: Macmillan, 1933, pp. 278-293.

835   "English Irony Before Chaucer." UNIVERSITY OF TORONTO QUARTERLY, 6 (July 1937), 538-57.

836   "Fiction of James T. Farrell." CANADIAN FORUM, 19 (Apr. 1939), 21-24.

837   "The Beginnings of Chaucer's Irony." PMLA, 54 (Sept. 1939), 637-55.

838   "To Arms with Canadian Poetry." CANADIAN FORUM, 19 (Jan. 1940), 322-24.

839   "Humour Old and New." ONTARIO LIBRARY REVIEW, 24 (May 1940), 133-35.

840   "Sherwood Anderson: A Memory." CANADIAN FORUM, 21 (June 1941), 82-83.

841   "War and the English Intellectuals." CANADIAN FORUM, 21 (July 1941), 110-12, 114.

842   "The Two Worlds of Geoffrey Chaucer." MANITOBA ARTS REVIEW, 2 (Wint. 1941), 3-16.

843   "Is Chaucer's Irony a Modern Discovery?" JOURNAL OF ENGLISH AND GERMAN PHILOLOGY, 41 (July 1942), 303-19.

844   "Has Poetry a Future in Canada?" MANITOBA ARTS REVIEW, 5 (Spr. 1946), 7-15.

845   "Canada Calling." CANADIAN FORUM, 26 (May 1946), 31-32; 26 (June 1946), 59-61.

846   "On Being a Canadian Author." CANADIAN LIBRARY ASSOCIATION BULLETIN, 9 (Nov. 1952), 77-79.

847   "Does Canada Owe Her Authors a Living?" MAYFAIR, 27 (Feb. 1953), 36, 73-75.

848   "The Writer and the H-Bomb: Why Create?" QUEEN'S QUARTERLY, 62 (Spr. 1955), 37-44.

849   "Poets and Painters: Rivals or Partners." CANADIAN ART, 14 (Sum. 1957), 148-50.

850   "North American Drama Today: A Popular Art?" PROCEEDINGS AND TRANSACTIONS OF THE ROYAL SOCIETY OF CANADA, 3rd ser., 51 (1957), sect. 2, 31-42.

851   "Why, You Can't Teach Creative Writing." By H. Quincy Bogholder, Ph.D., F.R.S.B.K., pseud. INLAND (Salt Lake City), 3 (Sum. 1959), 3-10.

852   "'After His Ymage'--The Central Ironies of the FRIAR'S TALE." MEDIEVAL STUDIES, 21 (1959), 17-35.

853   "E.J. Pratt and His Critics." In OUR LIVING TRADITION. 2nd and 3rd ser. Ed. Robert L. McDougall. Toronto: University of Toronto Press, in association with Carleton University, 1959, pp. 123-47.

854   "The Modern Face of Hubris." In HUBRIS, MAN & EDUCATION. Ed. J. Alan Ross. Bellingham, Wash.: Union Printing, 1959, pp. 46-60.

855   "Random Remarks on a Random World." HUMANITIES ASSOCIATION BULLETIN, No. 29 (Jan. 1960), pp. 10-11, 18-20.

856   "The Squire's Yeoman." REVIEW OF ENGLISH LITERATURE, 1 (July 1960), 9-18.

857   "The Inhibited and the Uninhibited: Ironic Structure in THE MILLER'S TALE." NEOPHILOLOGUS, 44 (Oct. 1960), 333-38.

858 "Chaucer's 'Gentil' Manciple and His 'Gentil' Tale." NEUPHILOLO-
GISCHE MITTEILUNGEN, 61 (1960), 257-67.

859 "Structural Irony within the SUMMONER'S TALE." ANGLIA, 78 (1960),
204-18.

860 "Glimpses into the Life of Malcolm Lowry." TAMARACK REVIEW, 19
(Spr. 1961), 35-41.

861 "The Writer and the Canadian University." HUMANITIES ASSOCIATION
BULLETIN, 12 (Spr. 1962), 85-91.

862 "TURVEY and the Critics." CANADIAN LITERATURE, No. 30 (Aut.
1966), pp. 21-25.

   Reprinted in no. 872.

863 "The Canadian Writer vs. the Canadian Education." EVIDENCE, 10
(1967), 97-113.

For articles by Birney, see also no. 2629.

Manuscripts

864 Archives of the Canadian Rockies, Banff, Alta.; Glenbow-Alberta Institute,
Calgary, Alta.; McGill University Library, Montreal; Queen's University
Library, Kingston, Ont.; University of British Columbia Library, Van-
couver; University of Calgary Library; University of Toronto Library.

SECONDARY MATERIAL

Bibliography

865 Noel-Bentley, Peter C., and Earle Birney, comps. "Earle Birney: A
Bibliography in Progress, 1923-1969." WEST COAST REVIEW, 5 (Oct.
1970), 45-53.

For bibliographies of Birney, see also no. 33.

Criticism

866 Aichinger, Peter. EARLE BIRNEY. Twayne's World Authors, 538. Boston:
Twayne, 1979. 180 p. Bibliog. Index.

867 [Birney, Esther.] "A Biography of Capt. Earle Birney by His Wife."
CANADIAN REVIEW OF MUSIC AND ART, 2 (Oct.-Nov. 1943), 30.

868   Cohen, Gerald. "Earle Birney: Beyond Canadian Regionalism." In THE OLD CENTURY AND THE NEW: ESSAYS IN HONOR OF CHARLES ANGOFF. Ed. Alfred Rosa. Rutherford, N.J.: Fairleigh Dickinson University Press, 1978, pp. 238-56.

869   Davey, Frank. EARLE BIRNEY. Studies in Canadian Literature. Toronto: Copp Clark, 1971. vii, 128 p. Bibliog.

870   David, Jack. Interview with Earle Birney. In OUT-POSTS/AVANT-POSTES. By Caroline Bayard and Jack David. Three Solitudes: Contemporary Literary Criticism in Canada, vol. 4. Erin, Ont.: Porcépic, 1978, pp. 109-21. Bibliog., pp. 126-28.

871   Nesbitt, Bruce. Introd., DOWN THE LONG TABLE. New Canadian Library, no. 117. Toronto: McClelland and Stewart, 1975, n. pag.

872   _____, ed. EARLE BIRNEY. Critical Views on Canadian Writers, 9. Toronto: McGraw-Hill Ryerson, 1974. ix, 222 p.

       Besides reviews and analysis of the poetry, includes nos. 285, 862, and 5147.

873   PERSPECTIVES ON EARLE BIRNEY. Canadian Perspectives, 3. Downsview, Ont.: ECW, 1981. 180 p.

       Includes an article by Woodcock.

874   Robillard, Richard. EARLE BIRNEY. Canadian Writers, 9. Toronto: McClelland and Stewart, 1972. 64 p.

For criticism of Birney, see also nos. 182 and 5147.

Book Reviews

875   TURVEY: BCan, 5 (Apr. 1976), 12; CanR, 3 (July 1976), 41; CBRA, 1976, pp. 150-51; CFM, 30-31 (1979), 211-13; CFor, 29 (Dec. 1949), 213-14; CFor, 56 (June 1976), 56-57; CRead, 17, No. 4 (1976), 5-7; DR, 43 (1963-64), 595, 597; JCF, 19 (1977), 160-62; MACLEAN'S, 8 Mar. 1976, pp. 61-62; MONTREALER, 37 (Sept. 1963), 41-42; Q&Q, 42, No. 5 (1976), 43; QQ, 56 (Wint. 1949-50), 608-09; RUL, 4 (Apr. 1950), 736-38; SatN, 22 Nov. 1949, p. 26; TLS, 11 Apr. 1958, p. 193; UTQ, 19 (Spr. 1950), 275-76.

876   DOWN THE LONG TABLE: CBRA, 1975, p. 114; CFor, 35 (Feb. 1956), 258-59; CRead, 16, No. 4 (1975), 2-3; UTQ, 25 (Apr. 1956), 308-09.

877   BIG BIRD IN THE BUSH: BCan, 8 (May 1979), 33; CFor, 59 (June 1979), 43; Q&Q, 45 (Apr. 1979), 27.

878   THE CREATIVE WRITER: CanL, 31 (Wint. 1967), 61-64; QQ, 73 (Wint. 1966), 612-13; UTQ, 36 (July 1967), 452; WCR, 1 (Wint. 1967), 54-55.

879   THE COW JUMPED OVER THE MOON: ALIVE, 28 (1973), 46; BCan, 2 (Jan. 1973), 24; CanL, 63 (Wint. 1975), 113-15; LaUR, 6 (Fall 1973), 269.

880   SPREADING TIME: MACLEAN'S, 8 Sept. 1980, pp. 56-57; SatN, 95 (July 1980), 57.

BLAISE, CLARK (1940--)

Born in Fargo, North Dakota, of Canadian parents, Clark Blaise spent his youth in Florida and the eastern and central United States. He attended Denison University (Ohio) and Harvard (where he worked under Bernard Malamud), received an M.F.A. in creative writing from the University of Iowa, taught at the University of Wisconsin, and presently teaches English at Concordia University in Montreal where he moved in 1966. He has spent some time in India and the Near East.

PRIMARY MATERIAL

Monographs

FICTION

881   NEW CANADIAN WRITING, 1968: STORIES. By David Lewis Stein, Clark Blaise, and Dave Godfrey. Toronto: Clarke, Irwin, 1968. 200 p.

882   A NORTH AMERICAN EDUCATION: A BOOK OF SHORT FICTION. Toronto: Doubleday, 1973. 230 p.

883   TRIBAL JUSTICE. Toronto: Doubleday, 1974. 224 p.

      Short stories.

884   LUNAR ATTRACTIONS. Garden City, N.Y.: Doubleday, 1979. 305 p.

NONFICTION PROSE

885   DAYS AND NIGHTS IN CALCUTTA. By Clark Blaise and Bharati Mukherjee. Garden City, N.Y.: Doubleday, 1977. 300 p.

EDITED WORK

886   HERE AND NOW. Ed. Clark Blaise and John Metcalf. [Ottawa]:
Oberon, 1977. 213 p.

887   BEST CANADIAN STORIES, 1979. Ed. Clark Blaise and John Metcalf.
[Ottawa]: Oberon, 1979. 139 p.

888   80: BEST CANADIAN STORIES. Ed. Clark Blaise and John Metcalf.
[Ottawa]: Oberon, 1980. 191 p.

For work edited by Blaise, see also no. 3139.

Shorter Work

SHORT STORIES

889   "The Mayor." TAMARACK REVIEW, 42 (Wint. 1967), 14-32.

890   "Extractions and Contractions." TRI-QUARTERLY, 16 (Fall 1969), 125-35.

891   "A Class of New Canadians." FIDDLEHEAD, No. 84 (Mar.-Apr. 1970),
pp. 26-33.

892   "Eyes." FIDDLEHEAD, No. 91 (Fall 1971), pp. 24-28.

893   "Is Oakland Drowning?" JOURNAL OF CANADIAN FICTION, 1 (Spr.
1972), 25-26.

894   "The Voice of the Elephant." JOURNAL OF CANADIAN FICTION, 1
(Spr. 1972), 26-27.

895   "Cut, Print." SATURDAY NIGHT, 90 (June 1975), 49-56.

896   "Identity." In 81: BEST CANADIAN STORIES. Ed. John Metcalf and
Leon Rooke. [Ottawa]: Oberon, 1981, pp. 7-19.

ARTICLES

897   "To Begin, To Begin." In THE NARRATIVE VOICE. Ed. John Metcalf.
Toronto: McGraw-Hill Ryerson, 1972, pp. 22-26.

SECONDARY MATERIAL

Criticism

898 "Blaise of Glory . . . Best First Novel of 1979." BOOKS IN CANADA, 9 (Apr. 1980), 3-4.

899 Clery, Val. "Clark Blaise." IMPERIAL OIL REVIEW, 58, No. 6 (1974), 18-23.

900 Davey, Frank. "Impressionable Realism: The Stories of Clark Blaise." OPEN LETTER, 3rd ser., No. 5 (Sum. 1976), pp. 65-74.

    Discusses TRIBAL JUSTICE and A NORTH AMERICAN EDU-CATION.

901 Hancock, Geoffrey. "Clark Blaise on Artful Autobiography: 'I Who Live in Dreams Am Touched by Reality.'" BOOKS IN CANADA, 8 (Mar. 1979), 30-31.

    An interview.

902 _____. "Interview with Clark Blaise." CANADIAN FICTION MAGA-ZINE, Nos. 34-35 (1980), pp. 46-64.

903 Metcalf, John. "Interview: Clark Blaise." JOURNAL OF CANADIAN FICTION, 2 (Fall 1973), 77-79.

904 Ryval, Michael. "Confessions of a Reluctant Patriot." QUILL AND QUIRE, 45 (Apr. 1979), 14, 21.

For criticism on Blaise, see also no. 400.

Book Reviews

905 A NORTH AMERICAN EDUCATION: BCan, 2 (Apr. 1973), 51-52; CanL, 58 (Aut. 1973), 114-16; CFor, 53, No. 1 (Jan. 1974), 42; EQ, 7, No. 2 (1974), 159-60; JCF, 2, No. 4 (1973), 105-06; NewR, 3 Mar. 1973, p. 26; QUARRY, 22 (Sum. 1973), 74-75; SatN, 88 (May 1973), 35, 37, 39; TLS, 14 May 1976, p. 588.

906 TRIBAL JUSTICE: BCan, 3 (Oct. 1974), 17; CFM, 19 (Aut. 1975), 92-94; CFor, 54 (Nov. 1974), 20-21; ECW, 2 (Spr. 1975), 54-56; MACLEAN'S, 87 (Sept. 1974), 88; NYTBR, 29 Sept. 1974, p. 40; OntarioR, 2 (Spr.-Sum. 1975), 100-102; TamR, 64 (Nov. 1974), 85-87; TLS, 14 May 1976, p. 588; UTQ, 44 (Sum. 1975), 305.

907   LUNAR ATTRACTIONS: BCan, 8 (Mar. 1979), 29; CanL, 84 (Spr. 1980), 112-13; CFor, 59 (Apr. 1979), 27-28; FIDDLEHEAD, 122 (Sum. 1979), 139-40; MACLEAN'S, 29 Jan. 1979, pp. 50-51; NatR, 13 Apr. 1979, p. 493; NYTBR, 22 Apr. 1979, p. 14; QQ, 86 (Wint. 1979-80), 722-23; SatN, 94 (May 1979), 47-50.

908   DAYS AND NIGHTS IN CALCUTTA: BCan, 6 (Mar. 1977), 4-7; CAB, 52 (Sum. 1977), 32-33; CanL, 76 (Spr. 1978), 111-13; CFor, 57 (Apr. 1977), 38-39; JCF, 24 ([1979]), 156-58; MACLEAN'S, 21 Feb. 1977, p. 62; NY, 11 Apr. 1977, p. 142; PacA, 51 (Fall 1978), 550-51; Q&Q, 2 (1977), 40; SatN, 92 (Apr. 1977), 73, 75; SatR, 5 Feb. 1977, p. 34.

BODSWORTH, FRED (1918--)

Charles Frederick Bodsworth, journalist and naturalist, was born and educated in Port Burnwell, Ontario. In addition to work on tugboats and in tobacco fields, he has done free-lance magazine writing, with numerous articles published in Canadian and American magazines. After several years as reporter for the St. Thomas TIMES JOURNAL, he spent ten years beginning in 1943 as reporter and editor of the Toronto STAR and Toronto STAR WEEKLY, and several more as assistant editor of MACLEAN'S magazine. He was president of the Federation of Ontario Naturalists from 1964 to 1967 and led nature tours to Europe, Asia, and Africa. Much of his writing grows out of a concern for wildlife and the natural environment.

PRIMARY MATERIAL

Monographs

FICTION

909   LAST OF THE CURLEWS. Illus. T.M. Shortt. New York: Dodd, Mead, 1955. 128 p.

910   THE STRANGE ONE. New York: Dodd, Mead, 1959. 400 p.; rpt. as THE MATING CALL. New York: Pocket Books, 1961. 371 p.

911   THE ATONEMENT OF ASHLEY MORDEN. New York: Dodd, Mead, 1964. 468 p. Also as ASHLEY MORDEN. London: Longmans, 1964. 468 p.

912   THE SPARROW'S FALL. Garden City, N.Y.: Doubleday, 1967. 255 p.

NONFICTION PROSE

913   THE PEOPLE'S HEALTH AND W.H.O. By Brock Chisholm and C. Fred

Bodsworth. Toronto: Canadian Association for Adult Education and Canadian Institute of International Affairs, 1949. 19 p. Bibliog.

914   THE STRANGE STORY BEHIND THE BIBLE. Toronto: Maclean-Hunter, 1956. 16 p.

915   THE PACIFIC COAST. Illustrated Natural History of Canada. Toronto: Natural Science of Canada, 1970. 160 p. Bibliog.

SECONDARY MATERIAL

Criticism

916   Cole, D.W. Introd., THE ATONEMENT OF ASHLEY MORDEN. New Canadian Library, no. 140. Toronto: McClelland and Stewart, 1977, pp. vii-xiii.

917   Hocke, Brigitte. "Fred Bodsworth: Lauft, Füsse, lauft." WEIMARER BEITRÄGE, 21, No. 2 (1975), 136-41.

918   Stevens, John. Introd., LAST OF THE CURLEWS. New Canadian Library, no. 37. Toronto: McClelland and Stewart, 1963, pp. vii-xiv.

For criticism on Bodsworth, see also no. 679.

Book Reviews

919   LAST OF THE CURLEWS: UTQ, 25 (Apr. 1956), 357-58.

920   THE STRANGE ONE: CanA, 22 (May 1960), 101; CanL, 5 (Sum. 1960), 78-79; CFor, 40 (June 1960), 71; NY, 20 Feb. 1960, p. 166; TLS, 24 June 1960, p. 397; UTQ, 30 (July 1961), 409-10.

921   THE ATONEMENT OF ASHLEY MORDEN: CAB, 40 (Spr. 1965), 15; CanL, 26 (Aut. 1965), 76, 78; MONTREALER, 39 (Jan. 1965), 34; TamR, [34] (Wint. 1965), 110; UTQ, 34 (July 1965), 379-80.

922   THE SPARROW'S FALL: CanL, 36 (Spr. 1968), 77-78; NYTBR, 30 July 1967, p. 27; SaskH, 20 (Aut. 1967), 117-18; UTQ, 37 (July 1968), 387-88.

BRUCE, CHARLES (1906-71)

Born in Port Shoreham, Nova Scotia, Charles Tory Bruce attended Mount Allison University, Sackville, New Brunswick, wrote for the Halifax CHRONICLE, and, after 1928, worked with Canadian Press in New York, Halifax, Toronto, and London, acting as overseas correspondent from 1944 to 1945 and becoming general superintendent in 1945. Mount Allison awarded him an honorary D. Litt. in 1952. As much a poet as a novelist, Bruce is best known in the area of fiction for THE CHANNEL SHORE.

PRIMARY MATERIAL

Monographs

FICTION

923   THE CHANNEL SHORE. Toronto: Macmillan, 1954. 398 p.

924   THE TOWNSHIP OF TIME: A CHRONICLE. Toronto: Macmillan, 1959. 234 p.

NONFICTION PROSE

925   NEWS AND THE SOUTHAMS. Toronto: Macmillan, 1968. vii, 429 p. Index.

POETRY

926   WILD APPLES. Introd. Robert Norwood. Sackville, N.B.: Tribune, 1927. 23 p.

927   TOMORROW'S TIDE. Toronto: Macmillan, 1932. 28 p.

928   PERSONAL NOTE. Toronto: Ryerson, 1941. 8 p.

929   GREY SHIP MOVING AND OTHER POEMS. Introd. Wilfred Gibson. Toronto: Ryerson, 1945. vii, 34 p.

930   THE FLOWING SUMMER. Illus. Winifred Fox. Toronto: Ryerson, 1947. 31 p.

931   THE MULGRAVE ROAD. Toronto: Macmillan, 1951. vii, 39 p.

Shorter Work

SHORT STORIES

932   "Year of the Stella." MACLEAN'S, 1 Jan. 1948, pp. 10-11, 44-46ff.

933   "Road to Town." SATURDAY NIGHT, 14 Feb. 1948, p. 29.

934   "Young Avenue." SATURDAY NIGHT, 16 Oct. 1948, pp. 32-33.

935   "Wind in the Juniper." MACLEAN'S, 1 Sept. 1949, pp. 28-29, 69-72.

936   "Suspense." DALHOUSIE REVIEW, 32 (Aut. 1952), 197-200.

937   "Sand." ATLANTIC ADVOCATE, 47 (Sept. 1956), 21-23.

938   "Cadence." ATLANTIC ADVOCATE, 47 (Dec. 1956), 27-30.

939   "People from Away." ATLANTIC ADVOCATE, 47 (Jan. 1957), 57-61.

940   "Jarvey and the Dolphin." ATLANTIC ADVOCATE, 47 (May 1957), 33-35, 94-97.

941   "A Matter for Spike." ATLANTIC ADVOCATE, 47 (July 1957), 59-62.

942   "Inheritance." ATLANTIC ADVOCATE, 48 (Jan. 1958), 84-88.

Manuscripts

943   Dalhousie University Library, Halifax, N.S.; Mount Allison University Library, Sackville, N.B.

SECONDARY MATERIAL

Criticism

944   Davis, Richard C.   "Tradition and the Individual Talent of Charles Bruce."
       DALHOUSIE REVIEW, 59 (Aut. 1979), 443-51.

For criticism on Bruce, see also no. 168.

223779

Book Reviews

945   THE CHANNEL SHORE: APBR, 2 (June 1975), 4; DR, 34 (Aut. 1954),
       319, 321; JCF, 4, No. 3 (1975), 153-57; NYTBR, 27 Mar. 1955, p.
       30; UTQ, 24 (Apr. 1955), 260-61.

946   THE TOWNSHIP OF TIME: AtlA, 50 (Nov. 1959), 89; CanL, 2 (Aut.
       1959), 79-80; UTQ, 29 (July 1960), 473-74.

BUCKLER, ERNEST (1908--)

Ernest Buckler, born in Dalhousie West, Nova Scotia, earned a B.A. at Dalhousie University, Halifax, and an M.A. in philosophy at the University of Toronto and spent five years as an actuary for a Toronto insurance company, before returning to Nova Scotia in 1936. In 1939, he settled near Bridgetown, N.S., where he has lived ever since, both writing and farming. He has published many short stories and articles, winning several short story awards and, for WHIRLIGIG, the 1977 Leacock Medal for Humour. His novel, THE MOUNTAIN AND THE VALLEY, a carefully detailed and finely wrought exploration of psychological and artistic frustration, is considered a Canadian classic.

PRIMARY MATERIAL

Monographs

FICTION

947   THE MOUNTAIN AND THE VALLEY. New York: Henry Holt, 1952. 373 p.

948   THE CRUELEST MONTH. Toronto: McClelland and Stewart, 1963. 298 p.

949   THE REBELLION OF YOUNG DAVID AND OTHER STORIES. Selected and arranged by Robert D. Chambers. Toronto: McClelland and Stewart, 1975. 138 p.

NONFICTION PROSE

950   OX BELLS AND FIREFLIES: A MEMOIR. Drawings by Walter Richards. Toronto: McClelland and Stewart, 1968. 302 p.

951   NOVA SCOTIA: WINDOW ON THE SEA. Photos. Hans Weber. Toronto: McClelland and Stewart, 1973. 127 p.

952   WHIRLIGIG: SELECTED PROSE AND VERSE.   Introd. Claude Bissell. Toronto: McClelland and Stewart, 1977. 128 p.

Shorter Work

SHORT STORIES

953   "On the Third Day. . . ." SATURDAY NIGHT, 24 Apr. 1943, p. 33.

954   "Finest Tree." SATURDAY NIGHT, 1 Jan. 1944, p. 17.

955   "David Comes Home." COLLIER'S, 4 Nov. 1944, p. 24.

956   "A Sort of Sign." LADIES' HOME JOURNAL, 62 (May 1945), 36-37.

957   "Yes, Joseph, There Was a Woman; She Said Her Name Was Mary." SATURDAY NIGHT, 8 Dec. 1945, pp. 48-49.

958   "You Wouldn't Believe Me." SATURDAY NIGHT, 6 Dec. 1947, pp. 48.

959   "Line Fence." BETTER FARMING, 125 (Feb. 1955), 32-33.

960   "The Eruption of Albert Wingate." ATLANTIC ADVOCATE, 47 (Nov. 1956), 27-29.

961   "By Any Other Name: A Holiday Romance." ATLANTIC ADVOCATE, 47 (June 1957), 48, 79-80.

962   "In Case of Emergency." ATLANTIC ADVOCATE, 47 (Aug. 1957), 69-72.

963   "The Concerto." ATLANTIC ADVOCATE, 48 (Feb. 1958), 65-67.

964   "The Echoing Hills." ATLANTIC ADVOCATE, 48 (May 1958), 75-77.

965   "The Doctor and the Patient." ATLANTIC ADVOCATE, 51 (July 1961), 65-66.

966   "Nettles Into Orchids." ATLANTIC ADVOCATE, 51 (Aug. 1961), 70-71.

967   "One Sweet Day." ATLANTIC ADVOCATE, 52 (Jan. 1962), 49-53.

968   "Choose Your Partners." ATLANTIC ADVOCATE, 52 (Aug. 1962), 62-64, 66-67, 69ff.

969   "Guilt on the Lily." ATLANTIC ADVOCATE, 53 (Aug. 1963), 61-69.

ARTICLES

970   "How to Write an Artistic Novel." SATURDAY NIGHT, 3 May 1941, p. 25.

971   "Alden Nowlan: An Appreciation." FIDDLEHEAD, No. 81 (Aug.-Oct. 1969), pp. 46-47.

Manuscripts

972   University of Toronto Library.

SECONDARY MATERIAL

Bibliography

For a bibliography of Buckler, see no. 33.

Criticism

973   Barbour, Douglas. "The Critic Criticized: A Reply to Bruce MacDonald." STUDIES IN CANADIAN LITERATURE, 2 (Wint. 1977), 127-28.

        A rejoinder to no. 983.

974   _____. "David Canaan: The Failing Heart." STUDIES IN CANADIAN LITERATURE, 1 (Wint. 1976), 64-75.

        See nos. 983 and 994.

975   Bissell, Claude. Introd., THE MOUNTAIN AND THE VALLEY. New Canadian Library, no. 23. Toronto: McClelland and Stewart, 1961, pp. vii-xii.

976   Cameron, Donald A. "Don Cameron Interviews Ernest Buckler." QUILL AND QUIRE, 38 (July 1972), 5, 8.

        Reprinted in no. 124.

977   Chapman, Marilyn. "The Progress of David's Imagination." STUDIES IN CANADIAN LITERATURE, 3 (Sum. 1978), 186-98.

978   Cook, Gregory M., ed. with introd. ERNEST BUCKLER. Critical on Candian Writers, 7. Toronto: McGraw-Hill Ryerson, 1972. 145 p.

Articles and reviews, including some of Buckler's own comments; reprints nos. 540-41, 569, and 987.

979   Deorksen, L.M.   "THE MOUNTAIN AND THE VALLEY: An Evaluation." WORLD LITERATURE WRITTEN IN ENGLISH, 19 (1980), 45-56.

980   Dooley, David Joseph.   "Style and Communication in THE MOUNTAIN AND THE VALLEY."   DALHOUSIE REVIEW, 57 (Wint. 1977-78), 671-83.

Revised and reprinted in no. 139.

981   Dyck, Sarah.   "In Search of a Poet: Buckler and Pasternak."   GERMANO-SLAVICA, 2 (Spr. 1978), 325-36.

982   Kertzer, J.M.   "The Past Recaptured."   CANADIAN LITERATURE, No. 65 (Sum. 1975), pp. 74-85.

983   MacDonald, Bruce F.   "Word-Shapes, Time and the Theme of Isolation in THE MOUNTAIN AND THE VALLEY."   STUDIES IN CANADIAN LITERATURE, 1 (Sum. 1976), 194-209.

A reply to no. 974; for rejoinder, see no. 973.

984   Noonan, Gerald.   "Egotism and Style in THE MOUNTAIN AND THE VALLEY."   In ATLANTIC PROVINCES LITERATURE COLLOQUIUM PAPERS/ COMMUNICATIONS DU COLLOQUE SUR LA LITTÉRATURE DES PROVINCES ATLANTIQUES.   Ed. Kenneth MacKinnon.   Marco Polo Papers, 1.   Saint John, N.B.: Atlantic Canada Institute, 1977, pp. 68-78.

985   Ricou, Laurence.   "David Canaan and Buckler's Style in THE MOUNTAIN AND THE VALLEY."   DALHOUSIE REVIEW, 57 (Wint. 1977-78), 684-96.

986   Sarkar, Eilen.   "Ernest Buckler's THE MOUNTAIN AND THE VALLEY: 'The Infinite Language of Human Relations.'"   REVUE DE L'UNIVERSITÉ D'OTTAWA, 44 (July-Sept. 1974), 354-61.   Bibliog.

987   Spettigue, Douglas O.   "The Way It Was: Ernest Buckler."   CANADIAN LITERATURE, No. 32 (Spr. 1967), pp. 40-56.

Reprinted in nos. 978 and 5113.

988   Thomas, Clara.   "New England Romanticism and Canadian Fiction." JOURNAL OF CANADIAN FICTION, 2 (Fall 1973), 80-86.

Discusses THE MOUNTAIN AND THE VALLEY and George Elliott's KISSING MAN.

989 Westwater, A.M. "Teufelsdrockh is Alive and Doing Well in Nova Scotia: Carlylean Strains in THE MOUNTAIN AND THE VALLEY." DALHOUSIE REVIEW, 56 (Sum. 1976), 291-98.

990 Young, Alan R. ERNEST BUCKLER. Canadian Writers, no. 15. Toronto: McClelland and Stewart, 1976. 64 p. Bibliog.

991 _____. "The Genesis of Ernest Buckler's THE MOUNTAIN AND THE VALLEY." JOURNAL OF CANADIAN FICTION, No. 16 (1976), pp. 89-96.

992 _____. Introd., OX BELLS AND FIREFLIES. New Canadian Library, no. 99. Toronto: McClelland and Stewart, 1974, pp. xi-xvi.

993 _____. Introd., THE CRUELEST MONTH. New Canadian Library, no. 139. Toronto: McClelland and Stewart, 1977, pp. vii-xiii.

994 _____. "A Note on Douglas Barbour's 'David Canaan: The Failing Heart.' (SCL, Winter 1976)." STUDIES IN CANADIAN LITERATURE, 1 (Sum. 1976), 244-46.

      See no. 974.

995 _____. "The Pastoral Vision of Ernest Buckler in THE MOUNTAIN AND THE VALLEY." DALHOUSIE REVIEW, 53 (Sum. 1973), 219-26.

For criticism on Buckler, see also nos. 81, 540-41, and especially no. 3783.

Book Reviews

996 THE MOUNTAIN AND THE VALLEY: CFor, 33 (July 1953), 94-95; DR, 32 (Wint. 1953), iii, v; DR, 41 (Wint. 1961-62), 565; NYTBR, 26 Oct. 1952, p. 5; SatN, 13 Dec. 1952, p. 38; SatR, 8 Nov. 1952, p. 54; UTQ, 22 (Apr. 1953), 290-92.

997 THE CRUELEST MONTH: CanL, 19 (Wint. 1964), 58-59; DR, 43 (Wint. 1963-64), 566-69; QQ, 71 (Sum. 1964), 277; TamR, [36] (Sum. 1965), 82-86; UTQ, 33 (July 1964), 396-97.

998 THE REBELLION OF YOUNG DAVID: BCan, 4 (July 1975), 6-7; CAB, 51 (Fall 1975), 26; CanL, 66 (Aut. 1975), 117-18; CBRA, 1975, pp. 122-23; DR, 55 (Sum. 1975), 385-87; JCF, 16 (1976), 182-84; QQ, 82 (Wint. 1975), 657-59; TamR, 69 (Sum. 1976), 85-86; UTQ, 44 (Sum. 1976), 326.

999 OX BELLS AND FIREFLIES: ALPHABET, 16 (Sept. 1969), 66-69; AtlA, 59 (Dec. 1968), 56; BCLQ, 32 (Apr. 1969), 19-21; CAB, 44 (Sum. 1969), 16; CanL, 40 (Spr. 1969), 91-92; DR, 48 (Aut. 1968), 413-14; QQ, 76 (Aut. 1969), 546-47; QUARRY, 18 (Sum. 1969), 53-54; UTQ, 38 (July 1969), 355-56.

1000 WHIRLIGIG: AntigR, 32 (Wint. 1978), 107-09; CAB, 54 (Jan. 1979), 24; CanL, 80 (Spr. 1979), 85-86; CFor, 57 (Dec. 1977), 39; CRead, 19 (Mar. 1978), 12; FIDDLEHEAD, 116 (Wint. 1978), 169-71; Q&Q, 43, No. 16 (1977), 6; UTQ, 47 (Sum. 1978), 445-48.

CALLAGHAN, MORLEY (1903--)

Morley Callaghan was born in Toronto where he has passed most of his life. After studying at the University of Toronto and Osgoode Hall Law School, he was called to the bar in 1928 but never practiced law. Instead he turned to journalism for the Toronto STAR (where he met Ernest Hemingway), and then in 1929 spent most of a year in Paris among other expatriate writers. He has been a writer and to a lesser extent a literary commentator on radio and television ever since.

For thirteen years his short stories were included annually in O'Brien's BEST SHORT STORIES; he received the Governor General's Award for THE LOVED AND THE LOST in 1951, the Lorne Pierce Medal in 1960, the Order of Canada Medal of Service in 1967 (which he refused in protest at the earlier lack of support for his writing within Canada), the $15,000 Molson Prize in 1969, and $50,000 Royal Bank of Canada Award in 1971. Particularly acclaimed for his short fiction and for the novels of his middle period, Callaghan is a major Canadian novelist whose deliberately flat, low-key, simple style and simplified action often conceal psychological complexity as well as convey a strongly moral vision.

PRIMARY MATERIAL

Monographs

FICTION

1001 STRANGE FUGITIVE. New York: Charles Scribner's Sons, 1928. 264 p. Rev. ed. Introd. Robert Weaver. Edmonton, Alta.: M.G. Hurtig, 1970. xii, 266 p.

1002 A NATIVE ARGOSY. New York: Charles Scribner's Sons, 1929. 371 p.
Short stories.

1003   IT'S NEVER OVER.   New York: Charles Scribner's Sons, 1930.   225 p.

1004   NO MAN'S MEAT.   Paris: E.W. Titus, 1931.   42 p.

      Reprinted as part of no. 1019.

1005   A BROKEN JOURNEY.   New York: Charles Scribner's Sons, 1932.
      270 p.

1006   SUCH IS MY BELOVED.   New York: Charles Scribner's Sons, 1934.
      288 p.

1007   THEY SHALL INHERIT THE EARTH.   Toronto: Macmillan, 1935. 337 p.

1008   NOW THAT APRIL'S HERE AND OTHER STORIES.   New York: Random
      House, 1936.   316 p.

1009   MORE JOY IN HEAVEN.   New York: Random House, 1937.   278 p.

1010   LUKE BALDWIN'S VOW.   Illus. Stanley Turner.   Philadelphia: John C.
      Winston, 1948.   iii, 187 p.

      For children.

1011   THE VARSITY STORY.   Illus. Eric Aldwinckle.   Toronto: Macmillan,
      1948.   172 p.

1012   THE LOVED AND THE LOST: A NOVEL.   New York: Macmillan,
      1951.   234 p.

1013   STORIES.   Toronto: Macmillan, 1959.   364 p.

1014   THE MANY COLORED COAT.   Toronto: Macmillan, 1960.   318 p.

1015   A PASSION IN ROME: A NOVEL. Toronto: Macmillan, 1961.   352 p.

1016   AN AUTUMN PENITENT: TWO NOVELS.   Laurentian Library, 16.
      Toronto: Macmillan, 1973.   171 p.

      Reprints "An Autumn Penitent" and "In His Own Country"
      from A NATIVE ARGOSY.

1017   A FINE AND PRIVATE PLACE: A NOVEL.   Toronto: Macmillan, 1975.
      213 p.

1018 CLOSE TO THE SUN AGAIN: A NEW NOVEL. Toronto: Macmillan, 1977. 169 p.

1019 NO MAN'S MEAT & THE ENCHANTED PIMP. Toronto: Macmillan, 1978. 170 p.

Two novellas, the first a slightly revised version of no. 1004.

NONFICTION PROSE

1020 THAT SUMMER IN PARIS: MEMORIES OF TANGLED FRIENDSHIPS WITH HEMINGWAY, FITZGERALD, AND SOME OTHERS. Toronto: Macmillan, 1963. 255 p.

1021 WINTER. Photos. John de Visser. Toronto: McClelland and Stewart, 1974. 128 p.

DRAMA

1022 SEASON OF THE WITCH. Toronto: House of Exile, 1976. N. pag.

Based on THEY SHALL INHERIT THE EARTH.

Shorter Work

SHORT STORIES

1023 "The Novice." CANADIAN MAGAZINE, 73 (Mar. 1930), 11, 30-31.

1024 "The Chiseller." NEW YORKER, 16 Aug. 1930, pp. 15-17.

1025 "Lady in a Green Dress." SCRIBNER'S, 88 (Aug. 1930), 173-78.

1026 "Poolroom." SCRIBNER'S, 92 (Oct. 1932), 209-12.

1027 "Emily." HOUSEHOLD, 33 (Jan. 1933), 6-7.

1028 "Northern Summer Twilight." HOUSEHOLD, 33 (Sept. 1933), 3, 12, 26.

1029 "The Bridegroom." ESQUIRE, 1 (Jan. 1934), 62, 102.

1030 "The Girl Who Was Easy." ESQUIRE, 1 (May 1934), 38, 159-60, 162.

1031 "She's Nothing to Me." STORY, 4 (June 1934), 17-23.

1032   "The Intellectual." LITERARY AMERICA, 2 (Mar. 1935), 223-27.

1033   "In the Big Town." ESQUIRE, 5 (Apr. 1936), 40-41.

1034   "Enemy of the People." SCRIBNER'S, 100 (Sept. 1936), 139-41.

1035   "A Pair of Long Pants." REDBOOK, 67 (Oct. 1936), 36-37, 118-19.

1036   "The Fiddler on Twenty-Third Street." MACLEAN'S, 15 Dec. 1936, pp. 16-17, 34.

1037   "This Man, My Father." MACLEAN'S, 15 Mar. 1937, pp. 15, 58, 60.

1038   "Rendezvous with Self." ESQUIRE, 7 (Mar. 1937), 46, 191.

1039   "Evening in Madison Square." ESQUIRE, 7 (June 1937), 56, 188, 190.

1040   "A Little Beaded Bag." HARPER'S BAZAAR, 71 (Sept. 1937), 69, 149.

1041   "A Night Out." HOUSEHOLD, 37 (Oct. 1937), 44, 14-15.

1042   "A Boy Grows Older." ESQUIRE, 8 (Dec. 1937), 88, 194.

1043   "The Fugitive." NORTH AMERICAN REVIEW, 245 (Sum. 1938), 330-39.

1044   "The Consuming Fire." HARPER'S BAZAAR, 72 (Aug. 1938), 76, 126-27.

1045   "The Sentimentalists." HARPER'S BAZAAR, 72 (Nov. 1938), 90, 133.

1046   "The New Coat." ESQUIRE, 10 (Dec. 1938), 66, 208, 210.

1047   "The Thing that Happened to Uncle Adolph." JOHN O'LONDON'S WEEKLY, 3 Nov. 1939, pp. 125-26.

1048   "Hello, America." JOHN O'LONDON'S WEEKLY, 26 July 1940, pp. 461-62.

1049   "Big Jules." YALE REVIEW, NS 30 (Sept. 1940), 150-57.

1050   "The Mexican Bracelets." MACLEAN'S, 15 Apr. 1947, pp. 24, 45-48.

1051   "I Knew Him When." AMERICAN, 143 (Apr. 1947), 34-35.

1052   "With an Air of Dignity." MACLEAN'S, 15 Jan. 1948, pp. 10-11, 29-32.

1053   "All Right, Flatfoot!" MACLEAN'S, 15 Aug. 1948, pp. 13, 26-27.

1054   "New Kid." SATURDAY EVENING POST, 11 Sept. 1948, pp. 28-29.

1055   "The Indulgent Lady." MADEMOISELLE, Nov. 1948, pp. 132-33, 206-11.

1056   "Bachelor's Dilemma." MACLEAN'S, 1 Aug. 1950, pp. 24-25.

1057   "On the Edge of a World." ESQUIRE, 35 (Jan. 1951), 106.

1058   "Keep Away from Laura." MACLEAN'S, 1 Nov. 1952, pp. 12-13, 35-37.

1059   "The Way It Ended." CANADIAN HOME JOURNAL, 50 (Sept. 1953), 12-13, 34-35, 39.

1060   "We Just Had To Be Alone." MACLEAN'S, 5 Mar. 1955, pp. 18-19, 59-61.

1061   "The Doctor's Son." In TEN FOR WEDNESDAY NIGHT. Ed. Robert Weaver. Toronto: McClelland and Stewart, 1961, pp. 95-104.

1062   "The Meterman, Caliban, and Then Mr. Jones." EXILE, 1, No. 3 (1973), 124-57.

   An early version of THE ENCHANTED PIMP.

ARTICLES

1063   "The Past Quarter Century." MACLEAN'S, 15 Mar. 1936, pp. 36-38.

1064   "A Criticism." NEW FRONTIER, Apr. 1936, p. 24.

1065   "The Plight of Canadian Fiction." UNIVERSITY OF TORONTO QUARTERLY, 7 (Jan. 1938), 152-61.

   See no. 1830. Reprinted in no. 136.

1066   "Thomas Wolfe's Appetite for Life." SATURDAY NIGHT, 15 July 1939, p. 8.

1067   "Writers and Critics: A Minor League." SATURDAY NIGHT, 6 Nov.
        1954, pp. 7-8.

1068   "An Ocean Away." TIMES LITERARY SUPPLEMENT, 4 June 1964,
        p. 493.

1069   "The Pleasures of Failure." MACLEAN'S, 6 Mar. 1965, pp. 12-13,
        34, 37.

1070   "The Imaginative Writer." TAMARACK REVIEW, 41 (Aut. 1966), 5-11.

1071   "Solzhenitsyn." TAMARACK REVIEW, No. 55 (3rd quarter 1970), pp.
        71-76.

1072   Excerpt from His Speech of Acceptance on Receiving the Royal Bank
        Award, June 15, 1970. In SIXTEEN BY TWELVE. Ed. John Metcalf.
        Toronto: Ryerson, 1970, pp. 20-21.

For articles by Callaghan, see also nos. 192, 209, and 1450.

Manuscripts

1073   New York Public Library.

SECONDARY MATERIAL

Bibliography

1074   Latham, David, and Sheila Latham. "A Callaghan Log." JOURNAL
        OF CANADIAN STUDIES, 15 (Spr. 1980), 18-29.

Criticism

1075   Beatty, Jerome, Jr.   "Trade Winds." SATURDAY REVIEW, 21 Jan. 1961,
        pp. 14, 16, 18.

1076   Boire, Gary A. "The Parable and the Priest." CANADIAN LITERA-
        TURE, No. 81 (Sum. 1979), pp. 154-62.

1077   Cameron, Donald A. "Defending the Inner Light: An Interview with
        Morley Callaghan." SATURDAY NIGHT, 87 (July 1972), 17-22.

        Reprinted in no. 124.

1078   Clever, Glen. "Callaghan's MORE JOY IN HEAVEN as a Tragedy."
        CANADIAN FICTION MAGAZINE, Nos. 2-3 (Spr.-Sum. 1971), pp.
        88-93.

1079   Conron, Brandon. MORLEY CALLAGHAN. Twayne World Authors, 1.
        New York: Twayne, 1966. 188 p.

1080   _____. "Morley Callaghan and His Audience." JOURNAL OF CA-
        NADIAN STUDIES, 15 (Spr. 1980), 3-7.

1081   _____. "Morley Callaghan as a Short Story Writer." JOURNAL OF
        COMMONWEALTH LITERATURE, 3 (July 1967), 58-75.

            Reprinted from no. 1079.

1082   _____, ed. with introd. MORLEY CALLAGHAN. Critical Views on
        Canadian Writers, 10. Toronto: McGraw-Hill Ryerson, 1975. v, 156 p.

            Includes nos. 1097, 1108, 1113, and 5148.

1083   Dahlie, Hallvard. "Destructive Innocence in the Novels of Morley
        Callaghan." JOURNAL OF CANADIAN FICTION, 1 (Sum. 1972), 39-42.

1084   Dunn, William. "Note on a Master Novelist." LOST GENERATION,
        3, No. 2 (1975), 24-25.

1085   Ferris, Ina. "Morley Callaghan and the Exultant Self." JOURNAL OF
        CANADIAN STUDIES, 15 (Spr. 1980), 13-17.

1086   Friesen, Victor Carl. "The Short Stories of Morley Callaghan." CA-
        NADIAN SHORT STORY, 3 (Spr. 1977), 78-80.

1087   Gouri, C.R. "Society and Solitude in THE LOVED AND THE LOST."
        In ENGLISH WRITING IN THE TWENTIETH CENTURY. Ed. S. Krishna
        Sarma. Guntur, India: English Association, 1974, pp. 97-103.

1088   Heintzman, Ralph. "Two Solitudes." JOURNAL OF CANADIAN STUDIES,
        15 (Spr. 1980), 1-2, 123-24.

1089   Hoar, Victor. MORLEY CALLAGHAN. Studies in Canadian Literature,
        no. 4. Toronto: Copp Clark, 1969. iv, 123 p. Bibliog.

1090   Kendle, Judith. "Callaghan and the Church." CANADIAN LITERATURE,
        No. 80 (Spr. 1979), pp. 13-22.

1091 ____. "Callaghan as Columnist, 1940-48." CANADIAN LITERATURE, No. 82 (Aut. 1979), pp. 6-20.

1092 ____. "Spiritual Tiredness and Dryness of the Imagination: Social Criticism in the Novels of Morley Callaghan." JOURNAL OF CANADIAN FICTION, No. 16 (1976), pp. 115-30.

1093 Koch, E.A. "Callaghan: Lend-Lease from the Bohemians." SATURDAY NIGHT, 21 Oct. 1944, pp. 16-17.

1094 Korte, D.M. "The Christian Dimension of Callaghan's THE MANY COLORED COAT." ENGLISH QUARTERLY, 8, No. 3 (1975), 11-15.

1095 McCormack, Robert. "Letter from Toronto." CANADIAN LITERATURE, No. 7 (Wint. 1961), pp. 54-58.

1096 McPherson, Hugo. Introd., MORE JOY IN HEAVEN. New Canadian Library, no. 17. Toronto: McClelland and Stewart, 1969, pp. v-x.

1097 ____. "The Two Worlds of Morley Callaghan: Man's Earthly Quest." QUEEN'S QUARTERLY, 64 (Aut. 1957), 350-65. Reprinted in no. 1082.

1098 Marshall, Tom. "Tragic Ambivalence: The Novels of Morley Callaghan." UNIVERSITY OF WINDSOR REVIEW, 12 (Fall-Wint. 1976), 33-48.

1099 Mathews, Robin D. "Morley Callaghan and the New Colonialism: The Supreme Individual in Traditionless Society." STUDIES IN CANADIAN LITERATURE, 3 (Wint. 1978), 78-92.

> Discusses STRANGE FUGITIVE and, especially, THEY SHALL INHERIT THE EARTH; reprinted in no. 163.

1100 Moon, Barbara. "The Second Coming of Morley Callaghan." MACLEAN'S, 3 Dec. 1960, pp. 19, 62-64.

1101 Morley, Patricia A. "Callaghan's Vision: Wholeness and the Individual." JOURNAL OF CANADIAN STUDIES, 15 (Spr. 1980), 8-12.

1102 ____. MORLEY CALLAGHAN. Canadian Writers, no. 16. Toronto: McClelland and Stewart, 1978. 72 p. Bibliog.

1103 Orange, J. "Luke Baldwin's Vow and Morley Callaghan's Vision." CANADIAN CHILDREN'S LITERATURE, 1 (Spr. 1975), 9-21.

1103a Ross, Malcolm. Introd., SUCH IS MY BELOVED. New Canadian Library, no. 2. Toronto: McClelland and Stewart, 1957, pp. v-xiii.

1104   Staines, David, ed, with introd. THE CALLAGHAN SYMPOSIUM.
Ottawa: University of Ottawa Press, 1981. 123 p. Bibliog.

1105   Steinhauer, H. "Morley Callaghan." CANADIAN FORUM, 12 (Feb.
1932), 177-78.

1106   Sutherland, Fraser. "Hemingway and Callaghan: Friends and Writers."
CANADIAN LITERATURE, No. 53 (Sum. 1972), pp. 8-17.

1107   _____. THE STYLE OF INNOCENCE: A STUDY OF HEMINGWAY
AND CALLAGHAN. Toronto: Clarke, Irwin, 1972. 120 p. Bibliog.
Index.

1108   Walsh, William. "Morley Callaghan." In his A MANIFOLD VOICE:
STUDIES IN COMMONWEALTH LITERATURE. London: Chatto and
Windus, 1970, pp. 185-212.

        Reprinted in no. 1082.

1109   Ward, Margaret Joan. "The Gift of Grace." CANADIAN LITERATURE,
No. 58 (Aut. 1973), pp. 19-25.

1110   Watt, Frank W. Introd., THEY SHALL INHERIT THE EARTH. New Canadian Library, no. 33. Toronto: McClelland and Stewart, 1962,
pp. v-x.

1111   _____. "Morley Callaghan as Thinker." DALHOUSIE REVIEW, 39
(Aut. 1959), 305-13.

        Reprinted in no. 195.

1112   Weaver, Robert. "A Talk with Morley Callaghan." TAMARACK REVIEW,
No. 7 (Spr. 1958), pp. 3-29.

1113   Wilson, Edmund. "Morley Callaghan of Toronto." NEW YORKER, 26
Nov. 1960, pp. 224, 226, 228, 230, 233-34, 236-37.

        Discusses THE LOVED AND THE LOST and THE MANY COL-
        OURED COAT; reprinted in nos. 210 and 1082.

For criticism of Callaghan, see also nos. 123, 139, 158, 168, 182, 1001, 5148,
and 5162.

Book Reviews

1114   STRANGE FUGITIVE: JCF, 2 (Fall 1973), 112-13; NATION, 10 Oct.
1928 supplement, p. 370; NYTBR, 2 Sept. 1928, p. 7.

1115 A NATIVE ARGOSY: CFor, 9 (Aug. 1929), 389-90; NATION, 29
May 1929, p. 654; NYTBR, 24 Mar. 1929, p. 9; SatR, 20 Apr. 1929,
p. 909.

1116 IT'S NEVER OVER: CB, Feb. 1930, p. 38; NATION, 2 Apr. 1930,
p. 399; NewR, 23 Apr. 1930, p. 280; NYTBR, 19 Mar. 1930, p. 9;
SatR, 21 June 1930, p. 1140.

1117 A BROKEN JOURNEY: CBRA, 1976, p. 150; CFor, 56 (June 1976),
51-52; IFR, 4 (Jan. 1977), 93; NewR, 16 Nov. 1932, p. 27; NYTBR,
18 Sept. 1932, p. 14; SatR, 17 Sept. 1932, p. 104.

1118 SUCH IS MY BELOVED: NATION, 11 Apr. 1934, p. 421; NewR, 28
Mar. 1934, p. 191; NYTBR, 11 Mar. 1934, p. 9; SatR, 10 Mar. 1934,
p. 535.

1119 THEY SHALL INHERIT THE EARTH: CFor, 15 (Dec. 1935), 398-99;
NATION, 25 Sept. 1935, p. 361; NewR, 13 Nov. 1935, p. 27; NYTBR,
6 Oct. 1935, p. 6; SatR, 28 Sept. 1935, p. 6; UTQ, 5 (Apr. 1936),
369-71.

1120 NOW THAT APRIL'S HERE: CB, Oct. 1936, pp. 5, 12; CFor, 16 (Oct.
1936), 27; NATION, 26 Sept. 1936, p. 370; NewR, 21 Oct. 1936,
p. 331; NYTBR, 13 Sept. 1936, p. 6; SatN, 38 (Oct. 1942), 16; SatR,
19 Sept. 1936, p. 7; TamR, 13 (Aut. 1959), 112-16; UTQ, 6 (Apr.
1937), 363-65.

1121 MORE JOY IN HEAVEN: CFor, 17 (Mar. 1938), 427; DR, 40 (Wint.
1960-61), 583; NYTBR, 28 Nov. 1937, p. 7; SatR, 4 Dec. 1937,
p. 6; UTQ, 7 (Apr. 1938), 348-51.

1122 THE VARSITY STORY: CFor, 28 (Nov. 1948), 189; DR, 29 (July 1949),
200-201; NY, 19 Mar. 1949, p. 102; NYTBR, 16 Jan. 1949, p. 4;
SatN, 25 Sept. 1948, pp. 2-3, 24; SatR, 5 Feb. 1949, p. 11; UTQ,
18 (Apr. 1949), 273.

1123 THE LOVED AND THE LOST: CFor, 31 (June 1951), 70; COMMON-
WEAL, 20 Apr. 1951, p. 42; CULTURE, 12 (June 1951), 195-96; NA-
TION, 14 Apr. 1951, p. 352; NS, 3 Nov. 1961, p. 66; RUL, 6 (Sept.
1951), 51-53; SatN, 27 Mar. 1951, p. 7; UTQ, 21 (Apr. 1952), 260-63.

1124 STORIES: CanL, 2 (Aut. 1959), 67-70; CFor, 39 (Mar. 1960), 276-
77; CFor, 47 (Feb. 1968), 259; DR, 39 (Wint. 1960), 573, 575; LIS-
TENER, 23 Aug. 1962, p. 293; LISTENER, 13 Aug. 1964, p. 245; NS,
17 Aug. 1962, p. 206; PUNCH, 22 Aug. 1962, p. 283; SPECTATOR,

17 Aug. 1962, p. 223; SPECTATOR, 7 Aug. 1964, p. 188; TamR, 13 (Aut. 1959), 112-16; TLS, 17 Aug. 1962, p. 629; UTQ, 29 (July 1960), 472.

1125   THE MANY COLORED COAT: CanL, 7 (Wint. 1959), 59-61; CDim, 1, Nos. 1-2 (1963), 22; LISTENER, 14 Feb. 1963, p. 307; NS, 1 Feb. 1963, p. 157; NYTBR, 28 Aug. 1960, p. 5; PR, 28 (Mar. 1961), 301; RUO, 31 (Apr. 1961), 343; SatN, 15 Oct. 1960, pp. 27-28; SatR, 27 Aug. 1960, p. 12; SPECTATOR, 1 Mar. 1963, p. 269; TamR, 17 (Aut. 1960), 65-66, 69-71; TLS, 1 Feb. 1963, p. 73; UTQ, 30 (July 1961), 402-04.

1126   A PASSION IN ROME: CanL, 12 (Spr. 1962), 60-64; CFor, 41 (Feb. 1962), 261-62; HM, 223 (Nov. 1961), 116; LISTENER, 26 Mar. 1964, p. 529; MONTREALER, 36 (Feb. 1962), 42; NS, 27 Mar. 1964, p. 497; NYTBR, 15 Oct. 1961, p. 4; QQ, 69 (Sum. 1962), 308-10; SatN, 9 Dec. 1961, pp. 43-45; SatR, 11 Nov. 1961, p. 28; SPECTATOR, 27 Mar. 1964, p. 422; TamR, 22 (Wint. 1962), 88-92; TLS, 2 Apr. 1964, p. 269; UTQ, 31 (July 1962), 455-57.

1127   A FINE AND PRIVATE PLACE: BCan, 4 (July 1975), 3-5; CanL, 73 (Sum. 1977), 116-18; CBRA, 1975, pp. 115-16; CFor, 55 (Aug. 1975), 35-36; CRead, 16, No. 9 (1975), 6-7; DR, 55 (Aut. 1975), 590-91; ECW, 4 (Spr. 1976), 56, 58-60; MACLEAN'S, 88 (July 1975), 77; QQ, 82 (Wint. 1975), 642-44; SatN, 90 (July 1975), 63-64; UTQ, 45 (Sum. 1976), 314-15.

1128   CLOSE TO THE SUN AGAIN: BCan, 6 (Oct. 1977), 10-11; BCan, 8 (June 1979), 28; CanL, 77 (Sum. 1978), 100-103; CFor, 57 (Dec. 1977), 36-37; CRead, 18 (Sept. 1977), 2-3; DR, 57 (Wint. 1977-78), 786-88; FIDDLEHEAD, 118 (Sum. 1978), 170-72; JCanS, 14 (Spr. 1979), 96-97; JCF, 24 ([1979]), 141-44; MACLEAN'S, 3 Oct. 1977, p. 72; NatR, 16 Mar. 1979, p. 369; NY, 28 Aug. 1978, p. 93; Q&Q, 43, No. 12 (1977), 6; QQ, 85 (Spr. 1978), 59-61; SatN, 92 (Nov. 1977), 55-57, 60; UTQ, 47 (Sum. 1978), 332-34.

1129   NO MAN'S MEAT & THE ENCHANTED PIMP: BCan, 7 (Oct. 1978), 12, 14; CanL, 84 (Spr. 1980), 120-22; DR, 58 (Wint. 1978-79), 793-95; FIDDLEHEAD, 124 (Wint. 1980), 124-26; MACLEAN'S, 13 Nov. 1978, pp. 60, 62; Q&Q, 44 (Oct. 1978), 42; SatN, 93 (Oct. 1978), 75-77.

1130   THAT SUMMER IN PARIS: Atl, 211 (Feb. 1963), 132; CanL, 16 (Spr. 1963), 55-57; CBRA, 1976, pp. 76-77; MONTREALER, 37 (Feb. 1963), 35; NatR, 14 Jan. 1969, p. 29; NewR, 9 Feb. 1963, pp. 26-28; NS, 22 Nov. 1963, p. 746; NYRB, 1, No. 1 (1963), 13; NYTBR, 7 Apr. 1963, p. 43; QQ, 70 (Aut. 1963), 464; QUARRY, 13 (1963-64), 52; SatN, 78 (Mar. 1963), 29; SatR, 12 Jan. 1963, p. 61; SPECTATOR, 15 Nov. 1963, pp. 631-32; TamR, 26 (Wint. 1963), 98; TLS, 1 Nov. 1963, p. 885; UTQ, 33 (July 1964), 424-26.

CHILD, PHILIP (1898--)

A poet and a novelist, Philip Child was born in Hamilton, Ontario, attended schools in Germany and Switzerland as well as Canada, and went on to study at the University of Toronto, Cambridge University, and Harvard University. He served in the army during World War I, worked as a reporter, and then taught at Harvard and the Universities of Toronto and British Columbia. Two of his novels, DAY OF WRATH and MR. AMES AGAINST TIME, received Ryerson Fiction Awards, the latter also a Governor General's Award. It is GOD'S SPARROWS, however, a sensitive study of a young man's place within his family and within a world at war, for which he is best known.

PRIMARY MATERIAL

Monographs

FICTION

1131 THE VILLAGE OF SOULS. London: Thornton Butterworth, 1933. 315 p.

1132 GOD'S SPARROWS. London: Thornton Butterworth, 1937. 319 p.

1133 BLOW WIND--COME WRACK. London: Jarrolds, 1945. 192 p.

1134 DAY OF WRATH. Toronto: Ryerson, 1945. 274 p.

1135 MR. AMES AGAINST TIME. Toronto: Ryerson, 1949. vi, 244 p.

NONFICTION PROSE

1136 "Evangelism and English Literature, 1798-1830: A Study in Literary, Religious, and Social Interrelations." Diss., Harvard University, 1928. Bibliog.

1137 POST-WAR ORGANIZATION: A REPORT OF A ROUND-TABLE DIS-
CUSSION HELD AT THE SEVENTH ANNUAL STUDY CONFERENCE OF
THE CANADIAN INSTITUTE OF INTERNATIONAL AFFAIRS IN LON-
DON, ONTARIO, MAY 27 AND 28, 1940. Toronto: Canadian In-
stitute of International Affairs, 1940. 181 p.

1138 DYNAMIC DEMOCRACY: A PROBLEM ON STRATEGY IN THE WORLD
WAR OF MORALE. By Philip Child and John W. Holmes. Foreword
by Robert Falconer. Toronto: Canadian Association for Adult Education
and the Canadian Institute of International Affairs, 1941. 24 p.

POETRY

1139 THE VICTORIAN HOUSE AND OTHER POEMS. Toronto: Ryerson, 1951.
54 p.

1140 THE WOOD OF THE NIGHTINGALE. Toronto: Ryerson, 1965. 152 p.

EDITED WORK

1141 LONGER POEMS FOR UPPER SCHOOL, 1964-1965. Ed. with notes by
Philip Child and Roy H. Allin. Toronto: Ryerson, 1964. 64 p.

Shorter Work

ARTICLES

1142 "The Function of Tragedy." QUEEN'S QUARTERLY, 32 (Nov. 1924),
137-53.

1143 "Portrait of a Woman of Affairs--Old Style." UNIVERSITY OF TORONTO
QUARTERLY, 3 (Oct. 1933), 87-102.

Discusses Hannah More.

1144 Introd., WHITE NARCISSUS, by Raymond Knister. New Canadian Library, no. 32. Toronto: McClelland and Stewart, 1962, pp. 7-16.

For articles by Child, see also no. 125.

Manuscripts

1145 Hamilton Public Library, Hamilton, Ont.; National Library of Canada,
Ottawa; New York Public Library; Queen's University Library, Kingston,
Ont.

SECONDARY MATERIAL

Criticism

1146 Duffy, Dennis. Introd., GOD'S SPARROWS. New Canadian Library, no. 150. Toronto: McClelland and Stewart, 1978, pp. 5-11.

1147 _____. "Memory = Pain: The Haunted World of Philip Child's Fiction." CANADIAN LITERATURE, No. 84 (Spr. 1980), pp. 41-56.

1148 Magee, William H. "Philip Child: A Re-Appraisal." CANADIAN LITERATURE, No. 24 (Spr. 1965), pp. 28-36.

Book Reviews

1149 THE VILLAGE OF SOULS: CFor, 28 (Jan. 1949), 237; DR, 28 (Oct. 1948), 308; QQ, 57 (Sum. 1950), 266-67; RUL, 5 (Oct. 1950), 158-59; SatN, 11 Sept. 1948, p. 25; UTQ, 18 (Apr. 1949), 270-71.

1150 GOD'S SPARROWS: UTQ, 7 (Apr. 1938), 351-52.

1151 DAY OF WRATH: DR, 25 (Jan. 1946), 515-16; QQ, 52 (Wint. 1945), 493; SatN, 1 Dec. 1945, p. 34; UTQ, 15 (Apr. 1946), 284-85.

1152 MR. AMES AGAINST TIME: RUL, 5 (Oct. 1950), 160-62; SatN, 15 Nov. 1949, p. 22; UTQ, 19 (Apr. 1950), 269-70.

CLARKE, AUSTIN (1934--)

A West Indian writer who has now spent over twenty years in Canada, Austin Chesterfield Clarke was born, educated, and taught school for several years in Barbados. After attending the University of Toronto, he worked at a number of jobs, including free-lance reporting and broadcasting. Since 1955 when he came to Canada, he has lived mostly in Toronto with excursions as a diplomat with the Embassy of Barbados in Washington, D.C., and as a visiting lecturer, particularly in black literature, at a number of American universities. His fiction, with its accurate rendering of dialect, explores the West Indian experience both of the native and of the expatriate in Canada.

PRIMARY MATERIAL

Monographs

FICTION

1153   THE SURVIVORS OF THE CROSSING. Toronto: McClelland and Stewart, 1964. 202 p.

1154   AMONGST THISTLES AND THORNS. Toronto: McClelland and Stewart, 1965. 183 p.

1155   THE MEETING POINT. Toronto: Macmillan, 1967. 249 p.

First volume in a trilogy; see nos. 1157-58.

1156   WHEN HE WAS FREE AND YOUNG AND HE USED TO WEAR SILKS: STORIES. Toronto: Anansi, 1971. 151 p.

1157   STORM OF FORTUNE: A NOVEL. Boston: Little, Brown, 1973. 312 p.

Second volume in a trilogy beginning with no. 1155.

1158   THE BIGGER LIGHT: A NOVEL. Boston: Little, Brown, 1975. 288 p.
Third volume in a trilogy beginning with no. 1155.

1159   THE PRIME MINISTER: A NOVEL. Don Mills, Ont.: General Publishing, 1977. 191 p.

NONFICTION PROSE

1160   ALI KAMAL AL KADIR SUDAN: BLACK MAN IN A WHITE LAND.
Burlington, Ont.: Al Kitab Sudan, 1967. N. pag.

1161   THE CONFESSED BEWILDERMENT OF MARTIN LUTHER KING AND THE
IDEA OF NON-VIOLENCE AS A POLITICAL TACTIC. An Al Kitab
Sudan Publication. Burlington, Ont.: T. Watkins, 1968. 14 p.

1162   GROWING UP STUPID UNDER THE UNION JACK: A MEMOIR. Toronto:
McClelland and Stewart, 1980. 192 p.

Shorter Work

SHORT STORIES

1163   "I Hanging on, Praise God." BIM (Barbados), 9, No. 36 (1961-63),
275-81.

1164   "The Woman with the BBC Voice." TAMARACK REVIEW, 29 (Aut. 1963),
27-35.

1165   "The Collector." TRANSATLANTIC REVIEW, No. 23 (Wint. 1966-67),
pp. 24-37.

1166   "Why Didn't You Use a Plunger?" TAMARACK REVIEW, 52 (3rd quarter
1969), 51-57, 60-62.

1167   "Griff!" TAMARACK REVIEW, No. 58 (1971), pp. 34-50.

1168   "Hammie and the Black Dean." In NEW AMERICAN REVIEW 14. New
York: Simon and Schuster, 1972, pp. 219-47.

ARTICLES

1169   "Some Speculations as to the Absence of Racialistic Vindictiveness in
West Indian Literature." In THE BLACK WRITER IN AFRICA AND THE
AMERICAS. Ed. Lloyd W. Brown. University of Southern California

Studies in Comparative Literature, 6. Los Angeles: Hennessey and Ingalls, 1973, pp. 165-94.

SECONDARY MATERIAL

Criticism

1170   Brown, Lloyd W. "Austin Clarke in Canadian Reviews." CANADIAN LITERATURE, No. 38 (Aut. 1968), pp. 101-04.

1171   _____. "The West Indian Novel in North America: A Study of Austin Clarke." JOURNAL OF COMMONWEALTH LITERATURE, No. 9 (July 1970), pp. 89-103.

1172   Kelly, Terry. "How Austin Clarke Found the Bigger Light Was Back in Canada After All." BOOKS IN CANADA, 5 (Oct. 1976), 37-38.

Interview.

1173   Morgan, John. "Austin Clarke." MONTREALER, 41 (Sept. 1967), 27, 32-33.

1174   Slopen, Beverley. "Caribbean Memories of Power and Privilege." QUILL AND QUIRE, 46, No. 5 (1980), 23.

For criticism on Clarke, see also no. 1701.

Book Reviews

1175   THE SURVIVORS OF THE CROSSING: CAB, 40 (Spr. 1965), 16; CanL, 23 (Wint. 1965), 74-76; FIDDLEHEAD, [75] (Spr. 1968), 69-70; MONTREALER, 38 (Dec. 1964), 42; SatN, 80 (Feb. 1965), 26; TamR, [38] (Wint. 1966), 89.

1176   AMONGST THISTLES AND THORNS: ALPHABET, 12 (Aug. 1966), 93-94; CAB, 41 ([Spr.] 1966), 13; CFor, 47 (Aug. 1967), 118-19; FIDDLEHEAD, [75] (Spr. 1968), 70-71; MACLEAN'S, 16 Oct. 1965, p. 68; MONTREALER, 39 (Dec. 1965), 30; PUNCH, 21 July 1965, p. 102; SatN, 80 (Nov. 1965), 59-60; TamR, [38] (Wint. 1966), 90-91; TLS, 8 July 1965, p. 573.

1177   THE MEETING POINT: CanL, 35 (Wint. 1968), 74-75, 77-78; CFor, 48 (Apr. 1968), 19-20; FIDDLEHEAD, [75] (Spr. 1968), 71-72; MACLEAN'S, 80 (Aug. 1967), 70; NY, 22 Apr. 1972, p. 142; NYTBR, 9 Apr. 1972, p. 42; TamR, [45] (Aut. 1967), 117, 120; TLS, 11 May 1967, p. 404; UTQ, 37 (July 1968), 383.

1178 WHEN HE WAS FREE AND YOUNG AND HE USED TO WEAR SILKS:
      BCan, 1 (Nov. 1971), 4; CFM, 7 (Sum. 1972), 59-60; FIDDLEHEAD,
      95 (Fall 1972), 117-18; MACLEAN'S, 85 (Apr. 1972), 108; NYTBR, 9
      Dec. 1973, p. 48; QQ, 79 (Spr. 1972), 120; SatN, 86 (Oct. 1971),
      33-34; UTQ, 41 (Sum. 1972), 316.

1179 STORM OF FORTUNE: BCan, 2 (Apr. 1973), 38; CanL, 61 (Sum.
      1974), 106-08; JCF, 1 (Fall 1973), 96-97; NY, 20 Aug. 1973, p. 89.

1180 THE BIGGER LIGHT: BCan, 4 (June 1975), 15; NATION, 1 Nov.
      1975, p. 440; NY, 24 Feb. 1975, p. 140; NYTBR, 16 Feb. 1975, p. 12;
      SatN, 90 (June 1975), 71-72.

1181 THE PRIME MINISTER: BCan, 6 (Nov. 1977), 32, 34; BCan, 8 (Jan.
      1979), 22; LISTENER, 15 June 1978, p. 774; Q&Q, 43, No. 14 (1977),
      7; QQ, 87 (Aut. 1980), 465-66.

1182 GROWING UP STUPID UNDER THE UNION JACK: BCan, 9 (June
      1980), 23; Q&Q, 46 (June 1980), 36.

COHEN, LEONARD (1934--)

Leonard Cohen was born and grew up in English Montreal, graduating in English from McGill University in 1955. After some work in the family clothing business and an attempt at law at Columbia, he became a writer, living much of the time on the island of Hydra in Greece. Cohen is internationally known as the composer and singer of plaintive, reflective folk songs. As a literary figure, he is primarily a poet. BEAUTIFUL LOSERS, the novel which has aroused greatest interest, is an experimental, deliberately provocative mixture of fantasy, eroticism, history, and popular culture.

PRIMARY MATERIAL

Monographs

FICTION

1183   THE FAVOURITE GAME. London: Secker and Warburg, 1963. 222 p.

1184   BEAUTIFUL LOSERS. Toronto: McClelland and Stewart, 1966. 243 p.

POETRY

1185   LET US COMPARE MYTHOLOGIES. Drawings by Freda Guttman. McGill Poetry Series. Toronto: Contact, 1956. 79 p.

1186   THE SPICE BOX OF EARTH. Drawings by Frank Newfeld. [Toronto]: McClelland and Stewart, 1961. vii, 99 p.

1187   FLOWERS FOR HITLER. Toronto: McClelland and Stewart, 1964. ix, 128 p.

1188   PARASITES OF HEAVEN. Toronto: McClelland and Stewart, 1966. 80 p. Index.

1189   SELECTED POEMS 1956-1968. Toronto: McClelland and Stewart, 1968.
        x, 245 p.   Index.

1190   THE ENERGY OF SLAVES. Toronto: McClelland and Stewart, 1972.
        127 p.

1191   DEATH OF A LADIES' MAN. Toronto: McClelland and Stewart, 1978.
        216 p.   Index.

1192   TWO VIEWS. SEVEN POEMS BY LEONARD COHEN; SEVEN LITHO-
        GRAPHS BY GIGINO FALCONI. Toronto: Madison Gallery, 1980.
        N. pag.

Shorter Work

SHORT STORIES

1193   "Trade." TAMARACK REVIEW, 20 (Sum. 1961), 59-65.

1194   "Luggage Fire Sale." PARALLEL, No. 2 (May-June 1966), pp. 40-44.

1195   "Barbers and Lovers." INGLUVIN, No. 2 (Jan.-Mar. 1971), pp. 10-19.

Manuscripts

1196   University of Toronto Library.

SECONDARY MATERIAL

Bibliography

1197   MacDonald, Ruth, comp. "Leonard Cohen, a Bibliography, 1956-1973."
        BULLETIN OF BIBLIOGRAPHY, 31 (July-Sept. 1974), 107-10.

For bibliographies of Cohen, see also no. 33.

Criticism

1198   Barbour, Douglas. "Down with History: Some Notes Towards an Under-
        standing of BEAUTIFUL LOSERS." OPEN LETTER, 2nd ser., No. 8 (Sum.
        1974), pp. 48-60.

        Reprinted in no. 1205.

1199 Batten, Jack, Michael Harris, and Don Owen. "Léonard Cohen: The Poet as Hero." SATURDAY NIGHT, 84 (June 1969), 23-32.

Includes an interview; reprinted in no. 1205.

1200 Bem, Jeanne. "Avec Léonard Cohen: Magic is Alive." LANGUES MODERNES, 65 (1971), 514-21.

1201 Cavanagh, David. "Magic in Leonard Cohen's THE FAVORITE GAME and BEAUTIFUL LOSERS." ALIVE, 28 (1973), 19-22.

1202 De Venster, Dagmar. "Leonard Cohen's Women." In MOTHER WAS NOT A PERSON. Ed. Margret Andersen. Montreal: Black Rose Books, 1972, pp. 96-97.

1203 Djwa, Sandra. "Leonard Cohen: Black Romantic." CANADIAN LIT-ERATURE, No. 34 (Aut. 1967), pp. 32-42.

Reprinted in nos. 1205 and 5112.

1204 Garebian, Keith. "Desire as Art: Leonard Cohen's THE FAVORITE GAME." LE CHIEN D'OR/GOLDEN DOG, 4 (Nov. 1974), 29-34.

1205 Gnarowski, Michael, ed. with introd. LEONARD COHEN: THE ARTIST AND HIS CRITICS. Critical Views on Canadian Writers. Toronto: McGraw-Hill Ryerson, 1976. 169 p. Bibliog.

Reprints nos. 1198-99, 1203, 1212-13, 1217, and 1219.

1206 Hutcheon, Linda. "BEAUTIFUL LOSERS: All the Polarities." CANA-DIAN LITERATURE, No. 59 (Wint. 1974), pp. 42-56.

Reprinted in no. 5113.

1207 _____. "The Poet as Novelist." CANADIAN LITERATURE, No. 86 (Aut. 1980), pp. 6-14.

Discusses Cohen and Davies.

1208 Lee, Dennis. SAVAGE FIELDS: AN ESSAY IN LITERATURE AND COS-MOLOGY. Toronto: Anansi, 1977. 125 p.

Discusses Ondaatje's COLLECTED WORKS OF BILLY THE KID and Cohen's BEAUTIFUL LOSERS.

1209 Macri, F.M. "BEAUTIFUL LOSERS and the Canadian Experience." JOURNAL OF COMMONWEALTH LITERATURE, 8 (June 1973), 88-96.

1210 Matos, Manuel Cadafaz de. LEONARD COHEN: REDESCOBERTA DA VIDA E UMA ALEGORIA A EROS. Lisbon: Livros E(co)logiar a Terra, 1975.

1211 Monkman, Leslie. "BEAUTIFUL LOSERS: Mohawk Myth and Jesuit Legend." JOURNAL OF CANADIAN FICTION, 3, No. 3 (1974), 57-59.

1212 Morley, Patricia A. "'The Knowledge of Strangerhood': 'The Monuments Were Made of Worms.'" JOURNAL OF CANADIAN FICTION, 1 (Sum. 1972), 56-60.

Discusses THE FAVOURITE GAME; reprinted in no. 1205.

1213 Pacey, Desmond. "The Phenomenon of Leonard Cohen." CANADIAN LITERATURE, No. 34 (Aut. 1967), pp. 5-23.

Reprinted in nos. 177 and 1205.

1214 Purdy, Alfred W. "Leonard Cohen: A Personal Look." CANADIAN LITERATURE, No. 23 (Wint. 1965), pp. 7-16.

1215 Saltzman, Paul. "Famous Last Words from Leonard Cohen: The Poet's Final Interview He Hopes." MACLEAN'S, 86 (June 1972), 6-7, 77-80.

1216 Scobie, Stephen. LEONARD COHEN. Studies in Canadian Literature. Vancouver: Douglas and McIntyre, 1978. xii, 192 p. Bibliog.

1217 _____. "Magic, not Magicians: BEAUTIFUL LOSERS and STORY OF O." CANADIAN LITERATURE, No. 45 (Sum. 1970), pp. 56-60.

Reprinted in no. 1205.

1218 Smith, Rowland J. Introd., THE FAVOURITE GAME. New Canadian Library, no. 73. Toronto: McClelland and Stewart, 1970. N. pag.

1219 Snider, Burr. "Zooey Glass in Europe." GYPSY, 1, [No. 1 (1971), 10-13].

Reprinted in no. 1205.

1220 Vassal, Jacques. LEONARD COHEN. Paris: Albin Michel, 1974. 189 p. Bibliog.

In French.

For criticism on Leonard Cohen, see also nos. 126, 162, 170, 174, 205, 297, 407, 667, 686, 3023, 5063, and, especially, 3063 and 3537.

Book Reviews

1221 THE FAVOURITE GAME: ALPHABET, 9 (Nov. 1964), 78; BCan, 2 (Apr. 1973), 32-33; CAB, 39 (Spr. 1964), 12; CanL, 19 (Wint. 1964), 69-70; MACLEAN'S, 5 Oct. 1963, p. 79; NS, 20 Sept. 1963, p. 364;

PUNCH, 2 Oct. 1963, p. 505; SatN, 78 (Nov. 1963), 41; SatR, 5
Oct. 1963, p. 42; SPECTATOR, 25 Oct. 1963, p. 538; TamR, [30]
(Wint. 1964), 95; TLS, 11 Oct. 1963, p. 813; TLS, 18 Oct. 1970,
p. 1027; UTQ, 33 (July 1964), 393-94.

1222 BEAUTIFUL LOSERS: ALPHABET, 13 (June 1967), 94-95; CanL, 29
(Sum. 1966), 61-63; CFor, 47 (July 1967), 91; JCL, 3 (July 1967),
112-13; MACLEAN'S, 14 May 1966, p. 46; MONTREALER, 40 (June
1966), 35-36; LISTENER, 9 Apr. 1970, p. 488; NS, 3 Apr. 1970,
p. 482; NYRB, 28 Apr. 1966, p. 17; NYTBR, 8 May 1966, p. 30; PUNCH,
15 Apr. 1970, p. 580; SatN, 80 [81] (May 1966), 47; SoR, 4 (Wint.)
1968), 236, 240-41; TamR, [40] (Sum. 1966), 75-77; TLS, 23 Apr.
1970, p. 445; UTQ, 36 (July 1967), 379-80; WCR, 1 (Fall 1966), 58-60.

COHEN, MATT (1942--)

Matt Cohen was born in Kingston, Ontario, grew up in Ottawa, and received a Ph.D. in political science from the University of Toronto. He taught in the department of religion at McMaster University, Hamilton, Ontario, and since 1971 has been devoting himself to his writing. Particularly in his early novels, Cohen creates surrealistic dislocations of time, point of view, and style. Recently, he has been engaged in a more realistic family chronicle in several volumes.

PRIMARY MATERIAL

Monographs

FICTION

1223 KORSONILOFF. Spiderline edition. Toronto: Anansi, 1969. 106 p.

1224 JOHNNY CRACKLE SINGS. Toronto: McClelland and Stewart, 1971. 108 p.

     A novella.

1225 COLUMBUS AND THE FAT LADY AND OTHER STORIES. Toronto: Anansi, 1972. 213 p.

     Reprinted in no. 1234.

1226 TOO BAD GALAHAD. Drawings by Margaret Hathaway. [Toronto]: Coach House, 1972. N. pag.

     Reprinted in nos. 1225 and 1234.

1227 THE DISINHERITED. Toronto: McClelland and Stewart, 1974. 240 p.

     First volume in a tetralogy.

1228   WOODEN HUNTERS. Toronto: McClelland and Stewart, 1975. 219 p.

1229   THE COLOURS OF WAR. Toronto: McClelland and Stewart, 1977. 234 p.

       Second volume in a tetralogy, beginning with no. 1227.

1230   THE LEAVES OF LOUISE. Illus. by Rikki. Toronto: McClelland and Stewart, 1978. 30 p.

       For children.

1231   NIGHT FLIGHTS: STORIES NEW AND SELECTED. Toronto: Doubleday Canada, 1978. 180 p.

       Reprinted in no. 1234.

1232   THE SWEET SECOND SUMMER OF KITTY MALONE. Toronto: McClelland and Stewart, 1979. 233 p.

       Third volume in a tetralogy, beginning with no. 1227.

1233   FLOWERS OF DARKNESS. Toronto: McClelland and Stewart, 1981. 251 p.

       Fourth volume in a tetralogy, beginning with no. 1227.

1234   THE EXPATRIATE: COLLECTED SHORT STORIES. Toronto: General, 1982. 298 p.

       Includes nos. 1225, 1226, and 1231.

POETRY

1235   PEACH MELBA. [Toronto: Coach House, 1974.] N. pag.

EDITED WORK

1236   THE STORY SO FAR/2. [Toronto]: Coach House, 1973. 128 p.

Shorter Work

SHORT STORIES

1237   "Amazing Grace." In 73: NEW CANADIAN STORIES. Ed. David Helwig and Joan Harcourt. [Ottawa]: Oberon, 1973, pp. 105-09.

1238   "'Franz.'" CANADIAN FORUM, 56 (Feb. 1977), 41-44.

1239 "Pat Frank's Dream." In AURORA. Ed. Morris Wolfe. Toronto: Doubleday, 1978, pp. 199-206.

1240 "A Love for the Infinite." NORTH AMERICAN REVIEW, 265 (June 1980), 24-27.

1241 "A Week in New York." SATURDAY NIGHT, 95 (Dec. 1980), 66-71.

ARTICLES

1242 "Nihilism or Insanity: The Strange Life of Ichabod Oise." THIS MAGAZINE IS ABOUT SCHOOLS, 1 (Aut. 1967), 49-56.

1243 "The Rise and Fall of Serious CanLit: The Golden Years May Be Over." SATURDAY NIGHT, 94 (May 1979), 39-40, 42.

Reprinted in no. 136.

1244 "Craft before Culture." QUILL AND QUIRE, 45 (July 1979), 34.

Discusses Hugh Garner.

Manuscripts

1245 McMaster University Library, Hamilton.

SECONDARY MATERIAL

Criticism

1246 Abley, M. "It's a Long Way to Salem Country." MACLEAN'S, 12 Mar. 1979, p. 54.

1247 Ewing, Betty Moore. "Matt Cohen's Monologue in Morality." CANADIAN LITERATURE, No. 72 (Spr. 1977), pp. 41-44.

Discusses KORSONILOFF and JOHNNY CRACKLE SINGS.

1248 Kertzer, Jon. "Time and Its Victims: The Writing of Matt Cohen." ESSAYS ON CANADIAN WRITING, No. 17 (Spr. 1980), pp. 93-101.

1249 "Matt Cohen: Perceiving is Believing." QUILL AND QUIRE, 40 (Aug. 1974), 20.

1250 Moss, John G. Introd., WOODEN HUNTERS. New Canadian Library, no. 149. Toronto: McClelland and Stewart, 1975, pp. v-xii.

1251   Naglin, Nancy. "Matt Cohen: Graduate of the Sixties." BOOKS IN CANADA, 3 (Mar. 1974), 12-13.

1252   Oughton, John. "Interview with Matt Cohen." WAVES, 5 (Spr. 1977), 4-9.

For criticism on Matt Cohen, see also nos. 170, 205, 1701, and 5203.

Book Reviews

1253   KORSONILOFF: CFor, 50 (June 1970), 149; FIDDLEHEAD, 84 (Mar. 1970), 106-07; SatN, 84 (Nov. 1969), 63; TamR, 53 (1970), 86.

1254   JOHNNY CRACKLE SINGS: BCan, 1 (Nov. 1971), 11-12; BCLQ, 35 (Apr. 1972), 69-70; CFM, 7 (Sum. 1972), 58-59; CFor, 51 (Jan. 1972), 80; JCF, 1 (Wint. 1972), 87-88; SatN, 87 (Feb. 1972), 37.

1255   COLUMBUS AND THE FAT LADY: BCan, 1 (Nov. 1972), 2, 48; CanL, 62 (Aut. 1974), 110-11; CFM, 11 (Aut. 1973), 84-88; MACLEAN'S, 86 (Mar. 1976), 96; OpenL, 2nd ser., 4 (1973), 86-90; OpenL, 2nd ser., 4 (1973), 91-92; Q&Q, 38, No. 12 (1972), 8; QQ, 80 (Aut. 1973), 469.

1256   TOO BAD GALAHAD: CanL, 62 (Aut. 1974), 111-12; CFM; 13 (Spr. 1974), 115-17.

1257   THE DISINHERITED: BCan, 3 (Apr. 1974), 17-18; CanL, 62 (Aut. 1974), 88-89; CanR, 2 (Jan. 1975), 32-33; CFM, 17 (Spr. 1975), 113-15; CFor, 54 (Mar. 1975), 39; DR, 54 (Aut. 1974), 576-77; FIDDLE-HEAD, 102 (Sum. 1974), 107-09, 111-12; JCF, 4, No. 1 (1975), 187-89; MACLEAN'S, 87 (May 1974), 100; Q&Q, 40, No. 5 (1974), 16; QQ, 81 (Aut. 1974), 477-78; SatN, 89, No. 5 (May 1974), 46-47; TamR, 63 (Oct. 1974), 78; UTQ, 44 (Sum. 1975), 305-06; UWR, 10 (Spr. 1975), 80.

1258   WOODEN HUNTERS: BCan, 4 (Apr. 1975), 8-9; CanL, 67 (Wint. 1976), 90-91; CBRA, 1975, p. 121; CFM, 20 (Wint. 1976), 101-02; FIDDLEHEAD, 107 (Fall 1975), 135-36; MACLEAN'S, 88 (May 1975), 98; SatN, 90 (May 1975), 69-79; UTQ, 45 (Sum. 1976), 317-18.

1259   THE COLOURS OF WAR: BCan, 6 (Aug. 1977), 16; CanL, 75 (Wint. 1977), 74-77; CFor, 57 (Dec. 1977), 41; ECW, 9 (Wint. 1977-78), 173-75; FIDDLEHEAD, 119 (Fall 1978), 123-24; Q&Q, 43, No. 12 (1977), 8; QUARRY, 27 (Wint. 1978), 94-96; SatN, 92 (Sept. 1977), 73-75; UWR, 13 (Spr. 1978), 108.

1260   NIGHT FLIGHTS: AntigR, 35 (Aut. 1978), 94-95; BCan, 7 (May
       1978), 15-16; CAB, 54 (Oct. 1978), 30; CanL, 82 (Aut. 1979), 80-
       81; CFor, 58 (June 1978), 48-49; ECW, 12 (Fall 1978), 56-59; FID-
       DLEHEAD, 120 (Wint. 1979), 113-14; IFR, 5 (July 1978), 157-58;
       QUARRY, 28 (Spr. 1979), 92; SR, 87 (Wint. 1979), xix-xxii; TamR,
       79 (Aut. 1979), 77.

1261   THE SWEET SECOND SUMMER OF KITTY MALONE: BCan, 8 (Apr.
       1979), 5; CanL, 86 (Aut. 1980), 122-23; CFM, 30-31 (1979), 202-06;
       CFor, 59 (May 1979), 30; FIDDLEHEAD, 122 (Sum. 1979), 137-39;
       MACLEAN'S, 12 Mar. 1979, p. 54; Q&Q, Update, 16 Feb. 1979,
       p. 12; QUARRY, 28 (Aut. 1979), 94-96; SatN, 94 (Apr. 1979), 67-68;
       TamR, 77-78 (Sum. 1979), 101; TamR, 79 (Aut. 1979), 77-79; UTQ,
       49 (Sum. 1980), 328-29.

DAVIES, ROBERTSON (1913--   )

Born in Thamesville, Ontario, and raised in Renfrew and Kingston, William Robertson Davies studied at Queen's University and received his B.Litt. from Oxford University in 1938. After two years of acting, teaching, and editing for the Old Vic Repertory Company, he returned to Canada to act as literary editor for two years for SATURDAY NIGHT, then as writer and soon as editor and publisher of the Peterborough EXAMINER, a position which he held until 1968. In 1960, he began teaching English at the University of Toronto and in 1963 became the first Master of Massey College, University of Toronto. Davies is the recipient of more than a half dozen honorary degrees and in 1972 became a Companion of the Order of Canada. LEAVEN OF MALICE has won the Leacock Medal for Humour, THE MANTICORE the Governor General's Award.

Beginning first as a journalist and then mainly a playwright, Davies has attained a prominence in Canadian literature which now rests primarily on his two fictional trilogies, the Salterton trilogy and particularly the later Deptford trilogy. His novels--witty, erudite, and satirical with a well-developed sense of character--display a strong commitment simultaneously to physical and spiritual realities. The early novels lean toward social satire, the later toward psychological exploration.

PRIMARY MATERIAL

Monographs

FICTION

1262   THE DIARY OF SAMUEL MARCHBANKS. Decorations by Clair Stewart. Toronto: Clarke, Irwin, 1947. 204 p.

1263   THE TABLE TALK OF SAMUEL MARCHBANKS. Decorations by Clair Stewart. Toronto: Clarke, Irwin, 1949. vi, 248 p.

1264   TEMPEST-TOST. Toronto: Clarke, Irwin, 1951. v, 376 p.

First volume in the Salterton trilogy.

1265   LEAVEN OF MALICE. Toronto: Clarke, Irwin, 1954. 312 p.

Second volume in the Salterton trilogy.

1266   A MIXTURE OF FRAILTIES. Toronto: Macmillan, 1958. 379 p.

Third volume in the Salterton trilogy.

1267   MARCHBANKS' ALMANACK. Toronto: McClelland and Stewart, 1967.
xiv, 205 p.

1268   FIFTH BUSINESS: A NOVEL. Toronto: Macmillan, 1970. 314 p.

First volume in the Deptford trilogy.

1269   THE MANTICORE: A NOVEL. Toronto: Macmillan, 1972. 280 p.

Second volume in the Deptford trilogy.

1270   WORLD OF WONDERS. Toronto: Macmillan, 1975. 358 p.

Third volume in the Deptford trilogy.

1271   THE REBEL ANGELS. Toronto: Macmillan, 1981. 326 p.

NONFICTION PROSE

1272   SHAKESPEARE'S BOY ACTORS. London: J.M. Dent, 1939. vii, 207 p.
Bibliog.

B. Litt. thesis.

1273   RENOWN AT STRATFORD: A RECORD OF THE SHAKESPEARE FESTIVAL
IN CANADA, 1953. By Tyrone Guthrie and Robertson Davies. Illus.
Grant Macdonald. Toronto: Clarke, Irwin, 1953. viii, 127 p.

1274   TWICE HAVE THE TRUMPETS SOUNDED: A RECORD OF THE STRAT-
FORD SHAKESPEAREAN FESTIVAL IN CANADA, 1954. By Tyrone
Guthrie and Robertson Davies. Illus. Grant Macdonald. Toronto: Clarke,
Irwin, 1954. xiv, 192 p.

1275   THRICE THE BRINDED CAT HATH MEW'D: A RECORD OF THE STRAT-
FORD SHAKESPEAREAN FESTIVAL IN CANADA, 1955. By Robertson
Davies, Tyrone Guthrie, Boyd Neel, and Tanya Moiseiwitsch. Toronto:
Clarke, Irwin, 1955. xii, 178 p.

1276 A VOICE FROM THE ATTIC. Toronto: McClelland and Stewart, 1960. ix, 360, x p. Bibliog.; rpt. as THE PERSONAL ART: READING TO GOOD PURPOSE. London: Secker and Warburg, 1961. 268 p. Bibliog.

1277 STEPHEN LEACOCK. Canadian Writers, no. 7. Toronto: McClelland and Stewart, 1970. 62 p. Bibliog.

1278 WHAT DO YOU SEE IN THE MIRROR? Searchlights. Agincourt, Ont.: Book Society, 1970. 8 p.

1279 ONE HALF OF ROBERTSON DAVIES: PROVOCATIVE PRONOUNCE-MENTS ON A WIDE RANGE OF TOPICS. Toronto: Macmillan, 1977. 286 p.

1280 THE ENTHUSIASMS OF ROBERTSON DAVIES. Ed. Judith Skelton Grant. Toronto: McClelland and Stewart, 1979. 320 p.

1281 THE WELL-TEMPERED CRITIC: ONE MAN'S VIEW OF THEATRE AND LETTERS IN CANADA. Ed. Judith Skelton Grant. Toronto: McClelland and Stewart, 1981. 285 p.

DRAMA

1282 OVERLAID: A COMEDY. Canadian Playwright Series. Toronto: Samuel French, 1948. 24 p.

1283 EROS AT BREAKFAST, AND OTHER PLAYS. Introd. Tyrone Guthrie. Toronto: Clarke, Irwin, 1949. xiv, 129 p.

1284 FORTUNE, MY FOE. Toronto: Clarke, Irwin, 1949. 99 p.

1285 AT MY HEART'S CORE. Toronto: Clarke, Irwin, 1950. viii, 91 p.

1286 A MASQUE OF AESOP. Decorations by Grant Macdonald. Toronto: Clarke, Irwin, 1952. vi, 47 p.

1287 A JIG FOR THE GYPSY. Toronto: Clarke, Irwin, 1954. viii, 98 p.

1288 A MASQUE OF MR. PUNCH. Toronto: Oxford University Press, 1963. xii, 58 p.

1289 AT MY HEART'S CORE; OVERLAID. Toronto: Clarke, Irwin, 1966. 124 p.

     Reprints nos. 1282 and 1285.

1290 FOUR FAVOURITE PLAYS. Preface by Robertson Davies. Toronto: Clarke, Irwin, 1968. vii, 157 p.

1291 THE VOICE OF THE PEOPLE. Searchlights. Agincourt, Ont.: Book Society, 1968. 12 p.

Reprinted from no. 1283.

1292 HUNTING STUART AND OTHER PLAYS. Toronto: New, 1972. 274 p.

1293 QUESTION TIME: A PLAY. Toronto: Macmillan, 1975. xv, 70 p.

EDITED WORK

1294 SHAKESPEARE FOR YOUNG PLAYERS: A JUNIOR COURSE. Illus. Grant Macdonald. Toronto: Clarke, Irwin, 1942. xv, 255 p.

1295 FEAST OF STEPHEN: AN ANTHOLOGY OF SOME OF THE LESS FAMILIAR WRITINGS OF STEPHEN LEACOCK. Ed. with a critical introd. by Robertson Davies. Toronto: McClelland and Stewart, 1970. 154 p. Bibliog.

Shorter Work

SHORT STORY

1296 "Vanishing Poplin." SATURDAY NIGHT, 3 Oct. 1942, p. 29.

ARTICLES

1297 "A Harp That Once." QUEEN'S QUARTERLY, 50 (Wint. 1943-44), 374-81.

On Canadian poet J.R. Ramsay.

1298 "Literary Letter from Canada." NEW YORK TIMES BOOK REVIEW, 19 Mar. 1950, p. 30; 1 Feb. 1953, p. 23.

1299 "The Theatre: A Dialogue on the State of the Theatre in Canada." In ROYAL COMMISSION STUDIES: A SELECTION OF ESSAYS PREPARED FOR THE ROYAL COMMISSION ON NATIONAL DEVELOPMENT IN THE ARTS, LETTERS AND SCIENCES. Ottawa: King's Printer, 1951, pp. 369-92.

1300 "The Double Life of Robertson Davies." By Samuel Marchbanks, pseud. LIBERTY, Apr. 1954, pp. 18-19, 53-58.

1301   "Week with MIDDLEMARCH." SATURDAY NIGHT, 28 May 1955, pp.
        24-26.

1302   "The Writer in Canada." PUBLISHERS' WEEKLY, 15 Oct. 1956, pp.
        1864-67.

1303   Introd., LITERARY LAPSES, by Stephen Leacock. New Canadian Library,
        no. 3. Toronto: McClelland and Stewart, 1957, pp. vii-ix.

1304   "Stephen Leacock." In OUR LIVING TRADITION: SEVEN CANADIANS.
        1st ser. Ed. Claude T. Bissell. Toronto: University of Toronto Press,
        in association with Carleton University, 1957, pp. 128-49.

            Reprinted in no. 195.

1305   "Battle Cry for Book Lovers." SATURDAY EVENING POST, 28 May
        1960, pp. 24-25.

1306   "Architects and Architecture." JOURNAL OF THE ROYAL ARCHITEC-
        TURAL INSTITUTE OF CANADA, 37 (Aug. 1960), 346-49.

1307   "Shakespeare Over the Port." In STRATFORD PAPERS ON SHAKES-
        PEARE, 1960. Ed. B.A.W. Jackson. Toronto: W.J. Gage, 1961,
        pp. 95-107.

1308   "Book Collecting." HOLIDAY, 31 (May 1962), 13-17.

1309   "Literature and Medicine." CANADIAN MEDICAL ASSOCIATION
        JOURNAL, 29 Sept. 1962, pp. 701-06.

1310   "The Theatre." In THE ARTS AS COMMUNICATION. Ed. David Carlton
        Williams. Toronto: University of Toronto Press, 1962, pp. 19-31.

1311   "Confessions of an Editor." In DATELINE CANADA, 1962. Ottawa:
        National Press Club of Canada, 1963, p. 17.

1312   "The Northern Muse." HOLIDAY, 35 (Apr. 1964), 10, 16-21. Bibliog.

1313   "Educating for the Future." ATLANTIC MONTHLY, 214 (Nov. 1964),
        140-44.

1314   Introd., MOONBEAMS FROM A LARGER LUNACY, by Stephen Leacock.
        New Canadian Library, no. 43. Toronto: McClelland and Stewart,
        1964, pp. vii-x.

1315   Introd., A THEATRICAL TRIP FOR A WAGER! THROUGH CANADA
        AND THE UNITED STATES. . . ., by Horton Rhys. Illus. Sam Black.
        Limited ed. Vancouver: Alcuin Society, 1966, pp. 9-12.

1316   "The Poetry of a People." In NOTES FOR A NATIVE LAND: A NEW
        ENCOUNTER WITH CANADA. Ed. Andy Wainwright. Ottawa: Oberon,
        1969, pp. 96-99.

1317   "Some Thoughts on the Present State of Canadian Literature." PRO-
        CEEDINGS AND TRANSACTIONS OF THE ROYAL SOCIETY OF CANADA,
        4th ser., 9 (1971), 261-70.

1318   "What Does Canada Expect from Writers?" FINANCIAL POST, 25 Nov.
        1972, p. 22.

1319   "Ben Jonson and Alchemy." In STRATFORD PAPERS, 1968-69. Ed.
        B.A.W. Jackson. Hamilton: McMaster University Library Press, 1972,
        pp. 40-60.

1320   "Canadian Nationalism in Arts and Science." PROCEEDINGS AND
        TRANSACTIONS OF THE ROYAL SOCIETY OF CANADA, 4th ser., 13
        (1975), 15-24.

1321   "Playwrights and Plays." In THE REVELS HISTORY OF DRAMA IN ENG-
        LISH. Vol. 6: 1750-1880. By Michael R. Booth, Richard Southern,
        Frederick Marker, Lise-Lone Marker, and Robertson Davies. London:
        Methuen, 1975, pp. 145-269. Bibliog.

1322   "Dark Hamlet with the Features of Horatio: Canada's Myths and Realities."
        In VOICES OF CANADA: AN INTRODUCTION TO CANADIAN CUL-
        TURE. Ed. Judith Webster. Burlington, Vt.: Association for Canadian
        Studies in the United States, 1977, pp. 42-47.

1323   "The Novels of Mavis Gallant." CANADIAN FICTION MAGAZINE,
        No. 28 (1978), pp. 68-73.

1324   "Return to Rhetoric: The Brockington Lecture." QUEEN'S QUARTERLY,
        87 (Sum. 1980), 183-97.

1325   "Fifty Years of Theatre in Canada." UNIVERSITY OF TORONTO QUAR-
        TERLY, 50 (Fall 1980), 69-80.

For articles by Davies, see also nos. 208 and 1356.

Manuscripts

1326   McGill University Library, Montreal; Queen's University Library, Kingston, Ont.

SECONDARY MATERIAL

Bibliography

1327   Roper, Gordon, and M. Whalon, comps. "A Davies Log." JOURNAL OF CANADIAN STUDIES, 12 (Feb. 1977), 4-19.

For bibliographies of Davies, see also no. 33.

Criticism

1328   "ACTA Interviews Robertson Davies." ACTA VICTORIANA, 47 (Apr. 1973), 68-87.

1329   Anthony, Geraldine. "Robertson Davies (1913-)." In STAGE VOICES: TWELVE CANADIAN PLAYWRIGHTS TALK ABOUT THEIR LIVES AND WORK. Ed. Geraldine Anthony. Toronto: Doubleday, 1978, pp. 55-84. Bibliog.

1330   Baltensperger, Peter. "Battle with the Trolls." CANADIAN LITERA-TURE, No. 71 (Wint. 1976), pp. 59-67.

1331   Birkett, Norman. Foreword, THE TABLE TALK OF SAMUEL MARCH-BANKS. London: Chatto and Windus, 1951, pp. v-vii.

1332   Bjerring, Nancy E. "Deep in the Old Man's Puzzle." CANADIAN LITERATURE, No. 62 (Aut. 1974), pp. 49-60.

    Discusses FIFTH BUSINESS; reprinted in no. 5113.

1333   Bonnycastle, Stephen. "Robertson Davies and the Ethics of Monologue." JOURNAL OF CANADIAN STUDIES, 12 (Feb. 1977), 20-40.

    Discusses the Deptford novels.

1334   Bowen, Gail. "Guides to the Treasure of Self: The Function of Women in the Fiction of Robertson Davies." WAVES, 5, No. 1 (1976), 64-77.

1335   Brown, Russell M., and Donna A. Bennett. "Magnus Eisengrim: The Shadow of the Trickster in the Novels of Robertson Davies." MODERN FICTION STUDIES, 22 (Aut. 1976), 347-63.

1336   Buitenhuis, Elspeth. ROBERTSON DAVIES. Canadian Writers and Their Works. Toronto: Forum House, 1972. 80 p. Bibliog.

1337   Chapman, M. "Female Archetypes in FIFTH BUSINESS." CANADIAN LITERATURE, No. 80 (Spr. 1979), 131-36ff.

1338   Cluett, Robert. "Robertson Davies: The Tory Mode." COMPUTERS AND THE HUMANITIES, 11 (Jan.-Feb. 1977), 13-23.

1339   Cockburn, Robert. Introd., A VOICE FROM THE ATTIC. New Canadian Library, no. 83. Toronto: McClelland and Stewart, 1972, pp. viii-xii.

1340   "Conversations with Robertson Davies." TIME CANADA, 3 Nov. 1975, p. 10.

1341   Cude, Wilfred. "'False as Harlots' Oaths': Dunny Ramsay Looks at Huck Finn." STUDIES IN CANADIAN LITERATURE, 2 (Sum. 1977), 164-87.

       Reprinted in no. 133.

1342   _____. "Historiography and Those Damned Saints: Shadow and Light in FIFTH BUSINESS." JOURNAL OF CANADIAN STUDIES, 12 (Feb. 1977), 47-67.

       Reprinted in no. 133.

1343   _____. "Miracle and Art in FIFTH BUSINESS or Who the Devil is Liselotte Vitzlipützli?" JOURNAL OF CANADIAN STUDIES, 9 (Nov. 1974), 3-16.

       Reprinted in no. 133.

1344   Davy, Paul. "The Structure of Davies' Deptford Trilogy." ESSAYS ON CANADIAN WRITING, No. 9 (Wint. 1977-78), pp. 123-33.

1345   Dean, John. "Magic and Mystery in Robertson Davies' Deptford Trilogy." WAVES, 7 (Fall 1978), 63-68.

1346   Dombrowski, Theo, and Eileen Dombrowski. "'Every Man's Judgement': Robertson Davies' Courtroom." STUDIES IN CANADIAN LITERATURE, 3 (Wint. 1978), 47-61.

1347   Gerson, Carole. "Dunstan Ramsay's Personal Mythology." ESSAYS ON CANADIAN WRITING, No. 6 (Spr. 1977), pp. 100-108.

1348   Grant, Judith Skelton. ROBERTSON DAVIES. Canadian Writers, no. 17. Toronto: McClelland and Stewart, 1978. 58 p. Bibliog.

1349   _____. "Robertson Davies, God and the Devil." BOOK FORUM, 4, No. 1 (1978), 56-63. Bibliog.

1350   Heintzman, Ralph R. "The Virtues of Reverence." JOURNAL OF CANADIAN STUDIES, 12 (Feb. 1977), 1-2, 92-95.

1351   Hoy, Helen. "Poetry in the Dunghill: The Romance of the Ordinary in Robertson Davies' Fiction." ARIEL, 10 (July 1979), 69-98.

1352   Keith, William J. "THE MANTICORE: Psychology and Fictional Technique." STUDIES IN CANADIAN LITERATURE, 3 (Wint. 1978), 133-36.

1353   Knelman, M. "The Masterful Actor Who Plays Robertson Davies." SATURDAY NIGHT, 90 (June 1975), 30-35.

1354   La Bossière, Camille R. "Justice Staunton in Toronto, London, and Zürich: The Case of THE MANTICORE." STUDIES IN CANADIAN LITERATURE, 5 (Fall 1980), 290-301.

1355   Lawrence, Robert G. "A Survey of the Three Novels of Robertson Davies." BRITISH COLUMBIA LIBRARY QUARTERLY, 32 (Apr. 1969), 3-9.

1356   Lawrence, Robert G., and Samuel L. Macey, eds. STUDIES IN ROBERTSON DAVIES' DEPTFORD TRILOGY: WITH AN INTRODUCTORY ESSAY BY ROBERTSON DAVIES. English Literary Studies, No. 20. Victoria: University of Victoria, 1980. 123 p.

1357   Lewis, Gertrud Jaron. "Vitzliputzli Revisited." CANADIAN LITERATURE, No. 76 (Spr. 1978), pp. 132-34.

1358   McPherson, Hugo. "The Mask of Satire: Character and Symbolic Pattern in Robertson Davies' Fiction." CANADIAN LITERATURE, No. 4 (Spr. 1960), pp. 18-30.

        Reprinted in nos. 195 and 5102.

1359   Monaghan, David M. "Metaphors and Confusions." CANADIAN LITERATURE, No. 67 (Wint. 1976), pp. 64-73.

        Discusses FIFTH BUSINESS.

1360   Monk, Patricia. "Beating the Bush: The Mandala and National Psychic Unity in RIDERS IN THE CHARIOT and FIFTH BUSINESS." ENGLISH STUDIES IN CANADA, 5 (Fall 1979), 344-54.

1361 _____. "Confessions of a Sorcerer's Apprentice: WORLD OF WONDERS and the Deptford Trilogy of Robertson Davies." DALHOUSIE REVIEW, 56 (Sum. 1976), 366-72.

1362 _____. "Psychology and Myth in THE MANTICORE." STUDIES IN CANADIAN LITERATURE, 2 (Wint. 1977), 69-81.

1363 _____. THE SMALLER INFINITY: THE JUNGIAN SELF IN THE NOVELS OF ROBERTSON DAVIES. Toronto: University of Toronto Press, 1982. 214 p.

1364 Moore, Mavor. "Robertson Davies." ENGLISH QUARTERLY, 5 (Fall 1972), 15-20.

1365 _____. "Robertson Davies." In his 4 CANADIAN PLAYWRIGHTS: ROBERTSON DAVIES, GRATIEN GÉLINAS, JAMES REANEY, GEORGE RYGA. Toronto: Holt, Rinehart and Winston, 1973, pp. 9-17.

1366 Morley, Patricia. "Davies' Salterton Trilogy: Where the Myth Touches Us." STUDIES IN CANADIAN LITERATURE, 1 (Wint. 1976), 96-104.

1367 _____. ROBERTSON DAVIES. Profiles in Canadian Drama. [Toronto]: Gage Educational Publishing, 1977. 74 p. Bibliog. Index.

1368 Murray, Glenn. "Who Killed Boy Staunton: An Astrological Witness Reports." STUDIES IN CANADIAN LITERATURE, 2 (Wint. 1977), 117-23.

1369 Neufeld, James. "Structural Unity in 'The Deptford Trilogy': Robertson Davies as Egoist." JOURNAL OF CANADIAN STUDIES, 12 (Feb. 1977), 68-74.

1370 Newman, Peter C. "The Master's Voice: The Table Talk of Robertson Davies." MACLEAN'S, 85 (Sept. 1972), 42-43.

1371 Owen, Ivon. "The Salterton Novels." TAMARACK REVIEW, No. 9 (Aut. 1958), pp. 56-63.

1372 Radford, F.L. "Heinrich Heine, the Virgin, and the Hummingbird: FIFTH BUSINESS--A Novel and Its Subconscious." ENGLISH STUDIES IN CANADA, 4 (Spr. 1978), 95-110.

1373 Roper, Gordon. Introd., MARCHBANKS' ALMANACK. New Canadian Library, no. 61. Toronto: McClelland and Stewart, 1968, pp. ix-xvi.

1374   _____. "Robertson Davies' FIFTH BUSINESS and 'That Old Fantastical Duke of Dark Corners, C.G. Jung.'" JOURNAL OF CANADIAN FICTION, 1 (Wint. 1972), 33-39.

> Reprinted in no. 171.

1375   Staton, Eleanor. "Discussing Robertson Davies: A Promising Lad." CANADIAN REVIEW, 3 (Oct. 1976), 45-46.

1376   Stone-Blackburn, Susan. "The Novelist as Dramatist: Davies' Adaptation of LEAVEN OF MALICE." CANADIAN LITERATURE, No. 86 (Aut. 1980), pp. 71-86.

1377   St. Pierre, Paul M. "Rounding the Ovoid." MOSAIC, 11 (Spr. 1978), 127-35.

> Discusses FIFTH BUSINESS.

1378   Sutherland, Ronald. "The Relevance of Robertson Davies." JOURNAL OF CANADIAN STUDIES, 12 (Feb. 1977), 75-81.

> Discusses FIFTH BUSINESS; reprinted in no. 200.

1379   Thomas, Clara. "The Two Voices of A MIXTURE OF FRAILTIES." JOURNAL OF CANADIAN STUDIES, 12 (Feb. 1977), 82-91.

1380   Warwick, Ellen D. "The Transformation of Robertson Davies." JOURNAL OF CANADIAN FICTION, 3, No. 3 (1974), 46-51.

> Discusses FIFTH BUSINESS and THE MANTICORE; reprinted in no. 171.

1381   Webster, David. "Uncanny Correspondence: Synchronicity in FIFTH BUSINESS and THE MANTICORE." JOURNAL OF CANADIAN FICTION, 3, No. 3 (1974), 52-56.

1382   Wood, Barry. "In Search of Sainthood: Magic, Myth, and Metaphor in Robertson Davies' FIFTH BUSINESS." CRITIQUE, 19, No. 2 (1977), 23-32.

For criticism on Davies, see also nos. 124, 133, 139, 170-71, 205, 1207, and 2347.

Book Reviews

1383   THE DIARY OF SAMUEL MARCHBANKS: CanL, 31 (1967), 82-83; CFor, 27 (Mar. 1948), 284; SatN, 13 Dec. 1947, p. 35; UTQ, 17 (Apr. 1948), 301-02.

1384   THE TABLE TALK OF SAMUEL MARCHBANKS: UTQ, 19 (Apr. 1950), 324-25.

1385   TEMPEST-TOST: CFor, 31 (Nov. 1951), 187-88; QQ, 59 (Spr. 1952), 138-40; RUL, 6 (Jan. 1952), 400-401; SatN, 27 Oct. 1951, pp. 4-5; SatR, 23 Aug. 1952, p. 36; TLS, 18 July 1952, p. 465; UTQ, 21 (Apr. 1952), 265-66.

1386   LEAVEN OF MALICE: CFor, 34 (Jan. 1955), 238-39; NYTBR, 10 July 1955, p. 6; SatN, 23 Oct. 1954, pp. 18-19; SatR, 30 July 1955, p. 15; SPECTATOR, 4 Mar. 1955, p. 266; TLS, 11 Mar. 1955, p. 145; UTQ, 24 (Apr. 1955), 266-67.

1387   A MIXTURE OF FRAILTIES: CFor, 38 (Jan. 1959), 237-38; DR, 38 (Wint. 1959), 531, 533; HudR, 32 (Wint. 1979-80), 579; NY, 6 Sept. 1958, p. 127; NYTBR, 31 Aug. 1958, p. 6; NYTBR, 21 Sept. 1980, p. 43; SatN, 13 Sept. 1958, pp. 29-31; UTQ, 28 (Apr. 1959), 370-71.

1388   MARCHBANKS' ALMANACK: AltA, 58 (Nov. 1967), 72; CFor, 47 (Jan. 1968), 235; SatN, 82 (Nov. 1967), 60; UTQ, 37 (July 1968), 501-02.

1389   FIFTH BUSINESS: AntigR, 7 (Aut. 1971), 114-15; AtlA, 61 (Apr. 1971), 59-60; CanL, 49 (Sum. 1971), 80-81; CFor, 50 (Mar. 1971), 443-44; COMMONWEAL, 7 Jan. 1972, pp. 328-29; FIDDLEHEAD, 88 (Wint. 1971), 109-10; JCF, 1 (Wint. 1972), 33; LISTENER, 15 Apr. 1971, p. 490; NS, 4 Apr. 1980, p. 521; NY, 26 Dec. 1970, p. 63; NYRB, 8 Feb. 1973, p. 21; NYTBR, 20 Dec. 1970, p. 17; NYTBR, 24 Apr. 1977, p. 49; QQ, 78 (Spr. 1971), 140; SatN, 85 (Dec. 1970), 35-36; SatR, 26 Dec. 1970, p. 25; SR, 87 (Wint. 1979), 180; TamR, 57 (1971), 76-80.

1390   THE MANTICORE: BCan, 1 (Nov. 1972), 1-2; CanL, 56 (Spr. 1973), 113-14; CDim, 9 (May 1973), 44-45; CFor, 52 (Feb. 1973), 44-45; COMMONWEAL, 8 Dec. 1972, p. 232; DR, 53 (Spr. 1973), 163-65; EJ, 68 (Mar. 1979), 61; JCF, 2 (Wint. 1973), 83-84; JCF, 3, No. 3 (1974), 44-45; LISTENER, 12 Apr. 1973, p. 489; MACLEAN'S, 85 (Dec. 1972), 105; MACLEAN'S, 6 Oct. 1975, p. 92; NS, 20 Apr. 1973, p. 591; NS, 4 Apr. 1980, p. 521; NY, 9 Dec. 1972, p. 176; NYRB, 8 Feb. 1973, p. 21; NYTBR, 19 Nov. 1972, p. 4; Q&Q, 38, No. 11 (1972), 12; QQ, 80 (Sum. 1973), 304-05; SatN, 87 (Dec. 1972), 50, 52; SR, 87 (Wint. 1979), 180; TLS, 13 Apr. 1973, p. 409; UTQ, 42 (Sum. 1973), 343-44.

1391   WORLD OF WONDERS: AntigR, 24 (Wint. 1975), 102-08; BCan, 4 (Dec. 1975), 7-9; CanL, 73 (Sum. 1977), 112-14; CanR, 2 (Christmas

1975), 51; CBRA, 1975, pp. 97-98; CFor, 55 (Dec. 1975), 30-31; EJ, 68 (March 1979), 61; FIDDLEHEAD, 113 (Spr. 1977), 123-26; IFR, 3 (Jan. 1976), 70-72; MACLEAN'S, 6 Oct. 1975, p. 92; NewR, 13 Mar. 1976, pp. 31-32; NS, 4 Apr. 1980, p. 521; NYTBR, 25 Apr. 1976, p.20; NYTBR, 24 Apr. 1977, p. 49; QQ, 83 (Spr. 1976), 157-58; SatN, 90 (Nov. 1975), 73-74; SatR, 3 Apr. 1976, p. 28; SR, 85 (Jan. 1977), 116; SR, 87 (Wint. 1979), 180; TLS, 14 May 1976, p. 588; UTQ, 45 (Sum. 1976), 315-16.

1392   SHAKESPEARE'S BOY ACTORS: N&Q, 25 Mar. 1939, pp. 215-16; QR, 272 (1939), 370; SatN, 18 Mar. 1939, p. 21; TLS, 4 Feb. 1939, p. 74; UTQ, 9 (Oct. 1939), 115-16.

1393   A VOICE FROM THE ATTIC: CanL, 7 (Wint. 1961), 65-68; COMMON-WEAL, 28 Oct. 1960, p. 133; DR, 41 (Spr. 1961), 119, 121, 123; HAB, 32 (Jan. 1961), 26-27; HM, 222 (Jan. 1961), 104; JCF, 1 (Spr. 1972), 95-96; MONTREALER, 35 (Mar. 1961), 41-42; NY, 10 Dec. 1960, p. 246; NYTBR, 20 Nov. 1960, p. 54; QQ, 68 (Apr. 1961), 183-84; SatN, 12 Nov. 1960, pp. 41-43; TamR, 17 (Aut. 1960), 78; UTQ, 30 (July 1961), 425-26; WatR, 6 (Wint. 1961), 59, 61.

1394   STEPHEN LEACOCK: CFor, 50 (Sept. 1970), 222.

1395   ONE HALF OF ROBERTSON DAVIES: BCan, 7 (Jan. 1978), 13-14; CanL, 80 (Spr. 1979), 86-89; CFor, 57 (Oct. 1977), 25-26; DR, 58 (Spr. 1978), 184-85; MACLEAN'S, 17 Oct. 1977, pp. 82-84; NewR, 15 Apr. 1978, pp. 22-25; NY, 29 May 1978, p. 120; Q&Q, 43, No. 13 (1977), 52; SatN, 92 (Nov. 1977), 52, 54-55; SR, 87 (Wint. 1979), 180; UTQ, 47 (Sum. 1978), 445-48.

1396   THE ENTHUSIASMS OF ROBERTSON DAVIES: BCan, 9 (Mar. 1980), 18-19; JCF, 28-29 (1980), 200-203; Q&Q, 46, No. 2 (1980), 42.

de la Roche, Mazo (1879-1961)

One of Canada's most widely known popular writers, Mazo de la Roche was born near Toronto, spent her childhood in rural southern Ontario, and studied art and English at the University of Toronto. She travelled abroad and lived for a dozen years in London, England, passing some winters in Italy and returning finally to the Toronto area. Her Jalna novels, a series of romances exploring the fortunes of the Whiteoak family, brought her international fame and have been translated into almost a score of languages. In 1927, JALNA won the $10,000 Atlantic Monthly Prize; de la Roche also received the Lorne Pierce Medal, the National Medal of the University of Alberta, and an honorary D.Litt. from the University of Toronto.

PRIMARY MATERIAL

Monographs

FICTION

1397 EXPLORERS OF THE DAWN. Foreword by Christopher Morley. New York: A.A. Knopf, 1922. 292 p.

Short stories.

1398 POSSESSION. New York: Macmillan, 1923. 289 p.

1399 DELIGHT. New York: Macmillan, 1926. 232 p.

1400 JALNA. Boston: Little, Brown, 1927. 347 p.

1401 WHITEOAKS OF JALNA. Atlantic Monthly Press Book. Boston: Little, Brown, 1929. 423 p. Also as WHITEOAKS. London: Macmillan, 1929. viii, 384 p.

1402 FINCH'S FORTUNE. London: Macmillan, 1931. viii, 399 p.

1403 LARK ASCENDING. Atlantic Monthly Press Book. Boston: Little, Brown, 1932. 301 p.

1404 THE THUNDER OF NEW WINGS. Boston: Little, Brown, 1932. 279 p. Lithographed, in a limited edition.

1405 THE MASTER OF JALNA. Toronto: Macmillan, 1933. viii, 331 p.

1406 BESIDE A NORMAN TOWER. Illus. A.H. Watson. London: Macmillan, 1934. ix, 229 p.

1407 YOUNG RENNY. Toronto: Macmillan, 1935. viii, 277 p.

1408 WHITEOAK HARVEST. Boston: Little, Brown, 1936. viii, 378 p.

1409 GROWTH OF A MAN. Boston: Little, Brown, 1938. 380 p.

1410 THE CHRONICLES OF THE WHITEOAK FAMILY. 6 vols. London: Macmillan, 1939; rpt. as WHITEOAK CHRONICLES. London: Macmillan, 1940. x, 1,390 p.

Includes nos. 1400-02, 1405, 1407-08.

1411 THE SACRED BULLOCK AND OTHER STORIES OF ANIMALS. Illus. Stuart Tresilian. London: Macmillan, 1939. ix, 221 p.

1412 WHITEOAK HERITAGE. Boston: Little, Brown, 1940. 325 p.

1413 WAKEFIELD'S COURSE. Atlantic Monthly Press Book. Boston: Little, Brown, 1941. 406 p.

1414 THE TWO SAPLINGS. London: Macmillan, 1942. 214 p.

1415 THE BUILDING OF JALNA. Atlantic Monthly Press Book. Boston: Little, Brown, 1944. 366 p.

1416 RETURN TO JALNA. Atlantic Monthly Press Book. Boston: Little, Brown, 1946. viii, 462 p.

1417 MARY WAKEFIELD. Atlantic Monthly Press Book. Boston: Little, Brown, 1949. 337 p.

1418 RENNY'S DAUGHTER. Atlantic Monthly Press Book. Boston: Little, Brown, 1951. 376 p.

1419 A BOY IN THE HOUSE. London: Macmillan, 1952. 123 p. Rev. ed. A BOY IN THE HOUSE AND OTHER STORIES. Boston: Little, Brown, 1952. 244 p.

1420 WHITEOAK BROTHERS: JALNA--1923. Toronto: Macmillan, 1953. 307 p.

1421 VARIABLE WINDS AT JALNA. Toronto: Macmillan, 1954. 359 p.

1422 THE SONG OF LAMBERT. Illus. Eileen A. Soper. Toronto: Macmillan, 1955. 51 p.

For children.

1423 BILL AND COO. Illus. Eileen H. Soper. Toronto: Macmillan, 1958. 40 p.

For children.

1424 CENTENARY AT JALNA. Toronto: Macmillan, 1958. vi, 302 p.

1425 MORNING AT JALNA. London: Macmillan, 1960. vi, 263 p.

1426 SELECTED STORIES OF MAZO DE LA ROCHE. Ed. with introduction by Douglas Daymond. Foreword by Dorothy Livesay. Ottawa: University of Ottawa Press, 1979. 199 p. Bibliog.

NONFICTION PROSE

1427 PORTRAIT OF A DOG. Illus. Morgan Dennis. Boston: Little, Brown, 1930. 199 p.

1428 THE VERY HOUSE. London: Macmillan, 1937. 257 p.

Autobiography.

1429 QUEBEC: HISTORIC SEAPORT. Garden City, N.Y.: Doubleday, Doran, 1944. xii, 212 p. Index.

1430 RINGING THE CHANGES: AN AUTOBIOGRAPHY. Toronto: Macmillan, 1957. xvi, 304 p.

DRAMA

1431 LOW LIFE: A COMEDY IN ONE ACT. Toronto: Macmillan, 1925. 37 p.

1432 COME TRUE. Toronto: Macmillan, 1927. 47 p.

1433 LOW LIFE AND OTHER PLAYS. Boston: Little, Brown, 1929. 109 p.

1434 WHITEOAKS: A PLAY. Boston: Little, Brown, 1936. 124 p.

Shorter Work

SHORT STORIES

1435 "The Thief of St. Loo." MUNSEY'S, 28 (Oct. 1902), 182-87.

1436 "The Year's [sic] at the Spring." METROPOLITAN, 35 (May 1911), 141-52.

1437 "Portrait of a Wife." CANADIAN NATION, 1 (Feb. 1928), 13-17, 24, 26, 28, 30.

1438 "She Went Abroad." BYSTANDER, 2 Apr. 1930, pp. 25-29, 40.

1439 "Dummy Love." HARPER'S BAZAAR, 67 (Apr. 1932), 86-87, 105-06.

1440 "Baby Girl." LONDON MERCURY, 26 (Oct. 1932), 489-507.

1441 "Love in the Highlands." HARPER'S BAZAAR, 68 (Aug. 1933), 30-31, 88, 94.

1442 "Sentimental Story of a Lady." GOOD HOUSEKEEPING, 98 (Apr. 1934), 32-33, 35, 98.

1443 "Pity Poor Me." REDBOOK, July 1937.

1444 "Mrs. Meade Savors Life." CANADIAN HOME JOURNAL, 35 (May 1938), 7-9, 38, 40-42.

1445 "Pamela." CANADIAN HOME JOURNAL, 37 (Dec. 1940), 8-9, 30, 32-35.

1446   "Come Fly with Me." ATLANTIC MONTHLY, 173 (Mar. 1944), 97-
        100.

1447   "Spring Song." CANADIAN HOME JOURNAL, 40 (Apr. 1944), 5-6,
        22-24.

1448   "The Artists." REDBOOK.

        No publishing details. Listed in 1462; incorrectly listed in
        1426.

1449   "The Sale at Clough Manor." GOOD HOUSEKEEPING.

        No publishing details. Listed in 1462; incorrectly listed in
        1426.

ARTICLES

1450   "The Past Quarter Century." By Mazo de la Roche, Stephen Leacock,
        and Morley Callaghan. MACLEAN'S, 15 Mar. 1936, pp. 36, 38.

1451   "My First Book." CANADIAN AUTHOR AND BOOKMAN, 28 (Spr.
        1952), 3-4.

1452   "'I Still Remember. . . .'" MACLEAN'S, 27 Apr. 1957, pp. 15-17,
        80, 82, 84-90.

Manuscripts

1453   Public Archives of Canada, Ottawa; Queen's University Library, Kingston,
        Ont.; University of British Columbia Library, Vancouver; University of
        Toronto Library.

SECONDARY MATERIAL

Criticism

1454   Brown, Edward Killoran. "The Whiteoaks Saga." CANADIAN FORUM,
        12 (Oct. 1931), 23.

1455   Daymond, Douglas M. "Mazo de la Roche's Forgotten Novel." JOUR-
        NAL OF CANADIAN FICTION, 3, No. 2 (1974), 55-59.

        Discusses GROWTH OF A MAN.

1456 _____. "Nature, Culture and Love: Mazo de la Roche's EXPLORERS OF THE DAWN and THE THUNDER OF NEW WINGS." STUDIES IN CANADIAN LITERATURE, 1 (Sum. 1976), 158-69.

1457 _____. "POSSESSION: Realism in Mazo de la Roche's First Novel." JOURNAL OF CANADIAN FICTION, 4, No. 3 (1975), 87-94.

1458 _____. "WHITEOAK CHRONICLES: A Reassessment." CANADIAN LITERATURE, No. 66 (Aut. 1975), pp. 48-62.

1459 Doig, Joan. "Mazo de la Roche's DELIGHT: An Unexpected Source." STUDIES IN CANADIAN LITERATURE, 5 (Fall 1980), 305-15.

1460 Edgar, Pelham. "The Cult of Primitivism." In YEARBOOK OF THE ARTS IN CANADA 1928/29. Ed. Bertram Brooker. Toronto: Macmillan, 1929, pp. 39-42.

1461 Fellows, Jo-Ann. "The 'British Connection' in the Jalna Novels of Mazo de la Roche: The Loyalist Myth Revisited." DALHOUSIE REVIEW, 56 (Sum. 1976), 283-90.

1462 Hambleton, Ronald. MAZO DE LA ROCHE OF JALNA. Toronto: General Publishing, 1966. 239 p. Bibliog. Index.

1463 _____. THE SECRET OF JALNA. Don Mills, Ont.: PaperJacks, 1972. 172 p.

1464 Hendrick, George. MAZO DE LA ROCHE. Twayne's World Authors Series, 129. New York: Twayne, 1970. 149 p. Bibliog.

1465 Le Normand, Michelle. "Mazo de la Roche." LECTURES, 8 (Oct. 1951), 113-17.

    In French.

1466 Livesay, Dorothy. "Getting it Straight." IMPULSE, 2, Nos. 3-4 (1973), 29-35.

1467 _____. "The Making of Jalna: A Reminiscence." CANADIAN LITERATURE, No. 23 (Wint. 1965), pp. 25-30.

    Reprinted in no. 5113.

1468 _____. "Mazo de la Roche: 1879-1961." In THE CLEAR SPIRIT:

TWENTY CANADIAN WOMEN AND THEIR TIMES. Ed. Mary Innis. Toronto: University of Toronto Press, 1966, pp. 242-59.

1469   Moore, Jocelyn. "Mazo de la Roche." CANADIAN FORUM, 12 (July 1932), 380-81.

1470   North, Sterling. THE WRITINGS OF MAZO DE LA ROCHE. Boston: Little, Brown, [1938]. 15 p.

1471   Pacey, Desmond. Introd., DELIGHT. New Canadian Library, no. 21. Toronto: McClelland and Stewart, 1961, pp. vii-x.

1472   Sandwell, Bernard Keble. "The Work of Mazo de la Roche." SATURDAY NIGHT, 8 Nov. 1952, p. 7.

1473   Snell, J.G. "The United States at Jalna." CANADIAN LITERATURE, No. 66 (Aut. 1975), pp. 31-40.

1474   Weeks, Edward. "Mazo de la Roche." In his FRIENDLY CANDOR. Boston: Little, Brown, 1959, pp. 86-97.

1475   Wuorio, Eva-Lis. "Mazo of Jalna." MACLEAN'S, 1 Feb. 1949, pp. 19, 39-41.

For criticism on de la Roche, see also nos. 123, 141, and 1426.

Book Reviews

1476   EXPLORERS OF THE DAWN: NYTBR, 5 Mar. 1922, p. 19.

1477   POSSESSION: CFor, 3 (May 1923), 250, 252; NYTBR, 25 Mar. 1923, p. 9; SatR, 19 May 1923, p. 670; SPECTATOR, 9 June 1923, p. 971; TLS, 10 May 1923, p. 317.

1478   DELIGHT: CFor, 6 (July 1926), 318-19; DR, 41 (Wint. 1961-62), 566-67; Nation&A, 28 Aug. 1926, p. 615; NYTBR, 16 May 1926, p. 8; SatR, 20 Mar. 1926, p. 651; SatR, 7 Aug. 1926, p. 156; TLS, 19 Aug. 1926, p. 548.

1479   JALNA: CFor, 8 (Jan. 1928), 510; NATION, 16 Nov. 1927, p. 550; NewR, 9 Nov. 1927, p. 320; NYTBR, 9 Oct. 1927, p. 6; SatR, 15 Oct. 1927, p. 196; TLS, 1 Dec. 1927, p. 912.

1480   WHITEOAKS OF JALNA: CFor, 10 (Dec. 1929), 94, 96; NYTBR, 8
        Sept. 1929, p. 6; SatR, 21 Sept. 1929, p. 153; SPECTATOR, 9 Nov.
        1929, p. 691; TLS, 28 Nov. 1929, p. 1000.

1481   FINCH'S FORTUNE: NYTBR, 13 Sept. 1931, p. 7; SatR, 3 Oct. 1931,
        p. 164; TLS, 10 Sept. 1931, p. 680.

1482   LARK ASCENDING: NS&N, 3 Sept. 1932, p. 262; NYTBR, 14 Aug.
        1932, p. 14; SatR, 13 Aug. 1932, p. 42; SPECTATOR, 17 Sept. 1932,
        p. 350; TLS, 1 Sept. 1932, p. 606.

1483   THE MASTER OF JALNA: NYTBR, 10 Sept. 1933, p. 6; SatR, 16
        Sept. 1933, p. 109; TLS, 28 Sept. 1933, p. 648.

1484   BESIDE A NORMAN TOWER: TLS, 22 Nov. 1934, p. 837.

1485   YOUNG RENNY: NYTBR, 19 May 1935, p. 6; SatR, 18 May 1935,
        p. 5; TLS, 2 May 1935, p. 286; UTQ, 5 (Apr. 1936), 377-78.

1486   WHITEOAK HARVEST: CFor, 16 (Dec. 1936), 35; NYTBR, 27 Sept.
        1936, p. 7; SatR, 3 Oct. 1936, p. 11; SPECTATOR, 16 Oct. 1936,
        p. 654; TLS, 10 Oct. 1936, p. 811; UTQ, 6 (Apr. 1937), 347-48.

1487   GROWTH OF A MAN: CFor, 18 (Dec. 1938), 281-82; NYTBR, 18
        Sept. 1938, p. 7; SatR, 10 Sept. 1938, p. 7; SPECTATOR, 14 Oct.
        1938, p. 626; TLS, 24 Sept. 1938, p. 617; UTQ, 8 (Apr. 1939), 304-05.

1488   THE SACRED BULLOCK: NYTBR, 26 Nov. 1939, p. 24; TLS, 23 Sept.
        1939 Supplement, p. 553.

1489   WHITEOAK CHRONICLES: COMMONWEAL, 8 Apr. 1938, p. 666; NA-
        TION, 2 Apr. 1938, p. 394.

1490   WHITEOAK HERITAGE: CFor, 20 (Dec. 1940), 290; DR, 20 (Jan.
        1941), 519-20; NYTBR, 25 Aug. 1940, p. 7; SPECTATOR, 8 Nov. 1940,
        p. 486; TLS, 9 Nov. 1940, p. 565; UTQ, 10 (Apr. 1941), 293-94.

1491   WAKEFIELD'S COURSE: NY, 27 Sept. 1941, p. 78; NYTBR, 28 Sept.
        1941, p. 7; UTQ, 11 (Apr. 1942), 302-03.

1492   THE TWO SAPLINGS: SatN, 12 Dec. 1942, p. 47; UTQ, 12 (Apr.
        1943), 316-18.

1493   THE BUILDING OF JALNA: COMMONWEAL, 1 Dec. 1944, p. 181;
        NYTBR, 19 Nov. 1944, p. 10; UTQ, 14 (Apr. 1945), 273.

1494   RETURN TO JALNA: NYTBR, 17 Nov. 1946, p. 50.

1495   MARY WAKEFIELD: RUL, 5 (Oct. 1950), 162-63; SatN, 1 Mar. 1949, p. 16; SatR, 29 Jan. 1949, p. 17; UTQ, 19 (Apr. 1950), 271.

1496   RENNY'S DAUGHTER: NYTBR, 23 Sept. 1951, p. 4; RUL, 7 (Dec. 1952), 371-72; SatN, 15 Dec. 1951, p. 56; SatR, 22 Sept. 1951, p. 17; UTQ, 21 (Apr. 1952), 259.

1497   A BOY IN THE HOUSE: DR, 32 (Wint. 1953), xxvii; NYTBR, 4 Jan. 1953, p. 23; SatR, 6 Dec. 1952, p. 37; UTQ, 22 (Apr. 1953), 286-87.

1498   WHITEOAK BROTHERS: NYTBR, 22 Nov. 1953, p. 4; RUL, 8 (June 1954), 945-47; SatR, 26 Dec. 1953, p. 35; UTQ, 23 (Apr. 1954), 269-70.

1499   VARIABLE WINDS AT JALNA: NYTBR, 7 Nov. 1954, p. 49.

1500   CENTENARY AT JALNA: NYTBR, 15 June 1958, p. 28; TLS, 25 July 1958, p. 421; UTQ, 28 (Apr. 1959), 367-68.

1501   MORNING AT JALNA: CAB, Sum. 1961, p. 12; CanL, 7 (Wint. 1961), 74-76; RUO, 31 ([Apr.] 1961), 346; TLS, 29 July 1960, p. 477; UTQ, 30 (July 1961), 412-13.

1502   SELECTED STORIES: Q&Q, 46 (July 1980), 58.

1503   PORTRAIT OF A DOG: NYTBR, 12 July 1931, p. 16.

1504   THE VERY HOUSE: NYTBR, 24 Oct. 1937, p. 7; TLS, 16 Oct. 1937, p. 756.

1505   RINGING THE CHANGES: Atl, 199 (May 1957), 78; SatN, 3 Aug. 1957, pp. 23-24; TLS, 17 May 1957, p. 307; UTQ, 27 (Apr. 1958), 486.

ENGEL, MARIAN (1933--   )

Born in Toronto, Marian Engel grew up in a variety of Ontario towns, received a B.A. from McMaster University, Hamilton, and an M.A. from McGill University (where she studied under Hugh MacLennan), and spent a year studying on a fellowship at the University of Aix-Marseille in France. After teaching in Montana and Montreal and working in London and Nicosia, Cypress, she returned in 1964 to Toronto where she has remained with the exception of two years in the late seventies as writer-in-residence at the University of Alberta. From 1980 to 1981 she was writer-in-residence at the University of Toronto. Her controversial novel, BEAR, won the Governor General's Award in 1976.

PRIMARY MATERIAL

Monographs

FICTION

1506   NO CLOUDS OF GLORY. [Don Mills, Ont.]: Longmans, 1968. 181 p.; rpt. as SARAH BASTARD'S NOTEBOOK. Don Mills, Ont.: PaperJacks, 1974. 181 p.

1507   THE HONEYMAN FESTIVAL: A NOVEL. Toronto: Anansi, 1970. 131 p.

1508   MONODROMOS. Toronto: Anansi, 1973. 250 p.; rpt. as ONE WAY STREET: A NOVEL. London: H. Hamilton, 1975. 250 p.

1509   ADVENTURE AT MOON BAY TOWERS. Illus. Patricia Cupples. Toronto: Clarke, Irwin, 1974. N. pag.

>   For children.

1510   INSIDE THE EASTER EGG. Toronto: Anansi, 1975. 172 p.

>   Short stories.

1511 JOANNE: THE LAST DAYS OF A MODERN MARRIAGE. Markham, Ont.: PaperJacks, 1975. 134 p.

1512 BEAR: A NOVEL. Toronto: McClelland and Stewart, 1976. 141 p.

1513 MY NAME IS NOT ODESSA YARKER. Illus. Laszlo Gal. Toronto: Kids Can, 1977. N. pag.

For children.

1514 THE GLASSY SEA. Toronto: McClelland and Stewart, 1978. 167 p.

1515 LUNATIC VILLAS. Toronto: McClelland and Stewart, 1981. 251 p. Also as THE YEAR OF THE CHILD. New York: St. Martin's, 1981. 251 p.

NONFICTION PROSE

1516 THE ISLANDS OF CANADA. By Marian Engel and J.A. Kraulis. Edmonton: Hurtig, 1981. 128 p. Index.

Shorter Work

SHORT STORIES

1517 "A Girl of Reputation." CHATELAINE, 45 (Oct. 1972), 52-53, 100-103.

1518 "Girl in a Blue Shirtwaist." CHATELAINE, 47 (Feb. 1974), 34-35, 59-62.

1519 "The Santa Claus Syndrome." CHATELAINE, 47 (Dec. 1974), 36-37, 83-84.

1520 "Atlas and Gazeteer of the West China Shore: Working Notes for a Novel." QUEEN'S QUARTERLY, 82 (Spr. 1975), 92-95.

1521 "The Last Happy Wife." CHATELAINE, 50 (Mar. 1977), 43, 64-66.

1522 "Forbesy." CHATELAINE, 50 (Sept. 1977), 53, 76-78ff.

1523 "Madame Hortensia, Equilibriste." SATURDAY NIGHT, 92 (Sept. 1977), 46-50.

1524 "Taped." UNIVERSITY OF WINDSOR REVIEW, 13 (Fall-Wint. 1977), 78-81.

1525   "Father Instinct." CHATELAINE, 52 (Aug. 1979), 32-33, 48, 50, 52.

1526   "Hob Selkie's Christmas." CHATELAINE, 53 (Dec. 1980), 59, 128, 130, 133-34, 136.
        For children.

ARTICLES

1527   "The Passionate George Sand." CHATELAINE, 45 (Sept. 1972), 56-57, 77-79.

1528   "Canadian Writing Today." In CREATIVE LITERATURE IN CANADA SYMPOSIUM, UNIVERSITY OF TORONTO, 1974. Toronto: Ontario Ministry of Colleges and Universities, 1974, pp. 2-9.

1529   "The Woman as Storyteller." COMMUNIQUÉ, 8 (May 1975), 6-7, 44-45.

1530   "Où en Est la Littérature Anglo-Canadienne?" LIBERTÉ, 19 (July-Oct. 1977), 67-72.

        In English.

1531   "Step to the Mythic: THE DIVINERS and A BIRD IN THE HOUSE." JOURNAL OF CANADIAN STUDIES, 13 (Fall 1978), 72-72.

1532   "Writing High." CHATELAINE, 52 (Jan. 1979), 39, 96ff.

For articles by Engel, see also no. 132.

SECONDARY MATERIAL

Criticism

1533   Cameron, Elspeth. "Midsummer Madness: Marian Engel's BEAR." JOURNAL OF CANADIAN FICTION, No. 21 (1977-78), pp. 83-94.

1534   Cowan, Doris. "The Heroine of Her Own Life." BOOKS IN CANADA, 7 (Feb. 1978), 7-10.

1535   Hutchinson [Hutchison], Ann. "Marian Engel, Equilibriste." BOOK FORUM, 4, No. 1 (1978), 46-55. Bibliog.

1536   Monk, Patricia. "Engel's BEAR: A Furry Tale." ATLANTIS, 5 (Fall 1979), 29-39.

1537 Osachoff, Margaret Gail. "The Bearness of BEAR." UNIVERSITY OF WINDSOR REVIEW, 5, Nos. 1-2 (1979-80), 13-21.

1538 Parker, Douglas H. "'Memories of My Own Patterns': Levels of Reality in THE HONEYMAN FESTIVAL." JOURNAL OF CANADIAN FICTION, 4, No. 3 (1975), 111-16.

1539 Van Herk, Aritha, and Diana Palting. "Beyond Kitchen Sink Realism." BRANCHING OUT, 5, No. 2 (1978), 12-13.

    An interview.

1540 Zonailo, C. "Canadian Novelty." CALEDONIAN, 7, No. 1 (1977), 1-5.

For criticism on Engel, see also nos. 205, 430, 1701, 1944, 4122, and 4302.

Book Reviews

1541 NO CLOUDS OF GLORY: CFor, 48 (July 1968), 94; NYTBR, 25 Feb. 1968, p. 38; UTQ, 38 (July 1969), 358-59.

1542 THE HONEYMAN FESTIVAL: AntigR, 1 (Wint. 1971), 108-09; NYTBR, 1 Oct. 1972, p. 40; QUARRY, 20 (Sum. 1971), 63-64; SatN, 85 (Oct. 1970), 34-35; WCR, 6 (June 1971), 53-54.

1543 MONODROMOS: BCan, 2 (Oct. 1973), 9-10; CanL, 61 (Sum. 1974), 80-81.

1544 INSIDE THE EASTER EGG: BCan, 5 (Feb. 1976), 8-9; CBRA, 1975, p. 128; CFM, 24-25 (Spr. 1977), 184-86; CFor, 56 (May 1976), 35-36; FIDDLEHEAD, 110 (Sum. 1976), 143-46.

1545 JOANNE: BCan, 4 (May 1975), 6-8; CFM, 21 (Spr. 1976), 105-07.

1546 BEAR: AntigR, 25 (Spr. 1976), 95-97; ARCS, 7 (Spr. 1977), 140-42; BCan, 5 (Apr. 1976), 6-8; BrO, 3, No. 2 (1976), 41-42; CanL, 7 (Wint. 1976), 105-07; CanR, 3 (Sept. 1976), 42-43; CBRA, 1976, p. 133; CFM, 24-25 (Spr. 1977), 186-90; CFor, 56 (May 1976), 35; CFor, 57 (Sept. 1977), 30; ContempR, 231 (July 1977), 45-48; DR, 56 (Sum. 1976), 389-91; ECW, 5 (Fall 1976), 97-99; FIDDLEHEAD, 110 (Sum. 1976), 127-29; HM, 253 (Oct. 1976), 100; LISTENER, 14 Apr. 1977, p. 494; MACLEAN'S, 19 Apr. 1976, p. 64; NS, 1 Apr. 1977, p. 439; NYTBR, 15 Aug. 1976, pp. 8, 10, 12; NYTBR, 10 July 1977, p. 41; OntarioR, 5 (Fall 1976), 94-95; Q&Q, 42, No. 7 (1976), 36; QQ, 84 (Apr. 1977), 99-102; QUARRY, 25 (Aut. 1976), 59-61;

SatN, 91 (May 1976), 70-71; SatR, 18 Sept. 1976, p. 31; STAND, 19, No. 1 (1979), 69-71; TLS, 1 Apr. 1977, p. 393; UTQ, 46 (Sum. 1977), 345-46; UWR, 15 (Fall-Wint. 1979), 13-21; WAVES, 6 (Wint. 1978), 83-85; WLWE, 16 (Nov. 1977), 359-60.

1547 THE GLASSY SEA: BCan, 7 (Aug. 1978), 14; BCan, 8 (Aug. 1979), 34; BrO, 6, No. 1 (1979), 52; CAB, 54 (Aug. 1979, 34-35; CFor, 58 (Mar. 1979), 30; CHATELAINE, 51 (Sept. 1978), 6; DR, 58 (Wint. 1978-79), 786-88; FIDDLEHEAD, 120 (Wint. 1978), 144-45; IFR, 6 (Sum. 1979), 189-91; MACLEAN'S, 9 Oct. 1978, p. 64; NYTBR, 9 Sept. 1979, p. 12; OntarioR, 11 (Fall 1979), 87-88; Q&Q, 44, No. 13 (1978), 12; QUARRY, 28 (Wint. 1979), 89-91; SatN, 93 (Nov. 1978), 61-63; UTQ, 48 (Sum. 1979), 320-22; UWR, 14 (Spr. 1979), 113-14.

FINDLEY, TIMOTHY (1930--)

Actor, scriptwriter, and novelist, Timothy Findley was born in Toronto and now lives in nearby Cannington, Ontario. He worked at the Stratford (Ontario) Festival Theatre, attended the Central School of Speech and Drama in London, spent fifteen years as a professional actor, and wrote radio and television drama for the Canadian Broadcasting Corporation. Since 1962, he has been a full-time writer and broadcaster. His novel, THE WAR, won the Governor General's Award in 1977. In this novel and in the earlier works with their more surreal quality, Findley explores the issue of emotional integrity in prose that is fresh and precise.

PRIMARY MATERIAL

Monographs

NOVELS

1548   THE LAST OF THE CRAZY PEOPLE. Toronto: General Publishing, 1967. 282 p.

1549   THE BUTTERFLY PLAGUE. New York: Viking, 1969. 376 p.

1550   THE WARS. Toronto: Clarke, Irwin, 1977. 226 p.

1551   FAMOUS LAST WORDS: A NOVEL. Toronto: Clarke Irwin, 1981. 396 p.

DRAMA

1552   CAN YOU SEE ME YET? A PLAY. Introd. Margaret Laurence. Vancouver: Talonbooks, 1977. 166 p.

Shorter Work

SHORT STORIES

1553   "About Effie." TAMARACK REVIEW, No. 1 (Aut. 1956), pp. 48-60.

1554   "Chronicle of the Nightmare." ESQUIRE, 71 (Apr. 1969), 140-42, 158, 160, 162.

1555   "Hello Cheeverland, Goodbye." TAMARACK REVIEW, 64 (Nov. 1974), 14-23, 25-31, 33-50.

1556   "The Book of Pins." In 74: NEW CANADIAN STORIES. Ed. David Helwig and Joan Harcourt. [Ottawa]: Oberon, 1974, pp. 111-24.

1557   "Losers, Finders: Strangers at the Door." In 75: NEW CANADIAN STORIES. Ed. David Helwig and Joan Harcourt. [Ottawa]: Oberon, 1975, pp. 57-75.

1558   "Island." In THE NEWCOMERS: INHABITING A NEW LAND. Gen. ed. Charles E. Israel. Toronto: McClelland and Stewart, 1979, pp. 85-95.

1559   "A Long Hard Walk." In THE NEWCOMERS: INHABITING A NEW LAND. Gen. ed. Charles E. Israel. Toronto: McClelland and Stewart, 1979, pp. 145-55.

SECONDARY MATERIAL

Criticism

1560   McFadden, David. "The Dead Stand Up in Their Graves." QUILL AND QUIRE, 43, No. 17 (1977), 17.

For criticism on Findley, see also nos. 124 and 1701.

Book Reviews

1561   THE LAST OF THE CRAZY PEOPLE: CanL, 36 (Spr. 1968), 78-79; CFor, 48 (June 1968), 70; FIDDLEHEAD, [76] (Sum. 1968), 91; SatN, 82 (May 1967), 39, 41; SatR, 5 Aug. 1967, p. 36; TamR, [45] (Aut. 1967), 120; UTQ, 37 (July 1968), 386.

1562   THE BUTTERFLY PLAGUE: TLS, 5 Mar. 1970, p. 241.

1563   THE WARS: BCan, 6 (Oct. 1977), 8-9; BCan, 8 (Feb. 1979), 31;
        BCan, 8 (Apr. 1979), 18; CanL, 78 (Aut. 1978), 99-100; COMMON-
        WEAL, 19 Jan. 1979, pp. 26-27; CRead, 18 (Oct. 1977), 6-7; FIDDLE-
        HEAD, 118 (Sum. 1978), 172-74; JCanS, 14 (Spr. 1979), 94-96; MAC-
        LEAN'S, 17 Oct. 1977, p. 84; NYTBR, 9 July 1978, p. 14; NYTBR,
        11 Nov. 1979, p. 43; OntarioR, 9 (Fall 1978), 107; Q&Q, 43, No.
        14 (1977), 7; SR, 87 (Wint. 1979), xix; UTQ, 47 (Sum. 1978), 326-27;
        WCR, 13 (Oct. 1978), 52-54.

FRASER, SYLVIA (1935--)

Sylvia Fraser was born in Hamilton, Ontario, and received a B.A. in English and philosophy from the University of Western Ontario (Hamilton) in 1957. Until 1968, she wrote for the Toronto STAR WEEKLY. As a journalist, she has travelled in North America, Europe, and Africa. Her fiction explores the politics of childhood, modern urban life, and male-female relationships.

PRIMARY MATERIAL

Monographs

FICTION

1564   PANDORA: A NOVEL. Drawings by Harold Town. Toronto: McClelland and Stewart, 1972. 255 p.

1565   THE CANDY FACTORY. Toronto: McClelland and Stewart, 1975. 294 p.

1566   A CASUAL AFFAIR: A MODERN FAIRY TALE. Toronto: McClelland and Stewart, 1978. 287 p.

1567   THE EMPEROR'S VIRGIN: A NOVEL. Toronto: McClelland and Stewart, 1980. 384 p.

SECONDARY MATERIAL

Criticism

1568   Staines, David. Introd., PANDORA. New Canadian Library, no. 123. Toronto: McClelland and Stewart, 1976, pp. vii-xii.

For criticism, see also no. 205.

Book Reviews

1569   PANDORA: BCan, 1 (June 1972), 6-7; CanL, 60 (Spr. 1974), 109-
        10; DR, 52 (Wint. 1972-73), 701, 703-04; JCF, 1 (Fall 1972), 92-93;
        NYTBR, 11 Feb. 1973, p. 28; SatN, 87 (July 1972), 41-42; UTQ, 42
        (Sum. 1973), 349; UWR, 8 (Spr. 1973), 100.

1570   THE CANDY FACTORY: BCan, 4 (May 1975), 10; BrO, 2 (Nov. 1975),
        42; CanL, 71 (Wint. 1976), 104-05; CBRA, 1975, pp. 109-10; DR, 55
        (Aut. 1975), 558-60; ECW, 4 (Spr. 1976), 86-87; FIDDLEHEAD, 108
        (Wint. 1976), 112-13; MACLEAN'S, 88 (May 1975), 98.

1571   A CASUAL AFFAIR: BCan, 7 (Apr. 1978), 14-15; BCan, 8 (Aug.
        1979), 34; BrO, 5, No. 3 (1978), 38-39; CanL, 81 (Sum. 1979), 137-
        38; DR, 58 (Sum. 1978), 370-72; ECW, 11 (Sum. 1978), 130-34; FID-
        DLEHEAD, 119 (Fall 1978), 121-23; MACLEAN'S, 20 Mar. 1978, p. 70;
        MACLEAN'S, 8 Jan. 1979, p. 46; Q&Q Update, 16 Mar. 1978, p. 9; SatN,
        93 (July 1978), 80.

1572   THE EMPEROR'S VIRGIN: BCan, 9 (Apr. 1980), 16; BrO, 7, No. 2
        (1980), 55; MACLEAN'S, 17 Mar. 1980, p. 59; Q&Q, 46 (May 1980),
        30.

GALLANT, MAVIS (1922--)

One of Canada's expatriate writers, Mavis Gallant was born in Montreal and moved about extensively through two provinces and two states when growing up, attending seventeen different schools. Since her newspaper work with the Montreal STANDARD as a young woman in the 1940s, she has supported herself as a writer, publishing particularly in the NEW YORKER. She has spent most of her life in Europe and lives presently in Paris. In 1981, Gallant was made an officer of the Order of Canada. Her fiction is pruned, urbane, and gently mocking.

PRIMARY MATERIAL

Monographs

FICTION

1573   THE OTHER PARIS: STORIES. Boston: Houghton Mifflin, 1956. 240 p.

1574   GREEN WATER, GREEN SKY. Boston: Houghton Mifflin, 1959. 154 p.

1575   MY HEART IS BROKEN: EIGHT STORIES AND A SHORT NOVEL. New York: Random House, 1964. 273 p.; rpt. as AN UNMARRIED MAN'S SUMMER: EIGHT STORIES AND A SHORT NOVEL. London: Heinemann, 1965. vii, 247 p.

1576   A FAIRLY GOOD TIME. New York: Random House, 1970. 308 p.

1577   THE PEGNITZ JUNCTION: A NOVELLA AND FIVE SHORT STORIES. New York: Random House, 1973. 193 p.

1578   THE END OF THE WORLD AND OTHER STORIES. Introd. Robert Weaver. New Canadian Library, no. 91. Toronto: McClelland and Stewart, 1974. 167 p.

1579 FROM THE FIFTEENTH DISTRICT: A NOVELLA AND EIGHT SHORT STORIES. Toronto: Macmillan, 1979. 243 p.

1580 HOME TRUTHS: SELECTED CANADIAN STORIES. Toronto: Macmillan, 1981. 330 p.

Shorter Work

SHORT STORIES

1581 "Good Morning and Goodbye." PREVIEW, 22 (Dec. 1944), 1-3.

1582 "Three Brick Walls." PREVIEW, 22 (Dec. 1944), 4-6.

1583 "The Flowers of Spring." NORTHERN REVIEW, 3 (June-July 1950), 31-39.

1584 "Madeline's Birthday." NEW YORKER, 1 Sept. 1951, pp. 20-24.

1585 "The Deceptions of Marie-Blanche." CHARM, No. 83 (Mar. 1953), pp. 90-91, 146-55.

1586 "By the Sea." NEW YORKER, 17 July 1954, pp. 27-30.

1587 "In Italy." NEW YORKER, 25 Feb. 1956, pp. 32-36.

1588 "Thieves and Rascals." ESQUIRE, 46 (July 1956), 82, 85-86.

1589 "The Emergency Case." NEW YORKER, 16 Feb. 1957, pp. 34-36.

1590 "Jesus D'Été." NEW YORKER, 27 July 1957, pp. 30-34.

1591 "The Old Place." TEXAS QUARTERLY, 1 (Spr. 1958), 66-80.

1592 "When We Were Nearly Young." NEW YORKER, 15 Oct. 1960, pp. 38-42.

1593 "Better Times." NEW YORKER, 3 Dec. 1960, pp. 59-65.

1594 "Rose." NEW YORKER, 17 Dec. 1960, pp. 34-37.

1595 "Two Questions." NEW YORKER, 10 June 1961, pp. 30-36.

1596   "Night and Day."   NEW YORKER, 17 Mar. 1962, pp. 48-50.

1597   "One Aspect of a Rainy Day."   NEW YORKER, 14 Apr. 1962, pp. 38-39.

1598   "The Hunter's Waking Thoughts."   NEW YORKER, 29 Sept. 1962, pp. 34-35.

1599   "Willi."   NEW YORKER, 5 Jan. 1963, pp. 29-31.

1600   "Careless Talk."   NEW YORKER, 28 Sept. 1963, pp. 41-47.

1601   "The Circus."   NEW YORKER, 20 June 1964, pp. 38-40.

1602   "In Transit."   NEW YORKER, 14 Aug. 1965, pp. 24-25.

1603   "The Statues Taken Down."   NEW YORKER, 9 Oct. 1965, pp. 53-56.

1604   "Paola and Renata."   SOUTHERN REVIEW, NS 1 (Wint. 1965), 199-209.

1605   "Questions and Answers."   NEW YORKER, 28 May 1966, pp. 33-38.

1606   "Vacances Pax."   NEW YORKER, 16 July 1966, pp. 26-29.

1607   "A Report."   NEW YORKER, 3 Dec. 1966, pp. 62-65.

1608   "The Sunday After Christmas."   NEW YORKER, 30 Dec. 1967, pp. 35-36.

1609   "April Fish."   NEW YORKER, 10 Feb. 1968, pp. 27-28.

1610   "The Captive Niece."   NEW YORKER, 4 Jan. 1969, pp. 28-32.

1611   "Good Deed."   NEW YORKER, 22 Feb. 1969, pp. 35-41.

1612   "The Rejection."   NEW YORKER, 12 Apr. 1969, pp. 42-44.

1613   "Speck's Idea."   NEW YORKER, 19 Nov. 1979, pp. 44-54, 57-58, 60, 63-64, 66, 69-70, 72, 75-76, 78, 83-84, 86, 91-95, 98-99.

1614   "The Burgundy Weekend." TAMARACK REVIEW, 76 (Wint. 1979), 3-39.

1615   "From Sunrise to Daybreak: (A Year in the Life of an Émigré Review)."
        NEW YORKER, 17 Mar. 1980, pp. 34-36.

1616   "Dido Flute, Spouse to Europe (Addenda to a Major Biography)." NEW
        YORKER, 12 May 1980, p. 37.

1617   "Assembly." HARPER'S, 260 (May 1980), 75-78.

1618   "From Gamut to Yalta." NEW YORKER, 15 Sept. 1980, pp. 40-41.

1619   "Europe by Satellite." NEW YORKER, 3 Nov. 1980, p. 47.

1620   "Mousse." NEW YORKER, 22 Dec. 1980, p. 31.

ARTICLES

1621   "Reflections: The Events in May: A Paris Notebook." NEW YORKER,
        14 Sept. 1968, pp. 58-62 ff; 21 Sept. 1968, pp. 54-58 ff.

1622   "Annals of Justice." NEW YORKER, 26 June 1971, pp. 47-52, 54, 56,
        58-70, 73-75.

1623   "Paul Léautaud, 1872-1956." NEW YORK TIMES BOOK REVIEW, 9
        Sept. 1973, pp. 6, 10, 12, 14, 16.

1624   Introd., THE WAR BRIDES, edited by Joyce Hibbert. Toronto: PMA,
        1978, pp. xi-xix.

SECONDARY MATERIAL

Bibliographies

1625   Malcolm, Douglas, comp. "An Annotated Bibliography of Works by and
        about Mavis Gallant." ESSAYS ON CANADIAN WRITING, No. 6
        (Spr. 1977), pp. 32-55.

1626   _____. "Annotated Bibliography of Works by and about Mavis Gallant."
        CANADIAN FICTION MAGAZINE, No. 28 (1978), pp. 115-33.

        Supplement to no. 1625..

Criticism

1627   Hancock, Geoffrey. "An Interview with Mavis Gallant." CANADIAN FICTION MAGAZINE, No. 28 (1978), pp. 18-67.

1628   _____. "Mavis Gallant: Counterweight in Europe." CANADIAN FICTION MAGAZINE, No. 28 (1978), pp. 5-7.

1629   _____. "Mavis Tries Harder." BOOKS IN CANADA, 7 (June-July 1978), 4-8.

1630   Hatch, Ronald B. "Mavis Gallant: Returning Home." ATLANTIS, 4 (Fall 1978), 95-102.

1631   _____. "The Three Stages of Mavis Gallant's Short Fiction." CANADIAN FICTION MAGAZINE, No. 28 (1978), pp. 92-114.

1632   Hofsess, John. "Citations for Gallantry." BOOKS IN CANADA, 7 (Nov. 1978), 21.

1633   Jantz, Ursula. "'Orphans' Progress' in Its Canadian and Universal Context." In ESSAYS IN HONOUR OF ERWIN STÜRZL ON HIS SIXTIETH BIRTHDAY. Ed. James Hogg. Salzburg: Inst. für eng. Spache & Lit., Univ. Salzburg, 1980, pp. 302-09.

1634   Knelman, Martin. "The Article Mavis Gallant Didn't Want Written: In Pursuit of Our Elegant, Expatriate Storyteller." SATURDAY NIGHT, 93 (Nov. 1978), 24-25, 27-31.

1635   Lawrence, Karen. "From the Other Paris: Interview with Mavis Gallant." BRANCHING OUT, 3 (Feb.-Mar. 1976), 18-19.

1636   McDonald, Marci. "Exile in Her Own Write." MACLEAN'S, 19 Nov. 1979, pp. 6, 9-10, 12.

1637   Merler, Grazia. MAVIS GALLANT: NARRATIVE PATTERNS AND DEVICES. Ottawa: Tecumseh, 1978. 82 p. Bibliog. Index.

1638   Stevens, Peter. "Perils of Compassion." CANADIAN LITERATURE, No. 56 (Spr. 1973), pp. 61-70.

   Reprinted in no. 5113.

1639   Weaver, Robert. Introd., THE END OF THE WORLD AND OTHER STORIES. New Canadian Library, no. 91. Toronto: McClelland and Stewart, 1974, pp. 7-13.

For criticism on Gallant, see also nos. 1323, 1578, and 5197.

Book Reviews

1640 THE OTHER PARIS: COMMONWEAL, 20 Apr. 1956, p. 79; NYTBR, 26 Feb. 1956, p. 28; SATR, 25 Feb. 1956, p. 17.

1641 GREEN WATER, GREEN SKY: LISTENER, 18 Aug. 1960, p. 273; NYTBR, 1 Nov. 1959, p. 41; SatR, 17 Oct. 1959, p. 19; TC, Oct. 1960, p. 382; TLS, 29 July 1960, p. 477; YR, NS 49 (Dec. 1959), 283.

1642 MY HEART IS BROKEN: LISTENER, 19 Aug. 1965, p. 281; MACLEAN'S, 5 Sept. 1964, p. 45; NS, 3 Sept. 1965, p. 329; NYRB, 25 June 1964, pp. 17-18; NYTBR, 3 May 1964, p. 4; SatR, 18 Apr. 1964, pp. 45-46; TLS, 28 Oct. 1965, p. 964.

1643 A FAIRLY GOOD TIME: HudR 23 (Sum. 1970), 337; NY, 19 Sept. 1970, pp. 132-33; NYTBR, 7 June 1970, pp. 5, 34; SoR, 9 (Sum. 1973), 736; SPECTATOR, 18 July 1970, p. 47; TLS, 31 June 1970, p. 857.

1644 THE PEGNITZ JUNCTION: NS, 8 Mar. 1974, p. 334; NY, 3 Dec. 1973, p. 192; NYTBR, 24 June 1973, p. 4; NYTBR, 2 Dec. 1973, p. 78; SatN, 88 (Sept. 1973), 33-36; TLS, 15 Mar. 1974, p. 253.

1645 FROM THE FIFTEENTH DISTRICT: BCan, 8 (Oct. 1979), 13-14; BCan, 8 (Nov. 1979), 33; BOT, 2 (Oct. 1979), 480; CanL, 85 (Sum. 1980), 153-55; CFM, 34-35 (1980), 172-74; CFor, 60 (June 1980), 30-31; CRead, 20, No. 7 (1978), 1-2; FIDDLEHEAD, 124 (Winter 1980), 108-10; MACLEAN'S, 19 Nov. 1979, p. 57; NATION, 29 Dec. 1979, p. 697; NewR, 25 Aug. 1979, p. 38; NYRB, 24 Jan. 1980, p. 31; NYTBR, 16 Sept. 1979, p. 13; NYTBR, 25 Nov. 1979, p. 50; OBSERVER, 20 Apr. 1980, p. 39; Q&Q, 45 (Nov. 1979), 31; QQ, 87 (Spr. 1980), 160-61; SatN, 94 (Oct. 1979), 72-74; SatR, 13 Oct. 1979, pp. 77-78; TLS, 14 Mar. 1980, p. 289; UTQ, 49 (Sum. 1980), 326-27; WCR, 15 (June 1980), 34-37.

GARNER, HUGH (1913-79)

Born in Yorkshire, England, Hugh Garner arrived in Toronto in 1919, grew up in its Cabbagetown district, and made Toronto his permanent home. He left school early, worked as a copy boy for the Toronto STAR, rode freight trains across North America during the Depression, served as a machine-gunner in the International Brigade during the Spanish Civil War, and served in the navy during World War II. He prided himself on being a working-class writer. Garner's reputation, built on the sociological accuracy of his depiction of working-class Toronto in CABBAGETOWN, is perhaps better served by some of his short stories-- BEST STORIES won a Governor General's Award. Many of his novels, while displaying a close attention to detail, are basically lighter works of popular entertainment.

PRIMARY MATERIAL

Monographs

FICTION

1646 STORM BELOW. Toronto: Collins, 1949. ix, 227 p.

1647 CABBAGETOWN. Toronto: Collins, 1950. 160 p. Rev. ed. Toronto: Ryerson, 1968. viii, 415 p.

> The 1968 edition is greatly expanded from the abridged format of the 1950 edition.

1648 PRESENT RECKONING. Toronto: Collins, 1951. 158 p.

1649 WASTE NO TEARS. By Jarvis Warwick, pseud. New Toronto: Export, 1951.

1650 THE YELLOW SWEATER AND OTHER STORIES. Toronto: Collins, 1952. 238 p.

1651   SILENCE ON THE SHORE. Toronto: McClelland and Stewart, 1962. 311 p.

1652   BEST STORIES. Toronto: Ryerson, 1963. 254 p.

1653   MEN AND WOMEN: STORIES. Toronto: Ryerson, 1966. 172 p. Rev. ed. Richmond Hill, Ont.: Simon and Schuster, 1973. 227 p.

1654   A NICE PLACE TO VISIT. Toronto: Ryerson, 1970. 255 p.

1655   THE SIN SNIPER: A NOVEL. Richmond Hill, Ont.: Simon and Schuster, 1970. 277 p.; rpt. as STONE COLD DEAD: A NOVEL. Markham, Ont.: PaperJacks, 1978. 277 p.

1656   VIOLATION OF THE VIRGINS, AND OTHER STORIES. Toronto: McGraw-Hill Ryerson, 1971. 259 p.

1657   DEATH IN DON MILLS: A MURDER MYSTERY. Toronto: McGraw-Hill Ryerson, 1975. 299 p.

1658   THE INTRUDERS: A NOVEL. Toronto: McGraw-Hill Ryerson, 1976. 328 p.

1659   THE LEGS OF THE LAME AND OTHER STORIES. Ottawa: Borealis, 1976. 167 p.

1660   A HUGH GARNER OMNIBUS. Toronto: McGraw-Hill Ryerson, 1978. 752 p. Bibliog.

1661   MURDER HAS YOUR NUMBER: AN INSPECTOR McDUMONT MYSTERY. Toronto: McGraw-Hill Ryerson, 1978. 263 p.

NONFICTION PROSE

1662   AUTHOR, AUTHOR! Toronto: Ryerson, 1964. xv, 157 p.

1663   ONE DAMN THING AFTER ANOTHER! Toronto: McGraw-Hill Ryerson, 1973. 293 p. Bibliog.
    Autobiography.

DRAMA

1664   THREE WOMEN: A TRILOGY OF ONE-ACT PLAYS. Toronto: Simon and Pierre, [1973?]. 64 p.

Shorter Work

SHORT STORY

1665 "Christmas Eve in Cabbagetown." CANADIAN FORUM, 17 (Jan. 1938), 354-55.

ARTICLES

1666 "Toronto's Cabbagetown." CANADIAN FORUM, 16 (June 1936), 13-15.

1667 "Book Reviewers Brought to Book." SATURDAY NIGHT, 7 Mar. 1953, pp. 9-10.

1668 "How (Not) to Begin a Short Story." SATURDAY NIGHT, 6 Nov. 1954, pp. 16-17.

1669 "Cabbagetown Revisited: The Story of a Slum." SATURDAY NIGHT, 9 Nov. 1957, pp. 10-11, 31.

1670 "Author's Commentary." In SIXTEEN BY TWELVE. Ed. John Metcalf. Toronto: Ryerson, 1970, pp. 33-35.

For articles by Garner, see also no. 3397.

Manuscripts

1671 Queen's University Library, Kingston, Ont.

SECONDARY MATERIAL

Criticism

1672 Amiel, Barbara. "A Beginning, A Middle--and the End." MACLEAN'S, 16 July 1979, p. 22.

1673 Anderson, Allan. "An Interview with Hugh Garner." TAMARACK RE-VIEW, 52 (3rd quarter 1969), 19-34.

1674 Clark, Wayne. "Hugh Garner: Still Touchy After All These Years." MACLEAN'S, 19 Mar. 1979, pp. 10, 12.

1675   Edwards, Eileen. "A Sense of Place in Hugh Garner's Fiction." WORLD LITERATURE WRITTEN IN ENGLISH, 18 (Nov. 1979), 353-67.

1676   Fetherling, Doug. HUGH GARNER. Canadian Writers and Their Works Series. Toronto: Forum House, 1972. 80 p. Bibliog.

1677   Fulford, R. "Soldier, Sailor, Hobo and Writer: Notes on Hugh Garner." SATURDAY NIGHT, 94 (Sept. 1979), 14.

1678   Morgan, B. "And May There Be No Moaning at the Bar as an Old Pro Puts out to Sea." BOOKS IN CANADA, 8 (Aug.-Sept. 1979), 8-9.

1679   Moss, John G. "A Conversation with Hugh Garner." JOURNAL OF CANADIAN FICTION, 1 (Spr. 1972), 50-55.

1680   Spettigue, Douglas O. "The Hugh Garner Papers at Queen's." DOUGLAS LIBRARY NOTES, QUEEN'S UNIVERSITY, 17 (Sum. 1969), 7-12.

For criticism on Garner, see also nos. 168 and 1244.

Book Reviews

1681   STORM BELOW: CAB, 44 (Spr. 1969), 18; CanL, 40 (Spr. 1969), 66-68; CFor, 29 (Apr. 1949), 21-22; SatN, 3 May 1949, p. 16; SatN, 83 (Nov. 1968), 41; UTQ, 19 (Apr. 1950), 267-68.

1682   CABBAGETOWN: CAB, 44 (Wint. 1968), 17; CanL, 40 (Spr. 1969), 66-68; SatN, 83 (Nov. 1968), 36, 41; UTQ, 21 (Apr. 1952), 268-69; UTQ, 38 (July 1969), 357-58.

1683   PRESENT RECKONING: UTQ, 21 (Apr. 1952), 268-69.

1684   THE YELLOW SWEATER: CFor, 33 (Oct. 1953), 164; RUL, 7 (June 1953), 916-17; SatN, 8 Nov. 1952, p. 33; UTQ, 22 (Apr. 1953), 287-88.

1685   SILENCE ON THE SHORE: CanL, 17 (Sum. 1963), 68-70; CanL, 40 (Spr. 1969), 66-68; MACLEAN'S, 9 Feb. 1963, p. 45; MONTREALER, 37 (May 1963), 39-40; SatN, 78 (Mar. 1963), 29-30; SatN, 83 (Nov. 1968), 41; TamR, [26] (Wint. 1963), 59-60, 63; UTQ, 32 (July 1963), 397-98.

1686   BEST STORIES: CAB, 39 (Wint. 1963), 20; CanL, 19 (Wint. 1964), 55-57; CFor, 43 (Feb. 1964), 261; MACLEAN'S, 2 Nov. 1963, pp. 73-74;

MONTREALER, 37 (Dec. 1963), 42; QQ, 71 (Sum. 1964), 276; TamR, [31] (Spr. 1964), 98; UTQ, 33 (July 1964), 400.

1687   MEN AND WOMEN: CAB, 42 (Aut. 1966), 19; CanL, 31 (Wint. 1967), 59-61; CFor, 47 (July 1967), 91-92; MACLEAN'S, 17 Sept. 1966, p. 59; TamR, [43] (Spr. 1967), 68-69.

1688   A NICE PLACE TO VISIT: AtlA, 61 (Dec. 1970), 45; CanL, 50 (Aut. 1971), 72-75; CFor, 50 (Feb. 1971), 403.

1689   THE SIN SNIPER: BCan, 8 (Aug. 1979), 34.

1690   VIOLATION OF THE VIRGINS: BCan, 1 (Nov. 1971), 19; CanL, 54 (Aut. 1972), 85; CFor, 52 (Apr. 1972), 53; JCF, 1 (Wint. 1972), 85-86; SatN, 86 (Dec. 1971), 49; UTQ, 41 (Sum. 1972), 317.

1691   DEATH IN DON MILLS: BCan, 4 (Apr. 1975), 11-12; CAB, 50 (Sum. 1975), 27; CanL, 76 (Spr. 1978), 120-21; CBRA, 1975, pp. 113-14; CDim, 12 (Apr. 1977), 38; JCF, 20 (1977), 156-58; NYTBR, 13 July 1975, p. 36; UTQ, 45 (Sum. 1976), 316-17.

1692   THE INTRUDERS: BCan, 5 (May 1976), 19-20; CAB, 52 (Wint. 1976), 30; CanL, 76 (Spr. 1978), 122-23; CBRA, 1976, p. 139; CFor, 56 (Dec. 1976), 55-56; ECW, 7-8 (Fall 1977), 113-15; IFR, 4 (Jan. 1977), 81-82; JCF, 20 (1977), 156-58; Q&Q, 42, No. 10 (1976), 41-42; SatN, 91 (July 1976), 60-62.

1693   THE LEGS OF THE LAME: BCan, 6 (Mar. 1977), 40; CBRA, 1976, pp. 157-58; JCF, 22 (1978), 129-31.

1694   A HUGH GARNER OMNIBUS: CRead, 20, No. 7 (1978), 10-11.

1695   MURDER HAS YOUR NUMBER: BCan, 7 (May 1978), 14; BCan, 8 (June 1979), 28; CRead, 19 (June 1978), 5-7; JCF, 24 ([1979]), 145-48; Q&Q, 44 (Apr. 1978), 35.

1696   AUTHOR, AUTHOR! CAB, 39 (Sum. 1964), 16; CanL, 19 (Wint. 1964), 55-57; CFor, 43 (Feb. 1964), 261; MONTREALER, 38 (Spr. 1964), 38; SatN, 79 (May 1964), 27-28; TamR, 31 (Spr. 1964), 98.

1697   ONE DAMN THING AFTER ANOTHER! BCan, 2 (Nov. 1973), 1-2, 11; CAB, 49 (Wint. 1973), 24; CanL, 59 (Wint. 1974), 95-97; JCF, 3 (Wint. 1974), 100-101; SatN, 88 (Nov. 1973), 40-41, 43-44; WCR, 9 (Oct. 1974), 51-53.

GIBSON, GRAEME (1934--)

Graeme Gibson was born in London, Ontario, lived for several years in the Maritimes and in Australia, attended the University of Western Ontario, and taught at Ryerson Collegiate in Toronto. He has spent time in England, Scotland, France, and Mexico. His fiction departs from conventional modes to experiment with fictional discontinuity and the bizarre.

PRIMARY MATERIAL

Monographs

FICTION

1698 FIVE LEGS. Toronto: Anansi, 1969. 194 p.

1699 COMMUNION: A NOVEL. Toronto: Anansi, 1971. 119 p.

1700 FIVE LEGS AND COMMUNION. Toronto: Anansi, 1979. 333 p.

NONFICTION PROSE

1701 ELEVEN CANADIAN NOVELISTS: INTERVIEWED BY GRAEME GIBSON. Toronto: Anansi, [1973]. 324 p.

> Interviews with Atwood, Clarke, Matt Cohen, Engel, Findley, Godfrey, Laurence, Ludwig, Munro, Richler, and Symons.

SECONDARY MATERIAL

Book Reviews

1702 FIVE LEGS: ALPHABET, 17 (Dec. 1969), 91-92; BCAN, 8 (Nov. 1979),

27; CanL, 42 (Aut. 1969), 93-96; CDim, 6 (Aut. 1969), 58-59; CFor, 49 (May 1969), 41-42; DR, 49 (Aut. 1969), 436-37, 439; MACLEAN'S, 82 (June 1969), 98; QUARRY, 19 (Spr. 1970), 55; SatN, 84 (May 1969), 46, 48-49; UTQ, 39 (July 1970), 339; WCR, 5 (June 1970), 35-37.

1703   COMMUNION: BCan, 1 (Jan. 1972), 9; CanL, 53 (Sum. 1972), 91-92; CFM, 7 (Sum. 1972), 61; SatN, 87 (Feb. 1972), 32.

GODFREY, DAVE (1938--)

Dave Godfrey was born in Winnipeg, Manitoba. He received a B.A. (1960) from the University of Iowa, an M.A. (1963) from Stanford University, and a Ph.D. (1966) from the University of Iowa, having also attended several other universities. After teaching English in Cape Coast, Ghana, between 1963 and 1965, he returned to Canada where he taught at the University of Toronto for a number of years, moving on to become chairman of the creative writing department at the University of Victoria, British Columbia. Godfrey has helped found and direct three small Canadian publishing companies--House of Anansi, New Press, and Press Porcépic.

THE NEW ANCESTORS, a complex, experimental, political-psychological novel, draws on his experiences of African life. It won the 1971 Governor General's Award. Like his other writing, it reflects his interest in "that portion of literature where myth meets social realities."

PRIMARY MATERIAL

Monographs

FICTION

1704   DEATH GOES BETTER WITH COCA-COLA. Toronto: Anansi, 1967. 117 p.

    Short stories.

1705   THE NEW ANCESTORS. Toronto: New, 1970. 392 p.

1706   I CHING KANADA. Erin, Ont.: Porcépic, 1976. N. pag.

1707   DARK MUST YIELD. Erin, Ont.: Porcépic, 1978. 190 p.

    Short stories.

EDITED WORK

1708   MAN DESERVES MAN: CUSO IN DEVELOPING COUNTRIES. Ed. Bill McWhinney and Dave Godfrey. Toronto: Ryerson, 1968. xxii, 461 p.

1709   GORDON TO WATKINS TO YOU, DOCUMENTARY: THE BATTLE FOR CONTROL OF OUR ECONOMY. Ed. Dave Godfrey and Mel Watkins. Toronto: New, 1970. 261 p.

1710   GUTENBERG 2: THE NEW ELECTRONICS AND SOCIAL CHANGE. Ed. Dave Godfrey and Douglas Parkhill. Victoria, B.C.: Porcépic, 1979. 240 p. Rev. ed. Toronto: Porcépic, 1980. 224 p.

1711   THE TELIDON BOOK. Ed. David Godfrey and Ernest Chang. Victoria, B.C.: Porcépic, 1981. 300 p. Bibliog.

Shorter Work

SHORT STORIES

1712   "Fragment." CANADIAN FORUM, 39 (Jan. 1960), 228-30.

1713   "Up in the Rainforest." SATURDAY NIGHT, 82 (Nov. 1967), 81-82.

1714   "Friday Afternoon at the Iowa City Airport." CANADIAN FORUM, 50 (Jan. 1971), 340-42.

For stories by Godfrey, see also no. 881.

ARTICLES

1715   "Letter from Africa, to an American Negro." TAMARACK REVIEW, 38 (Wint. 1966), 57-80.

1716   "Recognizing the Island: Some Notes on Canadian Fiction in the Seventies." CANADIAN FORUM, 51 (Oct. 1971), 2.

1717   "Once More with Feeling, Mr. Richler." CANADIAN FORUM, 53 (Apr. 1973), 5, 43.

1718   "The Canadian Publishers: All 217 of Them." CANADIAN LITERATURE, No. 57 (Sum. 1973), pp. 65-82.

1719   "On Choosing Bondage." CANADIAN FORUM, 56 (June-July 1976), 18-23.

1720 "The Cultural Object." CANADIAN FORUM, 57 (Sept. 1977), 6-7.

For articles by Godfrey, see also no. 22.

SECONDARY MATERIAL

Criticism

1721 Bayard, Caroline, and Nick Power. "Interview with Dave Godfrey." OPEN LETTER, 3rd ser., No. 3 (Late Fall 1975), pp. 81-91.

1722 Cameron, Donald A. "Don Cameron Interviews Dave Godfrey." QUILL AND QUIRE, 38 (Feb. 1972), 3, 10-11.

Reprinted in no. 124.

1723 _____. "The Three People inside Dave Godfrey." SATURDAY NIGHT, 86 (Sept. 1971), 20-22.

1724 Lecker, Robert A. "Relocating THE NEW ANCESTORS." STUDIES IN CANADIAN LITERATURE, 2 (Wint. 1977), 82-92.

1725 Margeson, Robert W. "A Preliminary Interpretation of THE NEW AN-CESTORS." JOURNAL OF CANADIAN FICTION, 4, No. 1 (1975), 96-110.

1726 Miles, Ron. "Collection of Us: Dave Godfrey's 'The Hard-Headed Collector.'" ESSAYS ON CANADIAN WRITING, No. 6 (Spr. 1977), pp. 109-14.

1727 New, William H. "Godfrey's Book of Changes." MODERN FICTION STUDIES, 22 (Aut. 1976), 375-85.

Discusses DEATH GOES BETTER WITH COCA-COLA.

1728 _____. "Godfrey's Uncollected Artist." ARIEL, 4 (July 1973), 5-15.

Discusses "The Hard-Headed Collector."

1729 Quigley, Theresia. "THE NEW ANCESTORS: A Critical Analysis." ANTIGONISH REVIEW, No. 30 (Sum. 1977), pp. 65-71.

1730 Smiley, Calvin L. "Godfrey's Progress." CANADIAN LITERATURE, No. 75 (Wint. 1977), pp. 27-40.

1731   Turner, Susan, ed. "GORDON TO WATKINS TO YOU: Press Con-
        ference." CANADIAN FORUM, 50 (July-Aug. 1970), 158-60.

        Transcript of a press conference on GORDON TO WATKINS
        TO YOU.

For criticism on Godfrey, see also nos. 170 and 1701.

Book Reviews

1732   DEATH GOES BETTER WITH COCA-COLA: BCan, 3 (Jan. 1974), 14-
        15; CAB, 44 (Spr. 1969), 18; CanL, 38 (Aut. 1968), 92; CFor, 47
        (Mar. 1968), 282; FIDDLEHEAD, 75 (Spr. 1968), 78-79; MFS, 22 (Aut.
        1976), 375; QUARRY, 17, No. 3 (1968), 47-48; QQ, 75 (Sum. 1968),
        347-50.

1733   THE NEW ANCESTORS: BCan, 1 (Aug. 1971), 7-8; CanL, 49 (Sum.
        1971), 78-80; CFor, 51 (Apr. 1971), 16-17; FIDDLEHEAD, 90 (Sum.
        1971), 108-09; JCL, 7 (June 1972), 109-113; MACLEAN'S, 84 (Feb.
        1971), 57, 59; MACLEAN'S, 84 (Aug. 1971), 64; ME, Fall Book Sup-
        plement 1970, pp. 6-10; NATION, 6 Sept. 1971, pp. 186-88; SatN,
        86 (Feb. 1971), 29; UTQ, 40, No. 4 (1971), 382.

1734   I CHING KANADA: BCan, 6 (Apr. 1977), 24-25; CFor, 56 (Mar.
        1977), 29; ECW, 6 (Spr. 1977), 115-18; FIDDLEHEAD, 114 (Sum. 1977),
        136-37; Q&Q, 43, No. 3 (1977), 9; QUARRY, 26 (Spr. 1977), 68-70.

1735   DARK MUST YIELD: BCan, 7 (June 1978), 16-17; CanL, 82 (Aut.
        1979), 81-82; CFor, 58 (Apr. 1978), 31-32; FIDDLEHEAD, 120 (Wint.
        1979), 111-13; QUARRY, 28 (Spr. 1979), 91; UTQ, 48 (Sum. 1979),
        327-30; UWR, 14 (Fall 1978), 77-78; WCR, 13 (Oct. 1978), 78-80.

GRAHAM, GWETHALYN (1913-65)

Gwethalyn Erichsen-Brown was born in Toronto, educated at the University of Toronto, a Swiss finishing school, and Smith College, Massachusetts, and lived in Montreal. She wrote under the pseudonym Gwethalyn Graham. Her novel, EARTH AND HIGH HEAVEN, was acclaimed for its sympathetic portrayal of tensions between Jew and Gentile in Montreal. Both it and her earlier novel, SWISS SONATA, received Governor General's Awards.

PRIMARY MATERIAL

Monographs

FICTION

1736   SWISS SONATA. London: Jonathan Cape, 1938. 383 p.

1737   EARTH AND HIGH HEAVEN. Philadelphia: J.B. Lippincott, 1944. 288 p.

NONFICTION PROSE

1738   DEAR ENEMIES: A DIALOGUE ON FRENCH AND ENGLISH CANADA. By Gwethalyn Graham and Solange Chaput-Rolland. Toronto: Macmillan, 1963. xi, 112 p.

SECONDARY MATERIAL

Criticism

1739   Aitken, Margaret A. "Gwethalyn Graham, a Canadian Author with a Crusading Spirit." SATURDAY NIGHT, 28 Oct. 1944, p. 36.

1740   Mandel, Eli. Introd., EARTH AND HIGH HEAVEN. New Canadian
        Library, no. 13. Toronto: McClelland and Stewart, 1960, pp. v-xi.

Book Reviews

1741   SWISS SONATA: NS&N, 26 Feb. 1938, p. 332; NYTBR, 17 Apr. 1938,
        p. 6; SatN, 4 June 1938, p. 8; SatR, 23 Apr. 1938, p. 5; SPEC-
        TATOR, 11 Mar. 1938, p. 444; TLS, 19 Feb. 1938, p. 123; UTQ, 8
        (Apr. 1939), 302-03.

1742   EARTH AND HIGH HEAVEN: CAB, June 1945, p. 16; CanL, 7 (Wint.
        1961), 84; CHR, 26 (Sept. 1945), 326-28; DR, 25 (July 1945), 173-76;
        DR, 40 (Wint. 1960-61), 583; FSt, 2 (Apr. 1945), 33-34; NYTBR, 15
        Oct. 1944, p. 6; SatN, 9 Dec. 1944, p. 28; SatR, 7 Oct. 1944, p. 9;
        SPECTATOR, 17 Nov. 1944, p. 464; UTQ, 14 (Apr. 1945), 267-69;
        YR, NS 34 (Wint. 1945), 382.

1743   DEAR ENEMIES: CanL, 20 (Spr. 1964), 75-76; CFor, 43 (Nov. 1963),
        187-88; QUARRY, 13 (1963-64), 14-18; UTQ, 33 (July 1964), 482.

GROVE, FREDERICK PHILIP (1879-1948)

IN SEARCH OF MYSELF, Frederick Philip Grove's autobiographical account of his early life as the son of wealthy Swedish landowners, has now been challenged. D.O. Spettigue has identified Grove as Felix Paul Greve, born in Radamno (on the Polish-Russian border) into a German working-class family. Greve studied in Bonn, Rome, and Munich, and became a translator and free-lance writer. After accumulating large debts and being imprisoned for fraud in Bonn from 1903 to 1904, he staged a suicide and sailed for North America in 1909.

From 1912 when Grove appeared in Manitoba as a schoolteacher, his life is better known. For the next dozen years he struggled with poverty and poor health as a teacher and writer, acquiring a B.A. from the University of Manitoba in 1922. After a lecture tour and a year as editor for the financially troubled Graphic Press in Ottawa in 1929, he moved permanently to a farm near Simcoe, Ontario.

Grove received the Gold Medal of the Royal Society of Canada in 1934, honorary degrees from the Universities of Manitoba and Western Ontario, and the Governor General's Award for IN SEARCH OF MYSELF. His novels, while sometimes clumsy, have an important place in the history of Canadian fiction in the first half of the century, exploring the dark, even-tragic side of struggles with the land and with human drives, struggles within families and between generations. His nonfiction prose shares with the fiction a sensitivity to the rural landscape.

Entries are tentative for Grove's early (German) work in various genres.

PRIMARY MATERIAL

Monographs

FICTION

1744   FANNY ESSLER: EIN ROMAN. By F.P. Greve. Stuttgart: Axel Juncker, 1905. vii, 563 p.

1745 MAURERMEISTER IHLES HAUS. By F.P. Greve. Berlin: Karl Schnabel, 1906. 247 p.; rpt. as THE MASTER MASON'S HOUSE. Trans. Paul P. Gubbins. Introd. A.W. Riley and Douglas O. Spettigue. [Ottawa]: Oberon, 1976. 243 p.

1746 SETTLERS OF THE MARSH. New York: George H. Doran, 1925. 341 p.

1747 A SEARCH FOR AMERICA. Ottawa: Graphic, 1927. 448 p.

1748 OUR DAILY BREAD: A NOVEL. Toronto: Macmillan, 1928. v, 390 p.

1749 THE YOKE OF LIFE. Toronto: Macmillan, 1930. vi, 355 p.

1750 FRUITS OF THE EARTH. Toronto: J.M. Dent and Sons, 1933. viii, 335 p.

1751 TWO GENERATIONS: A STORY OF PRESENT-DAY ONTARIO. Toronto: Ryerson, 1939. 261 p.

1752 THE MASTER OF THE MILL. Toronto: Macmillan, 1944. 393 p.

1753 CONSIDER HER WAYS. Toronto: Macmillan, 1947. xxxii, 298 p.

1754 TALES FROM THE MARGIN: THE SELECTED SHORT STORIES OF FREDERICK PHILIP GROVE. Ed. with introd. and notes by Desmond Pacey. Toronto: Ryerson, McGraw-Hill, 1971. x, 319 p.

NONFICTION PROSE

1755 OSCAR WILDE. By F.P. Greve. Moderne Essays, 29. Berlin: Gose and Tetzlaff, 1903. 46 p.

1756 RANDARABESKEN ZU OSCAR WILDE. By F.P. Greve. Minden, W.Ger.: J.C.C. Bruns, [1903]. iii, 50 p.

1757 HEINRICH HEINES BEZIEHUNGEN ZU CLEMENS BRETANO. By Eduard Thorn, pseud. Berlin: E. Ebering, 1913. 193 p.

1758 OVER PRAIRIE TRAILS. Illus. C.M. Manly. Toronto: McClelland and Stewart, 1922. 231 p.

1759 THE TURN OF THE YEAR. Illus. C.M. Manly. Foreword by Arthur L. Phelps. Toronto: McClelland and Stewart, 1923. 237 p.

1760 IT NEEDS TO BE SAID. Toronto: Macmillan, 1929. 163 p.

Discusses literary theory.

1761 FRAUEN UM DICHTER. By Eduard Thorn, pseud. Stuttgart: Deutsche, 1933. 266 p. Bibliog.

Earlier edition unknown.

1762 SCHWÄRMEREI DES HERZENS ERZÄHLUNG. By Eduard Thorn, pseud. Leipzig: Hesse and Becker, 1937. 114 p.

Earlier edition unknown.

1763 IN SEARCH OF MYSELF. Toronto: Macmillan, 1946. 457 p.

1764 KÜNSTLER ÜBER KUNST: EIN EWIGER DIALOG ÜBER DIE PROBLEME DER KUNST VON LEONARDO BIS PICASSO. By Eduard Thorn, pseud. Baden-Baden: W. Klein, 1951. 392 p.

Earlier edition unknown.

1765 THE LETTERS OF FREDERICK PHILIP GROVE. Ed. with introd. and notes by Desmond Pacey. Toronto: University of Toronto Press, 1976. xxix, 584 p. Index.

POETRY

1766 WANDERUNGEN: GEDICHTE. By F.P. Greve. Munich: I. Littauer, 1902.

VERSE-DRAMA

1767 HELENA UND DAMON: EIN SPIEL IN VERSEN. By F.P. Greve. Munich: I. Littauer, 1902.

EDITED WORK

1768 AUSERLESENE GEDICHTE. By Christian Hofman von Hofmanswaldau. Ed. with introd. by F.P. Greve. Leipzig: Insel, 1907. 41 p.

1769 PROSASCHRIFTEN. By Jonathan Swift. Ed. with introd. and commentary by F.P. Greve. 4 vols. Berlin: Erich Reiss, [1910].

TRANSLATIONS

1770 DAS BILDNIS DORIAN GRAYS. By Oscar Wilde. Trans. F.P. Greve. Minden, W. Ger.: J.C.C. Bruns, [1902]. vi, 367 p.

1771 APOLOGIA PRO OSCAR WILDE. By Oscar Wilde. Trans. F.P. Greve. Minden, W. Ger.: J.C.C. Bruns, [1903].

1772 DIE TRAGÖDIE EINER SEELE. By Robert Browning. Trans. F.C. Gerden, pseud. Leipzig: Insel, 1903. 67 p.

1773 DILEMMAS. By Ernest Christopher Dowson. Trans. F.P. Greve. Leipzig: Insel, 1903. 128 p.

1774 FINGERZEIGE. By Oscar Wilde. Trans. with introd. by F.P. Greve. Minden, W. Ger.: J.C.C. Bruns, [1903]. viii, 268 p.

1775 DAS BILDNIS DES MR. W.H.; LORD ARTHUR SAVILES VERBRECHEN. By Oscar Wilde. Trans. F.P. Greve. Minden, W. Ger.: J.C.C. Bruns, [1904]. I, 136 p.

1776 DAS GRANATAPFELHAUS. By Oscar Wilde. Trans. F.P. Greve. Leipzig: Insel, 1904. 100 p.

1777 DIE RIESEN KOMMEN!! By H.G. Wells. Trans. F.P. Greve. Minden, W. Ger.: J.C.C. Bruns, [1904]. 388 p.

1778 DIE ZEITMASCHINE, ROMAN. By H.G. Wells. Trans. F.P. Greve. Minden, W. Ger.: J.C.C. Bruns, 1904. 175 p.

1779 DOKTOR MOREAUS INSEL. By H.G. Wells. Trans. F.P. Greve. Minden, W. Ger.: J.C.C. Bruns, [1904]. iv, 220 p.

1780 HARRY RICHMONDS ABENTEUER. By George Meredith. Trans. F.P. Greve. 2 vols. Minden, W. Ger.: J.C.C. Bruns, [1904].

1780a PARACELSUS. By Robert Browning. Trans. F.P. Greve. Leipzig: Insel, [1904]. 259 p.

1781 AUSBLICKE AUF DIE FOLGEN DES TECHNISCHEN UND WISSENSCHAFT-LICHEN FORTSCHRITTS FÜR LEBEN UND DENKEN DES MENSCHEN. By H.G. Wells. Trans. F.P. Greve. Minden, W. Ger.: J.C.C. Bruns, 1905. xi, 384 p.

1781a BRIEFE VON ROBERT BROWNING UND ELIZABETH BARRETT BROWNING. Trans. F.P. Greve. Berlin: S. Fischer, 1905. 495 p.

1782 DER IMMORALIST. By André Gide. Trans. F.P. Greve. Minden, W. Ger.: J.C.C. Bruns, 1905.

1783   DIANA VOM KREUZWEG. By George Meredith. Trans. F.P. Greve.
       2 vols. Minden, W. Ger.: J.C.C. Bruns, 1905.

1784   DIE ERSTEN MENSCHEN IM MOND. By H.G. Wells. Trans. F.P.
       Greve. Minden, W. Ger.: J.C.C. Bruns, 1905. iv, 348 p.

1785   Entry deleted.

1786   PALUDES (DIE SÜMPTE). By André Gide. Trans. F.P. Greve. Minden,
       W. Ger.: J.C.C. Bruns, [1905]. 124 p.

1787   RICHARD FEVERELS PRÜFUNG: DIE GESCHICHTE EINES VATERS UND
       EINES SOHNES. By George Meredith. Trans. F.P. Greve. Minden,
       W. Ger.: J.C.C. Bruns, [1905]. 328 p.

1788   EINE FRAU OHNE BEDEUTUNG. By Oscar Wilde. Trans. F.P. Greve.
       In SÄMTLICHE WERKE IN DEUTSCHER SPRACHE, vol. 9. Berlin: Globus,
       [1905-06].

1789   VERA ODER DIE NIHILISTIN. By Oscar Wilde. Trans. with introd. by
       F.P. Greve. In SÄMTLICHE WERKE IN DEUTSCHER SPRACHE, vol. 7.
       Berlin: Globus, [1905-06]. 202 p.

1790   DIE BOHEME: SZENEN AUS DEM PARISER KÜNSTLERLEBEN. By Henri
       Murger. Trans. F.P. Greve. Leipzig: Insel, 1906. 280 p.

1791   DIE SPHINX. By Oscar Wilde. Trans. F.P. Greve. Minden, W. Ger.:
       J.C.C. Bruns, [1906]. 85 p.

1792   WENN DER SCHLÄFER ERWACHT. By H.G. Wells. Trans. F.P. Greve.
       Minden, W. Ger.: J.C.C. Bruns, [1906]. iv, 416 p.

1793   GESAMMELTE WERKE. By Gustave Flaubert. Ed. E.W. Fischer. Trans.
       F.P. Greve et al. 10 vols. Minden, W. Ger.: Bruns, [1906-07].

       Volumes 4 and 9 translated by F.P. Greve; volumes 7 and 8
       translated by E. Greve with commentary by F.P. Greve.

1794   DIE NOVELLEN. By Miguel de Cervantes Saavedra. Trans. Konrad
       Thorer, pseud., from old translations. Introd. Felix Poppenberg. 2 vols.
       Leipzig: Insel, [1907].

1795   DIE ERZÄHLUNGEN AUS DEN TAUSEND UND EIN NÄCHTEN. Trans.
       F.P. Greve. Introd. Hugo von Hofmannsthal. Essay by Karl Dryoff.
       12 vols. Leipzig: Insel, [1907-08].

1796   BUNBURY. By Oscar Wilde. Trans. F.P. Greve. Wien: Wiener, 1908.
       104 p.

1797 DER SCHARFSINNIGE RITTER DON QUIXOTE VON DER MANCHA. By Miguel de Cervantes Saavedra. Trans. Konrad Thorer, pseud., from old translations. Introd. Felix Poppenberg. 3 vols. Leipzig: Insel, [1908].

1798 DIE GESCHICHTE DES GIL BLAS VON SANTILLANA. By A.R. Le Sage. Trans. Konrad Thorer, pseud. Afterword by Reinhard Buchwald. 2 vols. Leipzig: Insel, 1908.

1799 MARIUS DER EPIKUREER. By Walter Pater. Trans. with introd. by F. P. Greve. 2 vols. Leipzig: Insel, 1908.

1800 BALZACS MENSCHLICHE KOMÖDIE. By Honoré de Balzac. Trans. F. P. Greve et al. 14 vols. Leipzig: Insel, [1908-09].

Volumes 1, 6, 7, and parts of 2 and 11 are translated by Grove.

1801 AUF EINEM BALKON. IN EINER GONDEL. By Robert Browning. Trans. F.C. Gerden, pseud. Leipzig: Insel, 1909.

1802 Entry deleted.

1803 DER GRAF VON MONTE CRISTO. By A. Dumas. Trans. F.P. Greve. Berlin: Reiss, 1909.

1804 DER LUFTKRIEG. By H.G. Wells. Trans. F.P. Greve. Minden, W. Ger.: J.C.C. Bruns, 1909.

1805 DIE BRIEFE DES JUNIUS. Trans. with foreword by F.P. Greve. Leipzig: Insel, 1909. xxx, 452 p.

1806 DIE ENGE PFORTE. By André Gide. Trans. F.P. Greve. Berlin: Reiss, 1909.

1807 Entry deleted.

1808 SAUL: SCHAUSPIEL IN FÜNF AUFZÜGEN. By André Gide. Trans. F. P. Greve. Berlin: Reiss, 1909. 100 p.

1809 DAVID COPPERFIELD. By Charles Dickens. Based on old translations; [no trans. named]. Preface by Stefan Zweig. Leipzig: Insel, 1910. xxx, 1,107 p.

1810 DIE BALLADE VOM ZUCHTHAUS ZU READING. By Oscar Wilde. Trans. Eduard Thorn, pseud. Minden, W. Ger.: J.C.C. Bruns, 1910. 47 p.

1811   THE LEGACY OF SUN YATSEN: A HISTORY OF THE CHINESE REVO-
LUTION. By Gustav Amann. Prefaces by Karl Haushofer and Engelbert
Krebs. New York: Louis Carrier, 1929. 302 p. Index.

1812   AUSWAHL AUS VITA NUOVA. By Dante Alighieri.

    Publishing details unknown; listed in no. 1888.

1813   BOUVARD ET PÉCUCHET. By Gustave Flaubert.

    Publishing details unknown; listed in no. 1888.

1814   MURDER CONSIDERED AS A FINE ART. By Thomas De Quincey.

    Publishing details unknown; listed in no. 1888.

Shorter Work

SHORT STORIES

1815   "Drama at the Crossroads." CANADIAN NATION, Apr. 1928, pp. 14-18.

1816   "Platinum Watch." CANADIAN BOOKMAN, 21 (Oct. 1939), 5-12.

1817   "The Adventure of Leonard Broadus." CANADIAN BOY, 7 Apr. 1940,
pp. 105-06, 110; 14 Apr. 1940, pp. 117-19; 21 Apr. 1940, pp. 123-
24, 128; 28 Apr. 1940, pp. 130-31; 5 May 1940, pp. 141-43; 12 May
1940, pp. 148-49; 19 May 1940, pp. 155-56; 26 May 1940, pp. 163-
64, 166; 2 June 1940, pp. 169-70, 174, 176; 9 June 1940, pp. 177-
78, 180; 16 June 1940, pp. 189-90; 23 June 1940, pp. 196-97.

    For children.

1818   "The Slough." MOSAIC, 3 (Spr. 1970), 149-53.

    Reprinted from SELKIRK WEEKLY RECORD, 23 Dec. 1926.

ARTICLES

1819   "George Meredith." BAUKUNST FREISTATT, 1904, p. 36.

1820   Entry deleted.

1821   "'Die Stadt am Strande' im Ton eines grossen Franzosen und ihm zu Ehren."
DIE SCHAUBÜHNE, 3 (1907), 570.

1822   "Die Übersetzungen von TAUSEND UND EINE NACHT." ZEITSCHRIFT FÜR BÜCHERFREUNDE, 11 (1907-08), 45-47.

1823   "Reise in Schweden." NEUE REVUE UND MORGEN, 3 (Jan.-July 1909), 760-66.

1824   "Jean Jacques Rousseau als Erzieher." DER NORDWESTEN, 15 Nov. 1914, p. 14; 2 Dec. 1914, p. 14; 9 Dec. 1914, p. 14; 16 Dec. 1914, pp. 13-14.

1825   "Realism and After." CANADIAN BOOKMAN, 10 (Nov. 1928), 389-402.

1826   "Apologia pro Vita et Opere Suo." CANADIAN FORUM, 11 (Aug. 1931), 420-22.

1827   Appendix, THE HISTORY OF EMILY MONTAGUE, by Frances Brooke. Introd. and notes by Lawrence J. Burpee. Canada series, vol. 2. Ottawa: Graphic, 1931, pp. 327-33.

1828   "A Writer's Classification of Writers and Their Work." UNIVERSITY OF TORONTO QUARTERLY, 1 (Jan. 1932), 236-53.

1829   "Thomas Hardy: A Critical Examination of a Typical Novel and His Shorter Poems." UNIVERSITY OF TORONTO QUARTERLY, 1 (July 1932), 490-507.

1830   "The Plight of Canadian Fiction? A Reply." UNIVERSITY OF TORONTO QUARTERLY, 7 (July 1938), 451-67.

      A reply to Callaghan (no. 1065).

1831   "A Postscript to A SEARCH FOR AMERICA." QUEEN'S QUARTERLY, 49 (Aut. 1942), 197-213.

1832   "Democracy and Education." UNIVERSITY OF TORONTO QUARTERLY, 12 (July 1943), 389-402.

1833   "Peasant Poetry and Fiction from Hesiod to Hémon." PROCEEDINGS AND TRANSACTIONS OF THE ROYAL SOCIETY OF CANADA, 3rd ser., 38 (1944), sect. 2, 89-98.

1834   "Morality in the Forsyte Saga." UNIVERSITY OF TORONTO QUARTERLY, 15 (Oct. 1945), 54-64.

1835   "Grove's Letters from the Mennonite Reserve: Introduced by Margaret
       Stobie." CANADIAN LITERATURE, No. 59 (Wint. 1974), pp. 67-80.

For articles by Grove, see also nos. 125, 1768-69, 1789, 1793, 1799, 1805, and
1862.

Manuscripts

1836   Acadia University Library, Wolfville, N.S.; Queen's University Library,
       Kingston, Ont.; University of Manitoba Library, Winnipeg.

SECONDARY MATERIAL

Bibliography

1837   Raths, Deborah, comp. REGISTER OF THE FREDERICK PHILIP GROVE
       COLLECTION. Winnipeg: Department of Archives and Rare Books, Uni-
       versity of Manitoba Libraries, 1979. 65 p.

See Spettigue's bibliographies of Grove's work (nos. 1888-89); see also no. 1900.

Criticism

1838   Ayre, Robert. "Frederick Philip Grove." CANADIAN FORUM, 12
       (Apr. 1932), 255-57.

       Reprinted in no. 1873.

1839   Birbalsingh, Frank. "Grove and Existentialism." CANADIAN LITERA-
       TURE, No. 43 (1970), pp. 67-76.

       Reprinted in no. 197.

1840   Cohn-Sfetcu, Ofelia. "At the Mercy of Winds and Waves?--OVER
       PRAIRIE TRAILS by F.P. Grove." UNIVERSITY OF WINDSOR REVIEW,
       11 (Spr.-Sum. 1976), 49-56.

1841   Collin, William Edward. "La Tragique Ironie de Frederick Philip Grove."
       GANTS DU CIEL, 10 (Wint. 1946), 15-40.

1842   Dewar, Kenneth C. "Technology and the Pastoral Ideal in Frederick Philip
       Grove." JOURNAL OF CANADIAN STUDIES, 8 (Feb. 1973), 19-28.

1843   Dudek, Louis. "The Literary Significance of Grove's Search." INSCAPE,
       11, No. 1 (1974), 89-99.

       Reprinted in no. 140.

1844   Eggleston, Wilfred. "F.P.G.: The Ottawa Interlude." INSCAPE, 11, No. 1 (1974), 101-10.

1845   _____. "Frederick Philip Grove." In OUR LIVING TRADITION. 1st ser. Ed. Claude T. Bissell. Toronto: University of Toronto Press, in association with Carleton University, 1957, pp. 105-27.

     Reprinted in no. 1873.

1846   Gide, André. "Conversation avec un Allemand." In OEUVRES COM-PLÈTES D'ANDRÉ GIDE. Ed. augmentée de textes inédits établie par L. Martin Chauffer. [Paris]: Nrf, [1935], pp. 133-43.

1847   Heidenreich, Rosmarin. "The Search for F.P.G." CANADIAN LITERA-TURE, No. 80 (Spr. 1979), pp. 63-70.

1848   Holliday, W.B. "Frederick Philip Grove: An Impression." CANADIAN LITERATURE, No. 3 (Wint. 1960), pp. 17-22.

     Reprinted in no. 197.

1849   Kaye, Frances W. "Hamlin Garland and Frederick Philip Grove: Self-Conscious Chroniclers of the Pioneers." CANADIAN REVIEW OF AMERICAN STUDIES, 10 (Spr. 1979), 31-39.

1850   Keith, William J. "The Art of Frederick Philip Grove: SETTLERS OF THE MARSH as an Example." JOURNAL OF CANADIAN STUDIES, 9 (Aug. 1974), 26-36.

1851   _____. "F.P. Grove's 'Difficult' Novel: THE MASTER OF THE MILL." ARIEL, 4 (Apr. 1973), 34-48.

1852   _____. "Grove's OVER PRAIRIE TRAILS: A Re-Examination." LITERARY HALF-YEARLY, 13 (July 1972), 76-85.

1853   _____. "Grove's SEARCH FOR AMERICA." CANADIAN LITERATURE, No. 59 (Wint. 1974), pp. 57-66.

1854   MacDonald, R.D. "The Power of F.P. Grove's THE MASTER OF THE MILL." MOSAIC, 7 (Wint. 1974), 89-100.

1855   McKenna, Isobel. "As They Really Were: Women in the Novels of Grove." ENGLISH STUDIES IN CANADA, 2 (Spr. 1976), 109-16.

1856   McMullen, Lorraine. "Women in Grove's Novels." INSCAPE, 11, No. 1 (1974), 67-76.

1857 McMullin, Stanley E. "Evolution Versus Revolution: Grove's Perception of History." INSCAPE, 11, No. 1 (1974), 77-87.

1858 _____. "Grove and the Promised Land." CANADIAN LITERATURE, No. 49 (Sum. 1971), pp. 10-19.

       Reprinted in nos. 197 and 5113.

1859 _____. Introd., A SEARCH FOR AMERICA. New Canadian Library, no. 76. Toronto: McClelland and Stewart, 1971, pp. ix-xv.

1860 Makow, Henry. "Grove's 'The Canyon.'" CANADIAN LITERATURE, No. 82 (Aut. 1979), pp. 141-48.

1861 _____. "Grove's Treatment of Sex: Platonic Love in THE YOKE OF LIFE." DALHOUSIE REVIEW, 58 (Aut. 1979), 528-40.

1862 _____, ed. "Letters from Eden: Grove's Creative Rebirth." UNIVERSITY OF TORONTO QUARTERLY, 49 (Fall 1979), 48-64.

1863 Middlebro', Tom J. "Animals, Darwin, and Science Fiction: Some Thoughts on Grove's CONSIDER HER WAYS." CANADIAN FICTION MAGAZINE, No. 7 (Sum. 1972), pp. 55-57.

1864 Mitchell, Beverley. "The 'Message' and the 'Inevitable Form' in THE MASTER OF THE MILL." JOURNAL OF CANADIAN FICTION, 3, No. 3 (1974), 74-79.

1865 Morley, Patricia. "OVER PRAIRIE TRAILS: 'A Poem Woven of Impressions.'" HUMANITIES ASSOCIATION REVIEW, 25 (Sum. 1974), 225-31.

1866 Nause, John, ed. with introd. THE GROVE SYMPOSIUM. Reappraisals, Canadian Writers. Ottawa: University of Ottawa Press, 1974. 110 p.

1867 Nesbitt, Bruce H. "'The Seasons': Grove's Unfinished Novel." CANADIAN LITERATURE, No. 18 (Aut. 1963), pp. 47-51.

1868 Noel-Bentley, Peter. "The Position of the Unpublished 'Jane Atkinson' and 'The Weatherhead Fortunes.'" INSCAPE, 11, No. 1 (1974), 13-33.

1869 Pacey, Desmond. "Frederick Philip Grove." MANITOBA ARTS REVIEW, 3 (Spr. 1943), 28-41.

       Reprinted in no. 177.

1870   _____. FREDERICK PHILIP GROVE. Toronto: Ryerson, 1945. ix, 150 p. Bibliog. Index.

1871   _____. "Frederick Philip Grove: A Group of Letters." CANADIAN LITERATURE, No. 11 (Wint. 1962), pp. 28-38.

1872   _____. "In Search of Grove in Sweden: A Progress Report." JOURNAL OF CANADIAN FICTION, 1 (Wint. 1972), 69-73.

1873   _____, ed. FREDERICK PHILIP GROVE. Critical Views on Canadian Writers, 5. Toronto: Ryerson, 1970. 202 p. Bibliog.

> Reprints articles by Knister, Ayre, Skelton, Pacey, Sandwell, McCourt, Phelps, Eggleston, Saunders, Frye, Pierce, and others, as well as reviews.

1874 Pacey, Desmond, and J.C. Mahanti. "Frederick Philip Grove: An International Novelist." INTERNATIONAL FICTION REVIEW, 1 (Jan. 1974), 17-26.

1875 Parks, M.G. Introd., FRUITS OF THE EARTH. New Canadian Library, no. 49. Toronto: McClelland and Stewart, 1965, pp. vii-xiii.

1876 Pierce, Lorne. "Frederick Philip Grove (1871-1948)." PROCEEDINGS AND TRANSACTIONS OF THE ROYAL SOCIETY OF CANADA, 3rd ser., 43 (1949), Appendix C, 113-19.

> Reprinted in no. 1873.

1877 Raudsepp, Enn. "Grove & the Wellsprings of Fantasy." CANADIAN LITERATURE, No. 84 (Spr. 1980), pp. 131-37.

1878 Riley, Anthony W. "The German Novels of Frederick Philip Grove." INSCAPE, 11, No. 1 (1974), 55-66.

1879 Ross, Malcolm. Introd., OVER PRAIRIE TRAILS. New Canadian Library, no. 1. Toronto: McClelland and Stewart, 1957, pp. v-x.

1880 Rubio, Mary. "Grove's Search for the Artist." JOURNAL OF CANADIAN FICTION, No. 16 (1976), pp. 163-67.

1881 Sandwell, Bernard Keble. "Frederick Philip Grove and the Culture of Canada." SATURDAY NIGHT, 24 Nov. 1945, p. 18.

> Reprinted in no. 1873.

1882   Saunders, Doris B. "The Grove Collection in the University of Manitoba: A Tentative Evaluation." PAPERS OF THE BIBLIOGRAPHICAL SOCIETY OF CANADA, 2 (1963), 7-20.

1883   Saunders, Thomas. "The Grove Papers." QUEEN'S QUARTERLY, 70 (Spr. 1963), 22-29.

1884   _____. Introd., SETTLERS OF THE MARSH. New Canadian Library, no. 50. Toronto: McClelland and Stewart, 1966, pp. vii-xiii.

1885   _____. "A Novelist as Poet: Frederick Philip Grove." DALHOUSIE REVIEW, 43 (Sum. 1963), 235-41.

        Reprinted in no. 1873.

1886   Sirois, Antoine. "Grove et Ringuet: Témoins d'une Époque." CANA-DIAN LITERATURE, No. 49 (Sum. 1971), pp. 20-27.

        Discusses FRUITS OF THE EARTH and Ringuet's TRENTES AR-PENTS.

1887   Skelton, Isabel. "Frederick Philip Grove." DALHOUSIE REVIEW, 19 (July 1939), 147-63.

        Reprinted in no. 1873.

1888   Spettigue, Douglas O. F.P.G.: THE EUROPEAN YEARS. [Ottawa]: Oberon, 1973. 254 p. Bibliog. Index.

1889   _____. FREDERICK PHILIP GROVE. Studies in Canadian Literature, 3. Toronto: Copp Clark, 1969. vi, 175 p. Bibliog.

1890   _____. "'Frederick Philip Grove': A Report from Europe." QUEEN'S QUARTERLY, 78 (Wint. 1971), 614-15.

1891   _____. "Frederick Philip Grove in Manitoba." MOSAIC, 3 (Spr. 1970), 19-33.

1892   _____. "The Grove Enigma Resolved." QUEEN'S QUARTERLY, 79 (Spr. 1972), 1-2.

1893   _____. Introd., CONSIDER HER WAYS. New Canadian Library, no. 132. Toronto: McClelland and Stewart, 1977, pp. xix-xlii.

1894   _____. Introd., IN SEARCH OF MYSELF. New Canadian Library, no. 94. Toronto: McClelland and Stewart, 1974, pp. ix-xiv.

1895 _____. Introd., OUR DAILY BREAD. New Canadian Library, no. 114. Toronto: McClelland and Stewart, 1975, n. pag.

1896 Spettigue, Douglas O., and Anthony W. Riley. "Felix Paul Greve Redivivus: Zum früheren Leben des kanadischen Schriftstellers Frederick Philip Grove." SEMINAR, 9 (June 1973), 148-55.

1897 Sproxton, Birk. E. "Grove's Unpublished 'Man' and Its Relation to THE MASTER OF THE MILL." INSCAPE, 11, No. 1 (1974), 35-54.

1898 Stenberg, Peter A. "Translating the Translatable: A Note on a Practical Problem with F.P. Greve's WANDERUNGEN." CANADIAN REVIEW OF COMPARATIVE LITERATURE, 7 (1980), 206-12.

1899 Stich, K.P. "F.P. Grove's Language of Choice." JOURNAL OF COMMONWEALTH LITERATURE, 14 (Aug. 1979), 9-17.

1900 Stobie, Margaret R. FREDERICK PHILIP GROVE. Twayne World Author Series, 246. New York: Twayne, 1973. 206 p. Bibliog. Index.

1901 _____. "'Frederick Philip Grove' and the Canadianism Movement." STUDIES IN THE NOVEL, 4 (Sum. 1972), 173-85.

1902 _____. "Grove and the Ants." DALHOUSIE REVIEW, 58 (Aut. 1979), 418-33.

       Discusses CONSIDER HER WAYS.

1903 Sutherland, Ronald. FREDERICK PHILIP GROVE. Canadian Writers, no. 4. Toronto: McClelland and Stewart, 1969. 62 p.

1904 _____. "What was Frederick Philip Grove?" INSCAPE, 11, No. 1 (1974), 1-11.

       Reprinted in no. 200.

1905 Thompson, Eric. "Grove's Vision of Prairie Man." ARIEL, 10 (Oct. 1979), 15-33.

1906 Thompson, J. Lee. "In Search of Order: The Structure of Grove's SETTLERS OF THE MARSH." JOURNAL OF CANADIAN FICTION, 3, No. 3 (1974), 65-73.

1907 Watters, Reginald Eyre. Introd., THE MASTER OF THE MILL. New Canadian Library, no. 19. Toronto: McClelland and Stewart, 1961, pp. vii-xiii.

1908   Webber, Bernard. "Grove in Politics." CANADIAN LITERATURE, No.
       63 (Wint. 1975), pp. 126-27.

For criticism on Grove, see also nos. 78, 123, 130, 139, 146, 158, 160, 163,
168, 182, 190, 1745, 1754, 1759, 1765, 1835, 2152, 2889, and 4233.

Book Reviews

1909   FANNY ESSLER: DK, 19 (1906), 549-50.

1910   THE MASTER MASON'S HOUSE: BCan, 5 (Dec. 1976), 26; CanL, 73
       (Sum. 1977), 91-92; CBRA, 1976, p. 131; CFor, 56 (Dec. 1976), 54;
       ECW, 6 (Spr. 1977), 148-51; ESC, 3 (Sum. 1977), 241-43; GERMANO-
       SLAVICA, 2 (Spr. 1978), 380-83; HAB, 28 (Sum. 1977), 297-99; Q&Q,
       42, No. 15 (1976), 32-33; SatN, 91 (Nov. 1976), 52-54; UTQ, 47
       (Sum. 1978), 442-43.

1911   SETTLERS OF THE MARSH: CAB, 41, No. 4 (1966), 18; SatR, 30 Jan.
       1926, p. 529.

1912   A SEARCH FOR AMERICA: CFor, 8 (Mar. 1928), 576-77; MHRev, 21
       (Jan. 1972), 126-27; NS, 12 Oct. 1929 Supplement, p. xii; NYTBR,
       15 Jan. 1928, p. 2; NYTBR, 30 Dec. 1928, p. 8; SatR, 21 Apr. 1928,
       p. 801; SatR, 16 Mar. 1929, p. 785; SatR, 31 Aug. 1929, p. 252;
       TLS, 28 June 1928, p. 490.

1913   OUR DAILY BREAD: CFor, 9 (Nov. 1929), 66; NYTBR, 7 Oct. 1928,
       p. 20; QQ, 36 (Wint. 1929), 182-83.

1914   THE YOKE OF LIFE: CFor, 11 (Feb. 1931), 185-86; NYTBR, 1 Feb.
       1931, p. 23; SatR, 25 Oct. 1930, p. 274.

1915   FRUITS OF THE EARTH: CFor, 13 (Apr. 1933), 271; CFor, 13 (May
       1933), 319.

1916   TWO GENERATIONS: CFor, 19 (Oct. 1939), 225; NYTBR, 7 Jan.
       1940, p. 18; QQ, 46 (Aut. 1939), 380-81; SatN, 5 Aug. 1939, p. 9;
       UTQ, 9 (Apr. 1940), 291-92.

1917   THE MASTER OF THE MILL: CAB, Sept. 1945, p. 32; CanL, 10 (Aut.
       1961), 75-77; CFor, 24 (Mar. 1945), 290; DR, 25 (July 1945), 173,
       176-81; QQ, 52 (Sum. 1945), 254-55; SatN, 20 Jan. 1945, p. 19;
       UTQ, 14 (Apr. 1945), 271-72.

1918   CONSIDER HER WAYS: CAB, Fall 1947, p. 46, Supplement, pp. 47-

48; CFor, 26 (Mar. 1947), 283-84; DR, 27 (Apr. 1947), 116-17; SatN, 26 Apr. 1947, p. 12.

1919 TALES FROM THE MARGIN: BCan, 1 (Aug. 1971), 21; CanL, 51 (Wint. 1972), 84-87; UTQ, 41 (Sum. 1972), 405-06.

1920 OVER PRAIRIE TRAILS: CFor, 3 (May 1923), 248-50; TamR, 6 (Wint. 1958), 99-100.

1921 THE TURN OF THE YEAR: CFor, 4 (Feb. 1924), 152, 154.

1922 IT NEEDS TO BE SAID: CFor, 9 (Aug. 1929), 388-89; DR, 9 (Oct. 1929), 399-400.

1923 IN SEARCH OF MYSELF: CAB, Dec. 1946, pp. 4-5; CFor, 26 (Dec. 1946), 212-13; JCF, 16 (1976), 163-67; SatN, 19 Oct. 1946, p. 24; UTQ, 16 (Jan. 1947), 202-06.

1924 THE LETTERS OF FREDERICK PHILIP GROVE: ARIEL, 7 (Apr. 1976), 76-79; BCan, 5 (Mar. 1976), 8, 10; CanL, 71 (Wint. 1976), 95-97; CBRA, 1976, p. 61; CFor, 55 (Mar. 1976), 36; DR, 56 (Aut. 1976), 574-79; ESC, 3 (Sum. 1977), 244-50; GERMANO-SLAVICA, 2 (Spr. 1978), 380-83; HAB, 28 (Sum. 1977), 295-97; JCF, 17-18 (1976), 307-09; Q&Q, 42, No. 2 (1976), 44; QQ, 84 (Spr. 1977), 135-37; SatN, 91 (Mar. 1976), 68-69, 71; TLS, 14 May 1976, p. 576; UTQ, 45 (Sum. 1976), 426-27.

HELWIG, DAVID (1938--)

David Helwig was born in Toronto and grew up in Toronto, Hamilton, and Niagara-on-the-Lake, Ontario. He received a B.A. from the University of Toronto and an M.A. from the University of Liverpool and taught in the English department of Queen's University, Kingston, Ontario, from 1962 to 1974. He has been literary manager of CBC-TV drama and is currently an editor for Oberon Press.

PRIMARY MATERIAL

Monographs

FICTION

1925 THE STREETS OF SUMMER. [Ottawa]: Oberon, 1969. 188 p.

Short stories.

1926 THE DAY BEFORE TOMORROW. [Ottawa]: Oberon, 1971. 183p.; rpt. as MESSAGE FROM A SPY. Don Mills, Ont.: PaperJacks, 1975. 183 p.

1927 THE GLASS KNIGHT: A NOVEL. [Ottawa]: Oberon, 1976. 190 p.

1928 JENNIFER. [Ottawa]: Oberon, 1979. 179 p.

1929 THE KING'S EVIL. [Ottawa]: Oberon, 1981. 130 p.

NONFICTION PROSE

1930 A BOOK ABOUT BILLIE. By Billie Miller and David Helwig. [Ottawa]: Oberon, 1972. 168 p.

POETRY

1931 FIGURES IN A LANDSCAPE. [Ottawa]: Oberon, 1967. x, 217 p.
Poetry and drama.

1932 THE SIGN OF THE GUNMAN. [Ottawa]: Oberon, 1969. 151 p.

1933 THE BEST NAME OF SILENCE: POEMS. [Ottawa]: Oberon, 1972.
138 p.

1934 ATLANTIC CROSSINGS. [Ottawa]: Oberon, 1974. N. pag.

1935 A BOOK OF THE HOURS: POEMS. [Ottawa]: Oberon, 1979. 90 p.

EDITED WORK

1936 FOURTEEN STORIES HIGH. Ed. David Helwig and Tom Marshall. [Ottawa]:
Oberon, 1971. 172 p.

1937 72: NEW CANADIAN STORIES. Ed. David Helwig and Joan Harcourt.
[Ottawa]: Oberon, 1972. 135 p.

1938 WORDS FROM INSIDE. Prison Arts, 1971. Kingston, Ont.: n.p.,
[1972?]. N. pag.

1939 73: NEW CANADIAN STORIES. Ed. David Helwig and Joan Harcourt.
[Ottawa]: Oberon, 1973. 175 p.

1940 74: NEW CANADIAN STORIES. Ed. David Helwig and Joan Harcourt.
[Ottawa]: Oberon, 1974. 155 p.

1941 75: NEW CANADIAN STORIES. Ed. David Helwig and Joan Harcourt.
[Ottawa]: Oberon, 1975. 208 p.

1942 THE HUMAN ELEMENTS: CRITICAL ESSAYS. [Ottawa]: Oberon, 1978.
163 p.

> Essays on the cultural landscape of Canada; includes no. 355
> and articles on Munro (no. 3444) and Laurence (no. 5196).

1943 LOVE AND MONEY: THE POLITICS OF CULTURE. [Ottawa]: Oberon, 1980. 187 p.

1944 THE HUMAN ELEMENTS: SECOND SERIES. [Ottawa]: Oberon, 1981. 160 p.

> Includes analysis of Canadian literary criticism, and Wood-cock on Engel's novels.

Shorter Work

SHORT STORIES

1945 "Heat of Summer." CANADIAN FORUM, 39 (Apr. 1959), 8-10.

1946 "The Way Things Are." CANADIAN FORUM, 40 (Jan. 1961), 228.

1947 "After School." QUARRY, 15 (Nov. 1965), 27-29.

1948 "A Road through Summer Fields." QUARRY, 16 (Sum. 1967), 21-28.

1949 "Swimming Out, Swimming Back." WEST COAST REVIEW, 6 (June 1971), 21-22.

1950 "Winners and Losers." CANADIAN FICTION MAGAZINE, No. 6 (Spr. 1972), pp. 37-47.

1951 "Prophecies for April." CANADIAN FICTION MAGAZINE, No. 7 (Sum. 1972), pp. 38-41.

1952 "Red Barn, Interior." JOURNAL OF CANADIAN FICTION, 1 (Fall 1972), 35-41.

1953 "The Widower Bird." JOURNAL OF CANADIAN FICTION, 1 (Wint. 1972), 8-10.

1954 "Presences." In THE NARRATIVE VOICE. Ed. John Metcalf. Toronto: McGraw-Hill Ryerson, 1972, pp. 70-75.

1955 "Things That Happened Before You Were Born." In THE NARRATIVE VOICE. Ed. John Metcalf. Toronto: McGraw-Hill Ryerson, 1972, pp. 75-79.

1956 "Adam on the Art of Dying." QUEEN'S QUARTERLY, 85 (Wint. 1978-79), 608-14.

ARTICLES

1957 "A Place to Grow." QUEEN'S QUARTERLY, 76 (Spr. 1969), 74-80.

1958 "Author's Commentary." In SIXTEEN BY TWELVE. Ed. John Metcalf.
      Toronto: Ryerson, 1970, pp. 177-78.

1959 "Time in Fiction." In THE NARRATIVE VOICE. Ed. John Metcalf.
      Toronto: McGraw-Hill Ryerson, 1972, pp. 80-82.

SECONDARY MATERIAL

For criticism on Helwig, see nos. 162 and 181.

Book Reviews

1960 THE STREETS OF SUMMER: CanL, 44 (Spr. 1970), 89-91; CFor, 49
      (Mar. 1970), 280-82; DR, 49 (Wint. 1969-70), 591; MHRev, 20 (Oct.
      1971), 140-41; NS, 6 Feb. 1970, p. 192; QQ, 77 (Sum. 1970), 293-
      94; QUARRY, 19 (Spr. 1970), 57-58; WCR, 5 (Jan. 1971), 60.

1961 THE DAY BEFORE TOMORROW: BCan, 1, No. 4 (1971), 7-8; CanL,
      53 (Sum. 1972), 90-91; CBRA, 1975, p. 99; CRead, 15, No. 1 (1974),
      8-9; FIDDLEHEAD, 93 (Spr. 1972), 103-07; JCF, 1 (Wint. 1972), 86-87;
      QUARRY, 21 (Wint. 1972), 71-74; SatN, 86 (Dec. 1971), 38, 41; UTQ,
      41 (Sum. 1972), 312-13; WCR, 6 (Apr. 1972), 19-20.

1962 THE GLASS KNIGHT: BCan, 5 (May 1976), 18-19; CanL, 78 (Aut.
      1978), 101-02; CBRA, 1976, p. 125; CFor, 56 (Dec. 1976), 56-57;
      DR, 56 (Sum. 1976), 391-92; ECW, 5 (Fall 1976), 106-07; Q&Q, 42,
      No. 8 (1976), 34; QUARRY, 26 (Wint. 1977), 62-63; WAVES, 4, No.
      3 (1976), 82-84.

1963 JENNIFER: BCan, 8 (Nov. 1979), 8; CFor, 59 (Dec. 1979), 33;
      FIDDLEHEAD, 126 (Sum. 1980), 134-35; MACLEAN'S, 22 Oct. 1979,
      pp. 58, 60; Q&Q, 45 (Aug. 1979), 33; QQ, 87 (Aut. 1980), 519-21.

HODGINS, JACK (1938--)

A newcomer to Canadian fiction who is attracting considerable attention, Jack Hodgins is a Vancouver Island resident, born and raised in Comox Valley, British Columbia. His studies at the University of British Columbia included Earle Birney's writing course. He taught high school in Nanaimo, Vancouver Island, from 1961 to 1979 and in 1981 became a visiting professor at the University of Ottawa. Hodgins' fiction, which constructs a sometimes bizarre Vancouver Island populated by very real eccentrics, is compassionate, energetic, often humorous. THE RESURRECTION OF JOSEPH BOURNE won the 1979 Governor General's Award.

PRIMARY MATERIAL

Monographs

FICTION

1964 SPIT DELANEY'S ISLAND: SELECTED STORIES. Toronto: Macmillan, 1976. 199 p.

1965 THE INVENTION OF THE WORLD: A NOVEL. Toronto: Macmillan, 1977. xii, 354 p.

1966 THE RESURRECTION OF JOSEPH BOURNE: OR A WORD OR TWO ON THOSE PORT ANNIE MIRACLES. Toronto: Macmillan, 1979. 271 p.

1967 THE BARCLAY FAMILY THEATRE. Toronto: Macmillan, 1981. 299 p.

NONFICTION PROSE

1968 TEACHERS' RESOURCE BOOK TO TRANSITIONS II: SHORT FICTION: A SOURCE BOOK OF CANADIAN LITERATURE. By Jack Hodgins and Bruce Nesbitt. Vancouver: CommCept, 1978. 71 p. Bibliog.

EDITED WORK

1969   VOICE AND VISION. Ed. Jack Hodgins and William H. New. Toronto: McClelland and Stewart, 1972. 255 p. Bibliog.

1970   THE FRONTIER EXPERIENCE. Themes in Canadian Literature Series. Toronto: Macmillan, 1975. 122 p. Bibliog.

1971   THE WEST COAST EXPERIENCE. Themes in Canadian Literature Series. Toronto: Macmillan, 1976. 120 p. Bibliog.

Shorter Work

SHORT STORIES

1972   "The God of Happiness." WESTERLY, No. 4 (Dec. 1968), pp. 5-9.

1973   "Promise of Peace." NORTH AMERICAN REVIEW, NS 6 (Wint. 1969), 27-32.

1974   "Yesterday's Green Summer." DESCANT (Texas), 13, No. 4 (1969), 39-47.

1975   "The Graveyard Man." DESCANT (Texas), 15, No. 4 (1971), 2-10.

1976   "Witness." ALPHABET, Nos. 18-19 (1971), pp. 67-73.

1977   "Open Line." ANTIGONISH REVIEW, 9 (Spr. 1972), 11-17.

1978   "The Importance of Patsy McLean." JOURNAL OF CANADIAN FICTION, 2 (Wint. 1973), 5-7.

1979   "Edna Pike, on the Day of the Prime Minister's Wedding." EVENT, 2, No. 1 (1973), 26-33.

1980   "In the Museum of Evil." JOURNAL OF CANADIAN FICTION, 3 (Wint. 1974), 5-10.

1981   "Great Blue Heron." PRISM INTERNATIONAL, 14 (Sum. 1975), 38-43.

1982   "More than Conquerors." JOURNAL OF CANADIAN FICTION, No. 16 (1976), pp. 49-88.

1983   "The Leper's Squint." In THE STORY SO FAR 5. Ed. Douglas Barbour.
        Toronto: Coach House, 1978, pp. 49-65.

ARTICLE

1984   "External Despairs: From Japan to Norway, There's a Growing Interest
        Abroad in Canlit. Now, If We Could Only Send Them Some Books."
        BOOKS IN CANADA, 9 (Jan. 1980), 6-8.

SECONDARY MATERIAL

Criticism

1985   Beckmann, Susan. "Canadian Burlesque: Jack Hodgins' THE INVEN-
        TION OF THE WORLD." ESSAYS ON CANADIAN WRITING, No. 20
        (Wint. 1980-81), pp. 106-25.

1986   David, Jack. "An Interview with Jack Hodgins." ESSAYS ON CANA-
        DIAN WRITING, 11 (Sum. 1978), 142-46.

1987   Hancock, Geoffrey. "Interview with Jack Hodgins." CANADIAN FIC-
        TION MAGAZINE, Nos. 32-33 (1979-80), pp. 33-63.

1988   Jeffrey, David L. "Jack Hodgins and the Island Mind." BOOK FORUM,
        4, No. 1 (1978), 70-78. Bibliog.

1989   Lecker, Robert. "Haunted by a Glut of Ghosts: Jack Hodgins' THE IN-
        VENTION OF THE WORLD." ESSAYS ON CANADIAN WRITING, No.
        20 (Wint. 1980-81), pp. 86-105.

1990   Twigg, Alan. "The Invention of Hodgins' World." QUILL AND QUIRE,
        45 (Dec. 1979), 11, 13.

For criticism on Hodgins, see also no. 205.

Book Reviews

1991   SPIT DELANEY'S ISLAND: BCan, 5 (July 1976), 8; CanL, 76 (Spr.
        1978), 116-17; CBRA, 1976, p. 154; ECW, 5 (Fall 1976), 93-95; IFR,
        4 (Jan. 1977), 88-89; Q&Q, 42, No. 10 (1976), 38; UTQ, 46 (Sum.
        1977), 351-52; WAVES, 5, No. 1 (1976), 60-63.

1992   THE INVENTION OF THE WORLD: BCan, 61 (Apr. 1977), 23-24;
        CanL, 73 (Sum. 1977), 90-91; CanR, 4 (Apr. 1977), 32-33; DR, 57

(Aut. 1977), 584-86; ECW, 9 (Wint. 1977-78), 142-46; JCanS, 14 (Spr. 1979), 102-04; MACLEAN'S, 21 Mar. 1977, pp. 76-77; MHRev, 43 (July 1977), 138-39; NYTBR, 5 Feb. 1978, p. 32; Q&Q, 43, No. 5 (1977), 39; SatN, 92 (Mar. 1977), 86; UTQ, 47 (Sum. 1978), 334-35.

1993 THE RESURRECTION OF JOSEPH BOURNE: BCan, 8 (Aug. 1979), 10-11; CFor, 59 (Dec. 1979), 34-36; DR, 59 (Aut. 1979), 575-77; MAC-LEAN'S, 1 Oct. 1979, p. 54; Q&Q, 45 (Aug. 1979), 33; SatN, 94 (Oct. 1979), 70, 72.

HOOD, HUGH (1928--)

Born and raised in Toronto, Hugh John Blagdon Hood received his B.A. (1950), M.A. (1952), and Ph.D. (1955) from the University of Toronto. He taught at St. Joseph's College, West Hartford, Connecticut, from 1955 to 1961 and since then has been a professor of English at the University of Montreal. WHITE FIGURE, WHITE GROUND won the 1965 Beta Sigma Phi Award. Hood has begun work on an ambitious roman fleuve in twelve volumes which he expects to complete in about the year 2000. Rejecting conventional dramatic action and psychological exploration but also modern experimental discontinuity, he conveys a serenely Christian vision in novels of social documentation and spiritual analysis.

PRIMARY MATERIAL

Monographs

FICTION

1994 FLYING A RED KITE: STORIES. Toronto: Ryerson, 1962. 239 p.

1995 WHITE FIGURE, WHITE GROUND. Toronto: Ryerson, 1964. 251 p.

1996 AROUND THE MOUNTAIN: SCENES FROM MONTREAL LIFE. Toronto: Peter Martin, 1967. 175 p.

1997 THE CAMERA ALWAYS LIES. New York: Harcourt, Brace and World, 1967. 246 p.

1998 PREDICTIONS OF ICE. Searchlights. Agincourt, Ont.: Book Society, 1968. 8 p.

Reprinted from no. 1996.

1999 A GAME OF TOUCH. Don Mills, Ont.: Longman, 1970. 188 p.

2000 THE FRUIT MAN, THE MEAT MAN & THE MANAGER: STORIES. [Ottawa]: Oberon, 1971. 207 p.

2001 YOU CAN'T GET THERE FROM HERE: A NOVEL. [Ottawa]: Oberon, 1972. 202 p.

2002 THE SWING IN THE GARDEN. The New Age/Le Nouveau Siècle, Part 1. [Ottawa]: Oberon, 1975. 210 p.

First volume in a planned twelve-volume series; see nos. 2004 and 2006.

2003 DARK GLASSES. [Ottawa]: Oberon, 1976. 143 p.

Short stories.

2004 A NEW ATHENS. The New Age/Le Nouveau Siècle, Part 2. [Ottawa]: Oberon, 1977. 226 p.

Second volume in a series beginning with no. 2002.

2005 SELECTED STORIES. [Ottawa]: Oberon, 1978. 232 p.

2006 RESERVOIR RAVINE. The New Age/Le Nouveau Siècle, Part 3. [Ottawa]: Oberon, 1979. 238 p.

Third volume in a series beginning with no. 2002.

2007 NONE GENUINE WITHOUT THIS SIGNATURE. Introd. Keith Garebian. Downsview, Ont.: ECW, 1980. 189 p.

Short stories.

NONFICTION PROSE

2008 STRENGTH DOWN CENTRE: THE JEAN BÉLIVEAU STORY. Scarborough, Ont.: Prentice-Hall, 1970. 192 p.

2009 CENTRAL CANADA: A VACATIONER'S VIEW OF ONTARIO AND QUÉBEC. By Al Purdy and Hugh Hood. Ottawa: Canadian Government Travel Bureau, 1972. 16 p.

2010 THE GOVERNOR'S BRIDGE IS CLOSED. [Ottawa]: Oberon, 1973. 144 p.

Includes literary theory.

2011 SCORING: THE ART OF HOCKEY. By Hugh Hood and Seymour Segal. [Ottawa]: Oberon, 1979. N. pag.

Shorter Work

SHORT STORIES

2012 "The Isolation Booth." TAMARACK REVIEW, No. 9 (Aut. 1958), pp. 5-12.

2013 "Three Halves of a House." TAMARACK REIVIEW, 20 (Sum. 1961), 5-26.

2014 "The Changeling." CANADIAN FORUM, 41 (Mar. 1962), 274-80.

2015 "A Season of Calm Weather." QUEEN'S QUARTERLY, 70 (Spr. 1963), 76-93.

2016 "Educating Mary." MONTREALER, 39 (Sept. 1965), 24-31.

2017 "It's a Small World: Paradise Retained?" TAMARACK REVIEW, [46] (Wint. 1968), 101-08.

2018 "Suites and Single Rooms, with Bath." QUEEN'S QUARTERLY, 79 (Aut. 1972), 366-73.

2019 "The Granite Club." JOURNAL OF CANADIAN FICTION, 1 (Wint. 1972), 10-14.

2020 "The Winner." JUBILEE, 3 (1977), 4-21.

ARTICLES

2021 "International Symposium on the Short Story: Canada." KENYON RE-VIEW, 30, Issue 4 (1968), 469-77.

2022 "Author's Commentary." In SIXTEEN BY TWELVE. Ed. John Metcalf. Toronto: Ryerson, 1970, pp. 86-87.

2023 "Letter." ESSAYS ON CANADIAN WRITING, No. 9 (Wint. 1977-78), pp. 139-41.

Reply to review of DARK GLASSES in ESSAYS ON CANA-DIAN WRITING.

2024 "Hugh Hood and John Mills in Epistolary Conversation." FIDDLEHEAD, 116 (Wint. 1978), 133-46.

2025   "Before the Flood." ESSAYS ON CANADIAN WRITING, Nos. 13-14 (Wint.-Spr. 1978-79), pp. 5-20.

        Reprinted in no. 2045.

SECONDARY MATERIAL

Bibliography

2026   Struthers, J.R. (Tim), comp. "A Bibliography of Works by and on Hugh Hood." ESSAYS ON CANADIAN WRITING, Nos. 13-14 (Wint.-Spr. 1978-79), pp. 230-94.

        Reprinted in no. 2045.

Criticism

2027   Allard, Kerry, ed. "Conversation: Jewish Layton Catholic Hood Protestant Bowering." OPEN LETTER, 2nd ser., No. 5 (Sum. 1973), pp. 30-39.

2028   Blandford, Patrick. "Hood à la mode: Bicultural Tension in the Works of Hugh Hood." ESSAYS ON CANADIAN WRITING, Nos. 13-14 (Wint.-Spr. 1978-79), pp. 145-70.

        Reprinted in no. 2045.

2029   Cloutier, Pierre. "An Interview with Hugh Hood." JOURNAL OF CANADIAN FICTION, 2 (Wint. 1973), 49-52.

2030   _____. "Space, Time and the Creative Imagination: Hugh Hood's WHITE FIGURE, WHITE GROUND." JOURNAL OF CANADIAN FICTION, 3 (Wint. 1974), 60-63.

2031   Duffy, Dennis. "Grace: The Novels of Hugh Hood." CANADIAN LITERATURE, No. 47 (Wint. 1971), pp. 10-25.

        Reprinted in no. 5113.

2032   _____. "Space/Time and the Matter of Form." ESSAYS ON CANADIAN WRITING, Nos. 13-14 (Wint.-Spr. 1978-79), pp. 131-44.

        Reprinted in no. 2045.

2033   Fulford, Robert. "An Interview with Hugh Hood." TAMARACK REVIEW, 66 (June 1975), 65-77.

2034   Hale, Victoria G., ed. "An Interview with Hugh Hood." WORLD LITERATURE WRITTEN IN ENGLISH, 11 (Apr. 1972), 35-41.

2035   . "Interview with Hugh Hood." LE CHIEN D'OR/THE GOLDEN DOG, 3 (Feb. 1974), 25-33.

2036   Hancock, Geoffrey. "Hugh Hood's Celebration of the Millenium's End." QUILL AND QUIRE, 46, No. 11 (1980), 40.

2037   Lecker, Robert. "A Spirit of Communion: THE SWING IN THE GARDEN." ESSAYS ON CANADIAN WRITING, Nos. 13-14 (Wint.-Spr. 1978-79), pp. 187-210.

     Reprinted in no. 2045.

2038   Mathews, Lawrence. "The Secular and the Sacral: Notes on A NEW ATHENS and Three Stories by Hugh Hood." ESSAYS ON CANADIAN WRITING, Nos. 13-14 (Wint.-Spr. 1978-79), pp. 211-29.

     Reprinted in no. 2045.

2039   Mills, John. "Hugh Hood and the Anagogical Method." ESSAYS ON CANADIAN WRITING, Nos. 13-14 (Wint.-Spr. 1978-79), pp. 94-112.

     Reprinted in no. 2045.

2040   Morley, Patricia A. THE COMEDIANS: HUGH HOOD & RUDY WIEBE. Toronto: Clarke, Irwin, 1977. ix, 134 p. Index.

2041   Moss, John G. "Man Divided Amongst Himself: Hood's Leofrica." JOURNAL OF CANADIAN FICTION, 3 (Wint. 1974), 64-69.

2042   Orange, John. "Lines of Ascent: Hugh Hood's Place in Canadian Fiction." ESSAYS ON CANADIAN WRITING, Nos. 13-14 (Wint.-Spr. 1978-79), pp. 113-30.

     Reprinted in no. 2045.

2043   Sedgwick, Don. "Hugh Hood Evaluated." QUILL AND QUIRE, 46, No. 1 (1980), 18-19.

2044   Struthers, J.R. (Tim). "An Interview with Hugh Hood." ESSAYS ON CANADIAN WRITING, Nos. 13-14 (Wint.-Spr. 1978-79), pp. 21-93.

     Reprinted in no. 2045.

2045   , ed. BEFORE THE FLOOD: HUGH HOOD'S WORK IN PROGRESS. Downsview, Ont.: ECW, 1979. 294 p. Bibliog.

     Reprints articles by and about Hood from ESSAYS ON CANADIAN WRITING.

2046   Tata, Sam. "Mother Goosed: Hugh Hood's Version of 'Diddle Diddle Dumpling.'" IMPULSE, 3 (Fall 1973), 19-21.

       A parody.

2047   Thompson, Kent. "Formal Coherence in the Art of Hugh Hood." STUDIES IN CANADIAN LITERATURE, 2 (Sum. 1977), 203-12.

       Discusses "The Village Inside" from no. 1996.

2048   _____. "Hugh Hood and His Expanding Universe." JOURNAL OF CANADIAN FICTION, 3 (Wint. 1974), 55-59.

For criticism on Hood, see also nos. 141, 2007, and 5199.

Book Reviews

2049   FLYING A RED KITE: CAB, 38 (Spr. 1963), 11; CanL, 16 (Spr. 1963), 72-73; CFor, 42 (Jan. 1963), 229-30; DR, 43 (Sum. 1963), 264-65; MONTREALER, 37 (Apr. 1963), 55; QQ, 70 (Aut. 1963), 451-52; TamR, [27] (Spr. 1963), 87-89; UTQ, 32 (July 1963), 391-94.

2050   WHITE FIGURE, WHITE GROUND: CAB, 40 (Wint. 1964), 16; CanL, 25 (Sum. 1965), 76-77; FIDDLEHEAD, 63 (Spr. 1965), 70-71; NYTBR, 16 Aug. 1964, p. 5; QQ, 72 (Spr. 1965), 204; SatN, 79 (Oct. 1964), 30; TamR, [35] (Spr. 1965), 96-101; UTQ, 34 (July 1965), 376-77.

2051   AROUND THE MOUNTAIN: CanL, 36 (Spr. 1968), 94-95; LIBERTÉ, 9 (July 1967), 133-34; MACLEAN'S, 80 (Aug. 1967), 70-71; QUARRY, 26 (Aut. 1977), 72-73; TamR, [45] (Aut. 1967), 116-17; WCR, 6 (June 1971), 53.

2052   THE CAMERA ALWAYS LIES: CAB, 43 (Wint. 1967), 23; CFor, 48 (May 1968), 46-47; HM, 235 (Oct. 1967), 116; NYTBR, 10 Sept. 1967, p. 61; NYTBR, 19 Sept. 1967; SatN, 82 (Nov. 1967), 58.

2053   A GAME OF TOUCH: CFM, 2-3 (Spr. 1971), 94-97; CFor, 50 (Mar. 1971), 443; SatN, 85 (Nov. 1970), 47, 49.

2054   THE FRUIT MAN, THE MEAT MAN & THE MANAGER: BCan, 1 (Nov. 1971), 19; CanL, 54 (Aut. 1972), 85; CFor, 52 (Apr. 1972), 53; FIDDLEHEAD, 92 (Wint. 1971), 116-23; QQ, 79 (Spr. 1972), 120; QUARRY, 21 (Wint. 1972), 75-77; SatN, 86 (Dec. 1971), 42-43; WCR, 6 (Apr. 1972), 18-19.

2055   YOU CAN'T GET THERE FROM HERE: BCan, 1 (Nov. 1972), 26-27;

CanL, 58 (Aut. 1973), 101-02; CFM, 15 (Aut. 1974), 105, 107, 109; CRead, 14, No. 6 (n.d.), 8-9; DR, 53 (Spr. 1973), 169-71; ES, 55, No. 6 (1974), 546; QQ, 80 (Spr. 1973), 138-39; SatN, 87 (Nov. 1972), 50; TLS, 30 Mar. 1973, p. 340; UTQ, 42 (Sum. 1973), 347; UWR, 8 (Spr. 1973), 99-100.

2056   THE SWING IN THE GARDEN: AntigR, 30 (Sum. 1977), 98-100; BCan, 4 (Dec. 1975), 5-7; CanL, 67 (Wint. 1967), 99-102; CBRA, 1975, pp. 116-17; CFM, 22 (Sum. 1976), 104-07; CFor, 55 (Feb. 1976), 30; CRead, 16, No. 10 ([1975]), 5-7; DR, 59 (Spr. 1979), 184-86; FIDDLE-HEAD, 112 (Wint. 1977), 143-46; FIDDLEHEAD, 116 (Wint. 1978), 133-37; Q&Q, 42, No. 1 (1976), 20-21; QQ, 83 (Aut. 1976), 518-19; QUARRY, 25 (Sum. 1976), 79-80; SatN, 90 (Oct. 1975), 78-79; UTQ, 45 (Sum. 1976), 316; WCR, 10 (Feb. 1976), 35-36.

2057   DARK GLASSES: BCan, 6 (Mar. 1977), 41; CBRA, 1976, pp. 155-56; CFor, 56 (Mar. 1977), 30-31; ECW, 7-8 (Fall 1977), 105-08; FIDDLE-HEAD, 115 (Fall 1977), 145-47; LISTENER, 8 Sept. 1977, p. 318; Q&Q, 42, No. 15 (1976), 32; QUARRY, 26 (Aut. 1977), 73-74; UTQ, 46 (Sum. 1977), 346-47.

2058   A NEW ATHENS: BCan, 6 (Oct. 1977), 13; CFM, 27 (1977), 145-48; CFor, 57 (Dec. 1977), 37-38; DR, 59 (Spr. 1979), 186-89; ECW, 11 (Sum. 1978), 138-41; FIDDLEHEAD, 117 (Spr. 1978), 101-08; JCanS, 14 (Spr. 1979), 97-99; JCF, 30 (1980), 165-68; Q&Q, 43, No. 14 (1977), 6-7; QQ, 85 (Spr. 1978), 63-65; UTQ, 47 (Sum. 1978), 327-28; UWR, 13 (Spr. 1978), 108-09.

2059   SELECTED STORIES: BCan, 8 (Feb. 1979), 22.

2060   RESERVOIR RAVINE: BCan, 8 (Aug. 1979), 15-16; CanL, 87 (Wint. 1980), 139-40; CFor, 59 (Oct. 1979), 29-30; MACLEAN'S, 22 Oct. 1979, pp. 57-58; Q&Q, 45 (Nov. 1979), 30; QUARRY, 29 (Spr. 1980), 93-96; SatN, 94 (Nov. 1979), 44-45; UTQ, 49 (Sum. 1980), 333-36.

2061   NONE GENUINE WITHOUT THIS SIGNATURE: BCan, 9 (Aug. 1980), 9-10; CFor, 60 (Oct. 1980), 27-29; Q&Q, 46 (Nov. 1980), 39.

2062   THE GOVERNOR'S BRIDGE IS CLOSED: CanL, 62 (Aut. 1974), 102-04; CFor, 54 (Apr. 1974), 37; HAB, 25 (Fall 1974), 364-65; Q&Q, 40, No. 1 (1974), 13; TamR, 61 (Nov. 1973), 75-76; UTQ, 49 (Sum. 1980), 333-36; WLWE, 13 (Nov. 1974), 253-55.

KLEIN, A.M. (1909-72)

Abraham Moses Klein is a major Canadian poet who has also published a cryptic poetic novel, THE SECOND SCROLL. He was born in Montreal, received a B.A. from McGill University in 1930, and was called to the bar in 1933 after studying law at the University of Montreal. In addition to his work as a lawyer, he edited YOUNG JUDAEAN and CANADIAN ZIONIST briefly and, for fifteen years, CANADIAN JEWISH CHRONICLE. He ran unsuccessfully for the CCF (Cooperative Commonwealth Federation) party in 1948, and has lectured on poetry at McGill University. His travels to Israel, Europe, and North Africa in 1949 provided some of the material for THE SECOND SCROLL. In the mid-1950s, he suffered a breakdown and permanently ceased all his professional activities and writing. Klein received the Lorne Pierce Medal in 1957.

PRIMARY MATERIAL

Monographs

FICTION

2063 THE SECOND SCROLL. New York: A.A. Knopf, 1951. 198 p.

POETRY

2064 HATH NOT A JEW. Foreword Ludwig Lewisohn. New York: Behrman's Jewish Book House, 1940. xii, 116 p.

2065 THE HITLERIAD. Poets of the Year. New York: New Directions, 1944. 30 p.

2066 POEMS. Philadelphia: Jewish Publication Society of America, 1944. 82 p.

2067 SEVEN POEMS. Montreal: Privately printed, [1947?]. 8 p.

2068 THE ROCKING CHAIR AND OTHER POEMS. Toronto: Ryerson, 1948. 56 p.

2069 THE COLLECTED POEMS OF A.M. KLEIN. Comp. with introd. by Miriam Waddington. Toronto: McGraw-Hill Ryerson, 1974. x, 373 p. Index.

TRANSLATIONS

2070 FROM PALESTINE TO ISRAEL. By Moishe Dickstein. Montreal: Eagle, 1951. 105 p.

2071 OF JEWISH MUSIC, ANCIENT AND MODERN. By Israel Rabinovitch. Montreal: Book Center, 1952. 321 p.

Shorter Work

SHORT STORIES

2072 "Conversations Celestial." By A.M. JUDAEAN, 2 (Mar. 1929), 2.

2073 "Prophet in Our Midst." By Ben Kalonymus, pseud. JUDAEAN, 3 (Apr. 1930), 8.

2074 "By the Profit of a Beard." By Ben Kalonymus, pseud. JUDAEAN, 3 (June 1930), 7-8.

2075 "The Triumph of Zalman Tiktiner." By Ben Kalonymus, pseud. JUDAEAN, 4 (Nov. 1930), 8.

2076 "The Meed of the Minnesinger." JEWISH TRIBUNE, 5 Dec. 1930, pp. 10-11, 31.

2077 "The Parrot and the Goat." By Ben Kalonymus, pseud. JUDAEAN, 4 (Mar. 1931), 7-8.

2078 "The Bald-Headed Monarch." By Ben Kalonymus, pseud. JUDAEAN, 4 (May 1931), 7-8.

2079 "Too Many Princes. . . ." By Ben Kalonymus, pseud. JUDAEAN, 5 (Nov. 1931), 7-8.

2080 "Once Upon a Time." By Ben Kalonymus, pseud. JUDAEAN, 5 (Apr. 1932), 5, 7.

2081   "The Anti-Hill." By Aben Kandel, pseud. CANADIAN JEWISH CHRONI-CLE, 9 Sept. 1932, pp. 7-8.

   Caplan (2114) attributes this tentatively to Klein.

2082   "Master of the Horn." CANADIAN JEWISH CHRONICLE, 30 Sept. 1932, pp. 14, 67-69.

2083   "The Seventh Scroll." JEWISH STANDARD, 22 Sept. 1933, pp. 119, 163-67.

2084   "Friends, Romans, Hungrymen." NEW FRONTIER, 1 (Apr. 1936), 16, 18.

2085   "The Tale of the Marvellous Parrot." CANADIAN ZIONIST, 4 (Mar. 1937), 106, 108.

2086   "Memoirs of a Campaigner." CANADIAN ZIONIST, 5 (May 1937), 21, 25.

2087   "The Chanukah Dreidel." By Ben Kalonymus, pseud. CANADIAN JEWISH CHRONICLE, 23 Dec. 1938, pp. 7, 23.

2088   "We Who Are About To Be Born." CANADIAN JEWISH CHRONICLE, 2 June 1944, p. 4.

2089   "No Traveller Returns. . . ." By Arthur Haktani, pseud. CANADIAN JEWISH CHRONICLE, 30 June 1944, pp. 4, 16.

2090   "One More Utopia." CANADIAN JEWISH CHRONICLE, 7 Sept. 1945, pp. 5, 87-88.

2091   "The Trail of the Clupea Harengus." CANADIAN JEWISH CHRONICLE, 28 June 1946, pp. 9-13.

2092   "Kapusitchka." CANADIAN JEWISH CHRONICLE, 15 Oct. 1948, p. 4.

2093   "And It Shall Come To Pass." CANADIAN JEWISH CHRONICLE, 29 Oct. 1948, p. 4.

ARTICLES

2094   "Jewish Humour." JUDAEAN, 7 (Feb. 1934), 36, 39.

2095   "Of Hebrew Humor." OPINION, 6 (Nov. 1935), 15-19.

2096   "The Bible as Literature." By Ben Kalonimas, pseud. CANADIAN
        JEWISH CHRONICLE, 11 Apr. 1941, pp. 8-9.

2097   "Notes on a 'Court Jew.'" CANADIAN JEWISH CHRONICLE, 12 Dec.
        1941, pp. 4, 15.

2098   "The Fuerher Furioso." CANADIAN JEWISH CHRONICLE, 1 May 1942,
        p. 4.

2099   "Writing in Canada." CANADIAN JEWISH CHRONICLE, 22 Feb. 1946,
        pp. 8, 16; 1 Mar. 1946, p. 8.

2100   "A Definition of Poetry." CANADIAN JEWISH CHRONICLE, 19 Apr.
        1946, pp. 8, 12.

2101   "Marginalia." CANADIAN JEWISH CHRONICLE, 11 June 1948, pp.
        8-9; 25 June 1948, p. 8; 24 Dec. 1948, p. 6; 28 Jan. 1949, p. 6.

2102   "Book Reviewing: In Seven Easy Lessons." CANADIAN JEWISH CHRONI-
        CLE, 10 Dec. 1948, p. 8.

2103   "The Oxen of the Sun." HERE AND NOW, 1 (Jan. 1949), 28-48.
        Discusses Joyce's ULYSSES.

2104   "And the Mome Raths Outgrabe." HERE AND NOW, 2 (June 1949), 31-37.

2105   "Notebook of a Journey." CANADIAN JEWISH CHRONICLE, 12 Aug.
        1949, pp. 3, 6--23 Dec. 1949, p. 8.
        Appeared weekly.

2106   "The Black Panther (A Study in Technique)." ACCENT, 10 (Spr. 1950),
        139-55.
        Discusses chapter 1 of Joyce's ULYSSES.

2107   "Excerpt from Letter: 'On First Seeing the Ceiling of the Sistine Chapel.'"
        CANADIAN JEWISH CHRONICLE, 28 Apr. 1950, p. 5; 5 May 1950,
        p. 5; 12 May 1950, p. 5.

2108   "The Bible Manuscripts." By Ben Kalonimas, pseud. CANADIAN JEWISH
        CHRONICLE, 28 Sept. 1951, p. 9; 5 Oct. 1951, p. 10; 12 Oct. 1951,
        p. 10; 19 Oct. 1951, p. 8; 26 Oct. 1951, p. 9.

2109   "A Shout in the Street--An Analysis of the Second Chapter of Joyce's ULYSSES." NEW DIRECTIONS, 13 ([1951]), 327-45.

2110   "In Praise of the Diaspora." CANADIAN JEWISH CHRONICLE, 9 Jan. 1953, p. 4; 16 Feb. 1953, p. 4; 23 Jan. 1953, p. 4; 6 Feb. 1953, p. 4; 13 Feb. 1953, p. 4; 20 Feb. 1953, p. 6; 27 Feb. 1953, p. 4.

2111   "The Bible's Archetypical Poet." CANADIAN JEWISH CHRONICLE, 6 Mar. 1953, p. 7; 13 Mar. 1953, p. 4; 20 Mar. 1953, p. 4.

2112   "Some Letters of A.M. Klein to A.J.M. Smith, 1941-1951." In THE A.M. KLEIN SYMPOSIUM. Ed. Seymour Mayne. Ottawa: University of Ottawa Press, 1975, pp. 1-13.

For articles by Klein, see also no. 192.

Manuscripts

2113   Public Archives of Canada, Ottawa.

SECONDARY MATERIAL

Bibliographies

2114   Caplan, Usher, comp. "A.M. Klein: A Bibliography and Index to Manuscripts." In THE A.M. KLEIN SYMPOSIUM. Ed. Seymour Mayne. Ottawa: University of Ottawa Press, 1975, pp. 87-122.

2115   Seibrasse, Glen, comp. "A.M. Klein: A Bibliography." JEWISH DIĀLŎG, Passover 1973, pp. 60-64.

Criticism

2116   Broad, Margaret I. "Art & the Artist: Klein's Unpublished Novella." JOURNAL OF CANADIAN FICTION, 30 (1980), 114-31.

2117   Edel, Leon. "Abraham M. Klein." CANADIAN FORUM, 12 (May 1932), 300-302.

2118   Fischer, Gretl K. IN SEARCH OF JERUSALEM: RELIGION AND ETHICS IN THE WRITING OF A.M. KLEIN. Montreal: McGill-Queen's University Press, 1975. 256 p. Index.

2119   Fisher, Esther Safer. "A.M. Klein: Portrait of the Poet as Jew." CA-
       NADIAN LITERATURE, No. 79 (Wint. 1978), pp. 121-27.

2120   Gibbs, Jean. "Klein's Fabled City." JEWISH DĪÁLŎG, Passover 1973,
       pp. 50-57.

2121   Gotlieb, Phyllis. "Klein's Sources." CANADIAN LITERATURE, No.
       26 (Aut. 1965), pp. 82-84.

2122   Greenstein, Michael. "History in THE SECOND SCROLL." CANADIAN
       LITERATURE, No. 76 (Spr. 1978), pp. 37-46.

2123   Hirano, Keiichi. "Abraham Moses Klein." STUDIES IN ENGLISH LIT-
       ERATURE (Tokyo), English number (1964), pp. 71-103.

2124   Kertzer, J.M. "A.M. Klein's Meditation on Life." JOURNAL OF
       COMMONWEALTH LITERATURE, 13 (Aug. 1978), 1-19.

2125   Marshall, Tom A. "Theorems Made Flesh: Klein's Poetic Universe."
       CANADIAN LITERATURE, No. 25 (Sum. 1965), pp. 43-52.

       Reprinted in no. 2126.

2126   _____, ed. A.M. KLEIN. Critical Views on Canadian Writers, 4.
       Toronto: Ryerson, 1970. xxv, 165 p. Bibliog.

       Mainly on Klein's poetry; includes reviews, and reprints nos.
       2125, 2127, and 2136.

2127   Matthews, John. "Abraham Klein and the Problem of Synthesis." JOUR-
       NAL OF COMMONWEALTH LITERATURE, No. 1 (Sept. 1965), pp. 49-
       63.

       Reprinted in nos. 206 and 2126.

2128   Mayne, Seymour, ed. with introd. THE A.M. KLEIN SYMPOSIUM. Re-
       appraisals: Canadian Writers. Ottawa: University of Ottawa Press, 1975.
       xi, 122 p. Bibliog.

       Includes articles on the manuscripts and fiction as well as the
       poetry.

2129   Middlebro', Tom. "Yet Another Gloss on A.M. Klein's THE SECOND
       SCROLL." JOURNAL OF CANADIAN FICTION, 4, No. 3 (1975), 117-
       22.

2130   Nadel, Ira Bruce. "A.M. Klein on Literature." JEWISH DĪÁLŎG, Hanuk-
       kah 1974, pp. 4-7.

2131 _____. "The Prose and Poetry of A.M. Klein: An Introduction." MIDSTREAM, 20 (Dec. 1974), 36-48.

2132 Page, P. "The Sense of Angels." JEWISH DIÁLŎG, Passover 1973, pp. 18-19.

2133 Pollock, Zailig. "The Myth of Exile and Redemption in 'Gloss Gimel.'" STUDIES IN CANADIAN LITERATURE, 4 (Wint. 1979), 26-42.

2134 _____. "Sunflower Seeds: Klein's Hero and Demagogue." CANADIAN LITERATURE, No. 82 (Aut. 1979), pp. 48-58.

2135 Popham, E.A. "A.M. Klein: The Impulse to Define." CANADIAN LITERATURE, No. 79 (Wint. 1979), pp. 5-17.

2136 Samuel, Maurice. "The Book of the Miracle." JEWISH FRONTIER, Nov. 1951, pp. 11-15.

Reprinted in no. 2126.

2137 Smith, Arthur James Marshall. "Abraham Moses Klein." GANTS DU CIEL, 11 (Spr. 1946), 67-81.

2138 Steinberg, M.W. "A.M. Klein as Journalist." CANADIAN LITERATURE, No. 82 (Aut. 1979), pp. 21-30.

2139 _____. "The Conscience of Art: A.M. Klein on Poets and Poetry." In A POLITICAL ART: ESSAYS AND IMAGES IN HONOUR OF GEORGE WOODCOCK. Ed. William H. New. Vancouver: British Columbia Press, 1978, pp. 82-93.

2140 _____. Introd., THE SECOND SCROLL. New Canadian Library, no. 22. Toronto: McClelland and Stewart, 1961, pp. vii-xvi.

2141 _____. "The Stature of A.M. Klein." RECONSTRUCTIONIST, 29 Nov. 1957, pp. 14-18.

2142 _____. "A Twentieth Century Pentateuch: A.M. Klein's THE SECOND SCROLL." CANADIAN LITERATURE, No. 2 (Aut. 1959), pp. 37-46.

Reprinted in no. 195.

2143 Steinberg, M.W., and Seymour Mayne., "A Dialogue on A.M. Klein." Taped by Seymour Levitan. JEWISH DIÁLŎG, Passover 1973, pp. 10-16.

2144   Sutherland, John. "Canadian Comment." NORTHERN REVIEW, 2 (Aug.-Sept. 1949), 30-34.

2145   Waddington, Miriam. A.M. KLEIN. Studies in Canadian Literature, 10. Toronto: Copp Clark, 1970. vi, 145 p. Bibliog.

2146   _____. "Signs on a White Field: Klein's SECOND SCROLL." CANADIAN LITERATURE, No. 25 (Sum. 1965), pp. 21-32.

   Reprinted in nos. 2145 and 5102.

2147   Weir, Lorraine. "Portrait of the Poet as Joyce Scholar: An Approach to A.M. Klein." CANADIAN LITERATURE, No. 76 (Spr. 1978), pp. 47-55.

For criticism on Klein, see also nos. 407 and 5167.

Book Reviews

2148   THE SECOND SCROLL: CanL, 2 (Aut. 1959), 37-46; CanL, 11 (Wint. 1962), 72-73; CanL, 13 (Sum. 1962), 87-88; CFor, 31 (Jan. 1952), 234; COMMENTARY, 69 (Mar. 1980), 46; NATION, 3 Nov. 1951, p. 379; NYTBR, 25 Nov. 1951, p. 58; RUL, 6 (Jan. 1952), 403-05; SatN, 13 Oct. 1951, p. 27; UTQ, 21 (Apr. 1952), 264-65.

KNISTER, RAYMOND (1899-1932)

Born near Blenheim, Ontario, Raymond Knister studied at the University of Toronto and Iowa State University in the early 1920s; acted briefly as associate editor of MIDLAND, an Iowa literary magazine; and worked as a farmhand in southern Ontario. A number of his stories were published in the Toronto STAR. With the support of Frederick Philip Grove, Knister's MY STAR PREDOMINANT won the Graphic Press Award, although bankruptcy of Graphic complicated the awarding of the prize and publishing of the work. Knister drowned while swimming.

PRIMARY MATERIAL

Monographs

FICTION

2149 WHITE NARCISSUS: A NOVEL. Toronto: Macmillan, 1929. 254 p.

2150 MY STAR PREDOMINANT. Toronto: Ryerson, [1934]. 319 p.

   A fictionalized life of Keats.

2151 SELECTED STORIES OF RAYMOND KNISTER. Ed. with introd. by Michael Gnarowski. Canadian Short Stories, vol. 2. Ottawa: University of Ottawa Press, 1972. 119 p.

2152 THE FIRST DAY OF SPRING: STORIES AND OTHER PROSE. Ed. with introd. by Peter Stevens. Literature of Canada: Poetry and Prose in Reprint, 17. Toronto: University of Toronto Press, 1976. xxx, 469 p. Bibliog.

   Fiction and literary criticism by Raymond Knister, including an article on Grove.

POETRY

2153 COLLECTED POEMS OF RAYMOND KNISTER. Ed. with a Memoir by Dorothy Livesay and a Bibliography by Margaret Ray. Ryerson Library of Canadian Poets. Toronto: Ryerson, 1949. xli, 45 p.

EDITED WORK

2154 CANADIAN SHORT STORIES. Ed. with introd. by Raymond Knister. Toronto: Macmillan, 1928. xix, 340 p. Bibliog.

Shorter Work

SHORT STORIES

2155 "The Practical Wife." MACLEAN'S, 1 May 1927, pp. 16-17, 94-95, 97.

2156 "A Plaster on the Rooftree." MACLEAN'S, 15 Mar. 1931, pp. 18 ff.

2157 "An Airman's Tale-Spinning." JOURNAL OF CANADIAN FICTION, 4, No. 2 (1975), 66-70.

2158 "The Black Fox." JOURNAL OF CANADIAN FICTION, 4, No. 2 (1975), 124-41.

2159 "Boquet [sic] and Some Buds: A Stable Anthology." JOURNAL OF CANADIAN FICTION, 4, No. 2 (1975), 107-15.

2160 "Cherry Time." JOURNAL OF CANADIAN FICTION, 4, No. 2 (1975), 43-54.

2161 "Congratulations." JOURNAL OF CANADIAN FICTION, 4, No. 2 (1975), 62-65.

2162 "Corn Cob Corners Folks." JOURNAL OF CANADIAN FICTION, 4, No. 2 (1975), 116-23.

2163 "The Dance at the Beach." JOURNAL OF CANADIAN FICTION, 4, No. 2 (1975), 55-61.

2164 "Dentistry Blues." JOURNAL OF CANADIAN FICTION, 4, No. 2 (1975), 81-85.

2165 "Eric Mirth, or the Larger I." JOURNAL OF CANADIAN FICTION, 4, No. 2 (1975), 97-106.

2166 "Fishers of Pike." JOURNAL OF CANADIAN FICTION, 4, No. 2 (1975), 77-80.

2167 "He's All Right." JOURNAL OF CANADIAN FICTION, 4, No. 2 (1975), 75-76.

2168 "Rear Road." JOURNAL OF CANADIAN FICTION, 4, No. 2 (1975), 86-96.

2169 "Stuart's Wife: Dedicated to Theodore Dreiser." JOURNAL OF CANADIAN FICTION, 4, No. 2 (1975), 27-38.

2170 "Well, Well, Bertha." JOURNAL OF CANADIAN FICTION, 4, No. 2 (1975), 71-74.

2171 "The Years of the Cankerworm." JOURNAL OF CANADIAN FICTION, 4, No. 2 (1975), 39-42.

ARTICLES

2172 "The Canadian Girl." JOURNAL OF CANADIAN FICTION, 4, No. 2 (1975), 154-59.

2173 "Canadian Literati." JOURNAL OF CANADIAN FICTION, 4, No. 2 (1975), 160-68.

2174 "Canadian Literature: A General Impression: 'O Frabjous Day.'" JOURNAL OF CANADIAN FICTION, 4, No. 2 (1975), 169-74.

2175 "Democracy and the Short Story." JOURNAL OF CANADIAN FICTION, 4, No. 2 (1975), 146-48.

For articles by Knister, see also nos. 122 and 2154.

Manuscripts

2176 Queen's University Library, Kingston, Ont.; University of Toronto Library.

SECONDARY MATERIAL

Bibliographies

2177   Burke, A., comp. "Raymond Knister: An Annotated Checklist." ESSAYS
       ON CANADIAN WRITING, No. 16 (Fall-Wint. 1979-80), pp. 20-61. Index.

2178   Ray, Margaret, comp. RAYMOND KNISTER: A BIBLIOGRAPHY OF HIS
       WORKS. Toronto: Bibliographical Society of Canada, 1950. 8 p.

For bibliographies of Knister, see also no. 33.

Criticism

2179   Clever, Glen. "Point of View in WHITE NARCISSUS." STUDIES IN
       CANADIAN LITERATURE, 3 (Wint. 1978), 119-23.

2180   Denham, Paul. "Beyond Realism: Raymond Knister's WHITE NARCISSUS."
       STUDIES IN CANADIAN LITERATURE, 3 (Wint. 1978), 70-77.

2181   Givens, Imogen. "Raymond Knister--Man or Myth?" ESSAYS ON CA-
       NADIAN WRITING, No. 16 (Fall-Wint. 1979-80), pp. 5-19.

2182   Kennedy, Leo. "Raymond Knister." CANADIAN FORUM, 12 (Sept.
       1932, 459-61.

2183   O'Halloran, Bonita, comp. "Chronological History of Raymond Knister."
       JOURNAL OF CANADIAN FICTION, 4, No. 2 (1975), 194-99.

2184   Waddington, Marcus. "Raymond Knister: A Biographical Note." JOUR-
       NAL OF CANADIAN FICTION, 4, No. 2 (1975), 175-92.

For criticism of Knister, see also nos. 1144, 2151-53.

Book Reviews

2185   WHITE NARCISSUS: CFor, 9 (Aug. 1932), 389-90; NYTBR, 25 Aug.
       1929, p. 9; TLS, 28 Feb. 1929, p. 164.

2186   SELECTED STORIES OF RAYMOND KNISTER: CanL, 62 (Aut. 1974),
       79-83; EA, 26 (Oct. 1973), 493.

2187   THE FIRST DAY OF SPRING: CBRA, 1976, p. 220; CFor, 57 (June
       1977), 44-45; ECW, 6 (Spr. 1977), 144-47; ESC, 4 (Wint. 1978), 505-
       09; OntarioR, 7 (Fall 1977), 106-08; WLWE, 16 (Nov. 1977), 363-65.

KREISEL, HENRY (1922--)

Kreisel fled his birthplace, Vienna, in 1938 after the Nazi invasion. Interned in England in 1940 and sent to Canada, he was released in 1942, completed a B.A. in English (1946) and an M.A. (1947) at the University of Toronto, and a Ph.D. (1954) at the University of London. Since the 1950s he has been an English professor, in the 1960s department head, and, in the 1970s, dean and vice-president at the University of Alberta. He has been visiting professor at the University of British Columbia and Cambridge. His novel, THE RICH MAN, sympathetically explores the miscalculation of a Jewish-Canadian immigrant attempting to impress his Viennese relatives.

PRIMARY MATERIAL

Monographs

FICTION

2188   THE RICH MAN: A NOVEL. Toronto: McClelland and Stewart, 1948. 263 p.

2189   KLANAK ISLANDS: A COLLECTION OF SHORT STORIES. By Henry Kreisel et al. Vancouver: Klanak, 1959. 79 p.

2190   THE BETRAYAL. Toronto: McClelland and Stewart, 1964. 218 p.

2191   THE ALMOST MEETING AND OTHER STORIES. Edmonton: NeWest, 1981. 147 p.

NONFICTION PROSE

2192   "The Problem of Exile and Alienation in Modern Literature." Diss., University of London, 1954.

EDITED WORK

2193 APHRODITE. By John Heath. Ed. with introd. by Henry Kreisel. Toronto: Ryerson, 1958. 24 p.

Shorter Work

ARTICLES

2194 "Hurdling the English Language." CANADIAN AUTHOR AND BOOK-MAN, 24 (Dec. 1948), 40.

2195 "Joseph Conrad and the Dilemma of the Uprooted Man." TAMARACK REVIEW, No. 7 (Spr. 1958), pp. 78-85.

2196 "The Arts--'Useless'--But Expensive." HUMANITIES ASSOCIATION BULLETIN, No. 24 (Apr. 1958), pp. 7-10.

2197 "The African Stories of Margaret Laurence." CANADIAN FORUM, 41 (Apr. 1961), 8-10.

2198 "Literature as Language." ENGLISH TEACHER, June 1962, pp. 100-105.

2199 "Are We Neglecting Modern Writers?" ENGLISH TEACHER, June 1964, pp. 34-40.

2200 "The Prairie: A State of Mind." PROCEEDINGS AND TRANSACTIONS OF THE ROYAL SOCIETY OF CANADA, 4th ser., 6 (1968), 171-80.

   Reprinted in no. 161.

2201 "Diary of an Internment." WHITE PELICAN, 4 (Sum. 1974), 5-40.

2202 "Sheila Watson in Edmonton." In FIGURES IN A GROUND: CANADIAN ESSAYS ON MODERN LITERATURE COLLECTED IN HONOR OF SHEILA WATSON. Ed. Diane Bessai and David Jackel. Saskatoon: Western Producer Prairie Books, 1978, pp. 4-6.

For articles by Kreisel, see also nos. 149 and 2193.

SECONDARY MATERIAL

Criticism

2203 Cherniavsky, Felix. "Certain Worldly Experiences: An Interview with Henry Kreisel." SPHINX, 2 (Wint. 1977), 10-22. Bibliog.

2204 Greenstein, Michael. "The Language of the Holocaust in THE RICH MAN." ÉTUDES CANADIENNES/CANADIAN STUDIES, 4 (1978), 85-96.

2205 Lecker, Robert A. "States of Mind: Henry Kreisel's Novels." CANADIAN LITERATURE, No. 77 (Sum. 1978), pp. 82-93.

2206 Stedmond, John. Introd., THE RICH MAN. New Canadian Library, no. 24. Toronto: McClelland and Stewart, 1961, pp. v-viii.

2207 Warhaft, Sidney. Introd., THE BETRAYAL. New Canadian Library, no. 77. Toronto: McClelland and Stewart, 1971, pp. v-x.

Book Reviews

2208 THE RICH MAN: CBRA, 1975, p. 117; CFor, 28 (Feb. 1949), 263-64; DR, 41 (Wint. 1961-62), 575, 577; QQ, 69 (Aut. 1962), 462; SatN, 18 Dec. 1948, p. 20; UTQ, 18 (Apr. 1949), 266-68.

2209 THE BETRAYAL: CAB, 40 (Wint. 1964), 16; CanL, 23 (Wint. 1965), 72, 74; CFor, 45 (May 1965), 45; SatN, 79 (Nov. 1964), 32-33; TamR, [34] (Wint. 1965), 107-08; UTQ, 34 (July 1965), 377-79.

KROETSCH, ROBERT (1927--)

A novelist and more recently a poet as well, Robert Kroetsch was born in Heisler, Alberta. He worked on the Fort Smith portage, on the Mackenzie riverboats, and at the Goose Bay, Labrador, Air Force Base. Kroetsch studied at the University of Alberta (B.A., 1948), Middlebury College, Vermont (M.A., 1956), McGill University (under the tutelage of Hugh MacLennan), and the University of Iowa (Ph.D., 1961). He helped edit the journal, BOUNDARY II. A professor of English at the State University of New York, Binghampton, until 1978, Kroetsch is now at the University of Manitoba. His fiction is exuberant, often comic and bawdy, playing freely with myth and the tall tale. THE STUDHORSE MAN won the 1969 Governor General's Award.

PRIMARY MATERIAL

Monographs

FICTION

2210   "When Sick for Home." Diss., University of Iowa, 1961. 210 1.
>   A novel.

2211   BUT WE ARE EXILES. Toronto: Macmillan, 1965. 145 p.

2212   THE WORDS OF MY ROARING. Toronto: Macmillan, 1966. 211 p.
>   First volume in the Out West trilogy.

2213   THE STUDHORSE MAN. Toronto: Macmillan, 1969. 168 p.
>   Second volume in the Out West trilogy.

2214   GONE INDIAN. Toronto: New, 1973. 158 p.
>   Third volume in the Out West trilogy.

2215 BADLANDS: A NOVEL. Toronto: New, 1975. 270 p.

2216 WHAT THE CROW SAID. Don Mills, Ont.: General Publishing, 1978. 218 p.

NONFICTION PROSE

2217 ALBERTA. Traveller's Canada. Toronto: Macmillan, 1968. 231 p.

2218 THE CROW JOURNALS. Edmonton: NeWest, 1980. 92 p.
      Journal kept during the writing of WHAT THE CROW SAID.

POETRY

2219 THE LEDGER. London, Ont.: Applegarth Follies, 1975. N. pag.

2220 THE STONE HAMMER POEMS: 1960-1975. Nanaimo, B.C.: Oolichan Books, 1975. 63 p.

2221 SEED CATALOGUE: POEMS. Poetry Series One, no. 7. Winnipeg: Turnstone, 1977. 75 p.

2222 THE SAD PHOENICIAN. Toronto: Coach House, 1979. 75 p.

2223 THE CRIMINAL INTENSITIES OF LOVE AS PARADISE. Lantzville, B.C.: Oolichan Books, 1981. 29 p.

2224 FIELD NOTES: THE COLLECTED POETRY OF ROBERT KROETSCH. Don Mills, Ont.: General Publishing, 1981. 144 p.

EDITED WORK

2225 CREATION: ROBERT KROETSCH, JAMES BACQUE, PIERRE GRAVEL INCLUDING THE AUTHORS' CONVERSATIONS WITH MARGARET LAURENCE, MILTON WILSON, J. RAYMOND BRAZEAU. Toronto: New, 1970. 213 p.

2226 SUNDOGS: STORIES FROM SASKATCHEWAN. Moose Jaw, Sask.: Thunder Creek, 1980. 179 p.

Shorter Work

SHORT STORIES

2227 "The Stragglers." MONTREALER, Apr. 1950, pp. 34, 60.

2228 "The Toughest Mile." MONTREALER, Nov. 1950, p. 38.

2229 "Who Would Marry a Riverman?" MACLEAN'S, 4 Feb. 1956, pp. 18-19, 28-29, 32, 34.

2230 "The Harvester." MACLEAN'S, 29 Sept. 1956, pp. 22-23, 36, 38, 42-43.

2231 "Mrs. Brennan's Secret." MACLEAN'S, 14 Sept. 1957, pp. 36-37, 94-98.

2232 "The Blue Guitar." CANADIAN FORUM, 37 (Feb. 1958), 250-51.

2233 "Defy the Night." UNIVERSITY OF KANSAS CITY REVIEW, 26 (Spr. 1960), 229-33.

2234 "Earth Moving." In STORIES FROM WESTERN CANADA: A SELECTION. Ed. Rudy Wiebe. Toronto: Macmillan, 1972, pp. 134-40.

2235 "Taking the Risk." SALT, 16 (1977), 3-5.

ARTICLES

2236 "The Canadian Writer and the American Literary Tradition." ENGLISH QUARTERLY, 4 (Sum. 1971), 45-49.

2237 "Unhiding the Hidden: Recent Canadian Fiction." JOURNAL OF CANADIAN FICTION, 3, No. 3 (1974), 43-45.

   Reprinted in 136.

2238 "voice/in prose: effing the ineffable." FREELANCE, 8 (Nov. 1976), 35-36.

2239 "Canada is a Poem." In DIVIDED WE STAND. Ed. Gary Geddes. Toronto: Peter Martin, 1977, pp. 13-16.

2240 "The Disappearing Father and Harrison's Born-Again and Again and Again West." ESSAYS ON CANADIAN WRITING, 11 (Sum. 1978), 7-9.

2241 "Fear of Women in Prairie Fiction: Erotics of Space." CANADIAN
FORUM, 58 (Oct.-Nov. 1978), 22-27.

Reprinted in no. 149.

2242 "Death is a Happy Ending: A Dialogue in Thirteen Parts." By Robert
Kroetsch and Diane Bessai. In FIGURES IN A GROUND: CANADIAN
ESSAYS ON MODERN LITERATURE COLLECTED IN HONOR OF SHEILA
WATSON. Ed. Diane Bessai and David Jackel. Saskatoon: Western
Producer Prairie Books, 1978, pp. 206-15.

2243 "Contemporary Standards in the Canadian Novel." ESSAYS ON CANA-
DIAN WRITING, No. 20 (Wint. 1980-81), pp. 7-18.

For reply, see no. 247.

Manuscripts

2244 University of Calgary Library, Calgary, Alta.

SECONDARY MATERIAL

Bibliography

2245 Lecker, Robert A., comp. "An Annotated Bibliography of Works by and
about Robert Kroetsch." ESSAYS ON CANADIAN WRITING, Nos. 7-8
(1977), pp. 74-96.

Criticism

2246 Brahms, Flemming. "Robert Kroetsch." KUNAPIPI, 2, No. 2 (1980),
117-25.

An interview.

2247 Brown, Russell M. "An Interview with Robert Kroetsch." UNIVERSITY
OF WINDSOR REVIEW, 7 (Spr. 1972), 1-18.

2248 Cameron, Donald A. "Robert Kroetsch: The American Experience and
the Canadian Voice." JOURNAL OF CANADIAN FICTION, 1 (Sum.
1972), 48-52.

An interview; reprinted in no. 124.

2249 Davidson, Arnold E. "Frustrated Sexuality in Robert Kroetsch's THE STUD-
HORSE MAN." AMERICAN REVIEW OF CANADIAN STUDIES, 7 (Aut.
1977), 23-32.

2250 _____. "History, Myth, and Time in Robert Kroetsch's BADLANDS." STUDIES IN CANADIAN LITERATURE, 5 (Spr. 1980), 127-37.

2251 Enright, Robert, and Dennis Cooley. "Uncovering Our Dream World: An Interview with Robert Kroetsch." ARTS MANITOBA, 1 (Jan.-Feb. 1977), 32-39. Rpt. in ESSAYS ON CANADIAN WRITING, Nos. 18-19 (Sum.-Fall 1980), pp. 21-32.

2252 Hancock, Geoff. "An Interview with Robert Kroetsch." CANADIAN FICTION MAGAZINE, Nos. 24-25 (Spr.-Sum. 1977), pp. 32-52. Correction, No. 26 (Aut. 1977), p. 14.

2253 Harvey, Connie. "Tear-Glazed Vision of Laughter." ESSAYS ON CANADIAN WRITING, 11 (Sum. 1978), 28-54.

   Discusses BADLANDS.

2254 Harvey, Roderick W. "The Limitations of Media." CANADIAN LITERATURE, No. 77 (Sum. 1978), pp. 20-27.

   Discusses THE STUDHORSE MAN and GONE INDIAN.

2255 McCaughy, G.S. "THE STUDHORSE MAN: A Madman's View of Canadian History." REVUE DE L'UNIVERSITÉ D'OTTAWA, 44 (July-Sept. 1974), 406-13.

2256 MacKendrick, Louis K. "Robert Kroetsch and the Modern Canadian Novel of Exhaustion." ESSAYS ON CANADIAN WRITING, 11 (Sum. 1978), 10-27.

2257 Mandel, Ann. "Uninventing Structures: Cultural Criticism and the Novels of Robert Kroetsch." OPEN LETTER, 3rd ser., No. 8 (Spr. 1978), pp. 52-71.

2258 Melnyk, George. "Kroetsch: Leaving a Comfortable Exile." QUILL AND QUIRE, 42 (Nov. 1976), 19-20.

2259 Nicolaisen, W.F.H. "Ordering the Chaos: Name Strategies in Robert Kroetsch's Novels." ESSAYS ON CANADIAN WRITING, 11 (Sum. 1978), 55-65.

2260 Sullivan, Rosemary. "The Fascinating Place Between: The Fiction of Robert Kroetsch." MOSAIC, 11 (Spr. 1978), 165-76.

2261 Surette, P.L. "The Fabular Fiction of Robert Kroetsch." CANADIAN LITERATURE, No. 77 (Sum. 1978), pp. 6-19.

2262   Thomas, D.P. "Robert Kroetsch, Rupert Brooke, the Voices of the Dead." STUDIES IN CANADIAN LITERATURE, 1 (Wint. 1976), 124-29.

2263   Thomas, Peter. "Keeping Mum: Kroetsch's 'Alberta.'" JOURNAL OF CANADIAN FICTION, 2 (Spr. 1973), 54-56.

2264   _____. "Priapus in the Danse Macabre." CANADIAN LITERATURE, No. 61 (Sum. 1974), pp. 54-64.

       Reprinted in no. 5113.

2265   _____. ROBERT KROETSCH. Studies in Canadian Literature. Vancouver: Douglas and McIntyre, 1980. 139 p. Bibliog.

2266   _____. "Robert Kroetsch and Silence." ESSAYS ON CANADIAN WRITING, Nos. 18-19 (Sum.-Fall 1980), pp. 33-53.

For criticism on Kroetsch, see also nos. 160, 170, 173, 197, 205, 324, 400, and 4246.

Book Reviews

2267   BUT WE ARE EXILES: NYTBR, 13 Mar. 1966, p. 38; SatN, 80 [81] (May 1966), 47, 49; TamR, [38] (Wint. 1966), 100-103; UTQ, 35 (July 1966), 389-90.

2268   THE WORDS OF MY ROARING: CanL, 31 (Wint. 1967), 66-67; NS, 18 Nov. 1966, p. 750; PUNCH, 14 Dec. 1966, p. 902; SPECTATOR, 18 Nov. 1966, p. 657; TamR, [43] (Spr. 1967), 65-66; TLS, 8 Dec. 1966, p. 1147; UTQ, 36 (July 1967), 386.

2269   THE STUDHORSE MAN: CanL, 45 (Sum. 1970), 88-90; LISTENER, 23 Oct. 1969, p. 577; NYTBR, 26 Apr. 1970, p. 44; NYTBR, 7 June 1970, p. 2; NYTBR, 6 Dec. 1970, p. 102; SPECTATOR, 25 Oct. 1969, p. 551; TLS, 11 Dec. 1969, p. 1431; UTQ, 39 (July 1970), 344.

2270   GONE INDIAN: BCan, 2 (Apr. 1973), 55; CanL, 61 (Sum. 1974), 103-04; CFM, 16 (Wint. 1975), 107-09; DR, 54 (Spr. 1974), 166; ECW, 1 (Wint. 1974), 48; JCF, 3 (Wint. 1974), 93-95; LaUR, 7 (Sum. 1974), 156-59; MACLEAN'S, 86 (July 1973), 72; MHRev, 29 (Jan. 1974), 133-36; Q&Q, 39 (Apr. 1973), 10.

2271   BADLANDS: AntigR, 24 (1975), 98-101; BCan, 4 (Oct. 1975), 13-14; CBRA, 1975, p. 103; CDim, 12 (Apr. 1977), 40-42; CFM, 22 (Sum. 1976), 100-102; CFor, 55 (Dec. 1975), 54-55; NWR, 1 (Jan. 1976), 8; UTQ, 45 (Sum. 1976), 322.

2272   WHAT THE CROW SAID: BCan, 7 (Dec. 1978), 17; BCan, 8 (Oct. 1979), 30; CFM, 32-33 (1979-80), 165-67; FIDDLEHEAD, 122 (Sum. 1979), 134-37; UTQ, 48 (Sum. 1979), 326-27.

2273   THE CROW JOURNALS: CFor, 60 (Sept. 1980), 35; PFor, 5 (Spr. 1980), 111-14; Q&Q, 46 (June 1980), 36.

LAURENCE, MARGARET (1926--   )

Jean Margaret Wemyss Laurence was born in Neepawa, Manitoba, the town which served as a model for the fictitious Manawaka of much of her fiction. After graduation from the University of Manitoba, she lived in the Somaliland desert (1950-52) and in Gold Coast, now Ghana (1952-57), an experience which inspired her editing and study of African writers and her first short stories and novel. After five years in Vancouver, British Columbia, and ten years in Buckinghamshire, England, and travels in Europe and the East, she settled near Peterborough, Ontario.

She has been writer-in-residence at the Universities of Toronto, Western Ontario (London) and Trent (Peterborough). Her fiction has earned her almost a dozen honorary degrees, the Beta Sigma Phi Award for her first novel, the Molson Prize (1974), and Governor General's Awards for A JEST OF GOD and THE DIVINERS. In 1972, she was named a companion of the Order of Canada. In 1981, she began a three-year term as chancellor of Trent University. A major Canadian novelist, Laurence has concentrated for the most part on the lives of women characters. She explores the inner worlds of her protagonists in prose which is emotionally powerful, precise in idiom, and rich in sensory detail.

PRIMARY MATERIAL

Monographs

FICTION

2274   THIS SIDE JORDAN. Toronto: McClelland and Stewart, 1960. xi, 281 p.

2275   THE TOMORROW-TAMER: SHORT STORIES. Toronto: McClelland and Stewart, 1963. vii, 243 p.

2276   THE STONE ANGEL. Toronto: McClelland and Stewart, 1964. 308 p.

2277   A JEST OF GOD. Toronto: McClelland and Stewart, 1966. 202 p.
Also as RACHEL, RACHEL. New York: A.A. Knopf, 1966. 213 p.;
rpt. as NOW I LAY ME DOWN. London: Panther Books, 1968. 188 p.

2278   THE FIRE-DWELLERS. Toronto: McClelland and Stewart, 1969. 308 p.

2279   A BIRD IN THE HOUSE: STORIES. Toronto: McClelland and Stewart,
1970. 207 p.

2280   JASON'S QUEST. Illus. Steffan Torell. Toronto: McClelland and
Stewart, 1970. 211 p.

        For children.

2281   THE DIVINERS. Toronto: McClelland and Stewart, 1974. 382 p.

2282   THE OLDEN DAYS COAT. Illus. Muriel Wood. Toronto: McClelland
and Stewart, 1979. N. pag.

        For children.

2283   SIX DARN COWS. Illus. Ann Blades. Toronto: James Lorimer, 1979.
N. pag.

        For children.

2284   THE CHRISTMAS STORY. Illus. Helen Lucas. Toronto: McClelland
and Stewart, 1980. N. pag.

        For children.

NONFICTION PROSE

2285   THE PROPHET'S CAMEL BELL. Toronto: McClelland and Stewart, 1963.
239 p. Bibliog.; rpt. as NEW WIND IN A DRY LAND. New York:
A.A. Knopf, 1964. 295 p. Bibliog.

2286   LONG DRUMS AND CANNONS: NIGERIAN DRAMATISTS AND NOV-
ELISTS 1952-1966. London: Macmillan, 1968. 209 p. Bibliog. Index.

2287   HEART OF A STRANGER. Toronto: McClelland and Stewart, 1976.
221 p.

EDITED WORK

2288   A TREE FOR POVERTY: SOMALI POETRY AND PROSE. Nairobi: Eagle
Press for the Somaliland Protectorate, 1954. 146 p.

Shorter Work

SHORT STORIES

2289   "Calliope." By Jean Margaret Wemyss. VOX (United College, now University of Winnipeg), 18, No. 3 (1945), 10-12; rpt. in JOURNAL OF CANADIAN FICTION, 27 (1980), 9-14.

2290   "Tal des Walde." By Jean Margaret Wemyss. VOX, 29, No. 3 (1946), 3-5, 39-40, 54; rpt. in JOURNAL OF CANADIAN FICTION, 27 (1980), 15-22.

2291   "Uncertain Flowering." In STORY: THE MAGAZINE OF THE SHORT STORY IN BOOK FORM. Ed. Whit. Burnett. New York: A.A. Wyn, 1953, IV, 9-34.

2292   "Mask of Beaten Gold." TAMARACK REVIEW, [29] (Aut. 1963), 3-21.

2293   "A Queen in Thebes." TAMARACK REVIEW, [32] (Sum. 1964), 25-37.

ARTICLES

2294   Introd., THE LAMP AT NOON AND OTHER STORIES, by Sinclair Ross. New Canadian Library, no. 62. Toronto: McClelland and Stewart, 1968, pp. 7-12.

2295   "Ten Years' Sentences." CANADIAN LITERATURE, No. 41 (Sum. 1969), pp. 10-16.

      Reprinted in nos. 197, 5106, and 5113.

2296   "Author's Commentary." In SIXTEEN BY TWELVE. Ed. John Metcalf. Toronto: Ryerson, 1970, pp. 71-73.

2297   "Time and the Narrative Voice." In THE NARRATIVE VOICE. Ed. John Metcalf. Toronto: McGraw-Hill Ryerson, 1972, pp. 126-30.

2298   Introd., ABOVE GROUND, by Jack Ludwig. New Canadian Library, no. 100. Toronto: McClelland and Stewart, 1974, n. pag.

2299   Introd., HOUSE OF HATE, by Percy Janes. New Canadian Library, no. 124. Toronto: McClelland and Stewart, 1976, pp. vii-xi.

2300   "Listen. Just Listen." In DIVIDED WE STAND. Ed. Gary Geddes. Toronto: Peter Martin, 1977, pp. 20-25.

2301   Introd., CRACKPOT: A NOVEL, by Adele Wiseman. New Canadian
        Library, no. 144. Toronto: McClelland and Stewart, 1978, pp. 3-8.

2302   "Ivory Tower or Grassroots?: A Novelist as Socio-Political Being." In
        A POLITICAL ART: ESSAYS AND IMAGES IN HONOUR OF GEORGE
        WOODCOCK. Ed. William H. New. Vancouver: University of British
        Columbia Press, 1978, pp. 15-25.

        Reprinted in no. 136.

2303   "Gadgetry or Growing: Form and Voice in the Novel." JOURNAL OF
        CANADIAN FICTION, 27 (1980), 54-62.

2304   "Letter to Bob Sorfleet." JOURNAL OF CANADIAN FICTION, 27
        (1980), 52-53.

2305   "W.L. Morton: A Personal Tribute." JOURNAL OF CANADIAN STUDIES,
        15 (Wint. 1980-81), 134.

For articles by Laurence, see also nos. 1552 and 3773.

Manuscripts

2306   McMaster University Library, Hamilton.

SECONDARY MATERIAL

Bibliographies

2307   Warwick, Susan J., comp. "A Laurence Log." JOURNAL OF CANA-
        DIAN STUDIES, 13 (Fall 1978), 75-83.

2308   _____. "Margaret Laurence: An Annotated Bibliography." In THE
        ANNOTATED BIBLIOGRAPHY OF CANADA'S MAJOR AUTHORS. Ed.
        Robert Lecker and Jack David. Downsview, Ont.: ECW, 1979, pp.
        47-102. Index.

Criticism

2309   Bailey, Nancy I. "Fiction and the New Androgyne: Problems and Pos-
        sibilities in THE DIVINERS." ATLANTIS, 4 (Fall 1978), 10-17.

2310   _____. "Margaret Laurence, Carl Jung and the Manawaka Women."
        STUDIES IN CANADIAN LITERATURE, 2 (Sum. 1977), 306-21.

2311   Baxter, John. "THE STONE ANGEL: Shakespearian Bearings." COM-
        PASS, 1 (Aug. 1977), 3-19.

2312   Bennett, Donna A.   "The Failures of Sisterhood in Margaret Laurence's
        Manawaka Novels."   ATLANTIS, 4 (Fall 1978), 103-09.

2313   Bevan, Allan R.   Introd., THE FIRE-DWELLERS.   New Canadian Library,
        no. 87.   Toronto: McClelland and Stewart, 1973, pp. viii-xiv.

2314   Blewett, David.   "The Unity of the Manawaka Cycle."   JOURNAL OF
        CANADIAN STUDIES, 13 (Fall 1978), 31-39.

2315   Boone, Laurel.   "Rachel's Benign Growth."   STUDIES IN CANADIAN
        LITERATURE, 3 (Sum. 1978), 277-81.

2316   Bowering, George.   "That Fool of a Fear: Notes on A JEST OF GOD."
        CANADIAN LITERATURE, No. 50 (Aut. 1971), pp. 41-56.

        Reprinted in nos. 197 and 5113.

2317   Callaghan, Barry.   "The Writings of Margaret Laurence."   TAMARACK
        REVIEW, [36] (Sum. 1965), 45-51.

2318   Cameron, Donald A.   "Don Cameron Interviews Margaret Laurence."
        QUILL AND QUIRE, 38 (Mar. 1972), 3, 10-11.

        Reprinted in no. 124.

2319   Carrington, Ildikó de Papp.   "'Tales in the Telling': THE DIVINERS as
        Fiction about Fiction."   ESSAYS ON CANADIAN WRITING, No. 9
        (Wint. 1977-78), pp. 154-69.

2320   Coldwell, Joan.   "Hagar as Meg Merrilies, the Homeless Gipsy."   JOUR-
        NAL OF CANADIAN FICTION, 27 (1980), 92-100.

2321   _____.   "Margaret Laurence: In Search of Ancestors."   BOOK FORUM,
        4, No. 1 (1978), 64-69.   Bibliog.

2322   Cooley, Dennis.   "Antimacassared in the Wilderness: Art and Nature in
        THE STONE ANGEL."   MOSAIC, 11 (Spr. 1978), 29-46.

2323   Davidson, Cathy N.   "Geography as Psychology in the Manitoba Fiction
        of Margaret Laurence."   KATE CHOPIN NEWSLETTER, 2, No. 2 (1976-
        77), 5-10.

2324   _____.   "Past and Perspective in Margaret Laurence's THE STONE AN-
        GEL."   AMERICAN REVIEW OF CANADIAN STUDIES, 8 (Aut. 1978),
        61-69.

2325 Djwa, Sandra. "False Gods and the True Covenant: Thematic Continuity between Margaret Laurence and Sinclair Ross." JOURNAL OF CANADIAN FICTION, 1 (Fall 1972), 43-50.

2326 Dombrowski, Theo Q. "WHO IS THIS YOU? Margaret Laurence and Identity." UNIVERSITY OF WINDSOR REVIEW, 13 (Fall-Wint. 1977), 21-38.

2327 _____. "Word and Fact: Laurence and the Problem of Language." CANADIAN LITERATURE, No. 80 (Spr. 1979), pp. 50-62.

2328 Forman, Denyse, and Una Parameswaran. "Echoes and Refrains in the Canadian Novels of Margaret Laurence." CENTENNIAL REVIEW, 16 (Sum. 1972), 233-53.

2329 Gibbs, Robert. Introd., A BIRD IN THE HOUSE. New Canadian Library, no. 96. Toronto: McClelland and Stewart, 1974, n. pag.

2330 Githae-Mugo, Micere. VISIONS OF AFRICA: THE FICTION OF CHINUA ACHEBE, MARGARET LAURENCE, ELSPETH HUXLEY AND NGUGI WA THIONG'O. Nairobi: Kenya Literature Bureau, 1978. 198 p.

2331 Gom, Leona M. "Laurence and the Use of Memory." CANADIAN LITERATURE, No. 71 (Wint. 1976), pp. 48-58.

2332 _____. "Margaret Laurence: The Importance of Place." WEST COAST REVIEW, 10 (Oct. 1975), 26-30.

2333 _____. "Margaret Laurence and the First Person." DALHOUSIE REVIEW, 55 (Sum. 1975), 236-51.

2334 Grace, Sherrill E. "Crossing Jordan: Time and Memory in the Fiction of Margaret Laurence." WORLD LITERATURE WRITTEN IN ENGLISH, 16 (Nov. 1977), 328-39.

2335 _____. "A Portrait of the Artist as Laurence Hero." JOURNAL OF CANADIAN STUDIES, 13 (Fall 1978), 64-71.

2336 Hehner, Barbara. "River of Now and Then: Margaret Laurence's Narratives." CANADIAN LITERATURE, No. 74 (Aut. 1977), pp. 40-57.

2337 Hughes, Kenneth James. "Politics and A JEST OF GOD." JOURNAL OF CANADIAN STUDIES, 13 (Fall 1978), 40-54.

2338   Jeffrey, David L. "Biblical Hermeneutic and Family History in Contemporary Canadian Fiction: Wiebe and Laurence." MOSAIC, 11 (Spr. 1978), 87-106.

>Discusses THE STONE ANGEL and THE BLUE MOUNTAINS OF CHINA; parts are incorporated into a longer article in no. 4246.

2339   Johnston, Eleanor. "The Quest of the Diviners." MOSAIC, 11 (Spr. 1978), 107-17.

2340   Kearns, Judy. "Rachel and Social Determinism: A Feminist Reading of A JEST OF GOD." JOURNAL OF CANADIAN FICTION, 27 (1980), 101-23.

2341   Kertzer, J.M. "THE STONE ANGEL: Time and Responsibility." DALHOUSIE REVIEW, 54 (Aut. 1974), 499-509.

2342   Killam, G.D. Introd., A JEST OF GOD. New Canadian Library, no. 111. Toronto: McClelland and Stewart, 1974, n. pag.

2343   _____. Introd., THIS SIDE JORDAN. New Canadian Library, no. 126. Toronto: McClelland and Stewart, 1976, pp. ix-xvii.

2344   Kirkwood, Hilda. "Revolution and Resolution: An Interview with Margaret Laurence." CANADIAN FORUM, 59 (Mar. 1980), 15-18.

2345   Labonté, Ronald N. "Disclosing and Touching: Revaluating the Manawaka World." JOURNAL OF CANADIAN FICTION, 27 (1980), 167-82.

2346   Leney, Jane. "Prospero and Caliban in Laurence's African Fiction." JOURNAL OF CANADIAN FICTION, 27 (1980), 63-80.

2347   Lennox, John Watt. "Manawaka and Deptford: Place and Voice." JOURNAL OF CANADIAN STUDIES, 13 (Fall 1978), 23-29.

2348   Lever, Bernice. "Literature and Canadian Culture: An Interview with Margaret Laurence." ALIVE, No. 41 ([1975]), pp. 18-19.

2349   _____. "Margaret Laurence: Morag Divined." CANADIAN REVIEW, 2 (Sept.-Oct. 1975), 34, 36-37.

2350   _____. "Margaret Laurence, November 20, 1974." WAVES, 3 (Wint. 1975), 4-12.

>An interview.

2351 _____. "Nature Imagery in the Canadian Fiction of Margaret Laurence." ALIVE, No. 41 ([1975]), pp. 20-22.

2352 McCallum, Pam. "Communication and History: Themes in Innis and Laurence." STUDIES IN CANADIAN LITERATURE, 3 (Wint. 1978), 5-16.

Discusses THE DIVINERS.

2353 McLay, Catherine M. "Every Man is an Island: Isolation in A JEST OF GOD." CANADIAN LITERATURE, No. 50 (Aut. 1971), pp. 57-68.

2354 Maesser, Angelika. "Finding the Mother: The Individuation of Laurence's Heroines." JOURNAL OF CANADIAN FICTION, 27 (1980), 151-66.

2355 Mane, Robert. "Pour une Lecture de Margaret Laurence: Les Deux Structures de THE FIRE-DWELLERS." COMMONWEALTH ESSAYS AND STUDIES, 2 (Dec. 1976), 134-49.

2356 Melnyk, George. "Literature Begins with Writer's Craft." QUILL AND QUIRE, 43 (May 1977), 9, 12.

2357 Miner, Valerie. "The Matriarch of Manawaka." SATURDAY NIGHT, 89 (May 1974), 17-20.

2358 Monkman, Leslie. "The Tonnerre Family: Mirrors of Suffering." JOUR-NAL OF CANADIAN FICTION, 27 (1980), 143-50.

2359 Morley, Patricia. "Canada, Africa, Canada: Laurence's Unbroken Journey." JOURNAL OF CANADIAN FICTION, 27 (1980), 81-91.

2360 _____. "The Long Trek Home: Margaret Laurence's Stories." JOURNAL OF CANADIAN STUDIES, 11 (Nov. 1976), 19-26.

2361 _____. MARGARET LAURENCE. Twayne's World Authors Series, 591. Boston: Twayne, 1981. 171 p. Bibliog. Index.

2362 _____. "Margaret Laurence's Early Writing: 'A World in Which Others Have to be Respected.'" JOURNAL OF CANADIAN STUDIES, 13 (Fall 1978), 13-18.

2363 Mortlock, Melanie. "The Religion of Heritage: THE DIVINERS as a Thematic Conclusion to the Manawaka Series." JOURNAL OF CANA-DIAN FICTION, 27 (1980), 132-42.

2364   Nettall, Stephanie. "Margaret Laurence." BOOKS AND BOOKMAN, 9 (Oct. 1963), 27-28.

       An interview.

2365   New, William H. Introd., THE STONE ANGEL. New Canadian Library, no. 59. Toronto: McClelland and Stewart, 1968, pp. iii-x.

       Reprinted in no. 173.

2366   _____. "Text and Subtext: Laurence's 'The Merchant of Heaven.'" JOURNAL OF CANADIAN STUDIES, 13 (Fall 1978), 19-22.

2367   _____, ed. with introd. MARGARET LAURENCE: THE WRITER AND HER CRITICS. Critical Views on Canadian Writers. Toronto: McGraw-Hill Ryerson, 1977. 224 p. Bibliog.

2368   Osachoff, Margaret Gail. "Moral Vision in THE STONE ANGEL." STUDIES IN CANADIAN LITERATURE, 4 (Wint. 1979), 139-53.

2369   Packer, Miriam. "The Dance of Life: THE FIRE DWELLERS." JOURNAL OF CANADIAN FICTION, 27 (1980), 124-31.

2370   Pesando, Frank. "In a Nameless Land: The Use of Apocalyptic Mythology in the Writings of Margaret Laurence." JOURNAL OF CANADIAN FICTION, 2 (Wint. 1973), 53-58.

       Reprinted in no. 171.

2371   Peterman, Michael. "Margaret Laurence." JOURNAL OF CANADIAN STUDIES, 13 (Fall 1978), 1-2, 100-104.

2372   Pollack, Claudette. "The Paradox of THE STONE ANGEL." HUMANITIES ASSOCIATION REVIEW, 27 (Sum. 1976), 267-75.

2373   Pollock, Zailig. "Angel and Bird in THE STONE ANGEL." ENGLISH STUDIES IN CANADA, 2 (Fall 1976), 345-52.

2374   Read, S.E. "The Maze of Life: The Work of Margaret Laurence." CANADIAN LITERATURE, No. 27 (Wint. 1966), pp. 5-14.

       Reprinted in no. 197.

2375   Ricou, Laurence. "Never Cry Wolfe: Benjamin West's THE DEATH OF WOLFE in PROCHAIN ÉPISODE and THE DIVINERS." ESSAYS ON CANADIAN WRITING, No. 20 (Wint. 1980-81), pp. 171-85.

       Discusses Hubert Aquin and Laurence.

2376   Rocard, Marcienne. "Margaret Laurence's Attempt at Audio-Visual
        Fiction." KUNAPIPI, 1, No. 2 (1979), 91-100.

2377   _____. "The Métis in Margaret Laurence's Manawaka Works." ÉTUDES
        CANADIENNES/CANADIAN STUDIES, 5 (1978), 113-17.

2378   Rosengarten, H.J. "Inescapable Bonds." CANADIAN LITERATURE, No.
        35 (Wint. 1968), pp. 99-100.

2379   Russell, K. "Margaret Laurence's Seekers After Grace." CHELSEA
        JOURNAL, 3, No. 5 (1977), 245-48.

2380   Scott, Jamie S. "Redemptive Imagination in Margaret Laurence's Mana-
        waka Fiction." STUDIES IN RELIGION, 9 (1980), 427-40.

2381   Sheppard, June. "June Sheppard Talks with Margaret Laurence." BRANCH-
        ING OUT, Preview Issue, Dec. 1973, pp. 20-21.

2382   Staines, David. Introd., THE DIVINERS. New Canadian Library, no.
        146. Toronto: McClelland and Stewart, 1978, pp. v-xiv.

2383   Stevenson, Warren. "The Myth of Demeter and Persephone in A JEST
        OF GOD." STUDIES IN CANADIAN LITERATURE, 1 (Wint. 1976),
        120-23.

2384   Stratford, Philip. "KAMOURASKA and THE DIVINERS." REVIEW OF
        NATIONAL LITERATURES, 7 (1976), 110-26.

            Reprinted in no. 178.

2385   Swayze, Walter. "The Odyssey of Margaret Laurence." ENGLISH
        QUARTERLY, 3 (Fall 1970), 7-17.

2386   Thomas, Clara. "The Chariot of Ossian: Myth and Manitoba in THE
        DIVINERS." JOURNAL OF CANADIAN STUDIES, 13 (Fall 1978), 55-63.

            Reprinted in no. 171.

2387   _____. "A Conversation about Literature: An Interview with Margaret
        Laurence and Irving Layton." JOURNAL OF CANADIAN FICTION, 1
        (Wint. 1972), 65-68.

2388   _____. Introd., THE TOMORROW-TAMER AND OTHER STORIES. New
        Canadian Library, no. 70. Toronto: McClelland and Stewart, 1970,
        pp. xi-xix.

2389 _____ . THE MANAWAKA WORLD OF MARGARET LAURENCE. Toronto: McClelland and Stewart, 1975. 212 p. Bibliog.

2390 _____ . MARGARET LAURENCE. Canadian Writers, 3. Toronto: McClelland and Stewart, 1969. 64 p.

2391 _____ . "The Novels of Margaret Laurence." STUDIES IN THE NOVEL, 4 (Sum. 1972), 154-64.

2392 _____ . "Proud Lineage: Willa Cather and Margaret Laurence." CANADIAN REVIEW OF AMERICAN STUDIES, 2 (Spr. 1971), 3-12.

2393 _____ . "The Short Stories of Margaret Laurence." WORLD LITERATURE WRITTEN IN ENGLISH, 11 (Apr. 1972), 25-33.

2394 _____ . "The Wild Garden and the Manawaka World." MODERN FICTION STUDIES, 22 (Aut. 1976), 401-11.

2395 Thompson, Anne. "The Wilderness of Pride: Form and Image in THE STONE ANGEL." JOURNAL OF CANADIAN FICTION, 4, No. 3 (1975), 95-110.

2396 Unitt, Doris. "Meeting Margaret Laurence." REVIEW, 3 Oct. 1974, p. 14.

    An interview.

2397 Wigmore, Donnalu. "Margaret Laurence: The Woman Behind the Mask." CHATELAINE, 44 (Feb. 1971), 28-29, 52, 54.

For criticism on Laurence, see also nos. 78, 139, 157, 160, 170-71, 180, 205, 407, 430, 481-82, 628, 662, 687, 1531, 1701, 2197, 2225, 5195-96.

Book Reviews

2398 THIS SIDE JORDAN: BCLQ, 25 (July 1961), 31, 34; CanL, 8 (Spr. 1961), 62-63; CFor, 41 (Apr. 1961), 8-10; HAB, 33 (Apr. 1961), 23; LISTENER, 5 Jan. 1961, p. 43; MONTREALER, 35 (Feb. 1961), 39; NS, 19 Nov. 1960, p. 800; SatR, 10 Dec. 1960, p. 23; TLS, 4 Nov. 1960, p. 705; UTQ, 30 (July 1961), 406-07.

2399 THE TOMORROW-TAMER: Atl, 214 (Sept. 1964), 116; CAB, 39 (Spr. 1964), 10; CanL, 21 (Sum. 1964), 53-55; CanL, 45 (Sum. 1970), 82-84; CFor, 41 (Apr. 1961), 8-10; CFor, 44 (July 1964), 94; CRead, Mar. 1964, pp. 2-3; HM, 229 (July 1964), 100; NewR, 20 June 1964,

p. 19; NYTBR, 14 June 1964, p. 5; SatR, 13 June 1964, p. 25; SPEC-TATOR, 3 Jan. 1964, p. 20; TamR, [31] (Spr. 1964), 92-93; TamR, 55 (3rd Quarter 1970), 91-92, 94; TLS, 25 Oct. 1963, p. 869; UTQ, 34 (July 1965), 375-76.

2400 THE STONE ANGEL: ALPHABET, 10 (July 1965), 85-86; BCLQ, 28 (July 1964), 41, 43-44; CAB, 40 (Aut. 1964), 17; CanL, 21 (Sum. 1964), 53-54; CFor, 44 (Aut. 1964), 117; HM, 229 (July 1964), 100; HudR, 17 (Wint. 1964-65), 608; KRev, 26 (Aut. 1964), 759; LISTENER, 12 Mar. 1964, p. 443; NewR, 20 June 1964, p. 19; NYTBR, 14 June 1964, pp. 5, 33; PROGRESSIVE, 28 (Oct. 1964), 50; SatR, 13 June 1964, pp. 25-26; SPECTATOR, 20 Mar. 1964, p. 394; TamR, [33] (Aut. 1964), 92-94; TLS, 19 Mar. 1964, p. 229; UTQ, 34 (July 1965), 373-75.

2401 A JEST OF GOD: AtlA, 57 (May 1967), 78; BCLQ, 30 (Oct. 1966), 23-25; JCL, 5 (1968), 133-35; LISTENER, 25 Aug. 1966, p. 283; MAC-LEAN'S, 1 Oct. 1966, p. 54; SatN, 81 (Nov. 1966), 57-58; SatR, 27 Aug. 1966, p. 29; SPECTATOR, 8 July 1966, p. 60; TamR, [42] (Wint. 1967), 80-82; UTQ, 36 (July 1967), 382.

2402 THE FIRE-DWELLERS: Atl, 223 (June 1969), 112-13; AtlA, 59 (May 1969), 56; CanL, 43 (Wint. 1970), 91-92; CFor, 49 (July 1969), 87; EQ, 3 (Fall 1970), 7-16; FIDDLEHEAD, 82 (Nov. 1969), 72-73; JCF, 2 (Fall 1973), 114; LISTENER, 1 May 1969, p. 618; MACLEAN'S, 82 (June 1969), 98; MHRev, 11 (July 1969), 124-25; MONTREALER, 43 (June 1969), 9; NY, 31 May 1969, pp. 115-16; NYTBR, 3 Aug. 1969, p. 30; QQ, 76 (Wint. 1969), 722-24; QUARRY, 19 (Spr. 1970), 56; SatN, 84 (May 1969), 38-39; TamR, 52 (3rd Quarter 1969), 76-78; TLS, 22 May 1969, p. 563; UTQ, 39 (July 1970), 344-45.

2403 A BIRD IN THE HOUSE: Atl, 225 (Mar. 1970), 144; CanL, 45 (Sum. 1970), 84; CFor, 50 (Sept. 1970), 221-22; FIDDLEHEAD, 84 (Mar. 1970), 108-11; LIBERTÉ, 12 (July 1970), 85-87; MHRev, 15 (July 1970), 113-14; NYTBR, 19 Apr. 1970, p. 40; SatN, 85 (Aug. 1970), 26-27; SatR, 5 Sept. 1970, p. 28; TamR, 55 (3rd Quarter 1970), 94; WCR, 5 (Oct. 1970), 68-70.

2404 THE DIVINERS: AntigR, 18 (Sum. 1974), 107-08; Atl, 233 (June 1974), 108; BCan, June 1974, p. 7; CAB, 50 (Fall 1974), 26; CanL, 62 (Aut. 1974), 89-91; CanR, 1 (Nov. 1974), 28; CDim, 10 (Mar. 1975), 41-45; CFor, 54 (May 1974), 15-16; CRead, 15 (June 1974), 5-6; DR, 54 (Sum. 1974), 360-63; EC, 1 (1975), 111-15; FIDDLEHEAD, 104 (Wint. 1975), 111-14; IFR, 2 (Jan. 1975), 61-64; JCF, 3, No. 3 (1974), 93-96; MFS, 22 (Aut. 1976), 401; NewR, 27 July 1974, p. 28; NS, 10 Jan. 1975, p. 50; NY, 8 July 1974, p. 79; NYTBR, 23 June 1974, p. 6; OntarioR, 2 (Spr. 1975), 95-97; OpenL, 3rd ser., 2 (Apr. 1975), 125-28; Q&Q, 40, No. 5 (1974), 16-17; QQ, 81 (Wint.

(1974), 639-40; QUARRY, 24 (Wint. 1975), 63-65; TamR, 63 (Oct. 1974), 80-81; TLS, 10 Jan. 1975, p. 29; UTQ, 44 (Sum. 1975), 304; WCR, 10 (June 1975), 44-46.

2405   THE PROPHET'S CAMEL BELL: Atl, 214 (Sept. 1964), 116; CFor, 43 (Feb. 1964), 259; GeoJ, 130 (Mar. 1964), 164; HM, 229 (July 1964), 100; MACLEAN'S, 19 Oct. 1963, pp. 81-82; NYTBR, 28 June 1964, p. 6; PROGRESSIVE, 28 (Oct. 1964), 50; QQ, 71 (Aut. 1964), 456-57; SatN, 79 (Jan. 1964), 25-26; SatR, 13 June 1964, p. 33; TamR, [31] (Spr. 1964), 98; TLS, 6 Sept. 1963, p. 675; UTQ, 33 (July 1964), 431-32.

2406   LONG DRUMS AND CANNONS: Atl, 224 (July 1969), 110; CanL, 42 (Aut. 1969), 91-93; CFor, 48 (Feb. 1969), 249; FIDDLEHEAD, 80 (May 1969), 105-06; JCL, 9 (July 1970), 109-11; JML, 1, No. 2 (1970), 249; TamR, [52] (3rd Quarter 1969), 78-79; TLS, 2 Jan. 1969, p. 8; UTQ, 40 (Sum. 1971), 359-60; WLWE, 20 (Nov. 1971), 116-18.

2407   HEART OF A STRANGER: BCan, 5 (Nov. 1976), 14-15; BCan, 9 (Aug. 1980), 34; CAB, 52 (Spr. 1977), 36; CanL, 67 (Wint. 1976), 87-89; CanL, 71 (Wint. 1976), 2; CanR, 3 (Dec. 1976), 56; CBRA, 1976, p. 221; CFM, 24-25 (Spr. 1977), 163-65; CFor, 56 (Feb. 1977), 54-55; CRead, 17 (Dec. 1976), 6-8; DR, 57 (Sum. 1977), 397-400; Q&Q, 42, No. 15 (1976), 30; SatN, 91 (Nov. 1976), 49-50; UTQ, 46 (Sum. 1977), 477-79.

LEACOCK, STEPHEN (1869-1944)

Canada's internationally known humorist Stephen Leacock was born in Swanmoor, Hampshire, England, and came to Canada, to the Lake Simcoe area of Ontario, at the age of six. He earned a B.A. from the University of Toronto in 1891, a Ph.D. from the University of Chicago in 1903, and taught at Upper Canada College, Toronto, between 1889 and 1899. From 1901 until his reluctant retirement in 1936, he was a professor of economics at McGill University, Montreal, acting as department head from 1908 on.

He received honorary degrees from half a dozen universities as well as the Mark Twain Medal for Humour and, for MY DISCOVERY OF THE WEST, the Governor General's Award. Using his formula of "half a gallon of meiosos with a pint of hyperbole" and tossing in a dash of irony, incongruity, or literary parody when it suits his purpose, Leacock affectionately satirizes human folly.

PRIMARY MATERIAL

Monographs

HUMOR

2408   LITERARY LAPSES: A BOOK OF SKETCHES. Montreal: Gazette Printing, 1910. 125 p.

2409   NONSENSE NOVELS. London: John Lane, 1911. 230 p.

2410   SUNSHINE SKETCHES OF A LITTLE TOWN. London: John Lane, 1912. xii, 264 p.

2411   BEHIND THE BEYOND AND OTHER CONTRIBUTIONS TO HUMAN KNOWL-EDGE. Illus. A.H. Fish. London: John Lane, 1913. 196 p.

2412 ARCADIAN ADVENTURES WITH THE IDLE RICH. London: John Lane, 1914. 310 p.

2413 THE METHODS OF MR. SELLYER: A BOOK STORE STUDY. New York: John Lane, 1914. N. pag.

2414 MY FINANCIAL CAREER AND HOW TO MAKE A MILLION DOLLARS. New York: Winthrop, 1914. 31 p.

2415 NUMBER FIFTY-SIX. New York: Winthrop, 1914. 31 p.

Reprinted from LITERARY LAPSES (no. 2408).

2416 MARIONETTES' CALENDAR 1916: RHYMES. Drawings by A.H. Fish. London: John Lane, 1915. N. pag.

Also published as an engagement book.

2417 MOONBEAMS FROM A LARGER LUNACY. London: John Lane, 1915. 282 p.

2418 "Q.": A FARCE IN ONE ACT. By Stephen Leacock and Basil Macdonald Hastings. New York: S. French, 1915. 23 p.

A play.

2419 FURTHER FOOLISHNESS: SKETCHES AND SATIRES ON THE FOLLIES OF THE DAY. London: John Lane, 1916. 312 p.

2420 MERRY CHRISTMAS. New York: W.E. Rudge, 1917. 15 p.

Reprinted in FRENZIED FICTION (no. 2421).

2421 FRENZIED FICTION. London: John Lane, 1918. 239 p.

2422 THE HOHENZOLLERNS IN AMERICA: WITH THE BOLSHEVIKS IN BERLIN AND OTHER IMPOSSIBILITIES. London: John Lane, 1919. 269 p. Also as THE HOHENZOLLERNS IN AMERICA AND OTHER IMPOSSI-BILITIES. London: John Lane, 1919. 254 p.

2423 WINSOME WINNIE AND OTHER NEW NONSENSE NOVELS. London: John Lane, 1920. 243 p.

2424 THE LETTERS OF SI WHIFFLETREE--FRESHMAN. Ed. Frank D. Genest, pseud. Preface by Stephen Leacock. Illus. G.E. Tremble. Montreal: n.p., 1921. 69 p.

2425 MY DISCOVERY OF ENGLAND. London: John Lane, 1922. 219 p.

2426 COLLEGE DAYS. New York: Dodd, Mead, 1923. vi, 169 p.

2427 OVER THE FOOTLIGHTS, AND OTHER FANCIES. London: John Lane, 1923. vi, 278 p.

2428 STEPHEN LEACOCK. Ed. Peter McArthur. Makers of Canadian Literature. Toronto: Ryerson, 1923. 176 p. Bibliog. Index.

2429 THE GARDEN OF FOLLY. Toronto: S.B. Gundy, 1924. xi, 282 p.

2430 WINNOWED WISDOM: A NEW BOOK OF HUMOUR. New York: Dodd, Mead, 1926. xii, 288 p.

2431 SHORT CIRCUITS. Toronto: Macmillan, 1928. ix, 336 p.

2432 THE IRON MAN & THE TIN WOMAN: WITH OTHER SUCH FUTURITIES: A BOOK OF LITTLE SKETCHES OF TODAY AND TOMORROW. New York: Dodd, Mead, 1929. vi, 309 p.

2433 LAUGH WITH LEACOCK: AN ANTHOLOGY OF THE BEST WORKS OF STEPHEN LEACOCK. New York: Dodd, Mead, 1930. x, 339 p.

2434 THE LEACOCK BOOK: BEING SELECTIONS FROM THE WORKS OF STEPHEN LEACOCK. Arranged with introd. by Ben Travers. London: John Lane, 1930. xx, 248 p.

2435 WET WIT AND DRY HUMOUR: DISTILLED FROM THE PAGES OF STEPHEN LEACOCK. New York: Dodd, Mead, 1931. vi, 260 p.

2436 AFTERNOONS IN UTOPIA: TALES OF THE NEW TIME. Toronto: Macmillan, 1932. vi, 240 p.

2437 THE DRY PICKWICK AND OTHER INCONGRUITIES. London: John Lane, 1932. v, 271 p.

2438 THE PERFECT SALESMAN. Ed. E.V. Knox. New York: Robert M. McBride, 1934. vii, 151 p. Also as STEPHEN LEACOCK. London: Methuen, 1934. vii, 151 p.

2439 FUNNY PIECES: A BOOK OF RANDOM SKETCHES. New York: Dodd, Mead, 1936. viii, 292 p.

2440 HELLEMENTS OF HICKONOMICS IN HICCOUGHS OF VERSE DONE IN OUR SOCIAL PLANNING MILL. New York: Dodd, Mead, 1936. xi, 84 p.

Mainly poetry.

2441 LAUGHTER & WISDOM OF STEPHEN LEACOCK: BEING TWO VOLUMES IN ONE: THE DRY PICKWICK AND WINNOWED WISDOM. London: John Lane, 1936. 271, xiv, 264 p.

2442 THE LEACOCK LAUGHTER BOOK CONTAINING SHORT CIRCUITS, AFTERNOONS IN UTOPIA. London: John Lane, 1936. 336, 240 p.

2443 HERE ARE MY LECTURES AND STORIES. New York: Dodd, Mead, 1937. x, 251 p.

2444 MODEL MEMOIRS AND OTHER SKETCHES FROM SIMPLE TO SERIOUS. New York: Dodd, Mead, 1938. viii, 316 p.

2445 LAUGH PARADE: A NEW COLLECTION OF THE WIT AND HUMOR OF STEPHEN LEACOCK. New York: Dodd, Mead, 1940. viii, 326 p.

2446 MY REMARKABLE UNCLE AND OTHER SKETCHES. New York: Dodd, Mead, 1942. vi, 313 p.

2447 HAPPY STORIES: JUST TO LAUGH AT. New York: Dodd, Mead, 1943. viii, 240 p.

2448 MEMORIES OF CHRISTMAS. Toronto: Privately printed, Charles Bush, 1943. 29 p.

Two Christmas essays from MY REMARKABLE UNCLE (no. 2446).

2449 LAST LEAVES. [Preface by Barbara Nimmo.] Toronto: McClelland and Stewart, 1945. xxi, 213 p.

2450 THE LEACOCK ROUNDABOUT: A TREASURY OF THE BEST WORKS OF STEPHEN LEACOCK. New York: Dodd, Mead, 1946. vii, 422 p.

2451 THE BODLEY HEAD LEACOCK. Ed. with introd. by J.B. Priestley. London: Bodley Head, 1957. 464 p. Also as THE BEST OF LEACOCK. Toronto: McClelland and Stewart, 1957. 464 p.

2452 THE UNICORN LEACOCK. Ed. James Reeves. Illus. Franciszka Themerson. London: Hutchinson Educational, 1960. 191 p.

2453 CAROLINE'S CHRISTMAS. Toronto: Cooper and Beatty, 1969. 11 p.

Reprinted from NONSENSE NOVELS (no. 2409).

2454 HOODO McFIGGIN'S CHRISTMAS. Toronto: Cooper and Beatty, 1970. N. pag.

Reprinted from NONSENSE NOVELS (no. 2409).

2455 A BOOK OF RIDICULOUS STORIES. Little Blue Book, no. 1115. Girard, Kans.: Haldeman-Julius, [1975]. 64 p.

2456 ESSAYS OF SERIOUS SPOOFING. Little Blue Book, No. 1120. Girard, Kans.: Haldeman-Julius, [1975]. 64 p.

2457 A BOOK OF FUNNY DRAMATICS. Little Blue Book, No. 1116. Girard, Kans.: [Haldeman-Julius], n.d. 64 p.

2458 FOLLIES IN FICTION. Little Blue Book, no. 1119. Girard, Kans.: Haldeman-Julius, n.d. 63 p.

2459 THE HUMAN ANIMAL AND HIS FOLLY. Little Blue Book, No. 1117. Girard, Kans.: Haldeman-Julius, n.d. 62 p.

2460 MY MEMORIES AND MISERIES AS A SCHOOLMASTER. Illus. C.W. Jefferys. Toronto: Upper Canada College Endowment Fund, n.d. 15 p.

Also in COLLEGE DAYS (no. 2426).

2461 THIS LIFE AS I SEE IT. Little Blue Book, no. 1118. Girard, Kans.: [Haldeman-Julius], n.d. 64 p.

For humor by Leacock, see also no. 1295.

Other Works

2462 "The Doctrine of Laissez Faire." Diss., University of Chicago, 1903.

2463 ELEMENTS OF POLITICAL SCIENCE. Boston: Houghton Mifflin, 1906. ix, 417 p. Index.

2464 BALDWIN, LAFONTAINE, HINCKS: RESPONSIBLE GOVERNMENT. Makers of Canada. Toronto: G.N. Morang, 1907. xii, 371 p. Rev. enl. ed. MACKENZIE, BALDWIN, LA FONTAINE, HINCKS. Illus. A. G. Doughty. Makers of Canada. London: Oxford University Press, 1926. x, 395 p.

2465　GREATER CANADA, AN APPEAL: LET US NO LONGER BE A COLONY. Montreal: Montreal News, 1907. 10 p.

2466　TRADE AND COMMERCE. By Simon Litman, Stephen Leacock et al. Business Administration: Theory, Practice and Application, vol. 4. Chicago: Lasalle Extension University, 1910-11. 492 p.

2467　THE GREAT VICTORY IN CANADA. London: n.p., [1911]. 12 p.

2468　ADVENTURES OF THE FAR NORTH: A CHRONICLE OF THE FROZEN SEAS. Chronicles of Canada, 20. Toronto: Glasgow, Brook, 1914. xi, 152 p.

2469　THE DAWN OF CANADIAN HISTORY: A CHRONICLE OF ABORIGINAL CANADA AND THE COMING OF THE WHITE MAN. Chronicles of Canada, 1. Toronto: Glasgow, Brook, 1914. xii, 112 p.

2470　THE MARINER OF ST. MALO: A CHRONICLE OF THE VOYAGES OF JACQUES CARTIER. Chronicles of Canada, 2. Toronto: Glasgow, Brook, 1914. xi, 125 p.

2471　THE TRUTH ABOUT PROHIBITION FROM THE VIEWPOINT OF AN EMINENT PROFESSOR. New York: Allied Printing Trades Council, [1915]. 8 p.

2472　ESSAYS AND LITERARY STUDIES. London: John Lane, 1916. 253 p.

2473　NATIONAL ORGANIZATION FOR WAR. Ottawa: King's Printer, 1917. 11 p.

2474　BAGDAD ON THE SUBWAY. [New York: n.p., 192-]. 21 p.

2475　HOW MR. BELLAMY LOOKED BACKWARDS. . . . Milwaukee: American Constitutional League of Wisconsin, 1920. 31 p.
　　　　Also in THE UNSOLVED RIDDLE OF SOCIAL JUSTICE (no. 2476).

2476　THE UNSOLVED RIDDLE OF SOCIAL JUSTICE. London: John Lane, 1920. 152 p.

2477　THE GOLD STANDARD: AN ADDRESS DELIVERED BEFORE THE 1924 LIFE INSURANCE EDUCATIONAL CONGRESS HELD AT TORONTO, ONTARIO. N.p.: n.p., [1924]. 11 p.

2478 THE PROPER LIMITATIONS OF STATE INTERFERENCE. Toronto: n.p., 1924. 14 p.

2479 ECONOMIC PROSPERITY IN THE BRITISH EMPIRE. Toronto: Macmillan, 1930. vii, 245 p.

2480 BACK TO PROSPERITY: THE GREAT OPPORTUNITY OF THE EMPIRE CONFERENCE. New York: Macmillan, 1932. 108 p.

2481 MARK TWAIN. London: Peter Davies, 1932. 167 p. Bibliog.

2482 CHARLES DICKENS: HIS LIFE AND WORK. London: Peter Davies, 1933. viii, 275 p.

2483 STEPHEN LEACOCK'S PLAN TO RELIEVE IN DEPRESSION IN 6 DAYS, TO REMOVE IT IN 6 MONTHS, TO ERADICATE IT IN 6 YEARS. Toronto: Macmillan, 1933. 18 p.

2484 LINCOLN FREES THE SLAVES. New York: G.P. Putnam's Sons, 1934. 178 p.

2485 THE PURSUIT OF KNOWLEDGE: A DISCUSSION OF FREEDOM AND COMPULSION IN EDUCATION. New York: Liveright, 1934. 48 p.

2486 THE GATHERING FINANCIAL CRISIS IN CANADA: A SURVEY OF THE PRESENT CRITICAL SITUATION. Toronto: Macmillan, 1936. 24 p.

2487 HUMOUR AND HUMANITY: AN INTRODUCTION TO THE STUDY OF HUMOUR. London: Thornton Butterworth, 1937. 254 p.

2488 MY DISCOVERY OF THE WEST: A DISCUSSION OF EAST AND WEST IN CANADA. Toronto: Thomas Allen, 1937. 272 p.

2489 WHAT NICKEL MEANS TO THE WORLD. Toronto: n.p., 1937. 25 p.

2490 ALL RIGHT, MR. ROOSEVELT (CANADA AND THE UNITED STATES). New York: Farrar and Rinehart, 1939. 40 p.

2491 TOO MUCH COLLEGE, OR EDUCATION EATING UP LIFE: WITH KIN-DRED ESSAYS IN EDUCATION AND HUMOUR. New York: Dodd, Mead, 1939. ix, 255 p.

2492 OUR BRITISH EMPIRE: ITS STRUCTURE, ITS HISTORY, ITS STRENGTH. London: John Lane, 1940. 280 p. Index. Also as THE BRITISH

EMPIRE: ITS STRUCTURE, ITS UNITY, ITS STRENGTH. New York: Dodd, Mead, 1940. vi, 263 p. Index.

2493 CANADA: THE FOUNDATIONS OF ITS FUTURE. Illus. by Canadian Artists. Montreal: Privately printed, [1941]. xxx, 257 p. Index.

2494 MONTREAL: SEAPORT AND CITY. Doubleday, Doran Seaport Series, no. 7. Garden City, N.Y.: Doubleday, Doran, 1942. xi, 340 p. Rev. ed. LEACOCK'S MONTREAL. Ed. John Culliton. Toronto: Mc-Clelland and Stewart, 1963. xx, 332 p.

2495 OUR HERITAGE OF LIBERTY: ITS ORIGINS, ITS ACHIEVEMENT, ITS CRISIS: A BOOK FOR WAR TIME. London: John Lane, [1942]. 75 p.

2496 HOW TO WRITE. New York: Dodd, Mead, 1943. vii, 261 p. Index.

2497 MY OLD COLLEGE, 1843-1943. [Montreal]: Privately printed, 1943. 16 p.

2498 CANADA AND THE SEA. Canada's War at Sea: In Two Volumes. Montreal: Alvah M. Beatty, 1944. I, 74 p. Index.

2499 WHILE THERE IS TIME: THE CASE AGAINST SOCIAL CATASTROPHE. Toronto: McClelland and Stewart, 1945. 136 p.

2500 THE BOY I LEFT BEHIND ME. Garden City, N.Y.: Doubleday, 1946. 184 p.

Autobiography.

2501 OTHER PEOPLE'S MONEY: AN OUTSIDE VIEW OF TRUSTS AND IN-VESTMENTS. [Montreal]: Royal Trust, 1947. 21 p.

2502 SELECTED WRITINGS OF STEPHEN LEACOCK: EDUCATION AND LIVING. Image of America, 4. New York: Tyrex, 1960. 31 p.

2503 THE SOCIAL CRITICISM OF STEPHEN LEACOCK: THE UNSOLVED RIDDLE OF SOCIAL JUSTICE AND OTHER ESSAYS. Ed. with introd. by Alan Bowker. Social History of Canada. Toronto: University of Toronto Press, 1973. xlviii, 145 p. Bibliog.

2504 BRITISH AND CANADIAN GOVERNMENTS. N.p.: n.p., n.d. 12 p.

EDITED WORK

2505   LAHONTAN'S VOYAGES. Ed. with introd. and notes by Stephen Leacock. Ottawa: Graphic, 1932. xvi, 348 p.

2506   THE GREATEST PAGES OF CHARLES DICKENS: A BIOGRAPHICAL READER AND A CHRONOLOGICAL SELECTION FROM THE WORKS OF DICKENS WITH A COMMENTARY ON HIS LIFE AND ART. Garden City, N.Y.: Doubleday, Doran, 1934. viii, 233 p.

2507   HUMOR: ITS THEORY AND TECHNIQUE, WITH EXAMPLES AND SAMPLES: A BOOK OF DISCOVERY. Toronto: Dodd, Mead, 1935. v, 268 p.

2508   THE GREATEST PAGES OF AMERICAN HUMOR: SELECTED AND DISCUSSED BY STEPHEN LEACOCK: A STUDY OF THE RISE AND DEVELOPMENT OF HUMOROUS WRITINGS IN AMERICA WITH SELECTIONS FROM THE MOST NOTABLE OF THE HUMORISTS. Garden City, N.Y.: Doubleday, Doran, 1936. viii, 293 p.

Shorter Work

ARTICLES

2509   "Humor as I See It and Something about Humor in Canada." MACLEAN'S, 29 (May 1916), 11-13, 111-13.

2510   "O. Henry and His Critics." NEW REPUBLIC, 2 Dec. 1916, pp. 120-22.

2511   "Edwin Drood is Alive." BELLMAN, 15 June 1918, pp. 655-62.

2512   "Stories and Storytellers." OUTLOOK, 1 Feb. 1922, pp. 183-84.

2513   "Drama as I See It: Studies in the Plays and Films of Yesterday and Today." HARPER'S, 146 (Feb. 1923), 290-306; (Mar. 1923), 430-39; (Apr. 1923), 567-75; (May 1923), 723-32; 147 (June 1923), 7-16; (July 1923), 178-87.

2514   "Two Humorists: Charles Dickens and Mark Twain." YALE REVIEW, NS 24 (Sept. 1934), 118-29.

2515   "Mark Twain and Canada." QUEEN'S QUARTERLY, 42 (Spr. 1935), 68-81.

2516 Preface, MARK TWAIN: WIT AND WISDOM. Ed. Cyril Clemens. New York: Fred A. Stokes, 1935, pp. vii-viii.

2517 "Emigration in English Literature." QUARTERLY REVIEW, 270 (Apr. 1938), 204-20.

2518 "Andrew MacPhail." QUEEN'S QUARTERLY, 45 (Wint. 1938), 445-52.

2519 "Charles Dickens and Canada." QUEEN'S QUARTERLY, 46 (Spr. 1939), 28-37.

For articles by Leacock, see also nos. 192 and 1450.

Manuscripts

2520 McGill University Library, Montreal; Metropolitan Toronto Central Library; Orillia Public Library, Orillia, Ont.; Public Archives of Canada, Ottawa; Queen's University Library, Kingston, Ont.; St. Francis Xavier University Library, Sydney, N.S.; Stephen Leacock Memorial Museum, Orillia, Ont.; University of British Columbia Library, Vancouver.

SECONDARY MATERIAL

Bibliographies

2521 Curry, Ralph Leighton, comp. "Stephen Butler Leacock: A Check-List." BULLETIN OF BIBLIOGRAPHY, 22 (Jan.-Apr. 1958), 106-09.

   A supplement to no. 2522.

2522 Lomer, Gerhard R., comp. STEPHEN LEACOCK: A CHECK-LIST AND INDEX OF HIS WRITINGS. Ottawa: National Library of Canada, 1954. 153 p. Index.

2523 McGill University. Library School. A BIBLIOGRAPHY OF STEPHEN BUTLER LEACOCK COMPILED BY THE CLASS OF 1935 UNDER THE DIRECTION OF MARION VILLIERS HIGGINS. Montreal: McGill Library, 1935. 31 p. Index.

2524 "Select Bibliography of Stephen Leacock's Contributions to the Social Sciences." CANADIAN JOURNAL OF ECONOMICS AND POLITICAL SCIENCE, 10 (May 1944), 228-30.

Criticism

2525   Allen, Carleton Kemp. OH, MR. LEACOCK. London: John Lane, 1925. 113 p.

2526   Beharriel, S. Ross. Introd., NONSENSE NOVELS. New Canadian Library, no. 35. Toronto: McClelland and Stewart, 1963, pp. vii-xii.

2527   Berger, Carl. "The Other Mr. Leacock." CANADIAN LITERATURE, No. 55 (Wint. 1973), pp. 23-40.

2528   Bissell, Claude. "Haliburton, Leacock and the American Humourous [sic] Tradition." CANADIAN LITERATURE, No. 39 (Wint. 1969), pp. 5-19.

2529   Bush, Douglas. "Stephen Leacock." In THE CANADIAN IMAGINA-TION: DIMENSIONS OF A LITERARY CULTURE. Ed. David Staines. Cambridge: Harvard University Press, 1977, pp. 123-51.

2530   Cameron, Donald A. "The Enchanted Houses: Leacock's Irony." CA-NADIAN LITERATURE, No. 23 (Wint. 1965), pp. 31-44.

       Discusses SUNSHINE SKETCHES; reprinted in no. 5113.

2531   _____. FACES OF LEACOCK: AN APPRECIATION. Toronto: Ryerson, 1967. 176 p. Bibliog.

2532   _____. Introd., BEHIND THE BEYOND. New Canadian Library, no. 67. Toronto: McClelland and Stewart, 1969, pp. v-viii.

2533   _____. "Stephen Leacock: The Boy Behind the Arras." JOURNAL OF CANADIAN LITERATURE, No. 3 (July 1967), pp. 3-18.

2534   _____. "Stephen Leacock: The Novelist Who Never Was." DALHOUSIE REVIEW, 46 (Spr. 1966), 15-28.

2535   Clever, Glenn. "Leacock's DUNCIAD." STUDIES IN CANADIAN LIT-ERATURE, 1 (Sum. 1976), 238-41.

       Discusses ARCADIAN ADVENTURES.

2536   Cole, D.W. Introd., FURTHER FOOLISHNESS. New Canadian Library, no. 60. Toronto: McClelland and Stewart, 1968, pp. v-xii.

2537   Collins, John Philip. "Professor Leacock, Ph.D.: Savant and Humorist." BOOKMAN (London), 51 (Nov. 1916), 39-44.

2538   Curry, Ralph Leighton. Introd., ARCADIAN ADVENTURES WITH THE
        IDLE RICH. New Canadian Library, no. 10. Toronto: McClelland
        and Stewart, 1959, pp. vii-xi.

2539   _____. "Leacock and Benchley: An Acknowledged Literary Debt."
        AMERICAN BOOK COLLECTOR, 7 (Mar. 1957), 11-15.

2540   _____. STEPHEN LEACOCK: HUMORIST AND HUMANIST. Garden
        City, N.Y.: Doubleday, 1959. 383 p. Index.

2541   Curry, Ralph Leighton, and Janet Lewis. "Stephen Leacock: An Early
        Influence on F. Scott Fitzgerald." CANADIAN REVIEW OF AMERICAN
        STUDIES, 7 (Spr. 1976), 5-14.

2542   Dooley, David Joseph. Introd., FRENZIED FICTION. New Canadian
        Library, no. 48. Toronto: McClelland and Stewart, 1965, pp. vii-xiii.

2543   _____. Introd., SHORT CIRCUITS. New Canadian Library, no. 57.
        Toronto: McClelland and Stewart, [1967], pp. ix-xiv.

2544   Edgar, Pelham. "Stephen Leacock." QUEEN'S QUARTERLY, 53 (Sum.
        1946), 173-84.
            Reprinted in nos. 192 and 4518.

2545   Ewart, John S. "A Perplexed Imperialist." QUEEN'S QUARTERLY, 15
        (Oct. 1907), 90-100.

2546   Feibleman, James K. "Criticism of Modern Theories of Comedy." In
        his IN PRAISE OF COMEDY: A STUDY IN ITS THEORY AND PRACTICE.
        London: Allen and Unwin, 1939, pp. 123-67.

2547   Ferris, Ina. "The Face in the Window: SUNSHINE SKETCHES Recon-
        sidered." STUDIES IN CANADIAN LITERATURE, 3 (Sum. 1978), 178-85.
            See no. 2554.

2548   Innis, Harold Adams. "Stephen Butler Leacock (1869-1944)." CANA-
        DIAN JOURNAL OF ECONOMICS AND POLITICAL SCIENCE, 10 (May
        1944), 216-26.

2549   Kimball, Elizabeth. THE MAN IN THE PANAMA HAT: REMINISCENCES
        OF MY UNCLE, STEPHEN LEACOCK. Toronto: McClelland and Stewart,
        1970. 174 p.

2550   Kushner, J., and R.D. MacDonald. "Leacock: Economist/Satirist in

ARCADIAN ADVENTURES and SUNSHINE SKETCHES." DALHOUSIE
REVIEW, 56 (Aut. 1976), 493-509.

2551   Legate, David M. STEPHEN LEACOCK: A BIOGRAPHY. Toronto:
Doubleday, 1970. 296 p. Bibliog. Index.

2552   Lower, Arthur. "The Mariposa Belle." QUEEN'S QUARTERLY, 58 (Sum.
1951), 220-26.

2553   Lucas, Alec. "Leacock Writes for TRUTH." STUDIES IN CANADIAN
LITERATURE, 1 (Sum. 1976), 254-58.

2554   MacLulich, T.D. "Mariposa Revisited." STUDIES IN CANADIAN LIT-
ERATURE, 4 (Wint. 1979), 167-76.

        A reply to no. 2547.

2555   Magee, William H. "Genial Humour in Stephen Leacock." DALHOUSIE
REVIEW, 56 (Sum. 1976), 268-82.

2556   _____. "Stephen Leacock: Local Colourist." CANADIAN LITERATURE,
No. 39 (Wint. 1969), pp. 34-42.

2557   Mantz, Douglas. "The Preposterous and the Profound: A New Look at
the Envoi of SUNSHINE SKETCHES." JOURNAL OF CANADIAN FIC-
TION, No. 19 (1977), pp. 95-105.

        Reprinted in no. 172.

2558   Marshall, Tom A. "False Pastoral: Stephen Leacock's Conflicting Worlds."
JOURNAL OF CANADIAN FICTION, No. 19 (1977), pp. 86-94.

        Discusses ARCADIAN ADVENTURES.

2559   Mikes, George. "Stephen Leacock." In his EIGHT HUMORISTS. London:
Wingate, 1954, pp. 41-65.

2560   Pacey, Desmond. "Leacock as a Satirist." QUEEN'S QUARTERLY, 58
(Sum. 1951), 208-19.

        Reprinted in no. 177.

2561   Robinson, J.M. Introd., LAST LEAVES. New Canadian Library, no.
69. Toronto: McClelland and Stewart, 1970, pp. vi-xii.

2562   Ross, Malcolm. Introd., SUNSHINE SKETCHES OF A LITTLE TOWN.
New Canadian Library, no. 15. Toronto: McClelland and Stewart,
1960, pp. ix-xi.

2563 Savage, David. "Leacock on Survival: SUNSHINE SKETCHES Sixty
      Years After." JOURNAL OF CANADIAN FICTION, 1 (Fall 1972),
      64-67.

2564 _____. "Leacock's Lectures at McGill." CANADIAN NOTES AND
      QUERIES, No. 12 (1973), p. 13.

2565 Sedgewick, G.G. "Stephen Leacock as Man of Letters." UNIVERSITY
      OF TORONTO QUARTERLY, 15 (Oct. 1945), 17-26.

2566 Sharman, Vincent. "The Satire of Stephen Leacock's SUNSHINE SKETCHES."
      QUEEN'S QUARTERLY, 78 (Sum. 1971), 261-67.

2567 Spettigue, Douglas. "A Partisan Reading of Leacock." LITERARY HALF-
      YEARLY, 13 (July 1972), 171-80.

2568 Stevens, John. Introd., MY REMARKABLE UNCLE AND OTHER SKETCHES.
      New Canadian Library, no. 53. Toronto: McClelland and Stewart,
      1965, pp. vii-xii.

2569 Watt, Frank W. "Critic or Entertainer? Stephen Leacock and the Growth
      of Materialism." CANADIAN LITERATURE, No. 5 (Sum. 1960), pp. 33-42.

2570 Watters, Ronald Eyre. "A Special Tang: Stephen Leacock's Canadian
      Humour." CANADIAN LITERATURE, No. 5 (Sum. 1960), pp. 21-32.

2571 Whalley, George. Introd., MY DISCOVERY OF ENGLAND. New Ca-
      nadian Library, no. 28. Toronto: McClelland and Stewart, 1961, pp.
      vii-xiv.

For criticism on Leacock, see also nos. 139, 158, 182, 1295, 1303-04, 1314,
2434, 2449, 2451, 2503, 3526, and especially 1277.

Book Reviews

2572 LITERARY LAPSES: SPECTATOR, 9 July 1910, p. 61.

2573 NONSENSE NOVELS: ATHENAEUM, 8 July 1911, p. 43; MONTREALER,
      37 (Sept. 1963), 40; NATION, 24 Aug. 1911, p. 165; NYTSR, 1 Oct.
      1911, p. 591; SPECTATOR, 27 May 1911, p. 816.

2574 SUNSHINE SKETCHES OF A LITTLE TOWN: BCan, 2 (Apr. 1973), 33;
      DR, 40 (Wint. 1960-61), 583; NYTSR, 29 Sept. 1912, p. 540; SPEC-
      TATOR, 24 Aug. 1912, p. 277.

2575 BEHIND THE BEYOND: CanL, 41 (Sum. 1969), 142; MACLEAN'S, 27 (Apr. 1914), 110-12; NYTBR, 9 Nov. 1913, p. 614; SPECTATOR, 15 Nov. 1913, p. 828.

2576 ARCADIAN ADVENTURES WITH THE IDLE RICH: ATHENAEUM, 23 Jan. 1915, p. 68; DR, 40 (Spr. 1960), 133; NATION, 17 Dec. 1914, p. 715; NYTBR, 13 Dec. 1914, p. 569; SatR, 19 Dec. 1914, p. 635; SPEC-TATOR, 28 Nov. 1914, p. 753.

2577 MOONBEAMS FROM A LARGER LUNACY: NATION, 18 Nov. 1915, p. 601; NYTBR, 12 Dec. 1915, p. 511; NYTBR, 16 Jan. 1916, p. 20; SPECTATOR, 11 Dec. 1915, p. 836.

2578 FURTHER FOOLISHNESS: NYTBR, 31 Dec. 1916, p. 580.

2579 FRENZIED FICTION: NYTBR, 23 Dec. 1917, p. 573.

2580 THE HOHENZOLLERNS IN AMERICA: NYTBR, 1 June 1919, p. 310; SatR, 26 July 1919, p. 84; SPECTATOR, 26 July 1919, p. 120; TLS, 10 July 1919, p. 375.

2581 WINSOME WINNIE: CFor, 1 (Feb. 1921), 154; NYTBR, 19 Dec. 1920, p. 11; TLS, 2 Dec. 1920, p. 795.

2582 MY DISCOVERY OF ENGLAND: CFor, 2 (Aug. 1922), 728, 730; NATION, 16 Aug. 1922, pp. 171-72; Nation&A, 15 July 1922, p. 357; QQ, 30 (Aug. 1962), 109-10; SatR, 24 July 1922, p. 658; SPEC-TATOR, 29 July 1922, p. 146; TLS, 22 June 1922, p. 409.

2583 COLLEGE DAYS: TLS, 22 Nov. 1923, p. 788.

2584 OVER THE FOOTLIGHTS: NS, 11 Aug. 1923, p. 528; NYTBR, 29 July 1923, p. 2; SPECTATOR, 11 Aug. 1923, p. 198; TLS, 28 June 1923, p. 438.

2585 THE GARDEN OF FOLLY: Nation&A, 12 Apr. 1924, p. 626; NS, 13 Sept. 1924, p. 656; NYTBR, 10 Aug. 1924, p. 5; SatR, 9 Aug. 1924, p. 30; SatR, 13 Sept. 1924, p. 268; TLS, 7 Aug. 1924, p. 486.

2586 WINNOWED WISDOM: NS, 31 July 1925, p. 445; NYTBR, 4 July 1926, p. 16; SatR, 26 June 1926, p. 884; SPECTATOR, 19 June 1926, p. 1054; TLS, 24 June 1926, p. 434.

2587 SHORT CIRCUITS: NS, 28 July 1928, p. 522; NYTBR, 22 July 1928, p. 12; SatR, 28 July 1928, p. 11.

2588 THE IRON MAN & THE TIN WOMAN: NYTBR, 8 Dec. 1929, p. 42; SPECTATOR, 30 Nov. 1929, p. 827; TLS, 5 Dec. 1929, p. 1030.

2589 LAUGH WITH LEACOCK: NYTBR, 19 Oct. 1930, p. 28.

2590 AFTERNOONS IN UTOPIA: NYTBR, 25 Sept. 1932, p. 12; SatR, 19 Nov. 1932, p. 536; TLS, 24 Nov. 1932, p. 884.

2591 THE PERFECT SALESMAN: NYTBR, 2 Sept. 1934, p. 18.

2592 FUNNY PIECES: NYTBR, 29 Nov. 1936, p. 6.

2593 HELLEMENTS OF HICKONOMICS: POETRY, 50 (July 1937), 211.

2594 HERE ARE MY LECTURES AND STORIES: NYTBR, 2 Jan. 1938, p. 4.

2595 MODEL MEMOIRS: NYTBR, 11 Dec. 1938, p. 2; SatR, 14 Jan. 1939, p. 10; UTQ, 8 (Apr. 1939), 325-26.

2596 LAUGH PARADE: NYTBR, 8 Dec. 1940, p. 39; UTQ, 10 (Apr. 1941), 325.

2597 MY REMARKABLE UNCLE: NYTBR, 8 Mar. 1942, p. 4; SatR, 4 Apr. 1942, p. 6; TLS, 25 July 1942, p. 370; UTQ, 12 (Apr. 1943), 368.

2598 HAPPY STORIES: NYTBR, 23 Jan. 1944, p. 21.

2599 LAST LEAVES: NYTBR, 30 Sept. 1945, p. 4; RUL, 5 (Oct. 1950), 172-74; SatR, 20 Oct. 1945, p. 28; UTQ, 15 (Apr. 1946), 298-300.

2600 THE LEACOCK ROUNDABOUT: NYTBR, 15 Dec. 1946, p. 24; SatN, 18 Jan. 1947, p. 20; SatR, 28 Dec. 1946, p. 17.

2601 THE BODLEY HEAD LEACOCK: SPECTATOR, 6 Dec. 1957, p. 808.

2602 ESSAYS AND LITERARY STUDIES: NATION, 18 May 1916, p. 546; SatR, 15 Aug. 1916, p. 137; SPECTATOR, 15 July 1916, pp. 76-77; TLS, 6 July 1916, p. 318.

2603 MARK TWAIN: AmR, 1 (June 1933), 363-67; NewR, 29 Mar. 1933, p. 191; SPECTATOR, 6 Jan. 1933, p. 26; TLS, 24 Nov. 1932, p. 886.

2604   CHARLES DICKENS: AmR, 2 (Mar. 1934), 625-29; CFor, 14 (Apr. 1934),
        268-69; NATION, 7 Feb. 1934, p. 161; NewR, 9 May 1934, p. 369;
        NS&N, 6 Jan. 1934, p. 18; SatR, 13 Jan. 1934, p. 405; TLS, 7 Dec.
        1933, p. 873; VQR, 10 (July 1934), 455-59.

2605   HUMOUR AND HUMANITY: CFor, 18 (Jan. 1939), 322; COMMON-
        WEAL, 8 Apr. 1938, p. 668; NYTBR, 13 Mar. 1938, pp. 2, 32; TLS,
        18 Dec. 1937, p. 961.

2606   TOO MUCH COLLEGE: NYTBR, 26 Nov. 1939, p. 22; SatN, 16
        Dec. 1939, p. 21; UTQ, 9 (Apr. 1940), 331-32.

2607   HOW TO WRITE: SatN, 23 Jan. 1943, p. 20; SatR, 6 Feb. 1943,
        p. 8; TLS, 30 Sept. 1944, p. 475; UTQ, 13 (Apr. 1944), 360-61.

2608   THE BOY I LEFT BEHIND ME: CHR, 27 (Dec. 1946), 441-42; SatR,
        23 Feb. 1946, p. 17; TLS, 10 Jan. 1948, p. 16; UTQ, 15 (Apr. 1946),
        300.

2609   THE SOCIAL CRITICISM OF STEPHEN LEACOCK: ARCS, 3, No. 2
        (1973), 128; CanL, 62 (Aut. 1974), 105-07; CHR, 57 (June 1976),
        208-10; CJPS, 8 (Dec. 1975), 563-64.

LOWRY, MALCOLM (1909-57)

Malcolm Lowry is a significant British novelist who spent much of the last third of his life in Canada. Born in Merseyside, Cheshire, England, he travelled as cabin boy on a freighter before completing a degree at Cambridge in 1932. After living in France and the United States, and visiting Mexico, he settled as a beach squatter at Dollerton on the British Columbia coast where he stayed until 1954, with periodic forays to Mexico, Europe, and the United States. In the midst of a tumultuous life complicated by alcoholism, he died from an overdose of barbiturates in Sussex, England.

Best known for his powerful and disturbing novel UNDER THE VOLCANO, completed while at Dollerton, Lowry, particularly in OCTOBER FERRY TO GABRIOLA and "The Forest Path to the Spring" (in HEAR US, O LORD), also wrote fiction reflecting his experiences in British Columbia. HEAR US, O LORD won the 1961 Governor General's Award.

PRIMARY MATERIAL

Monographs

FICTION

2610   ULTRAMARINE: A NOVEL. London: Jonathan Cape, 1933. 275 p.
Rev. ed. Introd. M.B. Lowry. London: Jonathan Cape, 1963. 203 p.

2611   UNDER THE VOLCANO. New York: Reynal and Hitchcock, 1947.
375 p.

2612   HEAR US, O LORD, FROM HEAVEN THY DWELLING PLACE. Philadelphia: J.B. Lippincott, 1961. 283 p.

Short stories.

2613   DARK AS THE GRAVE WHEREIN MY FRIEND IS LAID. Ed. Douglas
        Day and Margerie Lowry. Toronto: General Publishing, 1968. xxiii,
        255 p.

2614   LUNAR CAUSTIC. Ed. Earle Birney and Margerie Lowry. Foreword by
        Conrad Knickerbocker. London: Jonathan Cape, 1968. 78 p. Bibliog.

2615   OCTOBER FERRY TO GABRIOLA. Ed. Margerie Lowry. New York:
        World Publishing, 1970. 338 p.

2616   CHINA, AND KRISTBJORG'S STORY IN THE BLACK HILLS. New York:
        Aloe, 1974. N. pag.

        Reprinted in PSALMS AND SONGS.

2617   MALCOLM LOWRY: PSALMS AND SONGS. Ed. Margerie Lowry.
        New York: New American Library, 1975. xii, 308 p. Bibliog.

        Includes short stories by Lowry and criticism about him.

NONFICTION PROSE

2618   SELECTED LETTERS. Ed. Harvey Breit and Margerie Bonner Lowry. Phila-
        delphia: J.B. Lippincott, 1965. xix, 459 p.

2619   NOTES ON A SCREENPLAY FOR F. SCOTT FITZGERALD'S TENDER IS
        THE NIGHT. By Malcolm Lowry and Margerie Bonner Lowry. Introd.
        Paul Tiessen. Bloomfield Hills, Mich.: B. Clark, 1976. xix, 84 p.

POETRY

2620   SELECTED POEMS OF MALCOLM LOWRY. Ed. Earle Birney and Margerie
        Lowry. Pocket Poets Series, no. 17. San Francisco: City Lights, 1962.
        79 p. Rev. ed. San Francisco: City Lights, 1963. 79 p.

Shorter Work

SHORT STORIES

2621   "In Le Havre." LIFE AND LETTERS, 10 (July 1934), 462-66.

2622   "The Element Follows You Around, Sir." SHOW MAGAZINE, 4 (Mar.
        1964), 45-46, 96-103.

2623   "Bulls of the Resurrection." PRISM INTERNATIONAL, 5 (Sum. 1965),
        4-11.

ARTICLES

2624   "Preface to a Novel." CANADIAN LITERATURE, No. 9 (Sum. 1961),
        pp. 23-29.

        Discusses UNDER THE VOLCANO; reprinted in no. 5108.

2625   "Two Letters." CANADIAN LITERATURE, No. 44 (Spr. 1970), pp. 50-56.

2626   "Lettres Inédites." LETTRES NOUVELLES, Nos. 2-3 (May-June 1974),
        pp. 241-59.

Manuscripts

2627   McGill University Library, Montreal; University of British Columbia Library,
        Vancouver; University of Texas, Austin.

SECONDARY MATERIAL

Bibliographies

2628   "Bibliography." MALCOLM LOWRY NEWSLETTER, 7 (1980), 22-25.

2629   Birney, Earle, and Margerie Lowry, comps. "Malcolm Lowry (1909-1957):
        A Bibliography." CANADIAN LITERATURE, No. 8 (Spr. 1961), pp. 81-
        88; No. 9 (Sum. 1961), pp. 80-84. Supplements: No. 11 (Wint. 1962),
        pp. 90-95; No. 19 (Wint. 1964), pp. 83-89.

2630   A MALCOLM LOWRY CATALOGUE, WITH ESSAYS BY PERLE EPSTEIN
        AND RICHARD HAUER COSTA. Focus Series, 2. New York: J. Howard
        Woolmer, 1968. 64 p. Index.

2631   New, William H., comp. MALCOLM LOWRY: A REFERENCE GUIDE.
        Boston: G.K. Hall, 1978. xxix, 162 p. Index.

2632   Yandle, Anne. "Bibliography." MALCOLM LOWRY NEWSLETTER, 5
        (1979), 2-8.

For bibliographies of Lowry, see also no. 2663.

Criticism

2633   Aiken, Conrad. "Hambo Ici et Là." Trans. Clarisse Francillon. LETTRES
        NOUVELLES, Nos. 2-3 (May-June 1974), pp. 263-79.

2634 _____. "Malcolm Lowry: A Note." CANADIAN LITERATURE, No. 8 (Spr. 1961), pp. 29-30.

Reprinted in nos. 2617 and 5108.

2635 Arac, Jonathan. "The Form of Carnival in UNDER THE VOLCANO." PMLA, 92 (May 1977), 481-89.

2636 Austin, Paul W. "Russian Views of Lowry." CANADIAN LITERATURE, No. 62 (Aut. 1974), pp. 126-28.

2637 Bareham, Terence. "After the Volcano: An Assessment of Malcolm Lowry's Posthumous Fiction." STUDIES IN THE NOVEL, 6 (Fall 1974), 349-62.

Reprinted in no. 2801.

2638 Bareham, Tony. "The Englishness of Malcolm Lowry." JOURNAL OF COMMONWEALTH LITERATURE, 11 (Dec. 1976), 134-49.

2639 _____. "Paradigms of Hell: Symbolic Patterning in UNDER THE VOL-CANO." In ON THE NOVEL: A PRESENT FOR WALTER ALLEN ON HIS 60TH BIRTHDAY FROM HIS FRIENDS AND COLLEAGUES. Ed. Suheil B. Bushrui. London: Dent, 1971, pp. 113-27.

Reprinted in no. 2801.

2640 _____. "The Title of DARK AS THE GRAVE WHEREIN MY FRIEND IS LAID." MALCOLM LOWRY NEWSLETTER, 1 (1977), 5-6.

2641 Barnes, Jim. "The Myth of Sisyphus in UNDER THE VOLCANO." PRAIRIE SCHOONER, 42 (Wint. 1968-69), 341-48.

2642 Baxter, Charles. "The Escape from Irony: UNDER THE VOLCANO and the Aesthetics of Arson." NOVEL, 10 (Wint. 1977), 114-26.

2643 Benham, David. "Lowry's Purgatory: Versions of LUNAR CAUSTIC." CANADIAN LITERATURE, No. 44 (Spr. 1970), pp. 28-37.

Reprinted in nos. 2801 and 5108.

2644 Berl, Emmanuel. "Hommage à Malcolm Lowry." PREUVES, No. 143 (Jan. 1963), pp. 64-66.

2645 Binns, Ronald. "Beckett, Lowry and the Anti-Novel." In THE CON-TEMPORARY ENGLISH NOVEL. Ed. Malcolm Bradbury and David Palmer. Stratford-upon-Avon Studies, 18. New York: Holmes and Meier, 1979, pp. 88-111.

2646 _____. "Lowry's Anatomy of Melancholy." CANADIAN LITERATURE, No. 64 (Spr. 1975), pp. 8-23.

Discusses ULTRAMARINE.

2647 _____. "The Q-Ship Incident: A Possible Cinematic Source." MALCOLM LOWRY NEWSLETTER, 7 (1980), 20-21.

2648 Bonnefoi, Geneviève. "Souvenir de Quauhnahuac." LETTRES NOUVELLES, NS 5 (July-Aug. 1960), 94-108.

2649 Boyd, Wendy. "Malcolm Lowry's UNDER THE VOLCANO: La despedida." AMERICAN IMAGO, 37 (1980), 49-64.

2650 Bradbrook, Muriel C. MALCOLM LOWRY, HIS ART AND EARLY LIFE: A STUDY IN TRANSFORMATION. London: Cambridge University Press, 1974. xiii, 170 p. Bibliog. Index.

2651 _____. "Narrative Form in Conrad and Lowry." In PROCEEDINGS AND PAPERS OF THE SIXTEENTH CONGRESS OF THE AUSTRALIAN UNIVERSITIES LANGUAGE AND LITERATURE ASSOCIATION HELD 21-27 AUGUST 1974 AT THE UNIVERSITY OF ADELAIDE, SOUTH AUSTRALIA. Ed. H. Bevan, M. King, and A. Stephens. N.p.: n.p., n.d., pp. 20-34.

2652 B[ruccoli], M[atthew] J. "Malcolm Lowry's Film Treatment for TENDER IS THE NIGHT." FITZGERALD/HEMINGWAY ANNUAL, 1972, p. 337.

2653 Busch, Frederick. "But This is What it is to Live in Hell: William Gass's 'In the Heart of the Heart of the Country.'" MODERN FICTION STUDIES, 19 (Spr. 1973), 97-108.

2654 Calder-Marshall, Arthur. "A Portrait of Malcolm Lowry." LISTENER, 12 Oct. 1967, pp. 461-63.

2655 Carroy, Jean-Roger. "De Melville à Lowry, et Retour par Nos Abîmes." LETTRES NOUVELLES, Nos. 2-3 (May-June 1974), pp. 123-69.

2656 _____. "Obscur Présent, le Feu. . . ." LETTRES NOUVELLES, NS 5 (July-Aug. 1960), 83-88.

2657 Carstensen, Frederico B. "La cábala en BAJO EL VOLCÁN." LA PALABRA Y EL HOMBRE, 2 (1972), 40-45.

2658 Chittick, V.L.O. "USHANT's Malcolm Lowry." QUEEN'S QUARTERLY, 71 (Spr. 1964), 67-75.

Discusses Conrad Aiken's portrayal of Lowry.

2659　Christella Marie, Sister. "UNDER THE VOLCANO: A Consideration of the Novel by Malcolm Lowry." XAVIER UNIVERSITY STUDIES, 4 (Mar. 1965), 13-27.

2660　Clipper, Lawrence J. "Hugh Firmin as General Winfield Scott: A Note." MALCOLM LOWRY NEWSLETTER, 4 (1979), 10-11.

2661　＿＿＿＿. "Yvonne's Astronomy Magazine." MALCOLM LOWRY NEWS-LETTER, 6 (1980), 3-6.

2662　Collier, Graham. "On a Tooloose Lowrey-Trek." MALCOLM LOWRY NEWSLETTER, 5 (1979), 19-20.

2663　Combs, Judith O., ed. MALCOLM LOWRY, 1909-1957: AN INVEN-TORY OF HIS PAPERS IN THE LIBRARY OF THE UNIVERSITY OF BRITISH COLUMBIA. Vancouver: University of British Columbia Library, 1973. 24 p.

2664　Corrigan, Matthew. "Malcolm Lowry, New York Publishing, & the 'New Illiteracy.'" ENCOUNTER, 35 (July 1970), 82-93.

2665　＿＿＿＿. "Malcolm Lowry: The Phenomenology of Failure." BOUNDARY 2, 3 (Wint. 1975), 407-42.

2666　Costa, Richard Hauer. "Costa on Venuti." MALCOLM LOWRY NEWS-LETTER, 3 (1978), 2-3.

2667　＿＿＿＿. "The Lowry/Aiken Symbiosis." NATION, 26 June 1967, pp. 823-26.

2668　＿＿＿＿. "Lowry's Forest Path: Echoes of WALDEN." CANADIAN LIT-ERATURE, No. 62 (Aut. 1974), pp. 61-68.

2669　＿＿＿＿. MALCOLM LOWRY. Twayne World Author Series, 217. New York: Twayne, 1972. 208 p. Bibliog. Index.

2670　＿＿＿＿. "Malcolm Lowry and the Addictions of an Era." UNIVERSITY OF WINDSOR REVIEW, 5 (Spr. 1970), 1-10.

2671　＿＿＿＿. "The Northern Paradise: Malcolm Lowry in Canada." STUDIES IN THE NOVEL, 4 (Sum. 1972), 165-72.

2672 _____. "Pietà, Pelado, and 'The Ratification of Death': The Ten-Year Evolvement of Malcolm Lowry's VOLCANO." JOURNAL OF MODERN LITERATURE, 2, No. 1 (1971), 3-18.

2673 _____. "ULYSSES, Lowry's VOLCANO and the Voyage between: A Study of an Unacknowledged Literary Kinship." UNIVERSITY OF TORONTO QUARTERLY, 36 (July 1967), 335-52.

2874 _____. "UNDER THE VOLCANO: A 'New' Charting of the Way It Was." MALCOLM LOWRY NEWSLETTER, 4 (1979), 2-3.

2675 Crawford, John. "Primitiveness in 'The Bravest Boat.'" RESEARCH STUDIES OF WASHINGTON STATE UNIVERSITY, 37 (1969), 330-33.

2676 Creswell, Rosemary. "Malcolm Lowry's Other Fiction." In CUNNING EXILES: STUDIES OF MODERN PROSE WRITERS. Ed. Don Anderson and Stephen Knight. Sydney: Angus and Robertson, 1975, pp. 62-80.

2677 Cross, Richard K. "Malcolm Lowry and the Columbian Eden." CONTEMPORARY LITERATURE, 14 (Wint. 1973), 19-30.

Reprinted in no. 2801.

2878 _____. MALCOLM LOWRY: A PREFACE TO HIS FICTION. Chicago: University of Chicago Press, 1980. xii, 146 p. Index.

2679 _____. "MOBY-DICK and UNDER THE VOLCANO: Poetry from the Abyss." MODERN FICTION STUDIES, 20 (Sum. 1974), 149-56.

2680 Dahlie, Hallvard. "Lowry's Debt to Nordahl Grieg." CANADIAN LITERATURE, No. 64 (Spr. 1975), pp. 41-51.

Links Greig's THE SHIP SAILS ON and ULTRAMARINE.

2681 _____. "Malcolm Lowry and the Northern Tradition." STUDIES IN CANADIAN LITERATURE, 1 (Wint. 1976), 105-14.

2682 _____. "Malcolm Lowry's ULTRAMARINE." JOURNAL OF CANADIAN FICTION, 3, No. 4 (1975), 65-68.

2683 Day, Douglas. MALCOLM LOWRY: A BIOGRAPHY. New York: Oxford University Press, 1974. 483 p. Bibliog.

2684 _____. "Malcolm Lowry: OSCURO COMO LA TUMBA DONDE MI AMIGO YACE." Trans. Alicia Jurado. REVISTA NACIONAL DE CULTURA (Caracas), 29 (Oct.-Dec. 1968), 32-41.

2685 _____. "Of Tragic Joy." PRAIRIE SCHOONER, 37 (Wint. 1963), 354-62.

> Discusses UNDER THE VOLCANO.

2686 de Margerie, Diane. "Correspondance et Correspondances." LETTRES NOUVELLES, Nos. 2-3 (May-June 1974), pp. 205-17.

2687 Dodson, Daniel D. "Malcolm Lowry." In SIX CONTEMPORARY BRITISH NOVELISTS. Ed. George Slade. New York: Columbia University Press, 1976, pp. 115-64. Bibliog.

2688 _____. MALCOLM LOWRY. Essays on Modern Writers, 51. New York: Columbia University Press, 1970. 48 p.

2689 Dorosz, Kristofer. MALCOLM LOWRY'S INFERNAL PARADISE. Acta Universitatis Upsaliensia, Studia Anglistica Upsaliensia, 27. Stockholm: Uppsala, 1976. 166 p. Bibliog. Index.

2690 Doyen, Victor. "Elements Towards a Spatial Reading of Malcolm Lowry's UNDER THE VOLCANO." ENGLISH STUDIES, 50 (Feb. 1969), 65-74.

2691 _____. "La Genèse d'AU-DESSOUS DU VOLCAN." LETTRES NOU-VELLES, Nos. 2-3 (May-June 1974), pp. 87-122.

2692 Doyle, James. "Lowry and Jazz: Some Observations." MALCOLM LOWRY NEWSLETTER, 5 (1979), 16-17.

2693 _____. "A Lowry Jazz Discography: Part I." MALCOLM LOWRY NEWSLETTER, 7 (1980), 10-17.

2694 Durrant, Geoffrey. "Aiken and Lowry." CANADIAN LITERATURE, No. 64 (Spr. 1975), pp. 24-40.

> Discusses ULTRAMARINE and Aiken's BLUE VOYAGE.

2695 _____. "Death in Life: Neo-Platonic Elements in 'Through the Panama.'" CANADIAN LITERATURE, No. 44 (Spr. 1970), pp. 13-27.

> Reprinted in nos. 2801 and 5108.

2696 _____. "Heavenly Correspondences in the Later Work of Malcolm Lowry." MOSAIC, 11 (Spr. 1978), 63-77.

2697 Edelstein, J.M. "On Re-Reading UNDER THE VOLCANO." PRAIRIE SCHOONER, 37 (Wint. 1963-64), 336-39.

2698   Edmonds, Dale. "Lowry=Volcano=Mexico?" RIATA, Spr. 1965, pp. 11-20.

2699   _____. "Mescallusions or The Drinking Man's UNDER THE VOLCANO." JOURNAL OF MODERN LITERATURE, 6 (Apr. 1977), 277-88.

2700   _____. "The Short Fiction of Malcolm Lowry." TULANE STUDIES IN ENGLISH, 15 (1967), 59-80.

2701   _____. "UNDER THE VOLCANO: A Reading of the 'Immediate Level.'" TULANE STUDIES IN ENGLISH, 16 (1968), 63-105.

   Reprinted in no. 2801.

2702   Epstein, Perle S. THE PRIVATE LABYRINTH OF MALCOLM LOWRY: UNDER THE VOLCANO and THE CABBALA. New York: Holt, Rinehart and Winston, 1969. 241 p. Bibliog. Index.

2703   _____. "Swinging the Maelstrom: Malcolm Lowry and Jazz." CANADIAN LITERATURE, No. 44 (Spr. 1970), pp. 57-66.

   Reprinted in no. 5108.

2704   Fernandez, Diane. "Malcolm Lowry et le Feu Infernal." PREUVES, Nos. 215-16 (Feb.-Mar. 1969), pp. 129-34.

2705   Fouchet, Max-Pol. "Non se puede . . ." LETTRES NOUVELLES, NS 5 (July-Aug. 1960), 21-25.

   Discusses UNDER THE VOLCANO. In French.

2706   Francillon, Clarisse. "Malcolm, Mon Ami." LETTRES NOUVELLES, NS 5 (July-Aug. 1960), 8-19.

2707   _____. "Souvenirs sur Malcolm Lowry." LETTRES NOUVELLES, No. 54 (Nov. 1957), pp. 588-603.

   Reprinted in no. 2617.

2708   Gabrial, Jan. "Maguey." SCHOONER, 17 (1944), 229-36.

2709   _____. "Munich of the Heart." DECADE, 7 (4th quarter 1945), 28-31.

2710   _____. "Voyage to the Shores of Guautla." NEW MEXICO QUARTERLY REVIEW, 15 (1945), 472-80.

2711   Galaviz, Juan Manuel. "Las 25 estaciones de Malcolm Lowry." LA
        PALABRA Y EL HOMBRE, No. 1 (1972), pp. 37-47.

        Discusses UNDER THE VOLCANO and DARK AS THE GRAVE.

2712   Garnett, George Rhys. "UNDER THE VOLCANO: The Myth of the
        Hero." CANADIAN LITERATURE, No. 84 (Spr. 1980), pp. 31-40.

2713   Grace, Sherrill E. "The Creative Process: An Introduction to Time and
        Space in Malcolm Lowry's Fiction." STUDIES IN CANADIAN LITERA-
        TURE, 2 (Wint. 1977), 61-68.

2714   _____. "Outward Bound." CANADIAN LITERATURE, No. 71 (Wint.
        1976), pp. 73-79.

        Discusses ULTRAMARINE; reprinted in no. 2801.

2715   _____. "UNDER THE VOLCANO: Narrative Mode and Technique."
        JOURNAL OF CANADIAN FICTION, 2 (Spr. 1973), 57-61.

2716   Gunn, Drewey Wayne. "The Volcano and the Barranca." In his AMERICAN
        AND BRITISH WRITERS IN MEXICO 1556-1973. Austin: University of
        Texas Press, 1974, pp. 164-80.

2717   Hagen, W.M. "Hagen on Venuti." MALCOLM LOWRY NEWSLETTER,
        3 (1978), 3.

2718   _____. "UNDER THE VOLCANO: The Fort Bliss First Edition." MAL-
        COLM LOWRY NEWSLETTER, 3 (1978), 6-9.

2719   Heilman, Robert B. "The Possessed Artist and the Ailing Soul." CA-
        NADIAN LITERATURE, No. 8 (Spr. 1961), pp. 7-16.

        Discusses UNDER THE VOLCANO; reprinted in nos. 2801
        and 5108.

2720   Hill, Art. "The Alcoholic on Alcoholism." CANADIAN LITERATURE,
        No. 62 (Aut. 1974), pp. 33-48.

        Reprinted in nos. 2801 and 5113.

2721   Hirschman, Jack. "Kabbala/Lowry, etc." PRAIRIE SCHOONER, 37
        (Wint. 1963-64), 347-53.

2722   Hochschild, Adam. "Private Volcano of Malcolm Lowry." RAMPARTS,
        12 (Mar. 1974), 45-48.

2723   Huddleston, Joan. "From Short Story to Novel: The Language of UNDER THE VOLCANO." ACLALS BULLETIN, 5, No. 2 (1979), 80-90.

2724   _____. "Noun Modification as an Index of Style in Lowry's UNDER THE VOLCANO." LANGUAGE AND STYLE, 10 (1977), 86-108.

2725   Iconocrit [pseud.]. "Malcolm Lowry's Mysterious End." ICONOMA-TRIX, 1 (Sept. 1975), 5-10.

2726   "An Interview with Mrs. Malcolm Lowry." MALCOLM LOWRY NEWS-LETTER, 2 (1978), 11-18; 4 (1979), 22-26; 5 (1979), 30-40.

2727   Jewison, D.B. "The Platonic Heritage in UNDER THE VOLCANO." STUDIES IN CANADIAN LITERATURE, 3 (Wint. 1978), 62-69.

2728   Jokobsen, Arnt Lykke. INTRODUCTION AND NOTES TO MALCOLM LOWRY'S UNDER THE VOLCANO. Anglica et Americana, 11. Copenhagen: Dept. of English, University of Copenhagen, 1980. 108 p.

2729   Kilgallin, Anthony R. "Eliot, Joyce & Lowry." CANADIAN AUTHOR AND BOOKMAN, 41 (Wint. 1965), 3-4, 6.

2730   _____. "Faust and UNDER THE VOLCANO." CANADIAN LITERA-TURE, No. 26 (Aut. 1965), pp. 43-54.

        Reprinted in no. 5108.

2731   _____. LOWRY. Erin, Ont.: Porcépic, 1973. 211 p. Bibliog.

2732   Kim, Suzanne. "Les Lettres de Malcolm Lowry." ÉTUDES ANGLAISES, 22 (Jan.-Mar. 1969), 58-61.

2733   _____. "Les Oeuvres de Jeunesse de Malcolm Lowry." ÉTUDES AN-GLAISES, 18 (Oct.-Dec. 1965), 383-94.

2734   _____. "Par l'Eau et le Feu: Deux Oeuvres de Malcolm Lowry." ÉTUDES ANGLAISES, 18 (Oct.-Dec. 1965), 395-97.

        Discusses ULTRAMARINE and HEAR US, O LORD, FROM HEAVEN THY DWELLING PLACE.

2735   Kirk, Downie. "More than Music: Glimpses of Malcolm Lowry." CA-NADIAN LITERATURE, No. 8 (Spr. 1961), pp. 31-38.

        Reprinted in nos. 2617 and 5108.

2736   Knickerbocker, Conrad. "Lowry à Vingt Ans." LETTRES NOUVELLES, No. 58 (Mar.-Apr. 1967), pp. 68-94.

2737   _____. "Malcolm Lowry and the Outer Circle of Hell." PARIS REVIEW, 8 (Wint.-Spr. 1963), 12-13.

       Reprinted in no. 2617.

2738   _____. "Swinging the Paradise Street Blues: Malcolm Lowry in England." PARIS REVIEW, 10 (Sum. 1966), 12-38.

2739   _____. "The Voyages of Malcolm Lowry." PRAIRIE SCHOONER, 37 (Wint. 1963-64), 301-14.

2740   Kondo, Ineko. "Lowry Studies in Japan." MALCOLM LOWRY NEWS-LETTER, 2 (1978), 3-4.

2741   Leech, Clifford. "The Shaping of Time: NOSTROMO and UNDER THE VOLCANO." In IMAGINED WORLDS: ESSAYS ON SOME ENGLISH NOVELS AND NOVELISTS IN HONOUR OF JOHN BUTT. Ed. Maynard Mack and Ian Gregor. London: Methuen, 1968, pp. 323-41.

2742   Lent, John. "Wyndham Lewis and Malcolm Lowry: Contents of Style and Subject Matter in the Modern Novel." In FIGURES IN A GROUND: CANADIAN ESSAYS ON MODERN LITERATURE COLLECTED IN HONOR OF SHEILA WATSON. Ed. Diane Bessai and David Jackel. Saskatoon: Western Producer Prairie Books, 1978, pp. 61-75.

2743   Longo, Joseph A. "UNDER THE VOLCANO: Geoffrey Firmin's Tragic Epiphany." NOTRE DAME ENGLISH JOURNAL, 12 (1979), 15-25.

2744   Lorenz, Clarissa. "Call it Misadventure." ATLANTIC MONTHLY, June 1970, pp. 106-10.

       Reprinted in no. 2617.

2745   Lowry, Russell. "Childhood Agonies." MALCOLM LOWRY NEWSLETTER, 7 (1980), 17-19.

2746   McConnell, William. "Recollections of Malcolm Lowry." CANADIAN LITERATURE, No. 6 (Aut. 1960), pp. 24-31.

       Reprinted in nos. 195, 2617, and 5108.

2747   McMullen, Lorraine. "Malcolm Lowry's 'Forest Path to the Spring.'" CANADIAN FICTION MAGAZINE, No. 5 (Wint. 1972), pp. 71-77.

2748   McNeil, C.G. "A Memory of Malcolm Lowry." AMERICAN REVIEW (New York), 17 (May 1973), 35-39.

Reprinted in no. 2617.

2749   Maekawa, Yuichi. "'Drunken Divine Comedy': Malcolm Lowry Shoron." EIGO SEINEN, 121 (1975), 290-92.

2750   Magee, A. Peter. "The Quest for Love." EMERITUS, 1 (Spr. 1965), 24-29.

Discusses Lowry and Thomas Wolfe.

2751   Makowiecki, Stefan. "An Analysis of Humour in the Works of Malcolm Lowry." STUDIA ANGLICA POSNANIENSIA, 4 (1972), 195-201.

2752   _____. "Symbolic Pattern in UNDER THE VOLCANO." KWARTALNIK NEOFILOLOGICZNY, 23 (1976), 455-63.

2753   Markson, David. "Malcolm Lowry: A Reminiscence." NATION, 7 Feb. 1966, pp. 164-67.

Reprinted in no. 2617.

2754   _____. MALCOLM LOWRY'S VOLCANO: MYTH SYMBOL MEANING. New York: Times Books, 1978. 241 p.

2755   _____. "Myth in UNDER THE VOLCANO." PRAIRIE SCHOONER, 37 (Wint. 1963-64), 339-46.

2756   _____. "The Ones that Burn: A Memoir of Malcolm Lowry." BOOKS AND BOOKMEN, 12 (Nov. 1966), 22-23, 102.

2757   Maurey, Pierre. "Lowry's Library: An Annotated Catalogue of Lowry's Books at the University of British Columbia." MALCOLM LOWRY NEWS-LETTER, 7 (1980), 3-10.

2758   Micha, René. "Le Voyage Qui Ne Finit Jamais." CRITIQUE, 30 (1974), 1082-94.

2759   Miller, David. MALCOLM LOWRY AND THE VOYAGE THAT NEVER ENDS. London: Enitharmon, 1976. 55 p.

2760   Myrer, Anton. "Le Monde Au-dessous du Volcan." Trans. Clarisse Francillon. LETTRES NOUVELLES, NS 5 (July-Aug. 1960), 59-66.

2761   Nadeau, Maurice. "Lowry." LETTRES NOUVELLES, NS 5 (July-Aug. 1960), 3-7.

2762   New, William H. "Gabriola: Malcolm Lowry's Floating Island." LITERARY HALF-YEARLY, 13, No. 1 (1972), 115-25.

       Reprinted in nos. 173 and 2801.

2763   _____. "Lowry, the Cabbala and Charles Jones." CANADIAN LITERATURE, No. 43 (Wint. 1970), pp. 83-87.

       Reprinted in no. 173.

2764   _____. "Lowry's Reading: An Introductory Essay." CANADIAN LITERATURE, No. 44 (Spr. 1970), pp. 5-12.

       Reprinted in no. 5108.

2765   _____. MALCOLM LOWRY. Canadian Writers, no. 11. Toronto: McClelland and Stewart, 1971. 64 p. Bibliog.

2766   _____. "A Note on Romantic Allusions in HEAR US, O LORD." STUDIES IN CANADIAN LITERATURE, 1 (Wint. 1976), 130-36.

2767   Nimmo, D.C. "Lowry's Hell." NOTES AND QUERIES, NS 16 (July 1969), 265.

2768   Noxon, Gerald. "Le Jeune Malcolm." LETTRES NOUVELLES, Nos. 2-3 (May-June 1974), pp. 24-30.

2769   _____. "Malcolm Lowry: 1930." PRAIRIE SCHOONER, 37 (Wint. 1963), 315-20.

       Reprinted in no. 2617.

2770   Pagnoulle, Christine. MALCOLM LOWRY: VOYAGE AU FOND DE NOS ABIMES. Lausanne: L'Âge d'Homme, 1977. 173 p.

2771   _____. "Par-delà les Miroirs." LETTRES NOUVELLES, Nos. 2-3 (May-June 1974), pp. 170-83.

       Discusses UNDER THE VOLCANO.

2772   _____. "To Hell and Back: Violence in Lowry's UNDER THE VOLCANO." COMMONWEALTH NEWSLETTER, 11 (1977), 21-28.

2773   Perlmutter, Ruth. "Malcolm Lowry's Unpublished Filmscript of TENDER IS THE NIGHT." AMERICAN QUARTERLY, 28 (Wint. 1976), 561-74.

2774 Pindancet-Laude, Corrine. "Deux Miroirs d'un Mȇme Texte." CRITIQUE, 28 (1972), 1015-16.

Discusses UNDER THE VOLCANO and OCTOBER FERRY TO GABRIOLA.

2775 Pottinger, Andrew J. "The Consul's 'Murder.'" CANADIAN LITERATURE, No. 67 (Wint. 1976), pp. 53-63.

2776 Purdy, Alfred W. "Dormez-Vous? A Memoir of Malcolm Lowry." CANADA MONTH, 2 (Sept. 1962), 24-26.

2777 _____. "Lowry: A Memoir." BOOKS IN CANADA, 3 (Jan.-Feb. 1974), 3-4.

2778 Raab, Lawrence. "The Two Consuls: UNDER THE VOLCANO." THOTH, 12 (Spr.-Sum. 1972), 20-29.

2779 Rapin, René. "Sur l'Art de Malcolm Lowry dans UNDER THE VOLCANO." In MÉLANGES OFFERTS À MONSIEUR GEORGES BONNARD À L'OCCASION DE SON QUATRE-VINGTIÈME ANNIVERSAIRE. Geneva: Droz, 1966, pp. 99-104.

2780 Rasporich, Beverly. "The Right Side of Despair: Lowry's Comic Spirit in LUNAR CAUSTIC and DARK AS THE GRAVE WHEREIN MY FRIEND IS LAID." MOSAIC, 10 (Sum. 1977), 55-67.

2781 Richey, Clarence W. "'The Ill-Fated Mr. Bultitude': A Note Upon an Allusion in Malcolm Lowry's UNDER THE VOLCANO." NOTES ON CONTEMPORARY LITERATURE, 3, No. 3 (1973), 3-5.

2782 Richmond, Lee J. "The Pariah Dog Symbolism in Malcolm Lowry's UNDER THE VOLCANO." NOTES ON CONTEMPORARY LITERATURE, 6, No. 2 (1976), 7-9.

2783 Romijn, Meijer Henk. "Malcolm Lowry." TIRADE, 7 (1963), 918-22.

2784 Ruffinelli, Jorge. "Malcolm Lowry: El viaje que nunca termina." TEXTO CRÍTICO, 9 (1978), 9-36.

2785 Simpson, W.G. "Lowry and Greig." TIMES LITERARY SUPPLEMENT, 12 Apr. 1963, p. 249.

2786 Slade, Carole. "The Character of Yvonne in UNDER THE VOLCANO." CANADIAN LITERATURE, No. 84 (Spr. 1980), pp. 137-44.

2787   _____. "UNDER THE VOLCANO and Dante's INFERNO 1." UNIVER-
SITY OF WINDSOR REVIEW, 10 (Spr.-Sum. 1975), 44-52.

Reprinted in no 2801.

2788 Smith, Anne, ed. THE ART OF MALCOLM LOWRY. London: Vision,
1978. 173 p. Index.

Includes an article by Woodcock.

2789 Spender, Stephen. Introd., UNDER THE VOLCANO. Philadelphia:
J.B. Lippincott, 1965, pp. vii-xxvi.

2790 Spriel, Stéphen. "Le Cryptogramme Lowry." LETTRES NOUVELLES, NS
5 (July-Aug. 1960), 67-81.

2791 Stern, James. "Malcolm Lowry: A First Impression." ENCOUNTER, 29
(Sept. 1967), 58-64, 66-68.

Reprinted in no. 2617.

2792 Taylor, Chet. "The Other Edge of Existential Awareness: Reading of
Malcolm Lowry's UNDER THE VOLCANO." LITERARY HALF-YEARLY,
14, No. 1 (1973), 138-50.

2793 Tiessen, Paul G. "Malcolm Lowry and the Cinema." CANADIAN LIT-
ERATURE, No. 44 (Spr. 1970), pp. 38-49.

Reprinted in no. 5108.

2794 Veitch, Douglas W. LAWRENCE, GREENE AND LOWRY: THE FIC-
TIONAL LANDSCAPE OF MEXICO. Introd. George Woodcock. Waterloo, Ont.: Wilfrid Laurier University Press, 1978. 193 p. Bibliog.

2795 Wainwright, J.A. "The Book 'Being Written': Art and Life in DARK
AS THE GRAVE WHEREIN MY FRIEND IS LAID." DALHOUSIE REVIEW,
59 (Spr. 1979), 82-104.

2796 Walker, Ronald G. "The Barranca of History: Mexico as Nexus of
Doom in UNDER THE VOLCANO" and "UNDER THE VOLCANO: The
Mexican Voyages of Malcolm Lowry." In his INFERNAL PARADISE:
MEXICO AND THE MODERN ENGLISH NOVEL. Berkeley: University
of California Press, 1978, pp. 237-321.

2797 Widmer, Eleanor. "The Drunken Wheel: Malcolm Lowry and UNDER
THE VOLCANO." In THE FORTIES: FICTION, POETRY, DRAMA. Ed.
Warren French. Deland, Fla.: Everett/Edwards, 1969, pp. 217-26.

2798　Wild, Bernadette. "Malcolm Lowry: A Study of the Sea Metaphor in UNDER THE VOLCANO." UNIVERSITY OF WINDSOR REVIEW, 4 (Fall 1968), 46-60.

2799　Wood, Barry. "The Edge of Eternity." CANADIAN LITERATURE, No. 70 (Aut. 1976), pp. 51-58.

　　　　Discusses "The Forest Path to the Spring." Reprinted in no. 2801.

2800　_____. "Malcolm Lowry's Metafiction: The Biography of a Genre." CONTEMPORARY LITERATURE, 19 (Wint. 1978), 1-25.

　　　　Reprinted in no. 2801.

2801　_____, ed. with introd. ON MALCOLM LOWRY: THE WRITER & HIS CRITICS. Ottawa: Tecumseh, 1980. 278 p. Bibliog.

　　　　Reprints reviews and articles on Lowry, including nos. 2637, 2639, 2643, 2677, 2695, 2701, 2714, 2719-20, 2762, 2787, 2799, and 2800.

2802　Wright, Terence. "UNDER THE VOLCANO: The Static Art of Malcolm Lowry." ARIEL, 1 (Oct. 1970), 67-76.

2803　Yacoubovitch, Roger I. "Cassure, Canal, Baranquilla." LETTRES NOU-VELLES, Nos. 2-3 (May-June 1974), pp. 184-204.

2804　Yandle, Anne. "Malcolm Lowry Collection UBC." MALCOLM LOWRY NEWSLETTER, 1 (1977), 6-7.

For criticism on Lowry, see also nos. 128, 810, 860, 2610, 2614, 2617, 2619, 2630, 5063, 5130, 5141, 5143-44, and especially 5108.

Book Reviews

2805　ULTRAMARINE: BCLQ, 27 (Oct. 1963), 28-29; CanL, 17 (Sum. 1963), 83-84; CFor, 43 (May 1963), 43-44; EA, 18 (Oct. 1965), 395-97; NewR, 17 Nov. 1962, p. 22; NS, 15 Feb. 1963, p. 242; NS&N, 24 June 1933, p. 850; NYTBR, 14 Oct. 1962, p. 5; PUNCH, 29 Aug. 1979, p. 338; QQ, 70 (Aut. 1963), 453; SatR, 17 Nov. 1962, p. 30; SPECTATOR, 23 June 1933, p. 920; SPECTATOR, 25 Aug. 1961, p. 262; SPECTATOR, 5 Apr. 1963, p. 440; TLS, 13 July 1933, p. 481; TLS, 22 Mar. 1963, p. 197.

2806　UNDER THE VOLCANO: ArQ, 3 (Aut. 1947), 281-83; Atl, 179 (May 1947), 144, 146; CAB, 41 (Sum. 1966), 11; COMMONWEAL, 7 Mar.

1947, pp. 523-24; ContempR, 210 (Feb. 1967), 108-09; CritQ, 4 (Wint. 1962), 377; CROSSCURRENTS, 16 (Sum. 1966), 373; ESPRIT, 18 (Nov. 1950), 702-07; HM, May 1947; KR, 9 (Sum. 1947), 474-77; LISTENER, 30 Oct. 1947, p. 788; LISTENER, 9 Feb. 1967, p. 202; MACLEAN'S, 5 Feb. 1966, p. 42; NATION, 22 Mar. 1947, pp. 335-36; NewR, 24 Feb. 1947, pp. 35-36; NMQ, 17 (Sum. 1947), 264-65; NoR, 1 (Aug. 1947), 37-38; NoR, 6 (Dec. 1953), 15-21; NS, 4 May 1962, pp. 148-49; NS, 27 Jan. 1967, pp. 117-18; NS&N, 6 Dec. 1947, pp. 455-56; NYRB, 3 Mar. 1966, p. 16; NYTBR, 23 Feb. 1947, p. 5; PR, 14 (Mar. 1947), 198-200; PUNCH, 1 Feb. 1967, p. 174; SatN, 1 Nov. 1947, p. 15; SatR, 22 Feb. 1947, pp. 9-10; SatR, 4 Dec. 1965, pp. 39-40, SHENANDOAH, 13 (Wint. 1961-62), 65-68; SPECTATOR, 10 Oct. 1947, p. 474; SPECTATOR, 25 Aug. 1961, p. 262; SPECTATOR, 20 Jan. 1967, pp. 74, 76; SR, 55 (Sum. 1947), 483; TLS, 20 Sept. 1947, p. 477; TLS, 11 May 1962, p. 338; TLS, 26 Jan. 1967, p. 57; VQR, 23 (Sum. 1947), lxxviii; YR, 36 (Sum. 1947), 767.

2807 HEAR US, O LORD, FROM HEAVEN THY DWELLING PLACE: Atl, Aug. 1961, p. 96; BCLQ, 26 (Apr. 1963), 31-33; CFor, 41 (Jan. 1962), 235-36; COMMONWEAL, 20 Oct. 1961, pp. 102, 120; CRead, 2 (July 1961), 2-3; CritQ, 4 (Wint. 1962), 377-79; EA, 18 (Oct. 1965), 395-97; NATION, 27 May 1961, pp. 465-66; NewR, 5 June 1961, pp. 24-25; NS, 4 May 1962, p. 24; NYTBR, 21 May 1961, pp. 1, 16; NYTBR, 25 May 1961, p. 39; PR, 28, Nos. 5-6 (1961), 712-15; SatN, 24 June 1961, pp. 29-30; SatR, 27 May 1961, p. 19; SatR, 31 Jan. 1970, p. 36; SHENANDOAH, 13 (Wint. 1961-62), 68-69; SPECTATOR, 4 May 1962, p. 589; TLS, 11 May 1962, p. 338; UTQ, 31 (July 1962), 467-71.

2808 DARK AS THE GRAVE WHEREIN MY FRIEND IS LAID: Atl, 222 (Aug. 1968), 84; CanL, 39 (Wint. 1969), 81-83; ConL, 11 (Sum. 1970), 401; CRITIC, 27 (Oct. 1968), 95; DR, 48 (Aut. 1968), 419-21; ENCOUN-TER, 35 (July 1970), 82; HudR, 21 (Wint. 1968-69), 751; IFR, 5 (Jan. 1978), 59-60; LISTENER, 3 July 1969, p. 24; MACLEAN'S, 81 (Aug. 1968), 59; NATION, 2 Sept. 1968, pp. 188-89; NewR, 12 Oct. 1968, pp. 38-41; NS, 25 July 1969, p. 116; NS, 14 Apr. 1972, p. 498; NYTBR, 4 Aug. 1968, p. 4; PUNCH, 25 June 1969, p. 951; QQ, 75 (Wint. 1968), 746-48; SatR, 6 July 1968, pp. 19-20; SHENANDOAH, 19 (Sum. 1968), 89-93; SPECTATOR, 9 Aug. 1969, p. 177; TLS, 3 July 1969, p. 721; UTQ, 38 (July 1969), 356-57.

2809 LUNAR CAUSTIC: CanL, 39 (Wint. 1969), 80-81; CFor, 48 (July 1968), 88; NS, 23 Feb. 1968, p. 243; NS, 4 Mar. 1977, p. 292; NYTBR, 27 July 1969, p. 8; PUNCH, 6 Mar. 1968, p. 358; SatR, 4 May 1968, p. 23; SPECTATOR, 23 Feb. 1968, p. 234; SPECTATOR, 5 Mar. 1977, p. 24; TLS, 21 Mar. 1968, p. 285.

2810 OCTOBER FERRY TO GABRIOLA: CanL, 48 (Spr. 1971), 74-80; ConL, 13 (Sum. 1972), 361; ContempR, 219 (Oct. 1971), 211; Crit, 28 (Nov.

1972), 1015; ES, 53 (1972), 328; MHRev, 22 (Apr. 1972), 127; NA-
TION, 26 Oct. 1970, p. 408; NS, 27 Aug. 1971, p. 276; NYTBR, 25
Oct. 1970, p. 5; NYTBR, 6 Dec. 1970, p. 102; SPECTATOR, 4 Sept.
1971, p. 344; SNNTS, 6 (Fall 1974), 349; TLS, 27 Aug. 1971, p. 1020;
WCR, 6 (June 1971), 51-52.

2811 PSALMS AND SONGS: CanL, 72 (Spr. 1977), 91-92; SoR, 16 (Apr. 1980),
478-82.

2812 SELECTED LETTERS: AtlA, 56 (Mar. 1966), 56; CAB, 41 (Sum. 1966),
11; CanL, 29 (Sum. 1966), 56-58; CFor, 46 (May 1966), 40; COM-
MONWEAL, 15 Apr. 1966, p. 124; ContempR, 210 (Feb. 1967), 108;
Crit, 30 (Dec. 1974), 1082; DR, 46 (Spr. 1966), 118-19, 121; LISTENER,
(9 Feb. 1967), p. 202; MACLEAN'S, 5 Feb. 1966, p. 42; NewR, 15 Jan.
1966, pp. 23-24; NS, 27 Jan. 1967, p. 117; NYRB, 3 Mar. 1966, p. 16;
NYTBR, 12 Dec. 1965, p. 4; SATR, 4 Dec. 1965, p. 39; SatR, 31 Jan.
1970, p. 36; SPECTATOR, 20 Jan. 1967, p. 74; TLS, 26 Jan. 1967, p. 57.

LUDWIG, JACK (1922--)

An expatriate Canadian, Jack Barry Ludwig left Winnipeg, the home of his birth in 1944, after receiving his B.A. from the University of Manitoba. With a Ph.D. from UCLA (1953), he has taught at several American universities, since 1961 at State University of New York, Stony Brook, where he became chairman of the English department in 1965. In the early sixties, he was co-founder and editor of the literary review, THE NOBLE SAVAGE. He has also been writer-in-residence at the Banff Centre, Alberta, University of Toronto, and the Stratford Shakespearean Festival, Ontario. A WOMAN OF HER AGE, perhaps his best-known novel, is an ironic and sympathetic portrayal of Jewish life in Montreal.

PRIMARY MATERIAL

Monographs

FICTION

2813 CONFUSIONS. Toronto: McClelland and Stewart, 1963. 276 p.

2814 REQUIEM FOR BIBUL. Searchlights. Agincourt, Ont.: Book Society, 1967. 8 p.

2815 ABOVE GROUND: A NOVEL. Boston: Little, Brown, 1968. 364 p.

2816 A WOMAN OF HER AGE. Toronto: McClelland and Stewart, 1973. 197 p.

NONFICTION PROSE

2817 "The Peacock Tradition in English Prose Fiction." Diss., University of California, 1953. ii, 365 l. Bibliog.

2818   RECENT AMERICAN NOVELISTS. University of Minnesota Pamphlets on American Writers, no. 22. Minneapolis: University of Minnesota Press, 1962. 47 p. Bibliog.

2819   HOCKEY NIGHT IN MOSCOW. With Original Drawings by Aislin. Introd. Howie Meeker. Toronto: McClelland and Stewart, 1972. 184 p. Enl. ed. THE GREAT HOCKEY THAW: OR, THE RUSSIANS ARE HERE. Illus. by Aislin. Garden City, N.Y.: Doubleday, 1974. xxii, 259 p.

2820   FIVE-RING CIRCUS: THE MONTREAL OLYMPICS. Garden City, N.Y.: Doubleday, 1976. 248 p.

2821   GAMES OF FEAR AND WINNING: SPORTS WITH AN INSIDE VIEW. Toronto: Doubleday, 1976. 219 p.

2822   THE GREAT AMERICAN SPECTACULARS: THE KENTUCKY DERBY, MARDI GRAS AND OTHER DAYS OF CELEBRATION. Garden City, N.Y.: Doubleday, 1976. 247 p.

POETRY

2823   HOMAGE TO ZOLOTOVA. Banff: Banff Centre Press, 1974.

EDITED WORK

2824   STORIES: BRITISH AND AMERICAN. Ed. with introd. by Jack Barry Ludwig and W. Richard Poirier. Boston: Houghton Mifflin, 1953. xi, 505 p.

2825   SOUNDINGS: NEW CANADIAN POETS. Ed. Jack Ludwig and Andy Wainwright. Toronto: Anansi, 1970. 126 p.

Shorter Work

SHORT STORIES

2826   "Meesh." TAMARACK REVIEW, 21 (Aut. 1961), 3-19.

2827   "Death was the Glass." MIDSTREAM, 7 (Wint. 1961), 37-41.

2828   "Celebration on East Houston Street." TAMARACK REVIEW, [27] (Spr. 1963), 20-28.

2829   "Einstein and This Admirer." LONDON, 5 (Sept. 1965), 65-74.

2830   "A Death of One's Own." TAMARACK REVIEW, [46] (Wint. 1968), 79-84.

ARTICLES

2831   "Clothes in Search of an Emperor." CANADIAN LITERATURE, No. 5 (Sum. 1960), pp. 63-66.

2832   "A Mirror of Moore." CANADIAN LITERATURE, No. 7 (Wint. 1961), pp. 18-23.

>   Reprinted in no. 5113.

2833   "Brian Moore: Ireland's Loss, Canada's Novelist." CRITIQUE, 5 (Spr.-Sum. 1962), 5-13.

2834   "Exile from the Emerald Isle." NATION, 15 Mar. 1965, pp. 287-88.

>   Discusses Brian Moore.

2835   "On Thermostats, Super-Egos, Theatre Directors, and Cleaning Ladies." TAMARACK REVIEW, [45] (Aut. 1967), 106-10, 112-13.

>   Discusses the writing of CONFUSIONS.

2836   "You Always Go Home Again." MOSAIC, 3 (Spr. 1970), 107-11.

2837   "You Have To Go Home Again." MACLEAN'S, 85 (Mar. 1972), 26-28.

2838   Preface, WILLIAM S. BURROUGHS: AN ANNOTATED BIBLIOGRAPHY OF HIS WORKS AND CRITICISM. Comp. Michael B. Goodman. Garland Reference Libraries of Humanities, 24. New York: Garland, 1975, pp. 7-8, 9-13.

2839   "Winnipeggers--Before and After DUBLINERS." In A POLITICAL ART: ESSAYS AND IMAGES IN HONOUR OF GEORGE WOODCOCK. Ed. William H. New. Vancouver: University of British Columbia Press, 1978, pp. 3-14.

For articles by Ludwig, see also no. 2824.

SECONDARY MATERIAL

Criticism

2840   James, Esther. "Ludwig's CONFUSIONS." CANADIAN LITERATURE, No. 40 (Spr. 1969), pp. 49-53.

2841   Stonehewer, Lila. "Anatomy of Confusion: Jack Ludwig's Evolution."
        CANADIAN LITERATURE, No. 29 (Sum. 1966), pp. 34-42.

For criticism on Ludwig, see also nos. 124, 180, 1701, 2298, and 3722.

Book Reviews

2842   CONFUSIONS: ALPHABET, 7 (Dec. 1963), 89-90; CanL, 19 (Wint.
        1964), 49-50; CDim, 2 (Jan. 1965), 15-16; CFor, 44 (Apr. 1964), 22;
        COMMENTARY, 36 (Dec. 1963), 492; CULTURE, 26 (Mar. 1965), 107-
        08; HudR, 16 (Wint. 1963-64), 601; LISTENER, 5 Dec. 1963, p. 955;
        MACLEAN'S, 19 Oct. 1963, p. 81; MONTREALER, 38 (Feb. 1964),
        49; PR, 31 (Wint. 1964), 143; PUNCH, 25 Dec. 1963, p. 935; SatN,
        78 (Nov. 1963), 40-41; SPECTATOR, 6 Dec. 1963, p. 757; TamR,
        [29] (Aut. 1963), 100-102; UTQ, 33 (July 1964), 391-92; VQR, 40
        (Wint. 1964), x.

2843   ABOVE GROUND: AtlA, 58 (May 1968), 78; CanL, 39 (Wint. 1969),
        83-84; CFor, 48 (Jan. 1969), 231; FIDDLEHEAD, [76] (Sum. 1968),
        90; KR, 30, No. 5 (1968), 683; NY, 6 July 1968, p. 64; NYTBR, 28
        July 1968, p. 4; PR, 35 (Fall 1968), 612; QQ, 75 (Wint. 1968), 746-
        47; SatR, 1 June 1968, p. 42; TamR, [48] (Sum. 1968), 73, 76-79;
        UTQ, 38 (July 1969), 356.

2844   A WOMAN OF HER AGE: AntigR, 19 (Aut. 1974), 107-09; BCan,
        3 (Jan. 1974), 10-11; CanL, 61 (Sum. 1974), 123-24; CFM, 13 (Spr.
        1974), 117, 119, 121, 123; DR, 54 (Sum. 1974), 365-67; FIDDLEHEAD,
        100 (Wint. 1974), 83-86; JCF, 3, No. 3 (1974), 91-92; MACLEAN'S,
        86 (Nov. 1973), 118, 120; Q&Q, 40, No. 2 (1974), 12; SatN, 89
        (Mar. 1974), 38, 40; TamR, 61 (Nov. 1973), 76-77; UWR, 10 (Spr.
        1975), 79.

2845   RECENT AMERICAN NOVELISTS: MASJ, 4 (Spr. 1963), 82; TamR,
        [27] (Spr. 1963), 101; ZAA, 13 (1965), 204-05.

McCLUNG, NELLIE (1873-1951)

Born in Chatsworth, Ontario, Nellie Letitia McClung moved west as a child and lived in southern Manitoba, Winnipeg, Edmonton, and finally Vancouver Island. A feminist, politician, and writer, she began her working life as a teacher. She worked for the Women's Christian Temperance Union and the suffrage movement, was a delegate to the Great War Conference in 1916, acted as a liberal representative to the Alberta legislature from 1921 to 1925, with several others petitioned the Supreme Court in 1927 and had women legally declared "persons," and was appointed a Canadian delegate to the League of Nations in 1938. Her tales are simple, moral, often sentimental. The first, SOWING SEEDS IN DANNY, was particularly popular in its time.

PRIMARY MATERIAL

Monographs

FICTION

2846 SOWING SEEDS IN DANNY. New York: Doubleday, Page, 1908. xii, 313 p. Also as DANNY AND THE PINK LADY. London: Hodder and Stoughton, 1908. xii, 313 p.

2847 THE SECOND CHANCE. New York: Doubleday, Page, 1910. viii, 369 p.

2848 THE BLACK CREEK STOPPING-HOUSE AND OTHER STORIES. Toronto: William Briggs, 1912. 224 p.

2849 PURPLE SPRINGS. Toronto: Thomas Allen, 1921. 325 p.

2850 THE BEAUTY OF MARTHA. London: Hutchinson, 1923. 288 p.

2851 WHEN CHRISTMAS CROSSED "THE PEACE." Toronto: Thomas Allen, 1923. 149 p.

2852   PAINTED FIRES. New York: Dodd, Mead, 1925. 316 p.

2853   ALL WE LIKE SHEEP AND OTHER STORIES. Toronto: Thomas Allen, 1926. ix, 261 p.

2854   BE GOOD TO YOURSELF: A BOOK OF SHORT STORIES. Toronto: Thomas Allen, 1930. 179 p.

2855   FLOWERS FOR THE LIVING: A BOOK OF SHORT STORIES. Toronto: Thomas Allen, 1931. 212 p.

NONFICTION PROSE

2856   IN TIMES LIKE THESE: ADDRESSES. Toronto: McLeod and Allen, 1915. 217 p.

2857   THE NEXT OF KIN: THOSE WHO WAIT AND WONDER. Boston: Houghton Mifflin, 1917. 256 p.

2858   THREE TIMES AND OUT. Told by Private Simmons. Written by Nellie McClung. Boston: Houghton Mifflin, 1918. viii, 247 p.

2859   CLEARING IN THE WEST: MY OWN STORY. Toronto: Thomas Allen, 1935. 378 p. Rev. ed. Don Mills, Ont.: Thomas Allen, 1976. 378 p.

   Autobiography.

2860   LEAVES FROM LANTERN LANE. Toronto: Thomas Allen, 1936. 199 p.

2861   MORE LEAVES FROM LANTERN LANE. Toronto: Thomas Allen, 1937. 201 p.

2862   THE STREAM RUNS FAST: MY OWN STORY. Toronto: Thomas Allen, 1945. xvi, 316 p.

   Autobiography.

Shorter Work

SHORT STORIES

2863   "Wedding March." DELINEATOR, 73 (Jan. 1909), 75-77.

2864   "The Girl from God Knows Where." MACLEAN'S, 15 Jan. 1931, pp. 3-5, 39-41.

Manuscripts

2865   Provincial Archives of Alberta, Edmonton; Provincial Archives of British
        Columbia, Vancouver; University of British Columbia Library, Vancouver.

SECONDARY MATERIAL

Criticism

2866   Bassett, Isabel. "Writers for Reform." In her THE PARLOUR REBELLION:
        PROFILES IN THE STRUGGLE FOR WOMEN'S RIGHTS. Toronto: Mc-
        Clelland and Stewart, 1975, pp. 127-45.

2867   Benham, Mary Lile. NELLIE McCLUNG. The Canadians. Don Mills,
        Ont.: Fitzhenry and Whiteside, 1975. 61 p.

        Biography for children.

2868   Eggleston, Wilfred. "Nellie McClung: Crusader." CANADIAN AU-
        THOR AND BOOKMAN, 19 (Sept. 1943), 21.

2869   MacEwan, J.W. Grant. "Nellie McClung: 'Loved and Remembered.'"
        In his AND MIGHTY WOMEN TOO: STORIES OF NOTABLE WESTERN
        CANADIAN WOMEN. Saskatoon: Western Producers Prairie Books, 1975,
        pp. 159-68.

2870   McMullen, Melvin Justus Given. RECALLED TO LIFE: SOUVENIR
        PHOTO SUMMARY OF THE COLORED DRAMATIC PRESENTATION
        COVERING THE LIFE AND TIMES OF NELLIE McCLUNG. 1965. 2nd
        ed., rev. and enl. Winnipeg: Manitoba Travel and Convention Asso-
        ciation, 1965. 18 p.

2871   Matheson, Gwen, and V.E. Lang. "Nellie McClung: 'Not a Nice
        Woman.'" In WOMEN IN THE CANADIAN MOSAIC. Ed. Gwen Matheson.
        Toronto: Peter Martin, 1976, pp. 1-22.

2872   "Nellie McClung." CANADIAN AUTHOR AND BOOKMAN, 27 (Aut.
        1951), 34.

2873   nelliemcclung. "On Nellie McClung." 3¢ PULP, 1 Sept. 1973, n. pag.

2874   Savage, Candace. OUR NELL: A SCRAPBOOK BIOGRAPHY OF NELLIE
        L. McCLUNG. Saskatoon: Western Producer Prairie Books, 1979. 253 p.
        Bibliog. Index.

2875   Strong-Boag, Veronica. "Canadian Feminism in the 1920's: The Case of Nellie L. McClung." JOURNAL OF CANADIAN STUDIES, 12 (Sum. 1977), 58-68.

2876   Zieman, Margaret K. "Nellie was a Lady Terror." MACLEAN'S, 1 Oct. 1953, pp. 20-21, 62-66.

For criticism on McClung, see also nos. 131 and 2889.

Book Reviews

2877   SOWING SEEDS IN DANNY: BCLQ, 37 (Wint. 1973), 32-33; NYTSR, 13 June 1908, p. 341.

2878   PURPLE SPRINGS: CFor, 1 (Sept. 1921), 378; NYTBR, 5 Mar. 1922, p. 16; TLS, 16 Feb. 1922, p. 110.

2879   PAINTED FIRES: NYTBR, 10 Jan. 1926, p. 9.

2880   IN TIMES LIKE THESE: ARCS, 3, No. 2 (1973), 126; BCan, 1 (Oct. 1972), 10; CanL, 54 (Aug. 1972), 113; CDim, 10 (June 1975), 42-48; QQ, 80 (Wint. 1973), 626.

2881   CLEARING IN THE WEST: UTQ, 5 (Apr. 1936), 379.

2882   THE STREAM RUNS FAST: CAB, Mar. 1946, p. 16; SatN, 8 Dec. 1945, p. 37; UTQ, 15 (Apr. 1946), 290-91.

McCOURT, EDWARD (1907-72)

Edward McCourt came from his birthplace Millingar, Ireland, to a homestead near Kitscoty, Alberta, at the age of two. Educated at the University of Alberta and as a Rhodes scholar at Oxford University, he taught at several high schools and then at Queen's University, Kingston, Ontario, the University of New Brunswick, and, from 1944 until his retirement, in the English department of the University of Saskatchewan. His novel, MUSIC AT THE CLOSE, was joint winner of the Ryerson Fiction Award in 1947 and his work of criticism, THE CANADIAN WEST IN FICTION, is a pioneering effort in that area.

PRIMARY MATERIAL

Monographs

FICTION

2883   THE FLAMING HOUR. Toronto: Ryerson, 1947. 170 p.

2884   MUSIC AT THE CLOSE. Toronto: Ryerson, 1947. 228 p.

2885   HOME IS THE STRANGER. Toronto: Macmillan, 1950. 268 p.

2886   THE WOODEN SWORD. Toronto: McClelland and Stewart, 1956. 255 p.

2887   WALK THROUGH THE VALLEY. Toronto: McClelland and Stewart, 1958. 222 p.

2888   FASTING FRIAR. Toronto: McClelland and Stewart, 1963. 222 p.
Also as THE ETTINGER AFFAIR. London: Macdonald, 1963. 222 p.

NONFICTION PROSE

2889 THE CANADIAN WEST IN FICTION. Canadian Men of Letters. To-
      ronto: Ryerson, 1949. vi, 131 p. Bibliog. Index. Rev. and enl.
      Toronto: McGraw-Hill Ryerson, 1970. 128 p.

      Discusses Ralph Connor, Niven, Grove, McClung, Stringer,
      Stead, Salverson, Ross, Mitchell, and van der Mark.

2890 BUCKSKIN BRIGADIER: THE STORY OF THE ALBERTA FIELD FORCE.
      Illus. Vernon Mould. Great Stories of Canada. Toronto: Macmillan,
      1955. vii, 150 p.

      For children.

2891 REVOLT IN THE WEST: THE STORY OF THE RIEL REBELLION. Illus.
      Jack Ferguson. Great Stories of Canada. Toronto: Macmillan, 1958.
      159 p.

      For children.

2892 THE ROAD ACROSS CANADA. Illus. John A. Hall. Toronto: Mac-
      millan, 1965. 199 p.

2893 REMEMBER BUTLER: THE STORY OF SIR WILLIAM BUTLER. Toronto:
      McClelland and Stewart, 1967. xii, 276 p.

2894 SASKATCHEWAN. Traveller's Canada. Toronto: Macmillan, 1968.
      x, 238 p.

2895 THE YUKON AND NORTHWEST TERRITORIES. Traveller's Canada.
      Toronto: Macmillan, 1969. 236 p.

Shorter Work

SHORT STORIES

2896 "Spring Idyll." SATURDAY NIGHT, 2 May 1942, p. 13.

2897 "Horn of Roland." SATURDAY NIGHT, 26 Dec. 1942, p. 25.

2898 "Tom o' the Skies." QUEEN'S QUARTERLY, 50 (Spr. 1943), 64-78.

2899 "Room for a Guest." SATURDAY NIGHT, 23 Oct. 1943, p. 41.

2900 "Happy Warrior: The French Kid was Too Much Like Little Joe." SAT-
      URDAY NIGHT, 8 July 1944, p. 25.

2901 "The Ancient Strain." QUEEN'S QUARTERLY, 52 (Wint. 1945), 429–42.

2902 "A Garden is a Lovesome Thing--But Some People Can't Take it." SAT-URDAY NIGHT, 1 June 1946, p. 32.

2903 "High Sierra." MACLEAN'S, 1 Sept. 1948, pp. 22–23, 59–60.

2904 "Dance for the Devil." SATURDAY EVENING POST, 18 Oct. 1952, pp. 26–27.

2905 "The White Mustang." In CANADIAN SHORT STORIES. Ed. Robert Weaver and Helen James. Toronto: Oxford University Press, 1952, pp. 14–26.

2906 "Our Man on Everest." MONTREALER, 35 (Mar. 1961), 24–27.

2907 "A Man for the Drink." MONTREALER, 35 (Dec. 1961), 36–42.

2908 "The Maltese Piano." MONTREALER, 37 (June 1963), 29–31.

2909 "The Medicine Woman." QUEEN'S QUARTERLY, 73 (Spr. 1966), 75–84.

2910 "The Hired Man." QUEEN'S QUARTERLY, 78 (Spr. 1971), 60–69.

ARTICLES

2911 "Thomas Hardy and War." DALHOUSIE REVIEW, 20 (July 1940), 227–34.

2912 "The Invasion Theme in English Poetry." DALHOUSIE REVIEW, 22 (Apr. 1942), 13–20.

2913 "Tolstoi's WAR AND PEACE." QUEEN'S QUARTERLY, 49 (Sum. 1942), 147–56.

2914 "Rupert Brooke: A Re-Appraisal." DALHOUSIE REVIEW, 24 (July 1944), 148–56.

2915 "Roughing it with the Moodies." QUEEN'S QUARTERLY, 52 (Spr. 1945), 77–89.

Reprinted in no. 195.

2916 "The Canadian Historical Novel." DALHOUSIE REVIEW, 26 (Apr. 1946), 30-36.

    Reprinted in no. 136.

2917 "Home on the Range." SATURDAY REVIEW OF LITERATURE, 2 Nov. 1946, p. 23.

2918 "Mrs. Trollope among the Savages." DALHOUSIE REVIEW, 28 (July 1948), 124-32.

2919 "Dr. Cheadle's Journal." SASKATCHEWAN HISTORY, 2 (May 1949), 21-24.

2920 "Canadian Letters." In ROYAL COMMISSION STUDIES: A SELECTION OF ESSAYS PREPARED FOR THE ROYAL COMMISSION ON NATIONAL DEVELOPMENT IN THE ARTS, LETTERS AND SCIENCES. Ottawa: Edmond Cloutier, King's Printer, 1951, pp. 67-82.

2921 "Atmosphere in the Short Story." WRITER, 66 (Oct. 1953), 336-38.

2922 "The Climate of Politics (Prairie Sector)." MONTREALER, 36 (Feb. 1962), 30-31.

2923 "Ed McCourt's Canada: So Long Mother England, Farewell Uncle Sam." MACLEAN'S, 85 (Feb. 1972), 16-17, 48.

2924 "Prairie Literature and Its Critics." In A REGION OF THE WIND: IN-TERPRETING THE WESTERN CANADIAN PLAINS. Ed. Richard Allen. Regina: Canadian Plains Studies Centre, University of Saskatchewan, 1973, pp. 153-62.

Manuscripts

2925 Queen's University Library, Kingston, Ont.; University of Saskatchewan Library, Saskatoon.

SECONDARY MATERIAL

Criticism

2926 Baldwin, R.G. "Pattern in the Novels of Edward McCourt." QUEEN'S QUARTERLY, 68 (Wint. 1961-62), 574-87.

2927   Bevan, Allan. Introd., MUSIC AT THE CLOSE. New Canadian Library, no. 52. Toronto: McClelland and Stewart, 1966, pp. 7-11.

2928   Bogaards, Winnifred M. "Edward McCourt: A Reassessment." STUDIES IN CANADIAN LITERATURE, 5 (Fall 1980), 181-208.

2929   _____. "Edward McCourt, One Man's View of Alberta and Saskatchewan." PRAIRIE FORUM, 5 (Spr. 1980), 39-50.

2930   _____. Introd., THE WOODEN SWORD. New Canadian Library, no. 97. Toronto: McClelland and Stewart, 1975, pp. v-xi.

2931   Brewster, Elizabeth. "Memoirs of a Romantic Ironist." CANADIAN LITERATURE, No. 70 (Aut. 1976), pp. 23-31.

For criticism on McCourt, see also no. 51.

Book Reviews

2932   THE FLAMING HOUR: CFor, 27 (June 1947), 71; DR, 27 (Oct. 1947), 372-73.

2933   MUSIC AT THE CLOSE: DR, 28 (July 1948), 195-96; QQ, 55 (Aut. 1948), 372-73; SaskH, 1 (May 1948), 29-30; UTQ, 17 (Apr. 1948), 269-70.

2934   HOME IS THE STRANGER: CFor, 30 (Feb. 1951), 263; RUL, 6 (Sept. 1951), 56-58; SaskH, 4 (Spr. 1951), 77-79; SatN, 19 Dec. 1950, pp. 21-22; UTQ, 20 (Apr. 1951), 266-67.

2935   THE WOODEN SWORD: CAB, Fall 1956, p. 11; CFor, 36 (Jan. 1957), 239; QQ, 64 (Spr. 1957), 144-45; UTQ, 26 (Apr. 1957), 317.

2936   WALK THROUGH THE VALLEY: CanL, 1 (Sum. 1959), 78-80; QQ, 67 (Sum. 1960), 316-17; SatN, 14 Mar. 1959, pp. 32-33; UTQ, 29 (July 1960), 473.

2937   FASTING FRIAR: CanL, 20 (Spr. 1964), 73-75; CDim, 2 (Jan. 1965), 16; CFor, 44 (Apr. 1964), 21-22; MONTREALER, 38 (Feb. 1964), 49; SatN, 79 (Mar. 1964), 28; TamR, [31] (Spr. 1964), 91-92; UTQ, 33 (July 1964), 395.

2938   THE CANADIAN WEST IN FICTION: CHR, 32 (Mar. 1951), 82-83; QQ, 56 (Aut. 1949), 456-58; RUL, 4 (Apr. 1950), 745-47; UTQ, 19 (Apr. 1950), 305.

2939   REVOLT IN THE WEST: SaskH, 12 (Spr. 1959), 75-76.

2940   REMEMBER BUTLER: CAB, 43 (Wint. 1967), 20; ECONOMIST, 2 Dec. 1967 Supplement, p. xxi; SaskH, 21 (Wint. 1968), 38-39; TLS, 25 Jan. 1968, p. 86; UTQ, 37 (July 1968), 527-28.

MacEWEN, GWENDOLYN (1941--)

Gwendolyn MacEwen is known primarily as a poet and one who established herself at a very early age. She was born and lives in Toronto, left school at eighteen to concentrate on her writing, has written radio plays and documentaries for CBC radio, and has travelled to the Middle and Far East. Her fiction, which makes use of the exotic and bizarre, often draws heavily on Eastern history, myth, and mysticism.

PRIMARY MATERIAL

Monographs

FICTION

2941   JULIAN THE MAGICIAN: A NOVEL. Toronto: Macmillan, 1963. 151 p.

2942   KING OF EGYPT, KING OF DREAMS: A NOVEL. Toronto: Macmillan, 1971. 287 p.

2943   NOMAN. [Ottawa]: Oberon, 1972. 121 p.

Short stories and a novella.

NONFICTION PROSE

2944   MERMAIDS AND IKONS: A GREEK SUMMER. Toronto: Anansi, 1978. 110 p.

POETRY

2945   THE DRUNKEN CLOCK: POEMS. Toronto: Aleph, 1961. N. pag.

2946   SELAH. Toronto: Aleph, 1961. 12 p.

2947   THE RISING FIRE. Toronto: Contact, 1963. vii, 82 p.

2948   A BREAKFAST FOR BARBARIANS. Toronto: Ryerson, 1966. 53 p.

2949   THE SHADOW-MAKER. Toronto: Macmillan, 1969. 83 p.

2950   THE ARMIES OF THE MOON. Toronto: Macmillan, 1972. 75 p.

2951   MAGIC ANIMALS: SELECTED POEMS OLD AND NEW. Toronto: Macmillan, 1974. 154 p.

2952   THE FIRE-EATERS. [Ottawa]: Oberon, 1976. 63 p.

DRAMA

2953   THE TROJAN WOMEN: A PLAY. Toronto: Playwrights Co-Op, 1979. 83 p.

Shorter Work

SHORT STORIES

2954   "Animal Syllables." ALPHABET, No. 15 (Dec. 1968), pp. 16-20.

2955   "Fragments from a Childhood." ALPHABET, No. 15 (Dec. 1968), pp. 10-15.

Manuscripts

2956   University of Toronto Library.

SECONDARY MATERIAL

Criticism

2957   Barrett, Elizabeth. "A Tour de Force." EVIDENCE, 8 (1964), 40-43.

2958   Davey, Frank. "Gwendolyn MacEwen: The Secret of Alchemy." OPEN LETTER, 2nd ser., No. 4 (Spr. 1973), pp. 5-23.

2959 Gose, E.B. "They Shall Have Arcana." CANADIAN LITERATURE, No. 21 (Sum. 1964), pp. 36-45.

Discusses JULIAN THE MAGICIAN; reprinted in no. 5113.

2960 "An Interview with Gwendolyn MacEwen." MANNA, No. 4 ([1973]), pp. 6-10.

2961 Sowton, Ian. "To Improvise an Eden." EDGE, 2 (Spr. 1964), 119-24.

For criticism on MacEwen, see also nos. 162, 181, and 618.

Book Reviews

2962 JULIAN THE MAGICIAN: ALPHABET, 8 (June 1964), 95-96; CanL, 21 (Sum. 1964), 36-45; TamR, [31] (Spr. 1964), 90-91; UTQ, 33 (July 1964), 399-400.

2963 KING OF EGYPT, KING OF DREAMS: BCan, 1 (Nov. 1971), 8-9; CanL, 53 (Sum. 1972), 102-04; CFor, 51 (Jan. 1972), 77; JCF, 1 (Sum. 1972), 76-77; SatN, 87 (Jan. 1972), 37, 40; UTQ, 41 (Sum. 1972), 314.

2964 NOMAN: BCan, 1 (Nov. 1972), 53; CanL, 58 (Aut. 1973), 110-11; CFM, 11 (Aut. 1973), 75-77; CRead, 15 (Jan. 1974), 8; JCF, 2 (Wint. 1973), 93-94; MHRev, 28 (Oct. 1973), 141-42; Q&Q, 38, No. 11 (1972), 11-12; QUARRY, 22 (Spr. 1973), 71.

2965 MERMAIDS AND IKONS: BCan, 7 (Oct. 1978), 16, 18; BrO, 5, No. 4 (1978), 41; CanL, 84 (Spr. 1980), 122-23; ECW, 12 (Fall 1978), 72-78.

MacLENNAN, HUGH (1907--)

Born in Glace Bay, Cape Breton Island, and raised in Halifax, Nova Scotia, Hugh MacLennan earned a B.A. in 1928 from Dalhousie University, Halifax, an M.A. as Rhodes scholar at Oxford University in 1932, and an M.A. and Ph.D. in classics from Princeton in 1935. He taught classics and history for ten years at Lower Canada College in Montreal and from 1951 to 1979 was a professor of English at McGill University.

MacLennan has made a significant contribution to the development of Canadian fiction through his pioneering exploration of Canadian geographical, political, and, especially, social realities. Long considered a major Canadian novelist for his attempts to link his characters with their larger context, he has won numerous honorary degrees and the 1966 Molson Prize. He has received Governor General's Awards for three novels--TWO SOLITUDES, THE PRECIPICE, and his most ambitious work, THE WATCH THAT ENDS THE NIGHT--and for two of his prose collections, CROSS-COUNTRY and THIRTY & THREE. His novels have been translated into a dozen languages.

PRIMARY MATERIAL

Monographs

FICTION

2966   BAROMETER RISING. New York: Duell, Sloan, and Pearce, 1941. 326 p.

2967   TWO SOLITUDES. New York: Duell, Sloan, and Pearce, 1945. 370 p.

2968   THE PRECIPICE. Toronto: Collins, 1948. viii, 372 p.

2969   EACH MAN'S SON. Toronto: Macmillan, 1951. xi, 244 p.

2970   THE WATCH THAT ENDS THE NIGHT. Toronto: Macmillan, 1959.
373 p.

2971   RETURN OF THE SPHINX. Toronto: Macmillan, 1967. 303 p.

2972   VOICES IN TIME. Toronto: Macmillan, 1980. 313 p.

NONFICTION PROSE

2973   OXYRHYNCHUS: AN ECONOMIC AND SOCIAL STUDY. Princeton,
N.J.: Princeton University Press, 1935. 93 p. Bibliog.

        Ph.D. dissertation.

2974   WHAT IS A CANADIAN? AN ADDRESS DELIVERED TO THE ROTARY
CLUB OF MONTREAL, JUNE 2ND, 1942. Montreal: Federated, [1942].
14 p.

2975   CANADIAN UNITY AND QUEBEC. By Emile Vaillancourt, J.P. Humphrey,
and Hugh MacLennan. Montreal: n.p., 1942. 16 p.

2976   CROSS-COUNTRY. Toronto: Collins, 1949. ix, 172 p.; rpt. with
new introduction by the author. Canadiana Reprint Series. Edmonton:
Hurtig, 1972. xxiii, 172 p.

2977   THE PRESENT WORLD AS SEEN IN ITS LITERATURE. Fredericton: University of New Brunswick, 1952. 12 p.

2978   THIRTY & THREE. Ed. Dorothy Duncan. Toronto: Macmillan, 1954.
ix, 261 p.

2979   THE FUTURE OF THE NOVEL AS AN ART FORM. Toronto: University
of Toronto Press, [1959?]. 11 p.

        Reprinted in no. 136.

2980   SCOTCHMAN'S RETURN AND OTHER ESSAYS. Toronto: Macmillan,
1960. v, 279 p.; rpt. as SCOTSMAN'S RETURN AND OTHER ESSAYS.
London: Heinemann, 1961. vii, 272 p.

2981   SEVEN RIVERS OF CANADA: THE MACKENZIE, THE ST. LAWRENCE,
THE OTTAWA, THE RED, THE SASKATCHEWAN, THE FRASER, THE ST.
JOHN. Toronto: Macmillan, 1961. ix, 170 p.; rpt. as THE RIVERS
OF CANADA: THE MACKENZIE, THE ST. LAWRENCE, THE OTTAWA,
THE RED, THE SASKATCHEWAN, THE FRASER, THE ST. JOHN. Photos.
John De Visser. New York: Charles Scribner's Sons, 1962. 170 p. Rev.
enl. ed. Toronto: Macmillan, 1974. 270 p. Bibliog. Index.

2982 TEXT OF AN ADDRESS: CANADIAN CLUB, TORONTO, MARCH 26, 1962. N.p.: n.p., [1962]. 11 p.

2983 THE HISTORY OF CANADIAN-AMERICAN RELATIONS. Plainfield, Vt.: Goddard College, 1963. 16 l.

2984 AN ORANGE FROM PORTUGAL. Thornhill, Ont.: Village, [1964]. N. pag.

Reprinted from CROSS-COUNTRY.

2985 THE COLOUR OF CANADA. Canadian Illustrated Library. Toronto: McClelland and Stewart, 1967. 126 p. Rev. ed. Toronto: McClelland and Stewart, 1972. 126 p. 2nd rev. ed. Toronto: McClelland and Stewart, 1978. 126 p.

2986 THE OTHER SIDE OF HUGH MacLENNAN: SELECTED ESSAYS OLD AND NEW. Ed. Elspeth Cameron. Toronto: Macmillan, 1978. xii, 301 p.

EDITED WORK

2987 McGILL: THE STORY OF A UNIVERSITY. Illus. John Gilroy. London: George Allen and Unwin, 1960. 135 p.

Includes MacLennan's "McGill Today" and "The Origins of McGill."

Shorter Work

ARTICLES

2988 "Oxyrhynchus." DALHOUSIE REVIEW, 16 (Oct. 1936), 314-23.

2989 "Culture, Canadian Style." SATURDAY REVIEW OF LITERATURE, 28 Mar. 1942, pp. 3-4, 18-20.

2990 "How Do I Write." CANADIAN AUTHOR AND BOOKMAN, 21 (Dec. 1945), 6-7.

2991 "Canada between Covers." SATURDAY REVIEW OF LITERATURE, 7 Sept. 1946, pp. 5-6, 28-30.

2992 "Do We Gag Our Writers?" MACLEAN'S, 1 Mar. 1947, pp. 13, 50, 52, 54-55.

2993   "The Psychology of Canadian Nationalism." FOREIGN AFFAIRS, 27 (Apr. 1949), 413-25.

2994   "My First Book." CANADIAN AUTHOR AND BOOKMAN, 28 (Sum. 1952), 3-4.

2995   "Fiction in the Age of Science." WESTERN HUMANITIES REVIEW, 6 (Aut. 1952), 325-34.

2996   "The Artist and Critic in Society." PRINCETON ALUMNI WEEKLY, 30 Jan. 1953, pp. 85-91.

2997   "The Writer and His Audience." MONTREALER, 28 (June 1954), 27, 30-31.

2998   "The Older Quest." DALHOUSIE REVIEW, 35 (Sum. 1955), 120-26.

2999   "The Challenge to Prose." PROCEEDINGS AND TRANSACTIONS OF THE ROYAL SOCIETY OF CANADA, 3rd ser., 49 (1955), Sect. II, 45-55.

3000   "New Nationalism and How it Might Have Looked to Shakespeare." MACLEAN'S, 16 Feb. 1957, pp. 8, 49-52.

3001   "The Defence of LADY CHATTERLEY." CANADIAN LITERATURE, No. 6 (Aut. 1960), pp. 18-23.

3002   "The Story of a Novel." CANADIAN LITERATURE, No. 3 (Wint. 1960), pp. 35-39.

        Discusses THE WATCH THAT ENDS THE NIGHT; reprinted in no. 195.

3003   "Personal Brief to the Royal Commission on Publications." CANADIAN LIBRARY, 17 (Mar. 1961), 235-42.

3004   "One Canada: The Real Promise of Quebec's Revolution." MACLEAN'S, 26 Aug. 1961, pp. 14-15, 32-34.

3005   "Postscript on Odysseus." CANADIAN LITERATURE, No. 13 (Sum. 1962), pp. 86-87.

        A reply to no. 5145.

3006   "The Arts in Canada: A Search for Identity." MUSICAL AMERICA, 83 (Sept. 1963), 12-13 ff.

3007   "Two Solitudes Revisited." MACLEAN'S, 14 Dec. 1964, pp. 26-27, 54-57.

3008   "Reflections on Two Decades." CANADIAN LITERATURE, No. 41 (Sum. 1969), pp. 28-39.

      Reprinted in nos. 2986 and 5106.

3009   "Canada Consists of This: Two Solitudes That Meet and Greet in Hope and Hate." MACLEAN'S, 84 (Aug. 1971), 19-23, 49-51.

3010   "Address to the Montreal Symposium on De-Canadianization." In THE EVOLUTION OF CANADIAN LITERATURE IN ENGLISH: 1945-1970. Ed. Paul Denham. Toronto: Holt, Rinehart and Winston, 1973, pp. 50-56.

3011   "A Society in Revolt." In VOICES OF CANADA: AN INTRODUCTION TO CANADIAN CULTURE. Ed. Judith Webster. Burlington, Vt.: Association for Canadian Studies in the United States, 1977, pp. 29-30.

3012   "Fiction in Canada--1930 to 1980." UNIVERSITY OF TORONTO QUARTERLY, 50 (Fall 1980), 29-42.

For articles by MacLennan, see also nos. 192, 208, and 2987.

Manuscripts

3013   McGill University Library, Montreal; University of Calgary, Calgary, Alta.

SECONDARY MATERIAL

Bibliographies

3014   Cameron, Elspeth, comp. "Hugh MacLennan: An Annotated Bibliography." In THE ANNOTATED BIBLIOGRAPHY OF CANADA'S MAJOR AUTHORS. Ed. Robert Lecker and Jack David. Downsview, Ont.: ECW, 1979, pp. 103-53. Index.

3015   _____. "A MacLennan Log." JOURNAL OF CANADIAN STUDIES, 14 (Wint. 1979-80), 106-21.

Criticism

3016 Arnason, David. "Canadian Nationalism in Search of a Form: Hugh MacLennan's BAROMETER RISING." JOURNAL OF CANADIAN FICTION, 1 (Fall 1972), 68-71.

3017 Bissell, Claude T. Introd., TWO SOLITUDES. Arranged for School Reading. Toronto: Macmillan, 1951, pp. vii-xxiii.

3018 Blodgett, E.D. "Intertextual Designs in Hugh MacLennan's THE WATCH THAT ENDS THE NIGHT." CANADIAN REVIEW OF COMPARATIVE LITERATURE, 5 (Fall 1978), 280-88.

3019 Boeschenstein, Hermann. "Hugh MacLennan, ein kanadischer Romancier." ZEITSCHRIFT FÜR ANGLISTIK UND AMERIKANISTIK, 8, No. 2 (1960), 117-35.

    Translated by C. Maurice Taylor in no. 3044.

3020 Bonnycastle, Stephen. "The Power of THE WATCH THAT ENDS THE NIGHT." JOURNAL OF CANADIAN STUDIES, 14 (Wint. 1979-80), 76-89.

3021 Boone, Laurel. "EACH MAN'S SON: Romance in Disguise." JOURNAL OF CANADIAN FICTION, 28-29 (1980), 147-56.

3022 Buitenhuis, Peter. HUGH MacLENNAN. Canadian Writers and Their Works. Toronto: Forum House, 1971. 83 p. Bibliog.

3023 _____. "Two Solitudes Revisited: Hugh MacLennan and Leonard Cohen." LITERARY HALF-YEARLY, 13 (July 1972), 19-32.

3024 Cameron, Donald A. "Hugh MacLennan: The Tennis Racket is an Antelope Bone." JOURNAL OF CANADIAN FICTION, 1, No. 1 (1972), 40-47.

    An interview; reprinted in no. 124.

3025 Cameron, Elspeth. HUGH MacLENNAN: A WRITER'S LIFE. Toronto: University of Toronto Press, 1981. xv, 421 p.

3026 _____. "'A Late Germination in a Cold Climate': The Growth of MacLennan Criticism." JOUNAL OF CANADIAN STUDIES, 14 (Wint. 1979-80), 3-19.

3027 _____. "MacLennan's SPHINX: Critical Reception & Oedipal Origins." JOURNAL OF CANADIAN FICTION, 30 (1980), 141-59.

3028 _____. "Ordeal by Fire: The Genesis of MacLennan's THE PRECIPICE." CANADIAN LITERATURE, No. 82 (Aut. 1979), pp. 35-46.

3029 _____. "The Overlay Theme in MacLennan's THE PRECIPICE." JOURNAL OF CANADIAN FICTION, No. 20 (1977), pp. 117-24.

3030 Capone, Giovanna. "Il Realismo Mitico di Hugh MacLennan." SPICILEGIO MODERNO, No. 6 (1976), pp. 79-102.

  Reprinted in no. 126.

3031 Cavanagh, David. "Thematic and Structural Unity in TWO SOLITUDES." ALIVE, 32 (1973), 50-51.

3032 Chambers, Robert D. "Hugh MacLennan and Religion: THE PRECIPICE Revisited." JOURNAL OF CANADIAN STUDIES, 14 (Wint. 1979-80, 46-53.

3033 _____. "The Novels of Hugh MacLennan." JOURNAL OF CANADIAN STUDIES, 2 (Aug. 1967), 3-11.

  Reprinted in no. 3044.

3034 Clark, J. Wilson. "Hugh MacLennan's Comprador Outlook." LITERATURE AND IDEOLOGY, No. 12 (1972), pp. 1-8.

  Discusses THE WATCH THAT ENDS THE NIGHT.

3035 Cockburn, Robert. THE NOVELS OF HUGH MacLENNAN. Montreal: Harvest House, 1969. 165 p. Bibliog.

3036 Davis, Marilyn J. "Fathers and Sons." CANADIAN LITERATURE, No. 58 (Aut. 1973), pp. 39-50.

3037 Dooley, David Joseph. "EACH MAN'S SON: The Daemon of Hope and Imagination." JOURNAL OF CANADIAN STUDIES, 14 (Wint. 1979-80), 66-75.

3038 Duncan, Dorothy. BLUENOSE: A PORTRAIT OF NOVA SCOTIA. New York: Harper and Brothers, 1942. 273 p. Bibliog. Index.

  Includes some personal reminiscences by Dorothy Duncan, MacLennan's first wife.

3039 _____. "My Author Husband." MACLEAN'S, 15 Aug. 1945, pp. 7, 36, 38-40.

3040   Duran, Gillian. "Terrorism, Human Nature, and Hugh MacLennan's RETURN OF THE SPHINX." LITERATURE AND IDEOLOGY, No. 15 (1973), pp. 51-58.

3041   Farmiloe, Dorothy. "Hugh MacLennan and the Canadian Myth." MOSAIC, 2 (Spr. 1969), 1-9.

        Reprinted in no. 3044.

3042   Goetsch, Paul. DAS ROMANWERK HUGH MacLENNANS: EINE STUDIE ZUM LITERARISCHEN NATIONALISMUS IN KANADA. Hamburg: Cram, de Gruyter, 1961. 142 p. Bibliog.

3043   _____. "Too Long to the Courtly Muses: Hugh MacLennan as a Contemporary Writer." CANADIAN LITERATURE, No. 10 (Aut. 1961), pp. 19-31.

        Reprinted in no. 5113.

3044   _____, ed. with introd. HUGH MacLENNAN. Critical Views on Canadian Writers, 8. Toronto: McGraw-Hill Ryerson, 1973. 179 p. Bibliog.

        Reprints articles by Boeschenstein, Chambers, Farmiloe, Hirano, McPherson, New, O'Donnell, Thorne, and Woodcock.

3045   Heintzman, Ralph. "The Other Daemon." JOURNAL OF CANADIAN STUDIES, 14 (Wint. 1979-80), 1-2, 151-52.

3046   Hirano, Keiichi. "Jerome Martell and Norman Bethune: A Note on Hugh MacLennan's THE WATCH THAT ENDS THE NIGHT." STUDIES IN ENGLISH LITERATURE (University of Tokyo), 44, English Number (1968), 37-59.

        Reprinted in no. 3044.

3047   Hoy, Helen. "'The Gates Closed on Us Then': The Paradise-Lost Motif in Hugh MacLennan's Fiction." JOURNAL OF CANADIAN STUDIES, 14 (Wint. 1979-80), 29-45.

3048   Hyman, Roger Leslie. "Hugh MacLennan: His Art, His Society and His Critics." QUEEN'S QUARTERLY, 82 (Wint. 1975), 515-27.

3049   _____. "Return to RETURN OF THE SPHINX." ENGLISH STUDIES IN CANADA, 1 (Wint. 1975), 450-65.

3050   James, William C. "A Voyage into Selfhood: Hugh MacLennan's THE

WATCH THAT ENDS THE NIGHT." In RELIGION AND CULTURE IN CANADA/RELIGION ET CULTURE AU CANADA: ESSAYS BY MEMBERS OF THE CANADIAN SOCIETY FOR THE STUDY OF RELIGION/RECUEIL D'ARTICLES PAR DES MEMBRES DE LA SOCIÉTÉ CANADIENNE POUR L'ÉTUDE DE LA RELIGION. Ed. Peter Slater. N.p.: Corp. Canadienne des Sciences Religieuses/Canadian Corp. for Studies in Religion, 1977, pp. 315-32.

3051 Kattan, Naïm. "Deux Romanciers Canadiens-Anglais et Montréal." In CULTURE POPULAIRE ET LITTÉRATURES AU QUÉBEC. Ed. René Bouchard. Saratoga, Calif.: Anma Libri, 1980, pp. 257-63.

Discusses MacLennan and Richler.

3052 Kelly, Catherine. "The Unity of TWO SOLITUDES." ARIEL, 6 (Apr. 1975), 38-61.

3053 Lucas, Alec. HUGH MacLENNAN. Canadian Writers, No. 8. Toronto: McClelland and Stewart, 1970. 61 p. Bibliog.

3054 _____. Introd., EACH MAN'S SON. New Canadian Library, no. 30. Toronto: McClelland and Stewart, 1962, pp. 7-13.

3055 Lynn, S. "A Canadian Writer and the Modern World." MARXIST QUARTERLY, 1 (Spr. 1962), 36-43.

Discusses THE WATCH THAT ENDS THE NIGHT.

3056 MacGregor, Roy. "A Voice Out of Time." MACLEAN'S, 22 Sept. 1980, pp. 45-48, 50.

3057 MacLulich, T.D. "Oedipus and Eve: The Novels of Hugh MacLennan." DALHOUSIE REVIEW, 59 (Aut. 1979), 500-518.

3058 _____. "THE PRECIPICE: MacLennan's Anatomy of Failure." JOURNAL OF CANADIAN STUDIES, 14 (Wint. 1979-80), 54-65.

3059 McPherson, Hugo. Introd., BAROMETER RISING. New Canadian Library, no. 8. Toronto: McClelland and Stewart, 1958, pp. ix-xv.

3060 _____. "The Novels of Hugh MacLennan." QUEEN'S QUARTERLY, 60 (Sum. 1953), 186-98.

Reprinted in no. 3044.

3061 Marshall, Tom A. "Some Working Notes on THE WATCH THAT ENDS THE NIGHT." QUARRY, 17 (Wint. 1968), 13-16.

3062 Mathews, Robin D. "Hugh MacLennan: The Nationalist Dilemma in Canada." STUDIES IN CANADIAN LITERATURE, 1 (Wint. 1976), 49-63.

Reprinted in no. 163.

3063 Morley, Patricia A. THE IMMORAL MORALISTS: HUGH MacLENNAN AND LEONARD COHEN. Toronto: Clarke, Irwin, 1972. 144 p. Index.

3064 Murphy, Rosalie. "A Comparison of THE RISE OF SILAS LAPHAM and BAROMETER RISING." AMERICAN REVIEW OF CANADIAN STUDIES, 9 (Aut. 1979), 125-29.

3065 New, William H. "The Storm and After: Imagery and Symbolism in Hugh MacLennan's BAROMETER RISING." QUEEN'S QUARTERLY, 74 (Sum. 1967), 302-13.

Reprinted in nos. 173 and 3044.

3066 _____. "Winter and the Night-People." CANADIAN LITERATURE, No. 36 (Spr. 1968), pp. 26-33.

Discusses RETURN OF THE SPHINX; reprinted in nos. 173 and 3044.

3067 O'Donnell, Kathleen. "TWO SOLITUDES: The Vision of Canada." REVUE DE L'UNIVERSITÉ D'OTTAWA, 43 (Oct.-Dec. 1973), 557-65.

3068 _____. "The Wanderer in BAROMETER RISING." UNIVERSITY OF WINDSOR REVIEW, 3 (Spr. 1968), 12-18.

Reprinted in no. 3044.

3069 Pérez Botero, Luis. "El Mundo novelesco de Hugh MacLennan." REVISTA DE LETRAS, 3 (Dec. 1971), 495-510.

3070 Roberts, Ann. "The Dilemma of Hugh MacLennan." MARXIST QUARTERLY, 1 (Aut. 1962), 58-66.

Discusses THE WATCH THAT ENDS THE NIGHT.

3071 Ross, Catherine Sheldrick. "Hugh MacLennan's Two Worlds." CANADIAN LITERATURE, No. 80 (Spr. 1979), pp. 5-12.

3072 Staines, David. "Mapping the Terrain." MOSAIC, 11 (Spr. 1978), 137-51.

3073 Stevenson, Warren. "A Neglected Theme in TWO SOLITUDES." CANADIAN LITERATURE, No. 75 (Wint. 1977), pp. 53-60.

3074   Sutherland, Ronald. "Hugh MacLennan: Interviewed by Ronald Suther-
        land." CANADIAN LITERATURE, Nos. 68-69 (Spr.-Sum. 1976),
        pp. 40-48.

3075   Thorne, W.B. "The Relation of Structure to Theme in THE WATCH THAT
        ENDS THE NIGHT." HUMANITIES ASSOCIATION BULLETIN, 20 (Spr.
        1969), 42-45.

        Reprinted in no. 3044.

3076   Watters, Reginald Eyre. "Hugh MacLennan and the Canadian Character."
        In AS A MAN THINKS. . . . Ed. Edmund Morrison and William Robbins.
        Toronto: W.J. Gage, 1953, pp. 228-43.

3077   Wilson, Edmund. "A Reporter at Large: O Canada: An American's
        Notes on Canadian Culture--1." NEW YORKER, 14 Nov. 1964, pp.
        63-140.

        Reprinted in no. 210.

3078   Zezulka, Joseph M. "MacLennan's Defeated Pilgrim: A Perspective on
        RETURN OF THE SPHINX." JOURNAL OF CANADIAN FICTION, 4,
        No. 1 (1975), 121-31.

3079   Zichy, Francis. "'Shocked and Startled into Utter Banality': Characters
        and Circumstance in THE WATCH THAT ENDS THE NIGHT." JOURNAL
        OF CANADIAN STUDIES, 14 (Wint. 1979-80), 90-105.

For criticism on MacLennan, see also nos. 126, 129, 139, 168, 182, 205,
2986, 3743, 5126, 5145, 5206, and especially 5058.

Book Reviews

3080   BAROMETER RISING: CFor, 21 (Dec. 1941), 282; DR, 21 (Jan. 1942),
        512; NY, 4 Oct. 1941, p. 87; NYTBR, 5 Oct. 1941, p. 32; QQ, 48
        (Wint. 1941), 482; SatN, 11 Oct. 1941, p. 20; SatR, 25 Oct. 1941,
        p. 21; UTQ, 11 (Apr. 1942), 298-300.

3081   TWO SOLITUDES: CFor, 25 (May 1945), 46; CGJ, 31 (Sept. 1945),
        xii-xiii; CHR, 26 (Sept. 1945), 326-28; COMMONWEAL, 16 Mar. 1945,
        p. 546; DR, 25 (Oct. 1945), 378-79; NATION, 24 Feb. 1945, p. 227;
        NewR, 26 Feb. 1945, p. 310; NYTBR, 21 Jan. 1945, p. 5; NYTBR,
        22 July 1945, p. 2; QQ, 52 (Wint. 1945), 494-96; SatN, 7 Apr. 1945,
        p. 21; SatR, 10 Mar. 1945, pp. 13-14; UTQ, 15 (Apr. 1946), 280-83.

3082   THE PRECIPICE: CAB, 25 (Aut. 1949), 36; CFor, 28 (Nov. 1948),

190; COMMONWEAL, 1 Oct. 1948, p. 601; NY, 18 Sept. 1948, p. 107; NYTBR, 12 Sept. 1948, p. 5; RUL, 4 (Apr. 1950), 742-43; SatN, 28 Aug. 1948, p. 17; SatR, 18 Sept. 1948, p. 26; UTQ, 18 (1948-49), 263-65.

3083   EACH MAN'S SON: CFor, 31 (Sept. 1951), 140; COMMONWEAL, 20 Apr. 1951, p. 46; NewR, 20 Aug. 1951, p. 21; NoR, 5 (Oct. 1951), 40-42; NY, 14 Apr. 1951, p. 137; NYTBR, 15 Apr. 1951, p 5; RUL, 6 (Sept. 1951), 53-54; SatN, 24 Apr. 1951, p. 35; SatR, 9 June 1951, p. 11; UTQ, 21 (Apr. 1952), 263-64.

3084   THE WATCH THAT ENDS THE NIGHT: AtlA, 49 (Mar. 1959), 77; CanL, 1 (Sum. 1959), 80-81; CFor, 39 (June 1959), 66; COMMON-WEAL, 1 May 1959, pp. 133-34; CULTURE, 20 (1959), 360-61; CULTURE, 29 (Sept. 1978), 271-73; DR, 39 (Spr. 1959), 115, 117, 119; NS, 19 Dec. 1959, p. 888; NY, 28 Feb. 1959, p. 117; NYTBR, 15 Feb. 1959, pp. 4-5; QQ, 66 (Sum. 1959), 343-44; SatN, 28 Mar. 1959, pp. 29-31; SatR, 28 Feb. 1959, p. 15; TamR, 11 (Spr. 1959), 77-79; UTQ, 29 (July 1960), 461-63.

3085   RETURN OF THE SPHINX: AtlA, 57 (Aug. 1967), 88; CanL, 36 (Spr. 1968), 26-33; DR, 47 (Aut. 1967), 435, 437; HM, 235 (Sept. 1967), 118; MACLEAN'S, 80 (Sept. 1967), 90-91; NYTBR, 20 Aug. 1967, p. 4; QQ, 74 (Wint. 1967), 762-65; SatN, 82 (Oct. 1967), 49; SatR, 7 Oct. 1967, p. 44; TamR, [45] (Aut. 1967), 114-16; UTQ, 37 (July 1968), 383-84.

3087   VOICES IN TIME: BCan, 9 (Aug. 1980), 4-6; CFor, 60 (Dec. 1980), 22-23; MACLEAN'S, 22 Sept. 1980, pp. 50-51; Q&Q, 46 (Oct. 1980), 36; SatN, 95 (Sept. 1980), 51, 54-55.

3087   OXYRHYNCHUS: UTQ, 10 (Apr. 1941), 327.

3088   CROSS-COUNTRY: BCan, 2 (Jan. 1973), 23-24; CFor, 29 (Jan. 1950), 236; CULTURE, 10 (Dec. 1949), 392-96; QQ, 79 (Aut. 1972), 438; RUL, 4 (Apr. 1950), 743-45; UTQ, 19 (Apr. 1950), 32.

3089   THIRTY & THREE: DR, 34 (Wint. 1955), 447; QQ, 62 (Sum. 1955), 264-65; UTQ, 24 (Apr. 1955), 303.

3090   SCOTCHMAN'S RETURN: AtlA, 51 (Jan. 1961), 81; CanL, 6 (Aut. 1960), 67-69; DR, 41 (Spr. 1961), 121; SatN, 1 Oct. 1960, pp. 26, 28; SPECTATOR, 22 Sept. 1961, p. 395; UTQ, 30 (July 1961), 426.

3091   THE OTHER SIDE OF HUGH MacLENNAN: BCan, 7 (Nov. 1978), 12-14; CRead, 20, No. 1 ([1978]), 1-2; DR, 59 (Spr. 1979), 190-93; Q&Q, 44, No. 16 (1978), 5; SatN, 93 (Nov. 1978), 56-58; UTQ, 48 (Sum. 1979), 445-47.

MARSHALL, JOYCE (1913--)

Born in Montreal and educated in English at McGill University (B.A. 1935), Joyce Marshall has lived for much of her adult life in Toronto. She has worked as a sales clerk, governess, civil servant, market researcher, manuscript reader, and translator.

PRIMARY MATERIAL

Monographs

FICTION

3092 PRESENTLY TOMORROW. Boston: Little, Brown, 1946. 309 p.

3093 LOVERS AND STRANGERS: A NOVEL. Philadelphia: J.B. Lippincott, 1957. 246 p.

3094 A PRIVATE PLACE: STORIES. [Ottawa]: Oberon, 1975. 135 p.

TRANSLATIONS

3095 THE ROAD PAST ALTAMONT. By Gabrielle Roy. Toronto: McClelland and Stewart, 1966. 146 p.

3096 WORD FROM NEW FRANCE: THE SELECTED LETTERS OF MARIE DE L'INCARNATION. Trans. and ed. Joyce Marshall. Toronto: Oxford University Press, 1967. viii, 435 p. Bibliog.

3097 NO PASSPORT: A DISCOVERY OF CANADA. By Eugène Cloutier. Drawings by Bob Hohnstock. Toronto: Oxford University Press, 1968. 280 p.

3098   WINDFLOWER. By Gabrielle Roy. Toronto: McClelland and Stewart, 1970. 152 p.

3099   THE OCTOBER CRISIS. By Gérard Pelletier. Toronto: McClelland and Stewart, 1971. 247 p.

3100   A WOMAN IN A MAN'S WORLD. By Thérèse-Forget Casgrain. Foreword Frank R. Scott. Toronto: McClelland and Stewart, 1972. 190 p.

3101   ENCHANTED SUMMER. By Gabrielle Roy. Toronto: McClelland and Stewart, 1976. 125 p.

Shorter Work

SHORT STORIES

3102   "And the Hilltop was Elizabeth." QUEEN'S QUARTERLY, 45 (Sum. 1938), 186-94.

3103   "The Old Woman." In CANADIAN SHORT STORIES. Ed. Robert Weaver and Helen James. Toronto: Oxford University Press, 1952, pp. 48-60.

3104   "The Screaming Silence." NEW LIBERTY, 30 (Oct. 1953), 29, 48-50.

3105   "Rightly Call the Nymph." MONTREALER, 37 (May 1963), 30-35.

3106   "Summer." In '75: NEW CANADIAN STORIES. Ed. David Helwig and Joan Harcourt. [Ottawa]: Oberon, 1975, pp. 42-56.

3107   "The Accident." FIDDLEHEAD, No. 108 (Wint. 1976), pp. 63-69.

3108   "The Gradual Day." CANADIAN FICTION MAGAZINE, No. 20 (Wint. 1976), pp. 84-89.

3109   "Paul and Phyllis." TAMARACK REVIEW, 72 (Fall 1977), 28-53.

3110   "Windows." CANADIAN FICTION MAGAZINE, No. 27 (1977), pp. 102-12.

3111   "The Escape." In AURORA: NEW CANADIAN WRITING 1978. Ed. Morris Wolfe. Toronto: Doubleday, 1978, pp. 123-33.

3112   "So Many Have Died." In THE BEST MODERN CANADIAN SHORT

STORIES. Ed. Ivon Owen and Morris Wolfe. Edmonton, Alta.: Hurtig, 1978, pp. 218-235.

ARTICLES

3113   "How Not to Write." SATURDAY NIGHT, 30 Sept. 1939, p. 20.

3114   "Françoise Mallet-Joris: A Young Writer on Her Way." TAMARACK REVIEW, No. 8 (Sum. 1958), pp. 63-72.

3115   Introd., THE ROAD PAST ALTAMONT, by Gabrielle Roy. Trans. Joyce Marshall. New Canadian Library, no. 129. Toronto: McClelland and Stewart, 1976, pp. vii-xi.

3116   ". . . A Difficult Country, and Our Home." In DIVIDED WE STAND. Ed. Gary Geddes. Toronto: Peter Martin, 1977, pp. 186-91.

Manuscripts

3117   McGill University Library, Montreal.

SECONDARY MATERIAL

Book Reviews

3118   PRESENTLY TOMORROW: CAB, Dec. 1946, p. 47; CFor, 26 (Oct. 1946), 164; SatR, 10 Aug. 1946, p. 14; UTQ, 16 (Apr. 1947), 259-60.

3119   LOVERS AND STRANGERS: UTQ, 27 (Apr. 1958), 458-59.

3120   A PRIVATE PLACE: BCan, 4 (Aug. 1975), 18; BrO, Sept.-Oct. 1976, p. 43; CanL, 75 (Wint. 1977), 97-98; CBRA, 1975, p. 127; CFM, 22 (Sum. 1976), 102-03; CRead, 17 (Mar. 1976), 2-3; QUARRY, 25 (Spr. 1976), 76-77; TamR, 69 (Sum. 1976), 82-83.

METCALF, JOHN (1938--)

John Metcalf was born in Carlisle, County Cumberland, England, lived in various parts of England, received from the University of Bristol a degree in English (1957) and a Certificate in Education, and taught high school in England and, after 1962, in Montreal as well. He has also taught and been writer-in-residence at Loyola University (Montreal), University of Ottawa, University of New Brunswick, Vanier College (Montreal), and McGill University.

PRIMARY MATERIAL

Monographs

FICTION

3121 NEW CANADIAN WRITING, 1969: STORIES. By John Metcalf, D.O. Spettigue, and C.J. Newman. Toronto: Clarke, Irwin, 1969. 152 p.

3122 THE LADY WHO SOLD FURNITURE. Toronto: Clarke, Irwin, 1970. 150 p.

   Short stories.

3123 GOING DOWN SLOW. Toronto: McClelland and Stewart, 1972. 177 p.

3124 THE TEETH OF MY FATHER. [Ottawa]: Oberon, 1975. 146 p.

   Short stories.

3125 DREAMS SURROUND US: FICTION AND POETRY. By John Metcalf and John Newlove. Delta, Ont.: Bastard, 1977. 86 p.

3126 GIRL IN GINGHAM. [Ottawa]: Oberon, 1978. 154 p. Rpt. as

PRIVATE PARTS: A MEMOIR. Scarborough, Ont.: New American Library, 1980. 150 p.

Two novellas.

3127 GENERAL LUDD. Downsview, Ont.: ECW, 1980. 301 p.

NONFICTION PROSE

3128 WORDCRAFT. By Charles Rittenhouse, John Metcalf, and Juliette Dowling. Dent's Canadian Texts. 4 vols. Toronto: J.M. Dent, 1968-70, 1977.

POETRY

3129 RHYME AND REASON. By John Metcalf and Gordon Callaghan. Toronto: Ryerson, 1968. xv, 172 p.

EDITED WORK

3130 RAZOR'S EDGE. By W. Somerset Maugham. Agincourt, Ont.: Book Society, 1967. 316 p.

3131 DAUGHTER OF TIME. By Josephine Tey. Agincourt, Ont.: Book Society, 1968. 246 p.

3132 SIXTEEN BY TWELVE: SHORT STORIES BY CANADIAN WRITERS. Scarborough, Ont.: McGraw-Hill Ryerson, 1970. 224 p. Bibliog.

3133 SALUTATION. Ed. John Metcalf and Gordon Callaghan. Toronto: Ryerson, 1970. 192 p. Index.

3134 KALEIDOSCOPE: CANADIAN STORIES. Photos. John de Visser. Toronto: Van Nostrand Reinhold, 1972. 138 p.

3135 THE NARRATIVE VOICE: SHORT STORIES AND REFLECTIONS BY CANADIAN AUTHORS. Ed. with introd. by John Metcalf. Scarborough, Ont.: McGraw-Hill Ryerson, 1972. 277 p.

3136 THE SPEAKING EARTH: CANADIAN POETRY. Toronto: Van Nostrand Reinhold, 1973. 128 p. Indexes.

3137 76: NEW CANADIAN STORIES. Ed. John Metcalf and Joan Harcourt. [Ottawa]: Oberon, 1976. 156 p.

3138 77: BEST CANADIAN STORIES. Ed. John Metcalf and Joan Harcourt. [Ottawa]: Oberon, 1977. 217 p.

3139   78: BEST CANADIAN STORIES. Ed. John Metcalf and Clark Blaise.
[Ottawa]: Oberon, 1978. 176 p.

3140   STORIES PLUS: CANADIAN STORIES WITH AUTHORS' COMMENTARIES.
Toronto: McGraw-Hill Ryerson, 1979. 243 p. Bibliog.

3141   FIRST IMPRESSIONS. [Ottawa]: Oberon, 1980. 142 p.

3142   NEW WORLDS: A CANADIAN COLLECTION OF STORIES WITH NOTES.
Toronto: McGraw-Hill Ryerson, 1980. 169 p.

3143   81: BEST CANADIAN STORIES. Ed. John Metcalf and Leon Rooke.
[Ottawa]: Oberon, 1981. 158 p.

3144   MAKING IT NEW. Introd. Barry Cameron. Toronto: Methuen, 1982.
320 p.

For work edited by Metcalf, see also nos. 886-88.

Shorter Work

SHORT STORIES

3145   "I've Got It Made." CANADIAN FORUM, 45 (Apr. 1965), 12-13.

3146   "A Thing They Wear." FIDDLEHEAD, No. 88 (Wint. 1971), pp. 47-54.

3147   "The Strange Aberration of Mr. Ken Smythe." In 73: NEW CANA-
DIAN STORIES. Ed. David Helwig and Joan Harcourt. [Ottawa]: Oberon,
1973, pp. 9-22.

3148   "Beryl." CANADIAN FICTION MAGAZINE, No. 13 (Spr. 1974), pp.
14-27.

3149   "Gentle as Flowers Make the Stones." QUEEN'S QUARTERLY, 81 (Sum.
1974), 221-37.

3150   "The Practice of the Craft." FIDDLEHEAD, No. 100 (Wint. 1974), pp.
43-53.

3151   "The Years in Exile." TAMARACK REVIEW, 67 (Oct. 1975), 17-34.

3152   "Playground." QUEEN'S QUARTERLY, 85 (Spr. 1978), 17-31.

ARTICLES

3153   "Author's Commentary." In SIXTEEN BY TWELVE. Ed. John Metcalf.
       Toronto: Ryerson, 1970, pp. 198-203.

3154   "Soaping a Meditative Foot." In THE NARRATIVE VOICE. Ed. John
       Metcalf. Toronto: McGraw-Hill Ryerson, 1972, pp. 154-59.

3155   "Notes on Writing a Story." FIDDLEHEAD, No. 114 (Sum. 1977), pp.
       68-72.

           Discusses "Private Parts" from GIRL IN GINGHAM.

3156   "Whooping Cranes of the Publishing World: Literary Magazines and
       Their Survival, or, the Future of Fiction; Panel Discussion." By John
       Metcalf et al. CANADIAN FICTION MAGAZINE, Nos. 34-35 (1980),
       pp. 4-17.

SECONDARY MATERIAL

Criticism

3157   Cameron, Barry. "An Approximation of Poetry: The Short Stories of John
       Metcalf." STUDIES IN CANADIAN LITERATURE, 2 (Wint. 1977), 17-35.

3158   _____. "Invention in 'Girl in Gingham.'" FIDDLEHEAD, No. 114
       (Sum. 1977), pp. 120-29.

3159   _____. "The Practice of the Craft: A Conversation with John Metcalf."
       QUEEN'S QUARTERLY, 82 (Aut. 1975), 402-24.

3160   Smith, Michael. "John Metcalf Finds the Canadian Climate for Short
       Stories is Warm but Exclusive: Interview." BOOKS IN CANADA, 8
       (Jan. 1979), 23-24.

3161   Thompson, Kent. "John Metcalf: A Profile." FIDDLEHEAD, No. 114
       (Sum. 1977), pp. 56-63.

For criticism on Metcalf, see also no. 3144.

Book Reviews

3162   THE LADY WHO SOLD FURNITURE: CanL, 47 (Wint. 1971), 101-02;
       CFM, 6 (Spr. 1972), 80-82; CFor, 50 (Nov. 1970), 312; FIDDLEHEAD,
       86 (Aug. 1970), 167-69; TamR, 56 (1971), 87-88; WCR, 5 (Jan. 1971),
       59-60; WLWE, 2, No. 1 (1972), 67-69.

3163   GOING DOWN SLOW: BCan, 1 (Oct. 1972), 20-21; CanL, 58
(Aut. 1973), 102-04; CFM, 10 (Spr. 1973), 112-14; CFor, 53 (Sept.
1973), 41; CRead, 14, No. 2 (n.d.), 9-10; DR, 53 (Sum. 1973),
367-68; FIDDLEHEAD, 96 (Wint. 1973), 116-18; JCF, 2 (Wint. 1973),
91-92; QQ, 80 (Spr. 1973), 139-40; QUARRY, 22 (Wint. 1973), 77-78;
SatN, 87 (nov. 1972), 50-51.

3164   THE TEETH OF MY FATHER: BCan, 4 (Aug. 1975), 18; CanL, 75
(Wint. 1977), 95-97; CBRA, 1975, p. 125; CFor, 55 (Aug. 1975),
36-37; FIDDLEHEAD, 105 (Spr. 1975), 123-26; OntarioR, 4 (Spr.
1976), 99-100; QQ, 83 (Spr. 1976), 172-73; TamR, 69 (Sum. 1976),
83-85; UWR, 11 (Spr. 1976), 108.

3165   GIRL IN GINGHAM: BCan, 9 (Aug. 1980), 34; CanL, 84 (Spr.
1980), 130; CFor, 58 (Sept. 1978), 27-28; ECW, 16 (Fall-Wint. 1979-
80), 191-97; FIDDLEHEAD, 118 (Sum. 1978), 174-78; MACLEAN'S, 12
June 1978, p. 73; MHRev, 52 (Oct. 1979), 143; QQ, 85 (Wint. 1978-
79), 707-08; QUARRY, 28 (Spr. 1979), 92-93; UTQ, 48 (Sum. 1979),
323-24.

3166   GENERAL LUDD: BCan, 9 (Aug. 1980), 9; CFor, 60 (Dec. 1980),
39-40; Q&Q, 46 (Oct. 1980), 35.

MITCHELL, W.O. (1914--)

William Ormond Mitchell was born in Weyburn, Saskatchewan, grew up in western Canada, lived in Florida during his high school years, and attended the Universities of Manitoba (1932-34) and Alberta (B.A., 1942). He has worked as a deck hand, salesman, fiction editor (for MACLEAN'S magazine, 1948-50), and high school teacher and principal in High River, Alberta, where he made his home for many years. The Universities of Calgary, Alberta, and Toronto have received him as lecturer and writer-in-residence. The homespun humor of Mitchell's CBC radio drama series, "Jake and the Kid," earned him a wide audience between 1948 and 1958, and the novel of the same name later won the 1962 Stephen Leacock Medal for Humour. His reputation, though, rests most firmly on his lyrical account of a boy and the prairie wind in WHO HAS SEEN THE WIND.

PRIMARY MATERIAL

Monographs

FICTION

3167   WHO HAS SEEN THE WIND.   Toronto: Macmillan, 1947.   344 p.

3168   JAKE AND THE KID.   Toronto: Macmillan, 1961.   184 p.
        Short stories.

3169   THE KITE.   Toronto: Macmillan, 1962.   210 p.

3170   THE BLACK BONSPIEL OF WULLIE MACCRIMMON.   Calgary: Frontiers Unlimited, [1965].   55 p.

3171   THE VANISHING POINT: A NOVEL.   Toronto: Macmillan, 1973.   393 p.

3172   HOW I SPENT MY SUMMER HOLIDAYS. Toronto: Macmillan, 1981. 224 p.

Drama

3173   THE DEVIL'S INSTRUMENT. Toronto: Simon and Pierre, [1973]. 31 p. A radio play.

Shorter Work

SHORT STORIES

3174   "But as Yesterday." QUEEN'S QUARTERLY, 49 (Sum. 1942), 132–38.

3175   "Elbow Room." MACLEAN'S, 15 Sept. 1942, pp. 18–20, 39.

3176   "Gettin' Born." MACLEAN'S, 1 May 1943, pp. 10–11, 39–41.

3177   "'Somethin's Gotta Go!'" MACLEAN'S, 1 July 1945, pp. 20–22.

3178   "Shoparoon for Maggie." MACLEAN'S, 15 May 1948, pp. 22–23, 66–67 ff.

3179   "Air-Nest and La Belle Dame." MACLEAN'S, 1 Nov. 1948, pp. 20–21, 28–30.

3180   "Crocus at the Coronation." MACLEAN'S, 1 June 1953, pp. 18–19, 46–48, 50, 52–53.

3181   "How Crocus Got Its Seaway." MACLEAN'S, 20 June 1959, pp. 16–17, 55–56, 58–60.

3182   "Patterns." In TEN FOR WEDNESDAY NIGHT. Ed. Robert Weaver. [Toronto]: McClelland and Stewart, 1961, pp. 59–71.

3183   "Melvin Arbuckle's First Course in Shock Therapy." MACLEAN'S, 5 Oct. 1963, pp. 38, 40–41, 44–48, 50.

3184   "Hercules Salvage." In STORIES FROM WESTERN CANADA: A SELEC- TION. Ed. Rudy Wiebe. Toronto: Macmillan, 1972, pp. 41–51.

ARTICLES

3185   "Author Looks at the Problems of Writers in Contemporary Canada." CA- NADIAN LIBRARY ASSOCIATION BULLETIN, 4 (Dec. 1947), 58–59.

3186 "It's Your Wagon." WRITER, 61 (Oct. 1948), 328-30.

3187 "The Unfolding Drama of W.O. Mitchell." MACLEAN'S, 2 May 1964, pp. 21-24.

3188 "Debts of Innocence." SATURDAY NIGHT, 91 (Mar. 1976), 36-37.

3189 "Some of Today's Developers Have the Sensitivity of Fascist Book Burners." CANADIAN HERITAGE, Dec. 1980, p. 29.

    An interview.

Manuscripts

3190 University of Calgary Library, Calgary, Alta.

SECONDARY MATERIAL

Bibliography

For a bibliography of Mitchell, see no. 33.

Criticism

3191 Barclay, Patricia. "Regionalism and the Writer: A Talk with W.O. Mitchell." CANADIAN LITERATURE, No. 14 (Aut. 1962), pp. 53-56.

3192 Bartlett, Donald R. "Dumplings & Dignity." CANADIAN LITERATURE, No. 77 (Sum. 1978), pp. 73-80.

    Discusses THE VANISHING POINT.

3193 Cowan, Hugh, and Gabriel Kampf. "ACTA Interviews W.O. Mitchell." ACTA VICTORIANA, 98 (Apr. 1974), 15-26.

3194 McLay, Catherine. "Crocus, Saskatchewan: A Country of the Mind." JOURNAL OF POPULAR CULTURE, 14 (Fall 1980), 333-49.

3195 _____. "W.O. Mitchell's THE KITE: A Study in Immortality." JOURNAL OF CANADIAN FICTION, 2 (Spr. 1973), 43-48.

3196 Martell, George. "I Feeled Them and Feeled Them." THIS MAGAZINE, 9 (July-Aug. 1975), 15-16.

3197 Mitchell, Ken. "The Universality of W.O. Mitchell's WHO HAS SEEN THE WIND." LAKEHEAD UNIVERSITY REVIEW, 4 (Spr. 1971), 26-40.

3198   "Morris Surdin Says. . . ." CANADIAN COMPOSER, No. 48 (Mar. 1970), pp. 34-37.

3199   New, William H. "A Feeling of Completion: Aspects of W.O. Mitchell." CANADIAN LITERATURE, No. 17 (Sum. 1963), pp. 22-33.

>   Discusses WHO HAS SEEN THE WIND and THE KITE; reprinted in nos. 173, 197, and 5113.

3200   O'Rourke, David. "An Interview with W.O. Mitchell." ESSAYS ON CANADIAN WRITING, No. 20 (Wint. 1980-81), pp. 149-59.

3201   Ricou, Laurence. "Notes on Language and Learning in WHO HAS SEEN THE WIND." CANADIAN CHILDREN'S LITERATURE, No. 10 (1977-78), pp. 3-17.

For criticism on Mitchell, see also nos. 51, 124, 160, 163, 182, 190, 324, and 2889.

Book Reviews

3202   WHO HAS SEEN THE WIND: CBRA, 1976, p. 149; CFM, 30-31 (1979), 210-11; CFor, 27 (Apr. 1947), 22; CULTURE, 9 (Mar. 1948), 100; DR, 27 (July 1947), 249-50; NYTBR, 23 Feb. 1947, p. 5; QQ, 54 (Sum. 1947), 286; QQ, 84 (Aut. 1977), 437-38; UTQ, 17 (Apr. 1948), 265-67.

3203   JAKE AND THE KID: CanL, 11 (Wint. 1962), 68-70.

3204   THE KITE: CanL, 15 (Wint. 1963), 76-77; CDim, 1, Nos. 1-2 (1963), 22-23; MONTREALER, 37 (Jan. 1963), 33; QQ, 70 (Sum. 1963), 284; TamR, [26] (Wint. 1963), 67-68; UTQ, 32 (July 1963), 401.

3205   THE VANISHING POINT: BCan, 2 (Dec. 1973), 12; CanL, 61 (Sum. 1974), 109-11; CFor, 54 (May 1974), 26-27; ECW, 1 (Wint. 1974), 47-48; JCF, 3 (Wint. 1974), 95-97; LaUR, 7 (Sum. 1974), 155-56; MACLEAN'S, 86 (Nov. 1973), 118; QQ, 81 (Spr. 1974), 144-45; SatN, 89 (Jan. 1974), 31-32.

MONTGOMERY, LUCY MAUD (1874-1942)

The well-loved children's author, Lucy Maud Montgomery, was born in Clifton, Prince Edward Island, but grew up in Cavendish, Prince Edward Island. At sixteen, she received her teacher's certificate from Prince of Wales College, Charlottetown. She taught for several years, moved briefly to Prince Albert, Saskatchewan, wrote for the Halifax DAILY ECHO, and lived for most of a decade in Cavendish with her ailing grandmother. On her grandmother's death, she moved to Ontario and spent many years in Toronto. Awarded the Order of the British Empire in 1935, she is known chiefly for the creation of the imaginative, outspoken, stout-hearted, red-haired heroine of ANNE OF GREEN GABLES. Although primarily a writer of children's stories, Montgomery has also written two novels for adults.

PRIMARY MATERIAL

Monographs

FICTION

3206 ANNE OF GREEN GABLES. Illus. M.A. and W.A.J. Claus. Boston: L.C. Page, 1908. viii, 429 p.

3207 ANNE OF AVONLEA. Boston: L.C. Page, 1909. vii, 366 p.

3208 KILMENY OF THE ORCHARD. Illus. George Gibbs. Boston: L.C. Page, 1910. 256 p.

3209 THE STORY GIRL. Boston: L.C. Page, 1911. vi, 365 p.

3210 CHRONICLES OF AVONLEA. Boston: L.C. Page, 1912. 306 p.

3211 THE GOLDEN ROAD. Boston: L.C. Page, 1913. x, 369 p.

3212   ANNE OF THE ISLAND. Boston: L.C. Page, 1915. viii, 326 p.

3213   ANNE'S HOUSE OF DREAMS. New York: A.L. Burt, 1915. 346 p.

3214   RAINBOW VALLEY. Toronto: McClelland and Stewart, 1919. viii, 341 p.

3215   FURTHER CHRONICLES OF AVONLEA: WHICH HAVE TO DO WITH MANY PERSONALITIES AND EVENTS IN AND AROUND AVONLEA. Illus. John Goss. Boston: L.C. Page, 1920. xi, 301 p.

3216   RILLA OF INGLESIDE. Toronto: McClelland and Stewart, 1921. 370 p.

3217   EMILY OF NEW MOON. New York: Frederick A. Stokes, 1923. 351 p.

3218   EMILY CLIMBS. New York: Frederick A. Stokes, 1925. 312 p.

3219   THE BLUE CASTLE: A NOVEL. Toronto: McClelland and Stewart, 1926. 309 p.
            For adults.

3220   EMILY'S QUEST. New York: Frederick A. Stokes, 1927. 310 p.

3221   MAGIC FOR MARIGOLD. New York: Frederick A. Stokes, 1929. vii, 328 p.

3222   A TANGLED WEB. New York: Frederick A. Stokes, 1931. 324 p. Also as AUNT BECKY BEGAN IT. London: Hodder and Stoughton, 1931. 317 p.

            For adults.

3223   PAT OF SILVER BUSH. New York: Frederick A. Stokes, 1933. viii, 329 p.

3224   MISTRESS PAT: A NOVEL OF SILVER BUSH. New York: Frederick A. Stokes, 1935. 338 p.

3225   ANNE OF WINDY POPLARS. New York: Frederick A. Stokes, 1936. 301 p. Also as ANNE OF WINDY WILLOWS. London: G.G. Harrap, 1936. 296 p.

3226   JANE OF LANTERN HILL. Toronto: McClelland and Stewart, 1937. 297 p.

3227   ANNE OF INGLESIDE. New York: Frederick A. Stokes, 1939. 323 p.

3228   THE ROAD TO YESTERDAY. Toronto: McGraw-Hill Ryerson, 1974. 251 p.

     Short stories.

3229   THE DOCTOR'S SWEETHEART AND OTHER STORIES. Ed. with introd. by Catherine McLay. Toronto: McGraw-Hill Ryerson, 1979. 190 p. Bibliog.

NONFICTION PROSE

3230   COURAGEOUS WOMEN. By Lucy M. Montgomery, Marian Keith (pseud.), and Mabel Burns McKinley. Toronto: McClelland and Stewart, 1934. vi, 203 p.

3231   THE GREEN GABLE LETTERS: FROM L.M. MONTGOMERY TO EPHRAIM WEBER, 1905-1909. Ed. Wilfred Eggleston. Toronto: Ryerson, 1960. 102 p.

3232   THE ALPINE PATH: THE STORY OF MY CAREER. Don Mills, Ont.: Fitzhenry and Whiteside, 1974. 96 p.

     Reprinted from EVERYWOMAN'S WORLD, 1917.

3233   MY DEAR MR. M: LETTERS TO G.B. MACMILLAN. Ed. Francis W. P. Bolger and Elizabeth R. Epperly. Toronto: McGraw-Hill Ryerson, 1980. xii, 212 p. Index.

POETRY

3234   THE WATCHMAN AND OTHER POEMS. Toronto: McClelland, Goodchild, and Stewart, 1916. xii, 159 p.

DRAMA

3235   ANNE OF GREEN GABLES: A MODERN DRAMATIZATION OF L.M. MONTGOMERY'S MOST POPULAR NOVEL, IN THREE ACTS. By Wilbur Braun (Alice Chadwicke, pseud.). New York: Samuel French, 1937. 139 p.

Shorter Work

SHORT STORIES

3236   "The Girl and the Wild Race." ERA, 13 (Jan. 1904), 65-69.

3237   "Promise of Lucy Ellen." DELINEATOR, 63 (Feb. 1904), 268-71.

3238   "Aunt Cynthia's Persian Cat." READER, 4 (Sept. 1904), 392-98.

3239   "Case of Atavism." READER, 6 (Nov. 1905), 658-66.

3240   "The Quarantine at Alexander Abraham's." EVERYBODY'S, 16 (Apr. 1907), 495-503.

3241   "Each in His Own Tongue." DELINEATOR, 76 (Oct. 1910), 247.

3242   "Garden of Spices." MACLEAN'S, 31 (Mar. 1918), 28-30, 93-100.

3243   "Enter Emily." DELINEATOR, 106 (Jan. 1925), 10-11.

3244   "Too Few Cooks." DELINEATOR, 106 (Feb. 1925), 10.

3245   "Night Watch." DELINEATOR, 106 (Mar. 1925), 10-11.

3246   "Her Dog Day." DELINEATOR, 106 (Apr. 1925), 10.

3247   "Magic for Marigold." DELINEATOR, 108 (May 1926), 10-11.

3248   "Lost, a Child's Laughter." DELINEATOR, 108 (June 1926), 15.

3249   "Bobbed Goldilocks." DELINEATOR, 109 (July 1926), 10.

3250   "Playmate." DELINEATOR, 109 (Aug. 1926), 15.

3251   "The Mirror." CANADIAN HOME JOURNAL, Feb. 1930, p. 8.

3252   "The House." CHATELAINE, May 1932, p. 10.

3253   "I Know a Secret." GOOD HOUSEKEEPING, 101 (Aug. 1935), 22-25.

ARTICLE

3254   "A Girl's Place at Dalhousie College, 1898." ALTANTIS, 5 (Fall 1979), 146-53.

            Reprinted from HALIFAX HERALD, Apr. 1896.

Manuscripts

3255 University of Guelph, Ont.; Queen's University Library, Kingston, Ont.

SECONDARY MATERIAL

Criticism

3256 Bolger, Francis W.P. THE YEARS BEFORE "ANNE." [Charlottetown]: Prince Edward Island Heritage Foundation, 1974. v, 229 p. Bibliog.

A biography of Montgomery's early career.

3257 Burns, J. "Anne and Emily: L.M. Montgomery's Children." ROOM OF ONE'S OWN, 3, No. 3 (1977), 37-48.

3258 Chapman, Ethel M. "Author of Anne." MACLEAN'S, 32 (Oct. 1919), 102-04, 106.

3259 Coldwell, Joyce-Ione Harrington. "Folklore as Fiction: The Writings of L.M. Montgomery." In FOLKLORE STUDIES IN HONOUR OF HERBERT HALPERT: A FESTSCHRIFT. Ed. Kenneth S. Goldstein et al. St. John's: Memorial University of Newfoundland, 1980, pp. 125-36.

3260 Cowan, Ann S. "Canadian Writers: Lucy Maud & Emily Byrd." CANADIAN CHILDREN'S LITERATURE, 1 (Aut. 1975), 42-49.

Discusses Montgomery and Emily Byrd Starr; reprinted in no. 3272.

3261 Fitzpatrick, Helen. "Anne's First Sixty Years." CANADIAN AUTHOR AND BOOKMAN, 44 (Spr. 1969), 5-7, 13.

3262 Fredeman, Jane Cowan. "The Land of Lost Content: The Use of Fantasy in L.M. Montgomery's Heroines." CANADIAN CHILDREN'S LITERATURE, 1 (Aut. 1975), 60-70.

Reprinted in no. 3272.

3263 Gillen, Mollie. THE WHEEL OF THINGS: A BIOGRAPHY OF L.M. MONTGOMERY, AUTHOR OF ANNE OF GREEN GABLES. Don Mills, Ont.: Fitzhenry and Whiteside, 1975. 200 p. Bibliog. Index.

3264 Hill, Maude Petitt. "The Best Known Woman in Prince Edward Island: L.M. Montgomery." CHATELAINE, 1 (May 1928), 8-9, 65; 1 (June 1928), 23, 41-42.

3265   L.M. MONTGOMERY AS MRS. EWAN MACDONALD OF THE LEASK-
DALE MANSE, 1911-1926. Leaskdale, Ont.: St. Paul's Presbyterian
Women's Association, 1965. 20 p.

3266   Little, Jean. "But What about Jane?" CANADIAN CHILDREN'S LIT-
ERATURE, 1 (Aut. 1975), 71-81.

        Reprinted in no. 3272.

3267   LUCY MAUD MONTGOMERY: "THE ISLAND'S LADY OF STORIES."
Springfield, P.E.I.: Women's Institute, 1963. 20 p.

3268   Millen, Muriel. "Who Was Ephraim Weber?" QUEEN'S QUARTERLY,
68 (Sum. 1961), 333-36.

3269   Ridley, Hilda M. THE STORY OF L.M. MONTGOMERY. Toronto:
Ryerson, 1956. xiii, 137 p.

3270   Rubio, Mary. "Satire, Realism & Imagination in ANNE OF GREEN
GABLES." CANADIAN CHILDREN'S LITERATURE, 1 (Aut. 1975), 27-36.

        Reprinted in no. 3272.

3271   Sorfleet, John R. "L.M. Montgomery: Canadian Authoress." CANA-
DIAN CHILDREN'S LITERATURE, 1 (Aut. 1975), 4-7.

        Reprinted in no. 3272.

3272   _____, ed. L.M. MONTGOMERY: AN ASSESSMENT. Guelph, Ont.:
Canadian Children's Press, 1976. 81 p.

        Includes nos. 3260, 3262, 3266, 3270-71, 3273-74, and 3277.

3273   Thomas, Gillan. "The Decline of Anne: Matron vs. Child." CANA-
DIAN CHILDREN'S LITERATURE, 1 (Aut. 1975), 37-41.

        Reprinted in no. 3272.

3274   Waterston, Elizabeth. "Lucy Maud Montgomery: 1874-1942." In THE
CLEAR SPIRIT: TWENTY CANADIAN WOMEN AND THEIR TIMES. Ed.
Mary Innis. Toronto: University of Toronto Press, 1966, pp. 198-220.

        Reprinted in no. 3272.

3275   Weber, Ephraim. "L.M. Montgomery as a Letter Writer." DALHOUSIE
REVIEW, 22 (Oct. 1942), 300-310.

3276 _____. "L.M. Montgomery's Anne." DALHOUSIE REVIEW, 24 (Apr. 1944), 64-73.

3277 Whitaker, Muriel A. "'Queer Children': L.M. Montgomery's Heroines." CANADIAN CHILDREN'S LITERATURE, 1 (Aut. 1975), 50-59.

    Reprinted in no. 3272.

3278 Willis, Leslie. "The Bogus Ugly Duckling: Anne Shirley Unmasked." DALHOUSIE REVIEW, 56 (Sum. 1976), 247-51.

    Discusses ANNE OF GREEN GABLES.

For criticism on Montgomery, see also nos. 81, 182, 481, 3229, and 3231.

Book Reviews

3279 ANNE OF GREEN GABLES: AtlA, 54 (Aug. 1964), 94; NYTBR, 18 July 1908, p. 404.

3280 ANNE OF AVONLEA: NATION, 2 Sept. 1909, p. 212; TES, 22 Feb. 1980, p. 29.

3281 KILMENY OF THE ORCHARD: ATHENAEUM, 30 July 1910, p. 122; NATION, 9 June 1910, p. 587.

3282 THE STORY GIRL: NATION, 10 Aug. 1911, p. 122.

3283 CHRONICLES OF AVONLEA: NATION, 22 Aug. 1912, p. 171.

3284 ANNE OF THE ISLAND: NATION, 26 Aug. 1915, p. 263.

3285 ANNE'S HOUSE OF DREAMS: NYTBR, 26 Aug. 1917, p. 318; SatN, 88 (Jan. 1973), 34.

3286 RAINBOW VALLEY: NYTBR, 21 Sept. 1919, p. 484.

3287 RILLA OF INGLESIDE: NYTBR, 11 Sept. 1921, p. 23.

3288 EMILY OF NEW MOON: NYTBR, 26 Aug. 1923, p. 24; TLS, 13 Sept. 1923, p. 605.

3289 THE BLUE CASTLE: JCF, 2 (Fall 1963), 102-04; NYTBR, 26 Sept. 1926, p. 33; SatN, 88 (Jan. 1973), 34; TLS, 30 Sept. 1926, p. 657.

3290   EMILY'S QUEST: SatN, 88 (Jan. 1973), 34.

3291   MAGIC FOR MARIGOLD: TLS, 24 Oct. 1929, p. 484.

3292   A TANGLED WEB: JCF, 2 (Fall 1973), 102-04; NYTBR, 20 Dec. 1931,
       p. 9; SatN, 88 (Jan. 1973), 34.

3293   PAT OF SILVER BUSH: TLS, 24 Aug. 1933, p. 562.

3294   JANE OF LANTERN HILL: NYTBR, 15 Aug. 1937, p. 22.

3295   ANNE OF INGLESIDE: NYTBR, 30 July 1939, p. 7; SatN, 11 Nov.
       1939, p. 8; SatN, 88 (Jan. 1973), 34.

3296   THE ROAD TO YESTERDAY: CAB, 49 (Sum. 1974), 26; CanL, 63
       (Wint. 1975), 89-92; DR, 54 (Wint. 1974-75), 783-84; MACLEAN'S, 87,
       No. 6 (1974), 94; NY, 2 Dec. 1974, p. 191; Q&Q, 40, No. 7 (1974),
       19.

3297   THE DOCTOR'S SWEETHEART: BCan, 8 (May 1979), 22.

3298   THE GREEN GABLE LETTERS: AtlA, 50 (June 1960), 97; CanL, 5 (Sum.
       1960), 87-88; CFor, 40 (Sept. 1960), 142; DR, 41 (Aut. 1961), 429,
       431; UTQ, 30 (July 1961), 422.

MOORE, BRIAN (1921--)

Irish-born Brian Moore is a Canadian citizen who resides in the United States. A native of Belfast, Moore attended a Jesuit College there, travelled in North Africa and Italy with the British Ministry of War Transport during the war, acted as an official for the United Nations Relief and Rehabilitation Administration in Poland for two years, and came to Canada in 1948. Here he worked for the Montreal GAZETTE (1948-1952) and wrote his first few novels. In 1959, he moved to New York and five years later to Malibu, California, where he has remained.

His impressive early novel THE LONELY PASSION OF JUDITH HEARNE won several literary awards; both THE LUCK OF GINGER COFFEY and THE GREAT VICTORIAN COLLECTION received Governor General's Awards. With sympathy, wit, and polish he portrays his protagonists (often Irish exiles in Canada or Canadian expatriates in the States) struggling with confusion and uncertainty.

PRIMARY MATERIAL

Monographs

FICTION

3299   THE EXECUTIONERS. Toronto: Harlequin Books, 1951. 157 p.

3300   WREATH FOR A REDHEAD. Toronto: Harlequin Books, 1951. 128 p.; rpt. as SAILOR'S LEAVE. New York: Pyramid Books, 1953. 158 p.

3301   FRENCH FOR MURDER. By Bernard Mara, pseud. New York: Gold Medal Books, 1954. 144 p.

3302   A BULLET FOR MY LADY. By Bernard Mara, pseud. New York: Gold Medal Books, 1955. 156 p.

3303 JUDITH HEARNE. London: André Deutsch, 1955. 223 p.; rpt. as THE LONELY PASSION OF JUDITH HEARNE. Boston: Little, Brown, 1956. 223 p.

3304 INTENT TO KILL. By Michael Bryan, pseud. New York: Dell, 1956. 190 p.

3305 THIS GUN FOR GLORIA. By Bernard Mara, pseud. New York: Gold Medal Books, 1956. 144 p.

3306 THE FEAST OF LUPERCAL. Atlantic Monthly Press Book. Boston: Little, Brown, 1957. 246 p.; rpt. as A MOMENT OF LOVE. London: Long-acre, 1960.

3307 MURDER IN MAJORCA. By Michael Bryan, pseud. New York: Dell, 1957. 158 p.

3308 THE LUCK OF GINGER COFFEY. London: André Deutsch, 1960. 221 p.

3309 AN ANSWER FROM LIMBO: A NOVEL. Atlantic Monthly Press Book. Boston: Little, Brown, 1962. 322 p.

3310 THE EMPEROR OF ICE-CREAM: A NOVEL. Toronto: McClelland and Stewart, 1965. 250 p.

3311 I AM MARY DUNNE: A NOVEL. Toronto: McClelland and Stewart, 1968. 217 p.

3312 FERGUS: A NOVEL. Toronto: McClelland and Stewart, 1970. 228 p.

3313 THE REVOLUTION SCRIPT. Toronto: McClelland and Stewart, 1971. 261 p.

3314 CATHOLICS: A NOVEL. Toronto: McClelland and Stewart, 1972. 107 p.

3315 THE GREAT VICTORIAN COLLECTION. Toronto: McClelland and Stewart, 1975. 213 p.

3316 THE DOCTOR'S WIFE. Toronto: McClelland and Stewart, 1976. 277 p.

3317 TWO STORIES. California State University Northridge Libraries. N. p.: Santa Susana, 1978. 58 p.
    Limited edition. Reprints nos. 3327 and 3329.

3318 THE MANGAN INHERITANCE. Toronto: McClelland and Stewart, 1979. 335 p.

3319 THE TEMPTATION OF EILEEN HUGHES: A NOVEL. Toronto: McClelland and Stewart, 1981. 211 p.

NONFICTION PROSE

3320 CANADA. By Brian Moore and the editors of LIFE. Life World Library. New York: Time, 1963. 160 p. Bibliog.

Shorter Work

SHORT STORIES

3321 "Sassenach." NORTHERN REVIEW, 5 (Oct.-Nov. 1951), 2-8.

3322 "Holdup." AMERICAN, 155 (June 1953), 143.

3323 "A Vocation." TAMARACK REVIEW, No. 1 (Aut. 1956), pp. 18-22.

3324 "Lion of the Afternoon." ATLANTIC MONTHLY, 200 (Nov. 1957), 79-83.

3325 "Next Thing Was Kansas City." ATLANTIC MONTHLY, 203 (Feb. 1959), 77-79.

3326 "Grieve for the Dear Departed." ATLANTIC MONTHLY, 204 (Aug. 1959), 43-46.

3327 "Uncle T." GENTLEMAN'S QUARTERLY, Nov. 1960, pp. 118-19, 140, 142, 144-54, 158.

Reprinted in no. 3317.

3328 "Hearts and Flowers." SPECTATOR, 24 Nov. 1961, pp. 743, 745.

3329 "Preliminary Pages for a Work of Revenge." MIDSTREAM, 7 (Wint. 1961), 57-61.

Reprinted in no. 3317.

3330 "Off the Track." In TEN FOR WEDNESDAY NIGHT. Ed. Robert Weaver. [Toronto]: McClelland and Stewart, 1961, pp. 159-67.

3331   "The Sight." In IRISH GHOST STORIES. Ed. Joseph Hone. London
        Hamish Hamilton, 1977, pp. 100-119.

ARTICLES

3332   "Brian Moore Tells about I AM MARY DUNNE." LITERARY GUILD,
        July 1968, p. 5.

3333   "Bloody Ulster: An Irishman's Lament." ATLANTIC MONTHLY, 226
        (Sept. 1970), 58-62.

3334   "How Brian Moore Rewrote THE REVOLUTION SCRIPT." MACLEAN'S,
        84 (Sept. 1971), 68.

3335   "The Expatriate Writer." ANTIGONISH REVIEW, No. 17 (Spr. 1974),
        pp. 27-30.

3336   "The Writer as Exile." CANADIAN JOURNAL OF IRISH STUDIES, 2
        (Dec. 1976), 5-17.

Manuscripts

3337   University of Calgary Library, Calgary, Alta.

SECONDARY MATERIAL

Bibliography

3338   Studying, Richard, comp. "A BRIAN MOORE Bibliography." ÉIRE/
        IRELAND, 10 (Fall 1975), 89-105.

Criticism

3339   Bray, Richard T. "A Conversation with Brian Moore." CRITIC, 35
        (Fall 1976), 42-44, 46-48.

3340   Cameron, Donald A. "Don Cameron Interviews Brian Moore." QUILL
        AND QUIRE, 38 (Apr. 1972), 3, 12-13.

        Reprinted in no. 124.

3341   Chambers, Harry. "The Real World of Brian Moore." PHOENIX, Mar.
        1967, pp. 41-48.

3342   Cook, Bruce. "Brian Moore: Private Person." COMMONWEAL, 23
        Aug. 1974, pp. 457-59.

3343   Cronin, John. "Ulster's Alarming Novels." ÉIRE/IRELAND, 4 (Wint. 1969), 27-34.

3344   Dahlie, Hallvard. BRIAN MOORE. Studies in Canadian Literature Series, 2. Toronto: Copp Clark, 1969. 130 p. Bibliog.

3344a   _____. BRIAN MOORE. Twayne's World Author Series, 632. Boston: Twayne, 1981. 168 p. Bibliog. Index.
         An expansion of no. 3344.

3345   _____. "Brian Moore: An Interview: Malibu, California, June 12, 1967." TAMARACK REVIEW, [46] (Wint. 1968), 7-29.

3346   _____. "Brian Moore's Broader Vision: THE EMPEROR OF ICE-CREAM." CRITIQUE, 9, No. 1 (1966), 43-55. Bibliog.

3347   de Santana, Hubert. "Interview with Author Brian Moore." MACLEAN'S, 11 July 1977, pp. 4, 6-7.

3348   _____. "Who is Brian Moore?" BOOKS IN CANADA, 6 (Oct. 1977), 4-6.

3349   DeWitt, Henry. "The Novels of Brian Moore: A Retrospective." PLOUGH-SHARES, 2, No. 2 (1974), 7-27. Bibliog.

3350   Dorenhamp, J.H. "Finishing the Day: Nature and Grace in Two Novels by Brian Moore." ÉIRE/IRELAND, 13 (Spr. 1978), 103-12.
         Discusses CATHOLICS and I AM MARY DUNNE.

3351   Flood, Jeanne. BRIAN MOORE. Irish Writers Series. Lewisburg, Pa.: Bucknell University Press, 1974. 88 p.

3352   Foster, John Wilson. "Crisis and Ritual in Brian Moore's Belfast Novels." ÉIRE/IRELAND, 3 (Aut. 1968), 66-74.

3353   _____. "Passage Through Limbo: Brian Moore's North American Novels." CRITIQUE, 13, No. 1 (1970), 5-18.

3354   Fraser, Keath. Introd., THE LUCK OF GINER COFFEY. New Canadian Library, no. 80. Toronto: McClelland and Stewart, 1972, pp. iii-ix.

3355   Frayne, John P. "Brian Moore's Wandering Irishman--The Not-So-Wild Colonial Boy." In MODERN IRISH LITERATURE: ESSAYS IN HONOR OF WILLIAM YORK TINDALL. Ed. Raymond J. Porter and James D. Brophy. New York: Iona College Press and Twayne, 1972, pp. 215-34.

3356   French, Philip.   "The Novels of Brian Moore."   LONDON, NS 5 (Feb.
       1966), 86-91.

3357   Fulford, Robert.   "Robert Fulford Interviews Brian Moore."   TAMARACK
       REVIEW, 23 (Spr. 1962), 5-18.

3358   Gallagher, Michael P.   "Brian Moore Talks to Michael Paul Gallagher."
       HIBERNIA, 10 Oct. 1969, p. 18.

3359   _____.   "The Novels of Brian Moore."   STUDIES, 60 (Sum. 1971),
       180-94.

3360   Girson, Rochelle.   "The Author."   SATURDAY REVIEW, 13 Oct. 1962,
       p. 20.

3361   Graham, John.   "A Conversation with Brian Moore."   In THE WRITER'S
       VOICE: CONVERSATIONS WITH CONTEMPORARY WRITERS.   Ed.
       George Garrett.   New York: Morrow, 1973, pp. 51-76.

3362   Green, Robert.   "Brian Moore's JUDITH HEARNE: Celebrating the Com-
       monplace."   INTERNATIONAL FICTION REVIEW, 7 (Wint. 1980), 29-33.

3363   Hirschberg, Stuart.   "Growing up Abject as Theme in Brian Moore's
       Novels."   CANADIAN JOURNAL OF IRISH STUDIES, 1 (Nov. 1975),
       11-16.

           Discusses THE FEAST OF LUPERCAL and THE EMPEROR OF
           ICE-CREAM.

3364   Jones, D.A.N.   "Brian Moore: Profile."   NEW REVIEW, 2 (Oct. 1975),
       47-50.

3365   Kattim [Kattan], Naïm.   "Brian Moore."   CANADIAN LITERATURE, No.
       18 (Aut. 1963), pp. 30-39.

3366   Kennedy, Alan.   Introd., I AM MARY DUNNE.   New Canadian Library,
       no. 128.   Toronto: McClelland and Stewart, 1976, pp. vii-xiii.

3367   Kersnowski, Frank L.   "Exit the Anti-Hero."   CRITIQUE: STUDIES IN
       MODERN FICTION, 10, No. 3 (1968), 60-71.

3368   McSweeney, Kerry.   "Brian Moore: Past and Present."   CRITICAL QUAR-
       TERLY, 18 (Sum. 1976), 53-66.

3369 Merivale, Patricia. "Neo-Modernism in the Canadian Artist-Parable: Hubert Aquin and Brian Moore." CANADIAN REVIEW OF COMPARATIVE LITERATURE, 6 (Spr. 1979), 195-205.

> Discusses Aquin's L'ANTIPHONAIRE and Moore's GREAT VICTORIAN COLLECTION.

3370 Paulin, T. "A Necessary Provincialism: Brian Moore, Maurice Leitch, Florence Mary McDovell." In TWO DECADES OF IRISH WRITINGS: A CRITICAL SURVEY. Ed. D. Dunn. Chester Springs, Pa.: Dufour Editions, 1975, pp. 242-56.

3371 Porter, Raymond J. "Mystery, Miracle, Faith in Brian Moore's CATHOLICS." EIRE/IRELAND, 10 (Fall 1975), 79-88.

3372 Prosky, Murray. "The Crisis of Identity in the Novels of Brian Moore." EIRE/IRELAND, 6 (Fall 1971), 106-18.

3373 Rafroidi, Patrick. "The Great Brian Moore Collection." CAHIERS IRLANDAIS, 4-5 (1975-76), 221-34. Bibliog.

3374 Ryan, Stephen P. "Ireland and Its Writers." CATHOLIC WORLD, 192 (Dec. 1960), 149-55.

3375 Sale, Richard B. "An Interview in London with Brian Moore." STUDIES IN THE NOVEL, 1 (Spr. 1969), 67-80.

3376 Scanlan, John A. "The Artist-in-Exile: Brian Moore's North American Novels." EIRE/IRELAND, 12 (Sum. 1977), 14-33.

3377 Shepherd, Allen. "Place and Meaning in Brian Moore's CATHOLICS." EIRE/IRELAND, 15, No. 3 (1980), 134-40.

3378 _____. "Place in Brian Moore's CATHOLICS." NOTES ON CONTEMPORARY LITERATURE, 9, No. 4 (1979), 4-5.

3379 Simmons, James. "Brian Moore and the Fallacy of Realism." HONEST ULSTERMAN, No. 22 (Mar.-Apr. 1970), pp. 8-14.

3380 Staines, David. "Observance without Belief." CANADIAN LITERATURE, No. 73 (Sum. 1977), pp. 8-24.

3381 Stedmond, John. Introd., JUDITH HEARNE. New Canadian Library, no. 39. Toronto: McClelland and Stewart, 1964, pp. v-viii.

3382 Sullivan, Robert. "Brian Moore: A Clinging Climate." LONDON, 16 (Dec. 1976–Jan. 1977), 63–71.

3383 Taranath, Rajeev. "Deepening Experience: A Note on THE EMPEROR OF ICE-CREAM." LITERARY CRITERION, 6 (Sum. 1966), 68–72.

3384 Toolan, Michael J. "Psyche and Belief: Brian Moore's Contending Angels." ÉIRE/IRELAND, 15, No. 3 (1980), 97–111.

For criticism on Moore, see also nos. 2832–34 and 5063.

Book Reviews

3385 JUDITH HEARNE: CAB, Wint. 1956-57, p. 28; CFor, 36 (Aug. 1956), 111-12; COMMONWEAL, 3 Aug. 1956, p. 448; NS&N, 21 May 1955, pp. 727-28; NYTBR, 17 June 1956, pp. 4, 16; QQ, 63 (Spr. 1956), 129-30; SatN, 26 Nov. 1955, pp. 14-15; SatN, 10 Dec. 1955, pp. 35-36; SatR, 7 July 1956, p. 9; SPECTATOR, 27 May 1955, p. 688; UTQ, 25 (Apr. 1956), 307-08.

3386 THE FEAST OF LUPERCAL: Atl, 199 (May 1957), 84-85; COMMON-WEAL, 12 July 1957, pp. 380-81; NS, 18 Feb. 1966, p. 227; NYTBR, 21 Apr. 1957, p. 6; QQ, 64 (Aut. 1957), 446-47; SatN, 25 May 1957, p. 303; SatR, 27 Apr. 1957, pp. 15, 27; TamR, 4 (Sum. 1957), 72-73; TLS, 7 Feb. 1958, p. 73; UTQ, 27 (July 1958), 451-52.

3387 THE LUCK OF GINGER COFFEY: BCan, 2 (Apr. 1973), 32; CanL, 6 (Aut. 1960), 69-70; CDim, 1, Nos. 1-2 (1963), 22; CFor, 41 (May 1961), 47-48; COMMONWEAL, 30 Sept. 1960, pp. 20-21; CRITIC, 19 (Oct. 1960), 51-52; HM, Oct. 1960, pp. 107-08; JCF, 1 (Spr. 1972), 95; KR, 23 (Wint. 1961), 178-79; LISTENER, 1 Sept. 1960, p. 357; NS, 27 Aug. 1960, p. 282; NYTBR, 4 Sept. 1960, p. 16; QQ, 68 (Sum. 1961), 351-52; RUO, 31 ([Apr.] 1961), 344; SatN, 15 Oct. 1960, p. 31; SatR, 27 Aug. 1960, p. 12; SPECTATOR, 26 Aug. 1960, p. 316; TamR, 17 (Aut. 1960), 65-71; TLS, 2 Sept. 1960, p. 557; UTQ, 30 (July 1961), 404-06; WatR, 6 (Wint. 1961), 61.

3388 AN ANSWER FROM LIMBO: Atl, Nov. 1962, pp. 143-44; CanL, 16 (Spr. 1973), 70-72; COMMENTARY, 36 (Aug. 1963), 176-77; COM-MONWEAL, 9 Nov. 1962, p. 179; COMMONWEAL, 7 Dec. 1962, p. 286; CRITIC, 21 (Oct. 1962), 86; HudR, 16 (Spr. 1963), 144; LIS-TENER, 11 Apr. 1963, p. 645; MACLEAN'S, 20 Oct. 1962, pp. 95-96; NS, 29 Mar. 1963, pp. 465-66; NY, 27 Oct. 1962, p. 215; NYTBR, 14 Oct. 1962, p. 4; PUNCH, 24 Apr. 1963, pp. 609-10; SatR, 13 Oct. 1962, pp. 20, 47; SPECTATOR, 3 May 1963, pp. 572-73; TamR, [26] (Wint. 1963), 63-67; TLS, 29 Mar. 1963, p. 221; UTQ, 32 (July 1963), 395-96; YR, 52 (Dec. 1962), 265-66.

3389 THE EMPEROR OF ICE-CREAM: ALPHABET, 12 (Aug. 1966), 95-96;
CanL, 28 (Spr. 1966), 68-70; CFor, 45 (Feb. 1966), 263; CRITIC,
24 (Dec. 1965), 70; DR, 46 (Spr. 1966), 135, 137, 139; HM, 231
(Oct. 1965), 132; HudR, 19 (Spr. 1966), 124; LIBERTÉ, 8 (Jan. 1966),
77-78; LISTENER, 3 Feb. 1966, p. 181; NS, 18 Feb. 1966, pp. 227-
28; NYTBR, 24 Oct. 1965, p. 5; NYTBR, 5 Dec. 1965, p. 4; NYTBR,
29 May 1977, p. 23; PrS, 40 (Spr. 1966), 89-90; PUNCH, 9 Feb.
1966, p. 212; SatR, 18 Sept. 1965, pp. 97-98; SPECTATOR, 4 Feb.
1966, p. 142; TLS, 3 Feb. 1966, p. 77; VQR, 42 (Aut. 1966), x.

3390 I AM MARY DUNNE: Atl, 222 (July 1968), 100; AtlA, 58 (July
1968), 78; CanL, 38 (Aut. 1968), 81-84; CFor, 48 (Oct. 1968), 164-
65; COMMONWEAL, 27 Sept. 1968, pp. 662-64; ÉIRE, 3 (Wint.
1968), 136-40; LISTENER, 24 Oct. 1968, p. 556; MACLEAN'S, 81
(Aug. 1968), 59; NATION, 24 June 1968, p. 832; NS, 31 May 1968,
p. 737; NS, 25 Oct. 1968, pp. 550, 552; NewR, 17 Aug. 1968, pp.
29-30; NYTBR, 23 June 1968, p. 4; PUNCH, 23 Oct. 1968, p. 596;
PUNCH, 1 Jan. 1969, p. 34; SatN, 83 (Sept. 1968), 29-30; SatR,
15 June 1968, pp. 23-24; SatR, 6 Sept. 1969, p. 34; SPECTATOR,
25 Oct. 1968, pp. 592-93; TamR, [48] ([Sum.] 1968), 63-65; TLS, 24
Oct. 1968, p. 1192; UTQ, 38 (July 1969), 354.

3391 FERGUS: CanL, 49 (Sum. 1971), 81-83; COMMONWEAL, 12 Feb.
1971, pp. 477-78; ÉIRE, 6 (Sum. 1971), 179-80; ES, 53 (1972), 282-
85; HM, 24 (Oct. 1970), 131; LIBERTÉ, 12 (Sept. 1970), 100-101;
LISTENER, 1 Apr. 1971, p. 422; NATION, 12 Oct. 1970, pp. 346-47;
NS, 26 Mar. 1971, p. 434; NYTBR, 27 Sept. 1970, p. 4; QUARRY,
20 (Wint. 1971), 63-64; SatN, 85 (Nov. 1970), 51; TLS, 9 Apr. 1971,
p. 413; YR, 60 (Mar. 1971), 430-31.

3392 THE REVOLUTION SCRIPT: ARCS, 2, No. 1 (1972), 100; AtlA, 62
(Apr. 1972), 70-71; BCan, 1 (Nov. 1971), 6-7; BCLQ, 35 (Spr. 1972),
59; CanL, 51 (Wint. 1977), 74-75; CDim, 9 (May 1973), 43; CFor,
51 (Jan. 1972), 74; DR, 51 (Wint. 1971-72), 584-87; ECONOMIST,
22 Jan. 1972, p. 49; ES, 54 (1973), 260; JCF, 1 (Wint. 1972), 86-
87; LISTENER, 20 Jan. 1972, p. 90; MACLEAN'S, 84 (Oct. 1971), 88;
NATION, 15 Apr. 1972, p. 23; NS, 21 Jan. 1972, pp. 86-87; NYTBR,
28 Nov. 1971, p. 6; PR, 39 (Spr. 1972), 276-77, 279-81; QUARRY,
21 (Wint. 1972), 70-71; SatN, 86 (Dec. 1971), 36, 38; SatR, 12
Feb. 1972, pp. 77-78; TLS, 21 Jan. 1972, p. 57; UTQ, 41 (Sum. 1972),
311-12.

3393 CATHOLICS: BCan, 1 (Oct. 1972), 1-2; CAB, 48 (Wint. 1972), 23;
CanL, 58 (Aut. 1973), 100-101; CFM, 10 (Spr. 1973), 110-12; CFor,
53 (Apr. 1973), 40; CRead, 14, No. 2 (n.d.), 11; CRITIC, 32 (Sept.
1973), 78-79; ES, 54 (1973), 260; HudR, 26 (Fall 1973), 545; LaUR,
6 (Fall 1973), 257-58; LISTENER, 2 Nov. 1972, pp. 610-11; MQR, 14
(Wint. 1975), 101; NAR, 15 (1972), 9-10, 231-34; NewR, 9 June 1973,
p. 31; NS, 3 Nov. 1972, p. 647; NY, 5 May 1973, p. 149; NYRB,

7 Mar. 1974, p. 18; NYTBR, 18 Mar. 1973, p. 39; PrS, 50 (Fall 1976), 281; Q&Q, 38 (Nov. 1972), 11; QQ, 79 (Wint. 1972), 581-83; RUO, 43 (Jan. 1973), 169-70; SatN, 87 (Oct. 1972), 38, 40; SatR, 7 Apr. 1973, pp. 94-95; SPECTATOR, 4 Nov. 1972, p. 714; TLS, 10 Nov. 1972, p. 1357; UTQ, 42 (Sum. 1973), 345; YR, 63 (Oct. 1973), 87-88.

3394   THE GREAT VICTORIAN COLLECTION: Atl, 236 (July 1975), 81; BCan, 4 (Aug. 1975), 14-15; CAB, 51 (Fall 1975), 27; CanL, 66 (Aut. 1975), 101-04; CFM, 21 (Spr. 1976), 107-09; CFor, 55 (Oct. 1975), 37-39; CJIP, 1 (Nov. 1975), 41; CRead, 16, No. 6 ([1975]), 5-6; CritQ, 18 (Sum. 1976), 53; ECW, 4 (Spr. 1976), 70-72; IUR, 6 (Spr. 1976), 119-21; LISTENER, 30 Oct. 1975, p. 582; MassR, 17 (Spr. 1976), 170; NatR, 26 Sept. 1975, p. 1064; NS, 17 Oct. 1975, p. 479; NY, 4 Aug. 1975, p. 89; NYRB, 7 Aug. 1975, p. 34; NYTBR, 29 June 1975, p. 2; NYTBR, 7 Dec. 1976, p. 62; OntarioR, 3 (Fall 1975), 105-06; PLOUGHSHARES, 3, No. 1 (1976), 149-53; QQ, 83 (Wint. 1976), 688-89; SatN, 90 (July 1975), 64-65; SatR, 26 July 1975, p. 30; SPECTATOR, 1 Nov. 1975, p. 573; TLS, 17 Oct. 1975, p. 1225; TLS, 7 May 1976, p. 1225; UTQ, 45 (Sum. 1976), 319.

3395   THE DOCTOR'S WIFE: BCan, 5 (Oct. 1976), 8-9; CanL, 72 (Spr. 1977), 77-80; CanR, 3 (Dec. 1976), 57; CFor, 56 (Dec. 1976), 51; ECONOMIST, 18 Dec. 1976, p. 131; ECW, 6 (Spr. 1977), 128-30; ENCOUNTER, 48 (Mar. 1977), 83; FIDDLEHEAD, 112 (Wint. 1977), 138-40; HudR, 30 (Spr. 1977), 155; LISTENER, 25 Nov. 1976, p. 688; MACLEAN'S, 4 Oct. 1976, p. 84; NewR, 27 Nov. 1976, p. 22; NS, 19 Nov. 1976, p. 714; NYRB, 30 Sept. 1976, p. 40; NYTBR, 26 Sept. 1976, p. 7; NYTBR, 21 Apr. 1977, p. 33; PUNCH, 14 June 1978, p. 1026; Q&Q, 42, No. 14 (1976), 7; QQ, 85 (Spr. 1978), 62-63; SatN, 91 (Oct. 1976), 68-69; SatR, 18 Sept. 1976, p. 30; SPECTATOR, 20 Nov. 1976, p. 22; TLS, 19 Nov. 1976, p. 1445; UTQ, 46 (Sum. 1977), 347-48; UWR, 13 (Fall 1977), 91-92.

3396   THE MANGAN INHERITANCE: Atl, 244 (Oct. 1979), 107; BCan, 8 (Oct. 1979), 11-13; BCan, 8 (Nov. 1979), 33; BCan, 9 (Dec. 1980), 28; CFor, 59 (Mar. 1980), 34; CRead, 20, No. 10, ([1978]), 5-6; CRITIC, 1 Sept. 1979, p. 2; CRITIC, 1 Jan. 1980, p. 7; ENCOUNTER, 54 (June 1980), 62; FIDDLEHEAD, 126 (Sum. 1980), 123-27; JCF, 30 (1980), 160-64; LISTENER, 15 Nov. 1979, p. 686; MACLEAN'S, 17 Sept. 1979, pp. 46, 48; NS, 16 Nov. 1979, p. 772; NY, 31 Dec. 1979, p. 77; NYTBR, 9 Sept. 1979, p. 12; OntarioR, 11 (Fall 1979), 87-90; Q&Q, 45 (Oct. 1979), 33; QQ, 86 (Wint. 1979-80), 742-47; SatN, 94 (Nov. 1979), 55, 57; SPECTATOR, 10 Nov. 1979, p. 23; TLS, 23 Nov. 1979, p. 10; UTQ, 49 (Sum. 1980), 327-28.

MUNRO, ALICE (1931--)

Alice Munro was born in Wingham, Ontario, attended the University of Western Ontario from 1949 to 1951, then moved to the West Coast where she worked in the Vancouver Public Library and in the sixties helped establish a book store in Victoria. Since 1972, she has lived in southwestern Ontario. Her freshness of observation and precision of language have established her as a Canadian novelist of significance. DANCE OF THE HAPPY SHADES and WHO DO YOU THINK YOU ARE? won Governor General's Awards, and LIVES OF GIRLS AND WOMEN, a portrayal of a young girl's growing up and an investigation into the nature of "real life," has attracted much interest.

PRIMARY MATERIAL

Monographs

FICTION

3397   DANCE OF THE HAPPY SHADES: STORIES. Foreword by Hugh Garner. Toronto: Ryerson, 1968. xi, 224 p.

3398   LIVES OF GIRLS AND WOMEN: A NOVEL. Toronto: McGraw-Hill Ryerson, 1971. 254 p.

3399   SOMETHING I'VE BEEN MEANING TO TELL YOU: THIRTEEN STORIES. Toronto: McGraw-Hill Ryerson, 1974. 246 p.

3400   WHO DO YOU THINK YOU ARE? STORIES. Toronto: Macmillan, 1978. 206 p.; rpt. as THE BEGGAR MAID: STORIES OF FLO AND ROSE. New York: A.A. Knopf, 1979. 210 p.

Shorter Work

SHORT STORIES

3401 "Basket of Strawberries." MAYFAIR, Nov. 1953, pp. 32-33, 78-79, 80, 82.

3402 "The Idyllic Summer." CANADIAN FORUM, 34 (Aug. 1954), 106-07, 109-10.

3403 "At the Other Place." CANADIAN FORUM, 35 (Sept. 1955), 131-33.

3404 "The Edge of Town." QUEEN'S QUARTERLY, 62 (Aut. 1955), 368-80.

3405 "How Could I Do That?" CHATELAINE, Mar. 1956, pp. 16-17, 65-70.

3406 "The Dangerous One." CHATELAINE, July 1957, pp. 48-51.

3407 "Red Dress." McCALL'S, 100 (Mar. 1973), 66-67, 138-39, 140-41, 146.

3408 "Home." In 74: NEW CANADIAN STORIES. Ed. David Helwig and Joan Harcourt. [Ottawa]: Oberon, 1974, pp. 133-53.

3409 "Moons of Jupiter." NEW YORKER, 22 May 1978, pp. 32-39.

3410 "Connection." CHATELAINE, 51 (Nov. 1978), 66-67, 97-98, 101, 104, 106.

3411 "Characters." PLOUGHSHARES, 4, No. 3 (1978), 72-82.

3412 "The Stone in the Field." SATURDAY NIGHT, 94 (Apr. 1979), 40-45.

3413 "A Better Place Than Home." In THE NEWCOMERS: INHABITING A NEW LAND. Gen. ed. Charles E. Israel. Toronto: McClelland and Stewart, 1979, pp. 113-24.

3414 "Dulse." NEW YORKER, 21 July 1980, pp. 30-39.

3415 "Wood." NEW YORKER, 24 Nov. 1980, pp. 46-54.

3416 "Turkey Season." NEW YORKER, 29 Dec. 1980, pp. 36-44.

3417   Entry deleted.

ARTICLES

3418   "Author's Commentary." In SIXTEEN BY TWELVE. Ed. John Metcalf.
        Toronto: Ryerson, 1970, pp. 125-26.

3419   "The Colonel's Hash Resettled." In THE NARRATIVE VOICE: SHORT
        STORIES AND REFLECTIONS BY CANADIAN AUTHORS. Ed. John
        Metcalf. Toronto: McGraw-Hill Ryerson, 1972, pp. 181-83.

Manuscripts

3420   University of Calgary, Calgary, Alta.

SECONDARY MATERIAL

Bibliography

3421   Cooke, D.E., comp. "Alice Munro: A Checklist (To December 31,
        1974)." JOURNAL OF CANADIAN FICTION, No. 16 (1976), pp.
        131-36.

Criticism

3422   Allentuck, Marcia. "Resolution and Independence in the Work of Alice
        Munro." WORLD LITERATURE WRITTEN IN ENGLISH, 16 (Nov. 1977),
        340-43.

3423   Bailey, Nancy I. "The Masculine Image in LIVES OF GIRLS AND
        WOMEN." CANADIAN LITERATURE, No. 80 (Spr. 1979), pp. 113-18,
        120.

3424   Blodgett, E.D. "Prisms and Arcs: Structures in Hébert and Munro."
        In FIGURES IN A GROUND: CANADIAN ESSAYS ON MODERN LIT-
        ERATURE COLLECTED IN HONOR OF SHEILA WATSON. Ed. Diane
        Bessai and David Jackel. Saskatoon: Western Producer Prairie Books,
        1978, pp. 99-121.

        Discusses Anne Hébert and Munro.

3425   Conron, Brandon. "Munro's Wonderland." CANADIAN LITERATURE,
        No. 78 (Aut. 1978), pp. 109-12, 114-18, 120-23.

Discusses DANCE OF THE HAPPY SHADES and SOMETHING I'VE BEEN MEANING TO TELL YOU.

3426 Dahlie, Hallvard. "The Fiction of Alice Munro." PLOUGHSHARES, 4, No. 3 (1978), 56-71.

3427 _____. "Unconsummated Relationships: Isolation and Rejection in Alice Munro's Stories." WORLD LITERATURE WRITTEN IN ENGLISH, 11 (Apr. 1972), 43-48.

3428 Dombrowski, Eileen. "'Down to Death': Alice Munro and Transcience." UNIVERSITY OF WINDSOR REVIEW, 14 (Fall-Wint. 1978), 21-29.

3429 Hoy, Helen. "'Dull, Simple, Amazing and Unfathomable': Paradox and Double Vision in Alice Munro's Fiction." STUDIES IN CANADIAN LITERATURE, 5 (Spr. 1980), 100-115.

3430 Knelman, Martin. "The Past, the Present, and Alice Munro." SATUR-DAY NIGHT, Nov. 1979, pp. 16-18, 20, 22.

3431 Kroll, Jeri. "Interview with Alice Munro." LITERATURE IN NORTH QUEENSLAND, 8, No. 1 (1980), 47-55.

3432 Macdonald, Rae McCarthy. "A Madman Loose in the World: The Vision of Alice Munto." MODERN FICTION STUDIES, 22 (Aut. 1976), 365-74.

3433 _____. "Structure and Detail in LIVES OF GIRLS AND WOMEN." STUDIES IN CANADIAN LITERATURE, 3 (Sum. 1978), 199-210.

3434 Martin, W.R. "Alice Munro and James Joyce." JOURNAL OF CA-NADIAN FICTION, No. 24 ([1979]), pp. 120-26.

3435 Metcalf, John. "A Conversation with Alice Munro." JOURNAL OF CANADIAN FICTION, 1 (Fall 1972), 54-62.

3436 Monaghan, David. "Confinement and Escape in Alice Munro's 'The Flats Road.'" STUDIES IN SHORT FICTION, 14 (Spr. 1977), 165-68.

3437 Murch, Ken. "Name: Alice Munro, Occupation: Writer." CHATE-LAINE, 48 (Aug. 1975), 42-43, 69-72.

3438 New, William H. "Pronouns and Propositions: Alice Munro's Stories." OPEN LETTER, 3rd ser., No. 5 (Sum. 1976), pp. 40-49.

Discusses SOMETHING I'VE BEEN MEANING TO TELL YOU.

3439   Rasporich, Beverly J. "Child-Women and Primitives in the Fiction of Alice Munro." ATLANTIS, 1 (Spr. 1976), 4-14.

3440   Stainsby, Mari. "Alice Munro Talks with Mari Stainsby." BRITISH COLUMBIA LIBRARY QUARTERLY, 35 (July 1971), 27-31.

3441   Struthers, J.R. (Tim). "Alice Munro and the American South." CANADIAN REVIEW OF AMERICAN STUDIES, 6 (Fall 1975), 196-204.

        Reprinted in no. 171.

3442   _____. "Reality and Ordering: The Growth of a Young Artist in LIVES OF GIRLS AND WOMEN." ESSAYS ON CANADIAN WRITING, No. 3 (Fall 1975), pp. 32-46.

3443   Wallace, Bronwen. "Men, Women and Body English in Alice Munro." BOOKS IN CANADA, 7, No. 7 (1978), 13.

3444   _____. "Women's Lives: Alice Munro." In THE HUMAN ELEMENTS: CRITICAL ESSAYS. Ed. David Helwig. [Ottawa]: Oberon, 1978, pp. 52-67.

For criticism on Munro, see also nos. 170-71, 205, 481, 1701, 3835 and 3917.

Book Reviews

3445   DANCE OF THE HAPPY SHADES: CanL, 39 (Wint. 1969), 91-92; CFor, 48 (Feb. 1969), 260; FIDDLEHEAD, 82 (Nov. 1969), 71-72; LISTENER, 13 June 1974, p. 777; MHRev, 11 (July 1969), 126; NS, 3 May 1974, p. 633; NY, 5 Nov. 1973, p. 186; NYTBR, 23 Sept. 1973, p. 48; QQ, 77 (Spr. 1970), 127-28; SatN, 84 (Aug. 1969), 33; SatN, 87 (Jan. 1972), 36-37; TLS, 10 May 1974, p. 493.

3446   LIVES OF GIRLS AND WOMEN: AntigR, 15 (Aut. 1973), 99-100; BCan, 1 (Nov. 1971), 4-5; CanL, 54 (Aut. 1972), 102-04; CFM, 11 (Aut. 1973), 93-95, 97-98; CFor, 51 (Jan. 1972), 76-77; EJ, 63 (Apr. 1974), 90; JCF, 1 (Fall 1972), 95-96; LISTENER, 29 Nov. 1973, p. 752; NS, 26 Oct. 1973, pp. 618-19; NY, 6 Jan. 1973, p. 75; SatN, 87 (Jan. 1972), 36-37; TLS, 17 Mar. 1978, p. 302; UTQ, 41 (Sum. 1971), 313-24.

3447   SOMETHING I'VE BEEN MEANING TO TELL YOU: ATLANTIS, 1 (Fall 1975), 129-30; BCan, 3 (June 1974), 7-8; BCLQ, 38 (Sum. 1974), 56-57; CAB, 50 (Fall 1974), 26; CanL, 67 (Wint. 1976), 85-87; CanR, 1 (Nov. 1974), 23; CFM, 16 (Wint. 1975), 99-101; CFor, 55 (June

1975), 42; FIDDLEHEAD, 102 (Sum. 1974), 116-19; HudR, 28 (Spr. 1975), 156; JCF, 4, No. 1 (1975), 194-96; NYTBR, 27 Oct. 1974, p. 54; OntarioR, 1 (Fall 1974), 103-04; OpenL, 3rd ser., 3 (Late Fall 1975), 107-10; Q&Q, June 1974, p. 11; QQ, 82 (Spr. 1975), 136-37; SatN, 89 (July 1974), 28; TamR, 63 (Oct. 1974), 82-83; UTQ, 44 (Sum. 1975), 305; WCR, 10 (June 1975), 46-47.

3448 WHO DO YOU THINK YOU ARE? BCan, 7 (Oct. 1978), 15-16; BCan, 9 (Jan. 1980), 20; BOT, 3 (Jan. 1980), 18; BrO, 6, No. 3 (1979), 43; CRead, 20, No. 4 (1978), 3-4; FIDDLEHEAD, 121 (Spr. 1979), 125-27; MACLEAN'S, 11 Dec. 1978, p. 62; NATION, 29 Dec. 1979, p. 696; NewR, 13 Oct. 1979, p. 40; NS, 25 Apr. 1980, p. 630; NYBR, 6 Mar. 1980, pp. 43-45; NYTBR, 16 Sept. 1979, p. 12; OntarioR, 11 (Fall-Wint. 1979-80), 87-89; Q&Q, 44 (Oct. 1978), 43; QQ, 87 (Aut. 1980), 461-62; SatN, 94 (Jan. 1979), 62, 64; SatR, 13 Oct. 1979, p. 76; SR, 88 (Sum. 1980), 412-23; SSF, 17 (Sum. 1980), 353-54; TamR, 77-78 (Sum. 1979), 98; UTQ, 48 (Sum. 1979), 319-20.

NIVEN, FREDERICK (1878-1944)

Born in Valparaiso, Chile, Frederick Niven grew up in Scotland and attended the Glasgow School of Art. For much of his early adulthood, he moved between Canada and England, working on the railroad, in lumber camps in British Columbia, and as a journalist in Glasgow and London. In the two years preceding World War I, he travelled through western Canada writing about the West; during the war he worked with the Ministry of Information in London. After 1920, Niven settled in British Columbia. His trilogy on the development of the Canadian West, which begins with THE FLYING YEARS, accurately establishes the characters' historical and geographical context.

PRIMARY MATERIAL

Monographs

FICTION

3449   THE LOST CABIN MINE. London: John Lane, 1908. 254 p.

3450   THE ISLAND PROVIDENCE. London: John Lane, 1910. 310 p.

3451   ABOVE YOUR HEADS. London: Martin Secker, 1911. 299 p.

3452   A WILDERNESS OF MONKEYS. New York: John Lane, 1911. 283 p.

3453   DEAD MEN'S BELLS: A ROMANCE. London: Martin Secker, 1912. 309 p.

3454   ELLEN ADAIR. London: Eveleigh Nash, 1913. 320 p.

3455   HANDS UP! New York: John Lane, 1913. vi, 315 p.

3456 THE PORCELAIN LADY. London: Martin Secker, 1913. 354 p.

3457 JUSTICE OF THE PEACE. London: Eveleigh Nash, 1914. 434 p.

3458 THE S.S. GLORY. Illus. Fred Holmes. London: William Heinemann, 1915. 213 p.

3459 CINDERELLA OF SKOOKUM CREEK. London: Eveleigh Nash, 1916. viii, 319 p.

3460 TWO GENERATIONS. London: Eveleigh Nash, 1916. 358 p.

3461 SAGE-BRUSH STORIES. London: Eveleigh Nash, 1917. x, 304 p.

3462 PENNY SCOT'S TREASURE. London: Collins, 1918. 306 p.

3463 THE LADY OF THE CROSSING: A NOVEL OF THE NEW WEST. London: Hodder and Stoughton, 1919. xii, 305 p.

3464 A TALE THAT IS TOLD. Toronto: Collins, 1920. 338 p.

3465 TREASURE TRAIL. New York: Dodd, Mead, 1923. 254 p.

3466 THE WOLFER. New York: Dodd, Mead, 1923. vii, 314 p.

3467 QUEER FELLOWS. London: John Lane, 1927. 251 p. Also as WILD HONEY. New York: Dodd, Mead, 1927. 251 p.

3468 THE THREE MARYS. London: Collins, 1930. 284 p.

3469 THE PAISLEY SHAWL. New York: Dodd, Mead, 1931. 252 p.

3470 THE RICH WIFE. London: Collins, 1932. 256 p.

3471 MRS. BARRY. New York: E.P. Dutton, 1933. 256 p.

3472 TRIUMPH. New York: E.P. Dutton, 1934. 252 p.

3473 THE FLYING YEARS. London: Collins, 1935. 284 p.
        First volume in a trilogy; see nos. 3477 and 3480.

3474   OLD SOLDIER: A NOVEL. London: Collins, 1936. 250 p.

3475   THE STAFF AT SIMSON'S: A NOVEL. London: Collins, 1937. 318 p.

3476   THE STORY OF THEIR DAYS. London: Collins, 1939. 444 p.

3477   MINE INHERITANCE. New York: Macmillan, 1940. 432 p. Bibliog.
        Second volume in a trilogy beginning with no. 3473.

3478   BROTHERS IN ARMS: BEING THE ACCOUNT WRITTEN BY JAMES
        NIVEN, TOBACCO MERCHANT OF GLASGOW, IN THE EIGHTEENTH
        CENTURY, RECENTLY DISCOVERED AND NOW EDITED AND SEEN
        THROUGH THE PRESS BY FREDERICK NIVEN. London: Collins, 1942.
        255 p.

3479   UNDER WHICH KING. London: Collins, 1943. 192 p.

3480   THE TRANSPLANTED. Toronto: Collins, 1944. 310 p.
        Third volume in a trilogy beginning with no. 3473.

NONFICTION PROSE

3481   THE STORY OF ALEXANDER SELKIRK (THE REAL ROBINSON CRUSOE).
        London: Wells Gardner, Darton, [1929]. viii, 119 p.
        For children.

3482   CANADA WEST. Illus. John Innes. London: J.M. Dent and Sons,
        [1930]. xi, 188 p.

3483   COLOUR IN THE CANADIAN ROCKIES. By Frederick Niven and Walter
        Joseph Phillips. Toronto: Thomas Nelson and Sons, 1937. 125 p. Index.

3484   COLOURED SPECTACLES. London: Collins, 1938. 352 p.
        Autobiography.

3485   A LADY IN THE WILDERNESS: A TALE OF THE YUKON, NOT OF
        ITS GOLD BUT OF BEN-MY-CHREE, THE LONG FAMOUS GARDEN
        OF MRS. PARTRIDGE. N.p.: N.p., [193-?]. 10 p.

3486   GO NORTH, WHERE THE WORLD IS YOUNG. [Seattle]: White Pass
        and Yukon Route, n.d. N.pag.

POETRY

3487   MAPLE-LEAF SONGS. London: Sedgwick and Jackson, 1917. 44 p.

3488   A LOVER OF THE LAND AND OTHER POEMS. New York: Boni and
        Liveright, 1925. vi, 72 p.

Shorter Work

SHORT STORIES

3489   "A Wind-Blown Rose." ENGLISH REVIEW, 5 (June 1910), 456-64.

3490   "Train Across the Country." SATURDAY NIGHT, 18 Mar. 1939, p. 3.

ARTICLES

3491   "Note Upon Style." BOOKMAN, 51 (June 1920), 434-37.

3492   "Henley." LIBRARY REVIEW, No. 27 (1934), pp. 98-98.

3493   "Andrew Lang." LIBRARY REVIEW, No. 44 (1937), pp. 170-74.

Manuscripts

3494   Metropolitan Toronto Central Library; University of British Columbia Li-
        brary, Vancouver.

SECONDARY MATERIAL

Criticism

3495   Abcock, St. John. "Frederick Niven." In his THE GLORY THAT WAS
        GRUB STREET: IMPRESSIONS OF CONTEMPORARY AUTHORS. London:
        Low, Marston, 1928, pp. 247-57.

3496   de Bruyn, Jan. Introd., THE FLYING YEARS. New Canadian Library,
        no. 102. Toronto: McClelland and Stewart, 1974, n. pag.

3497   New, William H. "A Life and Four Landscapes: Frederick John Niven."
        CANADIAN LITERATURE, No. 32 (Spr. 1967), pp. 15-28.

        Reprinted in nos. 173 and 5113.

3498 Reid, Alexander. "A Scottish Chekhov?" SCOTLAND'S, 58 (Mar. 1962), 45-46.

3499 Singleton, M.K. "Frederick Niven, Redivivus: A Scots-Canadian's Pacific Northwest." In NORTHWEST PERSPECTIVES: ESSAYS ON THE CULTURE OF THE PACIFIC NORTHWEST. Ed. Edwin R. Bingham and Glen A. Love. Seattle: University of Washington Press, 1979, pp. 120-35.

3500 Stevenson, Y.H. "Frederick Niven, 'Kootenay Scribe.'" CANADIAN AUTHOR AND BOOKMAN, 17 (Apr. 1940), 7-8.

3501 Walpole, Hugh, and Christopher Morley. Introd., JUSTICE OF THE PEACE. New York: Boni and Liveright, 1923, pp. ix-xviii.

For criticism on Niven, see also nos. 131, 324, and 2889.

Book Reviews

3502 THE LOST CABIN MINE: NYTSR, 6 Mar. 1909, p. 134.

3503 ELLEN ADAIR: NewR, 14 Oct. 1925, p. 211; NYTBR, 30 Aug. 1925, p. 9; SatR, 3 Oct. 1925, p. 180.

3504 HANDS UP! NYTBR, 27 Apr. 1913, p. 246.

3505 JUSTICE OF THE PEACE: NewR, 2 Jan. 1924, p. 155; NYTBR, 6 Jan. 1924, p. 16.

3506 THE S.S. GLORY: SPECTATOR, 29 Jan. 1916, p. 165.

3507 THE LADY OF THE CROSSING: NYTBR, 14 Sept. 1919, p. 468.

3508 A TALE THAT IS TOLD: ATHENAEUM, 1 Oct. 1920, p. 439; NYTBR, 14 Nov. 1920, p. 18; REVIEW, 19 Jan. 1921, p. 57; TLS, 30 Sept. 1920, p. 633.

3509 TREASURE TRAIL: NYTBR, 16 Dec. 1923, p. 19.

3510 QUEER FELLOWS: CFor, 7 (May 1927), 252, 254.

3511 THE PAISLEY SHAWL: NYTBR, 26 Apr. 1931, p. 22; SatR, 25 Apr. 1931, p. 778; TLS, 19 Mar. 1931, p. 236.

3512 MRS. BARRY: NATION, 30 Aug. 1933, p. 248; NYTBR, 20 Aug. 1933, p. 15; SatR, 9 Sept. 1933, p. 98; TLS, 9 Mar. 1933, p. 164.

3513 TRIUMPH: COMMONWEAL, 4 Jan. 1935, p. 295; NewR, 8 Aug. 1934, p. 354; NYTBR, 27 May 1934, p. 6; SatR, 26 May 1934, p. 717; TLS, 15 Mar. 1934, p. 186.

3514 OLD SOLDIER: UTQ, 6 (Apr. 1937), 349.

3515 THE STORY OF THEIR DAYS: CAB, Apr. 1940, pp. 7-8; NYTBR, 18 Feb. 1940, p. 8; SatN, 8 July 1939, p. 16; UTQ, 9 (Apr. 1940), 290-91.

3516 MINE INHERITANCE: CAB, July 1940, p. 6; CFor, 20 (Aug. 1940), 154; DR, 20 (July 1940), 258; NYTBR, 12 Jan. 1941, p. 7; SatN, 22 June 1940, p. 8; TLS, 11 May 1940, p. 233; UTQ, 10 (Apr. 1941), 294-96.

3517 BROTHERS IN ARMS: UTQ, 12 (Apr. 1943), 320-21.

3518 THE TRANSPLANTED: CFor, 24 (Jan. 1945), 241-42; CGJ, 30 (Feb. 1945), ix; CGJ, 30 (June 1945), xi.

3519 COLOURED SPECTACLES: SatN, 14 May 1938, p. 15; UTQ, 8 (Apr. 1939), 322.

O'HAGAN, HOWARD (1902-82)

Howard O'Hagan was born in Lethbridge, Alberta, studied law at McGill University, Montreal, and practiced it briefly, worked as a guide in the Rockies, travelled to Australia, was publicity agent for two Canadian railways and the Central Argentinian Railway, and spent eleven years in Sicily. For the past several decades he has been living on Vancouver Island. His early work was overlooked when it first appeared and has been recognized only recently. TAY JOHN, an unusual work with a legendary even mythic hero, is of particular interest.

PRIMARY MATERIAL

Monographs

FICTION

3520 TAY JOHN. London: Laidlaw and Laidlaw, 1939. 263 p.

3521 THE WOMAN WHO GOT ON AT JASPER STATION AND OTHER STORIES. [Denver, Colo.]: Alan Swallow, 1963. 112 p.

3522 THE SCHOOL-MARM TREE: A NOVEL. Introd. P.K. Page. Vancouver: Talonbooks, 1977. 244 p.

NONFICTION PROSE

3523 WILDERNESS MEN. Garden City, N.Y.: Doubleday, 1958. 263 p.

Shorter Work

SHORT STORIES

3524 "'Savoir-Faire.'" MACLEAN'S, 1 Dec. 1939, pp. 7-9, 46-47.

3525 "Ursus." Illus. Margaret Peterson. MALAHAT REVIEW, No. 50 (Apr. 1979), pp. 49–64.

ARTICLE

3526 "Stephie." QUEEN'S QUARTERLY, 68 (Sum. 1961), 135–46.

Reminiscences of Stephen Leacock.

SECONDARY MATERIAL

Criticism

3527 Fergusson, Harvey. Introd., TAY JOHN. New York: Clarkson N. Potter, 1960. N. pag.

3528 Geddes, Gary. "The Writer That CanLit Forgot: Howard O'Hagan, Mountain Man, Sings the Mysteries of the Rockies." SATURDAY NIGHT, 92 (Nov. 1977), 84–87, 90–92.

3529 Morley, Patricia. Introd., TAY JOHN. New Canadian Library, no. 105. Toronto: McClelland and Stewart, 1974, pp. vii–xiv.

3530 Roberts, K. "Talking to Howard O'Hagan." EVENT, 5, No. 3 (1976), 42–48.

3531 Stow, G. "Discordant Heritage." JOURNAL OF CANADIAN FICTION, No. 16 (1976), pp. 178–81.

Discusses TAY JOHN.

For criticism on O'Hagan, see also nos. 3522 and 3548.

Book Reviews

3532 TAY JOHN: CanL, 9 (Sum. 1961), 65–66; JCF, 16 (1976), 178–81; NYTBR, 13 Mar. 1960, p. 34; UTQ, 30 (July 1961), 414–15.

3533 THE WOMAN WHO GOT ON AT JASPER STATION: BCan, 7 (Apr. 1978), 18–19; CanL, 81 (Sum. 1979), 116–17; CRead, 19 (July 1978), 7–8; FIDDLEHEAD, 120 (Wint. 1978), 126–28; Q&Q, 44 (Apr. 1978), 36.

3534 THE SCHOOL-MARM TREE: BCan, 7 (Apr. 1978), 18; CAB, 54 (Oct. 1978), 28–29; CanL, 81 (Sum. 1979), 117–18; CFor, 58 (June 1978),

27-28; COMPASS, 4 (Aut. 1978), 97-104; CRead, 19 (July 1978), 7-9; FIDDLEHEAD, 120 (Wint. 1978), 128-29; Q&Q, 44 (Apr. 1978), 36; UTQ, 47 (Sum. 1978), 331-32.

3535   WILDERNESS MEN: SaskH, 13 (Spr. 1960), 79.

ONDAATJE, MICHAEL (1943--)

Philip Michael Ondaatje was born in Colombo, Ceylon, and moved to England when he was eleven and to Canada in 1962. Educated at Bishop's University (Lennoxville, Quebec), University of Toronto (B.A., 1965), and Queen's University, Kingston (M.A., 1967), he has taught English at the University of Western Ontario and, since the early seventies, at York University, Toronto. He is also a filmmaker. Ondaatje is best known as a poet (especially for THE COLLECTED WORKS OF BILLY THE KID), but COMING THROUGH SLAUGHTER, a poetic novel based on the life of cornetist Buddy Bolden and constructed of impressionistic fragments and images, has also attracted favorable comment.

PRIMARY MATERIAL

Monographs

FICTION

3536   COMING THROUGH SLAUGHTER. Toronto: Anansi, 1976. 156 p.

NONFICTION PROSE

3537   LEONARD COHEN. Canadian Writers, no. 5. Toronto: McClelland and Stewart, 1970. 64 p. Bibliog.

POETRY

3538   THE DIRTY MONSTERS. [Toronto]: Coach House, 1967. 77 p.

3539   THE MAN WITH SEVEN TOES. [Toronto]: Coach House, 1969. N. pag.

3540   THE COLLECTED WORKS OF BILLY THE KID: LEFT-HANDED POEMS. Toronto: Anansi, 1970. 105 p.

3541 RAT JELLY. Toronto: Coach House, 1973. 71 p.

3542 THERE'S A TRICK WITH A KNIFE I'M LEARNING TO DO: POEMS
1963-78. Toronto: McClelland and Stewart, 1979. xi, 107 p.

3543 ELIMINATION DANCE. Ilderton, Ont.: Nairn Coldstream, 1978.
N. pag. Rev. ed. Ilderton, Ont.: Brick Books, 1980. N. pag.

EDITED WORK

3544 THE BROKEN ARK: A BOOK OF BEASTS. Drawings by Tony Urquhart.
[Ottawa]: Oberson, 1971. N. pag.; rpt. as A BOOK OF BEASTS.
Drawings by Tony Urquhart. [Ottawa]: Oberon, 1979. N. pag.

3545 PERSONAL FICTIONS: STORIES BY MUNRO, WIEBE, THOMAS, AND
BLAISE. Toronto: Oxford University Press, 1977. 230 p.

3546 LONG POEM ANTHOLOGY. Ed. with introd. by Michael Ondaatje.
Toronto: Coach House, 1979. 343 p. Bibliog.

Shorter Work

SHORT STORY

3547 "Austin." PERIODICS, 1 (1977), 44-46.

ARTICLES

3548 "O'Hagan's Rough-Edged Chronicle." CANADIAN LITERATURE, No. 61
(Sum. 1974), pp. 24-31.

   Discusses O'Hagan's TAY JOHN; reprinted in no. 5113.

3549 "García Márquez and the Bus to Aracataca." In FIGURES IN A GROUND:
CANADIAN ESSAYS ON MODERN LITERATURE COLLECTED IN HONOR
OF SHEILA WATSON. Ed. Diane Bessai and David Jackel. Saskatoon:
Western Producer Prairie Books, 1978, pp. 19-31.

SECONDARY MATERIAL

Criticism

3550 Abley, M. "Home Is Where the Hurt Is." MACLEAN'S, 23 Apr. 1979,
p. 62.

3551   Scobie, Stephen. "COMING THROUGH SLAUGHTER: Fictional Magnets and Spider's Webbs." ESSAYS ON CANADIAN WRITING, 12 (Fall 1978), 5-23.

3552   Solecki, Sam. "An Interview with Michael Ondaatje." RUNE, No. 2 (Spr. 1975), pp. 39-54.

3553   _____. "Making and Destroying: Michale Ondaatje's COMING THROUGH SLAUGHTER and Extremist Art." ESSAYS ON CANADIAN WRITING, 12 (Fall 1978), 24-47.

3554   Witten, Mark. "Billy, Buddy, and Michael: The Collected Writings of Michael Ondaatje are a Composite Portrait of the Artist as a Private 'I.'" BOOKS IN CANADA, 6 (June-July 1977), 9-10, 12-13.

For criticism on Ondaatje, see also nos. 162, 181, 4180, and especially 1208.

Book Reviews

3555   COMING THROUGH SLAUGHTER: BCan, 6 (Feb. 1977), 29-30; CanL, 73 (Sum. 1977), 92-94; CBRA, 1976, pp. 125-26; CFM, 24-25 (Spr. 1977), 165-67; CFor, 56 (Dec. 1976), 46-47; CRead, 18 (July 1977), 2-3; FIDDLEHEAD, 113 (Spr. 1977), 126-29; MHRev, 44 (Oct. 1977), 140-42; NY, 9 May 1977, p. 146; NYTBR, 24 Apr. 1977, p. 14; OntarioR, 7 (Fall 1977), 104-06; PR, 44 (Wint. 1977), 160; Q&Q, 42, No. 15 (1976), 32; QQ, 84 (Aut. 1977), 436-37; QUARRY, 26 (Wint. 1977), 78-80; SPECTATOR, 8 Sept. 1979, p. 25; UTQ, 46 (Sum. 1977), 356-58; WLWE, 17 (Nov. 1978), 505-06.

3556   LEONARD COHEN: CFor, 50 (Sept. 1970), 222.

OSTENSO, MARTHA (1900-1963)

Born near Bergen, Norway, and raised in Minnesota and North Dakota, Martha Ostenso came to Manitoba in 1915. She taught briefly at a rural school, attended the University of Manitoba from 1918 to 1919, worked for the FREE PRESS in Winnipeg for the following two years, and then returned to the United States. Her place in Canadian fiction derives mainly from WILD GEESE, a forthright sometimes melodramatic tale of prairie passion and family conflict, which won the $13,500 Dodd-Mead Prize in 1925.

PRIMARY MATERIAL

Monographs

FICTION

3557 WILD GEESE. New York: Dodd, Mead, [1925]. 356 p. Also as THE PASSIONATE FLIGHT. London: Hodder and Stoughton, [1925]. 320 p.

3558 THE DARK DAWN. New York: Dodd, Mead, 1926. 294 p.

3559 THE MAD CAREWS. New York: Dodd, Mead, 1927. 346 p.

3560 THE YOUNG MAY MOON. New York: Dodd, Mead, 1929. 301 p.

3561 THE WATERS UNDER THE EARTH. New York: Dodd, Mead, 1930. 319 p.

3562 PROLOGUE TO LOVE. New York: Dodd, Mead, 1932. 265 p.

3563 THERE'S ALWAYS ANOTHER YEAR. New York: Dodd, Mead, 1933. 268 p.

3564   THE WHITE REEF. New York: Dodd, Mead, 1934. 288 p.

3565   THE STONE FIELD. New York: Dodd, Mead, 1937. 310 p.

3566   THE MANDRAKE ROOT. New York: Dodd, Mead, 1938. 304 p.

3567   LOVE PASSED THIS WAY. New York: Dodd, Mead, 1942. 217 p.

3568   O RIVER, REMEMBER! New York: Dodd, Mead, 1943. 393 p.

3569   MILK ROUTE. New York: Dodd, Mead, 1948. 250 p.

3570   THE SUNSET TREE. New York: Dodd, Mead, 1949. 255 p.

3571   A MAN HAD TALL SONS. New York: Dodd, Mead, 1958. 368 p.

NONFICTION PROSE

3572   AND THEY SHALL WALK: THE LIFE STORY OF SISTER ELIZABETH
       KENNY: WRITTEN IN COLLABORATION WITH MARTHA OSTENSO.
       New York: Dodd, Mead, 1943. 282 p.

POETRY

3573   A FAR LAND: POEMS. New York: Thomas Seltzer, 1924. viii, 70 p.;
       rpt. as IN A FAR LAND: POEMS. New York: Dodd, Mead, 1942.
       70 p.

Shorter Work

SHORT STORIES

3574   "The Storm." AMERICAN SCANDINAVIAN REVIEW, 12 (Sept. 1924),
       549-56.

3575   "White Tryst." NORTH AMERICAN, 226 (Dec. 1928), 758-64.

3576   "Strange Woman." DELINEATOR, 115 (Oct. 1929), 13-14.

3577   "Bridge." PICTORIAL REVIEW, 36 (Dec. 1934), 8-9.

3578   "Last Mad Sky." GOOD HOUSEKEEPING, 101 (Oct. 1935), 44-47.

3579   "Gardenias in Her Hair." PICTORIAL REVIEW, 38 (Sept. 1937), 83-98.

3580   "Dreamer." COLLIER'S, 19 Mar. 1938, pp. 9-10.

3581   "Tumbleweed." WOMAN'S HOME COMPANION, 65 (July 1938), 12-13.

3582   "Tonka Squaw." GOOD HOUSEKEEPING, 107 (Sept. 1938), 30-33.

3583   "Prairie Romance." WOMAN'S HOME COMPANION, 70 (Apr. 1943),
        20-21.

3584   "Meet the Sergeant." NATIONAL HOME MONTHLY, 44 (Nov. 1943),
        10-11, 57-59.

3585   "And the Town Talked." COUNTRY GUIDE, 63 (Feb. 1944), 6-7;
        (Apr. 1944), 10-11.

3586   "The Calendar." CANADIAN HOME JOURNAL, 41 (Apr. 1945), 12-
        13, 61-62, 64, 72.

SECONDARY MATERIAL

Criticism

3587   Colman, Morris. "Martha Ostenso, Prize Novelist." MACLEAN'S, 1
        Jan. 1925, pp. 56-58.

3588   Keith, William J. "WILD GEESE: The Death of Caleb Gare." STUDIES
        IN CANADIAN LITERATURE, 3 (Sum. 1978), 274-76.

3589   King, Carlyle. Introd., WILD GEESE. New Canadian Library, no. 18.
        Toronto: McClelland and Stewart, 1961, pp. v-x.

3590   Lawrence, Robert. "The Geography of Martha Ostenso's WILD GEESE."
        JOURNAL OF CANADIAN FICTION, No. 16 (1976), pp. 108-14.

3591   MacLellan, W.E. "Real 'Canadian Literature.'" DALHOUSIE REVIEW,
        6 (Apr. 1926), 18-23.

        Discusses WILD GEESE.

3592   Mickleburgh, Brita. "Martha Ostenso: The Design of her Canadian
        Prose Fiction." ALIVE, 35 ([1974]), 17-19.

3593   Mullins, Stanley G. "Some Remarks on Theme in Martha Ostenso's
        WILD GEESE." CULTURE, 23 (Dec. 1962), 359-62.

3594   Overton, G. "Novelist from Nowhere." MENTOR, 15 (June 1927),
        56-57.

3595   Tallman, Lyn. "Martha Ostenso." WESTERN HOME MONTHLY, 28
        (Mar. 1927), 30.

For criticism on Ostenso, see also nos. 174, 190, and 197.

Book Reviews

3596   WILD GEESE: CanL, 10 (Aut. 1961), 74-75; NATION, 6 Jan. 1926,
        p. 14; NYTBR, 18 Oct. 1925, p. 8; SatR, 28 Nov. 1925, p. 335;
        TLS, 24 Dec. 1925, p. 898.

3597   THE DARK DAWN: CFor, 7 (Jan. 1927), 121; NewR, 22 Dec. 1926,
        p. 146; NYTBR, 24 Oct. 1926, p. 6; SatR, 16 Oct. 1926, p. 191.

3598   THE MAD CAREWS: CFor, 8 (May 1928), 656-57; NewR, 23 Nov.
        1927, p. 25; NYTBR, 9 Oct. 1927, p. 6; SatR, 15 Oct. 1927, p. 197.

3599   THE YOUNG MAY MOON: NYTBR, 1 Sept. 1929, p. 7; SatR, 26
        Oct. 1929, p. 324.

3600   THE WATERS UNDER THE EARTH: NYTBR, 23 Nov. 1930, p. 6; SatR,
        1 Nov. 1930, p. 284.

3601   PROLOGUE TO LOVE: NYTBR, 2 Oct. 1932, p. 13.

3602   THERE'S ALWAYS ANOTHER YEAR: NYTBR, 22 Oct. 1933, p. 19;
        SatR, 28 Oct. 1933, p. 222.

3603   THE WHITE REEF: NYTBR, 4 Nov. 1934, p. 22; SatR, 10 Nov. 1934,
        p. 278.

3604   THE STONE FIELD: COMMONWEAL, 14 May 1937, p. 81; NYTBR,
        21 Mar. 1937, p. 7; SatR, 20 Mar. 1937, p. 16; UTQ, 7 (Apr. 1938),
        352-53.

3605   THE MANDRAKE ROOT: NYTBR, 30 Oct. 1938, p. 6; SatR, 12 Nov.
        1938, p. 20; UTQ, 8 (Apr. 1939), 307.

3606   LOVE PASSED THIS WAY: NYTBR, 1 Mar. 1942, p. 25.

3607   O RIVER, REMEMBER!   COMMONWEAL, 14 Jan. 1944, p. 332; NYTBR, 26 Sept. 1943, p. 18; SatN, 30 Oct. 1943, p. 31; SatR, 13 Nov. 1943, p. 8.

3608   MILK ROUTE: NYTBR, 7 Mar. 1948, p. 22.

3609   THE SUNSET TREE: SatR, 17 Dec. 1949, p. 27.

RADDALL, THOMAS (1903--)

Thomas Head Raddall was born in Hythe, Kent, England, came to Halifax in 1913, and began work as a coastguard and wireless operator with the Canadian Merchant Marine at the age of fifteen. After work as a bookkeeper in Nova Scotia pulp and paper mills, he turned to full-time writing in 1938, making his permanent home in Liverpool, Nova Scotia. Raddall has won Doubleday's $10,000 Award for THE GOVERNOR'S LADY, Governor General's Awards for THE PIED PIPER OF DIPPER CREEK, HALIFAX, and THE PATH OF DESTINY, the 1956 Lorne Pierce Medal, and the Order of Canada Medal of Service in 1970. He is noted for THE NYMPH AND THE LAMP, a realistic story of romantic involvement set in a life-saving station, and, among his many historical novels, for HIS MAJESTY'S YANKEES.

PRIMARY MATERIAL

Monographs

FICTION

3610 THE PIED PIPER OF DIPPER CREEK AND OTHER TALES. With an Appreciation by Lord Tweedsmuir (John Buchan). Edinburgh: William Blackwood and Sons, 1939. vii, 317 p.

3611 HIS MAJESTY'S YANKEES. Garden City, N.Y.: Doubleday, Doran, 1942. xi, 409 p.

3612 ROGER SUDDEN. Toronto: McClelland and Stewart, 1944. vi, 358 p.

3613 TAMBOUR AND OTHER STORIES. Decorations by Stanley Turner. Toronto: McClelland and Stewart, 1945. 388 p.

3614 PRIDE'S FANCY. Toronto: McClelland and Stewart, 1946. vi, 308 p.

3615   THE WEDDING GIFT AND OTHER STORIES. Toronto: McClelland and Stewart, 1947. vii, 325 p.

3616   THE NYMPH AND THE LAMP: A NOVEL. Boston: Little, Brown, 1950. 376 p.

3617   SON OF THE HAWK. Illus. Stanley Turner. Philadelphia: John C. Winston, 1950. vii, 247 p.

        For children.

3618   TIDEFALL: A NOVEL. Toronto: McClelland and Stewart, 1953. 309 p.; rpt. as GIVE AND TAKE: A NOVEL OF THE SEA. New York: Popular Library, 1955. 221 p.

3619   A MUSTER OF ARMS & OTHER STORIES. Toronto: McClelland and Stewart, 1954. 236 p.

3620   THE WINGS OF NIGHT. Garden City, N.Y.: Doubleday, 1956. 319 p.

3621   AT THE TIDE'S TURN AND OTHER STORIES. Introd. Allan Bevan. New Canadian Library, no. 9. Toronto: McClelland and Stewart, 1959. ix, 178 p.

3622   THE GOVERNOR'S LADY. Garden City, N.J.: Doubleday, 1960. 474 p.

3623   HANGMAN'S BEACH. Garden City, N.Y.: Doubleday, 1966. vi, 421 p.

NONFICTION PROSE

3624   THE SAGA OF THE ROVER. Illus. Thomas W. Hayhurst. [Halifax: Royal, 1932]. 91 p.

3625   THE MARKLAND SAGAS, WITH A DISCUSSION OF THEIR RELATION TO NOVA SCOTIA. By Thomas Raddall and Charles Hugh Le Pailleur Jones. Illus. Thomas W. Hayhurst. Montreal: Gazette Printing, [1934]. 116 p.

3626   WEST NOVAS: A HISTORY OF THE WEST NOVA SCOTIA REGIMENT. Liverpool, N.S.: n.p., 1947. 326 p.

3627   HALIFAX, WARDEN OF THE NORTH. Illus. Donald C. MacKay. Toronto: McClelland and Stewart, 1948. xviii, 348 p. Bibliog. Index. Rev. ed. Toronto: McClelland and Stewart, 1971. xvi, 343 p. Bibliog. Index.

3628   THE LITERARY ART. Samuel Robertson Memorial Lecture, 1954. Char-
        lottetown, P.E.I.: Prince of Wales College, 1954. 8 p.

            Also as no. 3651.

3629   THE PATH OF DESTINY: CANADA FROM THE BRITISH CONQUEST
        TO HOME RULE: 1763-1850. Canadian History Series, vol. 3. To-
        ronto: Doubleday, 1957. x, 468 p. Index.

3630   THE ROVER: THE STORY OF A CANADIAN PRIVATEER. Illus. Vernon
        Mould. Toronto: Macmillan, 1958. 156 p.

            For children.

3631   FOOTSTEPS ON OLD FLOORS: TRUE TALES OF MYSTERY. Garden
        City, N.Y.: Doubleday, 1968. 239 p.

            Includes Grey Owl's story.

3632   A PICTORIAL GUIDE TO HISTORIC NOVA SCOTIA, FEATURING LOUIS-
        BOURG, PEGGY'S COVE, SABLE ISLAND. Halifax: Book Room, 1970.
        31 p.

3633   IN MY TIME: A MEMOIR. Toronto: McClelland and Stewart, 1976.
        viii, 365 p.

            Autobiography.

EDITED WORK

3634   TALES OF THE SEA. By Archibald MacMechan. Ed. with foreword by
        Thomas Raddall. Toronto: McClelland and Stewart, 1947. xiv, 230 p.

Shorter Work

SHORT STORIES

3635   "Three Wise Men." MACLEAN'S, 1 Apr. 1928, pp. 6-7, 56-61.

3636   "The Pay-Off at Duncan's." BLACKWOOD'S, 236 (Sept. 1934), 390-
        405.

3637   "A Matter of History." BLACKWOOD'S, 241 (May 1937), 575-95.

3638   "The Lower Learning." BLACKWOOD'S, 244 (Oct. 1938), 533-49.

3639　"Lupita."　MACLEAN'S, 1 June 1940, pp. 5-7, 34-35.

3640　"Mr. Embury's Hat."　MACLEAN'S, 1 July 1940, pp. 14-15, 28, 30-31.

3641　"Swan Dance."　MACLEAN'S, 15 Apr. 1941, pp. 14-15, 50-52.

3642　"Action at Sea."　COLLIER'S, 11 Apr. 1942, p. 22.

3643　"Miracle."　SATURDAY EVENING POST, 9 Jan. 1943, p. 19.

3644　"The Deserter."　MACLEAN'S, 15 Oct. 1944, pp. 16-18, 34, 37-38.

3645　"The Winter's Tale."　In NEARLY AN ISLAND: A NOVA SCOTIAN ANTHOLOGY. Ed. Alice Hale and Sheila Brooks. St. John's, Nfld.: Breakwater, 1979, pp. 53-74.

ARTICLES

3646　"For Beginners Only."　WRITER, 57 (Sept. 1944), 259-61.

3647　"The Importance of Things Past."　DALHOUSIE REVIEW, 29 (July 1949), 113-18.

3648　"The Literary Tradition."　CANADIAN AUTHOR AND BOOKMAN, 25 (Aut. 1949), 3-7.

3649　"My First Book."　CANADIAN AUTHOR AND BOOKMAN, 28 (Aut. 1952), 5-8.

3650　"Sword and Pen in Kent: 1903-1913."　DALHOUSIE REVIEW, 32 (Aut. 1952), 145-52.

3651　"The Literary Art."　DALHOUSIE REVIEW, 34 (Sum. 1954), 138-46.
　　　　Reprinted in nos. 136 and 3628.

3652　"To a Young Writer."　ATLANTIC ADVOCATE, 55 (Aug. 1965), 27-28.

Manuscripts

3653　Dalhousie University Library, Halifax, N.S.

SECONDARY MATERIAL

Criticism

3654   Cameron, Donald A.   "Thomas Raddall: The Art of Historical Fiction."
        DALHOUSIE REVIEW, 49 (Wint. 1969-70), 540-48.

3655   Cockburn, Robert.   "'Nova Scotia Is My Dwelen Plas':   The Life and
        Work of Thomas Raddall."   ACADIENSIS, 7 (Spr. 1978), 135-41.

3656   Cogswell, Frederick.   Introd., PRIDE'S FANCY.   New Canadian Library,
        no. 98.   Toronto: McClelland and Stewart, 1974, pp. iii-xii.

3657   Fowke, Edith.   "'Blind MacNair':   A Canadian Short Story and Its Sources."
        In FOLKLORE STUDIES IN HONOUR OF HERBERT HALPERT: A FEST-
        SCHRIFT.   Ed. Kenneth S. Goldstein.   St. John's: Memorial University
        of Newfoundland, 1980, pp. 173-86.

3658   Gray, James.   Introd., HIS MAJESTY'S YANKEES.   New Canadian Library,
        no. 133.   Toronto: McClelland and Stewart, 1977, pp. xi-xviii.

3659   Hawkins, W.J.   "Thomas Raddall: The Man and His Work."   QUEEN'S
        QUARTERLY, 75 (Spr. 1968), 137-46.

3660   Leitold, J.R.   Introd., ROGER SUDDEN.   New Canadian Library, no.
        85.   Toronto: McClelland and Stewart, 1972, n. pag.

3661   Matthews, John.   Introd., THE NYMPH AND THE LAMP.   New Canadian
        Library, no. 38.   Toronto: McClelland and Stewart, 1963, pp. v-ix.

3662   Nowlan, Alden.   "An Historical Novelist the Reader Can Trust."   AT-
        LANTIC ADVOCATE, 67 (Apr. 1977), 63.

3663   Sorfleet, John R.   "Thomas Raddall: I Was Always a Rebel Underneath."
        JOURNAL OF CANADIAN FICTION, 2 (Fall 1973), 45-64.

        Interview.

3664   Spicer, Stanley T.   "Great Stories To Tell: A Profile of Thomas H.
        Raddall."   ATLANTIC ADVOCATE, 54 (Dec. 1963), 44-46.

3665   Wright, Ethel Clark.   "A Conflict of Loyalties."   DALHOUSIE REVIEW,
        23 (Apr. 1943), 83-86.

        Discusses HIS MAJESTY'S YANKEES.

For criticism on Raddall, see also nos. 81, 124, 168, 182, 3610, and 3621.

Book Reviews

3666 THE PIED PIPER OF DIPPER CREEK: CAB, Sept. 1944, p. 26; CULTURE, 5 (Mar. 1944), 96; SatN, 29 Jan. 1929, p. 20; UTQ, 13 (Apr. 1944), 318.

3667 HIS MAJESTY'S YANKEES: Atl, 171 (Jan. 1943), 144; DR, 23 (Apr. 1943), 83-86; JCF, 20 (1977), 152-55; NYTBR, 15 Nov. 1942, p. 12; UTQ, 12 (Apr. 1943), 321.

3668 ROGER SUDDEN: DR, 24 (Jan. 1945), 489; JCF, 1 (Spr. 1972), 94-95; SatN, 16 Dec. 1944, p. 25; SatR, 14 Apr. 1945, p. 58.

3669 TAMBOUR: CAB, Mar. 1946, p. 33; DR, 25 (Jan. 1946), 506; UTQ, 15 (Apr. 1946), 288.

3670 PRIDE'S FANCY: NYTBR, 3 Nov. 1946, p. 16.

3671 THE NYMPH AND THE LAMP: BCan, 2 (Apr. 1973), 34; CAB, Sum. 1950, pp. 11, 18; COMMONWEAL, 1 Dec. 1950, p. 213; NYTBR, 10 Dec. 1950, p. 24; RUL, 6 (Sept. 1951), 54-56; SatN, 28 Nov. 1950, p. 24; SatR, 11 Nov. 1950, p. 15; UTQ, 20 (Apr. 1951), 262-64.

3672 TIDEFALL: CFor, 33 (Jan. 1954), 237; DR, 34 (Spr. 1954), [95]; NYTBR, 22 Nov. 1953, p. 44; RUL, 8 (May 1954), 858-59; UTQ, 23 (Apr. 1954), 270.

3673 A MUSTER OF ARMS: CFor, 34 (Feb. 1955), 263.

3674 THE WINGS OF NIGHT: NYTBR, 23 Sept. 1956, p. 30; SatR, 24 Nov. 1956, p. 34; TamR, 2 (Wint. 1957), 75; UTQ, 26 (Apr. 1957), 314-15.

3675 AT THE TIDE'S TURN: CanL, 5 (Sum. 1960), 74; DR, 40 (Spr. 1960), 133.

3676 THE GOVERNOR'S LADY: AtlA, 51 (Oct. 1960), 79, 81; BCan, 8 (Oct. 1979), 29; CanL, 6 (Aut. 1960), 75-76; NYTBR, 9 Oct. 1960, p. 54; SatN, 24 Dec. 1960, p. 34; UTQ, 30 (July 1961), 411-12.

3677 HANGMAN'S BEACH: AtlA, 57 (Nov. 1966), 64; BCan, 8 (Oct. 1979), 29; CAB, 42 (Aut. 1966), 19-20; QQ, 74 (Sum. 1967), 345-46; UTQ, 36 (July 1967), 387-88.

3678   THE PATH OF DESTINY: CHR, 39 (June 1958), 154-55; SatN, 9
Nov. 1957, pp. 42-43.

3679   FOOTSTEPS ON OLD FLOORS: CAB, 43 (Sum. 1968), 17; NYTBR, 25
Feb. 1968, p. 34.

3680   IN MY TIME: BCan, 5 (Nov. 1976), 3-5; CBRA, 1976, pp. 60-61;
CFM, 27 (1977), 151-52; CRead, 18 (Feb. 1977), 2-4; DR, 57 (Spr.
1977), 187-88; Q&Q, 43, No. 1 (1977), 29; SatN, 91 (Nov. 1976),
67, 69-70; UTQ, 46 (Sum. 1977), 476-77.

RICHLER, MORDECAI (1931--)

Mordecai Richler was born in Montreal and attended Sir George Williams University there before setting out for England at the age of nineteen. He lived briefly in Spain and in Paris, and passed about twenty years in England where he devoted himself to writing fiction, filmscripts, criticism, and lighter journalism. He was writer-in-residence at Sir George Williams University and Carleton University, Ottawa, and in 1972 returned to Montreal to live. Richler has won the Governor General's Award for COCKSURE, HUNTING TIGERS UNDER GLASS, and ST. URBAIN'S HORSEMAN. His fiction, which documents and satirizes the Jewish ghetto of his youth as well as contemporary trendiness and neuroses, moves between realism and comic fantasy and absurdity.

PRIMARY MATERIAL

Monographs

FICTION

3681 THE ACROBATS: A NOVEL. London: André Deutsch, 1954. 204 p. Also as WICKED WE LOVE. Popular Library edition. (Listed in no. 70.)

3682 SON OF A SMALLER HERO: A NOVEL. London: André Deutsch, 1955. 232 p.

3683 A CHOICE OF ENEMIES. London: André Deutsch, 1957. 256 p.

3684 THE APPRENTICESHIP OF DUDDY KRAVITZ. London: André Deutsch, 1959. 319 p.

3685 THE INCOMPARABLE ATUK. Toronto: McClelland and Stewart, 1963. 191 p. Also as STICK YOUR NECK OUT. New York: Simon and Schuster, 1963. 189 p.

3686 COCKSURE: A NOVEL. Toronto: McClelland and Stewart, 1968. 250 p.

3687 ST. URBAIN'S HORSEMAN: A NOVEL. Toronto: McClelland and Stewart, 1971. 467 p.

3688 JACOB TWO-TWO MEETS THE HOODED FANG. Illus. Fritz Wegner. Toronto: McClelland and Stewart, 1975. 83 p.

   For children.

3689 JOSHUA THEN AND NOW. Toronto: McClelland and Stewart, 1980. 435 p.

NONFICTION PROSE

3690 HUNTING TIGERS UNDER GLASS: ESSAYS AND REPORTS. Toronto: McClelland and Stewart, 1968. 160 p.

   Includes literary criticism.

3691 THE STREET. Toronto: McClelland and Stewart, 1969. 128 p.

3692 SHOVELLING TROUBLE. Toronto: McClelland and Stewart, 1972. 158 p.

   Includes literary criticism.

3693 NOTES ON AN ENDANGERED SPECIES, AND OTHERS. New York: A.A. Knopf, 1974. 212 p.

3694 CREATIVITY AND THE UNIVERSITY. Frank Gerstein Lectures, 1972. By Mordecai Richler, André Fortier, and Rollo May. Toronto: York University, 1975. 61 p.

3695 IMAGES OF SPAIN. Photos. Peter Christopher. Toronto: McClelland and Stewart, 1977. 191 p.

3696 THE GREAT COMIC BOOK HEROES AND OTHER ESSAYS. Ed. with introd. by Robert Fulford. New Canadian Library, no. 152. Toronto: McClelland and Stewart, 1978. 194 p.

EDITED WORK

3697 CANADIAN WRITING TODAY. Harmondsworth, Engl.: Penguin, 1970. 331 p.

Shorter Work

SHORT STORIES

3698   "The Secret of the Kugel." NEW STATESMAN, 15 Sept. 1956, p. 305.

3699   "Wally Sylvester's Canadiana." TAMARACK REVIEW, 17 (Aut. 1960), 27-32.

3700   "Mr. Soon." SPECTATOR, 24 Nov. 1961, pp. 745-47.

3701   "My Sort of War." NEW STATESMAN, 4 Sept. 1964, pp. 313, 315.

3702   "Manny Moves to Westmount." SATURDAY NIGHT, 92 (Jan.-Feb. 1977), 29-36.

ARTICLES

3703   "How I Became an Unknown with My First Novel." MACLEAN'S, 1 Feb. 1958, pp. 18-19, 40-42.

3704   "Canadian Outlook." NEW STATESMAN, 10 Sept. 1960, pp. 346-47.

3705   "The Apprenticeship of Mordecai Richler." MACLEAN'S, 20 May 1961, pp. 20-21, 44-48.

3706   "Canadiana: One Man's View." HOLIDAY, 35 (Apr. 1964), 41, 44-47.

3707   "The Uncertain World." CANADIAN LITERATURE, No. 41 (Sum. 1969), pp. 23-27.

      Reprinted in nos. 5106 and 5113.

3708   "Nationalism and Literature in Canada." In NATIONAL CONSCIOUS-NESS AND THE CURRICULUM: THE CANADIAN CASE. Ed. Geoffrey Milburn and John Herbert. Toronto: Ontario Institute for Studies in Education, 1974, pp. 105-17.

3709   "Canadian Conundrums." AMERICAN LIBRARIES, 8 (Jan. 1975), 24-27. Bibliog.

3710   "Oh! Canada! Lament for a Divided Country." ATLANTIC, 240 (Dec. 1977), 41-55; 241 (Mar. 1978), 109.

3711   "Writing JACOB TWO-TWO." CANADIAN LITERATURE, No. 78 (Aut. 1978), pp. 6-8.

Manuscripts

3712   University of Calgary Library, Calgary, Alta.

SECONDARY MATERIAL

Bibliographies

3713   Darling, Michael, comp. "Mordecai Richler: An Annotated Bibliography." In THE ANNOTATED BIBLIOGRAPHY OF CANADA'S MAJOR AUTHORS. Ed. Robert Lecker and Jack David. Downsview, Ont.: ECW, 1979, pp. 155-211. Index.

3714   "Mordecai Richler: A Selected Bibliography." INSCAPE, 11 (Spr. 1974), 51-61.

Criticism

3715   "Authors & Editors." PUBLISHERS' WEEKLY, 28 June 1971, pp. 29-31.

   Interview.

3716   Bevan, Allan R. Introd., THE APPRENTICESHIP OF DUDDY KRAVITZ. New Canadian Library, no. 66. Toronto: McClelland and Stewart, 1969, n. pag.

   Reprinted in no. 3755.

3717   Birbalsingh, Frank M. "Mordecai Richler and the Jewish-Canadian Novel." JOURNAL OF CANADIAN LITERATURE, 7 (June 1972), 72-82.

3718   Bowering, George. "And the Sun Goes Down: Richler's First Novel." CANADIAN LITERATURE, No. 29 (Sum. 1966), pp. 7-17.

   Reprinted in no. 3755.

3719   Brandeis, Robert C. "Up from St. Urbain: Mordecai Richler: An Informal Perspective." JEWISH DIALOG, Sum. 1973, pp. 46-47.

3720   Cameron, Donald A. "Don Mordecai and the Hardhats." CANADIAN FORUM, 51 (March 1972), 29-33.

3721 _____. "The Professional Canadian." CANADIAN LITERATURE, No. 50 (Aut. 1971), pp. 103-04.

3722 Carroll, John. "On Richler and Ludwig." TAMARACK REVIEW, 29 (Aut. 1963), 98-102.

3723 Cloutier, Pierre. "Mordecai Richler's Exiles: A CHOICE OF ENEMIES." JOURNAL OF CANADIAN FICTION, 1 (Spr. 1972), 43-49.

3724 Cohen, Nathan. "A Conversation with Mordecai Richler." TAMARACK REVIEW, No. 2 (Wint. 1957), pp. 6-23.

   Reprinted in no. 3755.

3725 _____. "Heroes of the Richler View." TAMARACK REVIEW, No. 6 (Wint. 1958), pp. 47-49, 51-60.

   Reprinted in no. 3755.

3726 Cohn-Sfetcu, Ofelia. "Of Self, Temporal Cubism, and Metaphor: Mordecai Richler's ST. URBAIN'S HORSEMAN." INTERNATIONAL FICTION REVIEW, 3 (Jan. 1976), 30-34.

3727 Cude, Wilfred. "The Golem as Metaphor for Art: The Monster Takes Meaning in ST. URBAIN'S HORSEMAN." JOURNAL OF CANADIAN STUDIES, 12 (Spr. 1977), 50-69.

   Reprinted in no. 133.

3728 Davidson, Arnold E. "THE INCOMPARABLE ATUK: Mordecai Richler's Satire on Popular Culture and the Canadian Dream." STUDIES IN CONTEMPORARY SATIRE, 7 (1980), 8-16.

3729 Evanier, David. "The Jewish Mordecai Richler." MIDSTREAM, 20 (Dec. 1974), 24-36.

3730 Ferns, John. "Sympathy and Judgement in Mordecai Richler's THE APPRENTICESHIP OF DUDDY KRAVITZ." JOURNAL OF CANADIAN FICTION, 3 (Wint. 1974), 77-82.

3731 Goodman, Walter. "Mordecai Richler Then and Now." NEW YORK TIMES BOOK REVIEW, 22 June 1980, pp. 11, 22-24.

   An interview.

3732 Greenstein, Michael. "The Apprenticeship of Noah Adler." CANADIAN LITERATURE, No. 78 (Aut. 1978), pp. 43-51.

3733 Herrmann, K. "Canadian Jewry and the Duddy Kravitz Problem." LE CHIEN D'OR/GOLDEN DOG, 4 (1975), 18-26.

3734 Kattan, Naïm. "Mordecai Richler: Craftsman or Artist." CANADIAN LITERATURE, No. 21 (Sum. 1964), pp. 46-51.

Reprinted in no. 3755.

3735 McGregor, Grant. "Duddy Kravitz: From Apprentice to Legend." JOURNAL OF CANADIAN FICTION, 30 (1980), 132-40.

3736 MacGregor, Roy. "The Boy from St. Urbain." MACLEAN'S, 9 June 1980, pp. 45-47, 49-51.

3737 McSweeney, Kerry. "Revaluing Mordecai Richler." STUDIES IN CANADIAN LITERATURE, 4 (Sum. 1979), 120-31.

3738 Marty, M.E. "What Do They Know in Montreal?" CHRISTIAN CENTURY, 10 May 1978, p. 519.

3739 Mathews, Robin D. "Messiah or Judas: Mordecai Richler Comes Home." CANADIAN REVIEW, 1 (Feb. 1974), 3-5.

3740 Metcalf, John. "Black Humour: An Interview With Mordecai Richler." JOURNAL OF CANADIAN FICTION, 3 (Wint. 1974), 73-76.

3741 Myers, David. "Mordecai Richler as Satirist." ARIEL, 4 (Jan. 1973), 47-61.

3742 Nettell, Stephanie. "Mordecai Richler." BOOKS AND BOOKMAN, 9 (Oct. 1965), 27.

An interview.

3743 New, William H. "The Apprenticeship of Discovery." CANADIAN LITERATURE, No. 29 (Sum. 1966), pp. 18-33.

Discusses THE WATCH THAT ENDS THE NIGHT by MacLennan and, especially, THE APPRENTICESHIP OF DUDDY KRAVITZ; reprinted in nos. 173 and 3755.

3744 Nodelman, Perry. "JACOB TWO-TWO and the Satisfactions of Paranoia." CANADIAN CHILDREN'S LITERATURE, Nos. 15-16 (1980), pp. 31-37.

3745 Ower, John. "Sociology, Psychology and Satire in THE APPRENTICESHIP OF DUDDY KRAVITZ." MODERN FICTION STUDIES, 22 (Aut. 1976), 413-28.

3746   Parr, J. "Richler Rejuvenated." CANADIAN CHILDREN'S LITERATURE, 1, No. 3 (1976), 96-102.

3747   Perrotin, Françoise. "Les Deux Solitudes de Noah Adler." ÉTUDES CANADIENNES/CANADIAN STUDIES, 4 (1978), 51-63.

3748   Pollock, Zailig. "The Trail of Jake Hersh." JOURNAL OF CANADIAN FICTION, No. 22 (1978), pp. 93-105.

3749   Rosenberg, Leah. THE ERRAND-RUNNER: REFLECTIONS OF A RABBI'S DAUGHTER. Toronto: John Wiley and Sons, 1981. 149 p.

        Autobiography of Richler's mother.

3750   Ross, Malcolm. Introd., THE INCOMPARABLE ATUK. New Canadian Library, no. 79. Toronto: McClelland and Stewart, 1963, pp. vi-xi.

3751   Ryval, Michael. "St. Urbain's Craftsman." FINANCIAL POST, 5 Apr. 1980, pp. 55-58.

3752   Sarkar, Eileen. "The Uncertain Countries of Jacques Ferron and Mordecai Richler." CANADIAN FICTION MAGAZINE, No. 13 (Spr. 1974), pp. 98-107.

3753   Scott, Peter. "A Choice of Certainties." TAMARACK REVIEW, No. 8 (Sum. 1958), pp. 73-82.

        Reprinted in no. 3755.

3754   Sheps, G. David. "Waiting for Joey: The Theme of the Vicarious in ST. URBAIN'S HORSEMAN." JOURNAL OF CANADIAN FICTION, 3 (Wint. 1974), 83-92.

        "Erratum." JOURNAL OF CANADIAN FICTION, 3, No. 2 (1974), after p. 92.

3755   _____, ed. with introd. MORDECAI RICHLER. Critical Views on Canadian Writers, 6. Toronto: McGraw-Hill Ryerson, 1971. xxvi, 124 p. Bibliog.

        Reprints reviews and articles on Richler, including nos. 297, 541, 3716, 3718, 3724-25, 3734, 3743, 3753, and 5151.

3756   Stovel, Brian. Introd., A CHOICE OF ENEMIES. New Canadian Library, no. 136. Toronto: McClelland and Stewart, 1977, pp. vii-xv.

3757   Tallman, Warren. "Need for Laughter." CANADIAN LITERATURE, No. 56 (Spr. 1973), pp. 71-83.

Discusses ST. URBAIN'S HORSEMAN; reprinted in no. 5113.

3758   Warkentin, Germaine. "COCKSURE: An Abandoned Introduction."
       JOURNAL OF CANADIAN FICTION, 4, No. 3 (1975), 81-86.

For criticism on Richler, see also nos. 124, 126, 133, 139, 170-71, 174, 1701,
1717, 3051, 3696, 5151, 5160, and especially 5062.

Book Reviews

3759   THE ACROBATS: CanL, 29 (Sum. 1966), 7; SatR, 2 Oct. 1954,
       p. 62; SPECTATOR, 23 Apr. 1954, p. 503; UTQ, 24 (Apr. 1955), 262.

3760   SON OF A SMALLER HERO: CAB, 41, No. 4 (1966), 18; CanL, 30
       (Aut. 1966), 77-79; QQ, 62 (Spr. 1956), 129; UTQ, 25 (Apr. 1956),
       305-06.

3761   A CHOICE OF ENEMIES: JCF, 1 (Spr. 1972), 43; UTQ, 27 (Apr. 1958),
       457.

3762   THE APPRENTICESHIP OF DUDDY KRAVITZ: CanL, 3 (Wint. 1960),
       62-64; CM, 18 (Sum. 1980), 206; DR, 40 (Spr. 1960), 129, 131, 133;
       MONTREALER, 38 (Oct. 1964), 43; NS, 7 Nov. 1959, p. 636, NYTBR,
       25 Oct. 1959, p. 64; NYTBR, 8 Sept. 1974, p. 34; QQ, 67 (Spr. 1960),
       130-31; TamR, 13 (Aut. 1959), 134; TC, Feb. 1960, p. 187; UTQ, 29
       (Apr. 1960), 463-65.

3763   THE INCOMPARABLE ATUK: AtlA, 54 (Dec. 1963), 71; CanL, 19
       (Wint. 1964), 50-51; CDim, 2 (Jan. 1965), 16; COMMENTARY, 36
       (Dec. 1963), 492; MONTREALER, 37 (Nov. 1963), 55-56; NewR, 12
       Oct. 1963, p. 27; NS, 18 Oct. 1963, p. 535; NYTBR, 11 Aug. 1963,
       p. 23; SatR, 24 Aug. 1963, p. 37; SPECTATOR, 25 Oct. 1963, p. 538;
       TamR, [29] (Aut. 1963), 98-100; TLS, 18 Oct. 1963, p. 822; UTQ,
       33 (July 1964), 389-91.

3764   COCKSURE: CanL, 39 (Wint. 1969), 85-86; CFor, 48 (Apr. 1968),
       19; ENCOUNTER, 31 (Oct. 1968), 76; FIDDLEHEAD, 76 (Sum. 1968),
       88-89; HudR, 21 (Sum. 1968), 364; JCL, 8 (Dec. 1969), 150-52; LIS-
       TENER, 30 May 1968, p. 708; MACLEAN'S, 81 (June 1968), 69-70;
       NATION, 1 Apr. 1968, p. 451; NS, 19 Apr. 1968, p. 520; NYRB,
       22 Aug. 1968, p. 34; NYTBR, 5 May 1968, p. 37; PUNCH, 17 Apr.
       1968, p. 584; SatN, 83 (May 1968), 37-38; SPECTATOR, 7 June 1968,
       p. 778; TLS, 16 May 1968, p. 497; UTQ, 38 (July 1969), 353-54;
       WCR, 4 (Fall 1969), 60-63.

3765 ST. URBAIN'S HORSEMAN: AtlA, 62 (Sept. 1971), 51; BLM, 42
(1973), 276-81; CanL, 5 (Wint. 1972), 83-84; COMMONWEAL, 7
Jan. 1972, p. 330; ConL, 13 (Sum. 1972), 361; ContempR, 219
(Oct. 1971), 211; HudR, 24 (Aut. 1971), 538; JCL, 7 (June 1972),
115-17; LHY, 13, No. 1 (1972), 183; LISTENER, 2 Sept. 1971, p. 312;
MACLEAN'S, 84 (May 1971), 80; MHRev, 21 (Jan. 1972), 118-19;
NATION, 14 June 1971, p. 759; NS, 3 Sept. 1971, p. 308; NYRB,
21 Oct. 1971, p. 3; NYTBR, 27 June 1971, pp. 7, 16; NYTBR, 5 Dec.
1971, p. 84; QUARRY, 22 (Wint. 1973), 77-79; SatN, 86 (June 1971),
25-26; SPECTATOR, 11 Sept. 1971, p. 377; TamR, 58 (1971), 65-72;
TLS, 3 Sept. 1971, p. 1045; UTQ, 41 (Sum. 1972), 308-09.

3766 JOSHUA THEN AND NOW: Atl, 246 (July 1980), 84; BCan, 9 (May
1980), 7-8; BOT, 3 (July 1980), 337; CFor, 60 (Aug. 1980), 27-28;
COMMENTARY, 70 (Oct. 1980), 70-71; COMMONWEAL, 21 Nov.
1980, pp. 667-68; ECW, 20 (Wint. 1980-81), 160-64; LISTENER, 9
Oct. 1980, p. 481; MACLEAN'S, 9 June 1980, p. 51; NATION, 5
July 1980, pp. 22-24; NewR, 14 June 1980, pp. 30-32; NS, 26 Sept.
1980, p. 28; NY, 16 June 1980, p. 79; NYRB, 17 July 1980, pp. 35-
36; NYTBR, 22 June 1980, pp. 11, 24, 25; OBSERVER, 21 Sept. 1980,
p. 29; PUNCH, 5 Nov. 1980, p. 826; Q&Q, 46 (June 1980), 33;
SatN, 95 (June 1980), 58-59; TLS, 26 Sept. 1980, p. 1056.

3767 HUNTING TIGERS UNDER GLASS: ALPHABET, 17 (Dec. 1969), 73-75;
BCLQ, 32 (Apr. 1969), 27; CanL, 42 (Aut. 1969), 77-81; LISTENER,
20 Mar. 1969, p. 393; NS, 31 Jan. 1969, p. 160; QQ, 76 (Aut. 1969),
547-48; SPECTATOR, 25 Apr. 1969, p. 551; TLS, 23 Jan. 1969, p. 83.

3768 THE STREET: ALPHABET, 17 (Dec. 1969), 75-76; CanL, 44 (Spr. 1970),
84-86; CDim, 6 (Aug. 1969), 59; CFor, 49 (Aug. 1969), 119; LIBERTÉ,
11 (Nov. 1969), 109-12; NS, 25 Feb. 1972, p. 246; NYTBR, 5 Oct.
1975, p. 6; NYTBR, 7 Dec. 1975, p. 60; QQ, 76 (Wint. 1969), 722;
SatN, 84 (July 1969), 36, 38; SPECTATOR, 25 Feb. 1972, p. 212;
TLS, 25 Feb. 1972, p. 212.

3769 SHOVELLING TROUBLE: BCan, 1 (Oct. 1972), 21-22; CanL, 57
(Sum. 1973), 118-20; HAB, 24 (Spr. 1973), 150-51; JCF, 2 (Wint. 1973),
95; LaUR, 6 (Fall 1973), 269-70; MACLEAN'S, 85 (Sept. 1972), 88;
Q&Q, 38, No. 10 (1972), 10-11; QQ, 79 (Wint. 1972), 584-85; SPEC-
TATOR, 9 June 1973, p. 714; TLS, 27 Oct. 1972, p. 1278; UTQ, 42
(Sum. 1973), 441.

3770 NOTES ON AN ENDANGERED SPECIES: NewR, 18 May 1974, p. 28;
NYTBR, 2 June 1974, pp. 42-43; NYTBR, 1 Dec. 1974, p. 66.

ROSS, SINCLAIR (1908--)

Born in Shellbrook, Saskatchewan, James Sinclair Ross left school at sixteen to become a bank clerk. He worked for the Royal Bank in several Saskatchewan towns, in Winnipeg, and in Montreal. From 1942 to 1945 he served in the Canadian army. After his retirement from the bank in 1968, he lived for three years in Athens and since then in Barcelona. Ross is the author of haunting stories of emotional hardship and prairie life, and most notably of the novel AS FOR ME AND MY HOUSE with its psychologically complex and intriguing revelations of marital and artistic frustration.

PRIMARY MATERIAL

Monographs

FICTION

3771   AS FOR ME AND MY HOUSE. New York: Reynal and Hitchcock, 1941. 296 p.

3772   THE WELL. Toronto: Macmillan, 1958. 256 p.

3773   THE LAMP AT NOON AND OTHER STORIES. Introd. Margaret Laurence. New Canadian Library, no. 62. Toronto: McClelland and Stewart, 1968. 134 p.

3774   WHIR OF GOLD. Toronto: McClelland and Stewart, 1970. 195 p.

3775   SAWBONES MEMORIAL. Toronto: McClelland and Stewart, 1974. 140 p.

Shorter Work

SHORT STORIES

3776 "Day with Pegasus." QUEEN'S QUARTERLY, 45 (Sum. 1938), 141-56.

3777 "Jug and Bottle." QUEEN'S QUARTERLY, 56 (Wint. 1949-50), 500-521.

3778 "Saturday Night." QUEEN'S QUARTERLY, 58 (Aut. 1951), 387-400.

3779 "Spike." Trans. Pierre Villon. LIBERTÉ, 11 (Mar.-Apr. 1969), 181-97.

3780 "The Flowers that Killed Him." JOURNAL OF CANADIAN FICTION, 1 (Sum. 1972), 5-10.

ARTICLE

3781 "On Looking Back." MOSAIC, 3 (Spr. 1970), 93-94.

SECONDARY MATERIAL

Bibliography

For a bibliography of Ross, see no. 33.

Criticism

3782 Bowen, Gail. "The Fiction of Sinclair Ross." CANADIAN LITERATURE, No. 80 (Spr. 1979), pp. 37-48.

3783 Chambers, Robert D. SINCLAIR ROSS AND ERNEST BUCKLER. Studies in Canadian Literature. Vancouver: Copp Clark, 1975. 109 p. Bibliog.

3784 Cude, Wilfred. "Beyond Mrs. Bentley: A Study of AS FOR ME AND MY HOUSE." JOURNAL OF CANADIAN STUDIES, 8 (Feb. 1973), 3-18.
       Reprinted in no. 133.

3785 _____. "'Turn it Upside Down': The Right Perspective on AS FOR ME AND MY HOUSE." ENGLISH STUDIES IN CANADA, 5 (Wint. 1979), 469-88.
       Reprinted in no. 133.

3786 Daniells, Roy. Introd., AS FOR ME AND MY HOUSE. New Canadian Library, no. 4. Toronto: McClelland and Stewart, 1957, pp. v-x.

3787   Denham, Paul. "Narrative Technique in Sinclair Ross's AS FOR ME
        AND MY HOUSE." STUDIES IN CANADIAN LITERATURE, 5 (Spr. 1980),
        116-24.

3788   Djwa, Sandra. "No Other Way: Sinclair Ross' Stories and Novels."
        CANADIAN LITERATURE, No. 47 (Wint. 1971), pp. 49-66.

        Reprinted in nos. 197 and 5113.

3789   Dubanski, Richard. "A Look at Philip's 'Journal' in AS FOR ME AND
        MY HOUSE." JOURNAL OF CANADIAN FICTION, No. 24 ([1979]),
        pp. 89-95.

3790   Fraser, Keath. "Futility at the Pump: The Short Stories of Sinclair
        Ross." QUEEN'S QUARTERLY, 77 (Spr. 1970), 72-80.

3791   Friesen, Victor Carl. "The Short Stories of Sinclair Ross." CANADIAN
        SHORT STORY MAGAZINE, 2 (Fall 1976), 71-73.

3792   Kostash, Myrna. "Discovering Sinclair Ross: It's Rather Late: All We
        Can Do Now is Stand Back and Watch with Respect." SATURDAY
        NIGHT, 87 (July 1972), 33-37.

3793   McMullen, Lorraine. Introd., SAWBONES MEMORIAL. New Canadian
        Library, no. 145. Toronto: McClelland and Stewart, 1978, pp. 5-11.

3794   _____. SINCLAIR ROSS. Twayne World Authors Series, 504. Boston:
        Twayne, 1979. 159 p. Bibliog. Index.

3795   Mitchell, Ken. SINCLAIR ROSS. Moose Jaw, Sask.: Thunder Creek
        Co-op, 1981. 120 p.

3796   New, William H. "Sinclair Ross's Ambivalent World." CANADIAN
        LITERATURE, No. 40 (Spr. 1969), pp. 26-32.

        Discusses AS FOR ME AND MY HOUSE; reprinted in nos.
        173 and 197.

3797   Pearson, Alan. "James Sinclair Ross: Major Novelist with a Banking
        Past." MONTREALER, 42 (Mar. 1968), 18-19.

3798   Ross, Morton L. "The Canonization of AS FOR ME AND MY HOUSE:
        A Case Study." In FIGURES IN A GROUND: CANADIAN ESSAYS
        ON MODERN LITERATURE COLLECTED IN HONOR OF SHEILA WATSON.
        Ed. Diane Bessai and David Jackel. Saskatoon: Western Producer
        Prairie Books, 1978, pp. 189-205.

3799 Stephens, Donald. "Wind, Sun and Dust." CANADIAN LITERATURE, No. 23 (Wint. 1965), pp. 17-24.

>   Discusses AS FOR ME AND MY HOUSE: reprinted in no. 197.

3800 Stouck, David. Introd., AS FOR ME AND MY HOUSE. Lincoln: University of Nebraska Press, 1978, pp. v-xiii.

3801 _____. "The Mirror and the Lamp in Sinclair Ross's AS FOR ME AND MY HOUSE." MOSAIC, 7 (Wint. 1974), 141-50.

For criticism on Ross, see also nos. 51, 133, 139, 168, 190, 2294, 2325, 2889, and 5211.

Book Reviews

3802 AS FOR ME AND MY HOUSE: CFor, 21 (July 1941), 124-25; DR, 22 (Apr. 1942), 130; NYTBR, 2 Mar. 1941, p. 25; QQ, 48 (Sum. 1941), 198-99; SatN, 29 Mar. 1941, p. 18; UTQ, 11 (Apr. 1942), 298-302.

3803 THE WELL: CULTURE, 19 (Dec. 1958), 458; DR, 38 (Wint. 1959), 529-30; TamR, 10 (Wint. 1959), 106; UTQ, 28 (Apr. 1959), 369-70.

3804 THE LAMP AT NOON: QQ, 77 (Spr. 1970), 72-80; UTQ, 38 (July 1969), 363.

3805 WHIR OF GOLD: CanL, 48 (Spr. 1971), 92-94; CFor, 50 (Mar. 1971), 443; FIDDLEHEAD, 90 (Sum. 1971), 126-28.

3806 SAWBONES MEMORIAL: ALIVE, 41 (1975), 35; BCan, 3 (Dec. 1974), 9-11; CanR, 2 (July 1975), 42-43; CFM, 19 (Aug. 1975), 95-97; CFor, 55 (Nov. 1975), 37; DR, 55 (Aut. 1975), 573-75; FIDDLEHEAD, 105 (Spr. 1975), 130-31; MACLEAN'S, 87 (Oct. 1974), 110; Q&Q, 40, No. 12 (1974), 22; QQ, 82 (Wint. 1975), 641-42; SPHINX, 2 (Wint. 1976), 45-47; UTQ, 44 (Sum. 1975), 305; WCR, 10 (June 1975), 47-48.

RULE, JANE (1931--)

Born in Plainfield, New Jersey, Jane Rule has lived in many parts of the south-western and eastern United States, and has travelled widely in Europe. She received a B.A. from Mills College, California, in 1952 and studied further at Stanford University and the Universities of Birmingham and London. For about twenty years after her arrival in Vancouver in the late 1950s, she taught creative writing and English at the University of British Columbia from time to time. She now lives on a small island in British Columbia. Her novels explore the emotional relationships of women and particularly of lesbians.

PRIMARY MATERIAL

Monographs

FICTION

3807 THE DESERT OF THE HEART. Toronto: Macmillan, 1964. 254 p.

3808 THIS IS NOT FOR YOU. New York: McCall, 1970. 284 p.

3809 AGAINST THE SEASON. New York: McCall, 1971. 218 p.

3810 THEME FOR DIVERSE INSTRUMENTS: STORIES. Vancouver: Talonbooks, 1975. 185 p.

3811 THE YOUNG IN ONE ANOTHER'S ARMS. Garden City, N.Y.: Doubleday, 1977. 204 p.

3812 CONTRACT WITH THE WORLD. New York: Harcourt Brace Jovanovich, 1980. 339 p.

3813 OUTLANDER: STORIES AND ESSAYS. [Tallahassee, Fla.]: Naiad, 1981. 207 p.

Rule, Jane

NONFICTION PROSE

3814   LESBIAN IMAGES. Garden City, N.Y.: Doubleday, 1975. vi, 246 p. Bibliog. Index.

Shorter Work

SHORT STORIES

3815   "Your Father and I." HOUSEWIFE, Aug. 1961.

3816   "No More Bargains." REDBOOK, 121 (Sept. 1963), 68-69.

3817   "Three Letters to a Poet." LADDER, May-June 1968.

3818   "Moving On." REDBOOK, 131 (June 1968), 86-87.

3819   "Houseguest." LADDER, Jan. 1969.

3820   "The List." CHATELAINE, 42 (Apr. 1969), 30-31, 94, 96, 98-99.

3821   "Not an Ordinary Wife." REDBOOK, 133 (Aug. 1969), 70-71.

3822   "Anyone Will Do." REDBOOK, 133 (Oct. 1969), 108-09.

3823   "The Secretary Bird." CHATELAINE, 45 (Aut. 1972), 22, 50-52, 54.

3824   "Brother and Sister." In 72: NEW CANADIAN STORIES. Ed. David Helwig and Joan Harcourt. [Ottawa]: Oberon, 1972, pp. 30-37.

3825   "The Bosom of the Family." In 75: NEW CANADIAN STORIES. Ed. David Helwig and Joan Harcourt. [Ottawa]: Oberon, 1975, pp. 153-69.

3826   "Outlander." CANADIAN FICTION MAGAZINE, No. 23 (Aut. 1976), pp. 8-30.

3827   "A Delicate Balance." CHATELAINE, 49 (Dec. 1976), 36-37, 58 ff.

3828   "Joy." CHATELAINE, 50 (Aug. 1977), 31, 46-52.

3829   "Lilian." CONDITIONS II, 1977, pp. 89-93.

3830 "In the Attic of the House." CHRISTOPHER STREET, July 1979, pp. 68-74.

3831 "A Migrant Christmas." CHATELAINE, 52 (Dec. 1979), 39, 58, 60, 64, 66, 69, 71.

3832 "Home Movie." SINISTER WISDOM, Sum. 1980, pp. 28-35.

3833 "First Love/Last Love." CHRISTOPHER STREET, 4 (Dec. 1980), 34-36.

3834 "The Day I Don't Remember." RARA AVIS, No. 5 (Sum.-Fall 1981), pp. 84-101.

Articles

3835 "The Credible Woman." BOOKS IN CANADA, 1, No. 4 (1971), 4-5.
     Discusses Alice Munro.

3836 "Like a Woman." AMAZON QUARTERLY, 1 (Feb. 1973), 18-23.

3837 "With All Due Respect: In Defense of All Lesbian Lifestyles." In AFTER YOU'RE OUT. Ed. Karla Jay and Allen Young. New York: Links, 1975, pp. 22-26.

3838 "Private Parts and Public Figures." BODY POLITIC, No. 24 (June 1976), pp. 1-3.

3839 "This Gathering." CANADIAN FICTION MAGAZINE, No. 23 (Aut. 1976), pp. 46-47.

3840 "Life, Liberty and the Pursuit of Normalcy: The Novels of Margaret Atwood." MALAHAT REVIEW, No. 41 (Jan. 1977), pp. 42-49.

3841 "The Practice of Writing." CANADIAN WOMEN'S STUDIES, 1 (Spr. 1979), 34-35.

3842 "Seventh Waves." BRANCHING OUT, 6, No. 1 (1979), 16-17.

3843 "Sexuality in Literature." FIREWEED, 5-6 (Wint.-Spr. 1980), 22-27.

SECONDARY MATERIAL

Bibliography

3844 Sonthoff, Helen W., comp. "A Bibliography." CANADIAN FICTION MAGAZINE, No. 23 (Aut. 1976), pp. 133-38.

Criticism

3845   Axten, Mary. "Jane Rule Talks with Mary Axten." ESPRIT (Toronto), 1 (Nov.-Dec. 1975), 11, 12, 56.

3846   Galana, Laurel. "Sylvia: British Columbia." In THE NEW LESBIANS: INTERVIEWS WITH WOMEN ACROSS THE U.S. AND CANADA. Ed. Laurel Galana and Gina Covina. Berkeley, Calif.: Moon Books, 1977, pp. 94-104.

3847   Hancock, Geoff. "An Interview with Jane Rule." CANADIAN FICTION MAGAZINE, No. 23 (Aut. 1976), pp. 57-112.

3848   Hofsess, John. "Calumnity Jane." BOOKS IN CANADA, 5 (Oct. 1976), 3-6.

3849   _____. "Goodbye to All That." CINEMA CANADA, No. 31 (Oct. 1976), pp. 46-48.

3850   _____. "Who Is Jane Rule?" CONTENT, No. 70 (Jan. 1977), pp. 6-8.

3851   Kennedy, Sarah. "A Time of Harvest: Interview with Jane Rule." BRANCHING OUT, 7, No. 2 (1980), 25-28.

3852   Neimi, Judith. "Jane Rule and the Reviewers." MARGINS, No. 23 (1975), pp. 34-37.

3853   Sonthoff, Helen W. "Celebration: A Study of Jane Rule's Fiction." CANADIAN FICTION MAGAZINE, No. 23 (Aut. 1976), pp. 121-32.

For criticism on Rule, see also no. 205.

Book Reviews

3854   THE DESERT OF THE HEART: CanL, 21 (Sum. 1964), 63-64; HudR, 18 (Wint. 1965-66), 587; NS, 14 Feb. 1964, p. 260; NYTBR, 1 Aug. 1965, p. 28; TamR, [33] (Aut. 1964), 95; TLS, 5 Mar. 1964, p. 201; UTQ, 34 (July 1965), 380-81.

3855   THIS IS NOT FOR YOU: CanL, 47 (Wint. 1971), 104-05; JCF, 1 (Spr. 1972), 87-88; SoR, 7 (Wint. 1971), 295.

3856 AGAINST THE SEASON: JCF, 1 (Spr. 1972), 87-88; WCR, 6 (Oct. 1971), 55-56.

3857 THEME FOR DIVERSE INSTRUMENTS: BCan, 4 (Sept. 1975), 3-4; BrO, 2 (Sept. 1975), 38-40; CanL, 72 (Spr. 1977), 88-89; CBRA, 1975, pp. 126-27; CRead, 17 (Sept. 1976), 11; Q&Q, Aug. 1975; TamR, 68 (Spr. 1976), 94-95; WLWE, 17 (Apr. 1978), 206-07.

3858 THE YOUNG IN ONE ANOTHER'S ARMS: BCan, 6 (Mar. 1977), 3-4; CAB, 52 (Spr. 1977), 35-36; CanL, 73 (Sum. 1977), 91; CanR, [4] (May 1977), 33-34; CFM, 27 (1977), 139-40; CFor, 57 (June 1977), 59; ECW, 6 (Spr. 1977), 125-27; FIDDLEHEAD, 117 (Spr. 1978), 131-32; IFR, 5 (Jan. 1978), 82-83; JCF, 24 ([1979]), 153-55; MACLEAN'S, 21 Mar. 1977, pp. 77-78; Q&Q Update, 43, No. 3 (1977), 7; YR, 67 (Wint. 1977-78), 260.

3859 LESBIAN IMAGES: BCan, 4 (Sept. 1975), 4-5; BCLQ, 38 (Spr. 1976), 37-39; CanL, 72 (Spr. 1977), 87-88; CFor, 55 (Sept. 1975), 61-62; MHRev, 36 (Oct. 1975), 143; ROO, 1, No. 3 (1975), 90-93; TamR, 68 (Spr. 1976), 92-93, 95; TLS, 23 July 1976, p. 904; WCR, 10 (Feb. 1976), 62-63; WLWE, 17 (Apr. 1978), 205-07.

RYGA, GEORGE (1932--)

George Ryga was born into a Ukrainian family in Deep Creek, Alberta. He attended a country school for seven years and worked on farms, in construction, and for an Edmonton radio station before turning to full-time writing (for radio, television, and the stage) in 1963. He studied at the University of Texas. Ryga's play about Indian life, THE ECSTASY OF RITA JOE, with its strong note of social protest, established him as a Canadian playwright. More recently, he has added fiction to his repertoire. Ryga now lives near Penticton, British Columbia.

PRIMARY MATERIAL

Monographs

FICTION

3860 HUNGRY HILLS. Toronto: Longmans, 1963. 180 p.

3861 BALLAD OF A STONEPICKER. Toronto: Macmillan, 1966. 159 p.
      Rev. ed. Vancouver: Talonbooks, 1976. 142 p.

3862 NIGHT DESK: A NOVEL. Vancouver: Talonbooks, 1976. 123 p.

NONFICTION PROSE

3863 BEYOND THE CRIMSON MORNING: REFLECTIONS ON A JOURNEY
      THROUGH CONTEMPORARY CHINA. Garden City, N.Y.: Doubleday,
      1979. x, 213 p.

DRAMA

3864 INDIAN. Searchlights. Agincourt, Ont.: Book Society, 1968. 8 p.

3865 THE ECSTASY OF RITA JOE. Vancouver: Talonbooks, 1970. 90 p.
Enl. ed. THE ECSTASY OF RITA JOE AND OTHER PLAYS. Ed. with
introd. by Brian Parker. Toronto: New, 1971. xxiii, 236 p.

Enlarged edition includes no. 3864.

3866 CAPTIVES OF THE FACELESS DRUMMER. Vancouver: Talonbooks, 1971.
78 p. Rev. ed. Vancouver: Talonbooks, 1974. 119 p.

3867 SUNRISE ON SARAH. Vancouver: Talonbooks, 1973. 73 p.

3868 PLOUGHMEN OF THE GLACIER: A PLAY. Vancouver: Talonbooks,
1977. 79 p.

3869 SEVEN HOURS TO SUNDOWN: A PLAY. Vancouver: Talonbooks,
1977. 110 p.

Shorter Work

SHORT STORIES

3870 "Black is the Colour. . . ." ATLANTIC ADVOCATE, 57 (Jan. 1967),
25-29.

3871 "Visit from the Pension Lady." In THE NEWCOMERS: INHABITING
A NEW LAND. Gen. ed. Charles E. Israel. Toronto: McClelland
and Stewart, 1979, pp. 177-88.

ARTICLE

3872 "The Need for a Mythology." CANADIAN THEATRE REVIEW, 16 (Fall
1977), 4-6.

Manuscripts

3873 University of Calgary Library, Calgary, Alberta.

SECONDARY MATERIAL

Criticism

3874 Carson, Neil. "George Ryga and the Lost Country." CANADIAN LIT-
ERATURE, No. 45 (Sum. 1970), pp. 33-40.

3875   _____. "Ryga Revisited." JOURNAL OF CANADIAN FICTION, No. 16 (1976), pp. 185-87.

Discusses HUNGRY HILLS.

3876   Hay, P. "George Ryga: Beginnings of a Biography." CANADIAN THEATRE REVIEW, No. 23 (Sum. 1979), pp. 36-44.

3877   McCaughey, G. GEORGE RYGA. Agincourt, Ont.: Gage, 1977. 112 p.

Book Reviews

3878   THE HUNGRY HILLS: AtlA, 54 (Dec. 1963), 70-71; BCan, 4 (July 1975), 15; BCLQ, 27 (Apr. 1964), 15, 17; BCLQ, 38 (Spr. 1976), 31-32; FIDDLEHEAD, 107 (Fall 1975), 133-35; JCF, 16 (1976), 185-87; QUARRY, 13 (1963-64), 50; TamR, [31] (Spr. 1964), 89-90; UTQ, 33 (July 1964), 397.

3879   BALLAD OF A STONEPICKER: CanL, 34 (Aut. 1967), 76-78; QQ, 73 (Wint. 1966), 606-07; SatN, [81] (May 1966), 49; SPECTATOR, 21 Jan. 1966, p. 80; UTQ, 36 (July 1967), 385-86.

3880   NIGHT DESK: BCan, 5 (Sept. 1976), 30-31; CBRA, 1976, p. 152; ECW, 6 (Spr. 1977), 119-21; SatN, 92 (Jan. 1977), 83-84.

3881   BEYOND THE CRIMSON MORNING: BCan, 8 (Dec. 1979), 27-28; CanL, 86 (Aut. 1980), [157]; Q&Q, 45 (Dec. 1979), 28; SatN, 95 (Jan. 1980), 50-53.

SALVERSON, LAURA (1890-1970)

Born in Winnipeg to Icelandic immigrants, Laura Salverson studied in the western United States and lived in many parts of Canada, particularly in Winnipeg and Toronto. Although she has written some historical romance, her fiction also portrays the life of Scandinavian settlers in less melodramatic and romantic terms. IMMORTAL ROCK received the Ryerson Fiction Award in 1954, and THE DARK WEAVER and CONFESSIONS OF AN IMMIGRANT'S DAUGHTER won Governor General's Awards. The latter, like the fictional VIKING HEART, draws on Salverson's personal experiences in an immigrant community.

PRIMARY MATERIAL

Monographs

FICTION

3882   THE VIKING HEART. New York: George H. Doran, 1923. viii, 326 p.

3883   WHEN SPARROWS FALL. Toronto: Thomas Allen, 1925. 292 p.

3884   LORD OF THE SILVER DRAGON: A ROMANCE OF LIEF THE LUCKY. Toronto: McClelland and Stewart, 1927. 343 p.

3885   THE DOVE OF EL-DJEZAIRE. Toronto: Ryerson, [1933]. 288 p. Also as THE DOVE. London: Skeffington and Son, 1933. 288 p.

3886   THE DARK WEAVER: AGAINST THE SOMBRE BACKGROUND OF THE OLD GENERATIONS FLAME THE SCARLET BANNERS OF THE NEW. Toronto: Ryerson, [1937]. 415 p.

3887   BLACK LACE. Toronto: Ryerson, [1938]. 256 p.

3888 IMMORTAL ROCK: THE SAGA OF THE KENSINGTON STONE BASED ON THE PAUL KNUTSON EXPEDITION TO GREENLAND AND AMERICA IN THE FOURTEENTH CENTURY. Toronto: Ryerson, 1954. xi, 267 p.

NONFICTION PROSE

3889 CONFESSIONS OF AN IMMIGRANT'S DAUGHTER. London: Faber and Faber, [1939]. 523 p.

Autobiography.

POETRY

3890 WAYSIDE GLEAMS. Toronto: McClelland and Stewart, 1925. 97 p.

Shorter Work

SHORT STORIES

3891 "When Blind Guides Lead." MACLEAN'S, 1 Feb. 1925, pp. 13, 50-52.

3892 "The Dream of New Empire." CANADIAN NATIONAL RAILWAYS MAGAZINE, Oct. 1932, p. 12.

3893 "Agidia's Christmas." WESTERN HOME MONTHLY, Dec. 1932, p. 7.

3894 "Queer Heart." In SELECTED SHORT STORIES: A COLLECTION OF NOTABLE SHORT STORIES BY CANADIAN WRITERS FIRST PUBLISHED IN THE CANADIAN MAGAZINE. Toronto: Hugh C. MacLean, 1937, pp. 1-21.

3895 "Song at Twilight." NATIONAL HOME MONTHLY, 45 (Dec. 1944), 8-9, 35-39.

ARTICLES

3896 "An Autobiographical Sketch." ONTARIO LIBRARY REVIEW, 14 (Feb. 1930), 69-73.

3897 "On Writing the Novel." CANADIAN AUTHOR AND BOOKMAN, 35 (Wint. 1959-60), 12-14.

3898 "I Discover My Birthplace." In A CENTURY OF CANADIAN LITERATURE/ UN SIÈCLE DE LITTÉRATURE CANADIENNE. Toronto: Ryerson, 1967, pp. 155-57.

Manuscripts

3899   Acadia University Archives, Wolfville, N.S.; Public Archives of Canada, Ottawa; Queen's University Library, Kingston, Ont.

SECONDARY MATERIAL

Criticism

3900   Einarsson, Stefán. "Laura Goodman Salverson." In his HISTORY OF ICELANDIC PROSE WRITERS, 1800-1940. Ithaca, N.Y.: Cornell University Press, 1948, pp. 252-55.

3901   Fuller, Muriel. "Laura Goodman Salverson." CANADIAN AUTHOR AND BOOKMAN, 35 (Wint. 1958-59), 12.

3902   Hopwood, Alison. Introd., THE VIKING HEART. New Canadian Library, no. 116. Toronto: McClelland and Stewart, 1975, pp. ix-xiv.

3903   Stich, K.P. Introd., CONFESSIONS OF AN IMMIGRANT'S DAUGHTER. Social History of Canada, 34. Toronto: University of Toronto Press, 1981, pp. v-xvi.

For criticism on Salverson, see also no. 2889.

Book Reviews

3904   THE VIKING HEART: CBRA, 1975, p. 115.

3905   LORD OF THE SILVER DRAGON: NYTBR, 29 Jan. 1928, p. 14.

3906   THE DARK WEAVER: CA, 16 (Aut. 1938), 13.

3907   IMMORTAL ROCK: UTQ, 24 (Apr. 1955), 264.

3908   CONFESSIONS OF AN IMMIGRANT'S DAUGHTER: DR, 20 (Apr. 1940), 133-34; QQ, 47 (Spr. 1940), 128-29; SatN, 30 Dec. 1939, p. 15; UTQ, 9 (Apr. 1940), 325-26.

SIMPSON, LEO (1934--)

Born in Limerick, Ireland, Leo Simpson was hospitalized for much of his youth. He emigrated to Canada in 1961 and wrote radio and television plays. In 1966, he was able to resign as editor and publicity director for a Toronto publisher, to move north of Belleville, Ontario, and to support himself as a free-lance writer. In 1973 he acted as writer-in-residence at the University of Ottawa. Simpson writes animated comic novels which place modern protagonists in extreme or absurd situations.

PRIMARY MATERIAL

Monographs

FICTION

3909 ARKWRIGHT: A NOVEL. Toronto: Macmillan, 1971. 442 p.

3910 THE PEACOCK PAPERS: A NOVEL. Toronto: Macmillan, 1973. 226 p.

3911 THE LADY AND THE TRAVELLING SALESMAN: STORIES. Ed. with introd. by Henry Imbleau. Canadian Short Story Library. Ottawa: University of Ottawa Press, 1976. xx, 155 p. Bibliog.

3912 KOWALSKI'S LAST CHANCE. Toronto: Clark, Irwin, 1980. 200 p.

EDITED WORK

3913 MANY MANSIONS: STORIES BY DOUGLAS O. SPETTIGUE. Ed. with introd. by Leo Simpson. Canadian Short Story Library. Ottawa: University of Ottawa Press, 1976. xiv, 130 p.

Shorter Work

SHORT STORIES

3914 "The Case of the Friendly Teller." MONTREALER, 35 (Nov. 1961), 55-57.

3915 "The Viking Professor Strikes Back!" MONTREALER, 36 (Mar. 1962), 36-37.

3916 "The Ferris Wheel." In 72: NEW CANADIAN STORIES. Ed. David Helwig and Joan Harcourt. [Ottawa]: Oberon, 1972, pp. 9-29.

SECONDARY MATERIAL

Criticism

3917 Clery, Val. "Private Landscapes: Leo Simpson . . . and Alice Munro." QUILL AND QUIRE, 40, No. 3 (1974), 3, 15.

3918 Dixon, Michael F.N. "Leo Simpson and the Comic Moment." STUDIES IN CANADIAN LITERATURE, 2 (Wint. 1977), 5-16.

   Discusses the short stories.

3919 McMullen, Lorraine. "A Conversation with Leo Simpson." JOURNAL OF CANADIAN FICTION, 4, No. 1 (1975), 111-20.

3920 Tausky, Thomas E. "Peacock and THE PEACOCK PAPERS." STUDIES IN CANADIAN LITERATURE, 5 (Spr. 1980), 5-22.

For criticism on Simpson, see also nos. 170 and 3911.

Book Reviews

3921 ARKWRIGHT: BCan, 1 (Nov. 1971), 24; CanL, 54 (Aut. 1972), 94-96; CDim, 9 (May 1973), 44; CFor, 51 (Jan. 1972), 75-76; JCF, 1 (Spr. 1972), 90-91; UTQ, 41 (Sum. 1972), 309-10.

3922 THE PEACOCK PAPERS: BCan, 2 (Dec. 1973), 4-5; CanR, 1 (Feb. 1974), 16; CFor, 54 (July 1974), 36-37; DR, 54 (Spr. 1974), 192-93; JCF, 3, No. 3 (1974), 100-101; MACLEAN'S, 86 (Nov. 1973), 118; OpenL, 2nd ser., 7 (1974), 128; Q&Q, 40, No, 1 (1974), 13-14.

3923   THE LADY AND THE TRAVELLING SALESMAN: BCan, 5 (Sept. 1976), 29-30; CBRA, 1976, p. 154; CFor, 57 (June 1977), 50; FIDDLEHEAD, 113 (Spr. 1977), 134-38; JCF, 22 (1978), 132-34; Q&Q, 42, No. 12 (1976), 10; QUARRY, 26 (Spr. 1977), 53-55; WLWE, 17 (Nov. 1978), 507-08.

3924   KOWALSKI'S LAST CHANCE: BCan, 9 (Apr. 1980), 18-19; MACLEAN'S, 21 Apr. 1980, pp. 56-57; Q&Q, 46 (June 1980), 34; SatN, 95 (July 1980), 58-59.

STEAD, ROBERT (1880-1959)

Robert James Campbell Stead was born in Middleville, Ontario, grew up near Cartwright, Manitoba, and worked as a newspaper editor there and in Calgary. From 1913 to 1946, he was a publicity director for the Canadian Pacific Railway, the Department of Immigration, and finally the Department of Mines and Resources (where he supervised publicity for the national parks). His initial sensational fiction gives way to GRAIN, a more realistic portrayal of early prairie life in transition.

PRIMARY MATERIAL

Monographs

FICTION

3925   THE BAIL JUMPER. Toronto: William Briggs, 1914.   335 p.

3926   THE HOMESTEADERS: A NOVEL OF THE CANADIAN WEST. Toronto: Musson, 1916.   347 p.

3927   THE COW PUNCHER. New York: Harper and Brothers, 1918.   331 p.

3928   DENNISON GRANT: A NOVEL OF TODAY. Toronto: Musson, 1920. 388 p.   Rev. ed. ZEN OF THE Y.D.: A NOVEL OF THE FOOTHILLS. London: Hodder and Stoughton, 1925.   320 p.

3929   NEIGHBOURS. Toronto: Hodder and Stoughton, 1922.   315 p.

3930   THE SMOKING FLAX. Toronto: McClelland and Stewart, 1924.   301 p.

3931   GRAIN. Toronto: McClelland and Stewart, 1926.   281 p.

3932   THE COPPER DISC. Crime Club. Garden City, N.Y.: Doubleday, Doran, 1931. 312 p.

NONFICTION PROSE

3933   CANADA'S MOUNTAIN PLAYGROUNDS. Montreal: Canadian National Railway, [193-?]. 20 p.

3934   CANADA'S PLAYGROUNDS. Ottawa: Department of Mines and Resources, National Parks Bureau, 1941.

> Includes PLAYGROUNDS OF THE PRAIRIES, CANADA'S MOUNTAIN PLAYGROUNDS, and PLAYGROUNDS OF EASTERN CANADA.

3935   WORDS. Winnipeg: Public, [1945]. 21 p.

3936   PEOPLE WHO WORK FOR ME. Calgary: John D. McAra, 1948. 10 p.

3937   CALGARY, CITY OF THE FOOTHILLS. Ottawa: Canadian Geographical Society, 1951. 15 p.

POETRY

3938   THE EMPIRE BUILDERS, AND OTHER POEMS. Toronto: William Briggs, 1908. vii, 100 p.

3939   PRAIRIE BORN AND OTHER POEMS. Toronto: William Briggs, 1911. ix, 95 p.

3940   SONGS OF THE PRAIRIE. Toronto: William Briggs, 1911. v, 96 p.

3941   KITCHENER AND OTHER POEMS. Introd. William T. Allison. Toronto: Musson, 1917. xiv, 163 p.; rpt. as WHY DON'T THEY CHEER? POEMS. Introd. William T. Allison. London: T. Fisher Unwin, 1918. 166 p.

3942   THE MAPLE'S PRAISE OF FRANKLIN DELANO ROOSEVELT 1882-1945: CANADIAN TRIBUTES. By Robert Stead, Dorothy Dumbrille, and Nathaniel A. Benson. Ottawa: Tower Books, 1945. 18 p.

Shorter Work

SHORT STORIES

3943   "Driver Dick's Last Run." CANADIAN, 23 (Aug. 1904), 359-62.

3944   "A Complicated Speculation." CANADA WEST, Apr. 1907, pp. 501-08.

3945   "A Hero of Ladysmith." CANADA WEST, Aug. 1909, pp. 737-41.

3946   "The Fellow Who Won't Be Beat." CANADIAN COURIER, 10 Dec. 1910, pp. 15, 16, 26.

3947   "Peverly's Deposit." CANADIAN CENTURY AND CANADIAN LIFE AND RESOURCES, July 1911, pp. 11-12, 28.

3948   "The First Big Fill." CANADIAN COURIER, 6 July 1912, pp. 12, 27.

3949   "How Simpson Cashed His Bluff." CANADIAN PROGRESS, May 1913, pp. 13-15.

3950   "Wigstock and Company." CANADIAN PROGRESS, July 1913, pp. 12-14.

3951   "Riley's Sympathetic Strike." CANADIAN PROGRESS, Nov. 1913, pp. 9-12.

3952   "To Professional Services." CANADA MONTHLY, 15 (Mar. 1914), 311-13.

3953   "As You Were." MAGNET, No. 8 (Oct. 1919), pp. 1-16.

3954   "The President of the Bar Y." CANADIAN BOY, Sept. 1920, pp. 5-6; Oct. 1920, pp. 11, 26; Nov. 1920, pp. 9, 26.

3955   "Breaking the Buyer's Strike." MAGNET, No. 13 (Sept. 1921), pp. 1-16.

3956   "The Spirit of Christmas." MAGNET, No. 16 (Dec. 1921), pp. 1-16.

3957   "Something Wrong with the Ka-Chinker." MAGNET, No. 18 (Aug. 1922), pp. 1-17.

3958   "The Whispering Tunnel." TRAIL MAKER'S ANNUAL, 1922, pp. 156-65.

3959   "A Holler of Hope." MAGNET, No. 21 (Feb. 1924), pp. 1-14.

3960   "Little Miss Happiness." BANKER'S MONTHLY, 41 (Nov. 1924), 14-15, 44-45.

3961   "Christmas Eve on Section Six." CANADIAN COUNTRYMAN, 13 Dec. 1924, pp. 6, 7, 65.

3962   "Peter Brand's Christmas." MAGNET, No. 23 (Dec. 1925), pp. 1-12.

3963   "Just for Christmas, You Know." MAGNET, No. 24 (Dec. 1926), pp. 1-11.

3964   "When the Prairie Gets Them." MAGNET, No. 26 (Dec. 1927), pp. 1-15.

3965   "Madam Rumor and Mr. Fact." MAGNET, No. 27 (June 1928), pp. 1-11.

3966   "Fed Up." CAPPER'S FARMER, 39 (Oct. 1928), 9, 24, 58, 59.

3967   "A Financial Handicap." CANADIAN COUNTRYMAN, 8 Dec. 1928, pp. 5, 28, 30.

3968   "Holy Night." CANADIAN HOME JOURNAL, Dec. 1928, pp. 10-11, 20, 69-71.

3969   "We Are Born Single." CANADIAN HOME JOURNAL, Oct. 1929, pp. 12-13, 104-05.

3970   "Opal." FARMER'S WIFE, 33 (Apr. 1930), 5-6, 49. Rpt. rev. as "There is No Place Like Home." ONTARIO FARMER, 27 (May 1930), 11, 94-95, 98.

3971   "Engineer Conley." CAPPER'S FARMER, 41 (Nov. 1930), 8, 9, 55; 41 (Dec. 1930), 8-9, 20; 42 (Jan. 1931), 6-7, 33, 35; 42 (Feb. 1931), 8-9, 49, 66.

3972   "The Berkeley Diamonds." MACLEAN'S, 15 July 1931, p. 12.

3973   "Barbed-Wire Radio." CANADIAN, 90 (Oct. 1938), 22-23, 36, 38, 40.

ARTICLES

3974   "Canadian Literature: A Message." LITTLEBURY'S MAGAZINE, Mar. 1919.

3975   "Literature as a National Asset: A Radiographed Message." CANADIAN BOOKMAN, 6 (Dec. 1923), 343.

3976   "Literature as Factor in Nation Building." CANADIAN GAZETTE, 16 Jan. 1930, p. 376.

Manuscripts

3977   Public Archives of Canada, Ottawa.

SECONDARY MATERIAL

Bibliography

3978   Varma, Prem. "Robert Stead: An Annotated Bibliography." ESSAYS
        ON CANADIAN WRITING, No. 17 (Spr. 1980), pp. 141-204.

Criticism

3979   Bowker, Kathleen K. "Robert Stead: An Interview." CANADIAN
        BOOKMAN, 5 (Apr. 1923), 99.

3980   Davey, Frank. "Rereading Stead's GRAIN." STUDIES IN CANADIAN
        LITERATURE, 4 (Wint. 1979), 7-25.

3981   Elder, A.T. "Western Panorama: Settings and Themes in Robert J.C.
        Stead." CANADIAN LITERATURE, No. 17 (Sum. 1963), pp. 44-56.

        Reprinted in nos. 197 and 5113.

3982   Glicksohn, Susan Wood. Introd., THE HOMESTEADERS. Literature of
        Canada: Poetry and Prose in Reprint. Toronto: University of Toronto
        Press, 1973, pp. vii-xxiv. Bibliog.

3983   Mundwiler, Leslie. "Robert Stead--Home in the First Place." ESSAYS
        ON CANADIAN WRITING, 11 (Sum. 1978), 184-203.

3984   Saunders, Thomas. Introd., GRAIN. New Canadian Library, no. 36.
        Toronto: McClelland and Stewart, 1963, pp. v-xiii.

3985   Stich, K.P. "European Immigrants in the Fiction of Robert Stead."
        STUDIES IN CANADIAN LITERATURE, 1 (Wint. 1976), 76-84.

        Discusses THE HOMESTEADERS and NEIGHBOURS.

3986   Turner, Gordon. "The Incest Bond in Stead's GRAIN." SPHINX, 2
        (Wint. 1977), 23-32.

For criticism on Stead, see also nos. 190 and 2889.

Book Reviews

3987   THE HOMESTEADERS: ARCS, 4 (Aut. 1974), 104-06; CANADA, 2 (Mar. 1975), 75-77; QQ, 81 (Aut. 1974), 478-79.

3988   THE COW PUNCHER: NYTBR, 29 Dec. 1918, p. 582.

3989   GRAIN: CFor, 7 (Jan. 1927), 121-22; NYTBR, 13 Feb. 1927, p. 14; SatR, 5 Feb. 1927, p. 567.

STRINGER, ARTHUR (1874-1950)

A native of Chatham, Ontario, Arthur John Arbuthnot Stringer was educated at the Universities of Toronto and Oxford. He worked as a railway clerk, a reporter, an Ontario fruit farmer, and an Albertan rancher before settling in New York and, after 1919, in nearby New Jersey. A successful journalist, Stringer wrote popular tales of adventure, detection, and sentiment. Although poetry is his medium for serious literary expression, he does attempt to move somewhat beyond the thriller and the romance in his "Prairie" trilogy and some of his other fiction of that period.

PRIMARY MATERIAL

Monographs

FICTION

3990   THE OCCASIONAL OFFENDER.

No publishing details; listed in Henry Morgan's CANADIAN MEN AND WOMEN OF THE TIME (1912).

3991   THE LOOM OF DESTINY. Boston: Small, Maynard, 1899. 208 p.

Short stories for children.

3992   THE SILVER POPPY: A NOVEL. New York: D. Appleton, 1903. vi, 291 p.

3993   LONELY O'MALLEY: A STORY OF BOY LIFE. Illus. Frank T. Merrill. Boston: Houghton Mifflin, 1905. xi, 383 p.

For children.

3994   THE WIRE TAPPERS. Illus. Arthur William Brown. Boston: Little, Brown, 1906. 324 p.

3995 PHANTOM WIRES: A NOVEL. Illus. Arthur William Brown. Boston: Little, Brown, 1907. 295 p.

3996 THE UNDER GROOVE: A NOVEL. New York: McClure, 1908. 335 p.; rpt. as NIGHT HAWK. New York: Bobbs-Merrill, 1923. 307 p.

3997 THE GUN RUNNER: A NOVEL. New York: B.W. Dodge, 1909. x, 370 p.; rpt. as RISK. London: Hutchinson, 1912.

3998 THE SHADOW. New York: Century, 1913. 302 p.; rpt. as NEVER-FAIL BLAKE. New York: A.L. Burt, 1924. 302 p.

3999 THE MASTER OF ARMS. Chicago: Volland, 1914.

A bibliographical ghost? Listed in no. 4084.

4000 THE HAND OF PERIL: A NOVEL OF ADVENTURE. New York: Macmillan, 1915. 331 p.

4001 THE PRAIRIE WIFE: A NOVEL. Illus. H.T. Dunn. Indianapolis: Bobbs-Merrill, 1915. 316 p.

First volume in his "Prairie" trilogy.

4002 THE DOOR OF DREAD: A SECRET SERVICE ROMANCE. Illus. M. Leone Bracker. Indianapolis: Bobbs-Merrill, 1916. 375 p.

4003 THE HOUSE OF INTRIGUE. Illus. Armand Both. Indianapolis: Bobbs-Merrill, 1918. 363 p.

4004 THE MAN WHO COULDN'T SLEEP. Indianapolis: Bobbs-Merrill, 1919. 351 p.

4005 THE STRANGER. Toronto: Dominion Publicity Committee Victory Loan, 1919. 16 p.

4006 THE PRAIRIE MOTHER. Illus. Arthur E. Becher. Toronto: McClelland and Stewart, 1920. 359 p.

Second volume in his "Prairie" trilogy beginning with no. 4001.

4007 TWIN TALES: ARE ALL MEN ALIKE AND THE LOST TITIAN. Indianapolis: Bobbs-Merrill, 1921. 288 p.

4008 THE WINE OF LIFE. New York: A.A. Knopf, 1921. 389 p.

4009 THE PRAIRIE CHILD. Illus. E.F. Ward. Indianapolis: Bobbs-Merrill, 1922. 382 p.

> Third volume in his "Prairie" trilogy beginning with no. 4001.

4010 THE CITY OF PERIL. New York: A.A. Knopf, 1923. 317 p.

4011 THE DIAMOND THIEVES. Indianapolis: Bobbs-Merrill, 1923. 416 p.

4012 EMPTY HANDS. Illus. Herbert M. Stoops. Indianapolis: Bobbs-Merrill, 1924. 360 p.

4013 MANHANDLED. By Arthur Stringer and Russell Holman. Illus. New York: Bobbs-Merrill, 1924. 312 p.

4014 THE STORY WITHOUT A NAME. By Arthur Stringer and Russell Holman. Illus. with Scenes from the Photoplay, a Paramount Picture. New York: Grosset and Dunlap, 1924. 316 p.

4015 POWER. Indianapolis: Bobbs-Merrill, 1925. 308 p.

4016 IN BAD WITH SINBAD. Indianapolis: Bobbs-Merrill, 1926. 185 p.

4017 WHITE HANDS. Indianapolis: Bobbs-Merrill, 1927. 302 p.

4018 THE WOLF WOMAN: A NOVEL. Indianapolis: Bobbs-Merrill, 1928. 331 p.

4019 CRISTINA AND I. Indianapolis: Bobbs-Merrill, 1929. 301 p.

4020 THE WOMAN WHO COULDN'T DIE. Indianapolis: Bobbs-Merrill, 1929. 314 p.

4021 A LADY QUITE LOST: A NOVEL. Indianapolis: Bobbs-Merrill, 1931. 303 p.

4022 THE MUD LARK. Indianapolis: Bobbs-Merrill, 1932. 331 p.

4023 MARRIAGE BY CAPTURE. Indianapolis: Bobbs-Merrill, 1933. 316 p.

4024 MAN LOST. Indianapolis: Bobbs-Merrill, 1934. 328 p.

4025 PRAIRIE STORIES: CONTAINING THE PRAIRIE WIFE, THE PRAIRIE MOTHER, THE PRAIRIE CHILD. New York: A.L. Burt, [1936]. 316, 359, 382 p.

4026 THE WIFE-TRADERS: A TALE OF THE NORTH. Indianapolis: Bobbs–Merrill, 1936. 319 p. Also as TOOLOONA: A NOVEL OF THE NORTH. London: Methuen, 1936. 248 p.

4027 HEATHER OF THE HIGH HAND: A NOVEL OF THE NORTH. Indianapolis: Bobbs–Merrill, 1937. 291 p.

4028 THE LAMP IN THE VALLEY: A NOVEL OF ALASKA. Indianapolis: Bobbs–Merrill, 1938. 314 p.

4029 THE DARK WING. Indianapolis: Bobbs–Merrill, 1939. 311 p.

4030 THE PRAIRIE OMNIBUS: CONTAINING THE COMPLETE NOVELS: THE PRAIRIE WIFE, THE PRAIRIE MOTHER. New York: Grosset and Dunlap, [1939]. 316, 359 p.

4031 THE GHOST PLANE: A NOVEL OF THE NORTH. Indianapolis: Bobbs–Merrill, 1940. 304 p.

4032 INTRUDERS IN EDEN: A NOVEL. Indianapolis: Bobbs–Merrill, 1942. 308 p.

4033 STAR IN A MIST: A NOVEL. Indianapolis: Bobbs–Merrill, 1943. 312 p.

4034 THE DEVASTATOR: A NOVEL. Toronto: McClelland and Stewart, 1944. 198 p.

NONFICTION PROSE

4035 A STUDY IN KING LEAR. New York: American Shakespeare, 1897.

4036 CONFESSIONS OF AN AUTHOR'S WIFE. New York: Bobbs–Merrill, 1927. 310 p.

4037 RED WINE OF YOUTH: A LIFE OF RUPERT BROOKE. Indianapolis: Bobbs–Merrill, 1948. 287 p.

POETRY

4038 WATCHERS OF TWILIGHT, AND OTHER POEMS. London, Ont.: T.H. Warren, printer, 1894. 43 p.

4039 PAULINE, AND OTHER POEMS. London, Ont.: T.H. Warren, printer, 1895. 64 p.

4040   EPIGRAMS. London, Ont.: T.H. Warren, printer, 1896. 42 p.

4041   HEPHAESTUS, PERSEPHONE AT ENNA, AND SAPPHO IN LEUCADIA.
Toronto: Grant Richards, 1903. 43 p.

4042   THE WOMAN IN THE RAIN AND OTHER POEMS. Boston: Little, Brown,
1907. ix, 264 p. Also as SAPPHO IN LEUCADIA. Boston: Little,
Brown, 1907. 264 p.

4043   IRISH POEMS. New York: Mitchell Kennerley, 1911. 110 p. Also
as IRISH SONGS. Toronto: McClelland and Goodchild, [1911]. 110 p.;
rpt. as OUT OF ERIN (SONGS IN EXILE). Indianapolis: Bobbs-Merrill,
1930. viii, 155 p.

4044   OPEN WATER. London: John Lane, 1914. viii, 132 p.

4045   A WOMAN AT DUSK, AND OTHER POEMS. Indianapolis: Bobbs-Merrill,
1928. 156 p.

4046   DARK SOIL. Indianapolis: Bobbs-Merrill, 1933. 123 p.

4047   THE OLD WOMAN REMEMBERS, AND OTHER IRISH POEMS. Indianapolis: Bobbs-Merrill, 1938. 57 p.

4048   THE KING WHO LOVED OLD CLOTHES, AND OTHER IRISH POEMS.
Indianapolis: Bobbs-Merrill, 1941. 105 p.

4049   SHADOWED VICTORY. Indianapolis: Bobbs-Merrill, 1943. 78 p.

4050   NEW YORK NOCTURNES. Ryerson Poetry Chap-Books, no. 132 [133].
[Toronto: Ryerson, 1948]. 12 p.

DRAMA

4051   THE BLOT: A DRAMA.

No publishing details; listed in H. Morgan's THE CANADIAN
MEN AND WOMEN OF THE TIME (1912).

4052   THE CLEVEREST WOMAN IN THE WORLD AND OTHER ONE-ACT PLAYS.
Indianapolis: Bobbs-Merrill, 1939. 272 p.

Shorter Work

SHORT STORIES

4053 "Through the Valley of Illusion." HARPER'S, 105 (Sept. 1902), 625-33.

4054 "The Kings of Hate." EVERYBODY'S, 17 (Dec. 1907), 810-21.

4055 "The Guarded House." EVERYBODY'S, 19 (Aug. 1908), 244-57.

4056 "Children of Spring." DELINEATOR, 73 (June 1909), 780.

4057 "When the Bank Moved." EVERYBODY'S, 21 (Dec. 1909), 739-52.

4058 "The Burglar." EVERYBODY'S, 22 (Mar. 1910), 327-37.

4059 "The Man Who Made Good." EVERYBODY'S, 23 (Dec. 1910), 784-99.

4060 "The Seventh Disappearance." EVERYBODY'S, 24 (May 1911), 690-703.

4061 "Cowgirl." SATURDAY EVENING POST, 9 Dec. 1922, pp. 8-9.

4062 "Manhandled." SATURDAY EVENING POST, 22 Mar. 1924, pp. 5-7;
      29 Mar. 1924, pp. 22-23.

4063 "Killer's Daughter." SATURDAY EVENING POST, 4 Apr. 1925, pp.
      5-7.

4064 "Ancient Feud." SATURDAY EVENING POST, 11 Apr. 1925, pp. 10-11.

4065 "Woman-Handled." SATURDAY EVENING POST, 2 May 1925, pp. 10-11.

4066 "Fifth Avenue." SATURDAY EVENING POST, 19 Sept. 1925, pp. 12-13.

4067 "Capture." SATURDAY EVENING POST, 6 Feb. 1926, pp. 10-11.

4068 "The Weaker Sex." SATURDAY EVENING POST, 18 Dec. 1926, pp.
      10-11.

4069 "Came the Viking." SATURDAY EVENING POST, 5 Feb. 1927, pp.
      14-15.

4070   "Dew of Suspicion." SATURDAY EVENING POST, 9 Apr. 1927, pp. 16-17.

4071   "Gun Play." GOLDEN BOOK, 6 (July 1927), 85-97.

4072   "Juggler." GOLDEN BOOK, 19 (June 1934), 761-68.

4073   "Music Box." SATURDAY EVENING POST, 17 Apr. 1937, pp. 18-19.

4074   "The Potboiler." QUEEN'S QUARTERLY, 50 (Spr. 1943), 25-27.

4075   "Reprisal." GOOD HOUSEKEEPING, 121 (Sept. 1945), 20-21.

4076   "The Case Against Santa Claus." SATURDAY NIGHT, 24 Nov. 1945, pp. 48-49.

ARTICLES

4077   "Our Authors Get Together." MACLEAN'S, 15 Apr. 1921, pp. 24-25, 42.

4078   "My Work and My Workshop: The Effect of His Environment on the Literary Product of a Noted American Novelist." ARTS AND DECORA-TION, 19 (Aug. 1923), 9-10, 62-63.

4079   "Copperheads and Critics." SATURDAY NIGHT, 23 Nov. 1940, pp. 29, 36.

4080   "Wild Poets I Have Known." SATURDAY NIGHT, 1 Mar. 1941, pp. 29, 36; 26 Apr. 1941, p. 33; 24 May 1941, p. 29; 14 June 1941, p. 41; 11 Oct. 1941, p. 29; 25 Oct. 1941, p. 33; 10 Jan. 1942, p. 25; 11 Apr. 1942, p. 25; 26 June 1943, p. 37; 30 Oct. 1943, p. 41; 11 Mar. 1944, pp. 32-33.

Manuscripts

4081   Acadia University Library, Wolfville, N.S.; McGill University Library, Montreal; University of Western Ontario, London, Ont.; University of Toronto Library.

SECONDARY MATERIAL

Criticism

4082   Deacon, William Arthur. "What a Canadian Has Done for Canada."

In his POTEEN: A POT-POURRI OF CANADIAN ESSAYS. Ottawa: Graphic, 1926, pp. 51-62.

Reprinted in no. 192.

4083   Lauriston, Victor. "Arthur Stringer." EDUCATIONAL RECORD, 58 (Oct.-Dec. 1942), 209-14.

4084   _____. ARTHUR STRINGER, SON OF THE NORTH: BIOGRAPHY AND ANTHOLOGY. Makers of Canadian Literature. Toronto: Ryerson, 1941. 178 p. Bibliog. Index.

4085   _____. POSTSCRIPT TO A POET: OFF THE RECORD TALES ABOUT ARTHUR STRINGER--INCLUDING SOME THE CENSOR SHOULD HAVE SUPPRESSED. Chatham, Ont.: Tiny Tree Club, 1941. 48 p.

4086   Porter, McKenzie. "The Purple Prose and Purple Life of Arthur Stringer." MACLEAN'S, 9 Feb. 1963, pp. 26, 28-30.

For criticism on Stringer, see also no. 2889.

Book Reviews

4087   THE WIRE TAPPERS: NYTBR, 24 Dec. 1922, p. 22; NYTSR, 12 May 1906, p. 308; NYTSR, 16 June 1906, p. 382.

4088   THE UNDER GROOVE: NATION, 18 June 1908, p. 557; NYTSR, 2 May 1908, p. 258; NYTSR, 13 June 1908, p. 346.

4089   THE GUN RUNNER: NYTSR, 8 May 1909, p. 294; NYTSR, 12 June 1909, p. 379.

4090   THE SHADOW: NATION, 6 Feb. 1913, p. 129; NYTBR, 2 Feb. 1913, p. 51.

4091   THE HAND OF PERIL: NATION, 27 May 1915, p. 600; NYTBR, 2 May 1915, p. 170.

4092   THE PRAIRIE WIFE: MACLEAN'S, 29 (Mar. 1916), 93; NATION, 7 Oct. 1915, p. 438; NYTBR, 31 Oct. 1915, p. 421.

4093   THE DOOR OF DREAD: NYTBR, 11 June 1916, p. 239.

4094   THE MAN WHO COULDN'T SLEEP: NYTBR, 6 Apr. 1919, p. 174.

4095 THE PRAIRIE MOTHER: NYTBR, 25 July 1920, p. 26.

4096 TWIN TALES: NYTBR, 11 Dec. 1921, p. 18.

4097 THE WINE OF LIFE: NYTBR, 12 June 1921, p. 24.

4098 THE CITY OF PERIL: NYTBR, 4 Feb. 1923, p. 14.

4099 THE DIAMOND THIEVES: NYTBR, 9 Dec. 1923, p. 9.

4100 POWER: NYTBR, 26 Apr. 1925, p. 9; SatR, 6 June 1925, p. 804.

4101 WHITE HANDS: NYTBR, 6 Nov. 1927, p. 20; SatR, 5 Nov. 1927. p. 287.

4102 CRISTINA AND I: NYTBR, 6 Oct. 1929, p. 6.

4103 THE WOMAN WHO COULDN'T DIE: SatR, 20 Apr. 1929, p. 935.

4104 A LADY QUITE LOST: NYTBR, 3 May 1931, p. 21; TLS, 19 Nov. 1931, p. 917.

4105 THE MUD LARK: NYTBR, 7 Feb. 1932, p. 13.

4106 MARRIAGE BY CAPTURE: NYTBR, 16 Apr. 1933, p. 17.

4107 MAN LOST: NYTBR, 7 Oct. 1934, p. 23.

4108 THE WIFE-TRADERS: NYTBR, 2 Feb. 1936, p. 17.

4109 HEATHER OF THE HIGH HAND: NYTBR, 13 June 1937, p. 18.

4110 THE LAMP IN THE VALLEY: NYTBR, 11 Dec. 1938, p. 26.

4111 THE DARK WING: NYTBR, 4 June 1939, p. 7; SatR, 10 June 1939, p. 19; SatR, 5 Aug. 1939, p. 9.

4112 THE GHOST PLANE: NYTBR, 20 Oct. 1940, p. 28.

4113 INTRUDERS IN EDEN: NYTBR, 3 May 1942, p. 16; SatN, 25 July 1942, p. 15.

4114   STAR IN A MIST: SatN, 5 Feb. 1944, p. 15; UTQ, 13 (Apr. 1944), 319-20.

4115   THE DEVASTATOR: NYTBR, 21 Jan. 1945, p. 23.

4116   RED WINE OF YOUTH: SatR, 4 Sept. 1948, p. 14; UTQ, 18 (Apr. 1949), 287-88.

SYMONS, SCOTT (1933--   )

Born in Toronto, Scott Symons received a B.A. from the University of Toronto (1955), an M.A. from Cambridge University (1957), and a "Diplome d'Études Supérieures" from the Sorbonne.   He was a journalist in Toronto, Quebec City, and Montreal, research curator for the Smithsonian Institute and the Canadiana Collection of the Royal Ontario Museum, and assistant professor in fine art for the University of Toronto.   In the early seventies, he travelled in Mexico and Morocco, and in 1976 spent a year as writer-in-residence at Simon Fraser University, British Columbia.   An enfant terrible in Canadian letters, Symons throws down the gauntlet to the establishment with his sexual (and homosexual) explicitness, political unorthodoxy, and narrative formlessness.   PLACE D'ARMES won the Beta Sigma Phi Award in 1968.

PRIMARY MATERIAL

Monographs

FICTION

4117   COMBAT JOURNAL FOR PLACE D'ARMES: A PERSONAL NARRATIVE.
Toronto: McClelland and Stewart, 1967.   279 p.

4118   PLACE D'ARMES.   Toronto: McClelland and Stewart, 1967.   279 p.

4119   CIVIC SQUARE.   Toronto: McClelland and Stewart, 1969.   848 l.

"A limited facsimile edition of the original manuscript";
unbound.

NONFICTION PROSE

4120   HERITAGE: A ROMANTIC LOOK AT EARLY CANADIAN FURNITURE.
Photos.   John de Visser.   Toronto: McClelland and Stewart, 1971.
N. pag.   Bibliog.

Shorter Work

ARTICLES

4121   "The Meaning of English Canada." CONTINUOUS LEARNING, 2 (Nov.-Dec. 1963), 250-60.

4122   "The Canadian Bestiary: Ongoing Literary Depravity." WEST COAST REVIEW, 11 (Jan.-Feb. 1977), 3-16.

Manuscripts

4123   Library of Parliament, Ottawa; McGill University Library, Montreal; University of Toronto Library.

SECONDARY MATERIAL

Criticism

4124   Brigg, Peter. "Insite: PLACE D'ARMES." CANADIAN LITERATURE, No. 73 (Sum. 1977), pp. 79-85.

4125   Cameron, Elspeth. "Journey to the Interior: The Journal Form in PLACE D'ARMES." STUDIES IN CANADIAN LITERATURE, 2 (Sum. 1977), 267-77.

For criticism on Symons, see also nos. 87, 141, and 1701.

Book Reviews

4126   PLACE D'ARMES: CanL, 33 (Sum. 1967), 84-85; CFor, 47 (May 1967), 46; LIBERTÉ, 9 (Mar. 1967), 89-90; WCR, 2 (Fall 1967), 46-48.

THOMAS, AUDREY C. (1935--)

A native of Binghampton, New York, with a B.A. (1957) from Smith College, Massachusetts, Audrey C. Thomas came to Vancouver in 1959 and received a Master's (1963) and did doctoral work at the University of British Columbia. From 1964 to 1966, she lived in Kumasi, Ghana, and since then in Vancouver and on Galiano Island, B.C. Particularly in works such as MRS. BLOOD and BLOWN FIGURES, Thomas employs the post-modern technique of fragmentation to explore psychological states.

PRIMARY MATERIAL

Monographs

FICTION

4127 TEN GREEN BOTTLES: SHORT STORIES. Indianapolis: Bobbs-Merrill, 1967. 182 p.

4128 MRS. BLOOD. Indianapolis: Bobbs-Merrill, 1970. 200 p.

   First volume in the Isobel Carpenter trilogy.

4129 MUNCHMEYER AND PROSPERO ON THE ISLAND. Indianapolis: Bobbs-Merrill, 1971. 157 p.

   Two novellas.

4130 SONGS MY MOTHER TAUGHT ME. Vancouver: Talonbooks, 1973. 232 p.

   Second volume in the Isobel Carpenter trilogy.

4131 BLOWN FIGURES: A NOVEL. Vancouver: Talonbooks, 1974. 547 p.

   Third volume in the Isobel Carpenter trilogy.

4132   LADIES & ESCORTS. [Ottawa]: Oberon, 1977. 159 p.

       Short stories.

4133   LATAKIA: A NOVEL. Vancouver: Talonbooks, 1979. 172 p.

4134   REAL MOTHERS: SHORT STORIES. Vancouver: Talonbooks, 1981.
       168 p.

Shorter Work

SHORT STORIES

4135   "Clean Monday, Or Wintering in Athens." CAPILANO REVIEW, No.
       13 (1978), pp. 68-75, 77-83, 85-87.

4136   Entry deleted.

ARTICLES

4137 "African Journal Entries." CAPILANO REVIEW, No. 7 (Spr. 1975),
       pp. 55-62.

4138 "'My Craft and Sullen Art': The Writers Speak." ATLANTIS, 4 (Fall
       1978), 152-54.

Manuscripts

4139   University of British Columbia Library, Vancouver.

SECONDARY MATERIAL

Bibliography

4140   "Audrey Thomas/Bibliography." CAPILANO REVIEW, No. 7 (Spr. 1975),
       pp. 110-12.

Criticism

4141   Bellette, A.F. "Some Observations on the Novels of Audrey Thomas."
       OPEN LETTER, 3rd. ser., No. 3 (Late Fall 1975), pp. 65-69.

4142   Bowering, George. "Snow Red: The Short Stories of Audrey Thomas." OPEN LETTER, 3rd ser., No. 5 (Sum. 1976), pp. 28-39.

4143   _____. "Songs & Wisdom: An Interview with Audrey Thomas." OPEN LETTER, 4th ser., No. 3 (Spr. 1979), pp. 7-31.

4144   Coupey, Pierre, et al. "Interview/Audrey Thomas." CAPILANO REVIEW, No. 7 (Spr. 1975), pp. 87-109.

4145   Diotte, Robert. "The Romance of Penelope: Audrey Thomas's Isobel Carpenter Trilogy." CANADIAN LITERATURE, No. 86 (Aut. 1980), pp. 60-68.

4146   Komisar, Elizabeth. "Audrey Thomas: A Review/Interview." OPEN LETTER, 3rd ser., No. 3 (Late Fall 1975), pp. 59-64.

4147   Matheson, Graeme. "Below the Surface." QUILL AND QUIRE, 40, No. 10 (1974), 3.

      An interview.

4148   Stape, John H. "Dr. Jung at the Site of Blood: A Note on BLOWN FIGURES." STUDIES IN CANADIAN LITERATURE, 2 (Wint. 1977), 124-26.

4149   Wachtel, E. "Guts of MRS. BLOOD." BOOKS IN CANADA, 8 (Nov. 1979), 3-6.

4150   _____. "The Image of Africa in the Fiction of Audrey Thomas." ROOM OF ONE'S OWN, 2, No. 4 (1976), 21-28.

Book Reviews

4151   TEN GREEN BOTTLES: CanL, 38 (Aut. 1968), 94-96; FIDDLEHEAD, 116 (Wint. 1978), 150-52; NYTBR, 10 Dec. 1967, p. 55; OntarioR, 8 (Spr. 1978), 106; QQ, 85 (Aut. 1978), 517-18; QUARRY, 27 (Wint. 1978), 91-94; UTQ, 37 (July 1968), 388; WCR, 12 (Jan. 1978), 49-50.

4152   MRS. BLOOD: CanL, 50 (Aut. 1971), 98-99; FIDDLEHEAD, 95 (Fall 1972), 113-17; JCL, 7 (June 1972), 109-10; MACLEAN'S, 84 (Aug. 1971), 64; NYTBR, 3 Jan. 1971, p. 23; Q&Q, 42, No. 2 (1976), 39.

4153   MUNCHMEYER AND PROSPERO ON THE ISLAND: CanL, 55 (Wint. 1973), 112-13; FIDDLEHEAD, 95 (Fall 1972), 113-17; SatN, 87 (July 1972), 44-45; UTQ, 42 (Sum. 1973), 348.

4154 SONGS MY MOTHER TAUGHT ME: BCan, 3 (Mar. 1974), 16-17; BrO, Preview Issue (Dec. 1973), 38-39; CanL, 60 (Spr. 1974), 97; CFor, 54 (May 1974), 18-19; JCF, 3, No. 3 (1974), 90-91; MAC-LEAN'S, 87 (Feb. 1974), 80; NYTBR, 23 Dec. 1973, p. 12; OpenL, 2nd ser., 9 (Fall 1974), 119-20; Q&Q, 40, No. 2 (1974), 12; SatN, 89 (May 1974), 46-47; WLWE, 13 (Nov. 1974), 259-60.

4155 BLOWN FIGURES: BCan, 4 (Aug. 1975), 9-10; CanL, 65 (Sum. 1975), 86-90; FIDDLEHEAD, 106 (Sum. 1975), 113-14; MACLEAN'S, 88 (Jan. 1975), 71; MHRev, 36 (Oct. 1975), 140-42; NYTBR, 1 Feb. 1976, p. 8; OpenL, 3rd ser., 5 (1976), 81-82; QUARRY, 24 (Aut. 1975), 60-61; TamR, 66 (June 1975), 109-10.

4156 LADIES & ESCORTS: BCan, 6 (June 1977), 14; BrO, 5, No. 1 (1978), 41; FIDDLEHEAD, 116 (Wint. 1978), 150-52; Q&Q, 43, No. 9 (1977), 5; QQ, 85 (Aut. 1978), 517-18; QUARRY, 27 (Wint. 1978), 91-94; UTQ, 47 (Sum. 1978), 328-29; WascanaR, 11 (Fall 1976), 98-100; WCR, 12 (Jan. 1978), 49-50.

4157 LATAKIA: BCan, 8 (Dec. 1979), 11; CFor, 60 (June 1980), 38; ECW, 20 (Wint. 1980), 201-19; FIDDLEHEAD, 126 (Sum. 1980), 121-23; Q&Q, 46 (Feb. 1980), 41.

VAN DER MARK, CHRISTINE (1917--)

Christine van der Mark has been a schoolteacher in the Peace River district of Alberta and then composition instructor at the University of Alberta. She won an Oxford University Press fellowship for Canadian writers. IN DUE SEASON, a realistic novel examining the effects of frontier life through exploration of character, won the I.O.D.E. (Imperial Order of the Daughters of the Empire) Prize for Alberta writers.

PRIMARY MATERIAL

Monographs

FICTION

4158   IN DUE SEASON. Toronto: Oxford University Press, 1947. 363 p.

4159   HONEY IN THE ROCK. Toronto: McClelland and Stewart, 1966. 224 p.

Shorter Work

SHORT STORIES

4160   "Catch-Colt." HERE AND NOW, 1 (May 1948), 26-35.

4161   "Brothers." MACLEAN'S, 1 June 1948, pp. 14-15, 30 ff.

SECONDARY MATERIAL

Criticism

4162   Livesay, Dorothy. Introd., IN DUE SEASON. Vancouver: New Star Books, 1979, pp. i-iv.

4163   Wise, Dorothy. "Afterword" to IN DUE SEASON. Vancouver: New
       Star Books, 1979, pp. 365-72.

       By van der Mark's daughter.

For criticism on van der Mark, see also no. 2889.

Book Reviews

4164   IN DUE SEASON: DR, 28 (July 1948), 196; QQ, 55 (Spr. 1948), 114-
       15; UTQ, 17 (Apr. 1948), 267-69.

4165   HONEY IN THE ROCK: CanL, 31 (Wint. 1967), 65-66; CFor, 47
       (May 1967), 46-47; MACLEAN'S, 6 Aug. 1966, p. 47; QQ, 73 (Wint.
       1966), 607; UTQ, 36 (July 1967), 386.

VIZINCZEY, STEPHEN (1933--)

Stephen Vizinczey escaped from his native Hungary after the 1956 uprising and came to Canada after a period in Italy. For three years he edited a literary magazine, EXCHANGE, in Montreal and then moved to Toronto where he wrote and produced public affairs programs for the CBC. Unable to interest commercial publishers in his novel IN PRAISE OF OLDER WOMEN, the account of a young man's coming of age, he published it himself and met immediate success.

PRIMARY MATERIAL

Monographs

FICTION

4166   IN PRAISE OF OLDER WOMEN: THE AMOROUS RECOLLECTIONS OF ANDRÁS VAJDA. Toronto: Contemporary Canada, 1965. 183 p.

4167   THE RULES OF CHAOS. London: Macmillan, 1969. 223 p.

Shorter Work

ARTICLES

4168   "Frankenstein for the Sophisticated." TAMARACK REVIEW, 20 (Sum. 1961), 73-77, 79-81.

4169   "Budapest, 1956: Memoirs of a Freedom Fighter." HORIZON, 18 (Aut. 1976), 56-63.

Vizinczey, Stephen

SECONDARY MATERIAL

Criticism

4170   Robinow, Tony. "Stephen Vizinczey." MONTREALER, 41 (Sept. 1967), 26, 33-34.

4171   Slopen, Beverley. "Word Processors and the Multi-National Medicis." QUILL AND QUIRE, 46, No. 2 (1980), 31.

Book Reviews

4172   IN PRAISE OF OLDER WOMEN: CanL, 28 (Spr. 1966), 57-61; CDim, 3 (Jan. 1966), 29-30; HudR, 19 (Sum. 1966), 305; JCL, 3 (July 1967), 111-12; LIBERTÉ, 7 (Sept. 1965), 442-44; LISTENER, 11 Aug. 1966, p. 213; MACLEAN'S, 4 Sept. 1965, p. 46; MONTREALER, 39 (Nov. 1965), 62; NS, 12 Aug. 1966, p. 235; PUNCH, 24 Aug. 1966, p. 304; SatN, 80 (Sept. 1965), 29-31; SatN, 93 (May 1978), 38; SatR, 23 Apr. 1966, p. 48; SatR, 17 Dec. 1966, p. 36; SPECTATOR, 12 Aug. 1966, p. 210; TamR, [38] (Wint. 1966), 97-100; TLS, 18 Aug. 1966, p. 737; UTQ, 35 (July 1966), 385-86.

4173   THE RULES OF CHAOS: CanL, 45 (Sum. 1970), 75-76; CFor, 49 (Mar. 1970), 294; LISTENER, 8 May 1969, p. 654; NS, 2 May 1969, p. 626; NYTBR, 4 Oct. 1970, p. 32; QQ, 77 (Spr. 1970), 128-29; SatN, 84 (Oct. 1969), 46, 48, 50; SPECTATOR, 9 May 1969, p. 619; TLS, 22 May 1969, p. 550.

WATSON, SHEILA (1909--)

Born in New Westminster, British Columbia, Sheila Watson attended the University of British Columbia, receiving a B.A. (1931) and an M.A. (1933) in English and an Academic Teaching Certificate (1932). She taught school in a number of small B.C. towns and in Toronto, lectured at UBC, lived in Edmonton and Paris, and, between 1957 and 1965, completed a Ph.D. at the University of Toronto, supervised by Marshall McLuhan. Between 1961 and her retirement in 1975, she was a professor of English at the University of Alberta. Her innovative symbolic novel THE DOUBLE HOOK, winner of the Beta Sigma Phi Award, used biblical cadences and a poetic denseness of imagery to create a rural western tale that is homely and representational and at the same time symbolically charged.

PRIMARY MATERIAL

Monographs

FICTION

4174   THE DOUBLE HOOK. Toronto: McClelland and Stewart, 1959. 127 p.

4175   FOUR STORIES: BROTHER OEDIPUS, THE BLACK FARM, ANTIGONE, THE RUMBLE SEAT. Toronto: Coach House, 1979. 62 p.

NONFICTION PROSE

4176   "Wyndham Lewis and Expressionism." Diss., University of Toronto, 1965. 2 vols. xxxiii, 535 l. Bibliog.

Shorter Work

ARTICLES

4177   "Swift and Ovid: The Development of Metasatire." HUMANITIES ASSOCIATION BULLETIN, 18 (Spr. 1967), 5-13.

Entries 4177 through 4180 are reprinted in OPEN LETTER, 3rd ser., No. 1 (Wint. 1974-75).

4178   "The Great War, Wyndham Lewis and the Underground Press." ARTS/ CANADA, 24 (Nov. 1967), 3-17. Bibliog.

4179   "Canada and Wyndham Lewis the Artist." CANADIAN LITERATURE, No. 35 (Wint. 1968), pp. 44-61.

4180   "Michael Ondaatje: The Mechanization of Death." WHITE PELICAN, 2 (Fall 1972), 56-64.

4181   "Artist-Ape as Crowd-Master." OPEN LETTER, 3rd ser., No. 1 (Wint. 1974-75), pp. 115-18.

Discusses Wyndham Lewis.

4182   "Gertrude Stein: The Style is the Machine." OPEN LETTER, 3rd ser., No. 1 (Wint. 1974-75), pp. 167-78.

4183   "Myth and Counter-Myth." OPEN LETTER, 3rd ser., No. 1 (Wint. 1974-75), pp. 119-36.

Discusses Wyndham Lewis.

4184   "Power: Nude or Naked." OPEN LETTER, 3rd ser., No. 1 (Wint. 1974-75), pp. 151-57.

Discusses Jonathan Swift.

4185   "A Question of Portraiture." OPEN LETTER, 3rd ser., No. 1 (Wint. 1974-75), pp. 43-49.

Discusses Wyndham Lewis.

4186   "Unaccommodated Man." OPEN LETTER, 3rd ser., No. 1 (Wint. 1974-75), pp. 97-114.

Discusses Wyndham Lewis.

4187   "What I'm Going to Do." OPEN LETTER, 3rd ser., No. 1 (Wint. 1974-75), pp. 181-83.

Discusses THE DOUBLE HOOK.

4188   "Wyndham Lewis and G.K. Chesterton." CHESTERTON REVIEW, 6 (1980), 254-71.

SECONDARY MATERIAL

Criticism

4189   Barbour, Douglas. "Editors and Typesetters: A Semi-Bibliographical Note Concerning THE DOUBLE HOOK." OPEN LETTER, 3rd ser., No. 1 (Wint. 1974-75), pp. 184-87.

4190   Corbett, Nancy J. "Closed Circle." CANADIAN LITERATURE, No. 61 (Sum. 1974), pp. 46-53.

4191   Coupey, Pierre, et al. "Interview/Sheila Watson." CAPILANO REVIEW, Nos. 8-9 (Fall 1975-Spr. 1976), pp. 351-60.

4192   Downton, Dawn Rae. "Messages and Messengers in THE DOUBLE HOOK." STUDIES IN CANADIAN LITERATURE, 4 (Sum. 1979), 137-46.

4193   Godard, Barbara. "Between One Cliché and Another: Language in THE DOUBLE HOOK." STUDIES IN CANADIAN LITERATURE, 3 (Sum. 1978), 149-65.

4194   Grube, John. Introd., THE DOUBLE HOOK. New Canadian Library, no. 54. Toronto: McClelland and Stewart, 1966, pp. 5-14.

4195   Lennox, John Watt. "The Past: Themes and Symbols of Confrontation in THE DOUBLE HOOK and 'Le Torrent.'" JOURNAL OF CANADIAN FICTION, 2 (Wint. 1973), 70-72.

   Discusses Watson and Anne Hébert.

4196   Livesay, Dorothy. "Two Women Novelists of Canada's West." REVIEW OF NATIONAL LITERATURES, 7 (1976), 127-32.

   Discusses Watson and Ethel Wilson; reprinted in no. 178.

4197   Marlatt, D. "Interview/Sheila Watson." CAPILANO REVIEW, 8-9 (1976), 351-60.

4198   Marta, Jan. "Poetic Structures in the Prose Fiction of Sheila Watson." ESSAYS ON CANADIAN WRITING, No. 17 (Spr. 1980), pp. 44-56.

4199   Mitchell, Beverley. "Association and Allusion in THE DOUBLE HOOK." JOURNAL OF CANADIAN FICTION, 2 (Wint. 1973), 63-69.

4200   Monkman, Leslie. "Coyote as Trickster in THE DOUBLE HOOK." CANADIAN LITERATURE, No. 52 (Spr. 1972), pp. 70-76.

4201 Morriss, Margaret. "The Elements Transcended." CANADIAN LITERA-
TURE, No. 42 (Aut. 1969), pp. 56-71.

Reprinted in no. 5113.

4202 Sandler, Linda. "Sheila Watson as Lewisite Critic." CANADIAN LIT-
ERATURE, No. 70 (Aut. 1976), pp. 91-93.

4203 "Sheila Watson: A Biography." In FIGURES IN A GROUND: CANA-
DIAN ESSAYS ON MODERN LITERATURE COLLECTED IN HONOR OF
SHEILA WATSON. Ed. Diane Bessai and David Jackel. Saskatoon:
Western Producer Prairie Books, 1978, pp. 1-3.

For criticism on Watson, see also nos. 160, 168, 174, and 2202.

Book Reviews

4204 THE DOUBLE HOOK: ALPHABET, 3 (Dec. 1961), 49-51; BCLQ, 23
(Oct. 1959), 34, 36; CAB, 41, No. 4 (1966), 18; CanL, ·1 (Sum. 1959),
78-80; CFor, 39 (July 1959), 78-80; DR, 39 (Sum. 1959), 233-36;
FIDDLEHEAD, 46 (Aut. 1960), 43-44, 46; TamR, 12 (Sum. 1959), 85-
88; TLS, 27 Jan. 1961, p. 62; UTQ, 29 (July 1960), 465-67.

4205 FOUR STORIES: BCan, 9 (Feb. 1980), 8; Q&Q, 46, No. 4 (1979),
35; Q&Q, 46 (Apr. 1980), 35.

WIEBE, RUDY (1934--)

Born on a homestead farm near Fairholme, Saskatchewan, Rudy Henry Wiebe grew up in Coaldale, Alberta. He received a Th.B. from the Mennonite Brethern Bible College (Winnipeg) and attended the Universities of Alberta, Manitoba (B.A., 1956; M.A., 1960), Tübingen (West Germany), and Iowa. From 1963 to 1967, he taught at Goshen College, Indiana, and since 1967, he has been a professor of English and creative writing at the University of Alberta.

His novels are characterized by largeness of scope, abundance (in character, image, and language), a moral emphasis, and a growing experimentation in style and in narrative viewpoint. Often they draw on historical material to present sagas of peoples--Mennonite, Canadian Indian, and Métis--and of threats to their values. THE TEMPTATIONS OF BIG BEAR won the 1973 Governor General's Award.

PRIMARY MATERIAL

Monographs

FICTION

4206 PEACE SHALL DESTROY MANY. Toronto: McClelland and Stewart, 1962. 239 p.

4207 THE FIRST AND VITAL CANDLE. Toronto: McClelland and Stewart, 1966. 354 p.

4208 THE BLUE MOUNTAINS OF CHINA. Toronto: McClelland and Stewart, 1970. 227 p.

4209 THE TEMPTATIONS OF BIG BEAR. Toronto: McClelland and Stewart, 1973. 415 p.

4210   WHERE IS THE VOICE COMING FROM? STORIES. Toronto: Mc-
        Clelland and Stewart, 1974. 157 p.

4211   THE SCORCHED-WOOD PEOPLE: A NOVEL. Toronto: McClelland
        and Stewart, 1977. 351 p.

4212   ALBERTA: A CELEBRATION. Ed. Tom Radford. Photos. by Harry
        Savage. Edmonton: Hurtig, 1979. 208 p.

        Fictional vignettes.

4213   THE MAD TRAPPER. Toronto: McClelland and Stewart, 1980. 189 p.

EDITED WORK

4214   THE STORY-MAKERS: A SELECTION OF MODERN SHORT STORIES.
        Toronto: Macmillan, 1970. xxx, 354 p.

4215   STORIES FROM WESTERN CANADA: A SELECTION. Toronto: Mac-
        millan, 1972. xiv, 274 p.

4216   STORIES FROM PACIFIC AND ARCTIC CANADA: A SELECTION. Ed.
        Andreas Schroeder and Rudy Wiebe. Toronto: Macmillan, 1974. xv,
        284 p.

4217   DOUBLE VISION: AN ANTHOLOGY OF TWENTIETH-CENTURY STORIES
        IN ENGLISH. Toronto: Macmillan, 1976. xii, 331 p.

4218   GETTING HERE: STORIES. Edmonton, Alta.: NeWest, 1977. 119 p.

4219   MORE STORIES FROM WESTERN CANADA. Ed. Rudy Wiebe and Aritha
        van Herk. Toronto: Macmillan, 1980. 296 p.

Shorter Work

SHORT STORIES

4220   "The Power." In NEW VOICES: CANADIAN UNIVERSITY WRITINGS
        OF 1956. Ed. Earle Birney et al. Toronto: J.M. Dent and Sons,
        1956, pp. 128-33.

4221   "Games for Queen Victoria." SATURDAY NIGHT, 91 (Mar. 1976),
        60-67.

4222   "Hunting McDougall: 1869." FIDDLEHEAD, No. 108 (Wint. 1976),
        pp. 17-24.

4223　"After Thirty Years of Marriage." CANADIAN FORUM, 58 (Oct.-Nov. 1978), 36-40.

4224　"In the Beaver Hills." In AURORA: NEW CANADIAN WRITING 1978. Ed. Morris Wolfe. Toronto: Doubleday, 1978, pp. 71-80.

4225　"An Indication of Burning." CANADIAN FICTION MAGAZINE, Nos. 32-33 (1979-80), pp. 150-64.

ARTICLES

4226　"An Author Speaks about His Novel." CANADIAN MENNONITE, 11 Apr. 1963, p. 8.

A reply to no. 4241; reprinted in no. 4246.

4227　"The Artist as a Critic and a Witness." CHRISTIAN LIVING, 12 (Mar. 1965), 20-23.

Reprinted in no. 4246.

4228　"Passage by Land." CANADIAN LITERATURE, No. 48 (Spr. 1971), pp. 25-27.

Reprinted in nos. 136 and 197.

4229　"Western Canada Fiction: Past and Future." WESTERN AMERICAN LITERATURE, 6 (Spr. 1971), 21-30.

4230　"On the Trail of Big Bear." JOURNAL OF CANADIAN FICTION, 3, No. 2 (1974), 45-48.

Reprinted in nos. 136 and 4246.

4231　"Riel: A Possible Film Treatment." NEWEST REVIEW, 1 (June 1975), 6.

Reprinted in no. 4246.

4232　"All That's Left of Big Bear: In a Small Bag, in a Small Room in New York City, the Great Spirit Rests." MACLEAN'S, 88 (Sept. 1975), 52-55.

Reprinted in a longer version in no. 4246.

4233　"A Novelist's Personal Notes on Frederick Philip Grove." UNIVERSITY OF TORONTO QUARTERLY, 47 (Spr. 1978), 189-99.

Reprinted in no. 4246.

4234   "The Death and Life of Albert Johnson: Collected Notes on a Possible Legend." In FIGURES IN A GROUND: CANADIAN ESSAYS ON MODERN LITERATURE COLLECTED IN HONOR OF SHEILA WATSON. Ed. Diane Bessai and David Jackel. Saskatoon: Western Producer Prairie Books, 1978, pp. 220-46.

4235   "New Land, Ancient Land." In THE NEW LAND: STUDIES IN A LITERARY THEME. Ed. Richard Chadbourne and Hallvard Dahlie. Calgary: Wilfrid Laurier University Press, for the Calgary Institute for the Humanities, 1978, pp. 1-4.

>   Discusses PEACE SHALL DESTROY MANY and THE TEMPTATIONS OF BIG BEAR.

Manuscripts

4236   University of Calgary Library, Calgary, Alta.

SECONDARY MATERIAL

Criticism

4237   Bergman, Brian. "Rudy Wiebe: Storymaker of the Prairies." GATEWAY (University of Alberta), 10 Nov. 1977, p. 9.

>   An interview; reprinted in no. 4246.

4238   Bevan, Allan R. Introd., THE TEMPTATIONS OF BIG BEAR. New Canadian Library, no. 122. Toronto: McClelland and Stewart, 1976, pp. ix-xv.

4239   Bilan, Robert P. "Wiebe & Religious Struggle." CANADIAN LITERATURE, No. 77 (Sum. 1978), pp. 50-63.

>   Discusses THE BLUE MOUNTAINS OF CHINA.

4240   Ferris, Ina. "Religious Vision and Fictional Form: Rudy Wiebe's THE BLUE MOUNTAINS OF CHINA." MOSAIC, 11 (Spr. 1978), 79-85.

>   Reprinted in no. 4246.

4241   Giesbrecht, Herbert. "O Life, How Naked and How Hard When Known!" CANADIAN MENNONITE, 20 Mar. 1963, p. 5.

>   Discusses PEACE SHALL DESTROY MANY; for reply, see no. 4226; reprinted in no. 4246.

4242   Hancock, M. "Wiebe: A Voice Crying in the Wilderness." CHRIS-
TIANITY TODAY, 16 Feb. 1979, pp. 30-31.

4243   Keith, William J. EPIC FICTION: THE ART OF RUDY WIEBE. Edmonton: University of Alberta Press, 1981. 158 p. Bibliog. Index.

4244   _____. "From Document to Art: Wiebe's Historical Short Stories and
Their Sources." STUDIES IN CANADIAN LITERATURE, 4 (Sum. 1979),
106-19.

4245   _____. Introd., THE BLUE MOUNTAINS OF CHINA. New Canadian
Library, no. 108. Toronto: McClelland and Stewart, 1970, n. pag.

4246   _____, ed. A VOICE IN THE LAND: ESSAYS BY AND ABOUT RUDY
WIEBE. Western Canadian Literary Documents, 2. Edmonton: NeWest,
1981. 256 p. Bibliog. Index.

        New and reprinted articles and interviews, including a joint
        interview with Kroetsch.

4247   Mandel, Eli. "Where the Voice Comes From." QUILL AND QUIRE,
40, No. 12 (1974), 4, 20.

        An interview; reprinted in no. 4246.

4248   Mansbridge, Francis. "Wiebe's Sense of Community." CANADIAN
LITERATURE, No. 77 (Sum. 1978), pp. 42-49.

        Discusses PEACE SHALL DESTROY MANY.

4249   Melnyk, George. "Rudy, Riel, and Other Rebels." QUILL AND QUIRE,
43 (Nov. 1977), 31.

4250   _____. "The Western Canadian Imagination: An Interview with Rudy
Wiebe." CANADIAN FICTION MAGAZINE, No. 12 (Wint. 1974),
pp. 29-34.

        Reprinted in no. 4246.

4251   Reimer, Margaret, and Sue Steiner. "Translating Life into Art: A Conversation with Rudy Wiebe." MENNONITE REPORTER, 26 Nov. 1973,
pp. A7-A8.

        Reprinted in no. 4246.

4252   Robinson, J.M. Introd., PEACE SHALL DESTROY MANY. New Canadian Library, no. 82. Toronto: McClelland and Stewart, 1972, pp.
1-6.

4253   Suderman, Elmer F.   "Universal Values in Rudy Wiebe's PEACE SHALL DESTROY MANY."   MENNONITE LIFE, 20 (Oct. 1965), 72-76.

   Reprinted in no. 4246.

4255   Taylor, Lauralyn.   "THE TEMPTATIONS OF BIG BEAR: A Filmic Novel?" ESSAYS ON CANADIAN WRITING, No. 9 (Wint. 1977-78), pp. 134-38.

4256   Tiessen, H.E.   "A Mighty Inner River: 'Peace' in the Fiction of Rudy Wiebe."   JOURNAL OF CANADIAN FICTION, 2 (Fall 1973), 71-76.

   Reprinted in no. 171.

4257   Whaley, Susan.   "Narrative Voices in THE TEMPTATIONS OF BIG BEAR."   ESSAYS ON CANADIAN WRITING, No. 20 (Wint. 1980-81), pp. 134-48.

4258   Zwarun, Suzanne.   "Lonely Are the Grave: Someday, Maybe, We'll Appreciate Rudy Wiebe."   MACLEAN'S, 4 Sept. 1978, pp. 34-37.

For criticism of Wiebe, see also nos. 124, 131, 170-71, 205, 2338, and, especially, 2040.

Book Reviews

4259   PEACE SHALL DESTROY MANY: AIHR, 11 (Spr. 1963), 29-30; CAB, 38 (Wint. 1962), 15-16; CanL, 16 (Spr. 1963), 73-76; JCF, 1 (Spr. 1972), 96; MONTREALER, 37 (Feb. 1973), 37; SaskH, 16 (Wint. 1963), 38-39; UTQ, 32 (July 1963), 399-400.

4260   THE FIRST AND VITAL CANDLE: BCan, 8 (Oct. 1979), 29; CAB, 42 (Aut. 1966), 19; CanL, 31 (Wint. 1967), 76-77; CFor, 47 (Jan. 1968), 235-36; QQ, 73 (Wint. 1966), 607-08; UTQ, 36 (July 1967), 386-87.

4261   THE BLUE MOUNTAINS OF CHINA: FIDDLEHEAD, 88 (Wint. 1971), 98-102; SatN, 86 (Apr. 1971), 26, 28; UTQ, 40 (July 1967), 384.

4262   THE TEMPTATIONS OF BIG BEAR: AntigR, 18 (Sum. 1974), 105; BCan, 3 (Nov. 1974), 17-18; CAB, 49 (Wint. 1973), 23; CanL, 61 (Sum. 1974), 82-84; CFM, 17 (Spr. 1975), 120-23; CFor, 53 (Nov. 1973), 30; DR, 54 (Sum. 1974), 377-79; ECW, 1 (Wint. 1974), 49-50; FIDDLEHEAD, 105 (Spr. 1975), 128-29; JCF, 2 (Fall 1973), 88-91; LaUR, 7, Nos. 2--8, Nos. 1-2 (1974-75), 101-03; MACLEAN'S, 86 (Nov. 1973), 116, 118; QQ, 81 (Spr. 1974), 142-44; SatN, 89 (Feb. 1974), 32-33; UWR, 10 (Spr. 1975), 81-82; WCR, 9 (June 1974), 45-47; WLWE, 13 (Nov. 1974), 263-65.

4263   WHERE IS THE VOICE COMING FROM? BCan, 3 (Nov. 1974), 17–18; CanL, 63 (Wint. 1975), 102–03; CFM, 20 (Wint. 1976), 104–07; Q&Q, 40, No. 10 (1974), 20; TamR, 64 (Nov. 1974), 85; UTQ, 44 (Sum. 1975), 313; WCR, 9 (Apr. 1975), 16.

4264   THE SCORCHED-WOOD PEOPLE: AntigR, 33 (Spr. 1978), 102–03; ARCS, 8 (Aut. 1978), 152–53; BCan, 7 (Jan. 1978), 14; CanL, 77 (Sum. 1978), 98–100; CDim, 13, No. 2 (1978), 51–52; CEStudies, 10, No. 2 (1978), 185–86; CFM, 30–31 (1979), 220–22; CFor, 57 (Dec. 1977), 34; CRead, 18 (Dec. 1977), 5–7; ECW, 10 (Spr. 1978), 129–33; FIDDLEHEAD, 117 (Spr. 1978), 117–20; JCF, 28–29 (1980), 248–51; MOSAIC, 11 (Sum. 1978), 155–58; Q&Q Update, 16 Feb. 1978, p. 11; QQ, 85 (Aut. 1978), 518–19; UTQ, 47 (Sum. 1978), 335–38; UWR, 14 (Fall 1978), 90–94; WAL, 14 (Fall 1979), 237–38.

4265   THE MAD TRAPPER: BCan, 9 (Nov. 1980), 12–13; CFor, 60 (Dec. 1980), 42–43; Q&Q, 46 (Nov. 1980), 39.

WILSON, ETHEL (1888-1980)

Ethel Davis Wilson was born in Port Elizabeth, South Africa, and taken to England and then, at the age of eight after the death of her parents, to Vancouver. She was educated at the Vancouver Normal School, taught in Vancouver from 1907 to 1920, and travelled in Europe and the East. She has received a D.Litt. from the University of British Columbia, the Lorne Pierce Medal, the Canada Council Medal, and the Order of Canada Medal of Service. Like Nell Severance in the novel SWAMP ANGEL, Wilson applies an "amused intelligence" to the observation of very ordinary people. She creates engaging stories enhanced often by vivid images of the British Columbia landscape and notable for careful modulations of the detached, tolerant, and wry narrative voice.

PRIMARY MATERIAL

Monographs

FICTION

4266 HETTY DORVAL. Toronto: Macmillan, 1947. 116 p.

4267 THE INNOCENT TRAVELLER. Toronto: Macmillan, 1949. x, 276 p.

4268 THE EQUATIONS OF LOVE: TUESDAY AND WEDNESDAY; LILLY'S STORY. Toronto: Macmillan, 1952. 280 p. Two novellas; one rpt. as LILLY'S STORY. New York: Harper, 1953. 208 p.

4269 SWAMP ANGEL. Toronto: Macmillan, 1954. v, 215 p. Rev. ed. New York: Harper, 1954. 215 p.

4270 LOVE AND SALT WATER. Toronto: Macmillan, 1956. ix, 202 p.

4271 MRS. GOLIGHTLY AND OTHER STORIES. Toronto: Macmillan, 1961. 209 p.

Shorter Work

SHORT STORIES

4272   "The Cigar and the Poor Young Girl." ECHOES, No. 180 (Oct. 1945), pp. 11, 46.

4273   "My Father's Teacher: Looking Back with Ethel Wilson." MONTREALER, 32 (July 1958), 27-28.

4274   "Simple Translation." SATURDAY NIGHT, 23 Dec. 1961, p. 19.

4275   "Journey to a Fair Land." READER'S DIGEST, 80 (Apr. 1962), 143-44.
        Revision of no. 4274.

4276   "A Visit to the Frontier." TAMARACK REVIEW, 33 (Aut. 1964), 55-65.

ARTICLES

4277   "Address to the Students of the School of Architecture, U.B.C." JOUR-NAL OF THE ROYAL ARCHITECTURAL INSTITUTE OF CANADA, 36 (Apr. 1959), 130-33.

4278   "A Cat Among the Falcons: Reflections on the Writer's Craft." CA-NADIAN LITERATURE, No. 2 (Aut. 1959), pp. 10-19.
        Reprinted in no. 195.

4279   "The Bridge or the Stokehold? Views of the Novelist's Art." CANA-DIAN LITERATURE, No. 5 (Sum. 1960), pp. 43-47.
        Reprinted in no. 136.

4280   "Reflections in a Pool." CANADIAN LITERATURE, No. 22 (Aut. 1964), pp. 20-33.
        Reprinted in no. 5113.

4281   "Of Alan Crawley." CANADIAN LITERATURE, No. 19 (Wint. 1964), pp. 33-42.

4282   Introd., SWAMP ANGEL. Vancouver: Alcuin Society, 1967, pp. 7-11.

Manuscripts

4283   University of British Columbia Library, Vancouver.

Wilson, Ethel

SECONDARY MATERIAL

Bibliography

4284   McComb, Bonnie Martyn, comp. "Ethel Wilson: A Bibliography 1919-1977, Part I." WEST COAST REVIEW, 14 (June 1979), 38-43; "Part II," 14 (Oct. 1979), 49-57; "Part III," 14 (Jan. 1980), 58-64; "Part IV, Conclusion," 15 (June 1980), 67-72.

Criticism

4285   Birbalsingh, Frank M. "Ethel Wilson: Innocent Traveller." CANADIAN LITERATURE, No. 49 (Sum. 1971), pp. 35-46.

4286   Davies, Barrie. "Lamia: The Allegorical Nature of Hetty Dorval." STUDIES IN CANADIAN LITERATURE, 1 (Wint. 1976), 137-40.

4287   Hinchcliffe, Peter M. "'To Keep the Memory of So Worthy a Friend': Ethel Wilson as an Elegist." JOURNAL OF CANADIAN FICTION, 2 (Spr. 1973), 62-67.

4288   Livesay, Dorothy. "Ethel Wilson: West Coast Novelist." SATURDAY NIGHT, 26 July 1953, pp. 2, 36.

4289   MacDonald, R.D. "Serious Whimsy." CANADIAN LITERATURE, No. 63 (Wint. 1975), pp. 40-51.

        Discusses HETTY DORVAL.

4290   MacKay, Constance. "Vancouver's New Novelist." MAYFAIR, Nov. 1947, pp. 67, 101.

4291   McLay, Catherine M. "The Initiation of Mrs. Golightly." JOURNAL OF CANADIAN FICTION, 1 (Sum. 1972), 52-55.

        Discusses "Mrs. Golightly and the First Convention."

4292   Mitchell, Beverley. "In Defense of Hetty Dorval." STUDIES IN CANADIAN LITERATURE, 1 (Wint. 1976), 26-48.

4293   _____. "'On the OTHER Side of the Mountains': The Westering Experience in the Fiction of Ethel Wilson." In WOMEN, WOMEN WRITERS, AND THE WEST. Ed. L.L. Lee and Merrill Lewis. Troy, N.Y.: Whitston, 1979, pp. 219-31.

4294 _____. "Ulysses in Vancouver: A Critical Approach to Ethel Wilson's 'Tuesday and Wednesday.'" ATLANTIS, 4 (Fall 1978), 111-22.

4295 New, William H. "The 'Genius' of Time and Place: The Fiction of Ethel Wilson." JOURNAL OF CANADIAN STUDIES, 3 (Nov. 1968), 39-48.

Reprinted in no. 173.

4296 _____. "The Irony of Order: Ethel Wilson's THE INNOCENT TRAVELLER." CRITIQUE, 10, No. 3 (1968), 22-30.

Reprinted in no. 173.

4297 Pacey, Desmond. ETHEL WILSON. Twayne's World Authors, 33. New York: Twayne, 1967. 194 p. Bibliog. Index.

4298 _____. "Ethel Wilson's First Novel." CANADIAN LITERATURE, No. 29 (Sum. 1966), pp. 43-55.

4299 _____. "The Innocent Eye: The Art of Ethel Wilson." QUEEN'S QUARTERLY, 61 (Spr. 1954), 42-52.

Reprinted in no. 177.

4300 _____. Introd., SWAMP ANGEL. New Canadian Library, no. 29. Toronto: McClelland and Stewart, 1962, pp. 5-10.

4301 Sonthoff, Helen W. "The Novels of Ethel Wilson." CANADIAN LITERATURE, No. 26 (Aut. 1965), pp. 33-42.

4302 _____. "The Stories of Wilson & Engel." CANADIAN LITERATURE, No. 86 (Aut. 1980), pp. 148-52.

4303 Stouck, David. "Ethel Wilson's Novels." CANADIAN LITERATURE, No. 74 (Aut. 1977), pp. 74-88.

4304 Urbas, Jeannette. "Equations and Flutes." JOURNAL OF CANADIAN FICTION, 1 (Spr. 1972), 69-73.

Discusses Wilson and Gabrielle Roy.

4305 _____. "The Perquisites of Love." CANADIAN LITERATURE, No. 59 (Wint. 1974), pp. 6-15.

Reprinted in no. 5113.

4306   Watters, Reginald Eyre. "Ethel Wilson, The Experienced Traveller."
        BRITISH COLUMBIA LIBRARY QUARTERLY, 21 (Apr. 1958), 21-27.

4307   Whitaker, Muriel. "Ethel Wilson at Lac Le Jeune." CANADIAN LIT-
        ERATURE, No. 86 (Aut. 1980), pp. 143-48.

For criticism on Wilson, see also nos. 168, 4196, and 5180.

Book Reviews

4308   HETTY DORVAL: CULTURE, 9 (June 1948), 214-15; DR, 27 (Oct. 1947),
        373; NYTBR, 14 Sept. 1947, p. 16; UTQ, 17 (Apr. 1948), 272.

4309   THE INNOCENT TRAVELLER: CFor, 29 (Dec. 1949), 214; DR, 29
        (Jan. 1950), 461; SatN, 11 Oct. 1949, p. 46; SatR, 10 Dec. 1949,
        p. 17; UTQ, 19 (Apr. 1950), 275.

4310   THE EQUATIONS OF LOVE: CFor, 32 (Aug. 1952), 117; LISTENER,
        27 Mar. 1952, p. 525; NoR, 6 (June-July 1953), 36-40; NYTBR, 3
        May 1953, p. 5; SatN, 5 Apr. 1952, p. 28; SatR, 16 May 1953, p.
        42; SPECTATOR, 21 Mar. 1952, p. 378; UTQ, 22 (Apr. 1953), 288-
        90, 292.

4311   SWAMP ANGEL: CFor, 34 (Feb. 1955), 263; LISTENER, 19 Aug. 1954,
        p. 295; NYTBR, 29 Aug. 1954, p. 17; QQ, 61 (Wint. 1954-55), 555-
        56; SatR, 4 Sept. 1954, p. 22; UTQ, 24 (Apr. 1954), 263.

4312   LOVE AND SALT WATER: QQ, 64 (Spr. 1957), 143-44; TamR, 2 (Wint.
        1957), 71-72; TLS, 5 Oct. 1956, p. 581; UTQ, 26 (Apr. 1957), 316-17.

4313   MRS. GOLIGHTLY: BCLQ, 26 (Oct. 1962), 29, 31; CanL, 11 (Wint.
        1962), 67-68; MONTREALER, 36 (May 1962), 40-41; SatN, 28 Oct.
        1961, pp. 41-42; TamR, 22 (Wint. 1962), 95-96; TLS, 19 Jan. 1962,
        p. 37; UTQ, 31 (July 1962), 472.

WISEMAN, ADELE (1928--)

Adele Wiseman was born in Winnipeg, received a B.A. from the University of Manitoba, acted as executive secretary for the Winnipeg Ballet, did social work in London, England, taught school in Italy, and travelled to the Far East. She taught English at Macdonald College (McGill University), and at Sir George Williams University, Montreal. THE SACRIFICE, the moving portrayal of a Jewish immigrant's adjustment to a new life, won numerous awards including the Beta Sigma Phi Award and Governor General's Award.

PRIMARY MATERIAL

Monographs

FICTION

4314   THE SACRIFICE: A NOVEL. Toronto: Macmillan, 1956. 346 p.

4315   CRACKPOT: A NOVEL. Toronto: McClelland and Stewart, 1974. 300 p.

NONFICTION PROSE

4316   OLD MARKETS, NEW WORLD. Drawings by Joe Rosenthal. Toronto: Macmillan, 1964. 64 p.

4317   OLD WOMAN AT PLAY. Toronto: Clarke, Irwin, 1978. 148 p.

DRAMA

4318   TESTIMONIAL DINNER. Erin, Ont.: Porcépic, 1976. 80 p.

Shorter Work

SHORT STORY

4319   "Duel in the Kitchen." MACLEAN'S, 7 Jan. 1961, pp. 22-23, 74, 76-79.

ARTICLES

4320   "English Writing in Canada: The Future." PROCEEDINGS AND TRANS-ACTIONS OF THE ROYAL SOCIETY OF CANADA, 4th ser., 5 (1967), 45-50.

4321   "A Brief Anatomy of an Honest Attempt at a Pithy Statement about the Impact of the Manitoba Environment on my Development as an Artist." MOSAIC, 3 (Spr. 1970), 98-106.

SECONDARY MATERIAL

Criticism

4322   Freedman, Adele. "The Stubborn Ethnicity of Adele W.: Wiseman's Novels Speak Out for Everyone Who's Tempted to Sell Out the Past to Gain Acceptance. What Else Could You Expect from a Daughter of Winnipeg's North End?" SATURDAY NIGHT, 91 (May 1976), 23-28.

4323   Greenstein, M. "Movement and Vision in THE SACRIFICE." CANA-DIAN LITERATURE, No. 80 (Spr. 1979), pp. 23-36.

4324   Landsberg, M. "Adele Wiseman." CHATELAINE, 50 (Oct. 1977), 123, 125.

4325   Morley, Patricia. "Artist at Play: Wiseman's Theory of Creativity." ATLANTIS, 6, No. 1 (1980), 104-09.

4326   _____. "Wiseman's Fiction: Out of Pain, Joy." ÉTUDES CANADIENNES/CANADIAN STUDIES, 4 (1978), 41-50.

4327   Mullins, Stanley G. "Traditional Symbolism in Adele Wiseman's THE SACRIFICE." CULTURE, 19 (Sept. 1958), 287-97.

4328   Sherman, Kenneth. "CRACKPOT: A Lurianic Myth." WAVES, 3 (Aut. 1974), 5-10.

For criticism on Wiseman, see also nos. 131, 197, 430, and 2301.

Book Reviews

4329 THE SACRIFICE: CFor, 36 (Feb. 1957), 264; COMMONWEAL, 21
Sept. 1956, p. 616; NewR, 12 Nov. 1956, pp. 20-21; NY, 29 Sept.
1956, p. 153; NYTBR, 16 Sept. 1956, p. 4; QQ, 63 (Wint. 1956-57),
632; SatN, 13 Oct. 1956, p. 29; SatR, 15 Sept. 1956, p. 20; TamR,
2 (Wint. 1957), 72-73; TLS, 9 Nov. 1956, p. 661; UTQ, 26 (Apr. 1957),
312, 317-18.

4330 CRACKPOT: ALIVE, 41 ([1975]), 35; BCan, 3 (Nov. 1974), 9-11;
CanL, 64 (Spr. 1975), 115-18; CFM, 19 (Aut. 1975), 99-102; CRead,
15, No. 10 ([1974]), 2-3; ECW, 1 (Wint. 1974), 56-59; JCF, 16 (1976),
158-62; MACLEAN'S, 87 (Oct. 1974), 110; Q&Q, 40, No. 11 (1974),
20; QUARRY, 24 (Wint. 1975), 71-72; TamR, 65 (Mar. 1975), 91-93;
UTQ, 44 (Sum. 1975), 304-05; WAVES, 3 (Aut. 1974), 5-10.

WRIGHT, RICHARD (1937--)

Born in Midland, Ontario, Richard Bruce Wright worked as a sales manager for the Macmillan Publishing Company in Toronto in the sixties and then moved to Peterborough, Ontario. His first novels explore with humor and sympathy the vacillations and impasses of middle-class suburbanites; with FARTHING'S FORTUNES, Wright turns to the lively and less-structured genre of the picaresque novel.

PRIMARY MATERIAL

Monographs

FICTION

4331 ANDREW TOLLIVER. Illus. Lewis Parker. Buckskin Books, no. 11. Toronto: Macmillan, 1965. 105 p.

For children.

4332 THE WEEKEND MAN: A NOVEL. Toronto: Macmillan, 1970. 261 p.

4333 IN THE MIDDLE OF A LIFE: A NOVEL. Toronto: Macmillan, 1973. 305 p.

4334 FARTHING'S FORTUNES. Toronto: Macmillan, 1976. xiv, 333 p.

4335 FINAL THINGS. Toronto: Macmillan, 1980. 145 p.

EDITED WORK

4336 EIGHT MEN SPEAK AND OTHER PLAYS FROM THE CANADIAN WORKERS' THEATRE. Ed. Richard Bruce Wright and Robin Endres. Introd. Robin Endres. Toronto: New Hogtown, 1976. xxxvi, 147 p.

SECONDARY MATERIAL

Criticism

4337 Campbell, Sheila. "The Two Wes Wakehams: Point of View in THE
WEEKEND MAN." STUDIES IN CANADIAN LITERATURE, 2 (Sum. 1977),
289-305.

4338 _____. "Wes Wakeham and the Masculine Mystique." ROOM OF
ONE'S OWN, 1, No. 4 (1975), 26-32.

4339 Doyle, James. "'Any Modern City': The Urban Canadian Fiction of
Richard B. Wright." In THE PRACTICAL VISION: ESSAYS IN ENGLISH
LITERATURE IN HONOR OF FLORA ROY. Ed. Jane Campbell and
James Doyle. Waterloo, Ont.: Wilfrid Laurier University Press, 1978,
pp. 151-63.

4340 Gibson, Shirley. "Life to Wright . . . Or the Observer Observed.
Five Revealing Hours with Canada's Proud, Gun-Shy Comic Novelist."
BOOKS IN CANADA, 5 (Dec. 1976), 8-10.

Book Reviews

4341 THE WEEKEND MAN: CanL, 51 (Wint. 1972), 91-92; FIDDLEHEAD,
95 (Fall 1972), 110-13; NewR, 29 May 1971, p. 37; NY, 12 June
1971, p. 114; PrS, 45 (Fall 1971), 268; QUARRY, 22 (Wint. 1973),
77-78; SatN, 93 (May 1978), 40-41; SatR, 3 July 1971, p. 19; TLS,
2 Apr. 1971, p. 369.

4342 IN THE MIDDLE OF A LIFE: Atl, 232 (Dec. 1973), 126; BCan, 2
(Nov. 1973), 26-27; HudR, 25 (Wint. 1973-74), 778; JCF, 3 (Wint.
1974), 114-15; LISTENER, 16 May 1974, p. 641; MACLEAN'S, 86
(Nov. 1973), 118; NYTBR, 23 Sept. 1973, p. 7; NYTBR, 2 Dec. 1973,
p. 76; QQ, 81 (Wint. 1974), 637-39; SatN, 88 (Nov. 1973), 35-36;
TamR, 63 (Oct. 1974), 85-87, TLS, 15 Feb. 1974, p. 149.

4343 FARTHING'S FORTUNES: BCan, 5 (Oct. 1976), 10-11; CanL, 72
(Spr. 1977), 69-71; CBRA, 1976, pp. 141-42; CFor, 56 (Dec. 1976),
53; ECW, 6 (Spr. 1977), 122-24; FIDDLEHEAD, 112 (Wint. 1977), 141-
42; IFR, 4 (July 1977), 194-95; MACLEAN'S, 18 Oct. 1976, p. 76;
NYTBR, 2 Jan. 1977, p. 12; Q&Q, 42, No. 15 (1976), 32; QUARRY,
26 (Spr. 1977), 52-53; SatN, 91 (Nov. 1976), 50-52; UTQ, 46 (Sum.
1977), 348-50.

4344 FINAL THINGS: BCan, 9 (Nov. 1980), 12; MACLEAN'S, 17 Nov.
1980, pp. 70, 72; NYTBR, 14 Dec. 1980, p. 10; Q&Q, 46 (Dec. 1980),
29.

B. NONFICTION PROSE

BELANEY, ARCHIBALD STANSFELD
[GREY OWL] (1888-1938)

Better known in his life by his Indian names of Grey Owl or Wa-Sha-Quon-Asin, Archibald Stansfeld Belaney was actually born and raised in Hastings, England. He came to Canada in 1906. After working in northern Ontario as a trapper, guide, and ranger and living among the Ojibway Indians, he adopted an Indian identity, claiming Scottish-Indian parentage. Belaney served as a sniper in World War I. In 1928, partly through the influence of Gertrude Barnard (Anahareo), he rejected trapping; his prose efforts to create an understanding of wildlife, and his two tours of England generated considerable popular acclaim.

PRIMARY MATERIAL

Monographs

NONFICTION PROSE

4345   THE MEN OF THE LAST FRONTIER. London: Country Life, 1931. viii, 253 p.

4346   PILGRIMS OF THE WILD. London: Lovat Dickson, 1934. xxii, 281 p.

4347   THE ADVENTURES OF SAJO AND HER BEAVER PEOPLE. Toronto: Macmillan, 1935, xix, 256 p.; rpt. as SAJO AND THE BEAVER PEOPLE. New York: Scribner, 1936. 187 p.

    For children.

4348   TALES OF AN EMPTY CABIN. Toronto: Macmillan 1936. xvi, 335 p.

4349   A BIOGRAPHICAL NOTE, AND A DAY AT BEAVER LODGE. London: Lovat Dickson, 1937. 13 p.

4350   THE TREE. Toronto: Macmillan, 1937. 62 p.

    An excerpt from TALES OF AN EMPTY CABIN.

4351   A BOOK OF GREY OWL: PAGES FROM THE WRITINGS OF WA-SHA-QUON-ASIN. Ed. E.E. Reynolds. Preface by Lovat Dickson. London: Peter Davies, 1938. xvi, 324 p.

4352   FAREWELL TO THE CHILDREN OF THE BRITISH ISLES. London: Lovat Dickson, 1938. N. pag.

4353   BEAVERS: PAGES FROM THE WRITINGS OF GREY OWL. Ed. E.E. Reynolds. Illus. Stuart Tresilian. Cambridge: Cambridge University Press, 1940. 127 p. Also as ON THE TRAIL: PAGES FROM THE WRITINGS OF GREY OWL. Horizon Readers. Cambridge: Cambridge University Press, 1940. 126 p.

4354   CRY OF THE ANCIENTS. By Grey Owl and Little Pigeon. Illus. Daniel Nicholas. Independence, Mo.: Herald Publishing House, 1974. 207 p. Bibliog.

Manuscripts

4355   Public Archives of Canada, Ottawa.

SECONDARY MATERIAL

Criticism

4356   Bernard, Gertrude [Anahareo, pseud.]. DEVIL IN DEERSKINS: MY LIFE WITH GREY OWL. Toronto: New, 1972. vii, 190 p. Also as GREY OWL AND I: A NEW AUTOBIOGRAPHY. London: Peter Davies, 1972. x, 190 p.

4357   _____. MY LIFE WITH GREY OWL. London: Peter Davies, 1940. x, 230 p.

4358   Cory, Harper. GREY OWL AND THE BEAVER PEOPLE: WITH AN AC-COUNT OF BEAVER ACTIVITIES BY GREY OWL, WRITTEN FOR THE NATIONAL PARKS OF CANADA AND REPRINTED BY THEIR PERMIS-SION. London: Thomas Nelson and Sons, 1935. 144 p.

4359   Dickson, Lovat. "The Double Identity: The Growth of the Grey Owl Myth." CANADA, 1 (Spr. 1974), 1-8.

4360   _____. HALF-BREED: THE STORY OF GREY OWL (WA-SHA-QUON-ASIN). London: Peter Davies, 1939. viii, 345 p.

4361 _____. WILDERNESS MAN: THE STRANGE STORY OF GREY OWL.
Toronto: Macmillan, 1973. 283 p. Bibliog. Index. Also as WIL-
DERNESS MAN: THE CURIOUS LIFE OF ARCHIE BELANEY, CALLED
GREY OWL. New York: Atheneum.

4362 _____, ed. THE GREEN LEAF: A TRIBUTE TO GREY OWL. London:
Lovat Dickson, 1938. 109 p.

Includes letters and writing by Belaney.

4363 Eayrs, Hugh. Foreword, PILGRIMS OF THE WILD. Toronto: Macmillan,
1934, pp. vii-xi.

4364 _____. Introd., A BOOK OF GREY OWL. Toronto: Macmillan,
1938, pp. ix-xxi.

4365 Godard, Barbara. "George Stansfeld Belaney (1888-1938), 'Grey Owl.'"
CANADIAN NOTES AND QUERIES, No. 10 (1972), p. 7.

4366 "Grey Owl Papers in National Archives Showing." CANADIAN COL-
LECTOR, 15 (July-Aug. 1980), 53.

4367 Leitch, A. "Trail to an Empty Cabin." CANADIAN AUDUBON, 23
(Sept.-Oct. 1961), 120-23.

4368 Polk, James. "Grey Owl." In his WILDERNESS WRITERS. Toronto:
Clarke, Irwin, 1972, pp. 100-147.

4369 Rashley, R.E. "Grey Owl and the Authentic Frontier." ENGLISH
QUARTERLY, 4 (Fall 1971), 58-64.

4370 Smith, Donald B. "'Grey Owl.'" ONTARIO HISTORY, 63 (Sept. 1971),
160-76.

For criticism on Belaney, see also nos. 3631 and 4351.

Book Reviews

4371 THE MEN OF THE LAST FRONTIER: CBRA, 1976, p. 69; JCF, 1 (Sum.
1972), 82-83; SatR, 28 May 1932, p. 757; TLS, 10 Mar. 1932, p. 163.

4372 PILGRIMS OF THE WILD: CHR, 16 (June 1935), 199; SatR, 20 July
1935, p. 19; TLS, 14 Feb. 1935, p. 95; TLS, 6 Apr. 1973, p. 378.

4373   THE ADVENTURES OF SAJO AND HER BEAVER PEOPLE: TLS, 19 Sept.
       1935, p. 577; TLS, 30 Nov. 1935, p. 807; UTQ, 5 (Apr. 1936), 368–
       69.

4374   TALES OF AN EMPTY CABIN: JCF, 1 (Sum. 1972), 82–83; TLS, 24
       Oct. 1936, p. 850; UTQ, 6 (Apr. 1937), 358–60.

BERTON, PIERRE (1920--)

Born in Whitehorse in the Yukon Territories and educated at the University of British Columbia, Pierre Berton is one of Canada's best known journalists. Between 1942 and 1947, he served on two Vancouver newspapers (becoming Canada's youngest city editor) and in the Canadian Infantry Corps in World War II. In 1947 he joined MACLEAN'S magazine, becoming managing editor in 1953 and staying with that magazine until 1958 when he began a four-year stint as associate editor and columnist with the TORONTO STAR. Berton is known also as a panelist, and radio and television host and commentator.

MYSTERIOUS NORTH, KLONDIKE, and THE LAST SPIKE received Governor General's Awards; JUST ADD WATER received the Leacock Medal for Humour; and in 1961, Berton received the National Newspaper Award for Feature Writing and Staff Corresponding. His work records significant events from the Canadian past for a general audience.

PRIMARY MATERIAL

Monographs

NONFICTION PROSE

4375 THE GOLDEN TRAIL: THE STORY OF THE KLONDIKE RUSH. Great Stories of Canada. Illus. Duncan MacPherson. Toronto: Macmillan, 1954. 147 p.

    For children.

4376 THE ROYAL FAMILY: THE STORY OF THE BRITISH MONARCHY FROM VICTORIA TO ELIZABETH. Toronto: McClelland and Stewart, 1954. viii, 273 p. Bibliog.

4377 THE MYSTERIOUS NORTH. Toronto: McClelland and Stewart, 1956. 345, xiv p. Index.

4378 "A Klondike Bibliography." Mimeographed. Kleinberg, Ont.: n.p., 1958. 23 p.

4379 KLONDIKE: THE LIFE AND DEATH OF THE LAST GREAT GOLD RUSH. Toronto: McClelland and Stewart, 1958. viii, 457, xix p. Bibliog. Index.; rpt. as KLONDIKE FEVER: THE LIFE AND DEATH OF THE LAST GREAT GOLD RUSH. New York: A.A. Knopf, 1959. viii, 457 p. Bibliog.; rev. ed. KLONDIKE: THE GREAT GOLD RUSH, 1896-1899. Toronto: McClelland and Stewart, 1972. xxiii, 472 p. Bibliog.

4380 JUST ADD WATER AND STIR. [Toronto]: McClelland and Stewart, 1959. 222 p.

4381 ADVENTURES OF A COLUMNIST. Toronto: McClelland and Stewart, 1960. 211 p.

4382 THE NEW CITY: A PREJUDICED VIEW OF TORONTO. Photos. Henri Rossier. Toronto: Macmillan, 1961. 137 p.

4383 THE SECRET WORLD OF OG. Illus. William Winters. Toronto: McClelland and Stewart, 1961. 146 p.

   For children.

4384 FAST FAST FAST RELIEF. Illus. George Feyer. Toronto: McClelland and Stewart, 1962. 185 p.

4385 THE BIG SELL: AN INTRODUCTION TO THE BLACK ARTS OF DOOR-TO-DOOR SALESMANSHIP & OTHER TECHNIQUES. Toronto: McClelland and Stewart, 1963. 239 p.

4386 THE COMFORTABLE PEW: A CRITICAL LOOK AT CHRISTIANITY AND THE RELIGIOUS ESTABLISHMENT IN THE NEW AGE. Foreword Ernest Wilfred Harrison. Toronto: McClelland and Stewart, 1965. 158 p. Index.

4387 MY WAR WITH THE TWENTIETH CENTURY. Cartoons by the Author. Foreword Al Capp. Garden City, N.Y.: Doubleday, 1965. x, 198 p.

4388 REMEMBER YESTERDAY: A CENTURY OF PHOTOGRAPHS. Canadian Centennial Library. Toronto: Canadian Centennial Publishing, 1965. 127 p.

4389 THE COOL, CRAZY, COMMITTED WORLD OF THE SIXTIES: TWENTY-ONE TELEVISION ENCOUNTERS. Toronto: McClelland and Stewart, 1966. xvii, 217 p.

4390 THE CENTENNIAL FOOD GUIDE: A CENTURY OF GOOD EATING. By Pierre Berton and Janet Berton. Toronto: Canadian Centennial Publishing, 1966. 123 p. Index. Rev. ed. PIERRE & JANET BERTON'S CANADIAN FOOD GUIDE. Toronto: McClelland and Stewart, 1974. 136 p. Index.

4391 THE SMUG MINORITY. Toronto: McClelland and Stewart, 1968. 160 p.

4392 THE NATIONAL DREAM: THE GREAT RAILWAY, 1871-1881. Toronto: McClelland and Stewart, 1970. xiii, 439 p.

    See no. 4393.

4393 THE LAST SPIKE: THE GREAT RAILWAY, 1881-1885. Toronto: McClelland and Stewart, 1971. xii, 478 p.

    THE NATIONAL DREAM and THE LAST SPIKE were reprinted together as THE IMPOSSIBLE RAILWAY: THE BUILDING OF THE CANADIAN PACIFIC (New York: A.A. Knopf, 1972, xx, 574, xvii p.). There was an abridged edition, with photographs by Michael Reichmann: THE NATIONAL DREAM: THE LAST SPIKE (Toronto: McClelland and Stewart, 1974, 511 p., index).

4394 DRIFTING HOME. Toronto: McClelland and Stewart, 1973. 174 p.

4395 THE EXODUS OF THE JAPANESE: STORIES FROM THE PIERRE BERTON SHOW. By Pierre Berton and Janice Patton. Toronto: McClelland and Stewart, 1973. 47 p.

4396 HOW THE DEPRESSION HIT THE WEST. By Pierre Berton and Janice Patton. Toronto: McClelland and Stewart, 1973. 48 p.

4397 HOLLYWOOD'S CANADA: THE AMERICANIZATION OF OUR NATIONAL IMAGE. Toronto: McClelland and Stewart, 1975. 303 p. Index.

4398 MY COUNTRY: THE REMARKABLE PAST. Toronto: McClelland and Stewart, 1976. 320 p. Index.

4399 CANADA: PICTURES OF A GREAT LAND. By Pierre Berton et al. Produced by Jürgen F. Boden and Hans Scherz. Photos. Peter d'Angelo et al. San Francisco: Chronicle Books, 1976. 214 p.

4400 THE DIONNE YEARS: A THIRTIES MELODRAMA. Toronto: McClelland and Stewart, 1977. 232 p. Bibliog. Index.

4401 THE CRYSTAL GARDENS: WEST COAST PLEASURE PALACE. By Pierre Berton et al. Victoria, B.C.: Crystal Gardens Preservation Society, 1977. 120 p.

4402 THE WILD FRONTIER: MORE TALES FROM THE REMARKABLE PAST. Toronto: McClelland and Stewart, 1978. 250 p. Bibliog. Index.

4403 THE INVASION OF CANADA: 1812-1813. Toronto: McClelland and Stewart, 1980. 363 p. Bibliog. Index.

4404 FLAMES ACROSS THE BORDER, 1813-1814. Toronto: McClelland and Stewart, 1981. 492 p.

EDITED WORK

4405 GREAT CANADIANS: A CENTURY OF ACHIEVEMENT. Selected by Vincent Massey et al. Illus. Franklin Arbuckle. Canadian Centennial Library. Toronto: Canadian Centennial Publishing, 1965. 122 p.

4406 HISTORIC HEADLINES: A CENTURY OF CANADIAN NEWS DRAMAS. Canadian Illustrated Library. Toronto: McClelland and Stewart, 1967. 128 p. Bibliog.

4407 VOICES FROM THE SIXTIES: TWENTY-TWO VIEWS OF A REVOLUTIONARY DECADE. Garden City, N.Y.: Doubleday, 1967. xviii, 242 p.

Shorter Work

ARTICLES

4408 "The Function of a Magazine." ONTARIO LIBRARY REVIEW, 37 (Aug. 1953), 171-75.

4409 "Gold Rush Writing: The Literature of the Klondike." CANADIAN LITERATURE, No. 4 (Spr. 1960), pp. 59-67.

4410 "Whither the Press and Periodicals?" In THE ARTS AS COMMUNICATION. Ed. David Carlton Williams. Toronto: University of Toronto Press, 1962, pp. 35-54.

4411 "Stand Clear! Here Comes a Writer, Writing." MACLEAN'S, 83 (Sept. 1970), 45-48, 51.

4412 "The Way of One Writer: Pierre Berton." CANADIAN LIBRARY JOURNAL, 31 (Oct. 1974), 406-09.

   Discusses THE NATIONAL DREAM and THE LAST SPIKE.

Manuscripts

4413   McMaster University Library, Hamilton.

SECONDARY MATERIAL

Criticism

4414   Berton, Laura Beatrice, et al. "'Man of the Century.'" CANADIAN
AUTHOR AND BOOKMAN, 42 (Sum. 1967), 8-9.

4415   Byfield, Edward Bartlett. JUST THINK, MR. BERTON, (A LITTLE HARDER).
Illus. Peter Kuch. Foreword William Pollard. Winnipeg: Company of
the Cross, 1965. 149 p.

>   Reply to THE COMFORTABLE PEW.

4416   Forrest, A.C. "A Churchman Talks Back to Critic Pierre Berton." MAC-
LEAN'S, 6 Feb. 1965, pp. 16-17, 32-33.

>   Reply to THE COMFORTABLE PEW.

4417   Franklin, Stephen. "Can You Make a Million Writing Canadian Books?"
FINANCIAL POST, 74 (Oct. 1980), 80-82, 87-88.

4418   Hofsess, John. "Pierre Berton." In his INNER VIEWS: TEN CANA-
DIAN FILM-MAKERS. Toronto: McGraw-Hill Ryerson, 1975, pp.
159-71.

4419   _____. "The Second Last Spike: On Location with Pierre Berton."
MACLEAN'S, 87 (Mar. 1974), 30-31, 48, 50.

4420   Katz, Sidney. "Pierre's Adventures in Bertonland." MACLEAN'S, 20
Oct. 1962, pp. 19-21, 80, 82, 84, 86, 89.

4421   Kilbourn, William, ed. THE RESTLESS CHURCH: A RESPONSE TO THE
COMFORTABLE PEW. Toronto: McClelland and Stewart, 1966. 196 p.

4422   MacDonald, David. "Popular, Prodigious Pierre Berton." READER'S
DIGEST (Canada), 117 (Oct. 1980), 133-34, 136, 138, 140.

4423   Myers, Jay. "'I Just Call Myself a Writer'--An Interview with Pierre
Berton." CANADIAN AUTHOR AND BOOKMAN, 54 (Oct. 1978),
20-23. Bibliog.

4424 Robson, E.W., and M.M. Robson. TERMITES IN THE SHAPE OF MEN: COMMONSENSE VERSUS MR. BERTON. Vancouver: North Star Books, [1966]. 159 p.

Reply to THE COMFORTABLE PEW.

4425 Sigman, Joseph. "Pierre Berton and the Romantic Tradition." CANADIAN CHILDREN'S LITERATURE, No. 7 (1977), pp. 21-27.

Discusses THE SECRET WORLD OF OG.

For criticism on Berton, see also nos. 4386-87.

Book Reviews

4426 THE GOLDEN TRAIL: BCan, 4 (Mar. 1975), 15.

4427 THE ROYAL FAMILY: NYTBR, 7 Mar. 1954, p. 10.

4428 THE MYSTERIOUS NORTH: CFor, 36 (May 1956), 40-41; DR, 36 (Wint. 1957), 423; QQ, 64 (Spr. 1957), 132-33; SatR, 10 May 1956, p. 20; UTQ, 26 (Apr. 1957), 369.

4429 KLONDIKE: BCan, 1 (Oct. 1972), 15; CanL, 61 (Sum. 1974), 124; DR, 39 (Spr. 1959), 133, 135; SatR, 8 Nov. 1958, p. 21; SPECTATOR, 29 Apr. 1960, p. 634; TLS, 6 May 1960, p. 290; UTQ, 28 (Apr. 1959), 440-41.

4430 JUST ADD WATER AND STIR: BCLQ, 23 (Jan. 1960), 33-34; SatN, 5 Dec. 1959, pp. 44-45; UTQ, 29 (July 1960), 499.

4431 ADVENTURES OF A COLUMNIST: SatN, 10 Dec. 1960, p. 58; UTQ, 30 (July 1961), 426-27.

4432 THE NEW CITY: CanL, 11 (Wint. 1962), 77-78; SatN, 23 Dec. 1961, p. 32; TamR, 22 (Wint. 1962), 93-94.

4433 FAST FAST FAST RELIEF: BCLQ, 27 (Oct. 1963), 33; CAB, 38 (Wint. 1962), 9; SatN, 77 (Dec. 1962), 35-36; UTQ, 32 (July 1963), 425-26.

4434 THE BIG SELL: NYTBR, 17 Nov. 1963, p. 61; UTQ, 33 (July 1964), 429-30.

4435 THE COMFORTABLE PEW: BCLQ, 28 (Jan. 1965), 19, 21; CAB, 40 (Spr. 1965), 11; CFor, 44 (Feb. 1965), 261-63; SatN, 80 (Feb. 1965), 11-13; SatN, 80 (Apr. 1965), 20; TamR, 35 (Spr. 1965), 80-86; UTQ, 35 (July 1966), 454-55.

4436   MY WAR WITH THE TWENTIETH CENTURY: NYTBR, 2 May 1965, p. 43.

4437   THE COOL, CRAZY, COMMITTED WORLD OF THE SIXTIES: SatN, 81 (Nov. 1966), 58, 65.

4438   THE SMUG MINORITY: AtlA, 58 (Mar. 1968), 78; CanL, 39 (Wint. 1969), 103; CFor, 47 (Mar. 1968), 281-82; NYTBR, 10 Aug. 1969, p. 28.

4439   THE NATIONAL DREAM: AHR, 77 (Apr. 1972), 600; AIHR, 19 (Spr. 1971), 31; AtlA, 61 (Oct. 1970), 60; BCLQ, 34 (Apr. 1971), 75; CFor, 50 (Nov. 1970), 270-72; CGJ, 83 (Spr. 1971), ix; CHR, 52 (Dec. 1971), 435-37; DR, 50 (Wint. 1970-71), 563-65; GeoJ, 137 (June 1971), 235; IJ, 26 (Wint. 1970-71), 278-79; NATION, 31 May 1971, p. 696; QQ, 78 (Sum. 1971), 327-28; QQ, 80 (Spr. 1973), 143-44; SaskH, 24 (Wint. 1971), 34-35; SatN, 85 (Nov. 1970), 39, 45, 47.

4440   THE LAST SPIKE: AntigR, 8 (Wint. 1972), 103-04; AIHR, 20 (Wint. 1972), 29; AtlA, 62 (Jan. 1972), 54-55; BCan, 1 (Oct. 1971), 1-2, 10; BCan, 8 (Apr. 1979), 18; CFor, 51 (Jan. 1972), 71-72; CGJ, 85 (Oct. 1972), iv-v, viii; CHR, 53 (Dec. 1972), 453-55; DR, 52 (Spr. 1972), 140-42; GeoJ, 138 (June 1972), 240; MACLEAN'S, 84 (Nov. 1971), 108; PacA, Sum. 1972, p. 326; QQ, 80 (Spr. 1973), 143-44; SatN, 86 (Nov. 1971), 52, 54-56.

4441   THE GREAT RAILWAY: BCan, 1 (Oct. 1972), 15.

4442   THE IMPOSSIBLE RAILWAY: JAH, 60 (June 1973), 188; NYTBR, 12 Nov. 1972, p. 48; SatR, 2 Dec. 1972, p. 82.

4443   DRIFTING HOME: AtlA, 64 (Oct. 1973), 43; BCan, 2 (Nov. 1973), 16-17; UWR, 10 (Spr. 1975), 90-91.

4444   HOLLYWOOD'S CANADA: AtlA, 68 [66] (Feb. 1976), 63; BCan, 4 (Nov. 1975), 3-7; CanL, 75 (Wint. 1977), 93-94; CanR, 2 (Christmas 1975), 25-27; CBRA, 1975, p. 67; CFor, 55 (Feb. 1976), 31-32; CHR, 58 (June 1977), 231-32; JQ, 53 (Wint. 1976), 769; MACLEAN'S, 6 Oct. 1975, pp. 92, 94; QQ, 85 (Aut. 1976), 504-05; SatN, 90 (Oct. 1975), 71-72.

4445   MY COUNTRY: BCan, 5 (Dec. 1976), 12, 14; BCan, 8 (Nov. 1979), 28; CBRA, 1976, p. 262; Q&Q, 42, No. 14 (1976), 8.

4446   Entry deleted.

4447   THE DIONNE YEARS: BCan, 6 (Aug. 1977), 12-13; CRead, 18 (Aug. 1977), 2-4; MACLEAN'S, 19 Sept. 1977, pp. 79-80; NewR, 23 Sept. 1978, pp. 38-39; NYRB, 26 Oct. 1978, p. 53; NYTBR, 10 Dec. 1978, p. 16; Q&Q, 43, No. 12 (1977), 8; SatN, 92 (Oct. 1977), 59-60, 62-63.

4448   THE WILD FRONTIER: BCan, 7 (Dec. 1978), 12; BCan, 9 (Aug. 1980), 34; CHR, 60 (Sept. 1979), 364-65; MACLEAN'S, 18 Sept. 1978, p. 75; Q&Q, 44, No. 13 (1978), 12; SatN, 93 (Nov. 1978), 55-56.

4449   THE INVASION OF CANADA: BCan, 9 (Aug. 1980), 7-8; MACLEAN'S, 15 Sept. 1980, pp. 54, 56; Q&Q, 46 (Sept. 1980), 64; SatN, 95 (Sept. 1980), 55-56.

CARR, EMILY (1871-1945)

Emily Carr is primarily a significant and original Canadian painter and secondarily a writer. After growing up in Victoria, British Columbia, she studied art in San Francisco (1889-92), England (1899-1904)--where she spent months in a sanatorium--and France (1910-11). Unrecognized as a painter, she gave up art from 1913 to 1927 to support herself running a boarding house, selling fruit and handicrafts, and raising animals. Stimulated by the Canadian Group of Seven painters and by greater national interest in her work, she then began travelling to remote parts of the British Columbia coast, painting the totem poles, people, and landscape. In her seventies, when failing health prohibited travel, she turned to writing, producing conversational accounts of her experience. The first of these, KLEE WYCK, won her a Governor General's Award in 1941.

PRIMARY MATERIAL

Monographs

NONFICTION PROSE

4450   KLEE WYCK. Foreword Ira Dilworth. Toronto: Oxford University Press, 1941. xi, 155 p.

4451   THE BOOK OF SMALL. Toronto: Oxford University Press, 1942. viii, 245 p.; rpt. in two parts, each with a Foreword by Ira Dilworth: A LITTLE TOWN AND A LITTLE GIRL (Toronto: Clarke, Irwin, 1952, xvii, 124 p.) and THE BOOK OF SMALL (Toronto: Clarke, Irwin, 1952, xvii, 104 p.)

4452   THE HOUSE OF ALL SORTS. Toronto: Oxford University Press, 1944. vii, 222 p.

4453   EMILY CARR: HER PAINTINGS AND SKETCHES. Toronto: Oxford University Press for the National Gallery of Canada and the Art Gallery of Toronto, 1945. 64 p.

4454 GROWING PAINS: THE AUTOBIOGRAPHY OF EMILY CARR. Foreword Ira Dilworth. Toronto: Oxford University Press, 1946. xvi, 381 p.

4455 THE HEART OF A PEACOCK. Ed. Ira Dilworth. Line Drawings by the Author. Toronto: Oxford University Press, 1953. xv, 234 p.

4456 PAUSE: A SKETCH BOOK. Toronto: Clarke, Irwin, 1953. viii, 148 p.

4457 AN ADDRESS. Introd. Ira Dilworth. Toronto: Oxford University Press, 1955. ix, 13 p.

4458 HUNDREDS AND THOUSANDS: THE JOURNALS OF EMILY CARR. Toronto: Clarke, Irwin, 1966. x, 332 p.

4459 FRESH SEEING: TWO ADDRESSES. Preface by Doris Shadbolt. Introd. by Ira Dilworth to the 1930 Address. Toronto: Clark, Irwin, 1972. 38 p.

Shorter Work

ARTICLE

4460 "Letters from Emily Carr." Ed. Ruth Humphrey. UNIVERSITY OF TORONTO QUARTERLY, 41 (Wint. 1972), 93-150.

Manuscripts

4461 University of British Columbia Library.

SECONDARY MATERIAL

Bibliography

4462 Turpin, Marguerite, comp. THE LIFE AND WORK OF EMILY CARR (1871-1945): A SELECTED BIBLIOGRAPHY. Western Canadian Contributions to Librarianship, 2. Vancouver: School of Librarianship, University of British Columbia, 1965. 19 p.

Criticism

4463 Amsden, Philip. "Memories of Emily Carr." CANADIAN FORUM, 27 (Dec. 1947), 206-07.

4464 Burns, Flora Hamilton. "Emily Carr and the Newcombe Collection."
BEAVER, 293 (Sum. 1962), 27-35.

Also in no. 4474.

4465 _____. "Emily Carr: 1870-1945." In THE CLEAR SPIRIT: TWENTY
CANADIAN WOMEN AND THEIR TIMES. Ed. Mary Innis. Toronto:
University of Toronto Press, 1966, pp. 221-41.

4466 Entry deleted.

4467 Colman, M.E. "Emily Carr and Her Sisters." DALHOUSIE REVIEW,
27 (Apr. 1947), 29-32.

4468 Daniells, Roy. "Emily Carr." In OUR LIVING TRADITION: FOURTH
SERIES. Ed. Robert L. McDougall. Toronto: University of Toronto
Press, in association with Carleton University, 1962, pp. 119-34.

4469 Dilworth, Ira. Foreword, KLEE WYCK. Canadian Classics. Toronto:
Clarke, Irwin, 1951, pp. v-xvi.

4470 EMILY CARR: A CENTENNIAL EXHIBITION CELEBRATING THE ONE
HUNDREDTH ANNIVERSARY OF HER BIRTH. Organized by the Van-
couver Art Gallery. [Vancouver: Vancouver Art Gallery, 1971]. 96 p.
Bibliog. Rev. ed. Vancouver: J.J. Douglas, 1975. 96 p. Bibliog.

4471 Harris, Lawren. "Emily Carr and Her Work." CANADIAN FORUM,
21 (Dec. 1941), 277-78.

4472 Hembroff-Schleicher, Edythe. EMILY CARR: THE UNTOLD STORY.
Saanichton, B.C.: Hancock House, 1978. 408 p. Bibliog. Index.

4473 _____. M.E.: A PORTRAYAL OF EMILY CARR. Toronto: Clarke,
Irwin, 1969. 123 p.

4474 HUDSON'S BAY COMPANY PRESENTS THE WORLD OF EMILY CARR:
A NEW EXHIBITION OF HER PAINTINGS FROM THE NEWCOMBE COL-
LECTION RECENTLY ACQUIRED BY THE PROVINCE OF BRITISH CO-
LUMBIA. N.p.: n.p., 1962. 15 p.

Text is from no. 4464.

4475 Humphrey, Ruth. "Emily Carr: An Appreciation." QUEEN'S QUAR-
TERLY, 65 (Sum. 1958), 270-76.

4476   Kearley, Mark H. A FEW HINTS AND SUGGESTIONS ABOUT EMILY CARR AND HER WORK. Victoria: Federation of Canadian Artists, 1946.

4477   Livesay, Dorothy. "Carr & Livesay." CANADIAN LITERATURE, No. 84 (Spr. 1980), pp. 144-47.

4478   McDonald, John A. "Emily Carr: Painter as Writer." BRITISH CO- LUMBIA LIBRARY QUARTERLY, 22 (Apr. 1959), 17-23.

4479   Neering, Rosemary. EMILY CARR. The Canadians. Don Mills, Ont.: Fitzhenry and Whiteside, 1975. 61 p. Bibliog.

          Biography for children.

4480   Owen, Glyn. "Emily Carr." FIRST STATEMENT, 1, No. 17 (n.d.), 3-4.

4481   Pearson, Carol. EMILY CARR AS I KNEW HER. Foreword by Kathleen Coburn. Toronto: Clark, Irwin, 1954. x, 162 p.

4482   Shadbolt, Doris. THE ART OF EMILY CARR. Vancouver: Douglas and McIntyre, 1979. 223 p. Bibliog.

4483   _____. "Emily Carr: Legend and Reality." ARTSCANADA, 28 (June-July 1971), 17-21.

4484   Tatranic, Joe. "Genius Growing." BOOKS IN CANADA, 1 (Feb. 1972), 1-2, 21.

4485   Tippett, Maria. EMILY CARR: A BIOGRAPHY. Toronto: Oxford University Press, 1979. xiii, 314 p. Index.

4486   _____. "Emily Carr's KLEE WYCK." CANADIAN LITERATURE, No. 72 (Spr. 1977), pp. 49-58.

4487   _____. "A Paste Solitaire in a Steel-Claw Setting: Emily Carr and Her Public." BRITISH COLUMBIA STUDIES, No. 20 (Wint. 1973-74), pp. 3-14.

For criticism on Carr, see also nos. 87, 482, 4450-51, 4454, 4457, and 4459.

Book Reviews

4488   KLEE WYCK: BCHQ, 6 (Apr. 1942), 149-51; CHR, 23 (Mar. 1942), 90; SatN, 8 Nov. 1941, p. 18; UTQ, 11 (Apr. 1942), 319-20.

4489   THE BOOK OF SMALL: BCHQ, 7 (Jan. 1943), 64; CFor, 22 (Dec. 1942), 284, 286; CULTURE, 4 (Sept. 1943), 441; DR, 23 (Apr. 1943), 127; SatN, 5 Dec. 1942, p. 23.

4490   THE HOUSE OF ALL SORTS: CAB, Dec. 1944, pp. 14, 38; CFor, 25 (Apr. 1945), 24; QQ, 52 (Spr. 1945), 128-29; SatN, 16 Dec. 1944, p. 25; UTQ, 14 (Apr. 1945), 303-04.

4491   GROWING PAINS: BCHQ, 11 (Jan. 1947), 63; CFor, 26 (Jan. 1947), 234-35; CHR, 28 (June 1947), 212-14; DR, 26 (Jan. 1947), 513; SatN, 14 Dec. 1946, p. 43; SPECTATOR, 17 Oct. 1947, p. 506; UTQ, 16 (Apr. 1947), 330-31.

4492   THE HEART OF A PEACOCK: CArt, 11 (Wint. 1954), 78; CFor, 33 (Feb. 1954), 260; CULTURE, 15 (June 1954), 223-24; DR, 33 (Wint. 1954), xxxix; NS&N, 18 Sept. 1954, p. 334; TLS, 9 July 1954, p. 436; UTQ, 23 (Apr. 1954), 302-03.

4493   AN ADDRESS: CArt, 13 (Aut. 1955), 214; CULTURE, 17 (Sept. 1956), 324-25; UTQ, 25 (Apr. 1956), 359.

4494   HUNDREDS AND THOUSANDS: ARTSCANADA, 24 (Feb. supplement 1967), 7; CanL, 33 (Sum. 1967), 72-75; MACLEAN'S, 19 Nov. 1966, pp. 62-63; SatN, 81 (Nov. 1966), 54-56; TamR, 43 (Spr. 1967), 73-77; UTQ, 36 (July 1967), 438.

FRYE, NORTHROP (1912--)

One of Canada's pre-eminent scholars and critics, Northrop Frye was born in Sherbrooke, Quebec, and grew up in Moncton, New Brunswick. He completed a B.A. in philosophy and English at the University of Toronto, was ordained a United Church minister in 1936 after attending Emmanuel College, University of Toronto, and received an M.A. from Oxford University in 1940. Having joined the English department of Victoria College, University of Toronto, in 1939, he acted as chairman of the department from 1952 to 1959 and as Principal of Victoria from 1959 to 1966. In the forties, he was also literary editor of CANADIAN FORUM.

Frye first received acclaim for his work on William Blake, FEARFUL SYMMETRY, and for ANATOMY OF CRITICISM, a major work of critical theory. He has been visiting professor at the Universities of Harvard, Princeton, Columbia, Washington, Indiana, and British Columbia. Acknowledged as Canada's high priest of the imagination, he has received the Lorne Pierce Medal (1958), the Molson Prize (1970), and numerous honorary degrees.

PRIMARY MATERIAL

Monographs

NONFICTION PROSE

4495   FEARFUL SYMMETRY: A STUDY OF WILLIAM BLAKE. Princeton, N.J.: Princeton University Press, 1947. 462 p.

4496   ANATOMY OF CRITICISM: FOUR ESSAYS. Princeton, N.J.: Princeton University Press, 1957. x, 383 p.

4497   CULTURE AND THE NATIONAL WILL: THE CONVOCATION ADDRESS AT CARLETON UNIVERSITY, 17 MAY 1957. Ottawa: Carleton University for Institute of Canadian Studies, 1957. N. pag.

4498 ADDRESS BY H. NORTHROP FRYE ON THE OCCASION OF HIS IN-
STALLATION AS PRINCIPAL OF VICTORIA COLLEGE: OCTOBER 21,
1959. [Toronto]: Clarke, Irwin, 1959. 23 p.; rpt. as BY LIBERAL
THINGS: ADDRESS BY H. NORTHROP FRYE ON THE OCCASION OF
HIS INSTALLATION AS PRINCIPAL OF VICTORIA COLLEGE: OCTOBER
21, 1959. Toronto: Clarke, Irwin, 1960. 23 p.

4499 THE EDUCATED IMAGINATION. Toronto: Canadian Broadcasting Corporation, 1963. 68 p.

4500 FABLES OF IDENTITY: STUDIES IN POETIC MYTHOLOGY. New York:
Harcourt, Brace and World, 1963. 264 p.

4501 T.S. ELIOT. Edinburgh: Oliver and Boyd, 1963. 106 p. Bibliog.

4502 THE WELL-TEMPERED CRITIC. Bloomington: Indiana University Press,
1963. 160 p.

4503 LEARNING IN LANGUAGE AND LITERATURE. By A.R. MacKinnon
and Northrop Frye. Cambridge, Mass.: Harvard University Press, 1963.
62 p.

4504 A NATURAL PERSPECTIVE: THE DEVELOPMENT OF SHAKESPEAREAN
COMEDY AND ROMANCE. New York: Columbia University Press,
1965. ix, 159 p.

4505 THE RETURN OF EDEN: FIVE ESSAYS ON MILTON'S EPICS. Toronto:
University of Toronto Press, 1965. viii, 143 p.; rpt. as FIVE ESSAYS
ON MILTON'S EPICS. London: Routledge and Kegan Paul, 1966. ix,
158 p.

4506 FOOLS OF TIME: STUDIES IN SHAKESPEAREAN TRAGEDY. Alexander
Lectures. Toronto: University of Toronto Press, 1967. vi, 121 p.

4507 THE MODERN CENTURY: THE WHIDDEN LECTURES, 1967. Toronto:
Oxford University Press, 1967. 123 p.

4508 A STUDY OF ENGLISH ROMANTICISM. Studies in Language and Literature, 21. New York: Random House, 1968. vi, 180 p.

4509 SILENCE IN THE SEA (THE PRATT LECTURE, 1968). St. John's, Nfld.:
Memorial University, 1969. 14 p.

4510 THE STUBBORN STRUCTURE: ESSAYS ON CRITICISM AND SOCIETY.
Studies in the Humanities. Ithaca, N.Y.: Cornell University Press,
1970. xii, 316 p.

4511 THE BUSH GARDEN: ESSAYS ON THE CANADIAN IMAGINATION. Toronto: Anansi, 1971. x, 256 p. Index.

4512 THE CRITICAL PATH: AN ESSAY ON THE SOCIAL CONTEXT OF LIT-ERARY CRITICISM. Don Mills, Ont.: Fitzhenry and Whiteside, 1971. 174 p.

4513 ON TEACHING LITERATURE. New York: Harcourt Brace Jovanovich, 1972. 33 p.

4514 THE SECULAR SCRIPTURE: A STUDY OF THE STRUCTURE OF ROMANCE. Charles Eliot Norton Lectures, 1974-1975. Cambridge, Mass.: Harvard University Press, 1976. viii, 199 p. Index.

4515 SPIRITUS MUNDI: ESSAYS ON LITERATURE, MYTH, AND SOCIETY. Bloomington: Indiana University Press, 1976. xvi, 296 p.

4516 NORTHROP FRYE ON CULTURE AND LITERATURE: A COLLECTION OF REVIEW ESSAYS. Ed. with introd. by Robert D. Denham. Chicago: University of Chicago Press, 1978. viii, 264 p. Index.

4516a CREATION AND RECREATION. Toronto: University of Toronto Press, 1980. 76 p.

EDITED WORK

4517 PARADISE LOST, AND SELECTED POETRY AND PROSE. By John Milton. Ed. with introd. by Northrop Frye. New York: Holt, Rinehart and Winston, 1951. xxxviii, 601 p.

4518 ACROSS MY PATH. By Pelham Edgar. Ed. with introd. by Northrop Frye. Toronto: Ryerson, 1952. xiv, 167 p.

4519 SELECTED POETRY AND PROSE OF WILLIAM BLAKE. Ed. with introd. by Northrop Frye. New York: Modern Library, 1953. xxx, 475 p. Index.

4520 I BROUGHT THE AGES HOME. By Charles Trick Currelly. Ed. with introd. by Northrop Frye. Toronto: Ryerson, 1956. xx, 312 p.

4521 SOUND AND POETRY. Ed. with introd. by Northrop Frye. English Institute Essays, 1956. New York: Columbia University Press, 1957. xxvii, 156 p.

4522 THE COLLECTED POEMS OF E.J. PRATT. Ed. with introd. by Northrop Frye. 2nd ed. enl. Toronto: Macmillan, 1958. xxviii, 395 p. Index.

4523 THE TEMPEST. By William Shakespeare. Ed. with introd. by Northrop Frye. Baltimore: Penguin, 1959. 112 p. Rev. ed. Baltimore: Penguin, 1971. 108 p.

4524 THE VALLEY OF VISION: BLAKE AS PROPHET AND REVOLUTIONARY. By Peter F. Fisher. Toronto: University of Toronto Press, 1961. xi, 261 p. Index.

4525 DESIGN FOR LEARNING: REPORTS SUBMITTED TO THE JOINT COMMITTEE OF THE TORONTO BOARD OF EDUCATION AND THE UNIVERSITY OF TORONTO. Ed. with introd. by Northrop Frye. [Toronto]: University of Toronto Press, 1962. x, 148 p.

4526 ROMANTICISM RECONSIDERED: SELECTED PAPERS FROM THE ENGLISH INSTITUTE. Ed. with foreword by Northrop Frye. New York: Columbia University Press, 1963. ix, 144 p.

4527 BLAKE: A COLLECTION OF CRITICAL ESSAYS. Ed. with introd. by Northrop Frye. Twentieth Century Views, 58. Englewood Cliffs, N.J.: Prentice-Hall, 1966. 183 p. Bibliog.

4528 SOME BRITISH ROMANTICS: A COLLECTION OF ESSAYS. Ed. James V. Logan, John E. Jordan, and Northrop Frye. [Columbus]: Ohio State University Press, 1966. 343 p. Index.

4528a THE PRACTICAL IMAGINATION: STORIES, POEMS, PLAYS. Ed. Northrop Frye, Sheridan Baker, and George Perkins. New York: Harper and Row, 1980. xxi, 1, 1,514 p. Index.

For work edited by Frye, see also 154.

Shorter Work

SHORT STORY

4529 "The Resurgent." CANADIAN FORUM, 19 (Jan. 1940), 357-59.

ARTICLES

4530 "The Anatomy in Prose Fiction." MANITOBA ARTS REVIEW, 3 (Spr. 1942), 35-47.

4531 "A Liberal Education." CANADIAN FORUM, 25 (Sept. 1945), 134-35; 25 (Oct. 1945), 162-64.

4532 "Canadian Dreiser." CANADIAN FORUM, 28 (Sept. 1948), 121-22.
    Discusses Frederick Philip Grove; reprinted in no. 1873.

4533 "The Church: Its Relation to Society." In THE LIVING CHURCH. Ed. Harold W. Vaughan. Toronto: United Church Publishing House, 1949, pp. 152-72.

4534 "Poetry and Design in William Blake." JOURNAL OF AESTHETICS AND ART CRITICISM, 10 (Sept. 1951), 35-42.

4535 "Blake's Treatment of the Archetype." In ENGLISH INSTITUTE ESSAYS, 1950. Ed. Alan S. Downer. New York: Columbia University Press, 1951, pp. 170-96.

4536 "Trends in Modern Culture." In THE HERITAGE OF MODERN CULTURE: ESSAYS ON THE ORIGIN AND DEVELOPMENT OF MODERN CULTURE. Ed. Randolph C. Chalmers. Toronto: Ryerson, 1952, pp. 102-17.

4537 "Characterization in Shakespearian Comedy." SHAKESPEARE QUARTERLY, 4 (July 1953), 270-77.

4538 "Oswald Spengler." In ARCHITECTS OF MODERN THOUGHT. 1st ser. Toronto: Canadian Broadcasting Corporation, 1955, pp. 83-90.

4539 "Notes for a Commentary on MILTON." In THE DIVINE VISION: STUDIES IN THE POETRY AND ART OF WILLIAM BLAKE. Ed. Vivian de Sola Pinto. London: Gollanz, 1957, pp. 97-137.

4540 "William Blake." In ENGLISH ROMANTIC POETS AND ESSAYISTS: A REVIEW OF RESEARCH AND CRITICISM. Ed. Carol W. Houtchens and Lawrence H. Houtchens. New York: Modern Language Association, 1957, pp. 1-31.

4541 "Poetry." In THE ARTS IN CANADA: A STOCK-TAKING AT MID-CENTURY. Ed. Malcolm Ross. [Toronto]: Macmillan, 1958, pp. 84-90.

4542 "Humanities in a New World." In 3 LECTURES. By Northrop Frye, Clyde Kluckhohn, and V.B. Wigglesworth. University of Toronto Installation Lectures: 1958. Toronto: University of Toronto Press, [1959], pp. 9-23.

4543 "Religion and Modern Poetry." In CHALLENGE AND RESPONSE: MODERN IDEAS AND RELIGION. Ed. Randolph C. Chalmers and John A. Irving. Toronto: Ryerson, 1959, pp. 23-36.

4544 "Sir James Frazer." In ARCHITECTS OF MODERN THOUGHT, 3RD AND 4TH SER.: TWELVE TALKS FOR CBC RADIO. Toronto: Canadian Broadcasting Corporation, 1959, pp. 22-32.

4545   "The Critical Discipline." In CANADIAN UNIVERSITIES TODAY: SYM-
POSIUM PRESENTED TO THE ROYAL SOCIETY OF CANADA IN 1960.
Ed. George Stanley and Guy Sylvestre. Toronto: University of Toronto
Press, 1961, pp. 30-37.

4546   "Appearance and Reality in Education." SATURDAY NIGHT, 17 Mar.
1962, pp. 20-24.

4547   "Haliburton: Mask & Ego." ALPHABET, No. 5 (Dec. 1962), pp. 58-63.
        Reprinted in no. 172.

4548   "How True a Twain." In THE RIDDLE OF SHAKESPEARE'S SONNETS:
THE TEXT OF THE SONNETS, WITH INTERPRETIVE ESSAYS. By Edward
Hubler, Northrop Frye, Leslie A. Fiedler, Stephen Spender, and R.P.
Blackmur. London: Routledge and Kegan Paul, 1962, pp. 23-53.

4549   "Shakespeare's Experimental Comedy." In STRATFORD PAPERS ON SHAKE-
SPEARE 1961. Ed. B.W. Jackson. Toronto: W.J. Gage, 1962, pp. 2-14.

4550   "The Tragedies of Nature and Fortune." In STRATFORD PAPERS ON
SHAKESPEARE 1961. Ed. B.W. Jackson. Toronto: W.J. Gage, 1962,
pp. 38-55.

4551   "Literary Criticism." In THE AIMS AND METHODS OF SCHOLARSHIP
IN MODERN LANGUAGES AND LITERATURES. Ed. James Thorpe.
New York: Modern Language Association, 1963, pp. 57-69.

4552   "The Classics and the Man of Letters." ARION, 3 (Wint. 1964), 49-52.

4553   "The Problem of Spiritual Authority in the Nineteenth Century." In
LITERARY VIEWS: CRITICAL AND HISTORICAL ESSAYS. Ed. Carroll
Camden. Chicago: University of Chicago Press, for William Marsh Rice
University, 1964, pp. 145-58.

4554   "Nature and Nothing." In ESSAYS ON SHAKESPEARE. Ed. Gerald W.
Chapman. Princeton, N.J.: Princeton University Press, 1965, pp. 35-58.

4555   "The Structure and Spirit of Comedy." In STRATFORD PAPERS ON
SHAKESPEARE 1964. Ed. B.W. Jackson. Toronto: W.J. Gage, 1965,
pp. 1-9.

4556   Foreword, 1984, by George Orwell. Ed. Joseph Blakey. Scarborough,
Ont.: Bellhaven, 1967, pp. vii-xii.

4557   "Il Mito Romantico." LETTERE ITALIANE, 19 (1967), 409-40.

4558   "Literature and Myth." In RELATIONS OF LITERARY STUDY: ESSAYS ON INTERDISCIPLINARY CONTRIBUTIONS. Ed. James Thorpe. New York: Modern Language Association, 1967, pp. 27-55.

4559   "The Social Importance of Literature." EDUCATIONAL COURIER, 39 (Nov.-Dec. 1968), 19-23.

4560   "The University and the Heroic Vision." WASCANA REVIEW, 3, No. 2 (1968), 83-87.

4561   "Contexts of Literary Evaluation." In PROBLEMS OF LITERARY EVALU-ATION. Ed. Joseph Strelka. Yearbook of Comparative Criticism, 2. University Park: Pennsylvania State University Press, 1969, pp. 14-21.

4562   "The Ethics of Change: The Role of the University." In THE ETHICS OF CHANGE: A SYMPOSIUM. By Arthur Koestler, René Dubös, Martin Myerson, and Northrop Frye. Toronto: Canadian Broadcasting Corpora-tion, 1969, pp. 44-55.

        Discussion follows, pp. 57-67.

4563   "Old and New Comedy." SHAKESPEARE SURVEY, 22 (1969), 1-5.

4564   "The University and Personal Life: Student Anarchism and the Educa-tional Contract." In HIGHER EDUCATION: DEMAND AND RESPONSE (THE QUAIL ROOST SEMINAR). Ed. W.R. Niblett. London: Tavistock, 1969, pp. 35-51.

4565   "The Definition of a University." In ALTERNATIVES IN EDUCATION, OISE FIFTH ANNIVERSARY LECTURES. Ed. Bruce Rusk. Toronto: General Publishing, 1971, pp. 71-90.

4566   "THE DECLINE OF THE WEST by Oswald Spengler." DAEDALUS, 103 (Wint. 1974), 1-13.

4567   "New World without Revolution." In PRESERVING THE CANADIAN HERITAGE/LA PRÉSERVATION DU PATRIMONIE CANADIEN. Royal Society of Canada, 4th Symposium. Ottawa: Royal Society of Canada, [1975], pp. 15-25.

4568   "The Responsibilities of the Critic." MODERN LANGUAGE NOTES, 91 (Oct. 1976), 797-813.

        See no. 4652.

4569   "History and Myth in the Bible." In THE LITERATURE OF FACT: SE-
        LECTED PAPERS FROM THE ENGLISH INSTITUTE. Ed. with foreword
        by Angus Fletcher. New York: Columbia University Press, 1976, pp.
        1-19.

4570   "National Consciousness in Canadian Culture." PROCEEDINGS AND
        TRANSACTIONS OF THE ROYAL SOCIETY OF CANADA, 4th ser., 14
        (1976), 57-69.

4571   "Haunted by Lack of Ghosts: Some Patterns in the Imagery of Canadian
        Poetry." In THE CANADIAN IMAGINATION: DIMENSIONS OF A
        LITERARY CULTURE. Ed. David Staines. Cambridge, Mass.: Harvard
        University Press, 1977, pp. 22-45.

4572   "Literature, History, and Language." BULLETIN OF THE MIDWEST
        MODERN LANGUAGE ASSOCIATION, 12 (Fall 1979), 1-7.

4573   "Across the River and out of the Trees." UNIVERSITY OF TORONTO
        QUARTERLY, 50 (Fall 1980), 1-14.

4574   "The Meaning of Recreation: Humanism in Society." IOWA REVIEW,
        11, No. 1 (1980), 1-9.

For articles by Frye, see also no. 208.

Manuscripts

4575   McGill University Library, Montreal; Queen's University Library, Kingston,
        Ont.; University of Toronto Library.

SECONDARY MATERIAL

Bibliographies

4576   Denham, Robert D., ed. NORTHROP FRYE: AN ENUMERATIVE BIB-
        LIOGRAPHY. Scarecrow Author Bibliographies, no. 14. Metuchen,
        N.J.: Scarecrow, 1974. vii, 142 p. Indexes.

4577   _____. "Northrop Frye: A Supplementary Bibliography." CANADIAN
        LIBRARY JOURNAL, 34 (June 1977), 181-83, 185-87, 189, 191, 193,
        195-97. Addendum, 34 (Aug. 1977), 301-02.

        Supplement to no. 4576.

4578 _____. "Northrop Frye: A Supplementary Bibliography." CEA CRITIC, 42, No. 4 (1980), 25-34.

Criticism

4579 Ahmad, Igbal. "Imagination and Image in Frye's Criticism." ENGLISH QUARTERLY, 3 (Sum. 1970), 15-24.

4580 Altieri, Charles F. "Northrop Frye and the Problem of Spiritual Authority." PMLA, 87 (Oct. 1972), 964-75.

4581 Balfour, I. "Can the Centre Hold? Northrop Frye and the Spirit of the World." ESSAYS ON CANADIAN WRITING, 7-8 (1977), 214-21.

4582 Barry, Jackson G. "Form or Formula: Comic Structure in Northrop Frye and Susanne Langer." EDUCATIONAL THEATRE REVIEW, 16 (Dec. 1964), 333-40.

4583 Bashford, Bruce. "Literary History of Northrop Frye's ANATOMY OF CRITICISM." CONNECTICUT REVIEW, 8, No. 1 (1974), 48-55.

4584 Bašić, Sonja. "Northrop Frye kao mitski i arhetipski Kritičar." UMJETNOST RIJEČI, 14, No. 3 (1970), 353-85.

4585 Bates, Ronald. NORTHROP FRYE. Canadian Writers, 10. Toronto: McClelland and Stewart, 1971. 64 p.

4586 Berry, Ralph. "Shakespearean Comedy and Northrop Frye." ESSAYS IN CRITICISM, 22 (Jan. 1972), 33-40.

4587 Bowering, George. "Why James Reaney is a Better Poet 1) Than Any Northrop Frye Poet 2) Than He Used To Be." CANADIAN LITERATURE, No. 36 (Spr. 1968), pp. 40-49.

4588 Brienza, Susan D., and Peggy A. Knapp. "Imagination Lost and Found: Beckett's Fiction and Frye's ANATOMY." MODERN LANGUAGE NOTES, 95 (1980), 980-94.

4589 Casey, John. "A 'Science' of Criticism: Northrop Frye." In his THE LANGUAGE OF CRITICISM. London: Methuen, 1966, pp. 140-51.

4590 Celati, Gianni. "Archetipologia sistemetica: Per una iniziazione all' opero di Northrop Frye." LINGUA E STILE (Bologna), 4 (1969), 23-41.

4591   Ceserani, Remo. "Northrop Frye utopico pianificatore della città let-
        teraria." STRUMENTI CRITICI, 1 (Oct. 1967), 431-36.

4592   Conville, Richard. "Northrop Frye and Speech Criticism: An Intro-
        duction." QUARTERLY JOURNAL OF SPEECH, 56 (Dec. 1970), 417-25.

4593   Crews, Frederick. "Anaesthetic Criticism." In PSYCHOANALYSIS AND
        LITERARY PROCESS. Ed. Frederick Crews. Cambridge, Mass.: Win-
        throp, 1970, pp. 1-24.

4594   Cummings, Peter M. "Northrop Frye and the Necessary Hybrid: Criti-
        cism as Aesthetic Humanism." In THE QUEST FOR IMAGINATION:
        ESSAYS IN TWENTIETH-CENTURY AESTHETIC CRITICISM. Ed. O.B.
        Hardison, Jr. Cleveland: Press of Case Western Reserve University,
        1971, pp. 255-76.

4595   Denham, Robert D. "Frye and the Social Context of Criticism." SOUTH
        ATLANTIC BULLETIN, 39 (Nov. 1974), 63-72.

4596   _____. "Frye's Theory of Symbols." CANADIAN LITERATURE, No.
        66 (Aut. 1975), pp. 63-79.

4597   _____. NORTHROP FRYE AND CRITICAL METHOD. University Park:
        Pennsylvania State University Press, 1978. xii, 262 p. Index.

4598   _____. "Northrop Frye and Rhetorical Criticism." XAVIER UNIVER-
        SITY STUDIES, 11 (Spr. 1972), 1-11.

4599   _____. "Science, Criticism, and Frye's Metaphysical Universe." SOUTH
        CAROLINA REVIEW, 7, No. 2 (1975), 3-18.

4600   Douglas, Crerar. "A Theological Problem in Northrop Frye's Analysis
        of THE WINTER'S TALE." CHRISTIANITY AND LITERATURE, 24, No.
        2 (1975), 9-35.

4601   Dudek, Louis. "The Psychology of Literature." CANADIAN LITERATURE,
        No. 72 (Spr. 1977), pp. 5-20.

            Reprinted in no. 140.

4602   Dyrkjøb, Jan Ulrik. NORTHROP FRYES LITTERATURTEORI. Copen-
        hagen: Berlingske, 1979. 240 p.

4603   Edgar, Pelham. "Northrop Frye." In his ACROSS MY PATH. Ed.
        Northrop Frye. Toronto: Ryerson, 1952, pp. 83-89.

4604   Ellis, Katherine. "The Function of Northrop Frye at the Present Time." COLLEGE ENGLISH, 31 (Mar. 1970), 541-47.

4605   Finholt, Richard. "Northrop Frye's Theory of Countervailing Tendencies: A New Look at the Mode and Myth Essays." GENRE, 13 (1980), 203-57.

4606   Fischer, Michael R. "The Imagination as a Sanction of Value: Northrop Frye and the Uses of Literature." CENTENNIAL REVIEW, 21 (Spr. 1977), 105-17.

4607   Fletcher, Angus. "Northrop Frye: The Critical Passion." CRITICAL INQUIRY, 1 (June 1975), 741-56.

4608   Fraser, John. "Mr. Frye and Evaluation." CAMBRIDGE QUARTERLY, 2 (Spr. 1967), 97-116.

4609   Golden, Leon. "Aristotle, Frye, and the Theory of Tragedy." COMPARATIVE LITERATURE, 27 (Wint. 1975), 47-58.

4610   Gottfried, Rudolf B. "Our New Poet: Archetypal Criticism and THE FAERIE QUEENE." PMLA, 83 (Oct. 1968), 1362-77.

        See no. 4634.

4611   Hallie, Philip. "The Master Builder." PARTISAN REVIEW, 31 (Fall 1964), 650-51, 653-58.

4612   Hanes, V.G. "Northrop Frye's Theory of Literature and Marxism." HORIZONS: THE MARXIST QUARTERLY, No. 24 (Wint. 1968), pp. 62-78.

4613   Hernadi, Paul. "Northrop Frye." In his BEYOND GENRE: NEW DIRECTIONS IN LITERARY CLASSIFICATION. Ithaca, N.Y.: Cornell University Press, 1972, pp. 131-51.

4614   Holloway, John. "The Critical Zodiac of Northrop Frye." In his COLOURS OF CLARITY: ESSAYS ON CONTEMPORARY LITERATURE AND EDUCATION. London: Routledge and Kegan Paul, 1964, pp. 153-60.

4615   Hough, Graham. "Myth and Archetype II." In his AN ESSAY ON CRITICISM. New York: Norton, 1966, pp. 148-56.

4616   Howard, Ben. "Fancy, Imagination, and Northrop Frye." THOTH, 9 (Wint. 1968), 25-36.

4617   Inglis, Fred. "Professor Northrop Frye and the Academic Study of Lit-
        erature." CENTENNIAL REVIEW, 9 (1965), 319-31.

4618   Jackel, David. "Northrop Frye and the Continentalist Tradition." DAL-
        HOUSIE REVIEW, 56 (Sum. 1976), 221-39.

4619   Jensen, Jørgen I. "Litteraturkritiske unfordringer til teologien: Bibelske
        formproblemer." FØNIX (Copenhagen), 1 (1976-77), 254-82.

4620   Jewkes, W.T. "Mental Fight: Northrop Frye and the Teaching of Lit-
        erature." JOURNAL OF GENERAL EDUCATION, 27 (1976), 281-98.

4621   Johnsen, William A. "The Sparagmos of Myth Is the Naked Lunch of
        Mode: Modern Language as the Age of Frye and Borges." BOUNDARY
        2, 8, No. 2 (1980), 297-311.

4622   Kogan, Pauline. NORTHROP FRYE: THE HIGH PRIEST OF CLERICAL
        OBSCURANTISM. Literature and Ideology Monographs, no. 1. Mon-
        treal: Progressive Books and Periodicals, 1969. 98 p.

4623   Korpan, Barbara D. "Literary Evolution as Style: The 'Intrinsic His-
        toricity' of Northrop Frye and Juri Tynianov." PACIFIC COAST PHI-
        LOLOGY, 2 (Apr. 1967), 47-52.

4624   Kostelanetz, Richard. "The Literature Professors' Literature Professor."
        MICHIGAN QUARTERLY REVIEW, 17 (1978), 425-42.

4625   Krieger, Murray, ed. with introd. NORTHROP FRYE IN MODERN
        CRITICISM: SELECTED PAPERS FROM THE ENGLISH INSTITUTE. New
        York: Columbia University Press, 1966. x, 203 p. Bibliog.

4626   Langman, F.H. "Anatomizing Northrop Frye." BRITISH JOURNAL OF
        AESTHETICS, 18 (1978), 104-19.

4627   Lee, Alvin A. "Old English Poetry, Mediaeval Exegesis and Modern
        Criticism." STUDIES IN THE LITERARY IMAGINATION, 8 (Spr. 1975),
        47-73.

4628   Lentricchia, Frank. "The Historicity of Frye's Anatomy." SALMAGUNDI,
        No. 40 (1978), pp. 97-121.

4629   Lenz, Günter H. "Von der Erkenntnis der literarischen Struktur zur
        Struktur der literaturwissenschaftlichen Erkenntnis: Metakritische Bemer-
        kungen zu R.S. Crane und Northrop Frye." JAHRBUCH FÜR AMERIKA-
        STUDIEN, 17 (1972), 100-127.

4630   Lindop, Grevel. "Generating the Universe through Analogy: The Criticism of Northrop Frye." PN REVIEW, 3 (1977), 41-45.

See also 4657.

4631   MacDonald, R.D. "Frye's MODERN CENTURY Reconsidered." STUDIES IN CANADIAN LITERATURE, 4 (Wint. 1979), 95-108.

4632   Mandel, Eli W. "Toward a Theory of Cultural Revolution: The Criticism of Northrop Frye." CANADIAN LITERATURE, No. 1 (Sum. 1959), pp. 58-67.

4633   Mugerauer, Robert. "The Form of Northrop Frye's Literary Universe: An Expanding Circle." MOSAIC, 12 (Sum. 1979), 135-47.

4634   Ohmann, Carol. "Northrop Frye and the MLA." COLLEGE ENGLISH, 32 (Dec. 1970), 291-300.

Reply to no. 4610.

4635   Pandeya, Shiva M. "Theory of Style: A Note on the Ideas of T.S. Eliot, Northrop Frye, and Mammata." In ESSAYS AND STUDIES: FESTSCHRIFT IN HONOUR OF PROF. K. VISWANATHAM. Ed. G.V.L. M. Sarma. Machilipatnam: Triveni, 1977, pp. 95-101.

4636   Pedersen, Bertel. "Northrop Frye: Mod en Kritik uden Vaegge." KRITIK: TIDSSKRIFT FOR LITERATUR, FORSKNING, UNDERVISNING, No. 9 (1969), pp. 52-73.

4637   Riccomini, Donald R. "Northrop Frye and Structuralism: Identity and Difference." UNIVERSITY OF TORONTO QUARTERLY, 49 (Fall 1979), 33-47.

4638   Robinson, B. "Northrop Frye: Critique Fameux, Critique Faillible." REVUE DE L'UNIVERSITÉ D'OTTAWA, 42 (Oct.-Dec. 1972), 608-14.

4639   Rockas, Leo. "The Structure of Frye's ANATOMY." COLLEGE ENGLISH, 28 (Apr. 1967), 501-07.

4640   Rodway, Allan. "Generic Criticism: The Approach through Type, Mode, and Kind." In CONTEMPORARY CRITICISM. Ed. Malcolm Bradbury and David Palmer. Stratford-on-Avon Studies, 12. London: Edward Arnold, 1970, pp. 83-105.

4641   Saunders, D. "Whatever Happened to the Wedding Feast? A Critical Look at Northrop Frye's System of Archetypal Comic Narrative and Its

Application to some Recent French Examples." In PROCEEDINGS AND PAPERS OF THE SIXTEENTH CONGRESS OF THE AUSTRALASIAN UNIVERSITIES LANGUAGE AND LITERATURE ASSOCIATION HELD 21-27 AUGUST 1974 AT THE UNIVERSITY OF ADELAIDE, SOUTH AUSTRALIA. Ed. H. Bevan, M. King, and A. Stephens. N.p.: n.p., n.d., pp. 158-68.

4642 Schroeter, James. "The Unseen Center: A Critique of Northrop Frye." COLLEGE ENGLISH, 33 (Feb. 1972), 543-57.

4643 Shibles, Warren. "Northrop Frye on Metaphor." In his AN ANALYSIS OF METAPHOR IN LIGHT OF W.M. URBAN'S THEORIES. The Hague: Mouton, 1971, pp. 145-50.

4644 Slan, Jon. "Writing in Canada: Innis, McLuhan and Frye: Frontiers of Canadian Criticism." CANADIAN DIMENSION, 8 (Aug. 1972), 43-46.

4645 Slopen, Beverley. "Frye on Creation." QUILL AND QUIRE, 46, No. 3 (1980), 12.

4646 Sparshott, Francis. "Frye in Place." CANADIAN LITERATURE, No. 83 (Wint. 1979), pp. 143-55.

4647 Spears, Munroe K. "The Newer Criticism." SHENANDOAH, 21 (1970), 110-37.

4648 Sutherland, John. "Old Dog Trait--An Extended Analysis." CONTEMPORARY VERSE, No. 29 (Fall 1949), pp. 17-23.

4649 Teeuwissen, W. John. "The ANATOMY OF CRITICISM as Parody of Science." SOUTHERN HUMANITIES REVIEW, 14 (1980), 31-42.

4650 Von Hendy, A. "Poetics for Demogorgon: Northrop Frye and Contemporary Criticism." CRITICISM, 8 (Fall 1966), 318-35.

4651 Watkins, Evans. "Criticism and Method: Hirsch, Frye, Barthes." SOUNDINGS, 58 (1975), 257-80.

4652 Weber, Samuel. "The Responsibilities of the Critic: A Response." MODERN LANGUAGE NOTES, 91 (1976), 814-16.

A reply to no. 4568.

4653 Webster, Grant T. "Critical Exchange: The Missionary Criticism of Northrop Frye." SOUTHERN REVIEW, 2, No. 2 (1966), 164-69.

4654 Weimann, Robert. "Literarische Wertung und historische Tradition: Zu ihrer Aporie im Werk von Northrop Frye." ZEITSCHRIFT FÜR ANGLISTIK UND AMERIKANISTIK, 21, No. 4 (1973), 341-59.

4655 White, David A. "Northrop Frye: Value and System." CRITICISM, 15 (Sum. 1973), 189-211.

4656 Yamoto, Sadamiki. "Shinwa Hihyo no Zushiki--N. Frye." EIGO SEINEN (Tokyo), 116 (1970), 526-27, 573-74, 641-43.

4657 Young, Dudley. "The Deep Wood's Woven Shade." PN REVIEW, 5 (1977), 65-66.

A reply to 4630.

For criticism on Frye, see also nos. 127, 158, 291, 348, 4516, and 5179.

Book Reviews

4658 FEARFUL SYMMETRY: CFor, 27 (July 1947), 90; DR, 27 (Oct. 1947), 381-83; ELH, 15 (1948), 9-10; JEGP, 49 (1950), 124-27; MLN, 64 (1949), 62-63; MLQ, 9 (1948), 248-49; NER, 16 (1948), 190, 192; Person, 29 (1948), 215-17; POETRY, 71 (Nov. 1947), 101-03; PR, 31 (Fall 1964), 650; QQ, 54 (Aut. 1947), 395-97; RES, 24 (1948), 334-35; SatN, 19 July 1947, p. 17; SatR, 19 July 1947, p. 19; SPECTATOR, 10 Oct. 1947, p. 466; SR, 55 (Oct. 1947), 710-15; THOMIST, 9 (1948), 257-59; TLS, 10 Jan. 1948, p. 25; UTQ, 17 (Jan. 1948), 204-07; VQR, 23 (1947), 628-30; YWES, 28 (1947), 219-20.

4659 ANATOMY OF CRITICISM: ASch, 28 (1959), 232, 238; CE, 19 (1958), 279-80; CFor, 38 (Sept. 1958), 128-29; COMMONWEAL, 20 Sept. 1957, pp. 618-19; CRITICISM, 1 (Wint. 1959), 72-75; EF, 6 (1969), 221-26; ENCOUNTER, 10 (Feb. 1958), 79-82; HudR, 10 (1957-58), 614-19; JA, 16 (1957), 533-34; JP, 10 Sept. 1959, pp. 745-55; MFS, 3 (1957-58), 366; MLR, 54 (1959), 107-09; MP, 56 (1958), 69-72; NATION, 17 Jan. 1959, pp. 57-58; POETRY, 91 (1958), 320-28; PR, 31 (Fall 1964), 650-51; QJS, 43 (1957), 313; RES, 10 (1959), 317-23; SAQ, 58 (Wint. 1958), 140-41; SCN, 16 (1957), 17-18; SPECTATOR, 8 Sept. 1973, p. 317; SYMPOSIUM, 12 (Spr. 1958), 211-15; TamR, 8 (Sum. 1958), 92-98, 100-101; TLS, 14 Feb. 1958, pp. 81-82; UTQ, 28 (Jan. 1959), 190-96; WHR, 13 (1959), 109-12; WR, 22 (1958), 309-15; YR, NS 47 (Aut. 1957), 130-33; YWES, 37 (1960), 12.

4660 THE EDUCATED IMAGINATION: CE, 26 (Jan. 1965), 330-31; CULTURE, 3 (1970), 361-62; EJ, 54 (Apr. 1965), 343-44; HudR, 18 (Wint. 1965-66), 607-12; MQR, 4 (1965), 72; NYTBR, 26 Feb. 1967, p. 28; PR, 32 (Sum. 1965), 461-64, 466; SoR, 1, No. 3 (1965), 85-88; TamR,

[29] (Aut. 1963), 82-89; UTQ, 33 (July 1964), 406-07; YWES, 45 (1964), 17-18.

4661 FABLES OF IDENTITY: CanL, 24 (Spr. 1965), 63-66; HudR, 18 (Spr. 1964), 138-42; NYRB, 6 Feb. 1964, pp. 18-19; POETRY, 104 (Sept. 1964), 364; PR, 31 (Fall 1964), 650-51, 653-58; TamR, [33] (Aut. 1964), 72-78; UTQ, 33 (July 1964), 401-06, 408; YR, 53 (June 1964), 592-94.

4662 T.S. ELIOT: CanL, 19 (Wint. 1964), 51-54; CFor, 43 (Dec. 1963), 207-08; NS, 16 June 1963, pp. 198-99; PoetR, 54 (Wint. 1963-64), 326, 328; SPECTATOR, 5 July 1963, p. 24; TamR, [29] (Aut. 1963), 82-85; TLS, 12 July 1963, p. 511; UTQ, 33 (July 1964), 403-05.

4663 THE WELL-TEMPERED CRITIC: CanL, 20 (Spr. 1964), 6-14; HudR, 16 (Aut. 1963), 467-70; KR, 26 (Spr. 1964), 416-22; PR, 31 (Fall 1964), 650-58; QJS, 49 (1963), 457-58; SHENANDOAH, 14 (1963), 62-65; TamR, [29] (Aut. 1963), 82-89; UTQ, 33 (July 1964), 407-08; YR, 52 (Sum. 1963), xx, xxii.

4664 A NATURAL PERSPECTIVE: CanL, 27 (Wint. 1966), 69-71; CL, 17 (Sum. 1965), 278-79; CRITICISM, 9 (Sum. 1967), 298-301; DR, 46 (Spr. 1966), 112-13; EA, 19 (1966), 292; ECONOMIST, 14 Aug. 1965, p. 615; ELN, 3 (Dec. 1965), 134-36; FIDDLEHEAD, 65 (Sum. 1965), 70; HudR, 18 (Wint. 1965-66), 609; N&Q, NS 13 (Apr. 1966), 152-55; NYRB, 22 Apr. 1965, pp. 10-12; Person, 47 (Sum. 1966), 430-33; PR, 33 (Wint. 1966), 132-36; QR, 303 (Oct. 1965), 467-68; SatN, 38, No. 2 (1970), 375; SELit, 6 (1966), 362-64; SHStud, 2 (1966), 330-32; SN, 38 (1966), 375-38; SQ, 22 (Wint. 1971), 68-70; TLS, 12 Aug. 1965, p. 698; UTQ, 35 (July 1966), 405-07; YR, 56 (Sum. 1967), 563-65.

4665 THE RETURN OF EDEN: ALPHABET, Dec. 1965, pp. 74-75; BJA, 7 (July 1967), 293-95; CanL, 28 (Spr. 1966), 65-67; CE, 27 (May 1966), 643-44; CRITICISM, 8 (Fall 1966), 389-94; DR, 46 (Aut. 1966), 411, 413; EA, 19 (1966), 450-51; ELN, 4 (Mar. 1967), 216-18; HudR, 19 (Aut. 1966), 498-99; JEGP, 66 (Jan. 1967), 146-49; LISTENER, 76 (1966), 137; MLQ, 27 (Dec. 1966), 477-80; NS, 2 Dec. 1966, p. 838; NYRB, 9 June 1966, pp. 27-28; QQ, 73 (Aut. 1966), 455-57; RES, 18 (Aug. 1967), 330-32; SAQ, 66 (Spr. 1967), 260-63; SCN, 24 (Spr. 1966), 2-3; SELit, 6 (Wint. 1966), 187-88; SR, 77 (Wint. 1969), 176-84; UTQ, 35 (July 1966), 392-95; YR, 55 (Spr. 1966), xiv, xviii.

4666 FOOLS OF TIME: ANGLIA, 89 (1971), 385-86; DR, 47 (Sum. 1967), 279-81; ENGLISH, 17 (Aut. 1968), 99-102; HAB, 25 (Spr. 1974), 185-86; LISTENER, 9 May 1968, pp. 610-11; NYRB, 12 Oct. 1967, pp. 14-17; QQ, 74 (Wint. 1967), 773-74; RES, NS 20 (Aug. 1969), 386; SELit, 8 (1968), 365-68; SHStud, 5 (1970), 329-31; SQ, 20 (Wint.

1969), 101; TLS, 25 July 1968, p. 779; UTQ, 37 (July 1968), 400-403; WascanaR, 3, No. 1 (1968), 95-98; YR, 67 (Wint. 1968), 295-98.

4667 THE MODERN CENTURY: ASch, 37 (Sum. 1968), 522; BrBN, Aug. 1968; CanL, 38 (Aut. 1968), 77-81; CE, 30 (Dec. 1968), 264-66; COMMENTARY, 46 (Sept. 1968), 97-100; CRead, 9 (1967), 8-9; DR, 47 (Wint. 1967-68), 595, 597; ELN, 6 (Mar. 1969), 230-35; LIBERTÉ, 10 (Mar. 1968), 39-41; LISTENER, 9 (May 1968), 610-11; PR, 36 (Wint. 1969), 153-56; SHR, 3 (1969), 109-10; TamR, [46] (Wint. 1968), 115, 117, 119-20; UTQ, 37 (July 1968), 439-41.

4668 A STUDY OF ENGLISH ROMANTICISM: MLJ, 54 (Feb. 1970), 131-32; SN, 43, No. 2 (1971), 590-93; UTQ, 38 (July 1969), 371-73.

4669 THE STUBBORN STRUCTURE: CamR, 7 May 1971, p. 177; CanL, 49 (Sum. 1971), 4-5; ConL, 15 (Wint. 1974), 131; DR, 51 (Spr. 1971), 109-13; ENGLISH, 20 (Sum. 1971), 62-63; LISTENER, 21 Jan. 1971, p. 88; MOSAIC, 5 (Sum. 1972), 179-84; Neophil, 55 (Oct. 1971), 466-67; NS, 18 Dec. 1970, pp. 844-45; NSoc, 3 Dec. 1970, pp. 1010-11; RES, NS 22 (Nov. 1971), 522-25; SAQ, 70 (Sum. 1971), 418-20; SHR, 8 (Wint. 1974), 85; SoR, 8 (1974), 85-92; SPECTATOR, 5 Dec. 1970, pp. 733-34; UTQ, 41 (Wint. 1972), 170-73; YR, 60 (Mar. 1971), vi, x, xiv.

4670 THE BUSH GARDEN: ARCS, 2, No. 1 (1972), 100; CanL, 49 (Sum. 1972), 5-7; CDim, 8 (Jan. 1972), 55; CRead, 22 Mar. 1971, pp. 5-6; LHY, 13, No. 2 (1972), 44-45; MACLEAN'S, 84 (Apr. 1971), 86, 88; MHRev, 22 (Apr. 1972), 123-25; Q&Q, 19 Mar. 1971, p. 8; QQ, 79 (Sum. 1972), 264-65; SatN, 86 (Mar. 1971), 7; TamR, 60 (Oct. 1973), 52-56; UTQ, 41 (Wint. 1972), 172-73; WascanaR, 6, No. 2 (1972), 76-78.

4671 THE CRITICAL PATH: BCan, 1 (Nov. 1971), 30; CL, 24 (Wint. 1972), 72-73; CLIO, 2, No. 1 (1972), 72-76; ELN, 10, suppl. to No. 1 (Sept. 1971), 12; JCF, 1 (Sum. 1972), 78-80; NATION, 20 Sept. 1971, pp. 247-48; PR, 39 (1972), 63-79.

4672 THE SECULAR SCRIPTURE: CFor, 56 (June 1976), 62-63; CLIO, 6 (Fall 1976), 97; CLS, 15 (Dec. 1978), 434-36; CRCL, 4 (Fall 1977), 363; ELN, 14 (Dec. 1976), 151-54; JAF, 92 (Jan. 1979), 80-82; MFS, 23 (Sum. 1977), 307-10; MQR, 16 (Sum. 1977), 350; NatF, 60 (Fall 1980), 54; NewR, 27 Nov. 1976, p. 30; NY, 26 Apr. 1976, p. 147; NYRB, 14 Apr. 1977, p. 33; NYTBR, 18 Apr. 1976, p. 21; PQ, 56 (Fall 1977), 531; Q&Q, 42, No. 5 (1976), 41; QQ, 85 (Spr. 1978), 66-77; SHR, 12 (Sum. 1978), 301; STYLE, 11 (Spr. 1977), 212; TLS, 5 Nov. 1976, p. 1399; UTQ, 46 (Sum. 1977), 415-18; WLT, 51 (Wint. 1977), 167; YR, 66 (Spr. 1977), xii-xiii.

4673 SPIRITUS MUNDI: BForum, 3 (Wint. 1977), 42; CFor, 57 (June 1977), 38-39; COMMONWEAL, 27 May 1977, p. 346; DQ, 13 (Spr. 1978), 81; ECW, 7-8 (Fall 1977), 214-21; ESC, 4 (Wint. 1978), 490-99; JES, 9 (Sept. 1979), 208-10; NatF, 60 (Fall 1980), 54; NYRB, 14 Apr. 1977, p. 33; Q&Q, 43, No. 6 (1977), 38-39; SCR, 11 (Nov. 1978), 123; SR, 88 (Wint. 1980), 121-25; UTQ, 47 (Sum. 1978), 395-98; WLT, 51 (Sum. 1977), 505.

4674 NORTHROP FRYE ON CULTURE AND LITERATURE: BCan, 7 (June 1978), 18; CanL, 79 (Wint. 1978), 132; JAAC, 37 (Fall 1978), 106; NS, 29 Sept. 1978, p. 412; SCR, 11 (Nov. 1978), 123; SR, 88 (Wint. 1980), 121-25; UTQ, 48 (Sum. 1979), 431-33; UWR, 14 (Spr. 1979), 96-100; WLT, 52 (Aut. 1978), 697.

4675 CREATION AND RECREATION: Q&Q, 46 (Dec. 1980), 29.

GLASSCO, JOHN (1909-81)

Poet, essayist, translator, fiction writer, and pornographer, John Glassco was born in Montreal and attended Bishop's College, Lennoxville, Quebec, and McGill University in Montreal. At eighteen, he travelled to Paris where he spent three years as an active participant in the decadence movement until a serious case of tuberculosis forced his return to Montreal. Since then he has lived in the Eastern Townships of Quebec, where he served in municipal politics for the village of Foster between 1950 and 1954. MEMOIRS OF MONTPAR-NASSE, a memoir of his Paris days written immediately after his return and while tuberculosis still threatened his life (though not published until years later), has become a classic of its kind.

PRIMARY MATERIAL

Monographs

FICTION

4676　CONTES EN CRINOLINE. Paris: Gaucher, 1930.

4677　UNDER THE HILL. By Aubrey Beardsley, Now Completed by John Glassco. Paris: Olympia, 1959. 122 p.

4678　THE ENGLISH GOVERNESS. By Miles Underwood, pseud. Paris: Olympia, 1960.; rpt. as UNDER THE BIRCH: THE STORY OF AN ENGLISH GOVERNESS. Paris: Ophelia, 1965. 187 p. Rev. ed. HARRIET MARWOOD: GOVERNESS. Don Mill, Ont.: General Publishing, 1976. 232 p.

4679　FETISH GIRL. By Sylvia Bayer, pseud. 1973.

　　　No publishing details, listed in no. 92.

4680　THE FATAL WOMAN: THREE TALES. Toronto: Anansi, 1974. iv, 172 p.

NONFICTION PROSE

4681   MEMOIRS OF MONTPARNASSE. Introd. Leon Edel. Toronto: Oxford
        University Press, 1970. xiii, 241 p.

POETRY

4682   CONAN'S FIG. Paris: Transition, 1928.

4683   THE DEFICIT MADE FLESH. Toronto: McClelland and Stewart, 1958.
        64 p.

4684   A POINT OF SKY. Toronto: Oxford University Press, 1964. 78 p.

4685   SELECTED POEMS. Toronto: Oxford University Press, 1971. 94 p.

4686   MONTREAL. Montreal: D.C. Books, 1973. 30 p.

EDITED WORK

4687   ENGLISH POETRY IN QUEBEC: PROCEEDINGS OF THE FOSTER POETRY
        CONFERENCE, OCTOBER 12-14, 1963. Montreal: McGill University
        Press, 1965. 136 p.

4688   THE POETRY OF FRENCH CANADA IN TRANSLATION. Ed. with in-
        trod. by John Glassco. Toronto: Oxford University Press, 1970. xxvi,
        270 p. Indexes.

TRANSLATIONS

4689   THE JOURNAL OF SAINT-DENYS-GARNEAU. Introd. Gilles Marcotte.
        [Toronto]: McClelland and Stewart, 1962. 139 p.

4690   COMPLETE POEMS OF SAINT-DENYS-GARNEAU. Trans. with introd. by
        John Glassco. [Ottawa]: Oberon, 1975. 172 p. Index.

4691   LOT'S WIFE. By Monique Bosco. Toronto: McClelland and Stewart,
        1975. 149 p.

4692   VENUS IN FURS. By Leopold Von Sacher-Masoch. Trans. with introd. by
        John Glassco. Burnaby, B.C.: Blackfish, 1977. 111 p.

4693   CREATURES OF THE CHASE. By Jean-Yves Soucy. Toronto: McClelland
        and Stewart, 1979. 161 p.

Shorter Work

SHORT STORIES

4694 "Mr. Noad." CANADIAN FORUM, 32 (Mar. 1953), 277-80.

4695 "A Season in Limbo." By Silas N. Gooch, pseud. TAMARACK REVIEW, 23 (Spr. 1962), 55-84.

4696 "Countess Isobel and the Torturer." JEWISH DĪÁLŎG, Sum. 1972, pp. 32-41.

4697 "The Pigtail Man." JEWISH DĪÁLŎG, Hanukah 1973, pp. 47-57.

ARTICLE

4698 "Euterpe's Honeymoon: Notes on the Poetic Process." WEST COAST REVIEW, 13 (Feb. 1979), 3-4.

Manuscripts

4699 McGill University Library, Montreal; Public Archives of Canada, Ottawa.

SECONDARY MATERIAL

Criticism

4700 Clark, W. "In the Embrace of an Erotic Muse." MACLEAN'S, 17 Dec. 1979, pp. 10-12.

4701 Dobbs, Kildare. "The Great Glassco: Memoirs of a Gentleman of Pleasure." MACLEAN'S, 88 (Aug. 1975), 48-50, 52.

4702 Jamieson, Maclean. "John Glassco: The Eye of the Stranger." AP-PLEGARTH'S FOLLY, 1 (1973), 68-76.

4703 _____. "John Glassco: The Eye of the Stranger. Part II." APPLE-GARTH'S FOLLY, 2 (1975), 141-52.

4704 Murdoch, Charles. "Essential Glassco." CANADIAN LITERATURE, No. 65 (Sum. 1975), pp. 28-41.

For criticism on Glassco, see also no. 4681.

Book Reviews

4705   UNDER THE HILL: Atl, 220 (Sept. 1967), 132; KR, 29 (Sept. 1967),
543; NS, 12 Aug. 1966, p. 235; SatR, 9 Sept. 1967, p. 32; SPEC-
TATOR, 30 Sept. 1966, pp. 415-16.

4706   HARRIET MARWOOD: CBRA, 1976, p. 126; Q&Q, 42, No. 4 (1976),
21; SatN, 91 (Apr. 1976), 10.

4707   THE FATAL WOMAN: BCan, 4 (Feb. 1975), 21-22; CanL, 65 (Sum.
1975), 108-10; CFor, 54 (Nov. 1974), 21-22; Q&Q, 42, No. 4 (1976),
21; TamR, 65 (Mar. 1975), 93-97.

4708   MEMOIRS OF MONTPARNASSE: CanL, 44 (Spr. 1970), 67-68; CRevAS,
5 (Spr. 1974), 67-71; JJQ, 7 (Sum. 1970), 358; JML, 1, No. 5 (1971),
653; ME, Fall Book Supplement 1970, pp. 37-38; NewR, 25 Dec. 1971,
pp. 27-28; NS, 29 May 1970, p. 776; NYTBR, 29 Nov. 1970, p. 28;
SatN, 85 (Apr. 1970), 35-36; SatR/WORLD, 9 Feb. 1974, p. 42; TamR,
54 (1970), 77-80; WORLD, 31 July 1973, p. 37.

HIEBERT, PAUL (1892--)

Born in Pilot Mound, Manitoba, Paul Gerhardt Hiebert received a B.A. in philosophy from the University of Manitoba (1916), an M.A. in German from the University of Toronto (1917), and an M.Sc. (1923) and Ph.D. in chemistry (1924) from McGill University, Montreal. He served as a professor of chemistry at the University of Manitoba from 1924 to 1953 and retired to Carman, Manitoba. SARAH BINKS, his parody of a literary biography, delightfully challenges Canadian and literary pretensions and won the Leacock Medal for Humour in 1947.

PRIMARY MATERIAL

Monographs

FICTION

4709   SARAH BINKS. Drawings by J.W. McLaren. Toronto: Oxford University Press, 1947. xix, 181 p.

4710   WILLOWS REVISITED. Toronto: McClelland and Stewart, 1967. 176 p.

NONFICTION PROSE

4711   TOWER IN SILOAM. Toronto: McClelland and Stewart, 1966. 213 p.

4712   DOUBTING CASTLE: A SPIRITUAL AUTOBIOGRAPHY. Winnipeg: Queenston House, 1976. 120 p.

4713   FOR THE BIRDS. Introd. Reynold Siemens. Winnipeg: Peguis, 1980. 98 p.

Shorter Work

ARTICLE

4714   "The Comic Spirit at Forty Below Zero."   MOSAIC, 3 (Spr. 1970), 58-68.

Manuscripts

4715   University of Saskatchewan Library, Saskatoon.

SECONDARY MATERIAL

Criticism

4716   Bond, C.C.J.   "A Haunting Echo."   CANADIAN LITERATURE, No. 16 (Spr. 1963), pp. 83-84.

   Discusses SARAH BINKS.

4717   Noonan, Gerald A.   "Incongruity and Nostalgia in SARAH BINKS." STUDIES IN CANADIAN LITERATURE, 3 (Sum. 1978), 264-73.

4718   Siemens, Reynold.   "Reactions to Sarah."   CANADIAN LITERATURE, No. 75 (Wint. 1977), pp. 111-15.

4719   _____.   "SARAH BINKS in Retrospect: A Conversation with Paul Hiebert." JOURNAL OF CANADIAN FICTION, No. 19 (1977), pp. 65-76.

4720   Wheeler, A. Lloyd.   Introd., SARAH BINKS.   New Canadian Library, no. 44.   Toronto: McClelland and Stewart, 1964, pp. vii-xiii.

4721   _____.   "Up from Magma and Back Again with Paul Hiebert."   MANI-TOBA ARTS REVIEW, 6 (Spr. 1948), 3-14.

For criticism on Hiebert, see also nos. 51, 131, and 4713.

Book Reviews

4722   SARAH BINKS: CAB, 41 (Wint. 1965), 14; CanP, 11 (Mar. 1948), 42-43; CFor, 27 (Mar. 1948), 284; DR, 28 (July 1948), 196; RUL, 4 (May 1950), 812-13; SatN, 20 Mar. 1948, p. 17; UTQ, 17 (Apr. 1948), 301.

4723　WILLOWS REVISITED:　QQ, 74 (Aut. 1967), 545-46; SatN, 82 (May 1967), 41; UTQ, 37 (July 1968), 502-05.

4724　TOWER IN SILOAM:　CAB, 42 (Wint. 1966), 18; DR, 47 (Wint. 1967-68), 601, 603; QQ, 73 (Wint. 1966), 598-99; UTQ, 36 (July 1967), 457-59.

HORWOOD, HAROLD (1923--)

Harold Andrew Horwood, a Newfoundlander, has worked as a longshoreman, union organizer, naturalist, teacher, and journalist for the St. John's EVENING TELEGRAM. In politics, he campaigned for Newfoundland's union with Canada and represented Labrador in the Newfoundland House of Assembly. Between 1946 and 1948, he helped publish the literary review, PROTOCOL. He has taught creative writing at Memorial University, Newfoundland, and been writer-in-residence for the University of Western Ontario, Hamilton. Horwood lives in Beachy Cove, Newfoundland, and has travelled widely to the less accessible areas of his province; his writing draws heavily on his experience with the Newfoundland environment. TOMORROW WILL BE SUNDAY won the 1967 Beta Sigma Phi Award.

PRIMARY MATERIAL

Monographs

FICTION

4725   TOMORROW WILL BE SUNDAY. Garden City, N.Y.: Doubleday, 1966. 375 p.

4726   WHITE ESKIMO: A NOVEL OF LABRADOR. Garden City, N.Y.: Doubleday, 1972. 228 p.

4727   SHORT STORIES OF HAROLD HORWOOD. Portugal Cove, Nfld.: Breakwater, 1977. 200 p.

4728   ONLY THE GODS SPEAK: TEN TALES FROM THE TROPICS, SEVEN PIECES FROM THE NORTH. St. John's, Nfld.: Breakwater, 1979. x, 130 p.

NONFICTION PROSE

4729 PAPER FROM THE FORESTS OF NEWFOUNDLAND. Montreal: Bowater, 1956. 24 p.

4730 "The Story of the Boethucks." Mimeographed, in five parts. [St. John's, Nfld.]: n.p., [1959?].

4731 THE FOXES OF BEACHY COVE. Illus. by the Author. Garden City, N.Y.: Doubleday, 1967. 190 p.

4732 NEWFOUNDLAND. Traveller's Canada. Toronto: Macmillan, 1969. x, 244 p.

4733 DEATH ON THE ICE: THE GREAT NEWFOUNDLAND SEALING DISASTER OF 1914. By Cassie Brown and Harold Horwood. Garden City, N.Y.: Doubleday, 1972. xii, 270 p.

4734 BEYOND THE ROAD: PORTRAITS AND VISIONS OF NEWFOUNDLANDERS. Photos. Stephen Taylor. Toronto: Van Nostrand Reinhold, 1976. 144 p.

4735 BARTLETT: THE GREAT CANADIAN EXPLORER. Photos. by Bartlett. Toronto: Doubleday Canada, 1977. xiv, 194 p. Bibliog. Index.

4736 THE COLONIAL DREAM 1497-1760. Canada's Illustrated Heritage. Toronto: Natural Science of Canada, 1978. 128 p. Index.

EDITED WORK

4737 VOICES UNDERGROUND: POEMS FROM NEWFOUNDLAND. Ed. with introd. by Harold Horwood. Toronto: New, 1972. 81 p.

Shorter Work

SHORT STORIES

4738 "The Raven's Nest." ATLANTIC ADVOCATE, 57 (July 1967), 41-43.

4739 "The Shell Collector." In 73: NEW CANADIAN STORIES. Ed. David Helwig and Joan Harcourt. [Ottawa]: Oberon, 1973, pp. 93-104.

4740 "The Lady Who Fought at the Seige of Jerusalem." QUEEN'S QUARTERLY, 81 (Aut. 1974), 412-18.

4741   "Coming to an End." In 74: NEW CANADIAN STORIES. Ed. David
        Helwig and Joan Harcourt. [Ottawa]: Oberon, 1974, pp. 85-96.

4742   "Men Like Summer Snow." In STORIES FROM PACIFIC AND ARCTIC
        CANADA. Ed. Andreas Schroeder and Rudy Wiebe. Toronto: Mac-
        millan, 1974, pp. 230-37.

4743   "The Sound of Thunder." JOURNAL OF CANADIAN FICTION, 4, No.
        3 (1975), 73-80.

ARTICLES

4744   "E.J. Pratt and William Blake: An Analysis." DALHOUSIE REVIEW,
        39 (Sum. 1959), 197-207.

4745   "Tales of the Labrador Indians." Introd. by Harold Horwood. NEW-
        FOUNDLAND QUARTERLY, 66 (Sept.-Nov. 1967), 17-20; (Wint. 1968),
        16-18; (June 1968), 17-19.

Manuscripts

4746   Provincial Reference Library, St. John's, Nfld.

SECONDARY MATERIAL

Criticism

4747   Cameron, Donald A.   "Don Cameron Interviews Harold Horwood." QUILL
        AND QUIRE, 38 (Aut. 1972), 3, 10-11.

        Reprinted in no. 124.

For criticism on Horwood, see also no. 81.

Book Reviews

4748   TOMORROW WILL BE SUNDAY: ALPHABET, 14 (Dec. 1967), 83-85;
        AtlA, 56 (Mar. 1966), 73; MACLEAN'S, 2 Apr. 1966, p. 46; NYTBR,
        6 Feb. 1966, p. 40; SatN, 80 [81] (May 1966), 45, 47; SatR, 29
        Jan. 1966, p. 39; UTQ, 36 (July 1967), 380-81.

4749   WHITE ESKIMO: BCan, 2 (Jan. 1973), 60-61; CanL, 58 (Aut. 1973),
        92-93; CRead, 15, No. 1 (1974), 9; JCF, 2 (Wint. 1973), 98-99;
        NORTH, 19 (Nov. 1972), 36; NYTBR, 5 Nov. 1972, Pt. 1, p. 40;
        Q&Q, 38, No. 9 (1972), 8; SatN, 87 (Nov. 1972), 39, 41; UTQ,
        42 (Sum. 1973), 350.

4750 ONLY THE GODS SPEAK: BCan, 8 (Nov. 1979), 15-16; FIDDLE-
HEAD, 126 (Sum. 1980), 140-41; NQ, 76 (Sum. 1980), 13-14; Q&Q,
45, No. 9 (1979), 35.

4751 THE FOXES OF BEACHY COVE: AtlA, 58 (Nov. 1967), 73; TLS, 13
Feb. 1969, p. 166.

4752 NEWFOUNDLAND: CanL, 41 (Sum. 1969), 140; DR, 49 (Wint. 1969-
70), 583; TLS, 16 Apr. 1970, p. 437; UTQ, 39 (July 1970), 379-80.

4753 BARTLETT: AntigR, 33 (Spr. 1978), 99-101; CAB, 53 (July 1978),
38; CanL, 84 (Spr. 1980), 90-93; CGJ, 96 (Feb. 1978), 75-76; CHR,
60 (Mar. 1979), 89-90; NORTH, 25 (Mar. 1978), 66-67; NQ, 73
(Dec. 1977), 14; Q&Q, 43, No. 13 (1977), 51.

McLUHAN, MARSHALL (1911-80)

Canada's prominent communications expert and cultural theorist, Herbert Marshall McLuhan was born in Edmonton and received a B.A. (1932) and M.A. (1934) in English from the University of Manitoba and a B.A. (1936), M.A. (1939), and Ph.D. in literature (1942) from Cambridge. After teaching at the Universities of Wisconsin and St. Louis and at Assumption College (Windsor, Ontario), he joined the English department of St. Michael's College, University of Toronto, where he remained until his retirement in 1980. In 1963 he also founded and became director of the university's Centre for Culture and Technology.

McLuhan has received many honorary degrees and awards, including the Governor General's Award for THE GUTENBERG GALAXY and the 1967 Molson Prize. He is noted for his original work on the effects of the media--his early works had a particularly strong impact--and for his speculative, startling, and often aphoristic "probes" into the nature of culture and society.

PRIMARY MATERIAL

Monographs

NONFICTION PROSE

4754   "George Meredith as a Poet and Dramatic Parodist." Master's thesis, University of Manitoba, 1934.

4755   "The Place of Thomas Nashe in the Learning of His Time." Diss., Cambridge University, 1942.

4756   THE MECHANICAL BRIDE: FOLK-LORE OF INDUSTRIAL MAN. New York: Vanguard, 1951. vii, 157 p.

4757   COUNTERBLAST. N.p.: n.p., [1954?]. N. pag. Rev. enl. ed. Designed by Harley Parker. Toronto: McClelland and Stewart, 1969. 141 p.

4758 THE GUTENBERG GALAXY: THE MAKING OF TYPOGRAPHIC MAN.
Toronto: University of Toronto Press, 1962. 293 p. Bibliog.

4759 UNDERSTANDING MEDIA: THE EXTENSIONS OF MAN. Toronto:
McGraw-Hill, 1964. vii, 359 p.

4760 VERBI-VOCO-VISUAL EXPLORATIONS WITH ADDITIONAL CONTRIBU-
TIONS BY V.J. PAPANEK. New York: Something Else, 1967. 61 p.

  Reprint of EXPLORATIONS, 8 (Oct. 1957), entire issue.

4761 THE MEDIUM IS THE MASSAGE: AN INVENTORY OF EFFECTS. By
Herbert Marshall McLuhan and Quentin Fiore. Coordinated by Jerome
Agel. New York: Bantam, 1967. 160 p.

4762 THROUGH THE VANISHING POINT: SPACE IN POETRY AND PAINTING.
By Herbert Marshall McLuhan and Harley Parker. World Perspectives,
vol. 37. New York: Harper and Row, 1968. xxiv, 267 p.

4763 WAR AND PEACE IN THE GLOBAL VILLAGE: AN INVENTORY OF
SOME OF THE CURRENT SPASTIC SITUATIONS THAT COULD BE ELIMI-
NATED BY MORE FEEDFORWORD. By Herbert Marshall McLuhan and
Quentin Fiore. Coordinated by Jerome Agel. New York: McGraw-
Hill, 1968. 190 p.

4764 THE INTERIOR LANDSCAPE: THE LITERARY CRITICISM OF MARSHALL
MCLUHAN, 1943-1962. Ed. Eugene McNamara. Toronto: McGraw-
Hill, in association with the University of Windsor Press, 1969. xiv,
239 p. Bibliog.

4765 EXPLORATIONS OF THE WAYS, MEANS AND VALUES OF MUSEUM
COMMUNICATION WITH THE VIEWING PUBLIC: SEMINAR. By Marshall
McLuhan, Harley Parker, Jacques Barzun. New York: Museum of the
City of New York, 1969. 80 p.

4766 SPECTRUM OF CATHOLIC ATTITUDES. By William F. Buckley and
Marshall McLuhan. Ed. Robert Campbell. Milwaukee: Bruce Publishing,
1969. xxx, 191 p.

4767 CULTURE IS OUR BUSINESS. New York: McGraw-Hill, 1970. 336 p.

4768 FROM CLICHÉ TO ARCHETYPE. By Marshall McLuhan and Wilfred Watson.
New York: Viking, 1970. 213 p.

4769 SHARING THE NEWS: FRIENDLY TEAMNESS, TEAMING FRIENDNESS.
New York: American Broadcasting Company, 1971. 9 l.

4770 TAKE TODAY: THE EXECUTIVE AS DROPOUT. By Marshall McLuhan and
Barrington Nevitt. Don Mills, Ont.: Logman, 1972. ix, 304 p. Bibliog.

4771 AUTRE HOMME, AUTRE CHRÉTIEN À L'ÂGE ÉLECTRONIQUE. By P. Babin and Marshall McLuhan. Lyon: Chalet, 1977. 191 p.

4772 CITY AS CLASSROOM: UNDERSTANDING LANGUAGE AND MEDIA. By Marshall McLuhan, Kathryn Hutchon, and Eric McLuhan. Agincourt, Ont.: Book Society, 1977. 184 p. Bibliog.

With an eight-page TEACHER'S GUIDE.

EDITED WORK

4773 SELECTED POETRY. By Alfred Tennyson. Ed. with introd. by Marshall McLuhan. Rinehart editions, no. 69. New York: Holt, Rinehart and Winston, 1956. xxxii, 394 p.

4774 EXPLORATIONS IN COMMUNICATION: AN ANTHOLOGY. Ed. Edmund Carpenter and Marshall McLuhan. Boston: Beacon, 1960. xii, 210 p.

4775 VOICES OF LITERATURE: AN ANTHOLOGY OF VERSE IN TWO VOL-UMES. Ed. Marshall McLuhan and Richard J. Schoeck. New York: Holt, Rinehart and Winston, vol. 1.: 1964. viii, 247 p. Vol. 2: 1965. xi, 275 p.

Shorter Work

ARTICLES

4776 "G.K. Chesterton: A Practical Mystic." DALHOUSIE REVIEW, 15 (Jan. 1936), 455-64.

4777 "Education of Free Man." STUDIES IN HONOR OF ST. THOMAS AQUINAS, 1 (1943), 47-50.

4778 "Dagwood's America." COLUMBIA, 23 (Jan. 1944), 3, 22.

4779 "Poetic vs. Rhetorical Exegesis: The Case for Leavis against Richards and Empson." SEWANEE REVIEW, 52 (Apr. 1944), 266-76.

4780 "The Analogical Mirrors." KENYON REVIEW, 6 (Sum. 1944), 322-32.

4781 "Kipling and Forster." SEWANEE REVIEW, 52 (July 1944), 332-43.

4782 "Wyndham Lewis: Lemuel in Lilliput." STUDIES IN HONOR OF ST. THOMAS AQUINAS, 2 (1944), 58-72.

4783 "The New York Wits." KENYON REVIEW, 7 (Wint. 1945), 12-28.

4784   "Out of the Castle into the Counting-House." POLITICS, 3 (Sept. 1946), 277-79.

4785   "Footprints in the Sands of Crime." SEWANEE REVIEW, 54 (Oct. 1946), 617-34.

4786   "The Southern Quality." SEWANEE REVIEW, 55 (July 1947), 357-83.

4787   "HENRY IV, A Mirror for Magistrates." UNIVERSITY OF TORONTO QUARTERLY, 17 (Jan. 1948), 152-60.

4788   Introd., PARADOX IN CHESTERTON, by Hugh Kenner. London: Sheed and Ward, 1948, pp. xi-xxii.

4789   "Mr. Eliot's Historical Decorum." RENASCENCE, 2 (Aut. 1949), 9-15.

4790   "The Psychopathology of TIME and LIFE." NEUROTICA, No. 5 (1949), pp. 5-16.

4791   "Joyce, Aquinas, and the Poetic Process." RENASCENCE, 4 (Aut. 1951), 3-11.

4792   "A Survey of Joyce Criticism." RENASCENCE, 4 (Aut. 1951), 12-18.

4793   "Defrosting Canadian Culture." AMERICAN MERCURY, 74 (Mar. 1952), 91-97.

4794   "Technology and Political Change." INTERNATIONAL JOURNAL, 7 (Sum. 1952), 189-95.

4795   "Comics and Culture." SATURDAY NIGHT, 28 Feb. 1953, pp. 19-20. Reprinted in no. 192.

4796   "The Later Innis." QUEEN'S QUARTERLY, 60 (Aut. 1953), 385-94.

4797   "Culture without Literacy." EXPLORATION, 1 (Dec. 1953), 117-27.

4798   "Sight, Sound and the Fury." COMMONWEAL, 9 Apr. 1954, pp. 7-11.

4799   "Media as Art Forms." EXPLORATIONS, 2 (Apr. 1954), 6-13.

4800   "New Media as Political Forms." EXPLORATIONS, 3 (Aug. 1954), 120-26.

4801 "Catholic Humanism and Modern Letters." In CHRISTIAN HUMANISM IN LETTERS. McAuley Lectures, 1954. By Howard R. Patch, Walter J. Ong, and H. Marshall McLuhan. West Hartford, Conn.: St. Joseph College, 1954, pp. 69-87.

4802 "Space, Time and Poetry." EXPLORATIONS, 4 (Feb. 1955), 56-62.

4803 "Radio and TV vs. the ABCED-Minded." EXPLORATIONS, 5 (June 1955), 12-18.

4804 "The Media Fit the Battle of Jericho." EXPLORATIONS, 6 (July 1956), 15-19.

4805 "David Riesman and the Avant-Garde." EXPLORATIONS, 7 (Mar. 1957), 112-16.

4806 "Jazz and Modern Letters." EXPLORATIONS, 7 (Mar. 1957), 74-76.

4807 "Media Alchemy in Art and Society." JOURNAL OF COMMUNICATION, 8 (Sum. 1958), 63-67.

4808 "The Electronic Revolution in North America." In INTERNATIONAL LITERARY ANNUAL NO. 1. Ed. John Wain. London: John Calder, 1958, pp. 165-69.

4809 "Knowledge, Ideas, Information, and Communication (A Canadian View)." YEARBOOK OF EDUCATION, 1958, pp. 225-32.

4810 "Myth and Mass Media." DAEDALUS, 88 (Spr. 1959), 339-48.

4811 "Analyst's Statement." CURRENT ISSUES IN HIGHER EDUCATION, 1959, pp. 176-81.

4812 "Printing and Social Change." In PRINTING PROCESS: A MID-CENTURY REPORT. Cincinnati: International Association of Printing House Craftsmen, 1959, pp. 81-112.

4813 "Electronics and the Changing Role of Print." AUDIO-VISUAL COMMUNICATION REVIEW, 8 (Sept.-Oct. 1960), 74-83.

4814 "Effects of the Improvement of Communication Media." JOURNAL OF ECONOMIC HISTORY, 20 (Dec. 1960), 566-75.

4815   REPORT ON PROJECT ON UNDERSTANDING NEW MEDIA. N.p.:
        U.S. Department of Health, Education and Welfare, 1960.

        Reprinted in no. 4940.

4816   "Tennyson and the Romantic Epic." In CRITICAL ESSAYS ON THE POETRY
        OF TENNYSON. Ed. John Kilham. London: Routledge and Kegan
        Paul, 1960, pp. 86-95.

4817   "Inside the Five Sense Sensorium." CANADIAN ARCHITECT, 6 (June
        1961), 49-54.

4818   "The Humanities in the Electronic Age." HUMANITIES ASSOCIATION
        BULLETIN, 34 [12] (Fall 1961), 3-11.

4819   "The Electronic Age--The Age of Implosion." In MASS MEDIA IN
        CANADA. Ed. John A. Irving. Toronto: Ryerson, 1962, pp. 179-205.

4820   "The Agenbite of Outwit." LOCATION, 1 (Spr. 1963), 41-44.

4821   "We Need a New Picture of Knowledge." In NEW INSIGHTS AND
        THE CURRICULUM DEVELOPMENT. Ed. Alexander Frazier. Washington,
        D.C.: National Education Association, 1963, pp. 57-70.

4822   "New Media and the Arts." ARTS IN SOCIETY, 3 (Sept. 1964), 239-42.

4823   "Notes on Burroughs." NATION, 28 Dec. 1964, pp. 517-19.

4824   Introd., THE BIAS OF COMMUNICATION, by Harold A. Innis. To-
        ronto: University of Toronto Press, 1964, pp. iii-xvi.

4825   "Radio: The Tribal Drum." AUDIO-VISUAL COMMUNICATION RE-
        VIEW, 12, No. 2 (1964), 133-45.

4826   "T.S. Eliot." CANADIAN FORUM, 44 (Feb. 1965), 243-44.

4827   "A New Journey for the Magi." DECISIVE YEARS, April 1965, pp.
        12-16.

4828   "Address at Vision 65." AMERICAN SCHOLAR, 35 (Spr. 1966),
        195-205.

4829   "Electronics and the Psychic Drop-Out: Marshall McLuhan on Schools."
        THIS MAGAZINE IS ABOUT SCHOOLS, 1 (Apr. 1966), 37-42.

4830   "Invisible Environment."   CANADIAN ARCHITECT, 11 (May 1966), 71–74; 11 (June 1966), 73–75.

4831   "Great Change-Overs for You."   VOGUE, July 1966, pp. 62–63, 114–15, 117.

4832   "The Relation of Environment to Anti-Environment."   UNIVERSITY OF WINDSOR REVIEW, 2 (Fall 1966), 1–10.

4833   "Cybernation and Culture."   In THE SOCIAL IMPACT OF CYBERNETICS. Ed. Charles R. Dechert.   Notre Dame: University of Notre Dame Press, 1966, pp. 95–108.

4834   "The Emperor's Old Clothes."   In THE MAN-MADE OBJECT.   Ed. Gyorgy Kepes.   New York: George Braziller, 1966, pp. 90–95.

4835   "Guaranteed Income in the Electric Age."   In THE GUARANTEED IN-COME: NEXT STEP IN ECONOMIC EVOLUTION?   Ed. Robert Theobald.   Garden City, N.Y.:   Doubleday, 1966, pp. 185–97.

4836   "The Future of Education: The Class of 1989."   By Herbert Marshall McLuhan and George B. Leonard.   LOOK, 21 Feb. 1967, pp. 23–25.

4837   "The Future of Morality: The Inner Versus the Outer Quest."   In THE NEW MORALITY: CONTINUITY AND DISCONTINUITY.   Ed. William Dunphy.   New York: Herder and Herder, 1967, pp. 175–89.

4838   Untitled Speech.   In TECHNOLOGY AND WORLD TRADE: PROCEED-INGS OF A SYMPOSIUM, 16–17 NOVEMBER 1966.   Ed. Robert L. Stern.   Washington, D.C.:   Government Printing Office, 1967, pp. 9–14.

4839   "Whole World is a Happening."   HARPER'S BAZAAR, Apr. 1968, pp. 152–61.

4840   MCLUHAN DEW-LINE NEWSLETTER.   New York: Human Development Corp., 1 (July 1968–July 1969), monthly; 2 (July–Aug. 1969 to Mar.-Apr. 1970), every two months.

         Sometimes as DEW-LINE NEWSPAPER or MARSHALL MCLUHAN DEW-LINE.

4841   "The Reversal of the Overheated Image."   PLAYBOY, Dec. 1968, pp. 131–34, 245.

4842 "Environment as Programmed Happening." In KNOWLEDGE AND THE FUTURE OF MAN: AN INTERNATIONAL SYMPOSIUM. Ed. Walter J. Ong. New York: Holt, Rinehart and Winston, 1968, pp. 113-24.

4843 "Wyndham Lewis." ATLANTIC MONTHLY, 224 (Dec. 1969), 93-94, 97-98.

4844 "Retribalized Makers." In NATURAL ENEMIES?? Ed. Alexander Klein. Philadelphia: J.B. Lippincott, 1969, pp. 341-46.

4845 "Cicero and the Renaissance Training for Prince and Poet." RENAISSANCE AND REFORMATION, 6, No. 3 (1970), 38-42.

4846 "The Ciceronian Program in Pulpit and in Literary Criticism." RENAISSANCE AND REFORMATION, 7, No. 1 (1970), 3-7.

4847 "Roles, Masks, and Performances." NEW LITERARY HISTORY, 2 (Spr. 1971), 517-31.

4848 "Innovation is Obsolete." EVERGREEN REVIEW, 15 (June 1971), 46-49, 64.

4849 "Discontinuity and Communication in Literature." In PROBLÈMES DE L'ANALYSE TEXTUELLE/PROBLEMS OF TEXTUAL ANALYSIS. Ed. Pierre R. Léon et al. Montréal: Didier, 1971, pp. 189-99.

4850 "Erasmus: The Man and the Masks." ERASMUS IN ENGLISH, 3 (1971), 7-10.

4851 Foreword, EMPIRE AND COMMUNICATIONS, by Harold Adams Innis. Rev. by Mary Quayle Innis. Toronto: University of Toronto Press, 1972, pp. v-xii.

4852 "Mr. Eliot and the St. Louis Blues." ANTIGONISH REVIEW, No. 18 (Sum. 1974), pp. 23-27.

4853 "At the Moment of Sputnik the Planet Became a Global Theater in Which There are no Spectators but Only Actors." JOURNAL OF COMMUNICATION, 24 (Wint. 1974), 48-58.

4854 "Francis Bacon: Ancient or Modern?" RENAISSANCE AND REFORMATION, 10, No. 2 (1974), 93-98.

4855 "The Violence in the Media." CANADIAN FORUM, 56 (Sept. 1976), 9-12.

4856 "Formal Causality in Chesterton." CHESTERTON REVIEW, 2 (1976), 253-59.

4857 "Cultures in the Electronic World: Can the Bottom Line Hold Quebec?" By Marshall McLuhan and Barrington Nevitt. PERCEPTION, 1 (Nov.-Dec. 1977), 66-69.

4858 "Alphabet, Mother of Invention." By Marshall McLuhan and R.K. Logan. INTERNATIONAL SOCIETY FOR GENERAL SEMANTICS, 34 (Dec. 1977), 373-83.

4859 "Canada: The Borderline Case." In THE CANADIAN IMAGINATION: DIMENSIONS OF A LITERARY CULTURE. Ed. David Staines. Cambridge, Mass.: Harvard University Press, 1977, pp. 226-48.

4860 "Rhetorical Spirals in FOUR QUARTETS." In FIGURES IN A GROUND: CANADIAN ESSAYS ON MODERN LITERATURE COLLECTED IN HONOR OF SHEILA WATSON. Ed. Diane Bessai and David Jackel. Saskatoon: Western Producer Prairie Books, 1978, pp. 76-86.

4861 "Pound, Eliot, and the Rhetoric of THE WASTE LAND." NEW LITERARY HISTORY, 10 (Spr. 1979), 557-80.

4862 "Living at the Speed of Light." MACLEAN'S, 7 Jan. 1980, pp. 32-33.

4863 "La Galaxie 80." L'ACTUALITÉ, 5 (Jan. 1980), 23-27.

4864 "Lewis's Prose Style." In WYNDHAM LEWIS: A REVALUATION: NEW ESSAYS. Ed. Jeffrey Meyers. Montreal: McGill-Queen's University Press, 1980, pp. 64-67.

For articles by McLuhan, see also no. 4940.

Manuscripts

4865 Public Archives, Ottawa.

SECONDARY MATERIAL

Bibliography

4866 THE WRITINGS OF MARSHALL McLUHAN: LISTED IN CHRONOLOGICAL ORDER FROM 1934 TO 1975: WITH AN APPENDED LIST OF REVIEWS

AND ARTICLES ABOUT HIM AND HIS WORK. Fort Lauderdale, Fla.: Wake-Brook House, 1975. 101 p.

Criticism

4867 Albanese, C.L. "Technological Religion: Life-Orientation and THE MECHANICAL BRIDE." JOURNAL OF POPULAR CULTURE, 10 (Sum. 1976), 14-27.

4868 Andrews, Cicily Isabel [Rebecca West, pseud.] McLUHAN AND THE FUTURE OF LITERATURE: THE ENGLISH ASSOCIATION PRESIDENTIAL ADDRESS 1969. London: Oxford University Press, 1969. 19 p.

4869 Arlen, M.J. "Marshall McLuhan and the Technological Embrace." NEW YORKER, 1 Apr. 1967, pp. 135-38.

Reprinted in nos. 4884 and 4934.

4870 Baldwin, Casey. "Interview with Professor Marshall McLuhan." MAC-LEAN'S, 7 Mar. 1977, pp. 4, 8-9.

4871 Barnett, J. "Architecture in the Electronic Age." ARCHITECTURAL RECORD, 141 (Mar. 1967), 151-52.

An interview.

4872 Becker, S.L. "McLuhan as Rorschach." JOURNAL OF BROADCASTING, 19 (Spr. 1975), 235-40. Reply: M.P. Breen, 20 (Fall 1976), 567-72.

4873 Behar, Jack. "McLuhan's FINNIGAN'S WAKE." DENVER QUARTERLY, 3 (Spr. 1968), 5-27.

4874 Bellegu, André. "Wiener, McLuhan et la Montée des Automates." LI-BERTÉ, 9 (Sept.-Oct. 1967), 38-50.

4875 Bermudo, José Manuel. EL McLUHANISMO: IDEOLOGIA DE LA TEC-NOCRACIA. Barcelona: Picazo, 1972. 219 p. Bibliog.

4876 Blake, R.W. "New English: Hot Stuff or Cool, Man, Cool." ENGLISH JOURNAL, 60 (Sept. 1971), 728-34.

4877 Bornstein, Eli. "An Interview with Marshall McLuhan." STRUCTURIST, No. 6 (1966), pp. 61-62, 64-68.

4878 Bourdin, Alain. MacLUHAN [sic]: COMMUNICATION, TECHNOLOGIE

ET SOCIÉTÉ. Paris: Éditions Universitaires, 1970. 142 p. Bibliog.

4879 Bronson, D.B. "Reading, Writing and McLuhan." ENGLISH JOURNAL, 57 (Nov. 1968), 1151-55.

4880 Burgess, Anthony. "The Modicum is the Messuage." SPECTATOR, 13 Oct. 1967, p. 427.

Reprinted in no. 4934.

4881 Cameron, E. "McLuhan, Youth and Literature." HORN BOOK, 48 (Oct. 1972), 433-40; 48 (Dec. 1972), 572-79.

4882 Carey, James W. "Harold Adams Innis and Marshall McLuhan." ANTIOCH REVIEW, 27 (Spr. 1967), 5-39.

Reprinted in no. 4934.

4883 Comstock, W. Richard. "Marshall McLuhan's Theory of Sensory Form: A Theological Reflection." SOUNDINGS, 51 (1968), 166-83.

4884 Crosby, Harry Herbert, and George R. Bond, eds. THE McLUHAN EXPLOSION: A CASEBOOK ON MARSHALL McLUHAN AND UNDERSTANDING MEDIA. New York: American Book, 1968. ix, 235 p.

Includes nos. 4869, 4885, 4889, 4900, 4903, 4910, and 4936.

4885 Culkin, John M. "A Schoolman's Guide to Marshall McLuhan." SATURDAY REVIEW, 18 Mar. 1967, pp. 51-53, 70-72.

Reprinted in nos. 4884 and 4934.

4886 Curtis, James M. "Marshall McLuhan and French Structuralism." BOUNDARY 2, 1 (Fall 1972), 134-46.

4887 de Kerckhove Varent, Derrick. "McLuhan: Art et Liberté." VIE DES ARTS, 18 (Aut. 1973), 19-23; English trans. p. 91.

4888 Demers, Pierre E. "Marshall McLuhan or the Return of the Nonliterate." FU JEN STUDIES, 4 (1971), 61-78.

4889 De Mott, Benjamin. "Against McLuhan." ESQUIRE, Aug. 1966, pp. 71-73.

Reprinted in nos. 4884 and 4940.

4890 Duffy, Dennis. MARSHALL McLUHAN. Canadian Writers, no. 1. Toronto: McClelland and Stewart, 1969. 64 p. Bibliog.

4891   Edwards, Thomas R. "The Soft Machine." PARTISAN REVIEW, 35 (Sum. 1968), 433-43.

4892   Efron, Arthur. "Making Peace with the Mechanical Bride." PAUNCH, No. 22 (Jan. 1965), pp. 65-73.

4893   Findlay, Peter R. "Clues to McLuhan." QUEEN'S QUARTERLY, 74 (Wint. 1967), 694-99.

4894   Finkelstein, Sidney. SENSE AND NONSENSE OF McLUHAN. New York: International, 1968. 122 p.

4895   Francks, Warren T. "The Normative Role of McLuhan: Paul Revere or Benedict Arnold?" JOURNALISM QUARTERLY, 45 (Spr. 1968), 25-30.

4896   Gamaleri, Gianpiera. LA GALASSIA McLUHAN: II MONDO PLAS-MATO DAI MEDIA? Rome: Armando Armando, 1976. 221 p. Bibliog.

4897   Gambino, Richard. "McLuhanism: A Massage That Muddles." MID-WEST QUARTERLY, 14 (Oct. 1972), 53-62.

4898   Girgus, Sam B. "The Mechanical Mind: Thoreau and McLuhan on Freedom, Technology and the Media." THOREAU JOURNAL QUARTERLY, 9, No. 4 (1977), 3-9.

4899   Hagler, Ronald. "Out of the Tribe. . . ." BRITISH COLUMBIA LI-BRARY QUARTERLY, 28 (July-Oct. 1964), 12-16.

4900   Hurley, N.P. "Marshall McLuhan: Communications Explorer." NA-TIONAL CATHOLIC WEEKLY, 18 Feb. 1967, pp. 241-43.

        Reprinted in no. 4884.

4901   "Interview de Herbert Marshall McLuhan." In THÉORIE DE L'IMAGE. Paris: R. Laffont, 1975, pp. 8-23.

4902   "Interview with Professor Marshall McLuhan." MACLEAN'S, 7 Mar. 1977, pp. 4, 8-9.

4903   Johansen, John M. "An Architecture for the Electronic Age." AMERICAN SCHOLAR, 35 (Sum. 1966), 461-71.

        Reprinted in nos. 4884 and 4940.

4904   Johnstone, Kenneth. "McLuhan's Art." OPEN LETTER, 3rd ser., No. 5 (Sum. 1976), pp. 75-79.

4905   Jones, Edward T. "Marshall McLuhan: Media Analyst." UNISA EN-
GLISH STUDIES, 2 (June 1968), 3-12.

4906   Kattan, Naïm. "Marshall McLuhan." LIBERTÉ, 9 (Sept.-Oct. 1967),
15-20.

4907   Kolb, Norman. "The New Education." BASILIAN TEACHER, 11 (Feb.
1967), 66-73.

An interview.

4908   Kostelanetz, Richard. "Il Pensiero di Marshall McLuhan." NUOVA
PRESENZA, 11 (1968), 13-33.

4909   _____. "Marshall McLuhan: A Hot Apostle in a Cool Culture." TWEN-
TIETH CENTURY, 175 (Aut. 1966), 38-45.

Reprinted in no. 4934.

4910   _____. "Marshall McLuhan: He Sees Significance Where Others See
Only Data." COMMONWEAL, 20 Jan. 1967, pp. 420-26.

Reprinted in no. 4884.

4911   Krutch, Joseph Wood. "If You Don't Mind My Saying So. . . ."
AMERICAN SCHOLAR, 36 (Aut. 1967), 532-35.

4912   Kuhn, H.B. "McLuhan: Hero or Heretic?" CHRISTIANITY TODAY,
13 Sept. 1968, pp. 8-9.

4913   Kushner, Eva. "Marshall McLuhan et la Survivance de la Littérature."
In ACTES DU VIe CONGRÈS DE L'ASSOCIATION INTERNATIONALE
DE LITTÉRATURE COMPARÉE/PROCEEDINGS OF THE 6TH CONGRESS
OF THE INTERNATIONAL COMPARATIVE LITERATURE ASSOCIATION.
Ed. Michel Cadot, Milan V. Dimić, David Malone, and Miklós Szabolcsi.
Stuttgart: Bieber, 1975, pp. 221-26.

4914   Leary, D.J. "Voices of Convergence: Teilhard, McLuhan and Brown."
CATHOLIC WORLD, 204 (Jan. 1967), 206-11.

4915   Lee, Richard. "The McLuhan Understanding of Man and History." CRES-
SET, 31 (Oct. 1968), 8-18.

4916   Lima, Lauro de Oliveira. MUTAÇÕES EM EDUÇAÇÃO SEGUNDO
McLUHAN. Petrópolis: Editôra Vozes, 1971. 63 p.

4917   Lindsey, Shelagh. "Understanding Marshall McLuhan." BRITISH CO-
        LUMBIA LIBRARY QUARTERLY, 28 (July-Oct. 1964), 5-11.

4918   Lohof, Bruce A. "Through a Shutter Brightly: Notes on the New Com-
        position." CENTENNIAL REVIEW, 16 (Spr. 1972), 180-91.

4919   Lueders, E. "McLuhan Thesis: Its Limits and Its Appeal." ENGLISH
        JOURNAL, 57 (Apr. 1968), 565-67.

4920   Michael, T.A. "McLuhan, Media and the Ministry." CHRISTIAN CEN-
        TURY, 29 May 1968, pp. 708-12.

4921   Miller, Jonathan. McLUHAN. London: Fontana/Collins, 1971. 139 p.
        Bibliog. Also as MARSHALL McLUHAN. New York: Viking, 1971.
        133 p. Bibliog.

4922   Milowicki, Edward J. "Some Medieval Light on Marshall McLuhan."
        STUDIES IN THE LITERARY IMAGINATION, 4 (Oct. 1971), 51-59.

4923   Mottram, Eric, Marshall McLuhan, George Steiner, Jonathan Miller,
        and Andrew Forge. "The World and Marshall McLuhan." JOURNAL
        OF CANADIAN STUDIES, 1 (Aug. 1966), 37-54.

            Includes an interview.

4924   Muggeridge, Malcolm. "The Medium is McLuhan." NEW STATESMAN,
        1 Sept. 1967, p. 253.

4925   Nairn, Tom. "Into McLuhan's Maelstrom." NEW STATESMAN, 22
        Sept. 1967, pp. 362-63.

4926   Newman, Peter C. "The Table Talk of Marshall McLuhan." MACLEAN'S,
        84 (June 1971), 42, 45.

4927   Newton-De Molina, David. "McLuhan: Ice-Cold." CRITICAL QUAR-
        TERLY, 12 (Spr. 1970), 78-88.

            Reply to no. 4940.

4928   Norden, Eric. "Playboy Interview: Marshall McLuhan: A Candid Con-
        versation with the High Priest of Popcult and Metaphysician of Media."
        PLAYBOY, Mar. 1969, pp. 53-74, 158. Rpt. Chicago: HMH, 1969.
        N. pag.

4929   Palmer, T. "Gadfly and the Dinosaur." ENGLISH JOURNAL, 58 (Jan.
        1969), 69-74.

4930   Petillon, Pierre-Yves. "Avant et Après McLuhan." CRITIQUE, 25 (June 1969), 504-11.

4931   Printz-Påhlson, Göran. "Anti-McLuhan." In his SLUTNA VÄRLDAR, ÖPPER RYMD: ESSÄER OCH KRITIKER 1956-1971 [CLOSED WORLDS, OPEN SPACE: ESSAYS AND CRITIQUES, 1956-1971]. Staffanstrop, Sweden: Cavefors, 1971, pp. 139-45.

4932   Richardson, Robert D., Jr. "McLuhan, Emerson and Henry Adams." WESTERN HUMANITIES REVIEW, 22 (Sum. 1968), 235-42.

4933   Rockman, Arnold. "McLuhanism: The Natural History of an Intellectual Fashion." ENCOUNTER, 31 (Nov. 1968), 28-36.

4934   Rosenthal, Raymond, ed. with introd. McLUHAN: PRO & CON. New York: Funk and Wagnalls, 1968. 308 p.

        Includes nos. 4869, 4880, 4882, 4885, 4909, and 4945.

4935   Saint-Martin, Fernande. "La Galaxie de Gutenberg ou le Point de Vue de Sirius sur l'Occident." LIBERTE, 9 (Sept.-Oct. 1967), 21-37.

4936   Schickel, Richard. "Marshall McLuhan: Canada's Intellectual Comet." HARPER'S, 231 (Nov. 1965), 62-68.

        Reprinted in no. 4884.

4937   Sheps, G. David. "Utopianism, Alienation and Marshall McLuhan." CANADIAN DIMENSION, 3 (Sept.-Oct. 1966), 23-26.

4938   Sidwell, Robert T. "Cooling Down the Classroom: Some Educational Implications of the McLuhan Thesis." EDUCATIONAL FORUM, 32 (Mar. 1969), 351-58.

4939   Stearn, Gerald Emanuel. "Conversations with McLuhan." ENCOUNTER, 28 (June 1967), 50-58.

        An interview.

4940   _____, ed. McLUHAN: HOT & COOL: A PRIMER FOR THE UN-DERSTANDING OF & A CRITICAL SYMPOSIUM WITH A REBUTTAL BY McLUHAN. New York: Dial, 1967. xviii, 312 p. Bibliog.

        Includes nos. 4815, 4889, 4903, and 4946; for reply, see no. 4927.

4941   Theall, Donald F. THE MEDIUM IS THE REAR VIEW MIRROR: UNDER-STANDING McLUHAN. Montreal: McGill-Queen's University Press, 1971. xviii, 261 p. Bibliog.

4942   Toeplitz, Krzysztof Teodor. "Marshall McLuhan, Prorok Elektronicznego Zbawiena (1)." DIALOG (Warsaw), 18, No. 12 (1973), 85-95.

4943   Travers, D. "But What if McLuhan Is Right?" CATHOLIC WORLD, 207 (June 1968), 111-15.

4944   Waddington, Raymond B. "Folklore of Electrical Man: Marshall McLuhan." NEW MEXICO QUARTERLY, 36 (Aut. 1966), 241-57.

4945   Wagner, Geoffrey. "Misunderstanding Media: Obscurity as Authority." KENYON REVIEW, 29 (Mar. 1967), 246-55.

>   Reprinted in no. 4934.

4946   Walker, Dean. "McLuhan Explains the Media." EXECUTIVE, 6 (Aug. 1964), 22-27.

>   Reprinted in no. 4940.

4947   Wasson, Richard. "Marshall McLuhan and the Politics of Modernism." MASSACHUSETTS REVIEW, 13 (Aut. 1972), 567-80.

4948   Watson, Wilfred. "Education in the Tribal/Global Village." TWEN-TIETH CENTURY LITERATURE, 16 (Jan.-Oct. 1970), 207-16.

4949   _____. "Marshall McLuhan and Multi-Consciousness: The Place Marie Dialogues." BOUNDARY 2, 3 (Fall 1974), 197-211.

4950   Watt, G. INDEX TO H.M. McLUHAN'S THE GUTENBERG GALAXY. N.p.: n.p., [196-?]. N. pag.

For criticism on McLuhan, see also nos. 126, 180, 291, 4644, and 5159.

Book Reviews

4951   THE MECHANICAL BRIDE: CFor, 32 (Oct. 1952), 166-67; ECONO-MIST, 30 Sept. 1967, p. 1201; LISTENER, 28 Sept. 1967, p. 386; NewR, 26 Nov. 1951, p. 21; NS, 22 Sept. 1967, p. 362; NYRB, 23 Nov. 1967, p. 6; PR, 35 (Sum. 1968), 433; PUNCH, 4 Oct. 1967, p. 520; UTQ, 21 (Apr. 1952), 314-15.

4952   COUNTERBLAST: ALPHABET, 18-19 (1971), 103-05; AntigR, 1 (Spr. 1970), 124-30; BCLQ, 33 (Jan. 1970), 21, 23; CanL, 47 (Wint. 1971), 91-93; NATION, 8 Dec. 1969, pp. 638-39; NewR, 7 Feb. 1970, p. 30; UTQ, 40 (Fall 1970), 103; WCR, 5 (June 1970), 38-40.

4953 THE GUTENBERG GALAXY: AA, 65 (Apr. 1963), 478; AAPSS, Nov. 1964, p. 219; ALPHABET, 6 (June 1963), 73-75; BCLQ, 26 (Jan. 1963), 25, 27-28; CanL, 14 (Aut. 1962), 65-67; CJEPS, 31 (May 1965), 269-73; DR, 43 (Spr. 1963), 121, 123, 125, 127; ECONOMIST, 30 Sept. 1967, p. 1201; ENCOUNTER, 20 (Feb. 1963), 76; ETC, 21 (Dec. 1964), 495; JQ, 39 (Aut. 1962), 528; LISTENER, 8 Nov. 1962, pp. 776, 779; LISTENER, 28 Sept. 1967, p. 386; MCMT, 22 (1965), 52; MLR, 58 (Oct. 1963), 542; NewR, 8 Oct. 1962, p. 12; NS, 21 Dec. 1962, p. 902; NS, 22 Sept. 1967, p. 362; NYTBR, 1 May 1966, p. 6; PUNCH, 4 Oct. 1967, p. 520; RUO, 32 (Oct. 1962), 502-03; SatN, 77 (Oct. 1962), 33-34; TC, 171 (Wint. 1962-63), 168; TLS, 1 Mar. 1963, p. 156; UTQ, 33 (Apr. 1964), 338-40; YR, 52 (Spr. 1963), 454.

4954 UNDERSTANDING MEDIA: CanL, 22 (Aut. 1964), 55-60; CFor, 44 (Oct. 1964), 165-66; CJEPS, 31 (May 1965), 269-73; CJPS, 2 (June 1969), 272-73; COMMENTARY, 39 (Jan. 1965), 79-81; ECONOMIST, 30 Sept. 1967, p. 1201; HAB, 16 (Spr. 1965), 96-98; JQ, 41 (1964), 595-96; LISTENER, 62 (1964), 895-96; LISTENER, 4 Dec. 1966, p. 35; LISTENER, 28 Sept. 1967, p. 386; MACLEAN'S, 20 June 1964, p. 53; NATION, 5 Oct. 1964, p. 194; NatR, 29 Nov. 1966, pp. 1224-25; NS, 11 Dec. 1964, p. 925; NS, 22 Sept. 1967, p. 362; NY, 27 Feb. 1965, p. 129; NYRB, 20 Aug. 1964, p. 15; NYTBR, 1 May 1966, p. 6; PUNCH, 4 Oct. 1967, p. 520; QJS, 51 (Feb. 1965), 86; QQ, 71 (Aut. 1964), 449-50; SatR, 26 Nov. 1966, p. 40; SatR, 17 Dec. 1966, p. 37; SoR, 4 (June 1968), 217-19; TamR, [33] (Aut. 1964), 79-86; TLS, 6 Aug. 1964, p. 693; UTQ, 34 (July 1965), 383-85.

4955 THE MEDIUM IS THE MASSAGE: COMMONWEAL, 23 June 1967, p. 395; CRITIC, 26 (Aug. 1967), 62; ECONOMIST, 30 Sept. 1967, p. 1201; EJ, 64 (May 1975), 98; HM, 234 (June 1967), 103; LISTENER, 28 Sept. 1967, p. 386; NATION, 15 May 1967, p. 631; NS, 22 Sept. 1967, p. 362; NYRB, 23 Nov. 1967, p. 6; NYTBR, 26 Mar. 1967, p. 6; PR, 35 (Sum. 1968), 433; PUNCH, 4 Oct. 1967, p. 520; QJS, 54 (Apr. 1968), 194; SatR, 11 Mar. 1967, p. 137; TLS, 28 Sept. 1967, p. 887.

4956 THROUGH THE VANISHING POINT: CFor, 48 (Feb. 1969), 255; Crit, 25 (June 1969), 504; NatR, 19 Nov. 1968, pp. 1174-76; NYRB, 2 Jan. 1969, p. 15; PR, 35 (Sum. 1968), 433; UTQ, 40 (Fall 1970), 104; VQR, 45 (Wint. 1969), 162-67.

4957 WAR AND PEACE IN THE GLOBAL VILLAGE: NatR, 19 Nov. 1968, pp. 1174-76; NYRB, 2 Jan. 1969, p. 15; UTQ, 40 (Fall 1970), 103.

4958 THE INTERIOR LANDSCAPE: CanL, 47 (Wint. 1971), 93-94; CRITI-CISM, 12 (Sum. 1970), 244; NYTBR, 21 Dec. 1969, p. 8; QQ, 78 (Sum. 1971), 321-33; QUARRY, 19 (Sum. 1970), 55-56; VQR, 46 (Sum. 1970), c; WCR, 5 (June 1970), 40.

4959 CULTURE IS OUR BUSINESS: NYTBR, 12 July 1970, p. 7; QJS, 57 (Apr. 1971), 239; SatR, 9 May 1970, p. 68.

4960 FROM CLICHÉ TO ARCHETYPE: JQ, 49 (1972), 180-81; NYTBR, 13 Dec. 1970, p. 7; SatR, 21 Nov. 1970, p. 32; UTQ, 41 (Sum. 1972), 413-14.

4961 TAKE TODAY: BCan, 1 (Aug. 1972), 6-7; CAB, 48 (Spr. 1973), 24; NatR, 31 Mar. 1972, p. 352; NewR, 10 June 1972, p. 25.

4962 CITY AS CLASSROOM: ETC, 35 (June 1978), 195-98; MACLEAN'S, 27 June 1977, pp. 57-58; Q&Q, 43, No. 13 (1977), 31-32.

MOWAT, FARLEY (1921--)

Born in Belleville, Ontario, Farley Mowat grew up in various parts of southern Ontario and in Saskatoon, Saskatchewan. He served in Sicily and Italy in World War II, then received a B.A. from the University of Toronto in 1949. Mowat has spent much time in remote parts of Canada, particularly in the Arctic and in Newfoundland. His writing, usually subjective nonfiction for a general audience, introduces unfamiliar regions and peoples, protests against social-ecological injustices, or more humorously shares personal experiences. LOST IN THE BARRENS won the Governor General's Award, THE BOAT WHO WOULDN'T FLOAT the Leacock Medal for Humour.

PRIMARY MATERIAL

Monographs

FICTION

4963 LOST IN THE BARRENS. Drawings by Charles Geer. Atlantic Monthly Press Book. Boston: Little, Brown, 1956. 244 p.

>   For children.

4964 OWLS IN THE FAMILY. Illus. Robert Frankenberg. Atlantic Monthly Press Book. Boston: Little, Brown, 1961. 103 p.

>   For children.

4965 THE BLACK JOKE. Illus. D. Johnson. Toronto: McClelland and Stewart, 1962. 177 p.

>   For children.

4966 THE CURSE OF THE VIKING GRAVE. Illus. Charles Geer. Toronto: McClelland and Stewart, 1966. x, 243 p.

>   For children.

4967   THE SNOW WALKER. Toronto: McClelland and Stewart, 1975. 222 p.
       Short stories.

NONFICTION PROSE

4968   PEOPLE OF THE DEER. Drawings by Samuel Bryant. London: Michael
       Joseph, 1952. 316 p. Rev. ed. PEOPLE OF THE DEER: DEATH OF
       A PEOPLE. Toronto: McClelland and Stewart, 1975. 318 p.

       First volume of Ihalmiut Series; see also no. 4972.

4969   THE REGIMENT. Toronto: McClelland and Stewart, 1955. xix, 312 p.

4970   THE DOG WHO WOULDN'T BE. Illus. Paul Galdone. Atlantic Monthly
       Press Book. Boston: Little, Brown, 1957. 238 p.

4971   THE GREY SEAS UNDER. Toronto: McClelland and Stewart, 1958.
       341 p.

4972   THE DESPERATE PEOPLE. Woodcuts by Rosemary Kilbourn. Atlantic
       Monthly Press Book. Boston: Little, Brown, 1959. xii, 305 p. Rev.
       ed. THE DESPERATE PEOPLE: DEATH OF A PEOPLE--THE IHALMIUT
       VOLUME II. Toronto: McClelland and Stewart, 1975. 271 p.

4973   THE SERPENT'S COIL. Drawings by F. Newfeld. Toronto: McClelland
       and Stewart, 1961. 189 p.

4974   NEVER CRY WOLF. Toronto: McClelland and Stewart, 1963. 247 p.

4975   WESTVIKING: THE ANCIENT NORSE IN GREENLAND AND NORTH
       AMERICA. Maps and Drawings by Claire Wheeler. Toronto: McClelland
       and Stewart, 1965. xiv, 494 p.

4976   FARLEY MOWAT SPEAKS OUT ON CANADA'S ROLE IN VIETNAM.
       N.p.: n.p., [1966?]. 13 p.

4977   CANADA NORTH. Toronto: McClelland and Stewart, 1967. 127 p.
       Rev. enl. ed. CANADA NORTH NOW: THE GREAT BETRAYAL. Photos.
       Shin Sugino. Toronto: McClelland and Stewart, 1976. 191 p. Rev.
       enl. ed. also as THE GREAT BETRAYAL: ARCTIC CANADA NOW. Photos.
       Shin Sugino. Boston: Little, Brown, 1976. 191 p.

4978   THE EXECUTIONERS. Searchlight. Agincourt, Ont.: Book Society,
       1967. 8 p.

4979   THIS ROCK WITHIN THE SEA: A HERITAGE LOST. Photos. John de
       Visser. Boston: Little, Brown, 1968. N. pag.

4980   THE BOAT WHO WOULDN'T FLOAT. Illus. Marc G.P. Berthier. To-
       ronto: McClelland and Stewart, 1969. 243 p.

4981   SIBIR: MY DISCOVERY OF SIBERIA. Toronto: McClelland and Stewart,
       1970. 313 p. Also as THE SIBERIANS. Boston: Little, Brown, 1970.
       x, 360 p.

4982   A WHALE FOR THE KILLING. Toronto: McClelland and Stewart, 1972.
       239 p.

4983   WAKE OF THE GREAT SEALERS. Illus. David Blackwood. Toronto:
       McClelland and Stewart, 1973. 159 p.

4984   AND NO BIRDS SANG. Toronto: McClelland and Stewart, 1979. 250 p.

       A memoir of World War II.

4985   THE WORLD OF FARLEY MOWAT: A SELECTION FROM HIS WORKS.
       Ed. with introd. by Peter Davison. Toronto: McClelland and Stewart,
       1980. xiv, 338 p. Bibliog.

EDITED WORK

4986   COPPERMINE JOURNEY: AN ACCOUNT OF A GREAT ADVENTURE,
       SELECTED FROM THE JOURNALS OF SAMUEL HEARNE BY FARLEY
       MOWAT. Boston: Little, Brown, 1958. 144 p.

4987   ORDEAL BY ICE. Toronto: McClelland and Stewart, 1960. 364 p.
       Bibliog. Index. Rev. ed. ORDEAL BY ICE: THE SEARCH FOR THE
       NORTHWEST PASSAGE. Toronto: McClelland and Stewart, 1973. 428 p.

       First volume in the trilogy, The Top of the World.

4988   THE POLAR PASSION: THE QUEST FOR THE NORTH POLE, WITH SE-
       LECTIONS FROM ARCTIC JOURNALS. Toronto: McClelland and Stewart,
       1967. 303 p. Bibliog. Rev. ed. Toronto: McClelland and Stewart,
       1973. 365 p. Bibliog.

       Second volume in the trilogy, The Top of the World, begin-
       ning with no. 4987.

4989   TUNDRA: SELECTIONS FROM THE GREAT ACCOUNTS OF ARCTIC
       LAND VOYAGES. Toronto: McClelland and Stewart, 1973. 415 p.
       Bibliog. Index.

Third volume in the trilogy, The Top of the World, beginning with no. 4987.

Shorter Work

SHORT STORIES

4990   "Fighting Memories Pale Beside 'Eving a Drink' in Bremen." SATURDAY NIGHT, 25 Aug. 1945, p. 33.

4991   "The Riddle of the Viking Bow." MACLEAN'S, 1 Sept. 1951, pp. 12-13, 37-41.

4992   "Blizzard in the Banana Belt." MACLEAN'S, 1 Feb. 1952, pp. 13, 45-48.

4993   "Blinding of André Maloche." SATURDAY EVENING POST, 15 Nov. 1952, pp. 38-39.

4994   "The Woman He Left to Die." SATURDAY EVENING POST, 31 Jan. 1953, p. 31.

4995   "Last Husky." SATURDAY EVENING POST, 2 Apr. 1955, p. 24.

ARTICLES

4996   "How to be a Canadian Writer--and Survive." SATURDAY NIGHT, 16 May 1953, pp. 22-23.

4997   "Battle Tactics." In STOP, LOOK AND LAUGH. By William B. Coates. Drawings by Alan Moyler. Toronto: T. Nelson, 1960, pp. 173-80.

4998   "On Being Mowat." MACLEAN'S, 84 (Aug. 1971), 24-25, 52-53.

4999   "Way of One Writer: Farley Mowat." CANADIAN LIBRARY JOURNAL, 32 (Feb. 1975), 56-57.

Manuscripts

5000   McMaster University Library, Hamilton, Ontario.

SECONDARY MATERIAL

Criticism

5001 Batten, Jack. "Quintessence of Farley Mowatism." SATURDAY NIGHT, 86 (July 1971), 15-17.

5002 Carver, Jos. E. "Farley Mowat: An Author for All Ages." BRITISH COLUMBIA LIBRARY QUARTERLY, 32 (Apr. 1969), 10-16.

5003 Guy, Ray. "Farley Mowat--The Fellow from Up-Along." In BAFFLES OF WIND AND TIDE: AN ANTHOLOGY OF NEWFOUNDLAND POETRY, PROSE AND DRAMA. Portugal Cove, Nfld.: Breakwater, 1974, pp. 41-42.

5004 Lister, Joan. "Mowat's Metamorphosis." FINANCIAL POST, 10 Feb. 1973 supplement, pp. 28-30.

　　　　An interview.

5005 Lucas, Alec. FARLEY MOWAT. Canadian Writers, no. 14. Toronto: McClelland and Stewart, 1976. 64 p.

5006 _____. "Farley Mowat: Writer for Young People." CANADIAN CHILDREN'S LITERATURE, Nos. 5-6 (1976), pp. 40-51.

5007 MacLulich, T.D. "The Alien Role: Farley Mowat's Northern Pastorals." STUDIES IN CANADIAN LITERATURE, 2 (Sum. 1977), 226-38.

5008 Martin, Betty. "The World of Farley Mowat." CANADIAN AUTHOR AND BOOKMAN, 45 (Wint. 1969), 1-3, 13.

5009 Myers, Jay. "Farley Mowat--Last of the Saga-Men." CANADIAN AUTHOR AND BOOKMAN, 52 (Sum. 1977), 4-7.

　　　　An interview.

5010 Ross, Alexander. "Farley Mowat: Interview." MACLEAN'S, 81 (Mar. 1968), 9, 64-68.

For criticism on Mowat, see also no. 4985.

Book Reviews

5011 OWLS IN THE FAMILY: CanL, 15 (Wint. 1963), 70-73; NY, 24 Nov. 1962, p. 248; NYTBR, 11 Mar. 1962, p. 30; TLS, 6 Apr. 1963, p. 381.

5012 THE CURSE OF THE VIKING GRAVE: AtlA, 57 (Nov. 1966), 63; CanL, 35 (Wint. 1968), 82; SatR, 12 Nov. 1966, p. 53.

5013 THE SNOW WALKER: BCan, 4 (Oct. 1975), 12-13; CanL, 76 (Spr. 1978), 129-30; CBRA, 1975, p. 124; CFor, 55 (Mar. 1976), 34; ContempR, 232 (Feb. 1978), 110-11; CRead, 17 (Jan. 1976), 2-4; MACLEAN'S, 6 Oct. 1975, p. 94; NYTBR, 22 Feb. 1976, p. 4; NYTBR, 6 Nov. 1977, p. 59; SatN, 90 (Nov. 1975), 78-80.

5014 PEOPLE OF THE DEER: CBRA, 1975, pp. 242-43; CFor, 32 (June 1952), 69; CGJ, 45 (Aug. 1952), v-vi; CHJ, 33 (Spr. 1952), 295-96; SatN, 12 Apr. 1952, p. 32; SatN, 18 Oct. 1952, pp. 16, 52; SatN, 25 Oct. 1952, pp. 17-19; SatN, 1 Nov. 1952, pp. 26-27; SPECTATOR, 21 Nov. 1952, pp. 661-62; UTQ, 22 (Apr. 1953), 318.

5015 THE REGIMENT: CRead, 14, No. 6 (n.d.), 7.

5016 THE DOG WHO WOULDN'T BE: NYTBR, 18 Aug. 1957, p. 10; SatN, 12 Oct. 1957, pp. 27-28; UTQ, 27 (Apr. 1958), 486-87.

5017 THE GREY SEAS UNDER: AtlA, 49 (Jan. 1959), 61; CAB, Wint. 1958-59, p. 13; NS, 31 Oct. 1959, p. 602; NYTBR, 19 Oct. 1958, p. 63; SatN, 3 Jan. 1959, p. 23; UTQ, 28 (Apr. 1959), 433-34.

5018 THE DESPERATE PEOPLE: ARCTIC, 14 (Dec. 1961), 266-68; AtlA, 50 (Feb. 1960), 73; CanL, 4 (Spr. 1960), 77-78; CBRA, 1975, p. 242; CFor, 39 (Jan. 1960), 233-34; CGJ, 60 (May 1960), x; GeoJ, 127 (Mar. 1961), 107; NS, 11 June 1960, p. 866; NYTBR, 1 Nov. 1959, p. 12; QQ, 66 (Wint. 1959-60), 677-78; SatR, 28 Nov. 1959, p. 27; SPECTATOR, 20 May 1960, p. 742; TLS, 24 June 1960, p. 399; UTQ, 29 (July 1960), 526-27; WatR, 5 (Sum. 1960), 74-78.

5019 THE SERPENT'S COIL: NORTH, 9 (Jan. 1962), 43-44; NY, 12 May 1962, p. 176; NYTBR, 13 May 1962, p. 10; SatN, 9 Dec. 1961, p. 42; TLS, 28 Sept. 1962, p. 767.

5020 NEVER CRY WOLF: Atl, 212 (Nov. 1963), 160; CanA, 26 (Jan. 1964), 27; CFor, 44 (Aug. 1964), 119-20; CGJ, 68 (May 1964), viii-ix; ECONOMIST, 19 Dec. 1964, p. 1357; EJ, 65 (Jan. 1976), 74; MONTREALER, 38 (Feb. 1964), 50-51; NORTH, 11 (Jan. 1964), 56; QQ, 71 (Sum. 1964), 276; SatN, 78 (Nov. 1963), 45; SatR, 20 Nov. 1965, p. 41; UTQ, 33 (July 1964), 439-40.

5021 WESTVIKING: AIHR, 14 (Wint. 1966), 31-32; ALPHABET, 13 (June 1967), 87-88; Atl, 216 (Nov. 1965), 195; AtlA, 56 (Dec. 1965), 11-16; CAB, 41 (Spr. 1966), 10-11; CanL, 33 (Sum. 1967), 63-67; CHR,

47 (Sept. 1966), 280-81; DR, 45 (Wint. 1965-66), 520-22; HISTORY,
52 (June 1967), 182; JCanS, 1 (Aug. 1966), 58-60, 62; LISTENER,
12 Jan. 1967, p. 69; NYRB, 25 Nov. 1965, p. 30; NYTBR, 7 Nov.
1965, p. 68; QQ, 73 (Wint. 1966), 601; SaskH, 19 (Wint. 1966),
38-39; SatR, 18 Dec. 1965, p. 33; TamR, 40 (Sum. 1966), 79-83;
TLS, 14 July 1966, p. 618; UTQ, 36 (July 1967), 486.

5022   CANADA NORTH: BCan, 5 (Oct. 1976), 15-16; CBRA, 1976, p. 303;
CFor, 57 (June 1977), 63; MACLEAN'S, 24 Jan. 1977, pp. 51-52;
NORTH, 24 (May 1977), 56; Q&Q, 42, No. 15 (1976), 31.

5023   THIS ROCK WITHIN THE SEA: CanL, 39 (Wint. 1969), 102; SatR,
26 Apr. 1969, p. 33; UTQ, 38 (July 1969), 408.

5024   THE BOAT WHO WOULDN'T FLOAT: AtlA, 60 (Dec. 1969), 58; BCLQ,
33 (Apr. 1970), 23, 25; DR, 49 (Wint. 1969-70), 585; MONTREALER,
[43] (Dec. 1969), 9; NYTBR, 10 May 1970, p. 18; SatR, 27 June
1970, p. 57; TLS, 19 Mar. 1971, p. 333; UTQ, 39 (July 1970), 385-86.

5025   SIBIR: CDim, 7 (Jan. 1971), 43-45; ECONOMIST, 15 Jan. 1972, p.
53; GeoJ, 138 (June 1972), 260; QQ, 79 (Sum. 1972), 278-79; SlavR,
31 (June 1972), 446.

5026   A WHALE FOR THE KILLING: AntigR, 12 (Wint. 1972 [1973]), 109-
10; BCan, 1 (Oct. 1972), 4; CanL, 57 (Sum. 1973), 120-24; DR, 52
(Wint. 1972-73), 682-83; EJ, 62 (Mar. 1973), 478; EJ, 65 (Jan. 1976),
74; SatR, 21 Oct. 1972, p. 80; TES, 30 Nov. 1979, p. 24; TLS, 16
Feb. 1973, p. 182.

5027   WAKE OF THE GREAT SEALERS: CFor, 54 (July 1974), 35; CGJ, 88
(June 1974), 46; NORTH, 21 (Jan. 1974), 35.

5028   AND NO BIRDS SANG: BCan, 8 (Oct. 1979), 20; BCan, 8 (Nov.
1979), 33; BOT, 3 (Apr. 1980), 149; CHR, 61 (Sept. 1980), 404-05;
CRead, 20, No. 10 ([1978]), [3-4]; CRITIC, 39 (Sept. 1980), part 1,
p. 7; MACLEAN'S, 8 Oct. 1979, p. 58; NewR, 8 Mar. 1980, p. 40;
NY, 17 Mar. 1980, p. 166; NYTBR, 24 Feb. 1980, pp. 12-13; Q&Q
45 (Dec. 1979), 28; SatN, 94 (Nov. 1979), 40-42.

5029   THE WORLD OF FARLEY MOWAT: BCan, 9 (Nov. 1980), 29; SatN,
95 (Nov. 1980), 68.

WOODCOCK, GEORGE (1921--)

Man of letters George Woodcock was born in Winnipeg, although he grew up in Shropshire and the Thames valley, England. In the 1930s and 1940s, he was active in anarchist and pacifist movements, and in the forties edited the little magazines NOW and FREEDOM. Woodcock returned to Canada, to Vancouver Island, in 1949. Between 1956 and 1963 he taught in the English department at the University of British Columbia; he also helped found the journal CANADIAN LITERATURE, which he edited from its beginnings in 1959 until 1977. He has travelled extensively in Europe, South America, India, and Asia.

A prolific critic, social historian, biographer, dramatist, scriptwriter, broadcaster, and poet, Woodcock has received several honorary degrees, the Molson Prize, the Order of Canada (which he refused), and, for CRYSTAL SPIRIT, the Governor General's Award.

This checklist selects, from among Woodcock's numerous articles, those on literary subjects.

PRIMARY MATERIAL

Monographs

NONFICTION PROSE

5030   NEW LIFE TO THE LAND: ANARCHIST PROPOSALS FOR AGRICULTURE. London: Freedom, 1942. 32 p.

5031   RAILWAYS AND SOCIETY. London: Freedom, 1943. 31 p.

5032   ANARCHY OR CHAOS. London: Freedom, 1944. 124 p.

5033   HOMES OR HOVELS: THE HOUSING PROBLEM & ITS SOLUTION. London: Freedom, 1944. 32 p.

5034   ANARCHISM AND MORALITY. London: Freedom, 1945. 16 p.

5035   WHAT IS ANARCHISM? London: Freedom, 1945. 13 p. Bibliog.

5036   WILLIAM GODWIN: A BIOGRAPHICAL STUDY. Foreword by Herbert Read. London: Porcupine, 1946. x, 266 p. Index.

5037   THE BASIS OF COMMUNAL LIVING. London: Freedom, 1947. 44 p.

5038   THE INCOMPARABLE APHRA. London: T.V. Boardman, 1948. 248 p.
       A biography of Aphra Behn.

5039   THE WRITER AND POLITICS. London: Porcupine, 1948. 248 p.

5040   THE PARADOX OF OSCAR WILDE. London: T.V. Boardman, 1949.
       239 p.

5041   BRITISH POETRY TODAY: AN ADDRESS DELIVERED TO THE STUDENTS
       AND PUBLIC AT THE UNIVERSITY OF BRITISH COLUMBIA, TUESDAY,
       JANUARY 24TH, 1950. Lecture Series, no. 7. Vancouver: University
       of British Columbia, 1950. 15 p.

5042   THE ANARCHIST PRINCE: A BIOGRAPHICAL STUDY OF PETER
       KROPOTKIN. By George Woodcock and Ivan Avakumovic. London:
       T.V. Boardman, 1950. 463 p. Bibliog.

5043   RAVENS AND PROPHETS: AN ACCOUNT OF JOURNEYS IN BRITISH
       COLUMBIA, ALBERTA, AND SOUTHERN ALASKA. London: Allan
       Wingate, 1952. 244 p.

5044   PIERRE-JOSEPH PROUDHON: A BIOGRAPHY. New York: Macmillan
       1956. 291 p. Bibliog.; rpt. as PIERRE-JOSEPH PROUDHON: HIS
       LIFE AND WORK. Studies in the Libertarian and Utopian Tradition.
       New York: Schocken Books, 1972. 295 p. Bibliog.

5045   PAPERS OF THE SHAW FESTIVAL. By S.N.F. Chant, George Woodcock,
       and David C. Corbett. Introd. M.W. Steinberg. Lecture Series, no.
       26. Vancouver: University of British Columbia, 1956. iii, 56 p.

5046   TO THE CITY OF THE DEAD: AN ACCOUNT OF TRAVELS IN MEXICO.
       London: Faber and Faber, 1957. 271 p.

5047   INCAS AND OTHER MEN: TRAVELS IN THE ANDES. London: Faber
       and Faber, 1959. 268 p.

5048 ANARCHISM: A HISTORY OF LIBERTARIAN IDEAS AND MOVEMENTS. Cleveland: Meridian Books, 1962. 504 p. Bibliog.; rpt. with a Post-script. Harmondsworth, Engl.: Penguin, 1975. 492 p. Bibliog. Index.

5049 FACES OF INDIA: A TRAVEL NARRATIVE. Illus. Ingeborg Woodcock. London: Faber and Faber, 1964. 280 p.

5050 ASIA, GODS AND CITIES: ADEN TO TOKYO. London: Faber and Faber, 1966. 340 p.

5051 CIVIL DISOBEDIENCE. Toronto: Canadian Broadcasting Corporation, 1966. 69 p.

5052 THE CRYSTAL SPIRIT: A STUDY OF GEORGE ORWELL. Boston: Little, Brown, 1966. vii, 366 p. Bibliog. Index.

5053 THE GREEKS IN INDIA. London: Faber and Faber, 1966. 199 p. Bibliog.

5054 KERALA: A PORTRAIT OF THE MALABAR COAST. London: Faber and Faber, 1967. 323 p. Bibliog.

5055 THE DOUKHOBORS. By George Woodcock and Ivan Avakumovic. Toronto: Oxford University Press, 1968. 382 p. Bibliog.

5056 THE BRITISH IN THE FAR EAST. Social History of the British Overseas. London: Weidenfeld and Nicolson, 1969. xxviii, 259 p. Bibliog.

5057 HENRY WALTER BATES: NATURALIST OF THE AMAZONS. Great Travel-lers. London: Faber and Faber, 1969. 269 p. Bibliog.

5058 HUGH MacLENNAN. Studies in Canadian Literature, 5. Toronto: Copp Clark, 1969. vi, 121 p. Bibliog.

5059 THE TRADE UNION AND THE COMMUNITY. Tavistock Lecture, 1968. London: Tavistock Institute of Human Relations, 1969. 14 p.

5060 CANADA AND THE CANADIANS. Photos. Ingeborg Woodcock. To-ronto: Oxford University Press, 1970. 344 p. Bibliog. Rev. ed. To-ronto: Macmillan, 1973. 346 p.

5061 THE HUDSON'S BAY COMPANY. New York: Crowell-Collier, 1970. 186 p.

5062 MORDECAI RICHLER. Canadian Writers, no. 6. Toronto: McClelland and Stewart, 1970. 62 p. Bibliog.

5063 ODYSSEUS EVER RETURNING: ESSAYS ON CANADIAN WRITERS AND WRITING. Introd. W.H. New. New Canadian Library, no. 71. Toronto: McClelland and Stewart, 1970. xv, 158 p.

    Includes general discussion of Canadian literature and articles on MacLennan, Callaghan, Moore, Wyndham Lewis, Lowry, Irving Layton, Leonard Cohen, A.J.M. Smith, and Birney.

5064 INTO TIBET: THE EARLY BRITISH EXPLORERS. Great Travellers. London: Faber and Faber, 1971. 277 p. Bibliog. Index.

5065 MOHANDAS GANDHI. Modern Masters, M15. New York: Viking, 1971. 133 p. Bibliog.; rpt. as GANDHI. London: Collins, 1972. 108 p. Bibliog.

5066 DAWN AND THE DARKEST HOUR: A STUDY OF ALDOUS HUXLEY. New York: Viking, 1972. 299 p. Bibliog. Index.

5067 HERBERT READ: THE STREAM AND THE SOURCE. London: Faber and Faber, 1972. 304 p. Bibliog. Index.

5068 THE REJECTION OF POLITICS AND OTHER ESSAYS ON CANADA, CANADIANS, ANARCHISM AND THE WORLD. Toronto: New, 1972. xiii, 192 p.

    Some literary criticism, including nos. 5159-60.

5069 WHO KILLED THE BRITISH EMPIRE? AN INQUEST. London: Cape, 1974. 339 p. Bibliog.

5070 AMOR DE COSMOS: JOURNALIST AND REFORMER. Canadian Lives. Don Mills, Ont.: Oxford University Press, 1975. ix, 177 p. Bibliog. Index.

5071 GABRIEL DUMONT: THE MÉTIS CHIEF AND HIS LOST WORLD. Edmonton, Alta.: Hurtig, 1975. 256 p. Bibliog.

5072 CANADIAN POETS, 1960-1973: A LIST. Ottawa: Golden Dog, 1976. x, 69 p.

5073 SOUTH SEA JOURNEY. Toronto: Fitzhenry and Whiteside, 1976. 341 p. Index.

5074   PEOPLES OF THE COAST: THE INDIANS OF THE PACIFIC NORTHWEST. Edmonton, Alta.: Hurtig, 1977. 223 p. Bibliog. Index.

5075   FACES FROM HISTORY: CANADIAN PROFILES & PORTRAITS. Edmonton, Alta.: Hurtig, 1978. 254 p. Index.

5076   GABRIEL DUMONT. Canadians. Don Mills, Ont.: Fitzhenry and Whiteside, 1978. 63 p. Bibliog.

5077   THOMAS MERTON, MONK AND POET: A CRITICAL STUDY. Vancouver: Douglas and McIntyre, 1978. 200 p. Bibliog. Index.

5078   THE CANADIANS. Don Mills, Ont.: Fitzhenry and Whiteside, 1979. 301 p. Index. Also as THE CANADIAN. Cambridge, Mass.: Harvard University Press, 1979. 301 p. Index.

        Includes a chapter "The Life of the Arts."

5079   A GEORGE WOODCOCK READER. Ed. with introd. by Doug Fetherling. Ottawa: Deneau and Greenberg, 1980. xiv, 238 p. Bibliog.

        Some previously unpublished material and a number of reprinted pieces, including nos. 5129, 5148, 5150, and 5174.

5080   A PICTURE HISTORY OF BRITISH COLUMBIA. Edmonton: Hurtig, 1980. 240 p. Index.

5081   THE WORLD OF CANADIAN WRITING: CRITIQUES & RECOLLECTIONS. Vancouver: Douglas and McIntyre, 1980. xi, 306 p.

        Reprints nos. 5159, 5162, 5165, 5167, 5177, 5179-80, 5184, 5192-93, 5195-97, 5199, and 5203.

5082   100 GREAT CANADIANS. Edmonton: Hurtig, 1980. 160 p.

5083   CONFEDERATION BETRAYED: THE CASE AGAINST TRUDEAU'S CANADA. Madeira Park, B.C.: Harbour, 1981. 198 p. Bibliog.

5084   IVAN EYRE. Preface by John Hirsch. Don Mills, Ont.: Fitzhenry and Whiteside, 1981. 191 p. Bibliog. Index.

5085   THE MEETING OF TIME AND SPACE: REGIONALISM IN CANADIAN LITERATURE. Edmonton: NeWest Institute for Western Canadian Studies, 1981. 38 p.

5086   TAKING IT TO THE LETTER. Dunvegan, Ont.: Quadrant Books, 1981. 159 p. Index.

        Correspondence with Canadian authors.

POETRY

5087   SIX POEMS. London: E. Lahr, 1938. N. pag.

5088   BALLAD OF AN ORPHAN HAND. London: E. Lahr, 1939. N. pag.

5089   THE WHITE ISLAND. London: Fortune, [1940]. 39 p.

5090   THE CENTRE CANNOT HOLD. Routledge New Poets, 10. London: Routledge, 1943. 44 p.

5091   IMAGINE THE SOUTH. Pasadena, Calif.: private printing, 1947. N. pag.

5092   SELECTED POEMS OF GEORGE WOODCOCK. Illus. Pat Gangnon. Toronto: Clarke, Irwin, 1967. N. pag.

5093   NOTES ON VISITATIONS: POEMS 1936-1975. Introd. Al Purdy. Toronto: Anansi, 1975. x, 101 p.

5094   ANIMA, OR, SWANN GROWN OLD: A CYCLE OF POEMS. Coatsworth, Ont.: Black Moss, 1977. 31 p.

5095   THE KESTREL AND OTHER POEMS OF PAST AND PRESENT. Sunderland, Engl.: Ceolfrith, 1978. 54 p.

5096   THE MOUNTAIN ROAD: POEMS. Fiddlehead Poetry Books, 296. Fredericton, N.B.: Fiddlehead, 1980. 70 p.

DRAMA

5097   GABRIEL DUMONT AND THE NORTHWEST REBELLION. Toronto: Playwrights Co-Op, 1976. 32 p.

        Originally a radio play entitled SIX DRY CAKES FOR THE HUNTED.

5098   TWO PLAYS: THE ISLAND OF DEMONS; SIX DRY CAKES FOR THE HUNTED. Vancouver: Talonbooks, 1977. 110 p.

EDITED WORK

5099   WILLIAM GODWIN: SELECTIONS FROM POLITICAL JUSTICE. By William Godwin. Ed. with introd. by George Woodcock. London: Freedom, 1943. 32 p.

5100 A HUNDRED YEARS OF REVOLUTION: 1848 AND AFTER. Ed with preface by George Woodcock. London: Porcupine, 1948. 286 p.

5101 LETTERS OF CHARLES LAMB. Selected, with introd. and notes by George Woodcock. London: Grey Walls, 1950. 227 p.

5102 A CHOICE OF CRITICS: SELECTIONS FROM CANADIAN LITERATURE. Toronto: Oxford University Press, 1966. xxi, 247 p. Bibliog.

> Reprints general discussions (nos. 540-41) and articles on poets and novelists, including MacLennan (no. 5145), Klein (no. 2146), Callaghan (no. 5148), and Davies (no. 1358).

5103 VARIATIONS ON THE HUMAN THEME. Toronto: Ryerson, 1966. 241 p.

5104 RURAL RIDES. By William Cobbett. Harmondsworth, Engl.: Penguin, 1967. 533 p.

5105 THE EGOIST. By George Meredith. Ed. with introd. by George Woodcock. Harmondsworth, Engl.: Penguin, 1968. 606 p.

5106 THE SIXTIES: WRITERS AND WRITING OF THE DECADE: A SYMPOSIUM TO CELEBRATE THE TENTH ANNIVERSARY OF CANADIAN LITERATURE. Vancouver: University of British Columbia Publications Centre, 1969. 138 p.

> Among the articles reprinted are ones by Laurence (no. 2295), Richler (no. 3707), MacLennan (no. 3008), and Norman Levine and articles on the novel, short story, and criticism (nos. 440, 508, 511).

5107 A TALE OF TWO CITIES. By Charles Dickens. Ed. with introd. by George Woodcock. Illus. Hablot L.[K.] Browne (Phiz'). Harmondsworth, Engl.: Penguin, 1970. 410 p.

5108 MALCOLM LOWRY: THE MAN AND HIS WORK. Canadian Literature Series, 3. Ed. with introd. by George Woodcock. Vancouver: University of British Columbia Press, 1971. ix, 174 p. Bibliog.

> Four original articles and reprints of others, particularly from CANADIAN LITERATURE.

5109 WYNDHAM LEWIS IN CANADA. Introd. Julian Symons. Canadian Literature Series, 1. Vancouver: University of British Columbia Publications Centre, 1971. vii, 110 p. Bibliog.

5110 TYPEE: A PEEP AT POLYNESIAN LIFE. By Herman Melville. Ed. with introd. and notes by George Woodcock. Harmondsworth, Engl.: Penguin, 1972. 367 p.

5111   COLONY AND CONFEDERATION: EARLY CANADIAN POETS AND
        THEIR BACKGROUND. Introd. Roy Daniells. Canadian Literature
        series, 6. Vancouver: University of British Columbia Press, 1974. vii,
        218 p.

5112   POETS AND CRITICS: ESSAYS FROM CANADIAN LITERATURE, 1966-74.
        Toronto: Oxford University Press, 1974. x, 246 p.

        Mainly on poetry; also reprints articles (nos. 716 and 1203)
        discussing Leonard Cohen's and Atwood's fiction.

5113   THE CANADIAN NOVEL IN THE TWENTIETH CENTURY: ESSAYS FROM
        CANADIAN LITERATURE. Ed. with introd. by George Woodcock. New
        Canadian Library, no. 115. Toronto: McClelland and Stewart, 1975.
        xi, 337 p. Bibliog.

        Reprints articles on twenty-four Canadian novelists.

5114   THE ANARCHIST READER. Hassocks, Engl.: Harvester, 1977. 383 p.
        Bibliog.

5115   THE RETURN OF THE NATIVE. By Thomas Hardy. Ed. with introd.
        and notes by George Woodcock. Harmondsworth, Engl.: Penguin, 1978.
        490 p.

Shorter Work

SHORT STORIES

5116   "Frail Lilies." SERPENT, Feb. 1938, p. 67.

5117   "Fungi." SERPENT, July 1938, pp. 166-67.

ARTICLES

5118   "William Godwin and Political Justice." NOW, 2nd ser., 2 (1943),
        20-29.

5119   "Herman Melville." FREEDOM, 1 Feb. 1947, pp. 6-7.

5120   "The Poetry of Alex Comfort." POETRY QUARTERLY, 9 (Sum. 1947),
        106-15.

5121   "A Study in Decline." NOW, 7 (July-Aug. 1947), 42-51.
        Discusses H.G. Wells.

5122   "Aldous Huxley: An Unrealized Novelist." GATE, 2 (June–Aug. 1948), 10–19.

5123   Introd. and notes, THE SOUL OF MAN UNDER SOCIALISM, by Oscar Wilde. London: Porcupine, 1948, pp. v–viii, 61–62.

5124   "Letter from North America: Reflections on a Colonial Culture." DELPHIC REVIEW, Spr. 1950, pp. 44–48.

5125   "Orwell and Conscience." WORLD REVIEW, Apr. 1950, pp. 28–33.

5126   "Hugh MacLennan." NORTHERN REVIEW, 3 (Apr.–May 1950), 2–10.
        Reprinted in no. 3044.

5127   "Aldous Huxley: The Growth of a Moralist." TOMORROW (New York), Feb. 1951, pp. 52–56.

5128   "Henry James and the Conspirators." SEWANEE REVIEW, 60 (Apr. 1952), 219–29.

5129   "Recollections of George Orwell." NORTHERN REVIEW, Aug.–Sept. 1953, pp. 17–27.
        Reprinted in no. 5079.

5130   "On the Day of the Dead." NORTHERN REVIEW, 6 (Dec.–Jan. 1953–54), 15–21.
        Discusses Lowry.

5131   "Dylan Thomas and the Welsh Environment." ARIZONA QUARTERLY, 10 (Wint. 1954), 293–305.

5132   "Koestler as Novelist." CANADIAN FORUM, 34 (Feb. 1955), 250–51.

5133   "The Intellectual Fury." NEW YORKER, 4 June 1955, pp. 104, 106, 109–13.

5134   "Proudhon, an Appreciation." DISSENT, 2 (Aut. 1955), 394–405.

5135   "A View of Canadian Criticism." DALHOUSIE REVIEW, 35 (Aut. 1955), 216–23.
        Reprinted in no. 5063.

5136   "Five Who Fear the Future." NEW REPUBLIC, 16 Apr. 1956, pp. 17-19.

5137   "Citizens of Babel: A Study of Joyce Cary." QUEEN'S QUARTERLY, 63 (Sum. 1956), 236-46.

5138   "Mexico and the English Novelist." WESTERN REVIEW, 21 (Aut. 1956), 21-32.

5139   "Utopias in Negative." SEWANEE REVIEW, 64 (Wint. 1956), 81-97.

5140   "The Disengaged: A Letter from France." TAMARACK REVIEW, No. 8 (Sum. 1958), pp. 46-54.

5141   "Malcolm Lowry's UNDER THE VOLCANO." MODERN FICTION STUDIES, 4 (Sum. 1958), 151-56.

        Reprinted in no. 5063.

5142   "The Tentative Confessions of a Prospective Editor." BRITISH COLUMBIA LIBRARY QUARTERLY, 23 (July 1959), 17-21.

5143   "Under Seymour Mountain." CANADIAN LITERATURE, No. 8 (Spr. 1961), pp. 3-6.

        Discusses Lowry; reprinted in nos. 5063 and 5108.

5144   "Malcolm Lowry as Novelist." BRITISH COLUMBIA LIBRARY QUARTERLY, 24 (Apr. 1961), 25-30.

        Reprinted in no. 5063.

5145   "A Nation's Odyssey: The Novels of Hugh MacLennan." CANADIAN LITERATURE, No. 10 (Aut. 1961), pp. 7-18.

        Reprinted in nos. 195, 5063, and 5102; for reply, see no. 3005.

5146   "Writing in Babel: Language & Literature in Modern India." TAMARACK REVIEW, 24 (Sum. 1962), 91-100.

5147   Introd., TURVEY, by Earle Birney. New Canadian Library, no. 34. Toronto: McClelland and Stewart, 1963, pp. ix-xv.

        Reprinted in nos. 872 and 5063.

5148   "Lost Eurydice: The Novels of Callaghan." CANADIAN LITERATURE, No. 21 (Sum. 1964), pp. 21-35.

        Reprinted in nos. 1082, 5063, 5079, 5102, and 5113.

5149   "Away from Lost Worlds." In ON CONTEMPORARY LITERATURE. Ed.
       Richard Kostelanetz. New York: Avon, 1964, pp. 97-109.

       Reprinted in nos. 206 and 5063.

5150   "Editorial Balance Sheet: Six Years of CANADIAN LITERATURE." BRITISH
       COLUMBIA LIBRARY QUARTERLY, 28 (Apr. 1965), 3-9.

       Reprinted in no. 5079.

5151   Introd., SON OF A SMALLER HERO, by Mordecai Richler. New Ca-
       nadian Library, no. 45. Toronto: McClelland and Stewart, 1966, pp.
       vii-xii.

       Reprinted in nos. 3755 and 5062.

5152   "Dylan Thomas: Flower of the Man." NEW LEADER, 5 June 1967, pp.
       18-20.

5153   "The Deepening Solitude: Notes on the Rebel in Literature." MALAHAT
       REVIEW, No. 5 (Jan. 1968), pp. 45-62.

5154   "On George Orwell." By John Wain and George Woodcock. COM-
       MENTARY, 47 (June 1969), 28, 30.

5155   "The Solitary Revolutionary: Proudhon's Notebooks." ENCOUNTER, 33
       (Sept. 1969), 46-55.

5156   "On Proudhon's WHAT IS PROPERTY?" ANARCHY, 106 (Dec. 1969),
       353-59.

5157   "COLONEL JACK and TOM JONES: Aspects of a Changing Century."
       WASCANA REVIEW, 5, No. 1 (1970), 67-73.

5158   "Life as a Mandala." NATION, 6 Sept. 1971, pp. 181-83.

       Discusses Herbert Read.

5159   "Inquest on McLuhan." NATION, 1 Nov. 1971, pp. 437-39.

       Reprinted in nos. 5068 and 5081.

5160   "The Wheel of Exile." TAMARACK REVIEW, 58 (1971), 65-72.

       Discusses Richler's ST. URBAIN'S HORSEMAN. Reprinted in
       no. 5068.

5161   "Margaret Atwood." LITERARY HALF-YEARLY, 13 (July 1972), 233-42.

5162 "Callaghan's Toronto: The Persona of a City." JOURNAL OF CANA-
DIAN STUDIES, 7 (Aug. 1972), 21-24.

Reprinted in no. 5081.

5163 "Nietzsche in the Thirties." MALAHAT REVIEW, No. 24 (Oct. 1972),
pp. 67-78.

5164 "On Being a Writer in Canada: A Personal Note." SATURDAY NIGHT,
87 (Nov. 1972), 57-59.

5165 Introd., SELECTED POEMS, by Al Purdy. Toronto: McClelland and
Stewart, 1972, pp. 8-15.

Reprinted in no. 5081.

5166 "On the Resources of Canadian Writing." In ROYAL COMMISSION
ON BOOK PUBLISHING: BACKGROUND PAPERS. Toronto: Queen's
Printer, 1972, pp. 61-85.

5167 "On A.M. Klein: A Tentative Note." JEWISH DIALOG, Passover
1973, pp. 58-59.

Reprinted in no. 5081.

5168 "The Critic as Mediator." SCHOLARLY PUBLISHING, 4 (Apr. 1973),
201-09.

5169 "The Darkness Violated by Light: A Revisionist View of H.G. Wells."
MALAHAT REVIEW, No. 26 (Apr. 1973), pp. 144-60.

5170 "De Mille and the Utopian Vision." JOURNAL OF CANADIAN FIC-
TION, 2 (Sum. 1973), 174-79.

Reprinted in no. 172.

5171 "Reprints and the Reading Public." CANADIAN LITERATURE, No. 57
(Sum. 1973), pp. 98-107.

5172 "Surfacing to Survive: Notes of the Recent Atwood." ARIEL, 4 (July
1973), 16-28.

Discusses SURFACING and SURVIVAL.

5173 "The Evergreen Maple Leaf." NATION, 1 Oct. 1973, pp. 309-13.

5174   "Poetry Magazines of the Thirties: A Personal Note." TAMARACK REVIEW, No. 60 (Oct. 1973), pp. 68-74.

       Reprinted in no. 5079.

5175   "Nietzsche, Camus and the Transcendence of Pessimism." EVENT, 2, No. 3 (1973), 18-27.

5176   "The Triumph of Talk in the Novels of Thomas Love Peacock." EVENT, 3, No. 1 (1973), 15-34.

5177   "The Dotted Points of Light." SATURDAY NIGHT, 89 (May 1974), 21, 23-24.

       Discusses Canadian writers; reprinted in no. 5081.

5178   "Alain-Fournier and the Lost Land." QUEEN'S QUARTERLY, 81 (Aut. 1974), 348-56.

5179   "Diana's Priest in the Bush Garden." BOUNDARY 2, 3 (Fall 1974), 185-96.

       Discusses Frye; reprinted in no. 5081.

5180   "Ethel Wilson." CANADIAN FICTION MAGAZINE, No. 15 (Aut. 1974), pp. 44-49.

       Reprinted in no. 5081.

5181   "Things as They Might Be: Things as They Are: Notes on the Novels of William Godwin." DALHOUSIE REVIEW, 54 (Wint. 1974-75), 685-97.

5182   "The Prose and Cons of 1974." BOOKS IN CANADA, 4 (Feb. 1975), 3-4, 6, 8.

5183   "A Fiction of Masks: Cocteau's Novels of Youth." ONTARIO REVIEW, No. 2 (Spr.-Sum. 1975), pp. 25-32.

5184   "Margaret Atwood: Novelist as Poet." In THE CANADIAN NOVEL IN THE TWENTIETH CENTURY. Ed. George Woodcock. Toronto: McClelland and Stewart, 1975, pp. 312-27.

       Based on nos. 5161 and 5172; reprinted in no. 5081.

5185   "On Kafka." JEWISH DIÁLŎG, Passover 1976, pp. 32-35.

5186 "Don Quixote's Dilemma, or, The Future of Fiction." CANADIAN FICTION MAGAZINE, No. 22 (Sum. 1976), pp. 65-73.

Reprinted in no. 136.

5187 "The Lure of the Primitive." AMERICAN SCHOLAR, 45 (Sum. 1976), 387-402.

5188 "Transformation Mask for Margaret Atwood." MALAHAT REVIEW, No. 41 (Jan. 1977), pp. 52-56.

5189 "From Up the Gum Tree: Wyndham Lewis and THE REVENGE FOR LOVE." QUEEN'S QUARTERLY, 84 (Sum. 1977), 210-17.

5190 "Intermittencies of Place and Poetry." CVII, 2, No. 4 (1977), 18-20.

5191 "Making the Poem." POETRY WINDSOR POÉSIE, 3, Nos. 1-2 (1977), 35-41.

5192 "Possessing the Land: Notes on Canadian Fiction." In THE CANADIAN IMAGINATION: DIMENSIONS OF A LITERARY CULTURE. Ed. David Staines. Cambridge, Mass.: Harvard University Press, 1977, pp. 69-96.

Reprinted in no. 5081.

5193 "We've Come a Long Way, Baby." BOOKS IN CANADA, 7 (Jan. 1978), 3-6.

Reprinted in no. 5081.

5194 "On Simone Weil." ATROPOS, 1 (Spr. 1978), 8-17.

5195 "Many Solitudes: The Travel Writings of Margaret Laurence." JOURNAL OF CANADIAN STUDIES, 13 (Fall 1978), 3-12.

Reprinted in no. 5081.

5196 "The Human Elements: Margaret Laurence's Fiction." In THE HUMAN ELEMENTS: CRITICAL ESSAYS. Ed. David Helwig. [Ottawa]: Oberon, 1978, pp. 134-61.

Reprinted in no. 5081.

5197 "Memory, Imagination, Artifice: The Late Short Fiction of Mavis Gallant." CANADIAN FICTION MAGAZINE, No. 28 (1978), pp. 74-91.

Reprinted in no. 5081.

5198 Preface, LAWRENCE, GREENE AND LOWRY: THE FICTIONAL LAND-

SCAPE OF MEXICO, by Douglas W. Veitch. Waterloo, Ont.: Wilfrid Laurier University Press, 1978, pp. xi–xiv.

5199 "Taming the Tiger of Power: Notes on Certain Fictions by Hugh Hood." ESSAYS ON CANADIAN WRITING, Nos. 13–14 (Wint.–Spr. 1978–79), pp. 171–86.

Reprinted in nos. 2045 and 5081.

5200 "The Sometime Sahibs: Two Post-Independence British Novelists of India." QUEEN'S QUARTERLY, 86 (Spr. 1979), 39–49.

Discusses Paul Scott and John Masters.

5201 "Meeting of the Muses: Recent Canadian Fiction and the Historical Viewpoint." CANADIAN HISTORICAL REVIEW, 60 (June 1979), 141–53.

5202 "On Patrick Anderson." CANADIAN LITERATURE, No. 81 (Sum. 1979), pp. 162–63.

5203 "Armies Moving in the Night: The Fiction of Matt Cohen." INTERNATIONAL FICTION REVIEW, 6 (Wint. 1979), 17–30.

Reprinted and expanded in no. 5081.

5204 "Nationalism and the Canadian Genius." ARTSCANADA, 36 (Dec. 1979–Jan. 1980), 2–10.

5205 "Servants of Clio: Notes on Creighton & Groulx." CANADIAN LITERATURE, No. 83 (Wint. 1979), pp. 131–41.

5206 "Surrogate Fathers and Orphan Sons." JOURNAL OF CANADIAN STUDIES, 14 (Wint. 1979–80), 20–28.

On Hugh MacLennan.

5207 "Two Great Commonwealth Novelists: R.K. Narayan and V.S. Naipaul." SEWANEE REVIEW, 87 (Wint. 1979), 1–28.

5208 "Literary Echoes." BOOKS IN CANADA, 9 (Mar. 1980), 6–8.

5209 "Voices Set Free." CANADIAN LITERATURE, No. 85 (Sum. 1980), pp. 158–66.

5210 "When the Past Becomes History: The Half-Century in Non-Fiction Prose." UNIVERSITY OF TORONTO QUARTERLY, 50 (Fall 1980), 90–101.

5211   "Rural Roots." BOOKS IN CANADA, 9 (Oct. 1980), 7-9.

        Discusses Sinclair Ross.

5212   "V.S. Naipaul and the Politics of Fiction." QUEEN'S QUARTERLY, 87 (Wint. 1980), 679-92.

For articles by Woodcock, see also nos. 157, 661, 873, 1944, and 2788.

Manuscripts

5213   University of British Columbia Library, Vancouver.

SECONDARY MATERIAL

Bibliography

5214   Avakumovic, Ivan, comp. "A Bibliography of the Writings of George Woodcock (1937-76)." In A POLITICAL ART: ESSAYS AND IMAGES IN HONOUR OF GEORGE WOODCOCK. Ed. William H. New. Vancouver: University of British Columbia Press, 1978, pp. 211-49.

Criticism

5215   Bilsland, John W. "George Woodcock, Man of Letters." BRITISH COLUMBIA LIBRARY QUARTERLY, 23 (July 1959), 23-28. Bibliog.

5216   Cameron, Silver Donald. "Pacific Anarchist: A Portrait of George Woodcock." In his SEASONS IN THE RAIN: AN EXPATRIATE'S NOTES ON BRITISH COLUMBIA. Toronto: McClelland and Stewart, 1978, pp. 125-36.

5217   Duffy, Dennis. "George Woodcock: Voyager of Liberty." CANADIAN LITERATURE, No. 83 (Wint. 1979), pp. 156-62.

5218   Fraser, Keath. "The Hinterland of Literature: Notes on the Travel Books of George Woodcock." ESSAYS ON CANADIAN WRITING, No. 3 (Fall 1975), pp. 21-31.

5219   Hancock, Geoffrey. "An Interview with George Woodcock." CANADIAN FICTION MAGAZINE, Nos. 30-31 (1979), pp. 129-49.

5220   Hughes, Peter. GEORGE WOODCOCK. Canadian Writers, no. 13. Toronto: McClelland and Stewart, 1974. 60 p.

5221   Nelles, Henry Vivian, and Abraham Rotstein, eds. NATIONALISM OR LOCAL CONTROL: RESPONSES TO GEORGE WOODCOCK. Toronto: New, 1973. viii, 97 p.

5222   New, William H., ed. A POLITICAL ART: ESSAYS AND IMAGES IN HONOUR OF GEORGE WOODCOCK. Vancouver: University of British Columbia Press, 1978. xv, 249 p. Bibliog.

5223   Stratford, Philip. "Writer at Play." CANADIAN LITERATURE, No. 85 (Sum. 1980), pp. 156–58.

For criticism on Woodcock, see also nos. 5036, 5063 and 5079.

Book Reviews

5224   THE INCOMPARABLE APHRA: CamJ, 2 (1949), 499–502; NS&N, 4 Dec. 1948, pp. 507–08; TLS, 6 Nov. 1948, p. 622.

5225   THE WRITER AND POLITICS: TLS, 25 Sept. 1948, p. 535.

5226   THE PARADOX OF OSCAR WILDE: NY, 11 Mar. 1950, p. 103; NYTBR, 26 Feb. 1950, p. 12; PR, 17 (Apr. 1950), 390–94; SatR, 4 Mar. 1950, p. 20; UTQ, 20 (Apr. 1951), 301.

5227   THE ANARCHIST PRINCE: APSR, 66 (Dec. 1972), 1398.

5228   RAVENS AND PROPHETS: BCHQ, 17 (Jan. 1953), 153–54; CFor, 32 (Feb. 1953), 260; DR, 33 (Aut. 1953), ix, xi; UTQ, 22 (Apr. 1953), 317–18.

5229   PIERRE–JOSEPH PROUDHON: AAPSS, 310 (Mar. 1957), 236; APSR, 51 (June 1957), 570; CFor, 36 (Feb. 1957), 263; JPE, 65 (Oct. 1957), 460; NS&N, 7 July 1956, p. 22; PSQ, 72 (Mar. 1957), 131; QQ, 63 (Wint. 1956–57), 637; SatR, 19 Jan. 1957, p. 55; SocS, 65 (Mar. 1974), 135; SPECTATOR, 12 Oct. 1956, p. 508; TLS, 3 Aug. 1956, p. 459.

5230   TO THE CITY OF THE DEAD: TamR, 5 (Aut. 1957), 91–92.

5231   INCAS AND OTHER MEN: CanL, 2 (Aut. 1959), 85–86; GeoJ, June 1960, p. 226; NS, 23 May 1959, p. 728; UTQ, 29 (July 1960), 517–18.

5232   ANARCHISM: AHR, 68 (Jan. 1963), 413; CHR, 44 (Sept. 1963), 258–

59; HISTORY, 49 (Oct. 1964), 404; NS, 7 Sept. 1962, pp. 287-88; TLS, 24 Dec. 1964, p. 1153; UTQ, 32 (July 1963), 450.

5233　FACES OF INDIA: BCLQ, 28 (July 1964), 54-56; NS, 20 Mar. 1964, p. 454; PacA, 39 (Spr. 1966), 187; SPECTATOR, 24 Apr. 1964, p. 558; TLS, 2 Apr. 1964, p. 275; UTQ, 34 (July 1965), 415-16.

5234　ASIA, GODS AND CITIES: ECONOMIST, 28 May 1966, p. 981; LISTENER, 12 Jan. 1967, p. 68; NS, 17 June 1966, p. 892; PUNCH, 11 May 1966, p. 707; SPECTATOR, 13 May 1966, p. 605; TLS, 12 May 1966, p. 402.

5235　THE CRYSTAL SPIRIT: BCLQ, 31 (July 1967), 37, 39-40; CAB, 43 (Aut. 1967), 16; CanL, 33 (Sum. 1967), 90-91; COMMENTARY, 43 (May 1967), 102; COMMONWEAL, 28 Apr. 1967, p. 180; ECONOMIST, 19 Apr. 1967, p. 656; LIBERTÉ, 10 (Jan. 1968), 56-58; LISTENER, 8 June 1967, p. 752; NS, 14 July 1967, p. 53; NYRB, 15 Dec. 1966, pp. 6-8; NYTBR, 13 Nov. 1966, p. 48; PUNCH, 7 June 1967, p. 849; SatN, 82 (June 1967), 33, 35; SPECTATOR, 23 June 1967, pp. 738-40; TamR, 58 (1973), 77; TLS, 13 July 1967, p. 614; UTQ, 37 (July 1968), 427-29; YR, 56 (Spr. 1967), xx.

5236　THE GREEKS IN INDIA: ClassR, 17 (Dec. 1967), 342; HiT, 16 (Sept. 1966), 655; NS, 20 Jan. 1967, p. 84; SPECTATOR, 15 July 1966, p. 87; TLS, 20 July 1967, p. 635; UTQ, 36 (July 1967), 427-28.

5237　KERALA: GeoJ, 134 (June 1968), 258; LISTENER, 28 Dec. 1967, p. 853.

5238　THE DOUKHOBORS: AA, 71 (Oct. 1969), 940; AHR, 74 (June 1969), 1753; CanL, 40 (Spr. 1969), 78-79; CHR, 50 (Dec. 1969), 454-55; COMMONWEAL, 4 Apr. 1969, p. 80; CSS, 4 (Sum. 1970), 300; HiT, 19 (Oct. 1969), 731; LaUR, 2 (Spr. 1969), 74-77; LISTENER, 19 June 1969, p. 868; NS, 14 Mar. 1969, p. 368; PHR, 38 (Nov. 1969), 497; QQ, 76 (Sum. 1969), 353-54; RusR, 29 (July 1970), 362; SaskH, 23 (Aut. 1970), 119-20; SatR, 18 Jan. 1969, p. 33; TamR, [49] (1969), 85-87; TLS, 24 Apr. 1969, p. 447; VQR, 45 (Spr. 1969), lxiv.

5239　THE BRITISH IN THE FAR EAST: ECONOMIST, 8 Nov. 1969, p. vi; ENCOUNTER, 35 (Nov. 1970), 90; GeoJ, 136 (Sept. 1970), 446; HiT, 20 (Jan. 1970), 65; NS, 24 Oct. 1969, p. 573; SPECTATOR, 15 Nov. 1969, p. 680; TLS, 11 Dec. 1969, p. 1423.

5240　HENRY WALTER BATES: AHR, 77 (June 1972), 854; CanL, 45 (Sum. 1970), 93; ECONOMIST, 30 Aug. 1969, p. 34; GeoJ, 135 (Sept. 1969), 456; HiT, 19 (June 1969), 437; PUNCH, 21 May 1969, p. 768; TLS, 5 June 1969, p. 607.

5241 HUGH MacLENNAN: CanL, 47 (Wint. 1971), 85; CFor, 50 (July 1970), 189; WascanaR, 5, No. 1 (1970), 96; WCR, 5 (Jan. 1971), 69-70; UTQ, 39 (July 1970), 375-76.

5242 CANADA AND THE CANADIANS: ARCS, 1, No. 1 (1971), 25; ARCS, 2, No. 1 (1972), 104; CanL, 49 (Sum. 1971), 92-94; CFor, 50 (Mar. 1971), 439-40; HiT, 21 (Feb. 1971), 147; LaUR, 4 (Spr. 1971), 69-71; MACLEAN'S, 83 (Dec. 1970), 83; ME, Fall Book Supplement 1970, pp. 28-29; NYTBR, 14 Feb. 1971, p. 2; TLS, 6 Nov. 1970, p. 1288; UTQ, 40 (Sum. 1971), 321-22.

5243 MORDECAI RICHLER: CanL, 47 (Wint. 1971), 85; CFor, 50 (Sept. 1970), 222-23.

5244 ODYSSEUS EVER RETURNING: CanL, 47 (Wint. 1971), 84-87; SatN, 85 (Apr. 1970), 33-34.

5245 INTO TIBET: AHR, 80 (Oct. 1975), 1033-34; GeoJ, 137 (Dec. 1971), 579; HiT, 21 (Aug. 1971), 599; TLS, 10 Sept. 1971, p. 1085.

5246 MOHANDAS GANDHI: TLS, 31 Mar. 1972, p. 351.

5247 DAWN AND THE DARKEST HOUR: CanL, 56 (Spr. 1973), 117-19; ConL, 15 (Wint. 1974), 148-53; EA, 26 (1973), 442; ENCOUNTER, 41 (July 1973), 66; ENGLISH, 22 (Spr. 1973), 33; JML, 3 (Feb. 1974), 652; LISTENER, 27 Apr. 1972, p. 555; NatR, 9 June 1972, p. 650; NewR, 1 July 1972, pp. 22-24; NYRB, 15 June 1972, p. 36; SPECTATOR, 25 Mar. 1972, p. 480; TLS, 12 May 1972, p. 544; UTQ, 42 (Sum. 1973), 417-18.

5248 HERBERT READ: NS, 24 Nov. 1972, p. 774; PrS, 49 (Spr. 1975), 86-87; SatN, 88 (June 1973), 37, 39-40; TLS, 1 Dec. 1972, p. 1457.

5249 THE REJECTION OF POLITICS: BCan, 2 (Jan. 1973), 25, 40; CDim, 10 (Mar. 1975), 57-59; CFor, 53 (Nov. 1973), 45-47; DR, 53 (Aut. 1973), 577-79; ECW, 5 (Fall 1976), 72-74; MHRev, 26 (Apr. 1973), 234; QQ, 80 (Sum. 1973), 288-89; UTQ, 42 (Sum. 1973), 418; UWR, 9 (Spr. 1974), 94-95.

5250 WHO KILLED THE BRITISH EMPIRE? APSR, 71 (June 1977), 868; AR, 33 (Spr. 1975), 117-18; BCan, 4 (Aug. 1975), 3-4; COMMENTARY, 60 (Nov. 1975), 78-79; CRead, 16, No. 6 (1975), 2-4; HISTORY, 3 (Mar. 1975), 114; HiT, 24 (Dec. 1974), 879; LISTENER, 21 Nov. 1974, p. 683; NY, 6 Jan. 1975, p. 82; PSQ, 90 (Fall 1975), 591; SatN, 90 (May 1975), 70-72; SPECTATOR, 16 Nov. 1974, p. 631; SPHINX, 2 (Wint. 1977), 47-53.

5251 AMOR DE COSMOS: CBRA, 1975, p. 51.

5252 GABRIEL DUMONT: ARCS, 7 (Aut. 1977), 90-92; BCan, 5 (Jan. 1976), 6-7; CBRA, 1975, pp. 48-49; CEStudies, 9, No. 1 (1977), 140-41; CFor, 55 (Dec. 1975), 28-29; CHR, 58 (Sept. 1977), 320-31; CJPS, 10 (Mar. 1977), 177-78; CRead, 16, No. 8 (1975), 2-4; ECW, 5 (Fall 1976), 72-74; Q&Q, 42, No. 2 (1976), 44; SaskH, 29 (Spr. 1976), 77-78; SPHINX, 2 (Sum. 1976), 42-46; UTQ, 45 (Sum. 1976), 410-11.

5253 SOUTH SEA JOURNEY: CBRA, 1976, pp. 279-80; HiT, 26 (Sept. 1976), 621; LISTENER, 27 May 1976, p. 686; PacA, 50 (Wint. 1977-78), 740-42; Q&Q, 42, No. 17 (1976), 26; SPECTATOR, 12 June 1976, p. 25; TLS, 27 May 1977, p. 662.

5254 PEOPLES OF THE COAST: AA, 81 (Sept. 1979), 664; BCStud, 40 (Wint. 1978-79), 57-75; BCStud, 41 (Spr. 1979), 59-60; CanL, 82 (Aut. 1979), 93-95; CEStudies, 10, No. 1 (1978), 161; CFor, 58 (June 1978), 49-50; Q&Q, 44, No. 2 (1978), 40; QQ, 86 (Aut. 1979), 513-14; RAn, 6 (Spr. 1979), 142; UTQ, 47 (Sum. 1978), 477-79; WHQ, 10 (Apr. 1979), 221-22.

5255 FACES FROM HISTORY: AIHR, 27 (Spr. 1979), 37-38; CHR, 60 (Sept. 1979), 358-59; Q&Q, 44, No. 17 (1978), 31.

5256 THOMAS MERTON: CanL, 82 (Aut. 1979), 126-27; CFor, 58 (Feb. 1979), 32-33; COMMONWEAL, 18 Jan. 1980, p. 23; COMMONWEAL, 29 Feb. 1980, p. 125; CRITIC, 37 (Mar. 1979), Part 1, 2; ECW, 16 (Fall 1979), 126-28; NATION, 6 Jan. 1979, pp. 21-22; NewR, 26 May 1979, p. 26; NYRB, 27 Sept. 1979, p. 25; QQ, 86 (Aut. 1979), 513-14; WascanaR, 13 (Fall 1978), 98-101.

5257 THE CANADIANS: BCan, 9 (Feb. 1980), 16; CanL, 85 (Sum. 1980), 180; CHist, 79 (Nov. 1980), 143; ECONOMIST, 12 July 1980, p. 101; NYRB, 17 July 1980, p. 29; Q&Q, 46 (Feb. 1980), 41-42; SMITHSONIAN, 11 (Apr. 1980), 146-48.

5258 A GEORGE WOODCOCK READER: MACLEAN'S, 20 Oct. 1980, p. 62; SatN, 95 (Oct. 1980), 61-62.

5259 THE WORLD OF CANADIAN WRITING: BCan, 9 (Dec. 1980), 10; CFM, 34-35 (1980), 178-80; CFor, 60 (Oct. 1980), 29-30; MACLEAN'S, 20 Oct. 1980, p. 62.

AUTHOR INDEX

This index includes authors, editors, compilers, and other contributors cited in the text. References are to entry numbers and alphabetization is letter by letter.

Author Index

544

C

Author Index

Duhamel, Roger 832
Dumas, A. 1803
Dumbrille, Dorothy 3942
Duncan, Dorothy 2978, 3038-39
Dunn, D. 3370
Dunn, H.T. 4001
Dunn, William 1084
Dunphy, William 4837
Duran, Gillian 3040
Durand, Régis 293, 667
Durrant, Geoffrey 2694-96
Dyck, Sarah 981
Dyrkjøb, Jan Ulrik 4602

E

Eayrs, Hugh 4363-64
Edel, Leon 2117, 4681
Edelstein, J.M. 2697
Edgar, Pelham 294-95, 834, 1460, 2544, 4518, 4603
Edmonds, Dale 2698-2701
Edwards, Eileen 1675
Edwards, Margaret H. 20
Edwards, Owen Dudley 578
Edwards, Thomas R. 4891
Efron, Arthur 4892
Eggleston, Wilfred 37, 142, 153, 1844-45, 2868, 3231
Egoff, Sheila A. 12, 143
Einarsson, Stefan 3900
Elder, A.T. 3981
Elliott, George 988
Elliott, Jean Leonard 420
Ellis, Katherine 4604
Endres, Robin 4336
Engel, Marian 1506-32
Enright, Robert 2251
Epperly, Elizabeth R. 3233
Epstein, Perle S. 2630, 2702-03
Erichsen-Brown, Gwethalyn. See Graham, Gwethalyn
Evanier, David 3729
Evans, Gwynneth 108
Ewart, John S. 2545
Ewing, Betty Moore 1247

F

Fairbanks, Carol 639
Falconer, Robert 1138
Falconi, Gigino 1192

Farmiloe, Dorothy 3041
Faxon, Frederick W. 97
Fee, Margery 21
Feibleman, James K. 2546
Fellows, Jo-Ann 1461
Ferguson, Jack 2891
Fergusson, Harvey 3527
Fernandez, Diane 2704
Ferns, John 3730
Ferraté, Juan 138
Ferres, John 296
Ferris, Ina 1085, 2547, 4240
Fetherling, Doug 1676, 5079
Feyer, George 4384
Fielder, Leslie A. 297, 4548
Findlay, Peter R. 4893
Findley, Timothy 1548-59
Finholt, Richard 4605
Finkelstein, Sidney 4894
Fiore, Quentin 4761, 4763
Fischer, E.W. 1793
Fischer, Gretl K. 2118
Fischer, Michael R. 4606
Fish, A.H. 2411, 2416
Fisher, Esther Safer 2119
Fisher, Peter F. 4524
Fitzpatrick, Helen 3261
Flaubert, Gustave 1793, 1813
Fletcher, Angus 4569, 4607
Flood, Jeanne 3351
Forge, Andrew 4923
Forman, Denyse 2328
Forrest, A.C. 4416
Fortier, André 3694
Foster, John Wilson 3352-53
Fouchet, Max-Pol 2705
Fowke, Edith 3657
Fox, Winifred 930
Francillon, Clarisse 2633, 2706-07, 2760
Francis, Wynne 298
Francks, Warren T. 4895
Frankel, Vivian 668
Frankenberg, Robert 4964
Franklin, Stephen 4417
Fraser, D.M. 669
Fraser, John 4608
Fraser, Keath 3354, 3790, 5218
Fraser, Nancy W. 299
Fraser, Sylvia 1564-67
Frayne, John P. 3355

Frazer, Frances M. 300
Frazier, Alexander 4821
Fredeman, Jane Cowan 3262
Freedman, Adele 4322
French, Donald G. 156
French, Philip 3356
French, W. 301
French, Warren 2797
Friesen, Victor Carl 302, 1086, 3791
Frizzell, Alan 583
Frum, Barbara 303
Frye, Northrop 4495-4575, 4603
Fulford, Robert 22, 304-05, 670,
  1677, 2033, 3357, 3696
Fuller, Muriel 3901
Fulton, E. Margaret 306
Fyfe, Janet 118

G

Gabrial, Jan 2708-10
Gal, Laszlo 1513
Galana, Laurel 3846
Galaviz, Juan Manuel 2711
Galdone, Paul 4970
Gallagher, Michael P. 3358-59
Gallant, Mavis 1573-1624
Gallup, Jennifer 6
Galt, George 671
Gamaleri, Gianpiera 4896
Gambino, Richard 4897
Gane, Margaret Drury 307
Gangnon, Pat 5092
Garebian, Keith 672, 1204, 2007
Garner, Hugh 1646-71, 3397
Garnett, George Rhys 2712
Garrett, George 3361
Geddes, Gary 308, 2239, 2300,
  3116, 3528
Geer, Charles 4963, 4966
Genest, Frank D. 2424
Gerden, F.C. 1772, 1801
Gerson, Carole 673, 1347
Gerstenberger, Donna 674
Gibbs, George 3208
Gibbs, Jean 2120
Gibbs, Robert 2329
Gibson, Graeme 1698-1701
Gibson, Mary Ellis 675
Gibson, Shirley 4340
Gibson, Wilfred 929

Gide, André 1782, 1786, 1806,
  1808, 1846
Giesbrecht, Herbert 4241
Gillen, Mollie 3263
Gilroy, John 2987
Girgus, Sam B. 4898
Girson, Rochelle 3360
Githae-Mugo, Micere 2330
Givens, Imogen 2181
Glassco, John 4676-99
Glicksohn, Susan Wood 3982
Gnarowski, Michael 23-24, 111,
  1205, 2151
Godard, Barbara 309-12, 4193,
  4365
Godfrey, Dave 22, 881, 1704-20
Godwin, William 5099
Goetsch, Paul 313, 3042-44
Goggio, Emilio 25
Golden, Leon 4609
Goldie, Terry 147
Goldstein, Kenneth S. 3259, 3657
Golysheva, Alisa Ivanovna 144
Gom, Leona M. 2331-33
Gooch, Silas N. 4695
Goodman, Michael B. 2838
Goodman, Walter 3731
Goodwin, K.L. 269, 416, 735
Gose, E.B. 2959
Goss, John 3215
Gotlieb, Phyllis 2121
Gottfried, Rudolf B. 4610
Gottleib, Lois C. 26, 314-16, 676
Gouri, C.R. 1087
Grace, Sherrill E. 317, 677, 2334-35,
  2713-15
Graham, Gwethalyn 1736-38
Graham, John 3361
Granatstein, J.L. 145, 318
Grant, Judith Skelton 1280-81, 1348-49
Gravel, Pierre 2225
Gray, James 3658
Grayson, J. Paul 319
Grayson, L.M. 319
Green, Robert 3362
Greene, Donald 320
Greening, W.E. 321
Greenstein, Michael 2122, 2204,
  3732, 4323
Greenwood, Thomas 322
Gregor, Ian 2741

Author Index

Greve, E. 1793
Greve, F.P. 1744-45, 1755-56,
1766-71, 1773-93, 1795-96,
1799-1800, 1803-08
Grey Owl 4345-55, 4358, 4362
Grieg, Peter E. 35
Griffith, Margaret 678
Gros-Louis, Dolores 323
Gross, Konrad 324
Grove, Frederick Philip 1744-1837
Grube, John 4194
Gubbins, Paul P. 1745
Gunn, Drewey Wayne 2716
Gustafson, Ralph 325
Guthrie, Tyrone 1273-75, 1283
Gutteridge, Don 679
Guttman, Freda 1185
Guy, Ray 5003
Gwyn, Sandra 326

H

Hagen, W.M. 2717-18
Hagler, Ronald 4899
Haktani, Arthur 2089
Hale, Alice 3645
Hale, Victoria G. 2034-35
Hall, John A. 2892
Hallie, Philip 4611
Halpenny, Francess G. 74, 146
Hambleton, Ronald 1462-63
Hamilton, L. 327
Hamilton, Robert M. 27
Hammond, Karla 680-81
Hancock, Geoffrey 328-30, 682,
901-02, 1627-29, 1987, 2036,
2252, 3847, 5219
Hancock, M. 4242
Hanes, V.G. 4612
Harcourt, Joan 1237, 1556-57,
1937, 1939-41, 3106, 3137-38,
3147, 3408, 3824-25, 3916,
4739, 4741
Hardison, O.B., Jr. 4594
Hardy, Thomas 5115
Harger-Grinling, Virginia 147
Harlow, Robert 331
Harlowe, Dorothy 119
Harris, J. Robert 98
Harris, Lawren 4471
Harris, Michael 1199

Harrison, Dick 148-49, 332-36
Harrison, Ernest Wilfred 4386
Harrison, J. 683
Harvard University. Library 28
Harvey, Connie 2253
Harvey, Roderick W. 2254
Hassan, Ihab 337
Hastings, Basil Macdonald 2418
Hatch, Ronald B. 1630-31
Hathaway, Margaret 1226
Haushofer, Karl 1811
Hawkins, W.J. 3659
Hay, P. 3876
Hayhurst, Thomas W. 3624-25
Hayne, David M. 29, 74
Hearne, Samuel 4986
Heath, Jeffrey M. 150
Heath, John 2193
Hedenstrom, Joanne 338
Hehner, Barbara 2336
Heidenreich, Rosmarin 1847
Heilman, Robert B. 2719
Heintzman, Ralph R. 1088, 1350,
3045
Helwig, David 355, 1237, 1556-57,
1925-59, 3106, 3147, 3408,
3444, 3824-25, 3916, 4739, 4741,
5196
Hembroff-Schleicher, Edythe 4472-73
Henderson, Diane 30
Hendrick, George 1464
Herbert, John 3708
Hermann, K. 3733
Hernadi, Paul 4613
Hertzel, Leo J. 339
Hibbert, Joyce 1624
Hicks, Granville 340
Hiebert, Paul 4709-15
Hill, Art 2720
Hill, Maude Petitt 3264
Hinchcliffe, Peter M. 4287
Hind-Smith, Joan 78
Hinz, Evelyn J. 684-85
Hirano, Keiichi 341, 2123, 3046
Hirsch, John 5084
Hirschberg, Stuart 3363
Hirschman, Jack 2721
Ho, Kwai Yiu 99
Hoar, Victor 1089
Hochschild, Adam 2722
Hocke, Brigitte 917

Author Index

McKenzie, Ruth 385-86
McKinley, Mabel Bums 3230
MacKinnon, A. R. 4503
MacKinnon, Kenneth 370, 984
McLaren, Duncan 102
McLaren, J. W. 4709
McLay, Catherine M. 697, 2353,
  3194-95, 3229, 4291
McLean, Isabel 31
McLean, Ken 387
MacLean, Susan 698
MacLellan, W. E. 3591
MacLennan, Hugh 2966-3013
McLeod, Alan Lindsey 564
McLuhan, Eric 4772
McLuhan, Herbert Marshall 4754-
  4865, 4923, 4940
MacLulich, T. D. 388-91, 699-700,
  2554, 3057-58, 5007
MacMechan, Archibald McKellar
  159, 3634
McMullen, Lorraine 392, 1856,
  2747, 3793-94, 3919
McMullen, Melvin Justus Given 2870
McMullin, Stanley E. 393, 1857-59
McNamara, Eugene 4764
McNeil, C. G. 2748
MacNutt, W. Stewart 204
MacPherson, Duncan 4375
McPherson, Hugo 394, 1096-97,
  1358, 3059-60
MacPike, E. F. 395
Macri, F. M. 701, 1209
McSweeney, Kerry 3368, 3737
McWhinney, Bill 1708
Maekawa, Yuichi 2749
Maes-Jelinek, Hena 266
Maesser, Angelika 2354
Magee, A. Peter 2750
Magee, William H. 396-99, 1148,
  2555-56
Mahanti, J. C. 1874
Makow, Henry 1860-62
Makowiecki, Stefan 2751-52
Malcolm, Douglas 1625-26
Malone, David 4913
Mandel, Ann 400, 2257
Mandel, Eli 160-61, 401-06, 702,
  1740, 4247, 4632
Mane, Robert 2355

Manheim, R. 632
Manly, C. M. 1758-59
Mansbridge, Francis 703, 4248
Mantz, Douglas 2557
Mara, Bernard 3301-02, 3305
Marchbanks, Samuel 1262-63, 1267,
  1300
Marchessou, Hélène 407
Marcotte, Gilles 4689
Margeson, Robert W. 1725
Marker, Frederick 1321
Marker, Lise-Lone 1321
Markson, David 2753-56
Marlatt, D. 4197
Marquis, Thomas Guthrie 408
Marshall, Joyce 3092-3117
Marshall, Tom A. 162, 704, 1098,
  1936, 2125-26, 2558, 3061
Marsland, Elizabeth 409
Marta, Jan 4198
Martell, George 3196
Martin, Betty 5008
Martin, George 96
Martin, Sandra 410, 794
Martin, W. R. 3434
Marty, M. E. 3738
Massey, Vincent 4405
Matheson, Graeme 4147
Matheson, Gwen 633, 2871
Matthews, Lawrence 2038
Matthews, Robin D. 163, 411-15,
  705, 1099, 3062, 3739
Matos, Manuel Cadafaz de 1210
Matthews, John 416-19, 2127, 3661
Matthews, William 38
Matthiasson, John S. 420
Maugham, Somerset 3130
Maurey, Pierre 2757
May, Rollo 3694
Mayne, Seymour 2112, 2114, 2128,
  2143
Meeker, Howie 2819
Melanson, Lloyd J. 81
Melnyk, George 2258, 2356,
  4249-50
Melville, Herman 5110
Mensenkampff, Ursula V. 164
Meredith, George 1780, 1783, 1787,
  5105
Merivale, Patricia 421, 3369
Merler, Grazia 1637

Author Index

Neel, Boyd 1275
Neering, Rosemary 4479
Neimi, Judith 3852
Nelles, Henry Vivian 5221
nelliemcclung 2873
Nesbitt, Bruce H. 42, 73, 871-72, 1867, 1968
Nettall, Stephanie 2364, 3742
Neufeld, James 1369
Nevitt, Barrington 4770, 4857
New, William H. 43, 173, 435-40, 1727-28, 1969, 2302, 2365-67, 2631, 2762-66, 2839, 3065-66, 3199, 3438, 3497, 3743, 3796, 4295-96, 5063, 5214, 5222
Newfeld, Frank 1186, 4973
Newlove, John 3125
Newman, C.J. 3121
Newman, Peter C. 1370, 4926
Newton, Norman 441
Newton-De Molina, David 4927
Niblett, W.R. 4564
nichol, b.p. 819
Nicholas, Daniel 4354
Nicolaisen, W.F.H. 2259
Nimmo, Barbara 2449
Nimmo, D.C. 2767
Niven, Frederick 3449-94
Niven, James 3478
Nodelman, Perry 711, 3744
Noel-Bentley, Peter C. 865, 1868
Noonan, Gerald A. 442, 984, 4717,
Norden, Eric 4928
Norris, Ken 712
North, Sterling 1470
Northey, Margot 174
Norwood, Robert 926
Nowlan, Alden 3662
Noxon, Gerald 2768-69

O

Oates, Joyce Carol 713-14
O'Broin, Padraig 443
O'Connor, John J. 444
O'Donnell, Kathleen 3067-68
O'Flaherty, Patrick 175, 445
O'Hagan, Howard 3520-26
O'Halloran, Bonita 2183
Ohmann, Carol 4634
Ondaatje, Michael 3536-49

Ong, Walter J. 4801, 4842
Onley, Gloria 715-16
Orange, John 1103, 2042
O'Rourke, David 3200
Orwell, George 4556
Osachoff, Margaret Gail 1537, 2368
Ostenso, Martha 3557-86
Oughton, John 1252
Overton, G. 3594
Owen, Don 1199
Owen, Glyn 4480
Owen, I.M. 355
Owen, Ivon 1371, 3112
Ower, John 3745

P

Pacey, Desmond 176-77, 446-57, 832, 1213, 1471, 1754, 1765, 1869-74, 2560, 4297-4300
Pache, Walter 458-60
Pachter, Charles 594
Packer, Miriam 2369
Page, P. 2132
Page, P.K. 627, 3522
Page, Sheila 717
Pagnoulle, Christine 2770-72
Palmer, David 2645, 4640
Palmer, T. 4929
Palting, Diana 1539
Pandeya, Shiva M. 4635
Paolucci, Ann 178, 461
Paolucci, Henry 461
Parameswaran, Una 2328
Park, Julian 179
Parker, Brian 3865
Parker, Douglas H. 1538
Parker, George 462
Parker, Harley 4757, 4762, 4765
Parker, Jack H. 25
Parker, Lewis 4331
Parkhill, Douglas 1710
Parks, M.G. 1875
Parr, John 180, 3746
Patch, Howard R. 4801
Pater, Walter 1799
Patton, Janice 4395-96
Paulin, T. 3370

U

Underwood, Miles 4678
Unitt, Doris 2396
Urbas, Jeannette 4304-05
Urquhart, Tony 3544

V

Vaillancourt, Emile 2975
van der Mark, Christine 4158-61
Van Herk, Aritha 1539, 4219
Van Varsveld, Gail 747
Varcoe, George 553
Varma, Prem 3978
Vassal, Jacques 1220
Vaughan, Harold W. 4533
Veitch, Douglas W. 2794, 5198
Villon, Pierre 3779
Vicenti, Fiora 748
Vipond, Mary 554-55
Vizinczey, Stephen 4166-69
Von Hendy, A. 4650
von Hofmannsthal, Hugo 1795
Von Sacher-Masoch, Leopold 4692
von Wilpert, Gero 337

W

Wachtel, E. 4149-50
Waddington, Marcus 2184
Waddington, Miriam 556, 2069,
  2145-46
Waddington, Raymond B. 4944
Wagner, Geoffrey 4945
Wain, John 4808, 5154
Wainwright, Andy 1316, 2825
Wainwright, J.A. 2795
Walker, Alan 616
Walker, Dean 4946
Walker, Ronald G. 2796
Wallace, Bronwen 3443-44
Wallace, William Stewart 67-68,
  89-90
Walpole, Hugh 3501
Walsh, William 206, 557, 1108
Ward, E.F. 4009
Ward, Margaret Joan 1109
Warhaft, Sidney 2207
Warkentin, Germaine 130, 3758
Warwick, Ellen D. 1380

Warwick, Jack 558-59
Warwick, Jarvis 1649
Warwick, Susan J. 2307-8
Wasson, Richard 4947
Waterston, Elizabeth 207, 560,
  3274
Watkins, Evans 4651
Watkins, Mel 1709
Watson, A.H. 1406
Watson, J. Wreford 561
Watson, Sheila 4174-88
Watson, Wilfred 4768, 4948-49
Watt, Frank W. 562-65, 1110-11,
  2569
Watt, G. 4950
Watters, Reginald Eyre 69-71, 566-69,
  1907, 2570, 3076, 4306
Weaver, Robert Leigh 570-72, 1001,
  1061, 1112, 1578, 1639, 2905,
  3103, 3182, 3330
Webb, Margaret Alice 17
Webb, Phyllis 749
Webber, Bernard 1908
Weber, Ephraim 3275-76
Weber, Hans 951
Weber, Samuel 4652
Webster, David 1381
Webster, Grant T. 4653
Webster, Judith 208, 1322, 3011
Weeks, Edward 1474
Wegner, Fritz 3688
Weimann, Robert 4654
Weir, Lorraine 2147
Wells, H.G. 1777-79, 1781, 1784,
  1792, 1804
Wemyss, Margaret 2289-90
West, Rebecca 4868
Westfall, William 573
Westwater, A.M. 989
Whaley, Susan 4257
Whalley, George 209, 574, 2571
Whalon, M. 1327
Wheeler, A. Lloyd 4720-21
Wheeler, Claire 4975
Whitaker, Muriel A. 575, 3277, 4307
White, David A. 4655
Whittaker, Ted 91
Widmer, Eleanor 2797
Wiebe, Rudy 2234, 3184, 4206-36,
  4742
Wigglesworth, V.B. 4542
Wigmore, Donnalu 2397

TITLE INDEX

This index includes book titles cited in the text. In some cases the titles have been shortened. References are to entry numbers and alphabetization is letter by letter.

A

Above Ground 2298, 2815, 2843
Above Your Heads 3451
Acrobats, The 3681, 3759
Across My Path 4518
Actes du VIIe Congrès de l'Association Internationale de Littérature Comparée 138
Address, An 4457, 4493
Address by H. Northrop Frye on the Occasion of His Installation as Principal of Victoria College 4498
Adventure at Moon Bay Towers 1509
Adventures of a Columnist 4381, 4431
Adventures of Sajo and Her Beaver People, The 4347, 4373
Adventures of the Far North 2468
Afternoons in Utopia 2436, 2590
After Survival 52
Against the Season 3809, 3856
Alberta 2217
Alberta: A Celebration 4212
Ali Kamal al Kadir Sudan 1160
All Right, Mr. Roosevelt 2490
All We Like Sheep and Other Stories 2853
Almost Meeting and Other Stories, The 2191
Alphabeing & Other Seasyours 825
Alpine Path, The 3232

"Alternative" Press in Canada, The 72
A.M. Klein (Marshall) 2126
A.M. Klein (Waddington) 2145
A.M. Klein Symposium, The 2128
Amongst Thistles and Thorns 1154, 1176
Amor de Cosmos 5070, 5251
Anarchism 5048, 5232
Anarchism and Morality 5034
Anarchist Prince, The 5042, 5227
Anarchist Reader, The 5114
Anarchy or Chaos 5032
Anatomy of Criticism 4496, 4659
And No Birds Sang 4984, 5028
Andrew Tolliver 4331
And They Shall Walk 3572
Anima, or, Swann Grown Old 5094
Animals in That Country, The 595
Anna's Pet 589
Anne of Avonlea 3207, 3280
Anne of Green Gables 3206, 3279
Anne of Green Gables: A Modern Dramatization of L.M. Montgomery's Most Popular Novel, in Three Acts 3235
Anne of Ingleside 3227, 3295
Anne of the Island 3212, 3284
Anne of Windy Poplars 3225
Anne of Windy Willows 3225
Anne's House of Dreams 3213, 3285

C

H

O

Title Index

SUBJECT INDEX

This index includes major topics covered in the text. References are to entry numbers and alphabetization is letter by letter. Main areas of interest within a subject have been underlined.

A

Aborigenes in Canadian literature 341
Achebe, Chinua 2330
Adams, Henry 4932
Africa in Canadian literature 287, 429,
      435, 2330, 2359, 4150
Aiken, Conrad 2659, 2694
Alain-Fournier, Henri 5178
Alberta in literature 254, 396, 2263
      2929
Alienation
   Kreisel on 2192
   in Munro's fiction 3427
Alighieri, Dante 2787
Allegory, in Wilson's fiction 4286
ALPHABET, criticism of 620
Alternative presses
   checklist of serials by 72
   "little magazines" as 298
   Watson on 4178
Alther, Lisa 649
Anderson, Patrick 5202
Anderson, Sherwood 840
Animal stories 575
Antiquarian book trade, guide to 13
Apocalyptic literature 672, 2370
Aquin, Hubert 2373, 3369
Aquinas, Thomas 4791
Aristotle 4609
Atlantic provinces in literature
   bibliographies on 4

biographies on 81
   criticism of 251, 272, 370, 488
Atwood, Margaret
   bibliographies on 33, 639-42
   criticism of 126, 129, 133, 139,
      157, 162-63, 170-71,
      174, 205, 481-82, 643-
      749, 1701, 3840, 5112,
      5161, 5172, 5184, 5188
   book reviews 750-55
   fiction by 584-90
      short stories 604-16
   manuscript collections 638, 725
   nonfiction prose by 591-92
      critical and other shorter prose
         196, 206, 617-37
   poetry by 593-603
Australian literature, compared to
      Canadian literature 211,
      224, 242, 566
Authors, Canadian 209, 365, 450,
      457, 462
   artists as 510
   bibliography of Indian-Inuit 54
   Birney on 846-47, 863
   collective biography of 74-92
   Davies on 1302, 1318
   Kroetsch on 2236
   of Manitoba 37
   Mitchell on 3185
   Mowat on 4996
   of Nova Scotia 83-84

fiction by 909-12
nonfiction prose by 913-15
Borges, Jorge Luis 4621
Bowering, George 2027
Brazeau, J. Raymond 2225
Bretano, Clemens 1757
British Columbia
    authors of 366
    bibliographies about 18, 20
    in literature 1971
Brooke, Frances 1827
Brooke, Rupert 2914, 4037
Brown, James Sutherland 87
Bruce, Charles
    criticism of 168, 944
        book reviews 945-46
    fiction by 923-24
        short stories 932-42
    manuscript collections 943
    nonfiction prose by 925
    poetry by 926-31
Buckler, Ernest
    bibliography on 33
    biography of 81
    criticism of 540-41, 973-95,
        3783
        book reviews 996-1000
    fiction by 947-49
        short stories 953-69
    manuscript collections 972
    nonfiction prose by 950-52
        critical and other shorter prose
        970-71
Burroughs, William S. 2838
Butler, William 2893
Byrd, Emily 3260

C

Callaghan, Morley
    bibliography on 1074
    criticism of 123, 139, 158, 163,
        168, 182, 195, 210,
        1075-1113, 5063, 5102,
        5148, 5162
        book reviews 1114-30
    drama by 1022
    fiction by 1001-19
        short stories 1023-62

manuscript collections 1073
nonfiction prose by 1020-21
    critical and other shorter prose
        192, 209, 1063-72,
        1450
Canadian Authors Association (Toronto
        Branch) 167
Canadian Broadcasting Corp. 125
CANADIAN FICTION MAGAZINE
    index to 105
CANADIAN FORUM
    criticism of 282
    index to 93
    selections from 145
CANADIAN LITERATURE 5150, 5193
    index to 96
Canadian literature (in English)
        1317, 2174, 5063, 5081,
        5166, 5201
    comparative studies 138, 227-28,
        262, 362, 364, 479, 551
        American literature 149, 211,
            262, 332-33, 359, 395,
            500, 684, 2236, 2528
        Australian literature 211, 224,
            242, 566
        French-Canadian literature 188,
            193, 200-201, 207, 290,
            292, 353, 362, 364, 424,
            461, 468, 483, 496, 518,
            521, 528-29, 531-37,
            558-59
            bibliographies on 29, 60,
            116
    critical reception, international
        1984
        American 53, 210
        Commonwealth 437
        French 515
        German 190a, 477
        Italian 255, 478
        Swedish 155
    influence of American literature
        on 2236, 2248, 2528
        of European literature on 226
        of Scotland on 560
    literary history, criticism, and
        theory 122-583
        articles 212-583. See also
        cross references following
        no. 583

monographs 88, 122-211, 591,
809, 1281, 1701, 1942,
1944, 2889, 4511, 5063,
5081, 5085-86, 5102,
5106, 5112-13
reference sources for 1-121
bibliographical and general
reference works 1-73
biographical references 37, 50,
74-92, 135, 203
indexes 93-121
to manuscripts and special
collections 117-21
to serials, anthologies, and
collections 93-107
to theses 43, 108-16
research in 446-47
translations of 60
See also Authors, Canadian; specific
genres (e.g., Fiction,
Canadian)
Canadian Writers Conference, proceedings (1955) 209
Carlyle, Thomas 989
Carr, Emily
autobiography and journals 4454,
4458
bibliography on 4462
biography of 87, 4472-73, 4479,
4485
correspondence 4460
criticism of 87, 482, 4463-87
book reviews 4488-94
manuscript collections 4461
nonfiction prose by 4450-59
shorter critical prose 192, 4460
Cary, Joyce 5137
Cather, Willa 2392
Characters and characterization 307
Beresford-Howe on 790, 792
Davies's 1358
Lowry's 2786
MacLennan's 3079
Moore's 3355
See also classes of characters (e.g.,
Heroes)
Chaucer, Geoffrey 835, 837, 842-
43, 852, 856-59
Cheadle, Dr. 2919
Chesterton, G.K. 4188, 4776, 4788,
4856

Child, Philip
criticism of 1146-48
book reviews 1149-52
fiction by 1131-35
manuscript collections 1145
nonfiction prose by 1136-38
critical and other shorter prose
125, 1142-44
poetry by 1139-40
poetry edited by 1141
Children's literature
bibliography of 36
criticism of 143, 489
See also Animal stories
Chopin, Kate 663
Cicero 4845-46
Cinema. See Films
City in literature 493, 496
in Klein's fiction 2120
in Wright's fiction 4339
Clarke, Austin
criticism of 1170-74, 1701
book reviews 1175-82
fiction by 1153-59
short stories 1163-68
nonfiction prose by 1160-62
shorter critical prose 1169
Climate, as an influence on Canadian
literature 455
Cocteau, Jean 5183
Cohen, Leonard
bibliographies on 33, 1197
criticism of 126, 162, 170, 174,
177, 205, 297, 407,
667, 686, 1198-1220,
3023, 3063, 3537, 5063,
5112, 5149
book reviews 1221-22
fiction by 1183-84
short stories 1193-95
manuscript collections 1196
poetry by 1185-92
Cohen, Matt
critical and other shorter prose by
1242-44
criticism of 170, 205, 1246-52,
1701, 5203
book reviews 1253-61
fiction by 1223-34
short stories 1237-41

Subject Index

H

Subject Index

Wit and humor 125, 185, 629
  Atwood's use of 658, 662, 738
  Birney on 839
  Hiebert on 4714
  Hodgins' use of 1985
  Klein on 2094-95
  Leacock on 2487, 2507-09
  Leacock's use of 2528, 2546,
        2555, 2570
  Lowry's use of 2751, 2780
  Richler's use of 3740
  Simpson's use of 3918
  Wright's use of 4340
  See also names of authors known
        mainly as humorists (e.g.,
        Leacock, Stephen)
Wolfe, Thomas 2750
Women as authors. See Authors,
        Canadian
Women in literature 188, 245, 314-
        16, 323, 338, 343-44,
        384, 392, 428, 430,
        481-82, 522, 545-46,
        579, 637
  Atwood's 648-49, 652-53, 663,
        686, 723, 726
  Cohen's (L.) 1202
  Davies's 1334, 1337

  Grove's 1855-56
  Kroetsch on 2241
  Laurence's 2309-10, 2312, 2340,
        2354
  in mass circulation magazines 555
  Munro's 3439, 3443-44
  See also Heroines
Woodcock, George
  bibliography on 5214
  criticism of 5215-23
    book reviews 5224-59
  drama by 5097-98
  manuscript collections 5213
  nonfiction prose by 5030-86
    critical and other shorter prose
        157, 195-96, 206, 661,
        873, 1944, 2788, 5118-
        5212
  poetry by 5087-96
  short stories by 5116-17
  works edited by 5099-5115
World War I in fiction 371
Wright, Richard
  criticism of 4337-40
    book reviews 4341-44
  fiction by 4331-35
  works edited by 4336
Writer's Union of Canada, directory
        to 91